Manfried Dietrich - Oswald Loretz

Word-List

of the

Cuneiform Alphabetic Texts
from Ugarit, Ras Ibn Hani and Other Places

(KTU: second, enlarged edition)

Abhandlungen zur Literatur
Alt-Syrien-Palästinas und Mesopotamiens

Band 12

herausgegeben von

Manfried Dietrich — Oswald Loretz

1996
Ugarit-Verlag
Münster

Word-List

of the

Cuneiform Alphabetic Texts
from Ugarit, Ras Ibn Hani and Other Places
(KTU: second, enlarged edition)

Manfried Dietrich - Oswald Loretz

EDP management
Hans-Werner Kisker

1996
Ugarit-Verlag
Münster

Herstellung: Weihert-Druck GmbH, Darmstadt
Printed in Germany
ISBN 3-927120-40-5
ISSN 0948-3144

Printed on acid-free paper

Preface

The following listing of all the word forms in the cuneiform alphabetic texts from Ugarit, Ras Ibn Hani etc. is intended to facilitate working with KTU^2 and to make the texts accessible in detail.

This book differs from the list of word forms by P. Zemánek (*Ugaritischer Wortformenindex.* Lexicographia orientalis 4. Hamburg 1995) and the concordance of word forms by J.-L. Cunchillos and J.-P. Vita (*Concordancia de Palabras Ugaríticas en morfología desplegada. Banco de datos filológicos semíticos noroccidentales.* Primera parte: Datos ugaríticos II.1-3. Madrid/Zaragoza 1995) above all by the fact that it is based on the improved and augmented edition KTU^2.

We would like to thank Hanspeter SCHAUDIG for his assistance.

Münster
May 1996

M. Dietrich - O. Loretz

Table of Contents

Preface v
Table of Contents vii
Introduction ix

A 1
I 18
U 28
B 33
G 54
D 58
Ḏ 65
H 66
W 70
Z 77
Ḥ 78
Ḫ 83
Ṭ 89
Ẓ 90
Y 91
K 105
L 117
M 127
N 141
S/Ś 150
ʿ 154
Ġ 166
P 168
Ṣ 174
Q 178
R 183
Š 189
T 199
Ṯ 212

Appendices 223
1. Words in Syllabic Cuneiform 223
2. Corrigenda to KTU^2 225
3. New Readings 226
4. Supplemented Words 228
5. Words in Erasures 228
6. Wrong Line Numbers 229
7. Lines Left Out 229
8. Words Crossing the Line Boundary 230
9. A Supplementary Text 232

Introduction

In the WORD-LIST we use the alphabet presently employed in the literature:

a i u b g d ḏ h w z ḥ ḫ ṭ ẓ y k l m n s/ś ʿ ġ p ṣ q r š t ṯ

Abbreviations and symbols:

\	Line-break, e.g.: a\lp 1.4 VIII 24f		
/	Variants, e.g.: a/ka[1.70 3 = aa[or ka[		
cor.	corrigendum,		
		e.g.:	al[yn 1.3 VI 24 cor. al[iyn;
			al[iyn 1.3 VI 24 (cor.)
(cor.)	correctum, see cor.		
lg.	legendum - with (!) certain, with (?) uncertain		
		e.g.:	abd 4.394 2 lg. kbd;
			kbd 4.394 2(!)
*	marks a line left out in KTU²		
		e.g.:	birt[n 4.692 13*

Following the Word-List we include the following Appendices — in the order of the numbers given to the texts in KTU²:

1. Corrigenda to KTU²
2. New readings
3. Supplemented words
4. Words in erasures
5. Wrong line numbers
6. Lines left out
7. Words crossing the line boundary
8. A supplementary text
9. New editions

A

ʾ 5.24 1
ʾẖmn 4.31 10
ʾs̱p 4.767 1
a 5.2 7, 5.6 1, 5.7 1, 5.8 1, 5.9 I 18, 5.9 II 3, 5.12 1, 5.12 5, 5.13 1, 5.13 2, 5.13 3, 5.13 7, 5.14 1, 5.15 3, 5.16 1, 5.16 8, 5.17 4, 5.19 1, 5.20 1, 5.20 4, 5.21 1, 6.73 2
a[1.5 IV 9, 1.13 34, 1.25 3, 1.67 4, 1.67 12, 1.107 36, 1.164 17, 1.166 2, 2.3 7, 2.49 7, 2.64 8, 2.83 5, 4.41 3, 4.69 V 14, 4.75 IV 1, 4.77 24, 4.106 16, 4.138 9, 4.201 5, 4.243 34, 4.335 7, 4.335 34, 4.366 2, 4.406 7, 4.422 35, 4.455 4, 4.469 5, 4.583 6, 4.596 3, 4.609 24, 4.673 1, 4.785 23, 5.11 15, 7.46 3, 7.176 12
]a 4.127 10
]\a 1.67 6f
]a[1.107 26, 3.1 40, 7.21 4
ax 2.34 21
ax[1.1 III 30, 1.12 II 42, 1.32 3, 1.59 7, 1.73 6, 1.159 2, 2.31 61, 2.77 2, 2.77 15, 4.10 8, 4.44 18, 4.248 7, 4.317 10, 4.318 10, 4.334 1, 4.434 8, 4.582 6, 4.619 9, 4.649 10, 7.2 5
]ax[7.13 4
xa[4.784 2 lg. ÉRIN.MEŠ
]xa 4.410 43
]xa[4.446 5
axdʿ 2.34 30
axm 1.64 2
axp 1.42 13
axxkx[1.86 18
a/n[1.107 21, 4.2 5, 4.17 7, 4.24 2, 4.69 V 2, 4.258 3, 4.650 4, 4.743 14, 7.114 2
]a/n 1.53 4, 2.35 19, 4.188 13, 4.328 1, 4.769 18, 4.769 70, 7.3 2
]a/n 7.222 1 cor.]n/at
]a/n[1.64 11
a/n/t[4.629 17
xa/n[4.97 8
a/ka[1.70 3
aupš 4.85 8, 4.102 12, 4.103 4, 4.769 59, 4.782 30
aup[š 1.87 58, 4.393 6, 4.617 12
au[pš 4.725 2
aupṯ 4.244 14
aupṯn[4.649 3
ab 1.1 III 24, 1.2 I 10, 1.3 V 8, 1.4 IV 24, 1.6 I 36, 1.14 I 37, 1.14 I 43, 1.14 III 32, 1.14 III 47, 1.14 VI 13, 1.14 VI 32, 1.16 I 3, 1.16 I 5, 1.16 I 6, 1.16 I 17, 1.16 I 19, 1.16 II 40, 1.16 II 42, 1.16 II 45, 1.17 VI 49, 1.19 III 15, 1.19 IV 29, 1.40 33, 1.40 41, 1.123 1, 4.147 13, 4.258 14, 7.45 3, 7.45 4
ab[1.2 I 16, 4.55 25, 4.69 V 22, 4.332 21, 4.335 32, 4.382 24, 4.448 4, 4.635 8, 4.706 1
]ab 4.443 8
abx[4.93 I 19
]xab 4.592 5, 4.609 8
]a/nba/n 4.682 6
abbl 4.309 3
abbly 4.377 20
abb[ly 4.431 7
ab]bly 4.368 17
abbt 4.778 18, 4.782 24
abg 4.309 12
abd 1.2 IV 3, 1.100 5, 1.100 11, 1.100 16, 1.100 22, 1.100 27, 1.100 32, 1.100 37, 1.100 42, 1.100 47, 1.100 54, 1.100 60, 1.107 35, 1.107 45, 4.635 48
abd 4.394 2 lg. kbd
abd[4.727 24
abdg 4.232 2
abdḥr 4.33 36
abdḥ[r 4.40 11
abdy 1.107 7
abdʿn 4.12 9, 4.33 31, 4.233 5
abḏr 1.81 19, 4.71 III 6
abḏr[4.422 38
abh 1.2 I 33, 1.2 I 36, 1.2 III 21, 1.3 IV 40, 1.3 V 10, 1.3 V 35, 1.4 IV

21.13 21, 1.14 I 41, 1.14 II 6, 1.14 IV 6, 1.16 I 12, 1.16 VI 40, 1.19 I 32, 1.19 II 10, 1.24 27, 1.92 15, 1.92 24, 1.114 14, 1.117 3

ab[h 1.1 III 26, 1.24 9

a]bh 1.18 I 5

a\bh 1.24 19f

[a]\bh 1.24 29f

abzn[1.64 6

aby 1.2 III 19, 1.17 I 23, 1.18 I 26, 1.82 9, 2.17 9, 4.7 12, 4.130 5

aby[4.332 1, 4.554 3, 4.593 8

ab[y 2.6 2

abyy 4.103 51

abyn 1.17 I 16, 1.22 I 27

abynm 4.70 6

abyt 4.611 3

abk 1.2 III 16, 1.2 III 17, 1.6 IV 10, 1.6 VI 27, 1.14 II 24, 1.16 VI 27

a]bk 1.16 VI 28

abky 1.19 III 5, 1.19 III 20, 1.19 III 34, 4.723 13

abkrn 1.15 III 16

abl 1.82 33, 4.371 10

]abl 1.17 V 2

ablḥ 4.412 I 30

ablm 1.18 I 30, 1.18 IV 8, 1.18 IV 8, 1.19 IV 1, 1.19 IV 1, 1.19 IV 3

a[blm 1.18 I 30

abm 4.63 II 2, 4.75 III 1, 4.75 VI 2, 4.780 1

abmlk 4.75 IV 10, 4.86 8

abmn 4.33 40, 4.63 II 31, 4.63 III 2, 4.115 6, 4.130 6, 4.134 11, 4.155 13, 4.281 25, 4.282 11, 4.307 3, 4.313 21, 4.350 9, 4.382 34, 4.782 13

abmn[4.281 3

ab<n> 1.6 I 2

abn 1.3 III 23, 1.3 III 26, 1.5 VI 17, 1.12 I 9, 1.14 III 13, 1.16 I 14, 1.16 II 36, 1.18 IV 40, 1.19 I 8, 1.100 1, 1.103 1, 1.133 18, 4.33 24, 4.182 10, 4.182 27, 4.335 25, 4.370 3, 4.423 21, 4.626 10, 4.715 2, 4.776 2, 5.22 13

abn[1.4 II 2, 1.7 31, 4.427 13

abn[1.135 14 lg. abn[d

ab[n 4.774 1

a[bn 4.206 6

a]bn 4.367 5

a\bn 1.24 36f

]a/nba/n 4.682 6

abn[d 1.116 28(!), 1.135 14(!)

abnm 1.1 V 11, 1.1 V 23, 1.23 66, 1.82 43

abġl 3.10 19, 4.75 II 3, 4.86 3, 4.134 12, 4.188 7, 4.281 20, 4.370 12, 4.635 26, 4.791 16

abġ[l 4.381 21

a]bġl 4.609 14

ab]ġl 4.75 IV 12

a]bṣdq 4.151 I 11

abṣkn 4.194 19

abṣn 4.609 5

abqn 4.778 8

abqṯ 1.6 IV 20

abq[4.127 10

abr[4.647 7

abrḫṭ 4.309 27

abrm 4.352 2, 4.352 4

a]brm 4.433 4

abrn 4.617 21

abrpu 4.96 10, 4.214 III 5

a]br[p]u 4.75 VI 4

abršd 1.44 6

abršn 4.45 8, 4.225 15, 4.281 7, 4.645 3

abršp 4.63 I 35

abrš[p 4.75 IV 6

abrt[4.748 11

abšḫr 4.723 14

abškn 4.141 I 14, 4.285 7

abšr 4.617 29

abšrkm 1.19 II 37

abšti 4.344 11, 4.720 5

abt[g 4.27 8

ag 1.116 4(!)

ag[1.82 21, 4.248 2, 4.563 2

agbṯr 4.286 7

agdyn 4.631 15

agdn 3.4 3

agdṯb 4.307 8, 4.658 12

agd[ṯ]b 4.632 2

ag]dṯb 4.35 I 2

agzw 4.7 8

[[agzry]] 1.23 60

agzrym 1.23 58, 1.23 61

a<g>zrt 1.13 30

agzrt 1.13 29

agy 4.761 3

agyx 4.753 1

agyn 4.70 2, 4.70 5, 4.75 IV 9, 4.80 22, 4.123 10, 4.313 25, 4.379 9, 4.609 36, 4.631 8

agyn[4.37 2, 4.50 16

agynt 4.33 35

agyt 4.55 12

a]gytn 3.2 6

aglby 4.69 VI 3, 4.344 13

aglr 1.68 24

a[g]lr 1.68 21

agm 1.91 31, 4.68 49, 4.365 28, 4.610 3

agm[4.539 2, 4.686 2

agmz 4.335 5, 4.350 10

agmy 4.98 3, 4.183 II 16, 4.355 11, 4.690 12

a]gmy 4.355 2

agmn 4.12 5, 4.93 IV 4, 4.313 8, 4.783 3

agmn[4.327 2

’gn 6.70 1

agn 1.23 15, 1.23 31, 1.23 36

agndy 1.116 4 lg. ag ndym

agny 4.379 9

agġd 1.128 10

agpt̲ 4.382 25

agpt̲n 4.97 4, 4.631 2

agpt̲r 1.141 1, 4.96 4, 4.374 4, 4.631 10, 4.696 9, 4.714 2, 6.62 1

agpt̲r[4.278 2, 4.644 7

agr 4.243 33

agrx 4.753 22

ag\ršk m 3.9 6f

agrtn 1.19 IV 51

agttp 4.320 3

ad 1.23 32, 1.23 32, 1.23 43, 1.23 43, 1.172 23, 2.26 20

]ad[1.2 III 1

]adx[7.73 1, 7.114 6

adbˤl 4.609 19, 4.753 20

adbˤ[l 4.727 3

add 1.65 9

adḥ[4.635 62

ady 4.63 I 41, 4.65 5, 4.93 I 3, 4.93 I 6, 4.124 10, 4.225 13, 4.412 II 31, 4.753 17

adld̲n 4.69 I 12, 4.340 19, 4.356 7

ad]ld̲n[4.451 2

adl[4.604 2

adm 1.3 II 8, 1.14 I 37, 1.14 III 32, 1.14 III 47, 1.14 VI 32, 1.107 3, 1.169 14, 1.169 15, 2.39 33

adm[1.14 I 43

ad]m 1.14 VI 13

admx 1.42 20

admd 1.116 23

admn 1.42 43, 4.63 III 3

adn 1.1 IV 17, 1.6 VI 58, 1.124 1, 2.18 4, 4.90 3, 4.122 18, 4.129 8, 4.609 33, 5.11 8, 6.16 2, 7.218 2

]adn 1.3 V 9

a]dn 2.39 5

adnh 1.24 13, 1.24 33

ad[nh 2.39 6

adnhm 4.360 3

adn<h>m 4.358 8(?)

adny 2.64 2

]adny 2.39 9

adnk 1.16 I 44, 1.16 I 57, 2.14 19

adnkm 1.2 I 17, 1.15 VI 5, 1.16 I 60

ad[nkm 1.2 I 45

ad]nkm 1.2 I 34

adnn 4.54 8

adnnˤm 4.171 5

adnˤm 4.141 II 26

adn[ˤm 4.141 I 1

adnṣdq 4.7 8

adnty 2.83 5

adˤ 4.86 14

adˤy 4.347 10

adˤl 4.63 II 46

adr 1.12 II 29, 1.16 I 8, 1.16 II 46, 1.17 VI 20, 1.17 VI 21, 1.17 VI 22, 1.17 VI 23, 1.176 19, 2.38 14, 4.195 5

adr[2.83 10

adrdn 4.147 9, 4.148 3, 4.264 5

adr[dn 4.141 I 10

a]drdn 4.183 I 22

adrm 1.17 V 7, 2.3 19, 4.4 2, 4.4 5, 4.158 8, 4.246 7

adrt 1.92 7, 4.102 4, 4.102 9, 4.102 16, 4.102 28, 4.411 7

adrtm 4.102 7, 4.102 18

adt[7.56 3

adty 2.12 2, 2.12 7, 2.12 12, 2.22 4, 2.24 2, 2.25 2, 2.33 4, 2.33 19, 2.68 1, 2.68 4, 2.68 8, 2.68 15, 2.82 2, 4.13 36, 4.69 III 13, 4.344 7, 4.410 7, 4.422 3, 4.616 4, 4.769 7
adt[y 4.494 4
a[d]ty 2.24 5
a[dty 2.24 10
a]dty 2.33 1, 2.33 3
ad]ty 2.56 1
adtny 2.11 1, 2.11 5, 2.11 15
aḏdd 4.709 2
aḏddy 4.96 3, 4.352 9, 4.635 8, 4.635 16, 4.635 20, 4.635 21, 4.635 22, 4.635 23, 4.635 24, 4.635 30, 4.635 31, 4.635 32, 4.635 33, 4.635 34, 4.635 35, 4.635 38, 4.635 39, 4.635 40, 4.635 42, 4.635 44
aḏ[ddy 4.635 25
a[ḏd]dy 4.635 29
a[ḏdd]y 4.635 27
a[ḏddy 4.635 26
aḏddym 4.721 3
aḏddn 4.214 IV 7
aḏdt 4.106 8
aḏmln 4.417 2
aḏml[4.83 1
aḏmny 4.15 2
aḏmr 1.69 4, 1.70 3, 1.70 4
aḏ[mr 1.67 20
aḏmṯn 4.70 4
aḏnn 1.42 43
aḏx[1.51 1
]xah 1.63 8
ahbt 1.3 III 7, 1.4 IV 39, 1.101 18
a]h[b]t 1.7 23
ahlh 1.17 V 32
ahlhm 1.15 III 18
<a>hlm 1.19 IV 52
ahlm 1.19 IV 50, 1.19 IV 60
ahpkk 1.5 III 12
ahq[6.42 3
awx 4.423 2
awl 1.12 II 56
awldn 4.54 9, 4.129 5
awpn 4.204 4
awṣ 1.3 IV 30 lg. arṣ
awr 4.332 11
awrnm 1.42 4
awrġl 1.42 30
az 4.205 6
azzlt 4.182 57
azml 5.23 3
az[mlm 4.390 10
azmr 1.41 51
aḥ 4.775 17
aḥ 4.62 1, lg. aḥ<d>(cor.)?
aḥ[1.37 4, 2.42 18
aḥ<d> 4.62 1(cor.,?), 4.349 4
aḥd 1.2 I 25, 1.6 I 46, 1.6 V 19, 1.6 V 22, 1.14 IV 21, 1.19 III 4, 1.19 III 19, 1.19 III 33, 1.115 14, 2.26 15, 4.5 1, 4.5 2, 4.5 3, 4.11 5, 4.73 5, 4.73 8, 4.78 6, 4.86 4, 4.102 3, 4.102 19, 4.102 20, 4.129 2, 4.129 3, 4.129 4, 4.129 5, 4.129 6, 4.129 7, 4.129 8, 4.129 9, 4.129 10, 4.129 11, 4.129 13, 4.137 10, 4.138 4, 4.138 5, 4.138 7, 4.141 III 3, 4.146 1, 4.151 II 4, 4.156 3, 4.156 4, 4.158 20, 4.169 6, 4.169 9, 4.182 36, 4.190 1, 4.190 2, 4.195 5, 4.195 9, 4.205 9, 4.209 1, 4.209 3, 4.209 5, 4.209 7, 4.209 8, 4.209 9, 4.209 10, 4.209 11, 4.209 13, 4.209 14, 4.209 15, 4.209 16, 4.209 17, 4.209 18, 4.209 19, 4.209 21, 4.209 22, 4.244 14, 4.244 15, 4.244 17, 4.249 3, 4.294 2, 4.295 6, 4.296 9(!), 4.296 10, 4.296 10, 4.296 11, 4.296 14, 4.303 3, 4.360 8, 4.367 8, 4.375 3, 4.375 5, 4.375 7, 4.375 9, 4.375 11, 4.380 28, 4.380 29, 4.380 30, 4.380 31, 4.420 5, 4.618 23, 4.618 24, 4.618 26, 4.630 1, 4.690 14, 4.750 8, 4.750 9, 4.750 10, 4.750 11, 4.751 3, 4.752 3, 4.752 7, 4.752 8, 4.775 10, 5.10 9
aḥd[4.231 8, 4.244 5, 4.244 6, 4.244 12, 4.244 14, 4.542 2
aḥ[d 1.6 V 26, 4.11 9, 4.86 17, 4.231 7, 4.243 37, 4.454 2, 4.483 2, 4.618 27, 4.618 28, 4.775 2
a[ḥ]d 4.618 32
a[ḥd 4.296 12
]aḥd 4.154 6, 4.765 3
aḥ]d 4.141 III 17, 4.195 5
a]ḥd 4.195 4, 4.228 8, 4.237 3, 4.419 5, 4.620 3, 4.765 2

aḥdh 1.71 10, 1.71 25, 1.72 20, 1.72 24, 1.72 35, 1.72 39, 1.85 6, 1.85 8, 1.85 11, 1.114 31
aḥd[h 1.85 32
aḥdh[1.49 5
aḥ[dh 1.72 8
a[ḥdh 1.85 28
a]ḥdh 1.71 6, 1.71 8
aḥdy 1.4 VII 49
aḥd<m> 4.384 14
aḥdm 4.89 4, 4.167 3, 4.208 6, 4.208 7, 4.302 2, 4.302 3, 4.384 12, 4.384 13
aḥdm[4.208 5, 4.532 1, 4.532 2, 4.532 3, 4.532 4
aḥd[m 4.532 5, 4.532 6
aḥ[dm 4.208 1
a[ḥdm 4.306 2
a]ḥdm 4.384 5
a/ṣḥ/m]dm 4.384 4, 4.384 6
aḥw 1.19 I 16, 1.82 19
aḥwy 1.17 VI 32, 1.18 IV 27
aḥẓx[1.6 V 23
aḥl 1.19 II 15, 1.19 II 22
aḥl 4.296 9 lg. aḥd
aḥrṯp 4.277 5
aḥš 1.82 2, 2.34 11
aḥ<t> 4.410 47
aḥt 1.48 12, 1.48 15, 1.48 16, 1.48 17, 1.48 20, 4.102 7, 4.102 10, 4.102 11, 4.102 21, 4.102 24, 4.102 26, 4.102 30, 4.136 4, 4.239 2, 4.349 3, 4.360 5, 4.410 6, 4.410 13, 4.410 25, 4.410 26, 4.410 27, 4.410 31, 4.410 35, 4.410 41, 4.410 43, 4.410 44, 4.410 45, 4.410 48, 4.625 6, 5.3 6
aḥ[t 4.410 18, 4.410 51
a[ḥt 4.102 28, 4.410 14
a]ḥt 4.410 24, 4.410 37
]aḥt 4.410 28, 4.410 29, 4.410 39
aḫ 1.10 II 9, 1.10 II 12, 1.16 II 17, 1.18 I 24, 4.103 5
aḫ[4.611 21, 4.754 8
]aḫ 4.127 4
aḫd 1.4 IV 60, 1.4 V 56, 1.4 VII 9, 1.10 II 6, 1.17 I 30, 1.17 II 5, 1.17 II 19, 1.85 15, 2.47 17, 4.296 8, 4.296 11, 4.296 14, 4.296 15, 4.296 16
aḫd[1.75 4
]aḫd 4.296 17
]aḫd[4.306 7
a]ḫd 2.33 16
a]\ḫd 1.18 I 17f lg. ti]\ḫd
aḫ<d> 4.62 1(?) cor. aḥ<d>
aḫdbn 4.90 6
aḫdhm 1.3 V 22, 1.18 I 9
aḫdy 4.281 21
aḫdt 1.4 II 3
aḫḏ 1.12 II 31, 1.12 II 32, 1.12 II 35
aḫḏ[1.12 II 33
aḫh 1.4 VI 44, 1.12 II 48, 1.16 I 53, 1.16 I 55, 1.17 I 19, 1.17 I 20, 1.96 2, 1.96 2, 3.4 4, 3.4 5, 5.9 I 10
a[ḫh 1.12 II 46
aḫ]h 1.6 VI 4
aḫy 1.5 I 23, 1.5 I 24, 1.5 I 25, 1.6 II 12, 1.17 II 15, 1.19 IV 34, 2.14 3, 2.14 10, 2.14 15, 2.38 2, 2.38 26, 4.739 9, 5.9 I 8
aḫy[2.67 4
]aḫy 1.4 VIII 38, 1.4 VIII 39
aḫyh 1.12 II 50
aḫym 1.6 VI 10, 1.6 VI 14
aḫyn 4.45 5, 4.86 10, 4.370 18, 4.635 41
aḫyn[4.105 4
aḫk 1.4 V 28, 1.6 V 20, 1.6 V 22, 1.10 II 25, 2.14 18, 2.38 3
aḫk[1.16 II 11
aḫm 1.22 I 5, 6.52 1
a]ḫm 1.14 I 9
aḫmlk 4.261 15, 4.609 33, 4.727 7, 4.727 9
aḫml[k 4.711 7
aḫmn 4.296 6
aḫn 4.356 11, 4.356 12
aḫny 4.103 55, 4.356 6
aḫnnn 2.15 9
aḫġl 4.297 5
aḫqm 4.86 23, 4.297 1
aḫr 1.2 I 30, 1.4 III 23, 1.4 V 44, 1.14 IV 32, 1.14 IV 46, 1.15 V 5, 1.16 I 31, 1.17 V 25, 1.20 II 5, 1.24 32, 4.65 8
aḫ]r 1.2 III 6, 1.4 III 36, 1.15 II 11, 1.16 I 50
aḫrm 1.163 5, 4.617 30, 4.734 10, 4.734 11

aḫršn 4.760 2
aḫršp 4.370 7
aḫšn 1.4 VII 32
aḫt 1.10 II 16, 1.10 II 20, 1.10 III 10, 1.16 VI 35, 1.16 VI 51, 1.82 36, 4.147 13, 4.410 54, 4.617 33
aḫth 1.3 IV 39, 1.16 I 51, 4.360 11, 4.658 46, 5.10 1
aḫty 4.75 VI 2
a]ḫty 2.21 3
aḫtk 1.16 I 28, 1.16 I 31, 1.16 I 32, 1.16 I 38, 5.11 12
a[ḫtk 1.18 I 24
aḫtmlk 2.11 4
aḫt{t}h 1.24 36
aṭṭ 4.635 43
aṭm 1.82 19
a]ṭm 1.82 7
aẓḥn 1.123 24
xay 1.19 II 36
ay 1.17 VI 3, 1.23 6, 1.23 6
ay[4.317 15
]ay 4.459 6
ayab 4.153 4, 4.214 III 10
ayaḫ 3.3 3, 4.79 6, 4.338 8
ayiḫ 4.86 28
aybyqt 1.70 39
ayḫ 4.214 II 6
ayy 4.611 6
ayl 4.617 14
]ayl 4.30 4
ayly 4.643 17, 4.645 2
aylm 1.6 I 24
ayln 4.309 22, 4.339 27
ayl[n/t 4.658 42
aylt 1.1 V 19, 1.5 I 17, 1.92 11, 1.133 8, 4.338 9
aym 4.595 3
aymr 1.2 IV 19, 1.2 IV 19
aymr[1.2 I 6
ak[6.65 1
]ak 7.7 1
ak/r[1.82 18
ak/r/p[1.166 5
]akd 1.54 7
akdn 1.54 2
akdṯb 4.307 22, 4.713 1
aky 4.170 13, 6.68 1
akyn 4.658 5
akl 1.14 II 28, 1.14 IV 9, 1.19 I 9, 1.19 IV 34, 1.72 21(!), 1.85 12, 1.85 15, 1.97 2, 1.107 35, 1.107 45, 1.112 12, 2.1 7, 2.39 17, 2.39 19, 2.39 30, 2.46 10, 2.46 15, 2.70 22, 2.71 18, 4.41 1, 4.271 1, 4.271 2, 4.271 3, 4.284 4, 4.636 1, 4.636 2, 4.636 5, 4.636 15, 4.688 2, 4.688 4, 6.13 3
akl[1.107 54
ak[l 1.104 10
a[kl 4.636 25
a]kl 4.636 10
akly 1.6 V 25
akly[1.6 V 24
aklm 1.12 I 26, 1.12 I 36, 1.12 II 35
akln 2.61 8
ak<l>t 1.19 II 20
aklt 1.19 II 23, 1.108 9
aklth 1.19 II 19
aktmy 4.63 IV 10
aktn 4.357 14
akṯn 1.107 48
al 1.2 I 14, 1.2 I 15, 1.2 I 15, 1.3 I 1, 1.3 V 21, 1.3 V 22, 1.3 VI 12, 1.4 III 5, 1.4 V 64, 1.4 VI 8, 1.4 VI 10, 1.4 VII 45, 1.4 VIII 1, 1.4 VIII 10, 1.4 VIII 15, 1.4 VIII 17, 1.5 III 11, 1.5 V 12, 1.6 VI 26, 1.14 III 12, 1.14 III 29, 1.14 VI 10, 1.16 I 25, 1.16 I 25, 1.16 I 26, 1.16 I 31, 1.16 I 34, 1.17 VI 34, 1.18 I 8, 1.18 IV 9, 1.19 III 53, 1.92 34, 1.164 19, 1.169 11, 1.169 11, 1.169 12, 1.169 18, 1.169 19, 1.176 26, 2.16 12, 2.18 3, 2.26 19, 2.30 21, 2.30 23, 2.31 14, 2.31 61, 2.38 27, 2.41 22, 2.47 16, 2.71 15, 2.79 4, 3.9 12, 4.62 2, 4.382 27, 5.9 I 14
al[1.5 V 23, 1.64 28, 1.107 22, 4.308 16
a[l 1.3 V 20
a]l 1.2 III 17, 1.92 35, 1.119 28
al/ṣ[4.69 V 23
aliy 1.3 III 14, 1.3 IV 7, 1.4 VIII 34, 1.5 II 10, 1.5 II 18
aliyn 1.1 IV 22, 1.2 I 4, 1.2 IV 28, 1.2 IV 31, 1.3 III 5, 1.3 III 13, 1.3 IV 7, 1.3 V 32, 1.4 II 22, 1.4 II 37, 1.4 III 10, 1.4 III 23, 1.4 III 37, 1.4 V 12, 1.4 V 35, 1.4 V 47, 1.4 V 59, 1.4 V

63, 1.4 VI 36, 1.4 VII 14, 1.4 VII 37, 1.4 VIII 33, 1.5 II 6, 1.5 II 10, 1.5 II 17, 1.5 V 1, 1.5 V 17, 1.5 VI 9, 1.6 I 12, 1.6 I 14, 1.6 I 19, 1.6 I 21, 1.6 I 23, 1.6 I 25, 1.6 I 29, 1.6 I 41, 1.6 I 58, 1.6 I 64, 1.6 II 21, 1.6 III 8, 1.6 III 20, 1.6 IV 4, 1.6 IV 15, 1.6 IV 20, 1.6 V 10, 1.6 VI 25, 1.10 II 13, 1.10 III 4, 1.10 III 37, 1.22 I 26, 1.92 39

ali\yn 1.4 VII 23f

al[i]yn 1.4 VI 4

aliy[n 1.4 IV 43, 1.15 II 12

ali[yn 1.3 I 2, 1.4 VI 7

al[iyn 1.3 VI 24(cor.), 1.4 V 49, 1.101 17

a[liyn 1.6 III 2

]aliyn 1.4 VII 2, 1.10 II 34, 1.92 31

al]iyn 1.6 I 27, 1.10 I 6

ali]yn 1.11 8

aliy]n 1.15 II 3

alit 1.90 19

a]lit 1.168 15

alb 4.700 4

alg 4.12 13

algbṯ 4.158 15

algp 1.66 3

alḏy 4.609 21

alḏyġ 1.125 6

alz 4.77 12, 4.93 II 14, 4.348 15, 4.412 I 27, 4.422 4, 4.755 7

]alz 4.498 7, 4.526 3

alzy 4.272 1

alḫb 4.243 16

alḫn 4.102 25, 4.337 11

alḫnm 4.392 4

aly 1.42 45, 1.42 45, 4.366 6

alyy 2.72 13, 4.753 3

al[yn 1.3 VI 24 cor. al[iyn

alk 1.19 IV 32, 1.19 IV 33, 1.21 II 6

alk[2.39 22

alkbl 4.369 16

al<l> 1.19 I 37

all 1.6 II 11, 1.12 II 47, 1.19 I 48, 4.182 5, 4.182 6

all[4.182 21

allm 4.168 9, 4.182 4

alm 1.82 8

almg 4.91 8

almdk 1.18 I 29

almnt 1.14 II 44, 1.14 IV 22, 1.16 VI 33, 1.16 VI 46, 1.16 VI 50, 1.17 V 8

aln 1.12 I 20

a/nln 1.42 51

alnb 1.116 21 lg. alnd

alnd 1.60 13, 1.116 21(!), 1.132 19, 1.132 23, 1.135 10

alnr 4.16 6, 5.7 3

alnṯr[4.391 18

a<l>p 1.10 III 16

alp 1.1 II 14, 1.1 III 2, 1.3 I 15, 1.3 IV 38, 1.3 IV 41, 1.3 IV 45, 1.3 VI 4, 1.3 VI 17, 1.4 V 24, 1.4 V 45, 1.4 V 56, 1.10 III 2, 1.10 III 15, 1.11 3, 1.14 III 18, 1.14 V 10, 1.17 II 29, 1.17 V 9, 1.18 I 21, 1.19 IV 43, 1.24 20, 1.39 2, 1.39 5, 1.41 14, 1.43 6, 1.43 16, 1.46 2, 1.56 4, 1.86 1, 1.86 2, 1.86 3, 1.90 5, 1.90 6, 1.105 8, 1.105 16, 1.105 23, 1.105 23, 1.109 9, 1.109 14, 1.109 17, 1.109 20, 1.109 27, 1.119 12, 1.130 14, 1.130 22, 1.148 2, 1.148 3, 1.148 4, 1.148 26, 1.148 27, 1.148 28, 1.162 3, 1.164 5, 1.168 10, 1.171 2, 1.173 3, 1.173 4, 1.175 2, 1.175 13, 3.8 11, 3.8 13, 4.14 2, 4.43 6, 4.91 3, 4.127 6, 4.127 6, 4.169 2, 4.169 2, 4.198 9, 4.201 5, 4.201 10, 4.202 2, 4.203 13, 4.203 15, 4.206 6, 4.212 1(!), 4.231 6, 4.231 7, 4.231 8, 4.247 16, 4.247 17, 4.247 19, 4.247 30(*bis*), 4.261 20, 4.261 23, 4.271 1, 4.272 5, 4.295 2, 4.295 6, 4.295 8, 4.295 17, 4.296 8, 4.296 11, 4.299 3, 4.299 4, 4.310 7, 4.337 2, 4.337 6, 4.337 21, 4.344 21, 4.353 2, 4.407 3, 4.548 2, 4.616 17, 4.636 2, 4.691 1, 4.709 5, 4.783 1, 4.783 3, 4.783 5, 4.783 7, 5.9 I 4, 6.13 3

alp[1.106 29, 4.23 1, 4.201 4, 4.231 5, 4.241 1, 4.247 14, 4.499 1, 4.508 3

al[p 1.41 11, 1.41 52, 1.130 25, 1.148 4, 1.148 10, 1.148 44, 4.211 2, 4.231 1, 4.231 2, 4.231 3

a[lp 1.27 9, 1.90 15, 1.126 5, 1.130 6, 4.247 24, 4.446 3

]alp 1.11 16, 1.134 1, 1.170 3, 4.198

5, 4.250 3, 4.250 4, 7.30 3
a]lp 1.46 5, 1.46 8, 1.91 8, 1.153 7, 4.14 14, 4.250 5, 4.271 2, 6.14 3
al]p 1.46 14, 1.134 2, 1.148 10, 1.148 44, 1.148 45, 1.170 9, 4.14 8, 4.296 12
]alp[4.572 2
a]l[p 1.139 16
a\lp 1.4 VIII 24f
[[alp]] 1.148 25
alph 4.417 5, 4.417 7
alpy 4.214 I 18
<alpm> 4.636 4
alpm 1.1 IV 30, 1.4 I 27, 1.4 VI 40, 1.4 VI 49, 1.6 I 20, 1.14 II 39, 1.14 IV 17, 1.19 IV 59, 1.22 I 12, 1.46 11, 1.105 5, 1.109 4, 1.109 27, 1.111 15, 1.111 17, 1.130 16, 1.148 9, 2.33 24, 2.33 32, 2.45 22, 2.45 24, 2.45 26, 2.81 25, 4.128 1, 4.132 1, 4.181 2, 4.181 6, 4.203 3, 4.203 5, 4.203 14, 4.247 25, 4.261 14, 4.261 15, 4.261 17, 4.261 18, 4.275 18, 4.295 13, 4.296 3, 4.358 1, 4.367 10, 4.387 17, 4.398 1, 4.402 5, 4.407 1, 4.422 1, 4.482 2, 4.618 15, 4.618 17, 4.618 19, 4.626 2, 4.626 8, 4.636 18, 4.658 48, 4.691 8, 4.721 5, 4.749 4
alp[m 1.162 5
al[pm 4.636 34
a[l]pm 4.618 10
a[lpm 4.636 9
]alpm 4.231 9
a]lpm 2.33 38, 4.304 4, 4.636 24
al]pm 4.636 14
a]lpm[4.306 8
alpnm 4.247 25
alt 1.6 VI 27, 1.82 2, 1.82 2
alt[1.55 5
]alt[7.101 2
a]lt 1.2 III 17
altġ 4.214 I 8
alṯd 1.131 7
a]lṯd 1.54 11
alṯy 1.40 29, 1.40 37, 1.84 15, 2.42 8, 4.149 8, 4.343 3, 4.705 9
al[ṯy 4.390 1
a]lṯy 4.155 3
alṯ]y 1.84 20
alṯyy 1.141 1, 4.352 2
alṯn 4.93 II 9, 4.232 14, 4.681 2
a]lṯn 4.526 1
alṯt 4.175 12
am 4.182 36
]a/nm 4.94 4, 4.94 5, 7.77 1
amxyx[1.51 17
amid 1.14 II 5
amd 1.19 III 47
amd[4.413 2
amdy[4.335 22
amdn 4.69 VI 30, 4.233 8
amd[n 4.633 13, 4.761 7
amḏy 4.48 11, 4.73 13, 4.346 6, 4.380 16
amḏ[y 4.68 43
a]mḏy 4.610 29
am]ḏy 4.693 27
amht 1.4 III 21, 1.4 III 22, 4.230 9
amḫ[ṣ 1.3 V 23
amy 4.693 55
amlk 1.6 I 62, 1.16 VI 37, 1.16 VI 53
am{.}lkn 1.6 I 46
amn 1.66 6, 2.23 21, 2.33 16
amn[1.66 5, 1.107 16, 5.11 21
amġy 1.21 II 7
amṣ 1.82 14, 2.33 5
a]mṣḫ.nn 1.3 V 1
amṣq[7.44 3
amr 1.2 I 31, 1.4 I 41, 1.13 27, 1.20 I 10, 1.22 II 17, 1.95 3, 1.107 16, 1.107 20, 2.58 3, 2.72 17, 2.72 24, 2.72 26, 2.72 29, 2.72 32
amr[4.93 I 20
]amr 1.107 17
am]r 2.72 35
]amr[4.94 14
am]\r 1.2 I 15f
amri[l 4.643 15
amrbˁl 4.116 16, 4.644 6
a/ḏmrbˁl 4.261 8
]amrw 1.125 6
amry 4.41 8, 4.44 32, 4.723 5
amry[4.415 5
]amry 1.77 1
amrk 1.16 IV 1, 2.33 13
am\rkm 1.13 28f
amrn 1.42 44, 1.42 45
amrr 1.3 VI 11, 1.4 IV 13, 1.4 IV 17,

1.123 26
amr[r 1.4 IV 3 , 1.4 IV 8
amr[t 1.2 IV 2
amšrt 1.162 15
amt 1.4 IV 61, 1.12 I 15, 1.12 I 16, 1.12 I 23, 1.14 II 3, 1.14 II 10, 1.14 III 25, 1.14 III 37, 1.14 VI 22, 1.17 VI 38, 1.17 VI 38, 4.659 7
amth 1.14 III 53
amtk 2.70 12, 2.70 19
amtm 1.5 I 6, 4.363 4
amtm[4.617 49
amtrn 3.2 10, 3.2 16, 4.344 8, 4.357 19, 4.410 8
amtr[n 4.357 29
an 1.2 I 45, 1.3 IV 33, 1.4 IV 59, 1.5 II 12, 1.5 II 19, 1.6 II 15, 1.6 IV 22, 1.6 IV 22, 1.6 IV 23, 1.6 IV 23, 1.16 VI 38, 1.16 VI 54, 1.17 VI 38, 1.18 I 24, 1.19 II 15, 1.19 II 22, 1.66 11, 1.66 33, 1.67 4, 1.82 6, 1.128 13, 1.128 13, 1.128 13, 1.128 14, 2.31 22, 7.164 7
an 1.12 II 37 lg. a{n}pnm
an[1.1 III 18, 1.69 15, 2.3 15, 2.23 15, 4.513 2, 4.545 II 2
]an 4.55 33, 4.127 8, 4.339 7, 7.108 3
a]n 1.3 IV 22, 1.13 11
xan 4.194 17, 4.734 3
anxx[1.3 V 16
anan 4.643 8
]anan[4.652 2
]ani[7.44 2
anbb 1.44 4
angḥ 1.172 8
ands 4.222 15
and[4.83 12
anhbm 1.3 II 3, 1.3 IV 45
anhb[m 1.3 III 1
anw 1.67 7(*bis*)
anḫ 1.17 I 17
anḫz 1.42 11
anḫn 1.6 III 18, 1.17 II 13
anḫr 1.5 I 15, 1.133 5
anẓ 1.73 11
any 1.3 V 35, 2.47 4, 4.390 1, 4.647 7, 4.689 1
an]y 1.4 IV 47
anyk 2.38 24
anykn 2.38 10
anyt 2.42 24, 2.42 26, 2.46 13, 2.47 3, 4.81 1, 4.125 1, 4.338 11, 4.338 12, 4.394 3, 4.421 2, 4.779 13
any[t 4.40 7, 4.40 10
anyth 4.338 16
ank 1.1 III 16, 1.1 IV 18, 1.2 I 28, 1.2 III 19, 1.3 III 28, 1.4 IV 60, 1.5 I 5, 1.6 II 21, 1.6 II 22, 1.6 III 18, 1.7 33, 1.13 10, 1.14 III 33, 1.14 VI 17, 1.17 II 12, 1.17 VI 32, 1.18 IV 26, 1.18 IV 40, 2.3 10, 2.3 11, 2.3 16, 2.3 17, 2.11 13, 2.16 13, 2.17 6, 2.26 7, 2.31 16, 2.31 23, 2.31 36, 2.31 39, 2.31 41, 2.31 48, 2.31 53, 2.31 57, 2.33 11, 2.33 15, 2.34 10, 2.38 18, 2.38 23, 2.41 17, 2.41 19, 2.48 6, 2.50 21, 2.63 11, 2.70 14, 2.72 23, 2.72 44, 2.76 5, 2.82 8, 2.82 21
ank[1.18 I 26, 2.42 25
an[k 1.3 IV 28, 1.18 IV 21, 2.31 3, 2.31 55
]ank 1.16 V 25, 2.31 17, 2.50 11
a]nk 1.17 VI 45(!), 2.31 40
]ank[2.31 6
]ankm[2.55 2
ankn 2.42 6
anm 1.6 I 50
ann 4.141 II 3, 4.149 18, 4.149 19, 4.222 16, 4.631 13, 4.631 19
ann[4.382 32, 4.658 40
anna 2.75 9
annd 4.412 III 10
anndn 4.148 7
annḏy 4.101 6, 4.245 II 2, 4.753 16
annḏr 3.2 5, 4.244 15, 4.295 15, 4.631 7
annḏr[4.84 9
ann[ḏ]r 4.292 1
annḫ 1.23 14
annḫb 4.707 17
anny 4.77 9, 4.93 I 10, 4.215 3, 4.769 55
anny[4.760 4
a]nny 4.112 II 6
annyn 4.12 12, 4.727 15
a]nnyn 4.412 II 17
annmn 4.339 25, 4.609 26, 4.631 11, 4.750 3

annmt 4.155 12

annpdgl 1.84 3

annš[n 4.633 14, 4.761 6

anntn 3.10 14, 4.93 IV 7, 4.141 II 4, 4.339 24, 4.370 8, 4.378 3, 4.623 4, 4.791 7

annt[n 4.84 3, 4.417 15

annṯb 4.115 3, 4.219 7, 4.226 1, 4.386 3

ansny 4.609 31

anġn 4.418 1

anp 1.126 2

a{n}pnm 1.12 II 37(!)

anry 4.727 4

anrmy 4.166 7, 4.337 18

anr[my 4.364 10

anš 1.2 I 38, 1.2 I 43, 1.3 III 35, 1.4 II 20, 1.19 II 47

anšq 1.2 IV 4

anšrm 4.204 2

anšt 1.6 V 21, 1.15 V 27, 1.16 VI 36, 1.16 VI 51, 1.18 I 16, 1.169 15

anšt[1.18 IV 10

anš[t 1.3 V 27

antn 4.70 7

a]ntn 4.658 3

asyy 4.611 4

ask 1.3 IV 24, 1.3 IV 29

asm 1.19 II 18, 1.19 II 25

ass 4.75 III 8

aspt 2.31 52

as]pt 1.107 45

asr 1.1 II 7, 1.19 II 32, 1.20 II 3, 1.22 II 22, 4.617 47

asr[4.635 52

a]sr 1.19 II 31

asrkm 1.2 I 37

asrm 1.39 11, 2.31 24

]asrm 4.260 2, 4.382 6

asrn 4.204 9, 4.233 3, 4.700 7

asrn[4.520 4

asṯ[1.59 3

a/tġ/t[4.769 62

aġwyn 1.82 42

aġzr[2.73 13

aġzt 1.24 3

]aġyn 4.461 2

aġl[4.506 1, 4.649 6

aġli 4.204 8, 4.769 40

]xaġli 4.260 7

aġld 4.71 IV 4, 4.382 32

aġlḏrm 4.276 13

aġlyn 4.63 III 19, 4.159 7, 4.696 7(!)

aġlkz 4.103 52

aġ]lkz 4.769 50

aġlltn 4.417 17

aġlmn 4.290 5, 4.296 12, 4.370 5, 4.370 17

aġltn 4.33 4, 4.69 VI 13, 4.115 1, 4.285 12, 4.295 7, 4.307 9, 4.313 20, 4.320 8, 4.370 39, 4.753 7

a]ġltn 4.122 23, 4.643 16, 4.659 3

a/i]ġlṯr 4.428 5

aġṣyn 4.696 7 lg. aġlyn

aġr 1.44 1, 1.44 8, 1.54 1, 1.54 13, 1.66 32, 1.128 1, 1.131 1

aġr[1.66 4, 7.40 3

]aġr[7.17 3

aġrl 1.128 19

aġrṯḫnd 1.125 14

aġt 4.49 5, 4.68 14, 4.244 16

aġt[1.112 25

aġ[t 4.610 40, 4.686 11

a]ġt 4.382 19, 4.553 5

aġty 4.748 10

ap 1.1 IV 26, 1.2 I 20, 1.2 I 38, 1.2 I 43, 1.2 IV 2, 1.3 IV 31, 1.3 V 27, 1.4 I 19, 1.4 V 6, 1.5 IV 6, 1.5 VI 21, 1.5 VI 25, 1.6 I 5, 1.6 V 21, 1.6 VI 43, 1.7 37, 1.15 III 24, 1.15 III 28, 1.16 I 3, 1.16 I 3, 1.16 I 9, 1.16 I 17, 1.16 I 17(?), 1.16 II 39, 1.16 II 40, 1.16 II 48, 1.16 VI 25, 1.17 V 6, 1.17 VI 32, 1.18 I 5, 1.18 IV 26, 1.19 I 16, 1.22 I 12, 1.23 24, 1.23 59, 1.23 61, 1.43 12, 1.43 15, 1.82 39, 1.90 2, 1.103 6, 1.103 41, 1.104 6, 1.164 4, 1.168 2, 1.168 9, 1.173 8, 2.3 20, 2.11 13, 2.17 2, 2.23 32, 2.30 22, 2.33 15, 2.33 20, 2.41 19, 2.49 13, 2.61 10, 2.73 16, 2.81 18, 2.81 29, 4.365 1, 4.380 1, 4.683 2, 4.693 1, 4.784 2, 7.2 2

ap[1.166 23, 4.35 II 7, 7.30 4

ap/r[7.46 2

ak/r/p[1.166 5

aph 1.18 IV 26, 1.71 6, 1.71 8, 1.71 10, 1.71 26, 1.72 40, 1.85 4, 1.85 6,

1.85 8, 1.85 11, 1.85 14, 1.85 17, 1.85 19, 1.85 29, 1.97 5, 1.103 41
a[ph 1.71 4, 1.72 26, 1.97 1, 1.97 7
aphm 1.2 I 13, 1.169 8
a<p>hn 1.17 V 5
ap{.}hn 1.17 II 28
aph<n> 1.17 I 1
aphn 1.17 V 14, 1.17 V 34, 1.19 I 20
apy 4.212 5, 4.362 4, 4.362 5
ap[y 4.387 26
apym 4.125 10
apk 1.16 I 41
apkxxm 1.148 14
apkm 1.40 31
apkn 1.40 22
ap[kn 1.40 39
apl 4.212 1 lg. alp
apm 1.103 6, 1.103 30
apn 1.3 I 24, 1.16 II 57, 4.370 43, 4.371 17, 4.424 22
apnk 1.5 VI 11, 1.6 I 56, 1.16 I 46, 1.17 II 27, 1.17 V 4, 1.17 V 13, 1.17 V 28, 1.17 V 33, 1.19 I 19, 1.19 I 38
a]pnk 1.15 II 8
ap]nk 1.14 V 12
apnm 4.88 3, 4.88 4, 4.88 5, 4.88 6, 4.88 7, 4.88 8, 5.22 26
apn[m 4.67 9
ap[nm 4.67 5, 4.67 6, 4.67 7, 4.67 8
apnnk 1.21 II 5
apnt 4.145 9, 4.169 7
a[pnt 4.67 10, 4.88 1
apnthn 4.145 3
apsh 1.6 I 61
apśny 3.8 5
apś[ny 3.8 8
apsny 4.295 1, 4.417 9
apsny[4.80 11
apʿ 1.19 I 13
]apġn 1.64 18
a]pġn[1.64 19
apq 1.4 IV 22, 1.6 I 34, 1.169 12
apq[1.4 II 30
ap]q 1.3 V 6, 1.17 VI 48
apr 1.15 III 30
apṯ 4.141 II 17, 4.377 11
]aṣ 4.111 8
al/ṣ[4.69 V 23
aṣd 1.6 II 15
aṣḥ 1.5 II 21, 1.22 II 19
aṣḥ[1.5 III 9
aṣ[ḥ 1.5 III 18, 1.5 III 25
aṣḥ.km 1.22 II 9
aṣḥkm 1.21 II 2
aṣ]ḥkm 1.21 II 10
aṣḥ]\km 1.22 II 3f
aṣṣ 1.117 10
aq[4.356 15
aqbrn 1.19 III 20
aqbrnh 1.19 III 5, 1.19 III 34
aqhr 4.14 3
aqh[r 4.61 4
aqht 1.17 V 36, 1.17 VI 20, 1.17 VI 26, 1.17 VI 33, 1.17 VI 33, 1.17 VI 42, 1.17 VI 51, 1.17 VI 54, 1.18 I 13, 1.18 IV 18, 1.18 IV 22, 1.18 IV 29, 1.18 IV 39, 1.19 I 1, 1.19 I 12, 1.19 II 17, 1.19 II 24, 1.19 II 42, 1.19 III 40, 1.19 III 47, 1.19 III 52, 1.19 IV 4, 1.19 IV 11
aq[h]t 1.19 IV 58
a]qht 1.18 I 21
aq\ht 1.19 IV 15f
aqny 1.14 II 4
]xa/nqr 4.198 3
aqrbk 1.24 27
aqry 1.3 IV 22, 1.3 IV 27
aqryk 1.17 VI 43
aqšr[1.82 20
ar 1.3 I 24, 1.3 III 6, 1.3 V 41, 1.4 I 16, 1.4 IV 55, 1.4 VI 10, 1.5 V 10, 1.24 38, 1.92 24, 1.111 20, 1.117 7, 2.26 10, 4.27 16, 4.68 48, 4.139 5, 4.214 I 4, 4.214 III 1, 4.365 4, 4.369 10, 4.375 4, 4.380 4, 4.382 23, 4.382 24, 4.384 3, 4.610 30, 4.684 7, 4.693 4, 4.777 3
ar[1.42 19, 1.51 3, 1.51 6, 1.51 8, 1.106 30, 2.37 8, 4.1 1, 4.8 6, 4.27 5, 4.44 2, 4.64 II 5, 4.75 IV 3, 4.80 2, 4.138 7, 4.244 31, 4.252 4, 4.300 4, 4.308 11, 4.683 6, 4.686 15, 4.726 1, 4.754 5, 7.42 2, 7.61 13, 7.130 3
]ar 4.382 22
arx 1.42 31
arx[4.412 I 25, 4.427 16
ak/r[1.82 18
ak/r/p[1.166 5

ap/r[7.46 2

]arxddrn 7.176 5

arbdd 1.3 III 17, 1.3 IV 10, 1.3 IV 30

ar[bdd 1.3 IV 25

arbḫ 1.92 10

arbn 4.133 1

ar<b>ˤ 4.34 5

arbˤ 1.16 II 23, 1.41 51, 1.48 18, 1.87 24, 1.91 24, 1.91 31, 1.106 19, 1.148 19, 2.26 9, 3.1 21, 4.14 14, 4.27 14, 4.27 17, 4.27 22, 4.40 17, 4.44 4, 4.44 5, 4.44 10, 4.44 14, 4.44 24, 4.44 30, 4.48 3, 4.48 4, 4.48 6, 4.48 7, 4.48 11, 4.52 10, 4.73 14, 4.91 2, 4.123 2, 4.123 8, 4.123 9, 4.141 III 5, 4.142 2, 4.142 3, 4.143 5, 4.152 9, 4.158 14, 4.163 2, 4.163 9, 4.167 10, 4.167 11, 4.169 7, 4.172 7, 4.173 8, 4.174 5, 4.174 14, 4.203 3, 4.203 5, 4.213 7, 4.216 8, 4.219 4, 4.243 18, 4.244 18, 4.246 6, 4.247 21, 4.266 6, 4.268 1, 4.268 4, 4.274 2, 4.274 4, 4.274 6, 4.282 1, 4.285 6, 4.288 8, 4.290 1, 4.296 5, 4.296 6, 4.299 3, 4.302 6, 4.313 4, 4.313 22, 4.319 1, 4.341 10, 4.349 1, 4.349 2, 4.355 5, 4.355 9, 4.355 11, 4.355 12, 4.355 16, 4.355 17, 4.355 18, 4.355 22, 4.355 33, 4.355 34, 4.355 37, 4.355 39, 4.358 6, 4.358 9, 4.360 3, 4.360 9, 4.362 3, 4.377 25, 4.380 3, 4.380 20, 4.380 21, 4.380 27, 4.380 34, 4.387 14, 4.387 18, 4.399 13, 4.407 1, 4.410 11, 4.411 5, 4.419 4, 4.421 4, 4.573 5, 4.575 2, 4.595 4, 4.618 5, 4.624 2, 4.624 8, 4.624 10, 4.626 2, 4.626 4, 4.627 3, 4.630 11, 4.697 6, 4.729 11, 4.749 3, 4.750 2, 4.752 5, 4.775 5, 4.777 13, 4.779 8, 4.783 8

arbˤ[2.47 7, 4.244 2, 4.396 13, 4.466 3

ar[b]ˤ 1.41 51, 4.34 7

arb[ˤ 1.41 22, 1.112 26, 4.20 3, 4.60 7, 4.63 II 45, 4.355 42, 4.362 5, 4.388 11, 4.530 2, 4.575 3, 4.632 18, 4.715 4, 4.715 5

ar[bˤ 1.13 5, 4.23 9, 4.127 3, 4.152 1, 4.227 II 5, 4.305 5, 4.380 20, 4.530 1, 4.624 2, 4.677 2, 4.683 18

a[r]bˤ 4.417 7

a[rb]ˤ 1.161 28

a[rbˤ 4.333 10, 4.387 25, 4.400 3

]arbˤ 2.29 1, 4.14 3, 4.306 5, 4.717 3

a]rbˤ 4.60 5, 4.60 9, 4.228 3, 4.230 1, 4.243 11, 4.285 2, 4.399 10, 4.624 14

ar]bˤ 4.63 II 45, 4.185 2, 4.380 3

]arb[ˤ 4.719 4

arb<ˤ> 4.73 9

arbˤm 1.76 7, 3.10 15, 3.10 17, 3.10 21, 4.91 15, 4.123 8, 4.142 3, 4.144 5, 4.158 3, 4.158 4, 4.169 1, 4.174 9, 4.179 16, 4.182 6, 4.212 4, 4.213 3, 4.213 4, 4.213 16, 4.213 22, 4.213 25, 4.213 28, 4.230 11, 4.243 5, 4.243 10, 4.243 12, 4.243 20, 4.243 22, 4.243 26, 4.280 11, 4.284 3, 4.290 6, 4.290 15, 4.290 18, 4.296 7, 4.310 3, 4.333 2, 4.338 10, 4.338 17(?), 4.341 15, 4.341 17, 4.341 18, 4.342 4, 4.344 8, 4.352 5, 4.369 11, 4.400 14, 4.630 2, 4.636 8, 4.636 13, 4.636 32, 4.658 46, 4.683 2, 4.697 5, 4.721 1, 4.777 9, 4.778 1, 4.778 9, 4.779 6, 4.782 1, 4.782 15, 4.791 9, 4.791 12, 4.791 17

arbˤm[4.257 4

arbˤ[m 4.44 12, 4.243 32, 4.417 7

ar[b]ˤm 4.396 2

ar[bˤ]m 4.340 7, 4.636 17

ar[bˤm 4.531 3, 4.636 28

a[r]bˤm 4.341 2

a[rbˤm 4.344 15

]arbˤm 1.76 2, 1.76 4, 4.197 25, 4.697 6

a]rbˤm 4.22 2, 4.340 14, 4.755 7

ar]bˤm 4.721 3

arb]ˤm 4.270 7

]arb[ˤm 4.197 21

a]rbˤ[m 4.257 2

ar<b>ˤt 4.101 1, 4.101 2

arbˤt 1.41 4, 1.87 4, 1.105 17, 1.109 1, 1.112 17, 4.98 17, 4.98 20, 4.146 7, 4.158 15, 4.226 10, 4.267 4, 4.270 4, 4.281 10, 4.341 16, 4.369 6, 4.658 13

arbˤt[1.57 2

arbˤ[t 4.386 10

ar[b]ʿt[7.176 4
ar[bʿt 4.276 10, 4.337 19
a]rbʿt 1.87 54
ar]bʿt 1.46 10, 4.258 6
[[arbʿt]] 4.709 7
argb 4.617 41
argd 4.749 1
argḏḏ 4.336 4, 4.753 19
argm 1.17 VI 39, 2.35 16
argmk 1.3 III 21, 1.3 IV 13, 1.4 I 20
argmn 1.3 IV 32, 3.1 18, 3.1 24, 4.43 3, 4.261 1, 4.610 1
arg[mn 1.87 5
a]rgmn 2.37 10
]argm[n 2.37 2
argmny 2.36 6
argmnk 1.2 I 37
argmnm 4.369 1
a]rgmnm 2.37 8
argn[4.694 2
argnd 4.386 11
ard 1.2 III 20, 1.5 VI 25
ardn 4.723 8
ardnd 1.110 9, 1.111 11, 1.116 15
]ardnd 1.135 6
a]r[dn]d 1.60 5
ardnm 1.42 4
arḏ<l>n 1.64 33
arḏln 1.64 25
arḏl[n 7.42 4
arḏln\ḫ 1.64 29f
arḏnm 1.42 31
arḏnnk 1.42 16, 1.42 28, 1.42 40
arḏn[n]k 1.42 34
a[r]ḏnnk 1.42 9
arw 6.62 2
]arwd 4.258 7
arwdn 4.45 3, 4.51 8, 4.55 4
arwn 4.783 1
arws 4.222 20
arwṯ 4.69 I 15, 4.129 11
arz 1.4 VII 41, 4.33 25, 4.63 II 45
arzh 1.4 VI 19, 1.4 VI 21
arzm 1.4 V 10
arḫ 1.6 II 28, 1.10 II 28, 1.10 III 19, 1.10 III 19, 1.13 22, 1.13 29, 1.15 I 5, 1.93 1
arḫ[1.10 III 23
ar[ḫ 1.6 II 6
a[rḫ 1.10 III 22
arḫh 1.3 V 37 lg. aryh
arḫl]b[1.113 20
arḫp 1.18 IV 21
arḫt 1.4 VI 50, 1.10 III 1
ary 4.33 12, 4.33 13, 4.33 14, 4.33 15, 4.49 3, 4.51 1, 4.53 4, 4.53 10, 4.55 14, 4.68 8, 4.80 5, 4.80 16, 4.113 4, 4.181 5, 4.244 16, 4.244 18, 4.317 7, 4.379 3, 4.379 7, 4.380 23, 4.762 6, 4.781 3
ar[y 4.80 3, 4.683 14
a]ry 4.553 9
aryh 1.3 V 37(!), 1.4 IV 50, 1.4 VI 44, 1.6 I 41, 1.12 II 47, 1.17 I 19, 1.17 I 21
ary]h 1.4 I 8
aryy 1.4 II 26, 1.5 I 23, 1.17 II 15
aryk 1.4 V 29
arym 4.310 6
aryn 1.123 23, 4.96 3
]a/tryn 1.52 7
ark 1.23 34, 4.63 II 42
arkbt 4.75 III 12
arkd 4.277 9
arkḏ 4.723 2
arkḏn 4.141 I 12
arkšt 4.631 4
arkty 1.3 V 23
ar[kty 1.18 I 10
arl 1.72 21 lg. akl
arm 1.148 17, 1.149 10, 4.232 5, 4.750 5
armgr 4.214 II 4
armḏr 1.131 14
armwl 4.7 4, 4.7 14, 4.102 9, 4.246 5, 4.364 6, 4.423 20, 4.423 22, 4.616 14
army 4.63 III 22, 4.232 7, 4.232 9, 4.309 10
armsġ 4.125 20
arn 3.1 19, 4.385 5
]arn 1.32 4
arnbt 4.412 II 7
arny 4.63 II 1, 4.68 27, 4.100 2, 4.123 7, 4.285 11, 4.365 10, 4.380 10, 4.610 11, 4.750 18
arny[4.80 6, 4.693 9
arnn 1.82 6
arśw 4.33 6, 4.69 II 14

arś[w 4.51 11
]arśw 4.331 5
arsw 4.54 2, 4.281 5
arśwn 4.35 II 4, 4.153 9
arswn 4.54 10
ar]swn 4.35 II 12
arspy 4.52 11
arġn 1.97 4
arpḫn 4.232 29
arpṯr 4.33 7
arp[4.196 8, 4.422 44
<arṣ> 1.5 V 18(?)
arṣ 1.1 II 10, 1.1 II 20, 1.1 V 28, 1.2 IV 5, 1.2 IV 23, 1.2 IV 26, 1.3 I 4, 1.3 II 39, 1.3 III 14, 1.3 III 16, 1.3 III 24, 1.3 III 28, 1.3 IV 8, 1.3 IV 10, 1.3 IV 24, 1.3 IV 28, 1.3 IV 30(!), 1.3 IV 36, 1.3 IV 43, 1.3 V 1, 1.3 V 5, 1.3 VI 16, 1.4 I 40, 1.4 V 9, 1.4 V 21, 1.4 VII 31, 1.4 VII 44, 1.4 VII 52, 1.4 VIII 4, 1.4 VIII 8, 1.4 VIII 9, 1.4 VIII 13, 1.5 II 5, 1.5 II 16, 1.5 III 4, 1.5 V 6, 1.5 V 15, 1.5 V 16, 1.5 VI 6, 1.5 VI 10, 1.5 VI 14, 1.5 VI 25, 1.5 VI 27, 1.6 I 8, 1.6 I 18, 1.6 I 43, 1.6 I 65, 1.6 II 16, 1.6 II 19, 1.6 II 19, 1.6 III 9, 1.6 III 21, 1.6 IV 5, 1.6 IV 16, 1.6 V 4, 1.10 I 9, 1.10 I 17, 1.10 II 24, 1.12 I 3, 1.15 III 3, 1.16 I 54, 1.16 III 2, 1.16 III 3, 1.16 III 5, 1.16 III 7, 1.17 I 27, 1.17 VI 15, 1.17 VI 46, 1.19 III 6(!), 1.19 III 35, 1.19 III 53, 1.23 62, 1.82 2, 1.82 38, 1.83 3, 1.107 34, 1.107 37, 1.107 44, 1.108 24, 1.114 22, 1.118 11, 1.148 5, 1.148 24, 1.161 9, 1.161 21, 1.161 21, 1.169 14, 1.174 2
arṣ[1.21 V 1
ar[ṣ 1.4 VII 34, 1.5 IV 4, 1.15 III 14, 1.107 33
a[rṣ 1.1 IV 7, 1.161 2
a]rṣ 1.3 IV 16, 1.3 IV 16, 1.3 V 50, 1.5 II 2, 1.5 VI 31, 1.17 I 45
a]r[ṣ 1.5 VI 4
a\rṣ 1.5 VI 8f
arṣh 1.14 I 29
arṣ<y> 1.4 IV 57
arṣy 1.3 III 7, 1.4 I 18, 1.7 24, 1.106 32, 1.118 22, 1.148 7
a]rṣy 1.47 23, 1.81 13
ar]ṣy 1.134 12
arr 1.10 III 29, 1.10 III 30, 4.355 32, 4.384 1, 4.683 1, 6.27 2
arr[1.166 22
arš 1.3 III 43, 1.6 VI 51, 5.11 12
arš[2.23 16
a]rš 2.23 18
aršḫ 1.100 63, 1.100 64
arš[ḫ 4.629 6
aršm 4.153 2
aršmg 4.194 3, 4.332 9, 4.339 11
arš[mg 4.332 2
a]ršmg 4.151 I 2
aršt 2.45 24, 5.9 I 7
art 4.68 10, 4.95 3, 4.235 3, 4.244 2, 4.247 26, 4.310 8, 4.610 8, 4.629 12, 4.631 1, 6.44 1
art[4.686 5, 7.46 4
art 1.19 III 6 lg. arṣ
arty 4.33 10, 4.33 11, 4.85 3, 4.244 8
arty[4.80 12
artyn 4.53 4, 4.214 I 6, 4.715 23
artn 4.129 3, 4.141 I 7, 4.609 30, 4.753 12
artn[4.504 3, 4.614 1
artṯb 4.102 4, 4.204 12, 4.281 28
arṯm 1.2 I 19, 1.2 I 35
ašisp 2.33 12
ašbḥ 4.232 21
ašhlk 1.3 V 24, 1.18 I 11
ašhl]k 1.3 V 2
ašk[1.114 15 lg. ašk[r
aškn 1.16 V 26, 1.16 V 27, 2.26 5
ašk[r 1.114 15(!)
aškrr 1.85 13
ašk[rr 1.72 18
ašlu 2.34 31 lg. aššu
ašld 1.23 65
ašlw 1.14 III 45
ašlḥk 1.17 VI 28
aš]lḥk 1.17 VI 18
ašmḫ 1.16 I 14 lg. nšmḫ
ašsprk 1.17 VI 28
ašʿrb 1.14 IV 41
ašʿt 4.247 22
ašṣi 1.2 IV 2
ašṣu 2.34 31(!), 2.34 33

ašṣuk 2.3 17
ašqlk 1.17 VI 44
ašr 1.24 1, 1.24 38, 1.24 40
ašrbˁ 1.17 V 3
]ašrh 4.359 6
ašt 1.3 IV 29, 1.4 V 61, 1.4 VI 5, 1.5 III 11, 1.19 III 6, 1.19 III 20, 2.33 12, 2.33 28
aš[t 1.2 III 13
a]št 2.33 12
aš]t 1.3 IV 23
]a/tšt 2.31 19
aštk 1.18 IV 17
aštm 1.4 VII 15
ašt.n 1.5 V 5
aštn 1.19 III 34, 2.32 10, 2.41 18
]aštn 2.32 7
at 1.1 III 16, 1.1 IV 17, 1.2 I 3, 1.2 IV 11, 1.2 IV 19, 1.5 V 6, 1.6 II 12, 1.12 I 14, 1.12 II 7, 1.12 II 23, 1.12 II 23, 1.13 11, 1.16 V 41, 1.17 I 16, 1.18 I 24, 1.18 IV 12, 1.18 IV 41, 1.103 1, 2.3 8, 2.3 18, 2.26 20, 2.30 20, 2.36 7, 2.36 10, 2.39 12, 2.42 26, 2.45 20, 2.45 28, 2.63 14, 2.71 13, 2.73 12, 2.73 14, 2.73 19, 2.80 9
at 1.14 I 38 lg. mn
at 1.1 V 25 lg. atzd
at 1.16 I 17 lg. ap?
at[1.4 II 40, 4.432 17
a[t 1.12 II 7
]at 2.8 4, 2.83 1
atxx[4.77 6
]a/nt 7.222 1(cor.)
a/tġ/t[4.769 62
atdb 1.123 25
atwt 1.4 IV 32
atzd 1.1 V 25(!)
atyn 4.69 III 2, 4.75 I 2, 4.75 IV 4
atynpṯ 1.42 3, 1.42 4
a]tk 1.17 VI 45 lg. a]nk
atl[4.754 3
atlg 2.26 16, 4.27 19, 4.348 2, 4.365 5, 4.369 12, 4.380 5, 4.625 1, 4.693 5
atlg[4.390 2
atl[g 4.68 44
a[tlg 4.683 7
]atlg 4.618 27
a]tlg 4.784 5
atlgy 4.45 9
atlgn 4.373 4
atm 1.1 III 18, 1.3 III 28, 1.3 IV 33, 1.22 II 13
atn 1.6 VI 55, 1.13 11, 1.14 IV 43, 1.24 19, 1.24 22, 1.42 1, 1.42 12, 1.125 2, 2.26 7, 2.31 66, 4.35 II 7, 4.70 5, 4.93 II 2, 4.261 18, 4.307 4, 4.348 13, 4.753 21
atn 2.42 20 lg. ttn?
atn[4.494 3
]atn 4.498 6
]atn[7.50 12
a/n/ttn 4.63 IV 3
atnb 4.46 13, 4.65 7, 4.93 IV 13, 4.106 9, 4.432 18, 4.692 4
a]tnb 4.422 5
atnd 1.110 2, 1.111 3, 1.125 5(!)
atn]d 1.60 1 lg. il]d
atnk 1.17 VI 17, 1.17 VI 27
atnnk 2.21 17
atnth 1.4 IV 12
atnt[y 1.4 IV 7
atnṯ]t 1.135 13(!)
atnṯtm 1.116 12
atġl 4.635 25
atšk 1.70 14
att 1.103 1
]a/ntṯ[1.107 53
]a/ttṯḫnm 1.64 32
aṯ 1.4 I 6, 1.66 9, 1.128 16, 1.131 10
aṯx[4.651 6
aṯb 1.16 VI 38, 1.16 VI 53, 1.82 37
aṯbn 1.6 III 18, 1.17 II 12
aṯbr[1.18 I 4
aṯbšmy 1.70 4
aṯb[šm]\y 1.70 4f
aṯbt 1.70 15
aṯḏ 1.131 11
aṯḫ 1.128 3
aṯy/ḫ[7.68 4
aṯ{ḫ}ḫlm 1.111 3
aṯḫlm 1.110 1, 1.111 8, 1.116 3, 1.116 9, 1.116 10, 1.125 1
aṯḫl[m 1.132 4
a[ṯḫlm 1.116 31
]aṯy 4.72 4
aṯy/ḫ[7.68 4

a/tṯyx 1.86 28
aṯm 1.51 17, 1.51 18, 1.51 19, 1.54 11
aṯ[m 1.51 4, 1.51 9, 1.51 11, 1.51 12, 1.51 13, 1.51 14
a[ṯm 1.51 15
a]ṯm 1.51 20
aṯ\m 1.44 6f
aṯnyk 1.3 III 22
aṯnyk[1.1 III 13
aṯ[nyk 1.7 30
aṯpṯ[1.64 23
aṯr 1.2 I 31, 1.4 IV 18, 1.5 VI 24, 1.6 I 7, 1.6 II 9, 1.6 II 30, 1.14 II 41, 1.14 II 42, 1.14 IV 19, 1.14 IV 20, 1.42 62, 1.43 24, 1.45 7, 1.45 8, 1.100 77, 1.107 28, 1.124 16, 1.161 20, 1.161 20, 2.39 34
aṯr 6.66 8 lg. m\aṯr
aṯr[1.16 V 6
aṯrh 1.17 I 28, 1.17 I 46, 1.20 II 2, 1.21 II 3, 1.21 II 11, 1.22 II 5, 1.22 II 11
aṯrh[1.22 II 21
aṯr[h 1.22 II 10
aṯ]rh 1.21 II 12
aṯr]h 1.21 II 4
aṯry 4.332 15
aṯr[y 1.17 II 17
aṯr[y]m 4.230 3
aṯryt 1.17 VI 36
aṯrk 1.22 I 3
aṯrm 1.45 7, 1.45 8
aṯrn 4.692 2
aṯrt 1.3 I 15, 1.3 V 4, 1.3 V 36, 1.3 V 40, 1.3 VI 10, 1.4 I 14, 1.4 I 21, 1.4 III 25, 1.4 III 27, 1.4 III 29, 1.4 III 34, 1.4 III 38, 1.4 IV 4, 1.4 IV 14, 1.4 IV 40, 1.4 IV 49, 1.4 IV 51, 1.4 IV 53, 1.4 IV 59, 1.4 IV 61, 1.4 V 1, 1.4 V 2, 1.4 VI 46, 1.6 I 40, 1.6 I 44, 1.6 I 47, 1.6 I 53, 1.6 V 1, 1.8 II 1, 1.8 II 5, 1.12 I 17, 1.14 IV 35, 1.14 IV 38, 1.15 III 25, 1.23 13, 1.23 24, 1.23 28, 1.39 6, 1.41 40, 1.46 6, 1.46 8, 1.65 5, 1.103 49, 1.112 24, 1.148 7, 1.148 31, 1.169 16, 2.31 42
aṯr[t 1.4 II 31, 1.4 II 41, 1.4 IV 2, 1.4 IV 31, 1.6 I 45, 2.31 63
aṯ[rt 1.4 II 28
a[ṯ]rt 1.15 II 26
a[ṯrt 1.3 IV 48
aṯ]\rt 1.87 38f
aṯš 1.128 17
aṯt 1.2 III 22, 1.3 I 14, 1.3 IV 40, 1.14 I 12, 1.14 I 14, 1.15 II 21, 1.15 II 21, 1.16 I 5, 1.16 I 19, 1.16 II 42, 1.19 IV 46, 1.23 42(*bis*), 1.23 49, 1.115 8, 1.127 26, 1.174 7, 4.102 5, 4.102 6, 4.102 8, 4.102 9, 4.102 10, 4.102 16, 4.102 19, 4.102 21, 4.102 22, 4.102 23, 4.102 24, 4.153 3, 4.153 4, 4.153 5, 4.349 2, 4.360 9, 4.386 19, 4.419 3, 4.419 6, 5.11 6
aṯt 1.23 43 cor. aṯtm
aṯt[1.94 29
aṯ[t 1.16 II 10, 1.23 48, 2.25 5
a[ṯt 1.140 5, 1.140 7, 1.140 9
a[[x]]ṯt 1.40 36
]a/xṯt 4.205 13
]a/tṯt 1.64 6
aṯtb 1.42 29, 1.42 31
aṯtbd 1.110 6, 1.116 15, 1.125 10, 1.135 5
<a>ṯth 4.339 4
aṯth 1.14 II 49, 1.14 IV 27, 1.16 IV 4, 1.16 IV 8, 1.17 I 39, 1.17 V 15, 4.295 2, 4.295 16, 4.339 3, 4.339 6, 4.339 7, 4.339 8, 4.339 9, 4.339 12, 4.339 15, 4.339 19, 4.339 23, 4.369 19, 4.417 3, 4.417 9, 4.625 20, 4.632 21, 4.644 4
aṯth[4.417 10, 4.644 9
aṯt[h 3.4 9, 4.417 11
aṯt\[h 1.14 V 13f
a[ṯth 4.295 3, 4.417 6, 4.417 15
aṯt]h 4.295 11, 4.295 12
aṯtḫ 1.42 58
aṯtḫ[n 1.42 55
aṯtḫnm 1.42 56
aṯty 2.33 28
aṯ[ty 1.23 52
aṯtyy 4.611 10
aṯtyn 4.696 4
aṯtk 1.15 V 23, 1.16 IV 12
aṯtm 1.2 I 10, 1.23 39(*bis*), 1.23 43(cor.), 1.23 46, 1.23 48, 4.102 7, 4.102 11, 4.102 18, 4.102 20

a[ṯ]tm 1.23 42
aṯtn 1.82 29
aṯtnṯ 1.66 29
aṯtn[ṯ 1.66 35
aṯtġṯḫḫṯnprt/n 1.68 23
]aṯry 4.58 4
]aṯrn 4.75 V 3
]aṯrt 1.3 V 39
a]ṯrt 1.4 II 26, 1.49 3, 1.118 19, 7.50 5
aṯ{t}rt 1.4 II 13
aṯtrt 1.41 15
]aṯr[t 1.4 I 11
]aṯt 1.14 V 15, 4.102 28
a]ṯt 4.102 12
aṯ]t 4.102 4, 4.102 13
aṯtbd 1.60 4(cor.)
a]ṯtbd 1.26 4
]aṯth 4.519 2, 4.519 4
a]ṯth 4.295 5
aṯtl 4.307 20(cor.)
a]ṯtnṯ 1.66 21
aṯtš 4.232 15
aṯṯ 1.23 64, 1.44 8, 1.54 13
aṯṯbd 1.60 4 cor. aṯtbd
aṯṯy 1.23 60
aṯṯl 4.307 20 cor. aṯtl

I

i 1.5 IV 6, 1.5 IV 7, 1.14 IV 38, 1.16 I 3, 1.16 I 20, 1.44 4, 1.66 9, 1.69 1, 4.358 3, 4.405 11, 4.734 7, 5.2 3, 5.2 6, 5.4 5, 5.5 1, 5.6 3, 5.12 4, 5.13 9, 5.15 4, 5.14 18, 5.15 1, 5.15 1, 5.15 1, 5.15 2, 5.15 4, 5.16 4, 5.17 3, 5.17 6, 5.19 4, 5.20 2, 5.20 3, 5.21 2
i 4.769 58 lg. i[š]dn
i[1.2 III 14, 1.16 II 7, 1.16 V 37, 1.64 28, 1.66 24, 1.93 5, 1.93 10, 1.123 2, 1.123 20, 1.157 7, 2.31 40, 2.31 54, 2.36 10, 2.62 2, 4.66 14, 4.69 V 18, 4.88 7, 4.178 11, 4.316 4, 4.335 10, 4.335 33, 4.393 11, 4.403 11, 4.427 2, 4.449 2, 4.617 13, 4.617 18, 4.647 2, 4.673 5, 7.3 2, 7.55 5, 7.109 2, 7.158 1, 7.163 5, 7.175 4, 7.189 1, 7.202 1, 7.207 5
]i 1.25 1, 1.64 21, 4.109 1, 4.382 4, 4.744 3
]i 7.37 3 cor.]l
]i[1.7 50, 7.64 1, 7.215 1
ix[1.64 17, 1.70 5, 1.149 6, 2.37 10, 2.49 4, 4.427 3, 7.53 6, 7.68 6
ixx[4.399 9
ixxxxx[4.748 7
]ix[7.157 1
]xi 4.182 54, 4.399 11, 4.658 4, 7.165 1
]xi[4.643 22, 7.59 1
xix[1.168 25
ixxˁm[4.273 10
ixnḏxxn 1.42 12
irxxi/hdrp 1.42 41
i/h 7.218 6
i/h[2.9 3, 4.178 10, 4.374 10
]i/h 1.10 II 32, 1.25 7, 7.46 6
]i/h[1.73 18, 1.167 14
i/hxxx 2.36 19
i/hxm 4.401 2
i/h/p[1.51 10
]i/hiḏ/šn 1.68 32
ib 1.3 III 37, 1.3 IV 4, 1.3 IV 5, 1.4 VII 35, 1.4 VII 38, 1.14 III 43, 1.14 VI 29, 1.19 I 31, 1.19 IV 59, 1.24 1, 1.24 18, 1.24 37, 1.103 17, 1.103 59, 1.111 21, 1.140 6, 2.33 10, 2.33 17, 2.33 29, 2.39 31, 4.261 23
]ib 2.33 11
i]b 1.103 33
ib/d[1.42 42, 4.462 2
ibh 1.2 IV 39, 1.103 10, 1.103 37, 1.103 54, 1.103 58
i]bh 1.103 11, 1.103 22
ib]h 1.103 15
iby 1.10 II 24
]iby 4.755 15
ibyḥ[6.37 1
ibyn 4.377 4, 4.607 21
ibyn[4.496 2
ibk 1.2 IV 8, 1.2 IV 9, 2.72 44
ibky 1.161 13
iblblhm 2.62 11
ibln 4.35 I 18, 4.93 IV 1, 4.311 10
ibln[4.545 II 7
ibm 2.33 27, 4.350 12, 4.610 8, 4.781 8
ibn 1.103 16, 1.103 51, 4.658 13
]i/hbn 4.28 8
ibnkl 1.42 47, 1.42 48
ibsn 3.9 5
ibˁl 4.141 I 4
ibˁlt 1.119 1
ib[ˁ]lt 1.119 11
ibˁr 2.31 55
ibˁr.nn 2.37 9
ibġyh 1.3 III 29
ibġ[yh 1.1 III 16
ib[ġyh 1.3 IV 19, 1.7 33
ibqˁ 1.19 III 3, 1.19 III 18, 1.19 III 32
ibr 1.4 VII 56, 1.8 II 9, 1.9 11, 1.10 III 20, 1.10 III 35, 1.12 II 55, 1.119 29, 4.136 3
ibrx[1.9 16
ibrd 4.33 26, 4.628 5
ib[r]d 4.424 23
]ibrd 4.217 3
ibrḏr 4.343 6

ibrh 1.14 III 16, 1.14 V 9
ibryn 4.222 21
ibrkḏ 2.21 7
ibrkyṯ 4.264 10
ibrm 1.12 I 32, 4.607 20
ibrmḏ 4.103 10, 4.103 51
ibrn 1.113 16, 1.113 19, 1.113 22, 1.113 24, 4.68 64, 4.103 37, 4.126 24, 4.752 7
ibrn[4.47 3, 4.99 12
ib[rn 4.105 1
i]br[n 4.610 44
i/h/pg[1.30 5
igd 1.42 61
igḏktḏ 1.64 7
igy 4.344 17, 4.410 9
igʿ 7.163 6
igr 2.34 12
ig[r 2.34 12
igty 1.64 7
igṯn[1.66 32
id 1.41 50, 1.90 1, 1.115 1, 1.149 4, 1.163 5, 1.164 1, 1.168 8, 2.82 3
i]d 1.164 3, 1.168 1
id 1.4 I 34 lg. il
ib/d[1.42 42, 4.462 2
idx 1.148 15
idbx 1.15 IV 12
]idd 2.31 42
idy 1.82 2
i]dy 1.82 2
idk 1.1 II 13(!), 1.1 III 21, 1.3 IV 37, 1.3 VI 12, 1.4 IV 20, 1.4 V 22, 1.4 VIII 1, 1.4 VIII 10, 1.5 I 9, 1.5 II 13, 1.5 V 11, 1.6 IV 7, 1.10 II 8, 1.14 VI 36, 1.17 VI 46, 1.18 I 20, 1.86 21, 1.100 63
id[k 1.3 V 5, 2.60 5
i[dk 1.2 I 19
]idk 1.63 2
id]k 1.6 I 32, 1.14 V 29
idly[4.383 7
idm 1.12 II 29, 1.12 II 30
]idmnn[1.55 4
]idmt 4.351 2
idn 2.15 5
idʿ 1.6 III 8
idp 1.149 8
idpd 1.149 7
idr 1.42 29
idr[4.452 2, 4.528 4
]idr[4.511 2
idrm 4.69 II 2, 4.377 8, 4.785 11
idrn 4.65 9
idrn[4.322 9, 4.694 3
idrp 1.148 32
idt[1.15 III 30
idṯ[4.118 7
idṯn 4.129 6, 4.277 12, 4.296 11
idṯn[4.649 5
idṯ[n 4.21 2
iš/ḏ[4.69 V 21
iḏt/m[1.66 8
iḏn 1.128 2
iḏr 1.42 1, 1.42 6, 1.42 17, 1.42 26, 1.42 29, 1.42 32, 1.42 35, 1.42 38, 1.42 44, 1.42 47, 1.42 50, 1.42 54, 1.42 57, 1.42 57, 1.42 60
iḏ[r 1.42 10, 1.42 15, 1.42 22
iḏ]r 1.42 41
iḏrn 4.64 V 8
iḏt/m[1.66 8
ih[1.167 9
i[h 7.222 3
ihbt 2.31 49
iht 1.3 VI 8
iwx[4.260 2
iwl[4.46 2
iwr 1.128 19
iwr[4.114 12, 4.289 2, 4.289 4, 4.289 7, 4.607 12, 4.678 2
iw[r 4.607 9, 4.607 10, 4.607 11, 4.725 1
iwrd 4.619 3
iwrdr 4.7 5
iwrḏ[4.678 3
iwrḏn 2.14 1, 4.243 30
iwrḏr 2.10 1
iwrḫz 4.367 7, 4.635 37
iwrḫt 4.103 13, 4.103 25
iwryn 4.307 14, 4.320 19
iwrkl 3.4 2, 3.4 13, 3.4 18, 4.282 2, 4.357 15
iwrm[4.357 20
iwrmḏ 4.7 12, 4.219 8, 4.417 14
i]wrmḏ 4.607 6
i]wrmḏ[4.675 5
i]wrmḫ 4.194 9

iwrn 1.42 51, 1.52 24, 1.110 4
iwrn[4.545 II 8
iw[r]n 1.42 51
iwrnr 4.16 5
i]wrġl[4.244 26
iwrpzn 2.14 2, 4.102 5, 4.102 10, 4.226 2, 4.336 3
iwrpzn[4.547 3
iw]rpzn 4.607 5
iwr]pzn 4.384 13
iwrtḏl 4.424 21, 4.607 8
iwrtn 4.70 7, 4.183 II 23
iwrṯġrn 4.607 7
iwrṯrm 2.33 2(?)
izl 4.35 I 17
izldn 4.320 5
izly 4.348 4
izml 4.284 2, 5.3 6
izmly 4.7 3
izr 1.91 8
]i/hṭ/ḥ[1.4 VI 11
iḥtrš 1.16 V 26
iḫd 2.15 10, 2.33 21
]iḫdl 7.51 4
iḫdn 2.15 7
iḫ<h> 4.780 2
iḫh 1.24 35, 4.123 23
iḫy 2.41 18, 2.44 2, 4.35 II 17, 4.170 4, 4.214 I 9, 4.366 7, 4.617 4
iḫy[4.427 15
iḫyx[4.114 11
iḫyn 4.75 II 6, 4.75 III 7, 4.75 IV 11, 4.175 13, 4.204 1, 4.692 3
iḫk 2.44 3
iḫmlk 4.339 22
iḫmn 4.282 4
iḫn 4.317 8
iḫny 4.65 13
iḫġl 4.130 4
iḫqm 2.4 21
iḫršp 3.9 18
]i/hṭ/ḥ[1.4 VI 11
iṭʿnk 1.5 I 26
iy 1.6 IV 4, 1.6 IV 5, 1.6 IV 15, 1.6 IV 16, 1.42 60, 1.148 13
]iy 4.75 VI 6
]i/hy 2.31 34
il/y[4.699 4
iyxx 1.2 I 47
iybʿl 4.168 2
iyb[ʿl 4.334 4
iyd 1.110 6, 1.116 14
iyd[1.111 10
i]yd 1.60 4
iy]d 1.135 5
iydm 1.125 11, 4.16 2
iykḏġ 1.42 15
iym 1.42 15
iynm 1.112 11
iyrḏ 4.147 18
iyry 4.222 18
iytlm 2.14 14, 4.165 2, 4.223 6, 4.223 7, 4.223 8, 4.223 9, 4.309 21, 4.344 9, 4.357 18, 4.367 9, 4.374 1, 4.379 6, 4.409 2, 4.410 28, 4.425 11
iytlm[4.680 2
iyt[lm 4.357 9
iyṯr 4.194 5, 4.364 2, 4.617 5
iyṯr[4.547 2
iyṯ[r 4.50 17
]iyṯr 4.615 1
i]yṯr 4.285 5
ik 1.2 I 40, 1.2 II 6, 1.3 III 36, 1.4 II 21, 1.4 II 23, 1.4 III 28, 1.4 IV 31, 1.4 IV 32, 1.5 II 21, 1.6 VI 24, 1.6 VI 26, 1.8 II 1, 1.18 IV 9, 1.176 22
ik[4.677 1
]xik 1.11 14
iky 2.14 6, 2.21 11, 2.26 5, 3.1 8
ikl 1.22 I 24
ikm 2.7 10
ikmy 2.82 17
ikrn[4.84 6, 4.289 6
<il> 1.40 34
il 1.1 III 22, 1.1 III 26, 1.1 IV 4, 1.1 IV 12, 1.1 IV 13, 1.1 V 22, 1.2 I 21, 1.2 I 30, 1.2 I 33, 1.2 I 36, 1.2 III 16, 1.2 III 19, 1.2 III 21, 1.3 III 29, 1.3 III 39, 1.3 III 39, 1.3 III 44, 1.3 III 46, 1.3 V 7, 1.3 V 26, 1.3 V 30, 1.3 V 35, 1.3 V 35, 1.3 V 39, 1.3 VI 14, 1.4 I 12, 1.4 I 30, 1.4 I 31, 1.4 I 33, 1.4 I 34(!), 1.4 I 36, 1.4 I 38, 1.4 I 41, 1.4 II 10, 1.4 II 34, 1.4 II 35, 1.4 II 36, 1.4 III 31, 1.4 IV 21, 1.4 IV 23, 1.4 IV 25, 1.4 IV 27, 1.4 IV 38, 1.4 IV 41, 1.4 IV 47, 1.4 IV 52, 1.4 IV 58, 1.4 VI 12, 1.4 VI 42, 1.4 VII

3, 1.4 VII 47, 1.4 VIII 32, 1.5 I 8, 1.5 I 13, 1.5 II 9, 1.5 IV 21, 1.5 VI 11, 1.6 I 35, 1.6 I 37, 1.6 I 43, 1.6 I 49, 1.6 I 65, 1.6 III 4, 1.6 III 10, 1.6 III 14, 1.6 III 22, 1.6 IV 2, 1.6 IV 10, 1.6 IV 13, 1.6 IV 23, 1.6 VI 27, 1.6 VI 31, 1.10 I 3, 1.10 II 5, 1.10 III 8, 1.10 III 33, 1.12 I 9, 1.12 I 12, 1.12 I 22, 1.12 I 41, 1.12 II 6, 1.12 II 9, 1.12 II 22, 1.12 II 44, 1.12 II 60, 1.13 20, 1.14 I 36, 1.14 I 41, 1.14 II 6, 1.14 II 9, 1.14 II 24, 1.14 III 31, 1.14 III 46, 1.14 III 49, 1.14 III 51, 1.14 IV 6, 1.14 VI 13, 1.14 VI 31, 1.14 VI 35, 1.15 II 16, 1.15 II 19, 1.15 II 20, 1.15 III 19, 1.15 V 17, 1.15 V 26, 1.16 I 10, 1.16 I 20, 1.16 IV 1, 1.16 IV 2, 1.16 IV 3, 1.16 IV 6, 1.16 IV 9, 1.16 IV 10, 1.16 V 23, 1.16 V 46, 1.17 I 23, 1.17 I 32, 1.17 I 34, 1.17 II 5, 1.17 II 22, 1.17 V 21, 1.17 V 31, 1.17 VI 23, 1.17 VI 29, 1.17 VI 47, 1.17 VI 48, 1.18 I 15, 1.19 I 13, 1.19 III 47, 1.19 IV 57, 1.22 I 5, 1.22 I 6, 1.22 I 7, 1.22 I 20, 1.23 31, 1.23 33, 1.23 34, 1.23 34, 1.23 35, 1.23 35, 1.23 37, 1.23 37, 1.23 39, 1.23 42, 1.23 42, 1.23 45, 1.23 45, 1.23 49, 1.23 52, 1.23 53, 1.23 59, 1.23 60, 1.27 8, 1.39 2, 1.39 7, 1.39 13, 1.40 25, 1.40 33, 1.40 34, 1.40 41, 1.40 42, 1.42 6, 1.42 7, 1.46 3, 1.47 1, 1.47 3, 1.47 26, 1.62 7, 1.65 1, 1.65 1, 1.65 2, 1.65 3, 1.65 5, 1.65 6, 1.65 7, 1.65 8, 1.65 9, 1.65 9, 1.65 12, 1.65 13, 1.65 14, 1.65 15, 1.65 16, 1.65 17, 1.65 18, 1.74 1, 1.81 7, 1.84 8, 1.87 2, 1.87 18, 1.87 42, 1.91 6, 1.92 15, 1.98 2, 1.100 3, 1.101 2, 1.102 1, 1.108 2, 1.108 3, 1.108 10, 1.108 11, 1.108 11, 1.108 12, 1.108 27, 1.109 13, 1.109 21, 1.109 24, 1.111 1, 1.111 18, 1.112 22, 1.113 15, 1.113 16, 1.113 17, 1.113 18, 1.113 19, 1.113 22, 1.113 23, 1.113 24, 1.113 25, 1.113 26, 1.114 1, 1.114 6, 1.114 12, 1.114 14, 1.114 14, 1.114 15, 1.114 17, 1.114 21, 1.114 22, 1.115 3, 1.115 7, 1.115 9, 1.117 3, 1.118 2, 1.118 25, 1.119 6, 1.119 14, 1.123 3, 1.123 15, 1.123 21, 1.123 29, 1.123 30, 1.128 1(*bis*), 1.128 2, 1.128 7, 1.128 7, 1.128 9, 1.128 13, 1.128 16, 1.133 17, 1.148 2, 1.148 8, 1.148 23, 1.148 25, 1.148 40, 1.148 43, 1.151 11, 1.153 6, 1.157 5, 1.162 1, 1.162 7(?), 1.162 12, 1.162 16, 1.164 7, 1.169 13, 1.169 13, 1.172 17, 1.174 1, 1.176 14, 2.23 22, 2.31 61, 2.42 8, 4.15 1, 4.63 II 41, 4.86 12, 4.149 17, 4.149 19, 4.341 5, 4.377 19, 4.610 30, 7.164 8

il 1.21 II 8 lg. <dn>il?

il[1.1 IV 18, 1.3 IV 54, 1.4 VII 5, 1.5 III 29, 1.14 I 5, 1.31 2, 1.67 21, 1.94 24, 1.123 18, 1.126 17, 1.137 2, 1.148 10, 1.157 9, 4.253 1, 4.405 9, 4.469 3, 4.583 5, 4.607 15, 4.609 16, 4.633 3, 4.732 2, 4.746 10, 4.763 4, 7.92 1, 7.104 2, 7.149 1

i[l 1.1 III 23, 1.1 IV 20, 1.2 III 5, 1.3 V 10, 1.16 V 10, 1.40 25, 1.49 2, 1.107 38, 1.152 4, 7.136 5

i[l(m) 7.164 4

]il 1.19 IV 57, 1.20 I 8, 1.41 11, 1.53 8, 1.83 2, 1.117 3, 4.155 4, 4.460 5, 4.635 5, 4.700 1, 4.701 13, 7.134 1

i]l 1.2 III 4, 1.2 III 17, 1.3 IV 19, 1.4 I 5, 1.4 IV 48, 1.6 I 33, 1.17 I 35, 1.46 6, 1.65 19, 1.113 20, 1.117 6

ilx[1.157 6, 4.64 IV 16, 4.200 11

i\l 1.24 44f

]i/hl 4.439 2

il/y[4.699 4

ila 1.19 IV 57

ilabn 4.226 3

ilak 1.4 VII 45, 2.21 11, 2.30 20, 2.42 21, 2.75 9

ilakk 2.31 44

ilan 1.42 7

il<i>b 1.130 9

ilib 1.47 2, 1.74 1, 1.91 5, 1.109 12, 1.109 15, 1.109 19, 1.109 35, 1.118 1, 1.138 2, 1.148 10, 1.148 23, 1.162 3, 1.162 6, 1.164 3, 1.164 6, 4.727 13

ilib[1.56 3, 1.56 5

ili[b 1.87 38

i[l]ib 1.41 35
i]lib 1.139 2
il]ib 1.130 27
ilibh 1.17 I 26
i]libh 1.17 I 44
iliby 1.17 II 16
]i/hlh/iṯdrn 7.23 4
ilb 1.128 14
ilb/d[4.593 9
ilbd 4.783 7
ilbʿl 4.261 21, 4.340 6, 4.377 7, 4.410 10, 4.609 3, 4.754 14, 4.775 17
ilbʿl[4.75 V 12
ilb[ʿl 4.381 22, 4.583 2
ilg 4.751 11
ilgdn 4.277 13
ilgn 4.63 I 34
ilgt 4.277 2
ild 1.42 7, 1.110 3, 1.111 4, 1.111 9, 1.116 13
ild[4.69 V 25
il]d 1.60 1(!)
ilb/d[4.593 9
il.dbḥ 1.1 IV 28
ildgn 4.63 III 9, 4.607 17, 4.609 20
ildy 4.130 3, 4.635 33
ildy[4.617 20
il.dm 1.125 1
il.dn 1.128 16
ildn 4.775 6
ilḏ 4.96 12
ilh 1.41 14, 1.108 13, 3.7 4
ilh[4.194 11
i]lh 1.39 5, 1.41 30
ilhd 4.63 I 7, 4.63 III 33, 4.609 7, 5.18 3, 5.18 7
i]lhd 5.18 1
ilhm 1.39 3, 1.39 5, 1.39 5, 1.39 9, 1.41 12, 1.87 16, 1.87 33
ilh[m 1.41 18, 1.87 30
il[hm 1.41 28, 1.87 33
i]lhm 1.41 14
ilhnm 4.182 1
ilht 1.3 V 28, 1.4 VI 48, 1.4 VI 50, 1.4 VI 52, 1.4 VI 54, 1.16 IV 8, 1.16 IV 12, 1.24 11, 1.25 2
ilh[t 1.24 40
i]lht 1.16 IV 4
]i/hlh/iṯdrn 7.23 4
ilwn 4.83 4
ilwn\y 1.128 17f
ilz 1.136 11
ilḥu 1.16 I 46, 1.16 I 58, 1.16 II 33
ilḥbn 4.63 III 44
ilḥm 1.5 I 20, 1.16 VI 18
ilḥmn 2.82 20
ily 2.16 4, 3.10 22, 4.63 II 22, 4.347 5, 4.625 22
ily[4.227 II 11, 4.334 3, 4.432 21, 4.488 2, 4.583 1
i\ly 5.18 3f
ilyy 4.244 24, 4.791 18
ilym 4.116 13
ilyn 3.3 11, 4.63 II 47, 4.229 11, 4.232 3, 4.232 37, 4.277 6, 4.340 1, 4.607 18, 4.759 9, 4.769 6
]ilyn 4.772 4, 4.785 28
ilysx[4.678 1
ilyqn 4.607 24
ilk 4.153 1
ilk 6.66 2 lg. ilr!mh 6.66 2
ilk 1.1 II 13 lg. idk
ilkšy 4.617 9
ill 1.128 14, 4.214 II 8
illay 1.69 16
illḏr 2.24 3
illḏrm 4.361 2, 4.362 1, 4.607 22
illm 4.93 IV 24
illsx[1.70 10
il<m> 1.6 III 24
ilm 1.1 III 19, 1.1 IV 6, 1.2 I 18, 1.2 I 20, 1.2 I 22, 1.2 I 23, 1.2 I 24, 1.2 I 26, 1.2 I 27, 1.2 I 29, 1.2 I 34, 1.2 I 37, 1.2 III 15, 1.2 III 19, 1.3 III 32, 1.3 III 43, 1.3 III 45, 1.3 IV 32, 1.3 IV 34, 1.3 V 3, 1.3 V 17, 1.3 V 20, 1.3 V 38, 1.4 I 22, 1.4 III 9, 1.4 III 14, 1.4 III 26, 1.4 III 30, 1.4 III 35, 1.4 IV 51, 1.4 V 1, 1.4 V 3, 1.4 VI 47, 1.4 VI 49, 1.4 VI 51, 1.4 VI 53, 1.4 VI 55, 1.4 VII 6, 1.4 VII 46, 1.4 VII 50, 1.4 VII 51, 1.4 VIII 15, 1.4 VIII 16, 1.4 VIII 21, 1.4 VIII 24, 1.4 VIII 30, 1.4 VIII 44, 1.5 I 7, 1.5 I 9, 1.5 I 12, 1.5 II 8, 1.5 II 11, 1.5 II 13, 1.5 II 14, 1.5 II 19, 1.5 II 20, 1.5 III 15, 1.5 III 20, 1.5 V 6, 1.5 V 16, 1.6 I 9, 1.6 I 11, 1.6 I 13, 1.6 I 18, 1.6 I

31, 1.6 II 13, 1.6 II 24, 1.6 II 25, 1.6 II 31, 1.6 IV 8, 1.6 IV 17, 1.6 V 9, 1.6 VI 7, 1.6 VI 9, 1.6 VI 24, 1.6 VI 30, 1.6 VI 48, 1.7 39, 1.8 II 2, 1.8 II 4, 1.12 I 28, 1.15 II 7, 1.15 II 11, 1.15 III 17, 1.15 III 18, 1.16 I 22, 1.16 II 43, 1.16 V 11, 1.16 V 16, 1.16 V 19, 1.16 V 20, 1.16 V 22, 1.17 I 2, 1.17 I 12, 1.17 I 21, 1.17 V 20, 1.17 V 29, 1.18 I 7, 1.19 III 6, 1.19 III 35, 1.19 IV 23, 1.19 IV 29, 1.19 IV 47, 1.19 IV 49, 1.20 II 9, 1.22 I 13, 1.23 1, 1.23 13, 1.23 19, 1.23 23, 1.23 28, 1.23 67, 1.24 25, 1.39 22, 1.41 6, 1.43 2, 1.43 8, 1.43 23, 1.43 24, 1.47 29, 1.53 5, 1.53 6, 1.82 42, 1.87 6, 1.103 41, 1.103 56, 1.104 2, 1.104 21, 1.105 26, 1.106 2, 1.107 2, 1.112 6, 1.112 8, 1.114 2, 1.114 3, 1.117 5, 1.118 28, 1.123 1, 1.123 32, 1.124 2, 1.128 12, 1.132 15, 1.132 21, 1.132 24, 1.133 2, 1.133 15, 1.139 17, 1.147 12, 1.148 9, 1.176 16, 1.176 20, 1.176 22, 2.4 20, 2.10 12, 2.11 7, 2.13 7, 2.14 4, 2.31 46, 2.34 3, 2.38 4, 2.44 4, 2.46 4, 2.63 5, 2.70 6, 2.71 4, 2.75 6, 4.149 1, 4.280 14, 4.284 6, 5.9 I 2

ilm[1.5 III 14, 1.19 III 21, 2.6 5, 2.7 10, 4.381 15

il[m 1.23 29, 1.106 8, 1.134 4, 2.30 6

i[lm 1.4 IV 32, 1.4 VI 16, 1.90 8, 1.123 31

i[l(m) 7.164 4

]ilm 1.17 I 6, 1.25 2, 7.37 2

i]lm 1.3 V 9, 1.17 I 9, 1.23 58, 1.107 51, 1.123 33, 2.21 5, 2.68 9

i]l[m 1.2 III 2

il]m 1.17 I 12, 2.4 4

ilmxxkl 4.391 13

ilmd 4.350 15, 4.354 3

ilmhr 4.63 I 9, 4.631 18, 4.775 10

ilmy 1.23 60

i]lmk 4.98 24

ilmlk 1.6 VI 54, 1.16 VI 59, 4.115 9, 4.133 2, 4.165 13, 4.261 10, 4.382 28, 4.607 16, 4.616 2, 4.659 8

ilml[k 4.386 11

i]lmlk 5.18 9

ilmn 4.141 I 13

]ilmn[4.658 26

iln 1.91 17, 1.112 30, 4.215 5, 4.350 11, 4.382 21, 4.609 21

iln[2.29 2

]iln 4.25 3, 7.30 5

]ilnx[1.75 5

ilnḥm 4.785 16

ilnym 1.3 IV 35, 1.6 VI 47, 1.20 I 2, 1.21 II 4

iln[ym 1.20 II 2

il[nym 1.22 II 6

i[ln]y[m 1.22 II 26

i[lnym 1.20 II 6, 1.21 II 12

[iln]\ym 1.22 II 13f(!)

ilnm 1.19 I 10

ilnnn 4.631 20

ilnqsd 4.715 24

ils 4.309 6

ilsk 4.102 8, 4.723 1

i]lsk 4.64 II 10

ilˁnt 4.617 43, 4.623 11

ilˁn[t 4.607 14

ilṣdq 4.215 4, 4.226 9, 4.628 1, 4.704 6

ilṣy 4.103 47

ilṣy[4.607 13

ilqṣm 1.4 V 17, 1.4 V 40

ilr[4.432 4, 4.574 6

]ilr[4.599 3

ilrb 3.3 11, 4.63 III 41, 4.63 IV 15

ilrm 4.607 19, 4.769 9

ilrˈmh 6.66 2(!)

ilrpi 4.347 7

ilrš 4.75 IV 10, 4.366 11, 4.371 2, 4.775 18

ilršp 4.313 5, 5.18 5

ilš 1.16 IV 3, 1.16 IV 6, 1.16 IV 7, 1.16 IV 11, 1.87 7, 4.232 17, 4.781 2

il[š 1.16 IV 3, 1.16 IV 10

ilšḥr 4.110 15

ilšlm 3.8 19, 4.382 27

ilšmḥ 4.781 8

ilšn 4.79 3, 4.609 36

ilšpš 4.65 12, 4.131 11, 4.219 6, 4.384 14, 4.425 13, 4.611 16, 4.775 21

ilšp[š 4.680 4

]ilšp[š 2.28 2 lg.]i l šp[š?

ilštmˁ 1.79 7, 1.80 1, 4.68 29, 4.110

1, 4.365 21, 4.369 14, 4.380 21, 4.382 26, 4.382 33, 4.610 15, 4.629 10, 4.693 19, 4.698 1, 4.750 9

ilštm[ʿ 4.685 9

]il[štmʿ 4.119 1

ilšt<m>ʿy 4.51 8

ilštmʿy 4.33 29, 4.33 30, 4.33 31, 4.181 7, 4.281 25

ilšt[mʿy 4.86 25, 4.86 26, 4.86 28

ilštmʿym 4.45 1, 4.124 3

ilšt[mʿy(m) 4.79 1

i{.}lt 1.4 I 7

ilt 1.3 II 18, 1.3 V 37, 1.4 IV 49, 1.6 I 40, 1.14 IV 35, 1.14 IV 39, 1.15 III 26, 1.39 11, 1.39 11, 1.41 24, 1.50 4, 1.67 6, 1.81 8, 1.81 21, 1.112 25, 1.117 4, 4.35 I 19

ilt[1.1 IV 14, 1.81 5, 4.512 3

il[t 1.50 2

i[lt 1.87 26

i]lt 1.81 12

iltḥm 2.49 9, 4.63 II 5, 4.180 6, 4.366 5, 4.366 12, 4.371 13, 4.690 8

il]tḥm 4.398 8

i]ltḥm[4.674 1

iltm 1.39 18, 1.102 13, 4.86 16

iltr[4.760 6

ilṯr 4.607 32

ilṯtmr 4.103 11

im 1.3 I 26, 1.6 V 21, 1.69 10, 2.15 8, 2.72 12, 2.72 13, 2.72 13, 2.72 20, 4.17 3

im[1.4 II 42

]im 1.2 III 22

]xim 4.373 3

imḫṣ 1.2 II 8, 1.19 IV 34

imḫṣh 1.19 I 14, 1.19 I 15

imm[1.70 18, 1.70 37

imnm 1.64 24

imr 1.1 IV 32, 1.3 V 1, 1.4 VI 43, 1.4 VIII 18, 1.6 II 22, 1.14 II 14, 1.14 III 56, 1.16 VI 17, 1.16 VI 20, 1.17 V 17, 1.17 V 22, 1.22 I 14, 1.86 16, 1.119 10, 1.131 5

im[r 1.14 II 13

]i/hmr 7.46 5

imrh 1.6 II 8, 1.6 II 29

]imr[n 4.542 2

imrt 4.75 III 10, 4.713 5

imt 1.5 I 18, 1.5 I 18, 1.5 I 19, 1.73 3

imtḫṣ 1.3 III 46

in 1.2 III 19, 1.2 III 22, 1.3 V 28, 1.3 V 33, 1.3 V 38, 1.4 IV 44, 1.4 IV 50, 1.10 II 4, 1.14 III 38, 1.14 VI 22, 1.16 V 16, 1.16 V 19, 1.16 V 22(!), 1.17 I 18, 1.19 II 27, 1.19 III 11, 1.19 III 11, 1.19 III 25, 1.19 III 25, 1.42 1, 1.42 3, 1.42 4, 1.42 54, 1.42 55, 1.42 55, 1.50 8, 1.60 6, 1.64 30, 1.64 30, 1.67 8, 1.67 8, 1.70 28, 1.82 2, 1.103 4, 1.103 7, 1.103 9, 1.103 10, 1.103 12, 1.103 14, 1.103 15, 1.103 26, 1.103 27, 1.103 28, 1.103 30, 1.103 31, 1.103 35, 1.103 37, 1.103 59, 1.110 1, 1.110 2, 1.110 9, 1.111 3, 1.111 5, 1.111 8, 1.111 11, 1.116 5(!*bis*), 1.116 6, 1.116 15, 1.116 16, 1.120 4, 1.124 16, 1.125 6, 1.125 7, 1.128 6, 1.132 18, 1.132 22, 1.176 9, 2.10 9, 3.2 18, 3.5 21, 4.136 5, 4.180 1, 7.43 7, 7.55 7

in[1.26 2, 1.67 15, 2.39 32, 2.73 9, 4.393 7, 7.1 3, 7.114 5, 7.130 1, 7.130 5

i[n 1.18 I 16, 1.103 6, 1.103 16, 1.103 52, 1.103 53, 1.103 55, 1.125 6

]in 4.643 10

i]n 1.2 III 14, 1.132 4, 4.298 1

]in[1.26b 4(!)

]i/hn 1.52 24

]i/hn[1.34 4

inbb 1.3 IV 34, 1.13 9, 1.13 32

]in{.}bb 1.1 II 14

inbbh 1.100 20

inḏ 1.42 39, 1.42 60, 1.42 61, 1.148 14, 1.148 15, 1.149 2

inḏr 1.128 4

in.ḏr 1.128 6

inḫzzy 1.116 5 lg. in ḫzzy

]i/hny 4.34 3

inm 2.82 10

inmṯy 1.116 5 lg. in mṯy

inn 2.39 20, 2.72 12, 3.4 16, 4.53 1, 4.145 7, 4.214 I 4, 4.379 1

innm 2.73 11

inr 1.16 I 2, 1.16 I 16, 1.16 II 39, 1.114 13, 4.715 4, 4.723 16

in[r 4.229 4

inš 1.39 22, 1.41 27, 1.46 8, 1.90 7, 1.105 26, 1.106 2, 1.123 31, 1.132 21, 1.132 24, 1.171 5, 1.173 7
in[š 1.112 5
i[nš 1.87 44
]inš 1.134 4
i]nš 1.87 6
i\nš 1.132 14f
inšk 2.81 7
inšr 4.110 10
inšt 1.6 VI 41, 4.38 5, 4.47 5, 4.99 3, 4.416 9
i]nšt 4.610 48
inṯt 1.116 11, 1.116 12
is 4.12 7, 4.123 8, 4.412 II 16
isg 4.83 3
isʿ 3.9 10
isp 1.107 44
]isp 1.107 33, 1.107 36
]isp[7.65 2
ispa 1.6 V 20
ispi 1.5 I 5
isr[1.8 II 13
]isrnn 1.61 4
iġyn 4.69 II 16
iġlyn 4.631 17
iġlkḏ 4.607 23
i/a]ġlṯr 4.428 5
iġr 2.33 13
ipd/b[4.594 5
ipd 1.5 V 2, 4.275 3, 4.707 13, 4.780 1, 4.780 3, 4.780 4, 4.780 7
ip[d 1.5 V 24, 1.136 1
i]pd 1.136 2
ipd/b[4.594 5
ipdk 1.5 I 5
ipd]k 1.5 I 31
ipdm 1.136 10, 4.707 22, 4.780 2
iph 2.25 4
iph[1.10 II 32
iphn 2.31 39
ipn 1.44 3, 1.131 5
ipt[4.289 3
iptt 4.707 11
ipṯ 4.734 5
ipṯl 4.125 11, 4.213 19, 4.215 2, 4.618 7, 4.625 13
ipṯ[l 4.182 25
i]pṯl 4.618 25
ip]ṯl 4.397 5
]ipṯl[4.522 1
ipṯn[4.84 4
iṣr 1.101 4
iṣ[r 1.160 1
iqḥ 1.14 IV 41
iqni 1.14 III 43, 1.14 VI 29, 3.1 28, 3.1 30, 3.1 32, 4.168 1, 4.182 6, 4.182 7, 4.182 8, 4.203 5, 4.778 14, 4.779 6
iq[ni 4.782 20
i]qni 4.182 31
iqn]i 3.1 38, 4.182 15, 4.182 18, 4.182 21
iqnim 1.4 V 19, 1.4 V 35
iqni[m 1.4 VII 1
i]qnim 1.1 II 5
i]qn[i]m 4.341 4
iq\nim 1.24 21f
iqnu 1.23 21, 3.1 23, 4.182 12, 4.182 16, 4.182 39, 4.247 28, 4.738 5, 4.778 17, 4.782 26
iq[nu 4.182 37
i[qnu 4.182 23
]iqnu 4.182 20
iqra 1.23 1
iqra 1.21 II 2 lg. iqra\[km
iqrakm 1.21 II 10
iqra\[km 1.21 II 2(!)
iqr[akm 1.22 II 4
i[qrakm 1.22 II 9
iqran 1.23 23
ir[4.619 6, 4.734 13, 7.42 1
]ir 4.401 17, 4.619 8
irx[1.68 28, 4.64 IV 11, 4.118 5, 4.619 4
]xir 4.258 12
irab 4.48 9
ir]ab 4.553 2
irb[7.130 4
irby 1.14 II 50, 1.14 IV 29
irbym 1.3 II 10
irbl 4.200 10
irbn 4.76 1, 4.355 34
irbṣ 4.122 1
irbṣ[4.788 6
irb[ṣ 4.358 5
ir[bṣ 4.125 15
irbt 1.69 3

irbtn 4.7 17
irgy 4.232 10
irgmn 4.181 1
irgm[n 4.390 12
irgn 4.129 9
irdyn 4.631 16
iry 1.87 61
iryn 4.35 I 21, 4.93 IV 16, 4.103 40, 4.229 6
iryn[4.512 1
irm 4.399 5
irn 1.103 33, 4.281 16
]i/hrn 1.12 I 7
irġn 1.72 23, 1.85 17, 1.85 28
irġ[n 1.72 34
ir]ġn 1.71 15
irpbn 4.187 2, 4.769 12
irpm 4.123 20
irpn 4.399 2
irpṯr 4.631 20
irṣ[4.382 35
irrṯrm 2.33 2 lg. iwrṯrm?
irš 1.17 VI 26, 1.17 VI 27
irš[1.62 2, 4.679 2
i]rš 1.17 VI 17
iršy 4.338 6
i]ršy 4.646 2
iršyn 4.69 II 12, 4.93 IV 19, 4.340 5
iršn 1.163 10, 4.77 17
iršpn 1.42 42
iršt 4.218 7, 4.626 1, 5.9 I 7
iršt[1.104 1
]iršt 2.22 4
irštk 2.41 16
iršt\[k] 1.108 20f
irt 1.22 I 25
irth 1.3 III 5, 1.5 V 25, 1.101 17
]i<r>tḥṣ 1.55 3
irty 1.6 III 19, 1.17 II 13
irtk 1.4 V 5, 1.18 I 19
irtm 1.2 IV 3
iš[4.235 2, 4.617 1, 7.68 3
iš/ḏ[4.69 V 21
išal 2.34 28
išalhm 2.32 4
išbʿl 4.617 35, 4.785 18
išbʿl[4.623 8
išdh 1.101 6
išdym 1.45 9
išdk 1.1 II 2, 1.3 III 20, 1.3 IV 12
iš[dk 1.1 III 11
išd]k 1.1 II 23
i[š]dn 4.769 58(!)
išḫn 1.161 18, 1.161 18
išḫrd 1.116 21
išḫry 4.149 13
iš[ḫry 1.119 14
išyy 4.7 20
i/h/pški/pr[4.53 16
išlḥ 1.14 V 21, 1.24 21
išm 1.106 30
išqb 1.1 V 19
išryt 1.22 I 19
išryt[1.18 I 28
iš[ryt 1.45 1
iš<t> 1.12 I 10
išt 1.2 I 32, 1.2 III 13, 1.3 III 45, 1.4 II 8, 1.4 VI 22, 1.4 VI 25, 1.4 VI 30, 1.4 VI 32, 1.6 II 33, 1.6 V 14, 1.23 14, 1.23 41, 1.23 44, 1.23 48, 1.48 8, 1.88 2
]išt 1.2 III 13
i]št 1.4 VI 27
ištir 1.18 IV 15, 4.290 3
i]štir 2.72 42
ištbm 1.3 III 40
ištynh 1.4 III 16
ištm 1.2 I 32, 1.3 III 40
ištmʿ 1.16 VI 42
ištm[ʿ 1.16 VI 29, 1.93 4
ištn 2.79 3, 5.9 I 16
ištnm 4.149 3
ištql 1.100 72
ištr 1.67 15
ištrmy 3.4 8
ištš 2.3 22
išttk 1.12 II 57
i<š>ttk 1.12 II 56
it 1.64 31, 1.66 31
]i/ht 4.22 6
itbd 1.14 I 8(!)
itbnnk 1.169 17
itg 1.42 18
itdb 1.14 I 8 lg. itbd
itḏnn 1.42 13
itḫm 1.66 3
itlk 1.6 II 15
]i/htm 4.210 3

itml 1.119 19
itn 2.15 4, 4.616 9
itnny 1.100 74
itnnk 1.100 76
its 1.2 IV 4
itp[p 1.18 I 33
itrḫ 1.23 64
itrṯ 1.3 III 47
iṯ 1.3 III 21, 1.6 III 3, 1.6 III 9, 1.6 III 21, 1.17 I 20, 1.18 I 18, 1.19 III 4, 1.19 III 19, 1.19 III 33, 1.19 III 33, 1.19 III 39, 1.19 III 39, 1.23 74, 1.41 55, 1.101 8, 2.39 34, 2.70 29, 2.73 18, 2.81 9, 4.296 1, 4.422 1, 4.616 11, 4.752 1
iṯ[1.19 III 19, 1.23 72
i[ṯ 1.19 III 4, 4.492 1
]iṯ 6.51 1, 7.75 2
]xiṯ[1.107 4
iṯb 4.219 15
iṯb[4.220 6
iṯ]bnm 4.182 19
iṯg 4.720 4
iṯk[7.68 2
iṯl 1.1 II 9, 1.18 IV 25, 1.19 II 39, 1.19 II 44
iṯm 1.5 III 24, 1.148 31
iṯmh 1.108 14
iṯp 1.149 3
iṯr 2.15 6
iṯrm 1.16 VI 18
iṯt 1.14 IV 38, 2.13 15, 2.30 14
iṯt[4.651 4
iṯtbnm 4.269 30
iṯtb[nm 4.609 1
iṯtb]nm 4.387 13
iṯtl 5.9 I 1, 5.9 IV 3
iṯt[l 4.556 2
iṯtqb 1.105 9
iṯtr[4.754 18
el 1.128 1 *sub* il

U

u 1.4 VII 43(*bis*), 1.9 13, 1.15 III 29, 1.16 I 4, 1.16 I 18, 1.16 I 22, 1.16 II 41, 1.16 II 43, 1.18 IV 26(!), 1.23 63, 1.23 64, 1.40 19, 1.40 22(*bis*), 1.40 23, 1.40 28, 1.40 30, 1.40 31(*ter*), 1.40 32, 1.40 36, 1.40 39, 1.40 39(!), 1.40 40, 1.67 16, 1.67 22, 1.69 9, 1.79 5, 1.79 7, 1.119 13(*bis*), 1.121 1, 1.121 2, 1.121 10, 1.161 12, 1.161 26, 1.169 5, 1.169 18(!), 2.23 2, 2.34 12, 2.36 15, 2.82 7, 5.4 5, 5.5 1, 5.6 3, 5.12 4, 5.13 9, 5.14 19, 5.15 3, 5.16 4, 5.17 3, 5.17 6, 5.19 4, 5.20 2, 5.20 3, 5.21 2
u[1.42 21, 1.126 14, 2.3 6, 4.243 9, 4.254 6, 4.262 8, 4.357 11, 4.395 1, 4.616 8, 7.130 2
]u 1.6 VI 8, 4.58 1, 4.619 10, 7.136 5
ux[1.103 33, 4.10 6
]xu 1.6 VI 42, 4.326 10, 4.619 11
uxmxx 4.377 32
u/d[1.69 8
]u/d[7.114 7
u/dx[4.396 7
u/d/b[4.654 2
u/d/l[4.44 16, 4.389 13
]u/d/l 1.35 7, 1.42 22
]ub[7.79 2
ub/d[4.629 1
uba 1.100 72
ubu 1.169 18 lg. u bu
ubdit 4.12 14
ubdy 4.7 1, 4.103 1, 4.110 1, 4.244 7, 4.389 3, 4.389 4, 4.389 7, 4.389 8, 4.389 9, 4.631 1, 4.692 1
ubdy[4.39 1
ubd[y 4.702 6
u]bdy 4.103 37, 4.103 39, 4.103 41, 4.103 44
ub]dy 4.103 7, 4.103 48
ubd]y 4.103 20
ubdym 4.164 3, 4.244 9, 4.309 1
ubd[ym 4.244 10
ubyn 4.93 IV 11, 4.399 12, 4.645 4, 4.728 5
ubyn[4.84 2
ubr/kš 4.611 17
ubl 1.42 3
ub[l 1.2 III 14
ubln 4.223 1
ubl[n 4.223 2
]ubln 4.57 4
ubn 4.7 6, 4.71 III 3, 4.98 5, 4.103 5, 4.115 4, 4.131 5, 4.141 II 8, 4.148 2, 4.165 15, 4.344 2, 4.609 9, 4.704 4, 4.723 7, 6.18 3
ubn[4.494 2
ubnyn 1.80 2, 4.137 11, 4.348 19
ubś 4.621 10
ubś[4.68 38
]ubś 4.302 8
ubs 4.693 49, 4.783 2, 4.783 4
ubr 4.371 19, 4.617 16
ubr/kš 4.611 17
ubrʿ 4.288 4
ubr[ʿ 4.693 11
ubrʿy 2.26 12, 4.27 15, 4.63 III 1, 4.68 28, 4.96 10, 4.100 1, 4.124 8, 4.375 12, 4.380 20, 4.610 14, 4.777 2
ubrʿy[4.685 8
ubr[ʿ(y) 4.622 2
ubr[ʿy 4.27 4
u]brʿy 4.33 18, 4.382 20
ub]rʿy 4.33 19
ubrʿym 4.616 7
ubr[ʿym 4.50 2
ubrʿn 4.110 3
ubrš 4.41 12, 4.214 III 3, 4.290 7
u]brš 4.769 34
u/d/lg 4.86 18
]xu/lgx[4.315 7
ugr 1.3 III 36, 1.4 VII 54, 1.4 VIII 47, 1.5 I 12, 1.8 II 7, 4.52 8, 4.54 11, 4.244 17
ugrm 1.12 I 25
]ugr<t> 1.40 26
ugrt 1.4 VIII 49, 1.6 VI 57, 1.40 10, 1.40 26, 1.40 35, 1.40 36, 1.42 11,

1.65 11, 1.84 1, 1.87 38, 1.105 6, 1.108 26, 1.109 11, 1.109 16, 1.109 36, 1.112 23, 1.119 2(?), 1.119 10(!), 1.119 12, 1.119 22, 1.131 9, 1.161 33, 2.3 7, 2.16 5, 2.19 7, 2.19 8, 2.20 2, 2.21 9, 2.35 17, 2.36 16, 2.38 1, 2.44 1, 2.46 2, 2.81 18, 3.1 25, 3.2 4, 3.4 11, 3.5 4, 4.141 III 8, 4.339 1, 4.355 30, 4.609 37, 4.709 3, 4.750 8, 6.23 3, 6.29 4, 6.75 3, 7.43 4, 7.63 3

ugrt[1.27 4, 1.119 3, 7.46 6

ugr[t 1.121 7, 1.130 26, 2.36 19, 2.59 2, 3.1 14

ug[rt 1.27 1, 1.109 34

u[g]rt 1.41 35

u[grt 1.40 2, 1.130 10, 1.130 24, 2.21 2

]ugrt 1.84 34, 7.162 3

u]grt 1.139 8

ugr]t 1.46 16

ug]rt[4.17 18

ugrtw[1.125 7

ugrty 4.33 8, 4.33 9, 4.750 3

ugrtym 2.81 27, 2.81 28

ugrtn 4.715 26

ud 3.10 1

ub/d[4.629 1

ul/dx[1.67 9

udasrp 1.66 2

udbr[4.248 4, 4.312 5

ud[br 4.312 9

udh 2.36 8

udm 1.14 III 4, 1.14 III 5, 1.14 III 30, 1.14 III 30, 1.14 III 31, 1.14 IV 47, 1.14 IV 48, 1.14 VI 11, 1.14 VI 12, 4.693 7

u[dm 1.14 VI 11

udmym 4.337 15, 4.394 5(?)

udmm 1.15 I 7

udmʿt 1.6 I 10, 1.16 I 28, 1.45 11

udmʿth 1.14 I 28, 1.161 16

udn 1.16 VI 42, 1.18 IV 23, 1.18 IV 34, 1.103 35, 1.103 37

ud[n 1.19 II 30

udnh 1.3 IV 2

u\[dnh] 1.6 VI 3f

udnk 1.13 23

udr 1.4 V 17, 1.4 V 40

udt 4.152 3

uḏn 1.149 1, 4.90 9

uḏnd 1.125 17

uḏn[d 1.116 27

uḏr 2.33 20, 4.769 18

uḏrh 2.30 15

uḏrn 4.428 8

uḏrn[4.86 13

uḏrnn 3.9 19

uwaḫ 4.364 7

uwil 4.75 II 8

uwyṯm 1.52 9, 1.52 11

u[wyṯm 1.52 13

uwln 1.128 19

uz 1.106 30, 4.247 20, 4.247 22, 4.296 5, 4.296 6

uzm 4.129 1, 4.247 21

uzʿrt 1.101 6

uzr 1.17 I 7, 1.17 I 9, 1.17 I 10, 1.17 I 11, 1.17 I 12

]uzr 1.17 I 2

uz]r 1.17 I 13

uzry 4.103 58

uzrm 1.17 I 21, 1.17 I 22

uḫ 4.643 13

uḫ<d> 4.635 5

uḫd 1.82 6, 1.82 14, 4.635 4, 4.635 9

uḫh 4.80 10, 4.759 4

uḫy 2.4 18, 2.41 20

u]ḫy 2.41 22

uḫl 4.723 11

uḫn 4.244 13, 4.393 10, 4.619 4

uḫn[4.39 7

uḫnp 1.91 34, 4.348 5, 4.355 14, 4.380 32, 4.610 7, 4.693 22, 4.777 7

uḫnp[4.27 2

]uḫnp 4.661 3

]uḫnp[4.414 5

uḫnpy 4.658 10

uḫn[p(y) 4.629 4

uḫry 1.12 II 27, 1.19 III 49, 1.19 III 56, 1.19 IV 7

uḫr\y 1.103 39f

uḫryt 1.17 VI 35

uṭ 1.2 I 13

uṭbm 4.337 11

uṭm 1.5 I 5, 1.18 IV 3

uṭpt 4.624 7

uy 2.3 13

uk 2.39 6, 2.39 8

uky 2.23 5
ul 1.14 II 35
ul[1.14 IV 15
]ul[1.66 25
ul/dx[1.67 9
]u/b/dṣ/l[7.79 4
ulb 4.281 13, 4.628 2
ulby 4.309 2
ulbt[4.383 3
ulbtyn 4.280 4
uldy 4.309 18
]ulh 1.5 V 24
ulkn 1.161 4
ull 4.68 19, 4.244 12
ully 2.81 14, 4.101 5, 4.245 II 5
ullym 4.70 6
ulm 1.79 3, 3.7 5, 3.7 6, 3.7 16, 4.27 20, 4.177 6, 4.213 10, 4.254 4, 4.307 2, 4.348 3, 4.365 7, 4.375 10, 4.380 7, 4.384 4, 4.625 4, 7.42 3, 7.42 5
ulm[4.160 10, 4.725 6
ul[m 4.160 6, 4.566 3, 4.566 4
u[lm 4.27 9
]ulm 4.618 26, 4.643 24
u]lm 4.63 I 1, 4.618 9
ul]m 4.784 8
u]lmx[4.414 8
ulmy 4.63 I 19, 4.339 5
ulmk 4.307 16
ulmn 1.23 9
uln 4.7 16, 4.63 I 39, 4.63 II 7, 4.63 II 8, 4.232 13, 4.778 2, 4.782 3
u[l]n 4.63 II 17
ulnhr 4.112 II 4
ulny 1.2 IV 5
ulġ[1.66 6, 1.66 7, 1.66 10
ulġn[1.66 18
ulp 1.40 3, 1.40 20, 1.40 20, 1.40 20, 1.40 21, 1.40 21, 1.40 21, 1.40 28, 1.40 29, 1.40 29, 1.40 29, 1.40 29, 1.40 30, 1.40 30, 1.40 36, 1.40 37, 1.40 37, 1.40 37, 1.40 38, 1.40 38, 1.40 38, 1.66 19, 1.66 33, 1.84 4, 1.84 15
ulp[1.154 5
ul[p 1.40 29, 1.40 37, 1.121 11, 1.154 3, 1.154 4
u[lp 1.40 4, 1.66 11, 1.66 26, 1.154 1, 1.154 2
u]lp 1.40 20, 1.40 38, 1.84 5, 1.84 16
u]l[p 1.154 6
ulpm 4.412 III 2
ulrm 4.759 6
ult̠ 1.4 IV 60, 4.390 7
um 1.14 I 9, 1.14 I 15, 1.19 III 29, 1.23 33, 1.23 33, 1.82 9, 1.100 1, 1.100 2, 1.100 8, 1.100 14, 1.100 19, 1.100 30, 1.100 35, 1.100 40, 1.100 45, 1.100 51, 1.100 57, 2.16 10, 2.31 46, 4.351 1
u[m 1.100 25
]um 4.237 2
umx[4.405 4
u/d/lm[4.252 5
umam[1.69 9
umdym 4.394 5 lg. udmym?
u<m>h 1.100 14
umh 1.24 34, 1.100 2, 1.100 8, 1.100 19, 1.100 25, 1.100 30, 1.100 35, 1.100 40, 1.100 45, 1.100 51, 1.100 57
umhthm 1.15 I 6
umḫ 4.35 I 6
umḫy 4.692 11
umy 1.6 VI 11, 1.6 VI 15, 2.11 1, 2.13 2, 2.13 5, 2.13 6, 2.13 11, 2.16 2, 2.16 6, 2.16 18, 2.30 4, 2.30 21, 2.34 2, 2.34 6, 2.34 8, 2.72 4, 2.72 5, 2.72 18, 2.82 1, 4.96 8, 5.10 3
umy[2.72 34
u[m]y 2.30 1, 2.30 5
u]my 2.30 9
u\[my] 2.72 42f
umm 1.70 25, 1.70 26, 1.70 28
ummt[4.64 V 4
umnd̠ 1.148 14
umt 1.14 I 6, 1.19 IV 40
umty 1.19 IV 35
umtk 1.6 IV 19
umtn 1.63 10, 1.131 12
un 1.5 VI 15, 1.19 I 40, 1.79 3
un[4.86 8
unil 1.17 II 8 lg. dnil
unk 5.11 3
unn 4.609 6, 4.615 4
unp 1.149 1, 4.281 10
unpt̠ 4.696 3
unr[4.161 4

unṯ 1.128 6, 1.128 7, 1.128 9, 2.19 2, 2.19 5, 3.5 20, 3.7 1, 4.86 4, 4.209 5, 4.209 7, 4.209 8, 4.209 9, 4.209 14, 4.209 15, 4.209 16, 4.209 17, 4.209 18, 4.209 19(!), 4.209 21, 4.209 22
unṯ[4.637 2
]unṯ 4.209 13
u]nṯ 3.2 18, 3.4 16, 4.209 10
un]ṯ 4.209 1, 4.209 11
unṯhm 3.4 19
unṯm 4.86 17
us 7.51 2
u/dsgr[1.64 3
usy 4.769 29
usyy 4.280 8
uss 4.658 18
usp 7.51 3
uġr 1.3 IV 34
updt 4.264 1
]yplṭ 4.638 2
upqt 1.1 V 11
u[pqt 1.2 III 9
]upqt 1.1 V 24
]u/b/dṣ/l[7.79 4
uṣb 4.93 IV 5
uṣbʿ[7.33 3
uṣ[bʿh 1.10 III 8 cor. uṣ[bʿth
uṣbʿ[t 1.15 V 16
uṣbʿ<t>h 1.19 I 8
uṣbʿth 1.2 IV 14, 1.2 IV 16, 1.2 IV 21, 1.2 IV 24, 1.3 II 33, 1.3 II 35, 1.4 IV 30, 1.14 III 54
uṣbʿth[1.101 15
uṣ[bʿth 1.10 III 8(cor.)
uṣb[ʿtk 1.14 II 11
]uq[7.112 1, 7.112 2
ur 1.10 I 11, 1.19 II 17, 1.19 II 24
ur[1.101 12
urx[1.104 23, 4.324 7, 4.635 13
urbt 1.4 V 61, 1.4 V 64, 1.4 VII 18, 1.4 VII 26, 1.109 19
ur[bt 1.4 VI 5, 1.171 6
u[rb]t 1.4 VI 8
u[rbt 1.41 11
u]rbt 1.82 25
urbtm 1.169 3
urgy 4.63 I 45
urgn 1.44 2
urḫ 4.131 2
uryy 4.12 8, 4.309 8
uryn 6.29 3
urk 2.23 20
urm 1.39 8, 1.76 12, 1.87 19, 1.119 13, 4.263 4
urmy 3.10 16, 4.791 11
urmn[7.42 6
urn 1.42 43, 4.90 5
urġnr 4.177 9
urġṯb 2.68 3, 4.410 30
urš[4.447 1
]urš[4.639 5
urt 4.617 44
urtn 4.115 2, 4.219 5, 4.337 4, 4.341 15
urt[n 4.332 3
uš[2.3 6
ušbš[1.2 III 11
ušbt[2.3 10
ušḫr 1.115 2, 1.131 1, 1.131 10
u<š>ḫr 1.115 12
]ušḫr[1.34 3
ušḫrd 1.60 12, 1.131 12, 1.135 10
]ušḫr[d 1.26b 3(!)
u[šḫrd 1.26 6(!)
ušḫry 1.39 13, 1.102 2, 1.118 23, 1.148 8, 4.168 10
uš[ḫr]y 1.81 22
u]šḫry 1.47 24
ušy 4.147 12
ušk 1.11 2
uškm 1.103 14
uškn 4.27 14, 4.119 5, 4.288 2, 4.296 16, 4.309 1, 4.365 19, 4.375 2, 4.380 18, 4.384 6, 4.693 17, 4.715 1, 4.750 6, 4.772 5, 4.777 5, 4.781 6
uškn[4.68 32, 4.685 6
ušk[n 4.27 3, 4.629 10
uškny 3.5 6, 3.10 5, 3.10 7, 4.33 22, 4.33 23, 4.33 24, 4.297 1, 4.339 13, 4.339 14, 4.386 12, 4.792 6
uškny[4.335 13
uš[kny 4.297 6
u]škny 4.33 21, 4.386 4
uš]kny 4.792 9
ušknym 4.261 13, 4.335 1
]ušknym 4.300 1
ušn 1.14 III 31, 1.14 VI 13
ušn[7.33 2

uššk 1.69 8
ušpġt 1.43 4, 1.92 26
ušpġtm 1.148 21
ušrh 1.103 47
ušry[n 4.75 II 9
uššk 1.67 21
uštyn 4.219 4
uštn 1.148 16
u/dt[4.631 22
utly 4.348 14
utllt 1.69 8
utṯb[1.70 16
uṯx[4.398 13
uṯḫt 1.47 31, 1.118 30
uṯkl 1.87 2
uṯpt 4.53 15, 4.145 7, 4.204 1, 4.204 2, 4.204 3, 4.204 4, 4.204 5, 4.204 6, 4.204 7, 4.204 8, 4.204 9, 4.204 10, 4.204 11, 4.204 12, 4.624 9
uṯp[t 4.670 2
u[ṯpt 4.624 4
u]ṯpt 4.624 3, 4.624 21
uṯp]t 4.624 23
uṯryn 3.1 30, 4.103 6
uṯryn[2.67 1
]uṯtx[1.68 18, 4.657 2

B

b 1.1 II 6, 1.1 II 14, 1.1 II 19, 1.1 III 2, 1.1 III 9, 1.1 III 28, 1.1 IV 4, 1.1 IV 7, 1.1 IV 8, 1.1 IV 10, 1.1 V 5, 1.1 V 6, 1.1 V 18, 1.1 V 26, 1.2 I 3, 1.2 I 6, 1.2 I 9, 1.2 I 24, 1.2 I 39, 1.2 I 43, 1.2 III 9, 1.2 III 11, 1.2 III 20(*bis*), 1.2 III 21, 1.2 IV 3(*bis*), 1.2 IV 6, 1.2 IV 14, 1.2 IV 16, 1.2 IV 21, 1.2 IV 24, 1.2 IV 28, 1.2 IV 32, 1.2 IV 38, 1.3 I 7, 1.3 I 11, 1.3 I 16, 1.3 I 17, 1.3 I 21, 1.3 II 5, 1.3 II 6, 1.3 II 13, 1.3 II 14(*bis*), 1.3 II 16, 1.3 II 19, 1.3 II 25, 1.3 II 26, 1.3 II 27, 1.3 II 28, 1.3 II 29, 1.3 II 31, 1.3 II 32, 1.3 II 34, 1.3 II 35, 1.3 III 2, 1.3 III 14, 1.3 III 15, 1.3 III 29, 1.3 III 30(*bis*), 1.3 III 31(*bis*), 1.3 IV 1, 1.3 IV 8, 1.3 IV 9, 1.3 IV 20, 1.3 IV 23, 1.3 IV 28, 1.3 IV 38, 1.3 IV 46, 1.3 V 11, 1.3 V 18, 1.3 V 21, 1.3 V 22, 1.3 V 23, 1.3 V 26(*bis*), 1.3 V 28, 1.3 VI 6, 1.3 VI 17, 1.4 I 31, 1.4 I 32, 1.4 I 34, 1.4 I 35, 1.4 II 4, 1.4 II 6, 1.4 II 7, 1.4 II 12, 1.4 II 34, 1.4 II 35, 1.4 II 42, 1.4 II 46, 1.4 III 13, 1.4 III 15, 1.4 III 16, 1.4 IV 36, 1.4 IV 37, 1.4 IV 37(!), 1.4 V 7, 1.4 V 8, 1.4 V 13, 1.4 V 14, 1.4 V 24, 1.4 V 30(*bis*), 1.4 V 36, 1.4 V 37, 1.4 V 55, 1.4 V 61, 1.4 V 62, 1.4 V 64, 1.4 V 65, 1.4 VI 5, 1.4 VI 6, 1.4 VI 8, 1.4 VI 9, 1.4 VI 22, 1.4 VI 23, 1.4 VI 25, 1.4 VI 26, 1.4 VI 27, 1.4 VI 28, 1.4 VI 31, 1.4 VI 32, 1.4 VI 33(*bis*), 1.4 VI 44, 1.4 VI 45, 1.4 VI 57, 1.4 VII 5, 1.4 VII 6, 1.4 VII 13(*bis*), 1.4 VII 17, 1.4 VII 18, 1.4 VII 26, 1.4 VII 27, 1.4 VII 41, 1.4 VII 48, 1.4 VII 49, 1.4 VIII 8, 1.4 VIII 18, 1.4 VIII 19, 1.4 VIII 23, 1.4 VIII 24, 1.5 I 7(*bis*), 1.5 I 16, 1.5 I 19, 1.5 I 21, 1.5 II 4(*bis*), 1.5 III 10, 1.5 III 19, 1.5 III 22, 1.5 III 26, 1.5 IV 9, 1.5 IV 14, 1.5 IV 16, 1.5 V 5, 1.5 V 15, 1.5 V 18, 1.5 V 19, 1.5 VI 17, 1.5 VI 18, 1.5 VI 25, 1.6 I 2, 1.6 I 8, 1.6 I 16, 1.6 I 17, 1.6 I 46, 1.6 I 57, 1.6 I 62, 1.6 I 65, 1.6 I 66, 1.6 I 67, 1.6 II 10, 1.6 II 11, 1.6 II 22, 1.6 II 23, 1.6 II 25, 1.6 II 31, 1.6 II 32, 1.6 II 33, 1.6 II 34(*bis*), 1.6 III 4, 1.6 III 5, 1.6 III 10, 1.6 III 11, 1.6 III 19, 1.6 IV 18, 1.6 V 2, 1.6 V 3, 1.6 V 8, 1.6 V 13, 1.6 V 14, 1.6 V 15, 1.6 V 16, 1.6 V 18, 1.6 V 19, 1.6 V 20, 1.6 V 22, 1.6 VI 32, 1.6 VI 51, 1.7 4, 1.7 9, 1.8 II 14, 1.9 13, 1.9 14, 1.10 II 4, 1.10 II 5, 1.10 II 6, 1.10 II 11, 1.10 II 23, 1.10 II 24, 1.10 II 25, 1.10 II 28, 1.10 II 29(*bis*), 1.10 II 30, 1.10 III 11, 1.10 III 12, 1.10 III 18(*bis*), 1.10 III 24, 1.10 III 27, 1.10 III 28, 1.10 III 29, 1.10 III 30, 1.10 III 31(*bis*), 1.11 1, 1.11 2, 1.12 I 20, 1.12 I 21, 1.12 I 40, 1.12 I 41, 1.12 II 36, 1.12 II 38, 1.12 II 52(*bis*), 1.12 II 55, 1.13 5, 1.13 11, 1.13 23, 1.14 I 20, 1.14 I 24, 1.14 I 25, 1.14 I 26, 1.14 I 27, 1.14 I 32, 1.14 I 35, 1.14 I 36, 1.14 I 38, 1.14 II 3, 1.14 II 7, 1.14 II 8, 1.14 II 19, 1.14 II 25, 1.14 II 26(!), 1.14 III 4, 1.14 III 7, 1.14 III 8, 1.14 III 9(*bis*), 1.14 III 15, 1.14 III 25, 1.14 III 37, 1.14 III 38, 1.14 III 45, 1.14 III 46, 1.14 III 47, 1.14 III 55, 1.14 III 56, 1.14 IV 1, 1.14 IV 2, 1.14 IV 7, 1.14 IV 8(!), 1.14 IV 33, 1.14 IV 46, 1.14 IV 51, 1.14 IV 52, 1.14 V 1(*bis*), 1.14 V 6, 1.14 V 38, 1.14 VI 8, 1.14 VI 21, 1.14 VI 23, 1.14 VI 31, 1.14 VI 32, 1.15 III 14, 1.15 III 15, 1.15 III 22, 1.15 IV 24, 1.15 IV 25, 1.15 V 7, 1.15 V 15, 1.15 V 27, 1.15 VI 8, 1.16 I 2, 1.16 I 14, 1.16 I 16, 1.16 I 34, 1.16 I 35, 1.16 I 41, 1.16 I 45, 1.16 I 47, 1.16 II 36, 1.16 II 38, 1.16 II 52, 1.16 III 1, 1.16 III 9, 1.16 III 14, 1.16 III 15, 1.16 III

16, 1.16 V 5, 1.16 V 11, 1.16 V 16, 1.16 V 19, 1.16 V 20, 1.16 V 22, 1.16 V 23, 1.16 V 30, 1.16 V 37, 1.16 V 45, 1.16 VI 10, 1.16 VI 25, 1.16 VI 32, 1.16 VI 45, 1.16 VI 57, 1.16 VI 58, 1.17 I 15, 1.17 I 16, 1.17 I 25(*bis*), 1.17 I 26, 1.17 I 30, 1.17 I 32, 1.17 I 33, 1.17 I 40, 1.17 I 43, 1.17 I 44, 1.17 II 5, 1.17 II 7, 1.17 II 8(*bis*), 1.17 II 13, 1.17 II 16, 1.17 II 19, 1.17 II 22, 1.17 II 23, 1.17 II 26, 1.17 II 39(*bis*), 1.17 V 4, 1.17 V 6, 1.17 V 7, 1.17 V 9(*bis*), 1.17 V 17, 1.17 V 23, 1.17 V 39, 1.17 VI 5, 1.17 VI 10, 1.17 VI 21(*bis*), 1.17 VI 22, 1.17 VI 23(*bis*), 1.17 VI 41, 1.17 VI 43, 1.17 VI 44, 1.18 I 14, 1.18 I 18, 1.18 I 21, 1.18 I 27, 1.18 IV 9, 1.18 IV 10(*bis*), 1.18 IV 15, 1.18 IV 17, 1.18 IV 18, 1.18 IV 26, 1.18 IV 28, 1.18 IV 29, 1.18 IV 38, 1.19 I 9, 1.19 I 13, 1.19 I 19, 1.19 I 30, 1.19 I 39, 1.19 I 41, 1.19 II 13, 1.19 II 14, 1.19 II 16(*bis*), 1.19 II 18, 1.19 II 20, 1.19 II 21, 1.19 II 23, 1.19 II 26(*bis*), 1.19 II 27, 1.19 II 28, 1.19 II 37, 1.19 II 56, 1.19 II 57, 1.19 III 6, 1.19 III 7(*bis*), 1.19 III 14, 1.19 III 20, 1.19 III 28, 1.19 III 35(*bis*), 1.19 III 36, 1.19 III 41, 1.19 III 41(?), 1.19 III 45, 1.19 III 53, 1.19 IV 9, 1.19 IV 10(*bis*), 1.19 IV 17, 1.19 IV 21, 1.19 IV 22, 1.19 IV 24(*bis*), 1.19 IV 30, 1.19 IV 31, 1.19 IV 41, 1.19 IV 42, 1.19 IV 43, 1.19 IV 44, 1.19 IV 45, 1.19 IV 51, 1.19 IV 52, 1.19 IV 54, 1.19 IV 56, 1.19 IV 57, 1.20 I 5, 1.20 II 1, 1.20 II 3, 1.20 II 9(*bis*), 1.22 I 6(?), 1.22 I 16(*bis*), 1.22 I 24, 1.22 I 25(*ter*), 1.22 II 20, 1.22 II 25, 1.23 4, 1.23 6(*bis*), 1.23 14(*bis*), 1.23 24, 1.23 27, 1.23 36, 1.23 38, 1.23 51, 1.23 56, 1.23 59, 1.23 61, 1.23 62, 1.23 63, 1.23 64, 1.23 74, 1.24 3, 1.24 18, 1.24 43, 1.24 43(!), 1.24 45, 1.24 46, 1.31 1, 1.39 8, 1.40 22(*bis*), 1.40 31(*ter*), 1.40 39(*bis*), 1.41 1, 1.41 3, 1.41 4, 1.41 11, 1.41 22, 1.41 38, 1.41 45, 1.41 47, 1.41 48, 1.41 50, 1.41 55, 1.43 2, 1.46 5, 1.48 8, 1.48 13, 1.49 8, 1.53 5, 1.55 6, 1.64 21, 1.65 12, 1.65 13, 1.65 14, 1.65 15, 1.65 16, 1.65 17, 1.65 18, 1.71 4, 1.71 6, 1.71 8, 1.71 10, 1.71 25, 1.71 26, 1.72 26, 1.72 40, 1.78 1(?), 1.79 7, 1.80 1, 1.80 4, 1.80 5, 1.82 4(*bis*), 1.82 9, 1.82 17, 1.82 26, 1.83 3, 1.85 3, 1.85 4(*bis*), 1.85 6, 1.85 8, 1.85 11, 1.85 14, 1.85 17, 1.85 19, 1.85 29, 1.86 22, 1.86 28, 1.87 1, 1.87 3, 1.87 4, 1.87 19, 1.87 24, 1.87 35, 1.87 51, 1.87 54, 1.88 2, 1.91 2, 1.91 15, 1.92 3, 1.92 8, 1.92 23, 1.93 2(*bis*), 1.93 3, 1.97 5, 1.97 7, 1.98 6, 1.100 3, 1.100 61, 1.100 64, 1.100 65, 1.101 2(*bis*), 1.101 7(*bis*), 1.101 14, 1.101 16, 1.103 1, 1.103 3, 1.103 5, 1.103 27, 1.103 48, 1.103 49, 1.103 51, 1.103 54(*bis*), 1.104 7, 1.104 11, 1.104 15, 1.105 3, 1.105 15, 1.105 17, 1.105 19, 1.105 21, 1.106 18, 1.106 23, 1.106 24, 1.106 25, 1.107 9, 1.107 10, 1.107 15, 1.107 42, 1.107 49, 1.108 2, 1.108 3, 1.108 4(*ter*), 1.108 5, 1.108 21, 1.108 22(*bis*), 1.108 23(*bis*), 1.108 25, 1.109 1, 1.109 3, 1.109 11, 1.109 19, 1.109 29, 1.111 15, 1.111 16, 1.111 20, 1.112 1, 1.112 8(*bis*), 1.112 11, 1.112 13, 1.112 15, 1.112 17, 1.112 21, 1.112 27, 1.112 29, 1.114 1(*bis*), 1.114 14, 1.114 15, 1.114 21, 1.115 7, 1.116 2, 1.116 10, 1.119 1(*bis*), 1.119 4, 1.119 11, 1.119 20(*bis*), 1.119 22(*bis*), 1.121 1, 1.124 6, 1.124 8, 1.124 9, 1.126 4, 1.126 19, 1.126 21, 1.127 23, 1.130 16, 1.132 1, 1.132 3, 1.132 22, 1.133 5, 1.133 11, 1.133 18, 1.136 9, 1.136 10, 1.138 1, 1.141 1, 1.142 3, 1.163 2, 1.163 5, 1.163 7, 1.163 10, 1.163 12, 1.163 14, 1.164 1, 1.164 4, 1.164 10, 1.166 28, 1.169 7(*bis*), 1.169 8(*ter*), 1.169 19(cor.), 1.169 15, 1.169 16(*bis*), 1.170 8, 1.171 6, 1.171 7, 1.172 21, 1.175 13, 1.175 17(*bis*), 1.176 18, 2.3 7, 2.3 9, 2.8 2, 2.10 19, 2.19 2, 2.19 5, 2.19

14, 2.23 13, 2.30 13, 2.30 23, 2.31 34, 2.31 46, 2.33 10, 2.33 14, 2.34 33, 2.36 7, 2.36 16, 2.36 17, 2.36 18, 2.38 12, 2.38 18, 2.38 27, 2.39 20, 2.40 9, 2.40 11, 2.42 23, 2.45 16, 2.47 9, 2.47 13, 2.49 13, 2.61 8, 2.62 5, 2.62 8, 2.62 12, 2.71 15, 2.71 17(?), 2.72 20, 2.72 30, 2.72 43, 2.73 2, 2.73 5, 2.73 9, 2.75 10, 2.79 10, 2.83 9, 3.2 7, 3.3 3, 3.3 4, 3.4 14, 3.5 6, 3.7 1, 3.7 5, 3.7 6, 3.7 7, 3.7 8, 3.7 9, 3.7 14, 3.7 15, 3.7 16, 3.8 6, 3.8 7, 3.8 9, 3.9 4, 3.9 8, 4.4 5, 4.31 1, 4.31 2, 4.31 3, 4.31 4, 4.31 5, 4.31 6, 4.31 10, 4.31 11, 4.80 13, 4.89 2, 4.89 3, 4.89 4, 4.96 11, 4.96 12, 4.101 1, 4.101 2, 4.101 3, 4.101 4, 4.101 5, 4.101 6, 4.102 1, 4.102 2, 4.102 3, 4.102 4, 4.102 5, 4.102 6, 4.102 7, 4.102 8, 4.102 9, 4.102 10, 4.102 11, 4.102 12, 4.102 13, 4.102 17, 4.102 19, 4.102 20, 4.102 21, 4.102 22, 4.102 23, 4.102 24, 4.102 25, 4.102 26, 4.102 27, 4.102 29, 4.102 30, 4.110 3, 4.111 9, 4.118 8, 4.118 10, 4.122 1, 4.124 2, 4.137 14, 4.139 4, 4.139 5, 4.139 6, 4.139 7, 4.141 III 1, 4.141 III 2, 4.141 III 6, 4.141 III 8, 4.141 III 11, 4.141 III 13, 4.141 III 15, 4.142 1, 4.142 2, 4.142 3, 4.142 5, 4.143 1(*bis*), 4.146 2, 4.146 3, 4.146 4, 4.146 5, 4.146 6, 4.146 7, 4.146 8, 4.149 12, 4.149 14, 4.149 16, 4.150 2, 4.150 4, 4.156 2, 4.156 3, 4.156 4, 4.156 5, 4.158 5, 4.158 6, 4.158 7, 4.158 8, 4.158 9, 4.158 20, 4.158 21, 4.158 22, 4.163 16, 4.164 4, 4.166 1, 4.167 2, 4.168 6, 4.168 12, 4.172 1, 4.172 2, 4.172 6, 4.178 2, 4.178 4, 4.182 1, 4.182 60, 4.185 8, 4.186 6, 4.189 7, 4.192 1, 4.193 1, 4.193 6, 4.195 8, 4.195 10, 4.198 3, 4.199 5, 4.200 8, 4.200 10, 4.213 3, 4.213 8, 4.213 10, 4.213 12, 4.213 13, 4.213 15, 4.213 18, 4.213 19, 4.213 20, 4.213 21, 4.213 23, 4.213 24, 4.225 17, 4.241 3, 4.243 10, 4.243 12, 4.243 14, 4.243 16, 4.243 18, 4.243 20, 4.243 22, 4.243 24, 4.243 26, 4.243 28, 4.244 9, 4.244 12, 4.244 13(*bis*), 4.244 23, 4.244 24, 4.246 1, 4.246 7, 4.266 1, 4.266 2, 4.266 6, 4.269 19, 4.269 30, 4.271 1, 4.271 2, 4.271 3, 4.274 3(!), 4.279 1, 4.279 3, 4.279 4, 4.279 5, 4.280 6, 4.290 7, 4.290 9, 4.290 11, 4.290 13, 4.295 1, 4.296 9, 4.296 10(*bis*), 4.296 11, 4.296 14, 4.296 16, 4.297 2, 4.297 3, 4.297 4, 4.297 7, 4.307 1, 4.307 2, 4.307 3, 4.307 21, 4.309 1, 4.313 22, 4.317 3, 4.317 9, 4.320 2, 4.320 8, 4.320 18, 4.329 3, 4.332 5, 4.336 1, 4.336 2, 4.336 8, 4.337 5, 4.337 7, 4.337 10, 4.337 11, 4.337 13, 4.337 15, 4.337 17, 4.337 19, 4.337 19, 4.337 20, 4.337 21, 4.337 22, 4.337 23, 4.337 24, 4.337 25, 4.338 3, 4.338 12, 4.341 2, 4.341 6, 4.341 8, 4.341 9, 4.341 11, 4.341 13, 4.341 15, 4.341 17, 4.341 18, 4.341 19, 4.345 2, 4.345 7, 4.345 9, 4.347 2, 4.347 4, 4.347 6, 4.347 8, 4.347 10, 4.355 8, 4.355 9, 4.355 10, 4.355 11, 4.355 12, 4.355 13, 4.355 14, 4.355 15, 4.355 16, 4.355 17, 4.355 18, 4.355 19, 4.355 20, 4.355 21, 4.355 22, 4.355 23, 4.355 24, 4.355 25, 4.355 26, 4.355 27, 4.355 28, 4.355 29, 4.355 30, 4.355 31, 4.355 32, 4.355 33, 4.355 34, 4.355 35, 4.355 36, 4.355 37, 4.355 38, 4.355 39, 4.355 41, 4.358 4, 4.358 5, 4.358 6, 4.358 7, 4.360 12, 4.361 1, 4.361 3, 4.367 1, 4.373 5, 4.373 7, 4.375 2, 4.375 4, 4.375 6, 4.375 8, 4.375 10, 4.375 12, 4.377 26, 4.377 32, 4.379 6, 4.379 7, 4.379 8, 4.382 14, 4.382 23, 4.382 24, 4.382 25, 4.382 26, 4.382 27, 4.382 28, 4.382 29, 4.382 32, 4.382 33, 4.382 34, 4.384 2, 4.384 3, 4.384 4, 4.384 5, 4.384 6, 4.387 1, 4.387 4, 4.387 13, 4.387 21, 4.388 11, 4.390 2, 4.394 3, 4.395 1, 4.397 1, 4.397 9, 4.397 13, 4.399 1, 4.399 9, 4.399 10, 4.400 2, 4.400 5, 4.400 10, 4.400 15, 4.401 16, 4.408 4, 4.408 5, 4.409 7, 4.409 8, 4.424 3, 4.424 4, 4.424 5, 4.430 4,

4.486 1, 4.542 1, 4.546 1, 4.557 1, 4.574 2, 4.574 9, 4.574 11, 4.589 3, 4.609 1, 4.616 1, 4.618 4, 4.619 4, 4.619 6, 4.625 1, 4.625 4, 4.625 7, 4.625 11, 4.625 13, 4.625 19, 4.630 2, 4.636 1, 4.636 2, 4.636 5, 4.636 10, 4.636 15, 4.636 20, 4.643 6, 4.643 7, 4.643 8, 4.643 9(*bis*), 4.643 10, 4.643 11, 4.643 12, 4.643 13, 4.643 14, 4.643 15, 4.643 16, 4.643 17, 4.643 18, 4.643 19, 4.643 25, 4.643 26, 4.644 5, 4.644 7, 4.645 2, 4.648 10, 4.648 11, 4.648 12, 4.648 13, 4.648 14, 4.648 15, 4.648 17, 4.648 18, 4.648 19, 4.648 20, 4.648 21, 4.648 22, 4.648 25, 4.658 1, 4.658 6, 4.658 7, 4.658 8, 4.658 9, 4.658 10, 4.658 11, 4.658 12, 4.658 13, 4.658 14, 4.658 15, 4.658 16, 4.658 17, 4.658 18, 4.658 19, 4.658 20, 4.658 21, 4.658 22, 4.658 23, 4.658 24, 4.658 25, 4.658 38, 4.658 39, 4.658 40, 4.658 41, 4.658 52, 4.664 4, 4.682 3, 4.682 12, 4.688 1, 4.691 6, 4.696 3, 4.696 4, 4.696 5, 4.696 6, 4.696 7, 4.696 8, 4.696 9(*bis*), 4.707 9, 4.707 12, 4.707 14, 4.707 16, 4.707 18, 4.707 20, 4.709 2, 4.709 3, 4.710 3, 4.710 5, 4.710 11, 4.710 12, 4.712 1, 4.720 4, 4.748 3, 4.748 4, 4.748 5, 4.748 11, 4.750 2, 4.750 5, 4.750 6, 4.750 7, 4.750 8, 4.750 9, 4.750 10, 4.750 11, 4.750 12, 4.750 13, 4.750 14, 4.750 15, 4.750 16, 4.750 17, 4.750 18, 4.765 9, 4.773 2, 4.779 11, 4.781 2, 4.783 2, 4.783 4, 4.783 6, 4.783 7, 5.4 1, 5.6 1, 5.8 1, 5.9 I 6, 5.9 I 17, 5.9 I 18, 5.9 II 1, 5.10 6, 5.11 5, 5.11 19, 5.12 1, 5.12 5, 5.13 1, 5.13 2, 5.13 3, 5.13 5, 5.13 6, 5.13 7, 5.14 2, 5.16 1, 5.16 2, 5.16 8, 5.17 4, 5.19 1, 5.20 1, 5.20 4, 5.21 1, 5.24 1, 5.25 15, 6.1 1, 6.14 3, 6.21 2, 6.26 3, 6.39 1, 6.39 2, 6.42 1, 6.45 1, 6.76 1, 7.51 5, 7.51 18, 7.52 6, 7.55 15, 7.64 4, 7.140 3, 7.197 5

b 1.18 IV 26 lg. u

b 4.274 3 lg. d

b 1.19 III 41 lg. bm?

b 1.93 1 lg. bġr?

b 5.18 9 lg. b<n>?

[[b]] 4.131 4

b[1.2 IV 30, 1.3 IV 26, 1.4 VII 3, 1.5 III 11, 1.10 III 17, 1.12 II 19, 1.12 II 20, 1.12 II 22, 1.16 II 2, 1.16 V 7, 1.16 V 14, 1.16 V 52, 1.18 IV 37, 1.24 10, 1.27 7, 1.41 32, 1.56 2, 1.72 24, 1.82 26, 1.104 8, 1.107 1 1.119 2, 1.126 12, 1.166 15, 2.2 6, 2.8 2, 2.21 23, 2.22 6, 2.23 25, 2.31 19, 2.73 3, 4.15 13, 4.31 7, 4.31 8, 4.33 2, 4.69 V 20, 4.86 22, 4.86 29, 4.205 12, 4.258 5, 4.258 14, 4.273 10, 4.275 10, 4.287 4, 4.287 5, 4.287 7, 4.312 6, 4.317 1, 4.317 6, 4.329 1, 4.387 15, 4.388 2, 4.388 3, 4.389 5, 4.393 13, 4.393 16, 4.405 7, 4.423 15, 4.439 1, 4.503 II 1, 4.574 8, 4.574 10, 4.585 2, 4.596 2, 4.600 2, 4.600 3, 4.619 1, 4.619 8, 4.620 3, 4.762 8, 4.764 1, 4.773 1, 4.785 7, 6.42 1, 7.7 2, 7.38 2, 7.107 5, 7.182 1, 7.184 10(*bis*), 7.202 2

]b 1.1 V 1, 1.1 V 15, 1.2 III 12, 1.3 VI 5, 1.15 II 9, 1.20 I 4, 1.30 2, 1.55 6, 1.58 4, 1.62 5, 1.64 2, 1.94 27, 1.97 1, 1.107 14, 1.137 7, 1.147 11, 1.175 3, 2.21 22, 2.23 15, 2.31 27, 2.74 1, 2.81 18, 4.102 15, 4.124 8, 4.124 9, 4.160 4, 4.214 III 4, 4.271 7, 4.357 11, 4.386 6, 4.397 5, 4.397 7, 4.401 9, 4.401 9, 4.410 1, 4.432 5, 4.461 1, 4.617 1, 4.754 10, 7.56 1, 7.141 1, 7.177 2

]\b 1.70 18f

]b[1.16 II 58, 4.185 10, 4.382 31, 4.435 14, 4.435 15, 4.658 25, 7.180 1, 7.213 1

bx 1.86 32

bx[1.2 II 1, 1.86 14, 1.94 21, 1.104 13, 1.107 52, 1.146 3, 2.5 4, 2.18 1, 4.77 22, 4.117 6, 4.273 9, 4.312 8, 4.393 22, 7.135 6, 7.171 3

]bx[4.247 9, 7.108 2, 7.176 3

bxx[2.46 20, 4.77 19

]bxx 4.196 5, 4.351 8

xb[7.54 1

xb/d 1.42 61, 1.70 10
]xb 1.15 IV 30, 1.146 8, 4.205 18, 4.275 8, 4.302 3, 7.50 8
]xb[4.396 23, 7.72 1, 7.123 1, 7.208 2
xxb 1.70 44, 4.785 21
]xxb 4.308 3
]xbx[4.247 10, 6.36 1
bxḫx 4.610 19
bxm 4.4 7
bxʿ 4.398 5
b/d 7.220 1
b/d[1.22 IV 2, 1.53 8, 1.58 4, 2.57 5, 4.254 1, 4.256 2, 4.312 3, 4.357 12, 4.446 2, 4.746 11, 4.769 20, 6.55 2, 7.210 1
]b/d 1.42 11, 1.139 17, 2.31 35, 4.60 2, 4.180 1, 4.275 6, 4.398 9, 6.46 1, 7.82 2
]b/d[4.427 8
]xb/d[7.19 1
xb/d[4.34 1
b/d/u[4.654 2
]b/d/l 4.769 5
]xb/s 1.74 2
b/ṣ[4.267 5, 4.434 9, 4.686 21, 7.98 4
]b/ṣ 4.258 16, 4.573 5, 4.717 4
]b/ṣ[7.84 6
]bxxxxa[2.57 10
bxḥxxxxṯar[1.86 31
]xxbxxḫy 4.612 8
]xxbxl 4.69 IV 28
]ba 1.153 5
badxxpn[1.70 8
bah 1.161 32 lg. bnh
baš 2.4 19 lg. bnš
bat 1.19 IV 51, 1.19 IV 52
]b/dat 1.172 3
biyx[4.649 9
bir 1.13 25, 1.91 29, 4.27 13, 4.68 30, 4.355 13, 4.365 29, 4.380 31, 4.397 13, 4.625 15, 4.683 19
bir[2.77 9, 4.629 5
b]ir 4.636 2, 4.661 2
biry 4.360 1, 4.690 6, 4.690 8
birt 4.771 10
birt[y 4.86 23
birtym 3.4 15, 4.337 3
birtn 4.77 13, 4.93 I 7, 4.422 5
birt[n 4.692 13*
bu 1.16 VI 3, 1.169 18(!)
bu 6.4 2 lg. bd?
bu/b/d[1.167 5
bul 4.214 III 1 lg. bdl
buly 4.366 8
buš[4.223 1
bb 2.31 27, 4.63 IV 9
]bb 1.14 V 25, 4.701 10
bbx[7.35 1
xxbbx[4.75 V 11
bb/d/u[1.167 5
]b/db/d[1.53 2, 7.195 2
]xbb/y/ṣ 4.214 II 16
bby 5.11 17 lg. byy
bbru 4.393 11
bbt 1.105 25, 1.115 3, 1.115 11, 1.171 3, 4.382 33
bbth 1.100 31
bbtm 1.46 9, 1.116 8
]bgzn[7.176 10
bgrt 4.93 IV 22
b.gt 4.625 9
bgt]n 4.141 I 2
bd 1.1 IV 22, 1.2 IV 13, 1.2 IV 15, 1.2 IV 21, 1.2 IV 23, 1.3 I 19, 1.4 I 24, 1.16 I 5, 1.16 I 19, 1.16 II 42, 1.17 V 26, 1.19 III 54, 1.25 7, 1.85 20, 1.91 1, 1.123 27, 2.4 21, 2.4 22, 2.38 21, 2.70 19, 2.79 5, 2.83 3, 3.2 14, 3.5 17, 3.5 19, 4.1 2, 4.43 2, 4.88 2, 4.91 1, 4.92 2, 4.103 2, 4.103 3, 4.103 4, 4.103 5, 4.103 6, 4.103 8, 4.103 9, 4.103 10, 4.103 11, 4.103 12, 4.103 13, 4.103 14, 4.103 15, 4.103 16, 4.103 17, 4.103 18, 4.103 19, 4.103 21, 4.103 22, 4.103 23, 4.103 24, 4.103 25, 4.103 26, 4.103 27, 4.103 28, 4.103 31, 4.103 35, 4.103 38, 4.103 40, 4.103 42, 4.103 43, 4.103 46, 4.103 47, 4.103 48, 4.103 50, 4.103 51, 4.103 52, 4.103 55, 4.103 56, 4.103 58, 4.110 2, 4.132 2, 4.132 5, 4.136 2, 4.138 2, 4.138 3, 4.138 4, 4.138 5, 4.138 6, 4.138 7, 4.138 8, 4.138 9, 4.141 I 1, 4.141 II 26, 4.143 3, 4.144 2, 4.145 9, 4.154 3, 4.154 4, 4.154 6, 4.166 7, 4.171 5, 4.177 1, 4.181 3, 4.181 5,

4.181 7, 4.184 4, 4.190 4, 4.191 13, 4.192 5, 4.193 10, 4.205 20, 4.217 9, 4.219 4, 4.223 1, 4.229 1, 4.244 7, 4.247 33, 4.248 2, 4.248 3, 4.264 2, 4.316 4, 4.316 6, 4.316 7, 4.317 13, 4.337 4, 4.337 7, 4.337 9, 4.337 11, 4.337 18, 4.341 3, 4.341 13, 4.341 15, 4.342 5, 4.356 16, 4.357 9, 4.357 12, 4.357 14, 4.357 15, 4.357 16, 4.357 17, 4.357 18, 4.357 19, 4.357 20, 4.357 21, 4.357 22, 4.357 23, 4.357 24, 4.357 25, 4.357 26, 4.357 27, 4.357 28, 4.357 29, 4.357 30, 4.357 31, 4.362 2, 4.374 1, 4.377 28, 4.377 29, 4.377 34, 4.379 2, 4.382 1, 4.382 2, 4.382 3, 4.398 8, 4.407 2, 4.410 16, 4.410 26, 4.410 27, 4.423 2, 4.423 4, 4.423 6, 4.423 8, 4.423 12, 4.423 14, 4.423 16, 4.423 18, 4.423 20, 4.423 24, 4.424 22, 4.425 4, 4.482 3, 4.548 4, 4.548 6, 4.579 2, 4.595 3, 4.595 4, 4.608 24, 4.609 9, 4.609 31, 4.618 9, 4.631 2, 4.631 3, 4.631 6, 4.631 7, 4.631 8, 4.631 10, 4.631 11, 4.631 14, 4.631 15, 4.631 18, 4.635 6, 4.635 8, 4.635 37, 4.635 58, 4.647 7, 4.705 5, 4.707 10, 4.707 13, 4.707 15, 4.707 17, 4.707 19, 4.710 1, 4.736 1, 4.749 1, 4.749 2, 4.752 1, 4.780 10, 4.780 11, 4.788 5, 4.788 6, 6.4 2(?)

bd[2.31 59, 4.93 I 30, 4.357 13, 4.423 10, 4.432 16, 4.544 1

b[d 4.88 3, 4.335 1, 4.357 32, 4.407 3, 4.702 4

]bd 4.177 3, 4.177 4, 4.177 5, 4.177 6, 4.177 7, 4.220 2, 4.424 8, 4.425 2, 4.425 6, 4.549 1, 4.635 1, 4.635 2, 4.635 3, 4.635 12, 4.647 3

b]d 3.2 17, 4.103 53, 4.177 2, 4.177 8, 4.177 9, 4.193 5, 4.357 5, 4.357 8, 4.357 10, 4.357 11, 4.423 22, 4.425 8, 4.635 11, 4.635 15, 4.635 55, 4.702 3, 6.18 3

]bd[1.135 1

b]d 4.631 12 lg. b]n

]xbd 4.239 3, 4.447 1

]xbd[7.176 8

]xxxbd 4.299 2

bd/b/u[1.167 5

]b/dd 1.63 9, 4.120 3

]b/dd[4.306 9, 4.702 2

]b/db/d[1.53 2, 7.195 2

]b/dl/d[7.166 2

bdil[4.75 II 2

bdd 7.222 5

bddy 1.19 II 28

bddn 4.69 V 7, 4.93 I 9, 4.318 5, 4.425 11, 4.769 37

bdh 1.3 I 10, 1.19 IV 55, 1.23 8, 1.23 8, 1.82 20, 1.107 3

bdhm 2.4 20, 4.386 13

bdy 1.19 IV 54, 4.277 9, 4.561 3

]bdy 4.320 16, 4.734 10

bdyn 4.191 14

bdk 1.4 II 32, 1.16 V 7

]bdk 1.1 II 24

bdl 4.69 III 6, 4.69 VI 17, 4.85 6, 4.96 1, 4.214 I 4, 4.214 III 1(!)

bdlm 4.86 21, 4.86 29, 4.116 20, 4.134 1, 4.232 42, 4.724 5

bdlm[4.312 4, 4.312 7

bdm 4.132 2

bdn 4.46 8, 4.63 III 30, 4.63 IV 12, 4.247 33, 4.343 1, 4.609 30, 4.609 34, 4.617 30, 4.631 7, 4.728 6, 4.779 10

]xbdn 4.197 10

bdqt 1.4 VII 19, 1.4 VII 28

bdrš[1.166 20

bḏm[4.556 3

bḏġb 4.690 2 cor. ḫḏġb

bh 1.3 III 32, 1.4 I 43, 1.4 II 16, 1.4 III 21, 1.4 III 22, 1.41 51, 1.103 9, 1.103 12, 1.103 14, 1.103 31, 1.103 52, 1.103 55, 1.103 58, 1.103 59, 1.111 22, 1.115 10, 1.140 12, 1.174 3, 3.2 18, 3.5 21, 4.132 4, 4.166 6, 4.401 4, 4.401 8, 4.401 14

bh[1.103 26

b[h 1.103 35, 1.103 37

]b/dh[7.195 1

bhl 4.240 4

bhm 1.12 I 30, 1.12 I 33, 1.19 III 39, 1.114 11, 1.114 27, 2.42 19, 4.136 5

bhmk 1.4 V 13 lg. bhtk

bhmt 1.103 8, 1.103 15, 1.103 16

bhm[t 1.103 34

bhmth 1.103 2
bhm[tn 1.163 1
]bhmtn 1.163 15
bht 1.2 III 7, 1.2 III 8, 1.3 II 4, 1.4 V 18, 1.4 V 19, 1.4 V 33, 1.4 V 34
bhth 1.4 V 36, 1.4 VI 16, 1.4 VI 44, 1.4 VII 42
bht[h 1.4 VI 38
bh]th 1.2 III 10
bhth{t} 1.10 II 4
bh\th 1.24 18f
<b>hty 1.4 VI 36
bhty 1.4 VIII 35
bhty[1.98 6
bh]ty 1.4 VIII 40
bhtk 1.4 V 13(!), 1.4 V 30
bh[t]k 1.3 V 20
bht\k 1.3 V 19f
bht{.}m 1.112 5
bhtm 1.4 V 51, 1.4 V 53, 1.4 VI 5, 1.4 VI 8, 1.4 VI 22, 1.4 VI 25, 1.4 VI 27, 1.4 VI 30, 1.4 VI 33, 1.4 VII 17, 1.4 VII 26, 1.39 21, 1.87 6, 1.87 29, 1.91 14, 1.100 70, 1.100 70, 1.105 9(?), 1.105 16, 1.109 31, 2.31 48, 4.35 I 16, 4.38 6, 4.47 10, 4.182 33, 4.183 I 1, 4.312 4, 4.312 7, 4.630 9, 4.750 2, 4.750 12
bhtm[1.57 6
bht[m 4.545 II 6
bh[tm 1.4 V 61, 1.53 7
b[htm 1.1 III 27, 4.609 18
bhṯ 1.5 II 11, 1.5 II 19
bw[4.106 14
bwtm 1.105 9 lg. bhtm?
bz 1.80 4
bḥ[4.17 20, 4.746 3
]bḥa 7.222 10
bḥ[lm 4.377 24
bḫr 1.15 V 22
b]ṭnm 1.15 VI 1
bṭr 4.382 1
]bṭr 4.382 2
by 1.2 III 19, 1.57 7, 2.2 7, 2.16 10, 2.38 13, 2.38 25, 2.60 4, 2.73 4, 4.181 5, 7.137 8
]by 1.126 4, 4.313 4, 4.431 5, 4.432 12, 4.480 1
]by[4.681 8
]b/dy 4.339 8
]b/dy[4.427 5
]xby/b/ṣ 4.214 II 16
byy 1.142 1, 4.170 25, 4.396 20, 5.10 1, 5.11 1, 5.11 17(!)
byy[4.334 2, 4.488 3, 4.617 11
]b/dymktmẓ$_2$k[1.77 5
byn 1.175 8, 4.86 30
byn[4.334 5 cor. gyn[
]byn 4.368 9
bk 1.3 I 12, 1.6 I 9, 1.14 II 7, 1.45 10, 1.82 10, 2.71 12
bk[2.7 3
]bk 4.262 10
bk 1.4 IV 37 lg. b k<s>
]b/dk 1.167 2
bkbtmx[1.70 20
]b/dkḫkyt[1.68 19
bky 1.16 I 14, 1.16 II 36, 1.16 II 41
bkyh 1.14 I 31
bkym 1.16 II 54
bkyt 1.19 IV 21
<b>kyt 1.19 IV 10
bkm 1.4 VII 42, 1.10 III 29, 1.16 II 50, 1.19 II 8, 1.19 II 9, 1.19 II 9, 1.107 12, 6.48 3
bk[r 1.13 28
bkrk 1.14 III 40, 1.14 VI 25
bkrm 1.82 9
bkt 1.16 VI 4
b<l> 1.100 30
bl 1.4 II 43, 1.4 V 61, 1.4 VI 5, 1.4 VII 43, 1.6 I 48, 1.12 II 7, 1.12 II 23, 1.14 II 37, 1.14 II 38, 1.14 V 21, 1.16 I 15, 1.16 II 31, 1.16 II 37, 1.17 I 20, 1.17 VI 27, 1.19 I 44, 1.19 I 44, 1.19 I 45, 1.19 I 45, 1.96 4, 1.96 5, 1.100 2, 1.100 8, 1.100 14, 1.100 19, 1.100 25, 1.100 35, 1.100 40, 1.100 45, 1.100 51, 1.100 57, 1.107 46, 1.169 7, 2.45 23, 2.45 27, 4.243 11, 4.309 4
bl[1.6 V 28, 1.16 II 29, 1.67 22, 4.662 2, 7.168 3
]bl 4.362 4
]bl[1.29 1, 4.708 1, 6.38 4
]b/dl/d[7.166 2
]b/d/uṣ/l[7.79 4
blblm 4.288 1
bld 1.22 I 18

bldn 1.91 6, 1.162 1
]bldn 4.307 11, 4.320 15
]b/dlḏ 1.42 27
blḫdrm 4.4 6
blẓn 4.63 II 9
bly 4.65 10, 4.69 I 2, 4.76 6, 4.93 II 3, 4.116 9, 4.356 13, 4.377 10, 4.386 2, 4.681 3, 4.710 1, 4.785 20
bly[1.69 11
blym 4.272 7
blkn 4.638 5
bln 1.72 26, 1.85 18
]bln 4.155 7, 4.320 14
blsmt 1.22 I 6 lg. b lsmt?
blʿ 1.174 4
]blʿd[n 4.498 4
blšpš 4.44 32
blšš 4.277 10
blt 1.5 I 18, 1.6 I 54, 1.67 6, 1.67 6, 1.67 15
blt[1.70 29, 1.107 17
bltn/wrḫ 1.67 16
bltn 1.67 18, 1.69 1, 1.70 27
bltn/wrḫ 1.67 16
xxblṯ 1.70 8
bm 1.2 I 39, 1.6 I 30, 1.10 II 7, 1.10 III 30, 1.12 I 12, 1.12 I 13, 1.14 I 31, 1.15 II 17, 1.16 I 42, 1.16 I 48, 1.16 III 10, 1.17 I 39, 1.19 I 34, 1.19 I 35, 1.19 II 25, 1.19 III 41(?), 1.22 I 5, 1.23 51, 1.23 56, 1.92 13, 2.13 14, 4.335 6
bm 1.14 II 26 lg. b
b[m 1.14 IV 8 lg. b
bm[1.82 22, 1.86 33
]bm 1.19 II 34, 1.42 36, 1.92 18, 4.103 33, 4.368 6, 7.51 9
bmx[1.160 3
b/ṣm[4.413 6
]b/dm 1.147 22, 1.172 29
]b/dmx[7.61 4
b/ṣm[4.65 14
]bmy[4.560 6
bmmt 4.412 III 14
xxxb/dmn[4.200 7
]b/dmr[7.89 1
bmt 1.4 IV 14, 1.4 IV 15, 1.4 VII 34, 1.5 VI 22, 1.6 I 5, 1.19 II 11, 4.247 17
b]mt 1.19 II 10
bmth 1.3 II 12, 1.19 I 17
]bmṯ$_2$kḫ$_2$tm 1.77 4
{bn} 1.5 II 18
<bn> 1.40 34
b<n> 1.4 VII 54, 4.754 18, 5.18 9(?)
bn 1.1 III 29, 1.1 V 23, 1.2 I 19, 1.2 I 21, 1.2 I 35, 1.2 I 37, 1.2 I 38, 1.2 I 42, 1.2 III 7, 1.2 III 14, 1.2 IV 14, 1.2 IV 16, 1.2 IV 22, 1.2 IV 25, 1.2 IV 40, 1.3 II 6, 1.3 II 20, 1.3 II 30, 1.3 IV 48, 1.3 V 4, 1.4 III 14, 1.4 IV 51, 1.4 V 1, 1.4 V 18, 1.4 V 33, 1.4 V 60, 1.4 VI 46, 1.4 VII 15, 1.4 VII 45, 1.4 VII 55, 1.4 VIII 16, 1.4 VIII 30, 1.5 I 7, 1.5 I 12, 1.5 I 13, 1.5 II 8, 1.5 II 11, 1.5 II 14, 1.5 II 19, 1.5 II 20, 1.5 III 6, 1.5 III 7, 1.5 VI 23, 1.6 I 6, 1.6 I 52, 1.6 II 13, 1.6 II 18, 1.6 II 25, 1.6 II 31, 1.6 V 1, 1.6 V 9, 1.6 VI 7, 1.6 VI 9, 1.6 VI 24, 1.6 VI 30, 1.8 II 4, 1.8 II 7, 1.8 II 8, 1.10 I 3, 1.10 II 16, 1.10 III 12, 1.10 III 14, 1.12 I 39, 1.12 II 25, 1.13 22, 1.14 I 9, 1.14 II 3, 1.14 II 25, 1.14 III 25, 1.14 III 37, 1.14 IV 7, 1.14 VI 22, 1.15 I 6, 1.15 III 20, 1.15 III 23, 1.16 I 20, 1.16 I 25, 1.16 I 26, 1.16 VI 55, 1.17 I 10, 1.17 I 13, 1.17 I 18, 1.17 I 20, 1.17 I 22, 1.17 II 14, 1.17 VI 29, 1.18 IV 19, 1.18 IV 21, 1.18 IV 30, 1.22 I 3, 1.22 I 3, 1.23 2, 1.23 59, 1.23 61, 1.23 65, 1.40 7, 1.40 25, 1.40 25, 1.40 26, 1.40 33, 1.40 34, 1.40 34, 1.40 41, 1.40 42, 1.45 12, 1.48 15, 1.62 7, 1.65 1, 1.65 2, 1.65 3, 1.79 4, 1.82 3, 1.82 16, 1.82 23, 1.82 23, 1.86 11, 1.86 15, 1.86 17, 1.86 25, 1.87 58, 1.87 58, 1.87 59, 1.100 74, 1.100 75, 1.101 5, 1.106 9, 1.107 6, 1.107 23, 1.112 6, 1.127 31, 1.133 1, 1.142 1, 1.143 2, 1.169 15, 2.8 6, 2.13 18, 2.61 3, 2.70 11, 2.70 17, 2.72 12, 2.72 13, 3.2 3, 3.2 6, 3.2 16, 3.3 3, 3.3 10, 3.3 11, 3.3 12, 3.4 3, 3.5 2, 3.5 12, 3.5 18, 3.7 2, 3.7 3, 3.7 4, 3.7 6, 3.7 7, 3.7 8, 3.7 9, 3.7 10, 3.7 15, 3.8 18, 3.8 20, 3.8 22, 3.9 19, 3.9 21, 3.10 2, 3.10 6, 3.10 14,

3.10 16, 3.10 18, 3.10 20, 3.10 22, 4.2 2, 4.2 4, 4.2 5, 4.7 2, 4.7 2, 4.7 3, 4.7 4, 4.7 5, 4.7 6, 4.7 6, 4.7 7, 4.7 8, 4.7 9, 4.7 10, 4.7 11, 4.7 12, 4.7 13, 4.7 14, 4.7 15, 4.7 17, 4.7 17, 4.7 18, 4.7 19, 4.7 20, 4.12 3, 4.12 4, 4.12 4, 4.12 5, 4.12 5, 4.12 6, 4.12 6, 4.12 7, 4.12 7, 4.12 8, 4.12 9, 4.12 10, 4.12 11, 4.12 12, 4.12 15, 4.12 16, 4.13 36, 4.13 36, 4.17 17, 4.21 1, 4.21 2, 4.24 4, 4.25 5, 4.30 7, 4.30 8, 4.31 8, 4.32 3, 4.33 3, 4.33 5, 4.33 8, 4.33 9, 4.33 11, 4.33 12, 4.33 13, 4.33 14, 4.33 15, 4.33 16, 4.33 17, 4.33 22, 4.33 23, 4.33 24, 4.33 25, 4.33 26, 4.33 28, 4.33 29, 4.33 30, 4.33 31, 4.33 32, 4.33 33, 4.33 34, 4.33 35, 4.33 36, 4.33 40, 4.33 41, 4.35 I 3, 4.35 I 4, 4.35 I 5, 4.35 I 6, 4.35 I 7, 4.35 I 8, 4.35 I 9, 4.35 I 13, 4.35 I 14, 4.35 I 15, 4.35 I 17, 4.35 I 18, 4.35 I 19, 4.35 I 21, 4.35 I 23, 4.35 I 24, 4.35 II 7, 4.35 II 9, 4.35 II 10, 4.35 II 12, 4.35 II 13, 4.35 II 14, 4.35 II 15, 4.35 II 16, 4.35 II 17, 4.35 II 18, 4.35 II 19, 4.35 II 22, 4.37 1, 4.37 2, 4.37 3, 4.37 4, 4.37 5, 4.39 2, 4.39 6, 4.39 7, 4.40 8, 4.40 11, 4.41 9, 4.41 10, 4.41 12, 4.45 2, 4.45 3, 4.45 5, 4.50 7, 4.50 10, 4.50 11, 4.50 12, 4.50 15, 4.50 16, 4.51 1, 4.51 5, 4.51 8, 4.51 9, 4.51 10, 4.51 11, 4.51 12, 4.51 13, 4.51 14, 4.51 15, 4.51 16, 4.52 1, 4.52 2, 4.52 3, 4.52 5, 4.52 8, 4.52 9, 4.52 13, 4.52 14, 4.52 15, 4.53 6, 4.53 7, 4.53 8, 4.53 12, 4.53 13, 4.54 7, 4.54 8, 4.54 11, 4.55 4, 4.55 6, 4.55 7, 4.55 8, 4.55 10, 4.55 12, 4.55 13, 4.55 23, 4.55 24, 4.55 24, 4.55 25, 4.55 25, 4.55 26, 4.55 27, 4.55 28, 4.55 29, 4.56 5, 4.63 I 5, 4.63 I 10, 4.63 I 12, 4.63 I 16, 4.63 I 17, 4.63 I 19, 4.63 I 21, 4.63 I 30, 4.63 I 31, 4.63 I 32, 4.63 I 40, 4.63 I 42, 4.63 I 43, 4.63 I 46, 4.63 I 47, 4.63 II 9, 4.63 II 23, 4.63 II 26, 4.63 II 36, 4.63 II 41, 4.63 II 43, 4.63 II 44, 4.63 II 45, 4.63 II 46, 4.63 III 4, 4.63 III 5, 4.63 III 7, 4.63 III 8, 4.63 III 10, 4.63 III 11, 4.63 III 12, 4.63 III 13, 4.63 III 15, 4.63 III 16, 4.63 III 17, 4.63 III 18, 4.63 III 19, 4.63 III 20, 4.63 III 21, 4.63 III 22, 4.63 III 23, 4.63 III 24, 4.63 III 25, 4.63 III 26, 4.63 III 27, 4.63 III 28, 4.63 III 29, 4.63 III 30, 4.63 III 31, 4.63 III 35, 4.63 III 36, 4.63 III 40, 4.63 III 43, 4.63 III 44, 4.63 IV 1, 4.63 IV 4, 4.63 IV 6, 4.63 IV 7, 4.63 IV 9, 4.63 IV 10, 4.63 IV 13, 4.63 IV 14, 4.63 IV 16, 4.64 II 1, 4.64 II 2, 4.64 II 3, 4.64 II 4, 4.64 III 5, 4.64 IV 8, 4.64 IV 9, 4.64 IV 10, 4.64 IV 11, 4.64 IV 12, 4.64 IV 13, 4.64 IV 17, 4.64 V 4, 4.64 V 5, 4.64 V 6, 4.64 V 7, 4.64 V 8, 4.64 V 10, 4.64 V 11, 4.64 V 12, 4.65 2, 4.65 3, 4.65 4, 4.65 7, 4.65 8, 4.65 9, 4.65 10, 4.65 14, 4.66 2, 4.66 5, 4.66 6, 4.66 7, 4.66 8, 4.66 9, 4.66 12, 4.66 13, 4.66 14, 4.66 15, 4.66 16, 4.66 17, 4.66 18, 4.66 19, 4.69 I 2, 4.69 I 5, 4.69 I 6, 4.69 I 9, 4.69 I 10, 4.69 I 12, 4.69 I 13, 4.69 I 14, 4.69 I 15, 4.69 I 16, 4.69 I 17, 4.69 I 18, 4.69 I 19, 4.69 I 20, 4.69 I 21, 4.69 I 22, 4.69 II 1, 4.69 II 2, 4.69 II 3, 4.69 II 4, 4.69 II 5, 4.69 II 6, 4.69 II 7, 4.69 II 8, 4.69 II 12, 4.69 II 13, 4.69 II 14, 4.69 II 15, 4.69 II 16, 4.69 II 18, 4.69 II 19, 4.69 II 20, 4.69 III 1, 4.69 III 2, 4.69 III 3, 4.69 III 4, 4.69 III 5, 4.69 III 7, 4.69 III 8, 4.69 III 9, 4.69 III 10, 4.69 III 12, 4.69 III 13, 4.69 III 14, 4.69 III 15, 4.69 III 16, 4.69 III 17, 4.69 III 19, 4.69 III 20, 4.69 III 21, 4.69 V 1, 4.69 V 2, 4.69 V 4, 4.69 V 7, 4.69 V 8, 4.69 V 9, 4.69 V 10, 4.69 V 11, 4.69 V 12, 4.69 V 13, 4.69 V 14, 4.69 V 15, 4.69 V 18, 4.69 V 19, 4.69 V 20, 4.69 V 21, 4.69 V 22, 4.69 V 23, 4.69 V 24, 4.69 V 25, 4.69 VI 10, 4.69 VI 11, 4.69 VI 12, 4.69 VI 13, 4.69 VI 14, 4.69 VI 15, 4.69 VI 16, 4.69 VI 18, 4.69 VI 19, 4.69 VI 20, 4.69 VI 23, 4.69 VI 26, 4.69 VI 27, 4.69 VI 28, 4.69 VI 29, 4.69 VI 30,

4.69 VI 31, 4.69 VI 32, 4.69 VI 33, 4.69 VI 34, 4.69 VI 35, 4.69 VI 36, 4.70 2, 4.70 4, 4.70 5, 4.70 7, 4.70 9, 4.71 III 6, 4.71 III 7, 4.71 III 8, 4.71 III 11, 4.71 III 12, 4.71 III 13, 4.75 I 1, 4.75 III 2, 4.75 III 3, 4.75 III 4, 4.75 III 7(!), 4.75 III 8, 4.75 III 9, 4.75 III 10, 4.75 III 11, 4.75 III 12, 4.75 IV 8, 4.75 IV 10, 4.75 IV 11, 4.75 IV 12, 4.75 IV 13, 4.75 IV 14, 4.75 V 14, 4.75 V 15, 4.75 V 16, 4.75 V 17, 4.75 V 20, 4.75 V 21, 4.75 V 22, 4.75 VI 1, 4.75 VI 4, 4.75 VI 5, 4.75 VI 6, 4.75 VI 7, 4.76 1, 4.76 2, 4.76 3, 4.76 4, 4.76 5, 4.76 6, 4.76 7, 4.77 2, 4.77 5, 4.77 6, 4.77 7, 4.77 9, 4.77 10, 4.77 11, 4.77 12, 4.77 13, 4.77 21, 4.77 22, 4.77 23, 4.77 24, 4.77 25, 4.77 26, 4.77 27, 4.77 28, 4.77 29, 4.77 30, 4.85 7, 4.86 5, 4.86 6, 4.86 7, 4.86 8, 4.86 9, 4.86 10, 4.86 11, 4.86 12, 4.86 12, 4.86 13, 4.86 25, 4.86 27, 4.88 5, 4.88 6, 4.88 7, 4.88 8, 4.90 1, 4.90 2, 4.90 3, 4.90 4, 4.90 5, 4.90 8, 4.90 9, 4.90 10, 4.93 I 2, 4.93 I 3, 4.93 I 4, 4.93 I 5, 4.93 I 7, 4.93 I 8, 4.93 I 9, 4.93 I 10, 4.93 I 12, 4.93 I 13, 4.93 I 14, 4.93 I 15, 4.93 I 16, 4.93 I 17, 4.93 I 18, 4.93 I 19, 4.93 I 20, 4.93 I 21, 4.93 I 22, 4.93 I 23, 4.93 I 24, 4.93 I 25, 4.93 I 26, 4.93 I 27, 4.93 I 28, 4.93 I 29, 4.93 I 31, 4.93 I 32, 4.93 II 1, 4.93 II 2, 4.93 II 3, 4.93 II 4, 4.93 II 5, 4.93 II 6, 4.93 II 7, 4.93 II 8, 4.93 II 9, 4.93 II 10, 4.93 II 12, 4.93 II 13, 4.93 II 14, 4.93 II 15, 4.93 II 16, 4.93 II 17, 4.93 III 2, 4.93 III 6, 4.93 IV 3, 4.93 IV 4, 4.93 IV 5, 4.93 IV 6, 4.93 IV 7, 4.93 IV 8, 4.93 IV 10, 4.93 IV 11, 4.93 IV 13, 4.93 IV 14, 4.93 IV 15, 4.93 IV 16, 4.93 IV 17, 4.93 IV 18, 4.93 IV 19, 4.93 IV 20, 4.93 IV 21, 4.93 IV 22, 4.93 IV 23, 4.93 IV 24, 4.93 IV 25, 4.93 IV 26, 4.93 IV 27, 4.93 IV 28, 4.93 IV 29, 4.93 IV 30, 4.93 IV 41, 4.96 1, 4.96 2, 4.96 8, 4.96 11, 4.97 2, 4.98 2, 4.98 4, 4.98 5, 4.98 7, 4.98 10, 4.98 11, 4.98 14, 4.98 15, 4.98 16, 4.98 18, 4.98 19, 4.98 20, 4.98 24, 4.101 2, 4.101 3, 4.101 4, 4.103 6, 4.103 8, 4.103 9, 4.103 10, 4.103 11, 4.103 16, 4.103 17, 4.103 18, 4.103 19, 4.103 21, 4.103 21, 4.103 22, 4.103 23, 4.103 26, 4.103 38, 4.103 38, 4.103 40, 4.103 42, 4.103 42, 4.103 43, 4.103 43, 4.103 49*, 4.103 50, 4.103 52, 4.103 53, 4.106 8, 4.106 9, 4.106 10, 4.106 11, 4.106 12, 4.106 14, 4.106 16, 4.106 17, 4.106 18, 4.106 19, 4.106 20, 4.106 21, 4.106 22, 4.108 3, 4.110 3, 4.110 4, 4.110 5, 4.110 6, 4.110 9, 4.110 10, 4.110 14, 4.110 15, 4.112 II 1, 4.112 III 1, 4.112 III 2, 4.112 III 3, 4.115 10, 4.115 12, 4.115 13, 4.116 6, 4.116 14, 4.116 21, 4.116 22, 4.122 4, 4.122 5, 4.122 6, 4.122 7, 4.122 8, 4.122 9, 4.122 10, 4.122 11, 4.122 12, 4.122 18, 4.122 20, 4.123 2, 4.123 4, 4.123 6, 4.123 10, 4.123 15, 4.124 2, 4.124 4, 4.124 5, 4.124 6, 4.125 5, 4.129 2, 4.129 12, 4.131 7, 4.131 9, 4.131 12, 4.133 1, 4.139 3, 4.141 II 1, 4.155 2, 4.155 10, 4.155 11, 4.155 13, 4.155 14, 4.155 15, 4.163 8, 4.170 5, 4.170 7, 4.170 9, 4.170 12, 4.170 13, 4.170 15, 4.170 17, 4.170 18, 4.170 19, 4.170 25, 4.172 4, 4.173 5, 4.181 5, 4.183 II 2, 4.183 II 3, 4.194 18, 4.197 7, 4.199 3, 4.200 8, 4.204 8, 4.204 10, 4.214 I 1, 4.214 I 2, 4.214 I 3, 4.214 I 8, 4.214 I 12, 4.214 I 13, 4.214 I 14, 4.214 I 16, 4.214 I 19, 4.214 I 20, 4.214 II 1, 4.214 II 2, 4.214 II 4, 4.214 II 10, 4.214 II 11, 4.214 II 15, 4.214 II 19(!), 4.214 III 2, 4.214 III 3, 4.214 III 4, 4.214 III 6, 4.214 III 7, 4.214 III 8, 4.214 III 11, 4.214 III 12, 4.214 III 18, 4.214 III 22, 4.214 IV 12, 4.214 IV 13, 4.215 3, 4.215 5, 4.222 15, 4.222 16, 4.222 17, 4.222 19, 4.222 20, 4.222 20, 4.222 21, 4.222 21, 4.224 6, 4.224 8, 4.224 9, 4.224 10, 4.224 11, 4.225 10, 4.225 13, 4.226 8, 4.226 9, 4.226 10, 4.227

I 11, 4.229 2, 4.229 3, 4.229 4, 4.229 5, 4.229 6, 4.230 9, 4.230 10, 4.232 2, 4.232 4, 4.232 5, 4.232 6, 4.232 6, 4.232 7, 4.232 8, 4.232 8, 4.232 9, 4.232 9, 4.232 10, 4.232 10, 4.232 11, 4.232 12, 4.232 14, 4.232 15, 4.232 16, 4.232 17, 4.232 18, 4.232 19, 4.232 21, 4.232 29, 4.232 30, 4.232 31, 4.232 32, 4.232 40, 4.232 43, 4.232 45, 4.232 46, 4.232 47, 4.232 48, 4.233 3, 4.233 4, 4.233 5, 4.233 6, 4.233 7, 4.233 8, 4.233 9, 4.240 2, 4.240 4, 4.243 6, 4.243 43, 4.245 I 3, 4.245 I 4, 4.245 I 5, 4.245 I 6, 4.245 I 8, 4.245 I 9, 4.245 I 13, 4.245 II 3, 4.245 II 4, 4.247 33, 4.248 3, 4.248 11, 4.255 2, 4.255 3, 4.255 5, 4.255 5, 4.259 7, 4.261 15, 4.261 23, 4.261 24, 4.263 2, 4.263 3, 4.263 4, 4.266 4, 4.273 9, 4.278 3, 4.278 4, 4.278 7, 4.278 10, 4.280 1, 4.280 4, 4.280 8, 4.280 10, 4.280 12, 4.281 4, 4.281 5, 4.281 10, 4.281 11, 4.281 13, 4.281 14, 4.281 16, 4.281 17, 4.281 18, 4.281 21, 4.281 23, 4.281 26, 4.281 29, 4.282 3, 4.283 4, 4.283 6, 4.283 8, 4.290 5, 4.290 7, 4.290 9, 4.290 11, 4.297 2, 4.297 7, 4.307 6, 4.307 18, 4.307 20, 4.309 2, 4.309 3, 4.309 4, 4.309 5, 4.309 6, 4.309 7, 4.309 8, 4.309 9, 4.309 10, 4.309 11, 4.309 12, 4.309 13, 4.309 14, 4.309 16, 4.309 17, 4.309 18, 4.309 19, 4.309 20, 4.309 21, 4.309 22, 4.309 23, 4.309 24, 4.309 25, 4.309 26, 4.309 27, 4.309 28, 4.309 29, 4.311 1, 4.311 2, 4.311 12, 4.311 13, 4.311 14, 4.313 5, 4.313 8, 4.313 25, 4.313 27, 4.315 9, 4.318 5, 4.320 11, 4.321 1, 4.321 2, 4.321 3, 4.322 7, 4.322 8, 4.322 9, 4.322 10, 4.322 11, 4.334 1, 4.334 2, 4.334 3, 4.334 4, 4.334 5*, 4.334 6*, 4.334 6, 4.334 7, 4.335 2, 4.335 3, 4.335 4, 4.335 5, 4.335 7, 4.335 8, 4.335 14, 4.335 15, 4.335 16, 4.335 17, 4.335 18, 4.335 19, 4.335 23, 4.335 24, 4.335 25, 4.335 26, 4.335 27, 4.335 28, 4.335 32, 4.335 33, 4.335 34, 4.335 35, 4.335 36, 4.335 37, 4.337 21, 4.338 9, 4.339 4, 4.339 13, 4.339 14, 4.339 18, 4.339 20, 4.339 21, 4.339 27, 4.340 1, 4.340 2, 4.340 3, 4.340 4, 4.340 5, 4.340 6, 4.340 7, 4.340 8, 4.340 10, 4.340 11, 4.340 13, 4.340 14, 4.340 16, 4.340 17, 4.340 18, 4.340 19, 4.340 20, 4.340 21, 4.341 13, 4.342 3, 4.343 1, 4.343 2, 4.343 5, 4.343 10, 4.344 7, 4.344 13, 4.344 14, 4.344 19, 4.347 7, 4.347 9, 4.348 6, 4.348 15, 4.348 16, 4.348 17, 4.348 18, 4.348 29, 4.350 2, 4.350 3, 4.350 5, 4.350 6, 4.350 7, 4.350 8, 4.350 9, 4.350 10, 4.350 11, 4.350 12, 4.350 13, 4.350 14, 4.350 15, 4.352 7, 4.352 8, 4.354 2, 4.354 3, 4.354 4, 4.354 5, 4.354 6, 4.354 7, 4.354 8, 4.356 1, 4.356 1, 4.356 2, 4.356 2, 4.356 3, 4.356 4, 4.356 5, 4.356 5, 4.356 6, 4.356 7, 4.356 7, 4.356 8, 4.356 8, 4.356 9, 4.356 10, 4.356 13, 4.356 14, 4.357 14, 4.357 23, 4.357 25, 4.357 26, 4.360 1, 4.360 6, 4.360 7, 4.360 10, 4.364 1, 4.364 2, 4.364 4, 4.366 2, 4.366 3, 4.366 4, 4.366 5, 4.366 6, 4.366 7, 4.366 8, 4.366 9, 4.366 10, 4.366 11, 4.366 12, 4.366 13, 4.366 14, 4.367 7, 4.369 16, 4.370 13, 4.371 2, 4.371 4, 4.371 6, 4.371 7, 4.371 8, 4.371 10, 4.371 15, 4.371 17, 4.371 19, 4.371 21, 4.371 22, 4.374 3, 4.374 13, 4.377 2, 4.377 3, 4.377 4, 4.377 5, 4.377 6, 4.377 7, 4.377 8, 4.377 9, 4.377 10, 4.377 11, 4.377 12, 4.377 13, 4.377 14, 4.377 18, 4.377 19, 4.377 20, 4.377 22, 4.379 3, 4.379 6, 4.379 8, 4.381 17, 4.382 19, 4.382 22, 4.382 23, 4.382 25, 4.382 26, 4.382 27, 4.382 29, 4.382 33, 4.382 34, 4.382 35, 4.383 2, 4.383 3, 4.383 5, 4.383 6, 4.383 7, 4.383 8, 4.383 9, 4.386 18, 4.388 9, 4.389 10, 4.389 11, 4.393 10, 4.393 17, 4.398 4, 4.399 8, 4.401 3, 4.403 12, 4.408 1, 4.408 3, 4.410 6, 4.410 7, 4.410 8, 4.410 9, 4.410 10, 4.410 37, 4.410 38, 4.410 39, 4.412 I 10, 4.412 I 11,

4.412 I 12, 4.412 I 13, 4.412 I 14, 4.412 I 23, 4.412 I 24, 4.412 I 27, 4.412 I 29, 4.412 I 30, 4.412 II 3, 4.412 II 4, 4.412 II 5, 4.412 II 6, 4.412 II 7, 4.412 II 9, 4.412 II 11, 4.412 II 12, 4.412 II 13, 4.412 II 14, 4.412 II 31, 4.412 II 33, 4.412 II 34, 4.412 III 1, 4.412 III 2, 4.412 III 3, 4.412 III 4, 4.412 III 5, 4.412 III 6, 4.412 III 7, 4.412 III 8, 4.412 III 10, 4.412 III 11, 4.412 III 13, 4.412 III 24, 4.412 III 25, 4.415 1, 4.415 2, 4.415 3, 4.415 4, 4.418 1, 4.422 2, 4.422 3, 4.422 4, 4.422 5, 4.422 6, 4.422 7, 4.422 8, 4.422 9, 4.422 10, 4.422 12, 4.422 13, 4.422 14, 4.422 28, 4.422 29, 4.422 31, 4.422 32, 4.422 33, 4.422 34, 4.422 35, 4.422 36, 4.422 37, 4.422 38, 4.422 39, 4.422 40, 4.422 41, 4.422 43, 4.422 44, 4.422 45, 4.422 46, 4.422 47, 4.422 48, 4.422 50, 4.422 51, 4.422 52, 4.423 3, 4.423 21, 4.423 23, 4.424 5, 4.424 18, 4.424 23, 4.425 4, 4.425 5, 4.425 12, 4.425 13, 4.427 2, 4.427 3, 4.427 18, 4.428 9, 4.429 4, 4.432 6, 4.432 7, 4.432 8, 4.432 9, 4.432 10, 4.432 12, 4.432 13, 4.432 14, 4.432 15, 4.432 16, 4.432 17, 4.432 18, 4.432 18, 4.432 19, 4.432 19, 4.432 20, 4.432 20, 4.432 21, 4.432 22, 4.432 23, 4.432 24, 4.432 25, 4.432 26, 4.434 3, 4.434 4, 4.434 5, 4.434 6, 4.434 7, 4.434 8, 4.434 9, 4.435 3, 4.435 5, 4.435 6, 4.435 7, 4.435 8, 4.435 9, 4.435 10, 4.435 11, 4.435 12, 4.435 13, 4.435 14, 4.435 15, 4.436 2, 4.436 3, 4.436 4, 4.436 5, 4.436 6, 4.441 2, 4.441 3, 4.441 4, 4.441 5, 4.441 6, 4.448 2, 4.448 4, 4.453 1, 4.453 2, 4.453 3, 4.455 1, 4.455 2, 4.455 3, 4.455 4, 4.455 5, 4.458 1, 4.458 2, 4.458 3, 4.458 4, 4.458 5, 4.458 6, 4.463 3, 4.485 5, 4.485 6, 4.495 2, 4.495 3, 4.502 2, 4.502 3, 4.518 3, 4.518 4, 4.520 1, 4.520 2, 4.520 5, 4.520 6, 4.524 1, 4.524 2, 4.524 3, 4.528 3, 4.537 2, 4.537 3, 4.537 4, 4.537 5, 4.539 1, 4.539 3, 4.545 II 1, 4.545 II 2, 4.545 II 3, 4.545 II 4, 4.545 II 5, 4.545 II 7, 4.545 II 8, 4.545 II 9, 4.545 II 10, 4.545 II 11, 4.547 2, 4.554 3, 4.561 3, 4.562 1, 4.562 2, 4.571 2, 4.571 3, 4.571 4, 4.571 5, 4.578 2, 4.578 3, 4.581 6, 4.581 7, 4.582 6, 4.586 3, 4.593 2, 4.593 4, 4.593 5, 4.593 6, 4.593 7, 4.593 8, 4.593 9, 4.605 2, 4.611 1, 4.611 2, 4.611 2, 4.611 3, 4.611 3, 4.611 4, 4.611 4, 4.611 5, 4.611 5, 4.611 6, 4.611 6, 4.611 7, 4.611 7, 4.611 9, 4.611 10, 4.611 10, 4.611 11, 4.611 11, 4.611 12, 4.611 12, 4.611 13, 4.611 13, 4.611 14, 4.611 14, 4.611 15, 4.611 15, 4.611 16, 4.611 16, 4.611 17, 4.611 18, 4.611 18, 4.611 19, 4.611 19, 4.611 20, 4.611 21, 4.611 22, 4.611 25, 4.611 26, 4.611 28, 4.611 29, 4.611 30, 4.615 4, 4.616 4, 4.616 9, 4.616 11, 4.616 15, 4.617 3, 4.617 3, 4.617 4, 4.617 4, 4.617 5, 4.617 5, 4.617 6, 4.617 6, 4.617 7, 4.617 7, 4.617 8, 4.617 8, 4.617 9, 4.617 9, 4.617 10, 4.617 10, 4.617 11, 4.617 11, 4.617 12, 4.617 12, 4.617 13, 4.617 13, 4.617 14, 4.617 14, 4.617 15, 4.617 16, 4.617 17, 4.617 18, 4.617 19, 4.617 21, 4.617 21, 4.617 24, 4.617 25, 4.617 25, 4.617 30, 4.617 31, 4.617 32, 4.617 32, 4.617 33, 4.617 33, 4.617 34, 4.617 35, 4.617 35, 4.617 36, 4.617 40, 4.617 41, 4.617 44, 4.617 47, 4.617 48, 4.617 49, 4.619 2, 4.623 2, 4.623 4, 4.623 5, 4.623 6, 4.623 7, 4.623 8, 4.623 9, 4.623 10, 4.623 11, 4.628 1, 4.628 2, 4.628 3, 4.628 4, 4.628 5, 4.628 5, 4.628 6, 4.628 7, 4.628 8, 4.631 4, 4.631 14, 4.631 16, 4.631 17, 4.631 18, 4.631 19, 4.631 20, 4.631 22, 4.632 23, 4.633 2, 4.633 3, 4.633 5, 4.633 6, 4.633 7, 4.633 8, 4.633 9, 4.633 10, 4.633 11, 4.633 12, 4.633 13, 4.635 9, 4.635 10, 4.635 11, 4.635 12, 4.635 13, 4.635 14, 4.635 15, 4.635 16, 4.635 17, 4.635 18, 4.635 19, 4.635 36, 4.635 45, 4.635

46, 4.635 48, 4.635 51, 4.635 52, 4.635 53, 4.635 54, 4.635 55, 4.635 56, 4.635 57, 4.635 58, 4.635 59, 4.635 60, 4.638 4, 4.638 6, 4.644 1, 4.644 3, 4.645 5, 4.645 6, 4.645 7, 4.645 9, 4.647 2, 4.647 6, 4.655 6, 4.655 8, 4.658 6, 4.658 9, 4.658 10, 4.658 11, 4.658 12, 4.658 13, 4.658 14, 4.658 15, 4.658 17, 4.658 18, 4.658 19, 4.658 20, 4.658 21, 4.658 42, 4.659 4, 4.659 5, 4.662 1, 4.662 3, 4.662 5, 4.672 2, 4.672 3, 4.672 4, 4.672 6, 4.677 5, 4.679 1, 4.679 3, 4.679 4, 4.679 6, 4.679 7, 4.681 2, 4.681 3, 4.681 4, 4.681 5, 4.681 6, 4.682 10, 4.687 1, 4.687 2, 4.687 3, 4.687 4, 4.690 2, 4.690 4, 4.690 10, 4.692 2, 4.692 3, 4.692 4, 4.692 4, 4.692 5, 4.692 7, 4.692 9, 4.692 10, 4.692 11, 4.692 12, 4.692 13*, 4.692 13, 4.692 15, 4.694 1, 4.694 2, 4.694 3, 4.694 4, 4.694 5, 4.695 2, 4.695 5, 4.700 2, 4.700 3, 4.700 4, 4.700 5, 4.700 6, 4.700 7, 4.700 8, 4.700 9, 4.700 10, 4.704 1, 4.704 2, 4.704 3, 4.704 4, 4.704 5, 4.704 6, 4.704 9, 4.704 10, 4.706 15, 4.711 6, 4.711 7, 4.713 1, 4.713 2, 4.713 3, 4.713 4, 4.713 5, 4.713 6, 4.714 2, 4.714 3, 4.714 4, 4.714 5, 4.714 6, 4.714 7, 4.715 2, 4.715 4, 4.715 5, 4.715 6, 4.715 7, 4.715 8, 4.715 9, 4.715 13, 4.715 14, 4.715 15, 4.715 16, 4.715 17, 4.715 18, 4.715 19, 4.715 20, 4.715 26, 4.720 1, 4.720 2, 4.720 3, 4.720 5, 4.723 1, 4.723 4, 4.723 6, 4.723 8, 4.723 9, 4.723 10, 4.723 11, 4.723 12, 4.723 13, 4.723 14, 4.723 15, 4.723 16, 4.724 1, 4.724 2, 4.724 3, 4.724 4, 4.724 5, 4.724 6, 4.724 9, 4.724 10, 4.724 11, 4.728 6, 4.732 2, 4.737 3, 4.739 4, 4.739 6, 4.739 8, 4.748 9, 4.750 1, 4.750 4, 4.752 8, 4.753 3, 4.753 10, 4.753 14, 4.753 16, 4.753 17, 4.753 18, 4.753 21, 4.753 22, 4.754 6, 4.754 7, 4.754 14, 4.754 15, 4.754 16, 4.754 17, 4.755 4, 4.755 6, 4.755 7, 4.755 8, 4.755 9, 4.759 1, 4.759 5, 4.759 6, 4.759 8, 4.759 9, 4.760 3, 4.760 4, 4.760 5, 4.760 6, 4.760 7, 4.760 8, 4.760 9, 4.761 2, 4.761 3, 4.761 4, 4.761 5, 4.761 7, 4.761 8, 4.761 9, 4.761 10, 4.761 11, 4.763 5, 4.763 6, 4.764 4, 4.764 5, 4.764 7, 4.769 3, 4.769 5, 4.769 6, 4.769 7, 4.769 11, 4.769 12, 4.769 14, 4.769 15, 4.769 16, 4.769 18, 4.769 19, 4.769 22, 4.769 41, 4.769 42, 4.769 45, 4.769 47, 4.769 55, 4.769 58, 4.769 59, 4.769 60, 4.769 61, 4.769 62, 4.769 69, 4.775 11, 4.778 6, 4.778 8, 4.778 11, 4.778 15, 4.778 18, 4.780 1, 4.780 6, 4.780 7, 4.780 17, 4.782 9, 4.782 14, 4.782 17, 4.782 22, 4.782 25, 4.782 30, 4.785 6, 4.785 8, 4.785 9, 4.785 10, 4.785 11, 4.785 12, 4.785 13, 4.785 14, 4.785 15, 4.785 16, 4.785 17, 4.785 18, 4.785 19, 4.785 20, 4.785 21, 4.785 22, 4.785 24, 4.785 30, 4.787 1, 4.787 4, 4.787 7, 4.787 8, 4.787 9, 4.787 10, 4.787 11, 4.787 12, 4.791 8, 4.791 11, 4.791 14, 4.791 16, 4.791 18, 4.792 8, 5.10 1, 5.11 1, 5.18 1, 5.18 3, 5.18 5, 5.18 7, 6.16 2, 6.55 1, 6.61 1, 6.62 1, 6.68 1, 7.220 2

bn[1.1 III 7, 1.17 V 37, 1.18 I 13, 1.24 7, 3.7 11, 4.17 8, 4.33 21, 4.35 I 2, 4.50 1, 4.64 III 1, 4.64 III 2, 4.64 III 3, 4.64 III 4, 4.75 V 13, 4.118 8, 4.190 3, 4.240 3, 4.255 1, 4.262 10, 4.322 3, 4.327 4, 4.354 1, 4.359 5, 4.372 4, 4.372 5, 4.381 18, 4.382 21, 4.386 6, 4.388 6, 4.388 7, 4.396 14, 4.406 3, 4.406 4, 4.406 6, 4.417 9, 4.420 2, 4.423 7, 4.514 2, 4.537 6, 4.560 2, 4.560 3, 4.560 4, 4.565 1, 4.565 2, 4.565 3, 4.565 4, 4.565 5, 4.611 23, 4.611 24, 4.619 10, 4.635 49, 4.662 6, 4.729 4, 4.733 2, 7.135 1

b[n 1.3 V 39, 1.5 III 21, 4.2 1, 4.12 13, 4.24 5, 4.33 18, 4.33 20, 4.39 5, 4.52 16, 4.63 II 47, 4.66 20, 4.66 21, 4.66 22, 4.66 23, 4.69 II 9, 4.69 II 24, 4.75 V 18, 4.75 V 19, 4.77 14, 4.79 5, 4.79 6, 4.93 IV 31, 4.93 IV 35, 4.93 IV 36, 4.93 IV 39, 4.93 IV

40, 4.97 1, 4.137 4, 4.190 1, 4.214 III 15, 4.214 III 17, 4.219 4, 4.224 2, 4.225 16, 4.232 4, 4.255 6, 4.290 13, 4.315 3, 4.322 12, 4.335 29, 4.382 32, 4.382 36, 4.412 I 15, 4.412 I 21, 4.412 I 22, 4.412 II 16, 4.412 II 30, 4.412 III 23, 4.422 16, 4.422 21, 4.422 22, 4.422 23, 4.422 24, 4.422 25, 4.422 27, 4.422 30, 4.422 42, 4.432 4, 4.432 5, 4.437 3, 4.437 5, 4.449 3, 4.449 4, 4.458 8, 4.502 1, 4.509 2, 4.514 1, 4.514 3, 4.514 4, 4.518 1, 4.518 2, 4.543 1, 4.543 2, 4.543 3, 4.543 4, 4.543 5, 4.544 3, 4.544 4, 4.544 5, 4.544 6, 4.560 5, 4.581 1, 4.631 21, 4.633 1, 4.658 41, 4.682 7, 4.682 8, 4.711 5, 4.728 8, 4.760 2

]bn 1.3 VI 3, 1.14 V 20, 1.17 I 3, 1.133 15, 1.171 1, 2.22 3, 4.46 1, 4.67 5, 4.101 5, 4.101 6, 4.101 7, 4.103 29, 4.103 62, 4.117 2, 4.127 12, 4.182 54, 4.223 1, 4.324 6, 4.325 2, 4.327 2, 4.327 3, 4.350 1, 4.373 6, 4.382 36, 4.389 2, 4.389 5, 4.410 36, 4.422 2, 4.422 3, 4.428 7, 4.428 8, 4.435 1, 4.435 2, 4.462 2, 4.462 3, 4.522 3, 4.528 4, 4.563 1, 4.569 2, 4.569 3, 4.587 1, 4.587 2, 4.587 3, 4.587 4, 4.596 2, 4.601 1, 4.601 2, 4.612 5, 4.612 6, 4.612 7, 4.643 17, 4.666 1, 4.666 2, 4.669 2, 4.702 5, 4.742 9, 4.769 49, 4.769 71, 4.785 29, 7.71 2, 7.110 2, 7.113 2, 7.168 3

b]n 1.4 VIII 44, 1.17 I 8, 1.94 25, 4.35 I 11, 4.35 I 12, 4.35 II 3, 4.55 23, 4.55 31, 4.57 9, 4.57 10, 4.64 IV 16, 4.69 VI 7, 4.69 VI 8, 4.69 VI 9, 4.75 IV 7, 4.98 21, 4.98 22, 4.103 58, 4.106 15, 4.112 II 2, 4.117 6, 4.159 9, 4.170 21, 4.200 9, 4.214 II 6, 4.229 10, 4.232 22*, 4.232 22, 4.232 23, 4.232 28, 4.234 4, 4.245 II 2, 4.261 12, 4.311 11, 4.318 7, 4.325 5, 4.335 20, 4.340 15, 4.382 24, 4.386 2, 4.389 12, 4.412 III 14, 4.434 2, 4.441 1, 4.445 1, 4.445 2, 4.449 1, 4.449 2, 4.452 1, 4.453 4, 4.462 1, 4.463 1, 4.464 1, 4.464 2, 4.473 3, 4.494 2, 4.495 1, 4.502 4, 4.537 1, 4.563 2, 4.563 3, 4.563 5, 4.574 6, 4.583 2, 4.583 3, 4.583 4, 4.583 5, 4.596 1, 4.596 3, 4.599 5, 4.615 3, 4.617 2, 4.624 2, 4.624 6, 4.624 9, 4.624 11, 4.631 12(!), 4.631 13, 4.658 22, 4.666 4, 4.666 5, 4.667 1, 4.679 8, 4.681 7, 4.682 2, 4.682 12, 4.737 2, 4.769 54, 4.785 23, 6.38 1

]bn[4.201 9, 4.424 12, 4.424 14, 4.769 2, 4.785 3

]bn[1.116 28 lg. abn[d

]b[n 4.432 1, 4.432 2, 4.432 3, 4.463 4

b]n[4.243 31, 4.543 6, 4.543 7, 4.737 1

[[bn]] 3.7 8, 4.281 28, 4.371 20, 4.617 15, 4.695 3

bnx[4.762 4

xbn 1.42 60

]xbn 4.613 23, 4.766 8, 7.125 2

]xxbn 4.139 8

]b/dn 4.217 4, 4.715 9

]b/dn[4.725 8

bnil 3.10 17, 4.297 3, 4.609 8, 4.609 19, 4.616 10, 4.623 6, 4.791 13

bn.dtn 4.422 53

bn.h 1.117 4

bnh 1.1 IV 12, 1.3 IV 49, 1.3 V 37, 1.4 I 13, 1.4 IV 49, 1.4 IV 52, 1.6 I 40, 1.17 I 25, 1.17 I 42, 1.117 6, 1.161 32(!), 2.82 16, 3.2 11, 3.2 17, 3.4 6, 3.5 14, 3.5 19, 4.16 12, 4.80 7, 4.102 1, 4.102 5, 4.102 21, 4.127 13, 4.243 11, 4.295 2, 4.295 4, 4.295 6, 4.295 8, 4.295 10, 4.295 13, 4.295 16, 4.332 7, 4.339 6, 4.339 19, 4.339 26, 4.339 27, 4.360 4, 4.360 10, 4.360 13, 4.364 8, 4.373 6, 4.417 8, 4.417 13, 4.417 16, 4.420 11, 4.519 2, 4.625 21, 4.644 5

bn[h 1.1 IV 29

b[nh 1.3 V 40, 4.417 14

b]nh 4.417 6

bnwn 1.16 IV 13

bnwt 1.4 II 11, 1.4 III 32, 1.6 III 5, 1.6 III 11, 1.17 I 24

bnwth 1.100 62

bny 1.1 IV 14, 1.4 II 11, 1.4 II 25, 1.4

III 32, 1.6 III 5, 1.6 III 11, 1.16 V 24, 1.17 I 24, 1.19 III 44, 2.2 10, 2.14 3(!), 2.14 11, 2.14 16, 2.46 9, 2.46 12, 7.63 7
]bny 2.46 7
]bnym 4.396 10
]b/dnyn 4.57 8
bnk 1.6 I 46, 1.22 I 2, 2.13 4, 2.30 3, 2.64 5, 2.82 6, 5.11 3
bnk[2.2 11
b]nk 1.5 V 5
bnkm 1.13 28
bnm 1.4 VII 16, 1.6 VI 11, 1.6 VI 15, 1.15 II 23, 1.15 III 21, 1.16 I 10, 2.2 8, 2.2 9, 4.561 2
bn[m 1.16 II 48
bnn 4.247 27, 4.377 16
bnn[4.258 10
bnny 2.33 34
bnʿnt 4.320 4
bnr 1.19 III 50, 1.19 III 52
bnš 1.86 8, 1.86 12, 1.127 15, 1.127 30, 1.127 31, 2.2 2, 2.2 5, 2.4 19(!), 2.9 6, 2.17 16, 2.33 33, 2.35 18, 2.45 25, 2.45 27, 2.77 9, 3.2 6, 3.5 16, 4.22 3, 4.44 23, 4.44 24, 4.44 25, 4.44 28, 4.46 2, 4.103 52, 4.125 2, 4.125 3, 4.125 6, 4.125 11, 4.125 18, 4.137 13, 4.141 I 1, 4.141 II 25, 4.144 1, 4.151 II 6, 4.163 15, 4.169 6, 4.182 56, 4.243 32, 4.277 1, 4.343 6, 4.343 7, 4.351 1, 4.358 3, 4.367 1, 4.367 9, 4.370 1, 4.380 19, 4.380 23, 4.380 24, 4.380 26, 4.398 1, 4.420 5, 4.609 1, 4.618 2, 4.618 5, 4.762 6
bnš[1.86 26, 4.44 3, 4.44 6, 4.44 7, 4.44 11, 4.161 6, 4.258 7, 4.380 9, 4.762 9, 7.55 6
bn[š 4.44 4, 4.44 8, 4.380 16, 4.609 51, 4.609 52
b[n]š[4.380 15
b[nš 4.44 9
b]nš 4.40 9, 4.380 17
bn]š 4.125 16, 4.766 12
bn]š[4.380 10
bnšx[7.197 4
bnšhm 4.347 2
bnšm 1.86 30, 1.163 2, 3.5 16, 4.29 2, 4.29 4, 4.243 8, 4.243 13, 4.243 15, 4.243 17, 4.243 19, 4.243 21, 4.243 23, 4.243 25, 4.301 1, 4.339 1, 4.339 17, 4.355 8, 4.355 9, 4.355 10, 4.355 11, 4.355 12, 4.355 13, 4.355 14, 4.355 15, 4.355 16, 4.355 17, 4.355 18, 4.355 19, 4.355 20, 4.355 21, 4.355 22, 4.355 33, 4.355 34, 4.355 35, 4.355 36, 4.355 37, 4.355 38, 4.355 39, 4.355 40, 4.355 41, 4.358 2, 4.363 2, 4.380 3, 4.380 4, 4.380 7, 4.380 18, 4.380 20, 4.380 21, 4.393 13, 4.395 1, 4.422 1, 4.618 8, 4.618 14, 4.655 1, 4.659 6, 4.752 1
bnšm[4.40 13, 4.138 1, 4.355 3, 4.355 4, 4.355 5
bnš[m 2.62 4, 4.40 15, 4.355 6
b[n]šm[4.355 7
b[n]š[m 4.380 8
b[nšm 4.40 17
]bnšm 4.243 2, 4.355 23, 4.355 24, 4.355 26, 4.355 32
b]nšm 4.243 4, 4.243 27, 4.355 25, 4.355 29, 4.355 30, 4.380 5, 4.380 6, 4.618 20
bn]šm 4.355 2, 4.355 27, 4.355 28, 4.355 31, 4.617 1, 4.618 16, 4.618 18, 4.618 22
b<n>t 1.40 35
bn{.}t 1.15 III 6
<bnt> 1.24 15
bnt 1.3 II 2, 1.3 V 20, 1.4 VI 36, 1.4 VIII 35, 1.12 II 43, 1.15 III 24, 1.17 II 26, 1.17 II 31, 1.17 II 33, 1.17 II 36, 1.17 II 38, 1.17 II 40, 1.17 VI 13, 1.24 6, 1.24 41, 1.82 13, 1.82 18, 1.82 18, 1.82 41, 1.82 41, 1.107 13, 1.124 8, 2.2 9
bn[t 1.7 35, 1.112 6
[bn]\t 1.24 40f
bnth 1.3 I 23, 4.360 3
bnṯyn 1.64 31
bs 1.87 58
bs[7.142 3
bśwn 4.14 11 cor. ḫśwn
bsn 4.15 11, 4.229 3, 4.300 3
xbsn 4.65 6
bʿ[1.176 10, 2.78 9, 4.356 16, 4.432 15, 7.149 6
]bʿ[4.200 2, 7.69 1, 7.200 1

]xbᶜ[4.742 1
bᶜd 1.16 VI 49, 1.119 9, 2.31 47, 4.17 16, 4.373 3
]bᶜd 1.20 I 2
bᶜd 1.65 10 lg. bᶜl
bᶜdh 1.45 6, 1.100 70, 1.100 70, 1.100 71
bᶜdhm 1.23 70
bᶜdy 6.4 2
bᶜdn 1.3 III 33
bᶜ]dn 1.4 II 17
bᶜyn 4.33 3, 4.51 14, 4.53 8, 4.55 12
<bᶜl> 1.19 III 12
bᶜl 1.2 I 4, 1.2 I 21, 1.2 I 24, 1.2 I 35, 1.2 I 36, 1.2 I 36, 1.2 I 38, 1.2 I 43, 1.2 IV 8, 1.2 IV 13, 1.2 IV 15, 1.2 IV 21, 1.2 IV 23, 1.2 IV 27, 1.2 IV 31, 1.3 I 3, 1.3 I 3, 1.3 I 21, 1.3 I 22, 1.3 III 6, 1.3 III 13, 1.3 III 37, 1.3 III 47, 1.3 IV 4, 1.3 IV 6, 1.3 IV 7, 1.3 IV 26, 1.3 IV 37, 1.3 IV 39, 1.3 V 3, 1.3 V 32, 1.3 V 38, 1.4 II 13, 1.4 II 22, 1.4 III 10, 1.4 III 17, 1.4 III 23, 1.4 III 37, 1.4 IV 19, 1.4 IV 50, 1.4 IV 62, 1.4 V 7, 1.4 V 12, 1.4 V 23, 1.4 V 26, 1.4 V 36, 1.4 V 48, 1.4 V 59, 1.4 V 63, 1.4 VI 2, 1.4 VI 4, 1.4 VI 7, 1.4 VI 15, 1.4 VI 36, 1.4 VII 2, 1.4 VII 11, 1.4 VII 12, 1.4 VII 13, 1.4 VII 15, 1.4 VII 24, 1.4 VII 24, 1.4 VII 28, 1.4 VII 29, 1.4 VII 30, 1.4 VII 35, 1.4 VII 38, 1.4 VII 40, 1.4 VII 42, 1.4 VII 53, 1.4 VIII 33, 1.5 I 10, 1.5 I 22, 1.5 I 26, 1.5 II 4, 1.5 II 6, 1.5 II 10, 1.5 II 18, 1.5 V 17, 1.5 VI 8, 1.5 VI 9, 1.5 VI 10, 1.5 VI 23, 1.5 VI 25, 1.5 VI 30, 1.6 I 1, 1.6 I 6, 1.6 I 7, 1.6 I 12, 1.6 I 14, 1.6 I 20, 1.6 I 21, 1.6 I 23, 1.6 I 25, 1.6 I 27, 1.6 I 29, 1.6 I 42, 1.6 I 42, 1.6 I 51, 1.6 I 59, 1.6 I 64, 1.6 II 9, 1.6 II 21, 1.6 II 30, 1.6 III 8, 1.6 III 9, 1.6 III 20, 1.6 III 21, 1.6 IV 3, 1.6 IV 4, 1.6 IV 5, 1.6 IV 14, 1.6 IV 15, 1.6 IV 16, 1.6 IV 20, 1.6 V 1, 1.6 V 5, 1.6 V 10, 1.6 VI 10, 1.6 VI 12, 1.6 VI 14, 1.6 VI 17, 1.6 VI 18, 1.6 VI 20, 1.6 VI 22, 1.6 VI 25, 1.6 VI 33, 1.6 VI 58, 1.8 II 3, 1.8 II 6, 1.9 12, 1.9 14, 1.9 17, 1.10 I 6, 1.10 II 3, 1.10 II 4, 1.10 II 13, 1.10 II 16, 1.10 II 22, 1.10 II 23, 1.10 II 31, 1.10 III 7, 1.10 III 11, 1.10 III 13, 1.10 III 32, 1.10 III 33, 1.10 III 35, 1.10 III 37, 1.11 8, 1.12 I 33, 1.12 I 34, 1.12 I 38, 1.12 I 40, 1.12 II 5, 1.12 II 21, 1.12 II 31, 1.12 II 33, 1.12 II 53, 1.12 II 55, 1.13 30, 1.14 II 24, 1.14 IV 7, 1.15 II 3, 1.15 II 12, 1.16 I 6, 1.16 II 45, 1.16 III 5, 1.16 III 7, 1.16 IV 7, 1.16 IV 11, 1.16 VI 56, 1.17 I 16, 1.17 I 31, 1.17 II 21, 1.17 V 20, 1.17 V 30, 1.17 VI 28, 1.17 VI 30, 1.19 I 43, 1.19 I 46, 1.19 III 2, 1.19 III 2, 1.19 III 8, 1.19 III 9, 1.19 III 13, 1.19 III 17, 1.19 III 17, 1.19 III 22, 1.19 III 23, 1.19 III 26, 1.19 III 27, 1.19 III 31, 1.19 III 31, 1.19 III 37, 1.19 III 43, 1.19 III 43, 1.19 IV 5, 1.22 I 8, 1.22 I 8, 1.22 I 26, 1.24 26, 1.24 27, 1.24 42, 1.27 4, 1.39 6, 1.39 7, 1.39 10, 1.39 14, 1.41 15, 1.41 41, 1.46 3, 1.46 6, 1.46 6, 1.46 8, 1.46 14, 1.47 5, 1.47 26, 1.48 2, 1.63 12(?), 1.65 10, 1.65 10(!), 1.77 3, 1.82 1, 1.82 3, 1.82 10, 1.82 38, 1.84 8, 1.84 47, 1.86 3, 1.87 45, 1.91 14, 1.92 14, 1.92 29, 1.92 31, 1.92 36, 1.92 39, 1.93 4, 1.98 8, 1.100 9, 1.101 1, 1.101 18, 1.102 3, 1.105 6, 1.105 17, 1.105 24, 1.108 18, 1.109 9, 1.109 11, 1.109 13, 1.109 16, 1.109 16, 1.109 20, 1.109 22, 1.109 29, 1.109 32, 1.112 22, 1.112 23, 1.114 20, 1.118 4, 1.118 25, 1.119 2, 1.119 3, 1.119 9, 1.119 12, 1.119 15, 1.119 21, 1.119 25, 1.119 27, 1.119 30, 1.119 30, 1.119 31, 1.119 32, 1.119 32, 1.119 33, 1.123 4, 1.124 8, 1.130 10, 1.130 11, 1.130 17, 1.130 24, 1.134 8, 1.139 6, 1.147 14, 1.148 8, 1.148 10(!), 1.148 26, 1.148 27, 1.151 10, 1.151 11, 1.151 12, 1.151 13, 1.156 2, 1.162 8, 1.162 13, 1.162 17, 1.169 2, 1.170 9, 1.173 2, 1.173 5, 2.4 23, 2.42 6, 2.44 8, 2.44 10, 2.44 16, 2.75 12, 2.81 3, 4.15 2, 4.15 3, 4.15 4, 4.15 5, 4.15 6,

4.15 7, 4.15 8, 4.63 IV 17, 4.153 2, 4.153 3, 4.153 4, 4.153 5, 4.153 6, 4.153 7, 4.153 8, 4.153 9, 4.153 10, 4.153 11, 4.172 5, 4.183 I 1, 4.224 6, 4.232 6, 4.321 3, 4.332 10, 4.332 19, 4.370 13, 4.520 3, 4.609 35, 4.609 36, 4.609 53, 4.647 7, 4.728 1, 4.778 4, 4.782 5, 5.11 2, 6.48 5, 7.63 4

bʿl[1.2 I 18, 1.2 II 5, 1.2 II 12, 1.22 II 7, 1.31 3, 1.86 17, 1.109 35, 1.114 24, 1.129 5, 1.166 9, 2.5 6, 2.23 31, 2.31 58, 2.35 1, 4.412 II 10, 4.635 48, 4.725 3

bʿ[l 1.5 IV 6, 1.5 IV 8, 1.6 III 3, 1.10 II 34, 1.12 II 24, 1.19 III 36, 1.109 5, 1.130 3, 2.3 5, 2.23 19, 2.31 65

b[ʿ]l 1.130 22

b[ʿl 1.1 IV 22, 1.2 IV 28, 1.10 III 10, 1.41 33, 1.77 2, 1.87 18, 1.87 36, 1.130 26

]bʿl 1.4 IV 43, 1.109 34, 1.137 4, 1.172 10, 4.474 2, 4.701 7

b]ʿl 1.9 5, 1.11 3, 1.119 34, 1.151 13, 1.173 3, 7.222 5

bʿ]l 1.4 VI 38, 1.5 V 23, 4.15 9, 4.15 11, 4.183 II 10

]bʿl[1.173 10, 4.509 3, 4.590 4, 4.757 1, 7.132 11

b]ʿ[l 1.46 17

bʿlx[4.50 4

bʿld[4.86 11

bʿldn 4.134 13

b]ʿldn 4.307 13

bʿldʿ 4.376 1

bʿlh 1.2 I 42, 1.48 9, 2.47 2, 3.1 12, 3.1 13, 3.1 26, 4.16 2, 6.14 2

b[ʿlh 2.39 8

bʿlhn 1.103 34

bʿlz 4.356 3

<b>ʿly 2.33 26

bʿly 2.17 8, 2.23 2, 2.23 19, 2.23 20, 2.23 24, 2.33 22, 2.33 31, 2.33 33, 2.35 5, 2.35 19, 2.40 1, 2.40 5, 2.40 18, 2.42 4, 2.42 10, 2.42 13, 2.45 11, 2.49 14, 2.61 2, 2.64 10, 2.64 13, 2.64 17, 2.75 5, 2.76 4, 2.76 6, 2.76 7, 2.81 6, 2.81 22, 2.81 24, 4.69 VI 4, 4.80 14, 4.116 3, 4.360 7, 4.389 6, 5.11 16

bʿly[2.76 8

bʿl[y 2.2 12, 2.23 8, 2.23 10

bʿ[ly 2.42 11, 2.77 6

b[ʿly 2.42 1, 2.51 2, 2.63 1

]bʿly 2.55 3, 4.75 V 5

]bʿly[4.757 3

bʿ]ly 2.35 16, 2.50 2

bʿl]y 2.23 17

bʿlyx[4.75 I 6

bʿlyskn 4.75 III 9

bʿlytn 4.628 2

bʿlk 1.1 IV 6, 1.161 20, 1.161 21, 2.23 4, 2.39 11, 2.39 13, 2.39 15, 2.39 19, 2.81 21

bʿl[k 2.73 8

bʿlkm 1.2 I 17, 1.2 I 33, 1.2 I 45, 1.15 IV 28, 4.17 16, 5.10 3

bʿlm 1.2 IV 9, 1.2 IV 36, 1.6 V 11, 1.10 II 32, 1.39 9, 1.47 6, 1.47 7, 1.47 8, 1.47 9, 1.82 6, 1.82 14, 1.87 20, 1.118 5, 1.118 6, 1.118 7, 1.118 8, 1.118 9, 1.118 10, 1.119 6, 1.119 28, 1.148 3, 1.148 4, 1.148 11, 1.148 11, 1.148 11, 1.148 12, 1.148 12, 1.148 44, 4.360 2, 4.360 5, 4.360 6, 4.360 7, 4.360 11, 4.691 7

bʿlm[4.262 4

b]ʿlm 1.47 10, 1.148 11

bʿl]m 1.47 11

]bʿl[m 1.148 4

bʿlmʿḏr 4.172 3, 4.266 3, 6.16 1

bʿlmtpṭ 4.214 II 5

bʿln 1.103 39, 3.4 5, 3.5 12, 3.5 18, 4.7 17, 4.35 II 17, 4.98 11, 4.133 3, 4.141 II 22, 4.159 1, 4.188 17, 4.281 8, 4.332 16, 4.358 6, 4.360 1, 4.609 12, 4.609 21, 4.609 23, 4.609 28, 4.617 2, 4.636 5, 4.729 2, 4.753 10, 4.787 5

bʿln[4.496 3

]bʿln 4.320 17

bʿl<n>y 2.70 28

bʿlny 1.15 V 20, 2.70 1, 2.70 6, 2.70 8

bʿlsip 4.80 3

bʿlskn 4.214 I 15, 4.377 28

bʿlṣdq 4.180 7

bʿlṣn 4.22 3, 4.183 II 21

bʿlrm 4.370 9

bʿlšlm 4.293 2
bʿlšm[4.679 5
bʿlt 1.39 21, 1.41 37, 1.48 4, 1.53 7, 1.87 5, 1.91 14, 1.105 8, 1.105 16, 1.108 6, 1.108 7, 1.109 31, 2.31 48, 4.54 1
bʿlt[1.81 6
bʿl[t 1.112 4
b]ʿlt 1.91 20
bʿ]lt 1.108 8
bʿ\lt 1.108 6f
bʿ]\lt 1.87 28f
bʿltn 4.611 2
]bʿm 4.682 1
bʿṣ 1.63 12 lg. bʿl?
bʿr 2.31 57, 2.61 9
bʿrm 2.71 17 lg. b ʿrm?
bʿrm 4.338 17 lg. arbʿm?
bġr 1.93 1(?)
b/dpr 4.750 15
]xbb/y/ṣ 4.214 II 16
]b/d/uṣ/l[7.79 4
b/ṣp/tx[1.20 II 12
bṣy 4.754 17
bṣl 1.44 5
bṣmy 4.408 4
bṣmn 4.183 II 29, 4.364 13, 4.658 21
bṣql 1.19 II 13, 1.19 II 14, 1.19 II 16, 1.85 5
bṣq[l 1.19 II 13
bṣ[ql 1.19 II 15
b[ṣql 1.71 5
bṣr 1.91 23, 4.355 39, 4.370 3, 4.610 18, 4.621 4, 4.750 16, 4.777 11
bṣr[4.68 45, 4.684 2
bṣ[r 4.693 41
bṣry 4.261 18
bṣry[4.33 6
bṣ]ry 4.51 11
bq[4.235 8, 7.15 2
bql 1.71 25, 1.85 32
bql[2.7 6
bq[l 4.520 3
]b/dq/tn 4.769 29
bqʿ 4.247 21, 4.247 23, 4.693 13
bqʿt 1.24 48, 4.48 8, 4.63 II 21, 4.100 6, 4.380 12, 4.643 9, 4.683 16, 4.777 4
b[q]ʿt 4.355 9
bqʿty 4.25 6
bqr 1.92 12, 4.691 1
bqr 1.14 III 9 lg. mqr
bqš 4.75 IV 13
bqtm 1.87 35 lg. dqtm
bqṯ 2.39 34
br 1.4 I 35, 2.19 4, 4.81 2, 4.81 3, 4.81 6, 4.608 3, 4.647 1, 4.647 4, 4.647 6, 4.769 18
br[1.55 7, 4.81 11, 4.81 12, 4.81 13, 4.81 14, 4.81 15, 4.81 16, 4.81 17, 4.81 18, 4.81 19, 4.382 34, 4.434 6, 4.702 3
b[r 4.81 10
]br[1.167 1
brxxx 1.20 II 12
]b/drx[4.457 2
bri 4.103 38
brd[4.255 4
brdd 4.7 3, 4.103 31, 4.763 9
brdn 4.356 13, 4.713 3
brḏl 4.91 6
brzn 4.66 6, 4.103 17, 4.623 5, 4.623 7, 4.631 22, 4.785 22
brzn[4.436 2
brzt 4.617 13
brḥ 1.5 I 1, 1.19 III 48, 1.19 III 55, 1.82 38
b]rḥ 1.5 I 28
]b/drḥn 7.50 2
brḥm 7.219 1
bry 2.14 3 lg. bny
]bry[1.107 50
]brk 1.15 V 11
b]rk 1.7 9
brkh 1.17 V 27, 1.18 IV 24, 1.172 25
brky 1.5 I 16
brkm 1.3 II 13, 1.3 II 27, 1.15 II 18
brkn 1.22 I 7
brkt 1.133 6
brkthm 1.2 I 23, 1.2 I 29
brktkm 1.2 I 25, 1.2 I 27
brktm 1.19 IV 32
brlt 1.5 I 15, 1.17 I 37, 1.17 V 18, 1.17 V 24
brlth 1.16 VI 12, 1.18 IV 25, 1.18 IV 37, 1.19 II 44
brlthm 1.19 II 39
b]rltk 1.16 I 42

brm 4.421 3
brn 4.281 26, 4.410 6
br[n 4.488 4
brś 4.759 8
brśm 4.69 II 19, 4.106 11
brsm 4.785 17
brsn 4.69 I 10
brq 1.3 III 26, 1.17 VI 11, 1.17 VI 12, 1.101 4, 4.98 15, 4.181 3, 4.300 2, 4.313 9, 4.350 5, 4.724 4
brq[4.262 9
b]rq 4.64 IV 4
brqd 4.377 15
brqm 1.4 V 9, 1.101 3
brqn 3.8 23, 4.53 5, 4.53 11, 4.141 I 9, 4.232 46, 4.278 8, 4.410 32, 4.753 11
brqt 4.787 7
brr 1.41 7, 1.46 10, 1.87 49, 1.87 51, 1.87 55, 1.105 20, 1.106 27, 1.112 11, 1.112 17, 1.119 5, 4.91 12, 4.203 2, 4.203 15, 4.272 3, 4.337 4
brr[4.268 3
br[r 1.87 4
b[rr 1.109 2
b]rr 1.48 21
br\r 1.87 7f
brrn 1.123 23, 4.200 9, 4.631 21
brt 2.3 5, 2.8 4, 2.19 3
]brt 7.50 6
]b/drt 4.103 56
brtk 1.82 5
bš[7.53 8
]bš 4.734 13
b/dš 4.627 2, 4.627 3, 4.627 4
]b/dš 4.627 8
b/d]š 4.627 11, 4.627 13
bšl 1.147 7
bšr 1.10 III 34, 1.15 IV 25, 7.163 5
]bš[r 1.15 V 8
bšrh 1.4 II 5, 1.24 9
]bšry 1.63 6
b]šrk 1.92 34
bšrt 1.10 III 33, 1.10 III 33
bšrtk 1.4 V 27
bštm 1.1 III 18, 1.3 IV 33
b<t> 1.4 I 16
bt 1.1 IV 6, 1.1 IV 21, 1.2 III 19, 1.3 I 24, 1.3 II 29, 1.3 II 31, 1.3 III 6, 1.3 III 7, 1.3 III 8, 1.3 III 46, 1.3 IV 47, 1.3 IV 51, 1.3 IV 52, 1.3 V 3, 1.3 V 27, 1.3 V 38, 1.3 V 41, 1.4 I 17, 1.4 I 18, 1.4 IV 50, 1.4 IV 55, 1.4 IV 56, 1.4 IV 57, 1.4 IV 62, 1.4 V 10, 1.4 V 11, 1.4 V 28, 1.4 V 56, 1.4 VI 10, 1.4 VI 11, 1.4 VII 13, 1.4 VII 14, 1.4 VIII 7, 1.5 IV 21, 1.5 V 10, 1.5 V 11, 1.5 V 15, 1.7 24, 1.8 II 3, 1.12 II 60, 1.12 II 61, 1.14 I 7, 1.14 II 29, 1.14 IV 10, 1.15 IV 21, 1.16 I 29, 1.16 III 17, 1.16 IV 7, 1.16 IV 11, 1.16 VI 3, 1.17 I 25, 1.17 I 31, 1.17 I 32, 1.17 II 4, 1.17 II 5, 1.17 II 21, 1.17 II 22, 1.18 I 16, 1.18 I 17, 1.19 I 32, 1.19 III 47, 1.22 I 24, 1.23 45, 1.23 45, 1.24 1, 1.24 5, 1.24 29, 1.39 12, 1.39 13, 1.41 20, 1.41 24, 1.41 32, 1.43 2, 1.43 2, 1.43 10, 1.43 16, 1.53 8, 1.63 12, 1.70 3, 1.79 7, 1.80 2, 1.87 26, 1.87 40, 1.87 42, 1.91 7, 1.91 10, 1.91 11, 1.100 1, 1.100 1, 1.100 1, 1.100 71, 1.100 72, 1.102 1, 1.104 13, 1.104 13, 1.104 14, 1.104 21, 1.105 6, 1.106 10, 1.106 12, 1.109 11, 1.114 12, 1.115 3, 1.115 7, 1.115 9, 1.116 10, 1.117 7, 1.119 3, 1.119 8, 1.119 9, 1.119 14, 1.119 22, 1.119 33, 1.123 29, 1.124 8, 1.124 9, 1.127 14, 1.127 31, 1.130 26, 1.132 3(!), 1.139 14, 1.148 18, 1.157 3, 1.171 1, 2.2 5, 2.26 6, 2.36 5, 2.36 14, 2.70 24, 2.72 17, 2.72 24, 2.72 32, 3.2 5, 3.2 14, 3.4 9, 3.4 11, 4.15 1, 4.15 2, 4.15 3, 4.15 4, 4.15 5, 4.15 6, 4.15 7, 4.15 8, 4.15 9, 4.15 11, 4.16 1, 4.42 5, 4.54 1, 4.75 III 5, 4.75 III 6, 4.75 III 13, 4.75 VI 2, 4.80 7, 4.98 13, 4.102 1, 4.102 2, 4.102 3, 4.102 4, 4.102 5, 4.102 6, 4.102 8, 4.102 9, 4.102 10, 4.102 11, 4.102 12, 4.102 13, 4.102 15, 4.102 17, 4.102 21, 4.102 22, 4.102 23, 4.102 24, 4.102 25, 4.102 26, 4.102 27, 4.102 29, 4.102 30, 4.123 16, 4.128 4, 4.137 14, 4.145 2, 4.149 1, 4.149 17, 4.149 19, 4.163 16, 4.168 6, 4.195 8, 4.195 9, 4.195 10, 4.199 5, 4.219 2, 4.254 1, 4.254 3, 4.269 1,

4.269 29, 4.274 5, 4.274 7, 4.337 16, 4.338 2, 4.341 5, 4.341 21, 4.358 1, 4.361 1, 4.382 31, 4.392 2, 4.392 3, 4.392 4, 4.430 4, 4.644 5, 4.644 7, 4.659 7, 4.688 3, 4.705 4, 4.710 6, 4.721 7, 4.727 2, 4.727 3, 4.727 4, 4.727 5, 4.727 6, 4.727 7, 4.727 8, 4.727 9, 4.727 10, 4.727 11, 4.727 12, 4.727 13, 4.727 14, 4.727 15, 4.727 16, 4.727 17, 4.727 18, 4.727 19, 4.727 20, 4.727 21, 4.727 22, 4.727 23, 4.734 5, 4.750 5, 4.750 6, 4.750 7, 4.750 8, 4.750 9, 4.750 10, 4.750 11, 4.750 14, 4.750 15, 4.755 2, 4.764 2, 4.766 12, 4.781 2, 5.11 5, 6.24 2, 6.66 9, 6.66 10, 7.63 5, 7.136 5

bt[1.4 II 1, 1.22 IV 5, 1.24 26, 1.27 3, 1.81 7, 4.269 2, 7.137 2, 7.140 3

b[t 1.3 I 25, 1.41 55, 1.81 8, 4.727 1

]bt 1.2 III 10, 1.117 5, 1.137 5, 1.169 18, 2.72 43, 4.94 13, 4.195 6, 4.197 13, 4.249 5, 4.270 2, 4.529 1, 4.529 2, 4.592 3, 6.47 3, 7.107 3

]\bt 1.69 6f

b]t 1.2 III 11, 1.41 37, 1.124 6, 4.219 3, 4.529 3, 4.529 4, 4.572 11, 4.727 24

]bt[4.572 4, 6.56 3, 7.90 1, 7.216 2

bt 4.214 II 19 lg. bn

bt 1.101 7 lg. dt?

btx[2.31 5

]xbt 1.107 27

xbt[4.253 2

[[bt]] = bt<h> 1.19 IV 10

]b/dt 1.82 3, 7.185 5

]b/dt[4.64 V 1

b/ṣt 4.769 42

b/ṣp/tx[1.20 II 12

btbt 1.105 22, 1.112 28, 4.182 18

btbt[1.112 24

]btdx[7.24 3

]btdp[1.68 18

bth 1.3 II 17, 1.7 3, 1.14 II 43, 1.14 IV 21, 1.15 II 9, 1.17 II 24, 1.17 II 26, 1.17 II 39, 1.19 I 49, 1.19 IV 8, 1.23 36, 1.100 67, 1.114 1, 1.114 17, 1.161 33, 2.2 4, 3.4 7, 4.80 15, 4.102 22, 4.102 25, 4.102 27, 4.258 3, 4.519 4, 4.617 1, 4.659 2

bt[h 1.19 IV 27, 1.92 14

]bth 4.420 12, 4.519 1, 4.519 5

b]th 1.15 II 10

[[bt]] = bt<h> 1.19 IV 10

btw 3.9 4, 4.700 10

btwm 4.320 13

bty 1.14 III 28, 1.14 III 38, 1.14 IV 40, 1.14 VI 14, 1.14 VI 23, 1.21 II 1, 1.21 II 9, 1.22 II 3, 2.31 66, 2.73 9, 3.9 8, 4.371 15

bt[y 1.22 II 8

bt\[y 1.21 II 7f

b[t]y 1.19 IV 20

]bty 4.646 4

b]ty 1.21 II 2, 4.682 7

xbty 4.77 16

]xbty 4.676 2

btk 1.15 II 22, 1.16 I 2, 1.16 I 16, 1.16 II 38, 1.82 12, 1.82 40, 1.127 23, 2.5 4, 2.31 58

btl 4.609 25

btlyn 4.72 3

btlt 1.3 III 11, 1.3 IV 21, 1.3 V 19, 1.3 V 29, 1.3 V 29, 1.4 II 14, 1.4 II 38, 1.4 III 24, 1.4 III 33, 1.4 IV 18, 1.4 V 20, 1.4 V 25, 1.6 II 14, 1.6 III 22, 1.6 III 23, 1.6 IV 6, 1.6 IV 21, 1.10 II 10, 1.10 II 15, 1.10 II 21, 1.10 II 26, 1.10 III 2, 1.10 III 9, 1.10 III 9, 1.13 19, 1.15 II 27, 1.17 VI 25, 1.18 I 14, 1.18 I 22, 1.18 IV 5, 1.18 IV 12, 1.18 IV 16, 1.19 II 43, 1.25 7, 1.101 15

bt\lt 1.3 II 32f

btl[t 1.7 25

b[t]lt 1.4 II 23

]btlt 1.4 III 39, 1.10 I 1, 1.19 I 5

b]tlt 1.11 4, 1.92 29

bt]lt 1.7 13, 1.10 II 35, 1.11 7, 1.18 I 20, 1.18 IV 4

btltm 1.17 VI 34

btm 1.23 45, 1.48 4, 1.94 24, 4.370 14, 4.750 13, 4.750 16, 4.750 17, 4.750 18

bt[m 1.41 37

]btm 1.10 I 20

b]tm 1.116 30(!)

]xbtm[4.30 5

]btmny[7.164 6

btn 1.124 14, 4.315 2, 4.708 5, 4.769 47

btn[4.80 8

]b/dtn 4.69 II 9

]b/dq/tn 4.769 29

btr 4.335 2

btry 4.122 20, 4.681 4

btšy 3.4 7

bṯ 1.2 IV 28, 1.2 IV 29

bṯ[7.56 4

]bṯ 7.50 1

bṯy 1.96 6, 1.96 11, 1.96 12

bṯn 1.3 III 41, 1.5 I 1, 1.5 I 2, 1.17 VI 14, 1.19 IV 61, 1.100 74, 1.100 75, 1.166 28, 1.169 3, 1.175 11

]b/dṯn 1.55 5

bṯnm 1.6 VI 19, 1.82 6

]bṯnm 1.82 35

bṯnt 1.82 35

bṯt 1.1 IV 5, 1.4 III 19, 1.4 III 21, 1.96 6, 1.96 13

bṯṯ 1.78 1 lg. b ṯṯ?

G

g 1.23 14, 5.4 1, 5.6 1, 5.8 1, 5.9 I 17, 5.9 I 18, 5.12 1, 5.12 5, 5.13 1, 5.13 2, 5.13 3, 5.13 4, 5.13 5, 5.13 6, 5.13 7, 5.14 3, 5.15 1(*quater*), 5.15 4, 5.16 1, 5.16 2, 5.16 8, 5.17 4, 5.19 1, 5.20 1, 5.20 4, 5.21 1, 5.24 1, 5.25 15
g[1.7 34, 1.69 3, 2.27 3, 4.205 11, 4.214 III 13, 4.424 18, 4.563 5, 7.109 1
]g 4.247 11, 4.521 2, 7.4 1, 7.212 1
]g[7.28 1
g 5.13 2 lg. z
gxxx 1.42 43
gx[1.20 II 3, 1.82 17, 4.357 8, 4.399 16
]xg 7.130 4
gxxy 4.245 I 6
./g[7.135 3
g/z/ḫ[1.176 13, 4.422 51
]g/m 4.234 2
xxga 4.399 4
gan 1.17 VI 44
gb 1.1 V 13, 1.24 43, 1.43 1, 1.43 2, 1.172 23
gb 1.24 43 lg. . b
gb[3.7 10, 4.381 23, 4.422 45, 4.764 7
]xgb 4.198 8, 4.708 10
]gbd 4.224 5
gbh 1.1 V 28, 1.114 5, 1.175 13, 1.175 17
gby 4.110 4
gbk 1.169 5
gbl 1.3 VI 7, 1.16 VI 57, 2.44 8, 4.338 13, 4.338 15, 7.137 5
gb[l 1.2 I 9
g]bl 2.44 3
]gbl 4.618 28
gbly 4.321 2
gbln 4.63 III 14
]gbn 4.151 I 10
]g/ṣbn 4.57 7
gbʿ 1.3 III 31, 1.5 VI 27, 1.6 II 16, 4.63 II 10
gbʿhd[1.9 10
gbʿl 4.750 11
gbʿly 4.33 27, 4.33 28, 4.51 5, 4.68 6, 4.177 2, 4.365 6, 4.380 6, 4.386 2, 4.693 6
gbʿl[y 4.317 5
gbʿ]ly 4.784 7
gbʿlym 4.40 16
gbʿm 1.4 V 16, 1.4 V 32, 1.4 V 39
gbʿn 4.769 16
gbry 4.296 13
gbrn 4.141 II 19, 4.309 17, 4.730 6
gbṯt 1.12 I 31
gg 1.13 11, 1.41 50, 4.102 2
gg[4.17 19, 4.678 5
ggh 1.17 I 32
ggy 1.17 II 22, 4.429 3
ggk 1.17 II 7
ggn 1.92 16
ggnh 1.16 VI 26
ggʿt 4.364 4
gg[ʿt 4.337 9
ggt 1.14 II 27, 1.14 IV 9
gd 1.23 14, 1.85 20, 1.89 4, 1.97 13
gd[1.85 25, 1.123 21, 4.258 4, 7.52 7
]gd[7.13 2
g]d 1.89 3
gl/d[4.658 23
gdaḫ 1.87 59
gdy 1.79 4, 4.150 3, 4.423 23
gdl 4.14 1, 4.14 7, 4.14 13, 4.240 2, 4.786 2
gdl[4.426 4, 4.788 3, 7.46 8, 7.140 1
gd]l 1.103 47
gdlm 4.152 6
g<d>lt 1.119 7, 1.132 20
gdlt 1.3 V 23, 1.18 I 10, 1.39 3, 1.39 8, 1.39 8, 1.39 13, 1.39 13, 1.39 13, 1.39 14, 1.39 14, 1.39 15, 1.39 15, 1.39 15, 1.39 19, 1.39 21, 1.41 12, 1.41 17, 1.41 30, 1.41 33, 1.41 34, 1.41 44, 1.41 46, 1.46 4, 1.46 5, 1.46 9, 1.53 8, 1.87 28, 1.87 33, 1.87 36,

1.87 37, 1.106 3, 1.106 4, 1.106 5, 1.106 18, 1.106 21, 1.106 31, 1.109 13, 1.109 32, 1.109 35, 1.112 26, 1.119 6, 1.119 6, 1.119 7, 1.132 5, 1.132 6, 1.132 7, 1.132 18, 1.132 19, 1.148 9, 1.162 18, 1.162 19

gdl[t 1.39 5, 1.87 16, 1.138 5

gd[]t 1.41 26, 1.41 14, 1.41 41, 1.126 3, 1.130 27, 1.138 2

g[dlt 1.87 45

g\[dlt 1.46 6f

]gdlt 1.46 7, 1.139 9

g]dlt 1.39 18

gd]lt 1.58 2

gdl]t 1.46 9, 1.87 31

g]dlt[1.28 2

gdm 1.3 II 2, 1.17 VI 21, 1.111 7

gdn 4.63 III 12, 4.75 IV 12, 4.96 8, 4.244 17, 4.658 18, 4.710 2

gdr[4.617 19

gdrn 3.7 7, 4.63 I 43

gdrt 1.19 I 13

gdš 4.7 9

gh 1.2 III 15, 1.2 IV 6, 1.3 III 36, 1.4 II 21, 1.4 IV 30, 1.4 V 26, 1.4 VII 22, 1.5 VI 22, 1.6 I 39, 1.6 II 11, 1.6 III 17, 1.6 IV 9, 1.6 V 11, 1.6 VI 13, 1.10 II 19, 1.15 III 27, 1.16 I 13, 1.16 II 36, 1.16 VI 15, 1.16 VI 40, 1.17 II 12, 1.18 I 23, 1.19 III 11, 1.19 III 16, 1.19 III 25, 1.19 III 30, 1.19 III 42, 1.19 III 51, 1.19 IV 2, 1.19 IV 20

gh[1.5 IV 5

]gh 1.5 II 21, 1.17 VI 53

]gh[7.209 4

ghl 1.45 3

ghm 1.5 II 17, 1.14 VI 39, 1.19 II 40

gw[1.54 4

]xgw[7.39 3

gwl 4.124 9, 4.213 18, 4.348 23, 4.397 7, 4.618 4, 4.618 24, 4.625 11

gz/ḫ̮[4.160 7

gzzm 4.213 30, 4.269 4, 4.269 26

gzl 2.22 3, 4.63 I 5, 4.75 III 4, 4.356 14, 4.389 2

<g>zr 1.23 63

gzr 1.23 63

gzry 4.69 III 1

gz/ḫ̮[4.160 7

gḫ̮t 4.127 5

gy 2.4 19, 2.82 14

gyx 7.218 5

gyn 4.340 8

gyn[4.334 5(cor.)

gynm 4.44 28

gk[1.136 2

]gk 4.104 3

gl 1.14 II 19, 1.14 IV 1, 1.14 IV 2, 4.356 3

gl[4.308 15

g]l 1.14 II 18

gl[1.13 35

]glx[4.699 1, 7.161 2

gl/d[4.658 23

glb 2.62 5, 4.610 28

glbm 4.269 29, 4.275 16

glbt 4.303 2

glbty 4.267 4, 4.610 27

glbty[4.621 11

glgl 1.13 33, 4.339 13

gld 4.75 III 5

gld[4.617 3

gldy 4.110 17

gl[ḥ]t 1.19 II 32

glyt/n 4.106 18

glyṯlymxxw 1.70 2

gll 4.683 31

glln 4.110 19

gllr 4.787 1

glltky 4.643 11, 4.643 12

gllt[ky 4.408 5

]glm 4.148 9

gln 4.12 6, 4.63 I 27, 4.309 11, 4.327 3, 4.379 3, 4.635 43, 4.759 9

g/sln 4.86 6

glʿd 4.93 I 14, 4.125 2, 4.412 III 11

glṯ 1.4 V 7, 1.8 II 13, 1.101 7

gm 1.1 IV 2, 1.3 V 12, 1.4 II 29, 1.4 VII 52, 1.6 I 10, 1.6 I 43, 1.6 III 22, 1.8 II 5, 1.14 V 22, 1.15 IV 2, 1.16 IV 16, 1.17 V 15, 1.19 I 49, 1.103 3

gm[1.4 II 47, 4.214 III 11, 7.116 2

]gm 2.3 25, 2.81 24

g]m 1.14 V 13

g]mx 1.17 VI 41

]xgm[4.116 1

gmdr 4.7 10

gmz 4.350 14
gmḥ 4.51 3
gmḥn 4.55 28, 4.214 III 8
gml 1.24 42
gml[m 1.104 22
gmm 4.55 10
gmn 1.6 I 19, 1.6 I 21, 4.280 8, 4.410 29
g]mn 1.6 I 23
gm]n 1.6 I 29
gmnpk 4.638 3
gmr 1.2 I 46, 1.6 VI 6
gmr[4.74 4
gmrd 4.7 11, 4.7 15, 4.103 14, 4.103 23, 4.103 24, 4.103 48, 4.103 50, 4.165 10, 4.425 15, 4.692 6
gm]rd 4.692 7
gmrhd 4.75 VI 7, 4.753 6
gmrm 1.6 VI 16
gmrn 4.127 11, 4.335 27
gmrš 4.75 IV 7, 4.313 18
gmrš[4.422 41
gmrt 4.63 I 10, 4.277 7, 4.368 19, 4.377 18
gmš 4.611 18, 4.713 2
gn 1.5 VI 21, 1.6 I 4, 1.106 18, 1.106 23, 1.165 3, 4.75 V 17, 4.219 3, 4.219 14, 6.62 2
gn[4.220 5, 4.567 3
]gn 4.69 IV 21
]gnx[4.623 12
gnb 4.50 7, 4.52 1
gngnh 1.4 VII 49
gngnt 1.91 22
gnh 1.106 22
gny 4.54 12
gnym 4.55 13
gnʿ 4.382 14
gnʿy 4.68 56, 4.213 23, 4.297 4, 4.365 26, 4.380 17
g]nʿy 4.48 12
gnʿym 3.3 13
gnryn 2.15 1, 2.15 7
gntn[4.422 47
g/ḫ/zslrš 4.63 II 15
gsn 4.382 27, 4.616 13
gssn 6.63 1
gʿyn 4.33 33, 4.50 12, 4.55 31, 4.214 II 2
gʿl 1.98 7
gʿr 1.114 14, 4.103 21, 4.611 16
]gʿr[4.653 3
gʿt 1.14 III 18
gp 1.23 30, 1.23 30
]gp[1.68 12
gpn 1.3 III 36, 1.4 IV 7, 1.4 IV 12, 1.5 I 12, 1.8 II 6, 1.23 9, 1.23 10, 1.23 11, 2.6 3, 2.31 35, 4.261 24, 4.339 20, 4.358 7, 5.23 11
gpnx[4.245 I 13
gpny 1.19 II 4, 4.125 17
gpnm 1.4 IV 10
gp[nm 1.2 I 43
gpp 4.706 4
gprh 1.19 I 11
gprm 1.19 I 11
gpt 1.4 VII 36
gr 1.19 III 47, 1.40 35, 1.84 12, 1.119 26, 4.655 6, 5.22 28
gr[4.69 V 13, 4.114 15, 4.542 1, 4.785 8
g[r 1.40 18
]gr 2.2 3, 7.140 2
]gr[7.11 2
]grx[7.150 3
grb 4.366 13
grbzhm 4.363 2
grbn 4.75 VI 3, 4.101 3, 4.245 II 4, 4.263 6, 4.371 8, 4.412 I 13, 4.775 5
grgyn 4.337 24
g]rgyn 4.244 27, 4.763 8
grgmš 2.75 8
grg[mš 2.36 21
g]rgmš 2.20 1
grgmšh 4.779 13
grgs 4.33 29, 4.51 9
grgs[4.695 2
g]rgs 4.52 13
g]rgrh 1.16 I 48
grgš 4.50 14, 4.123 15, 4.187 3, 4.194 1, 4.214 III 21, 4.377 9, 4.787 4
g]rgš 2.67 2
grdy 4.309 28
grdn 4.93 IV 18, 4.422 3
grdš 1.14 I 11, 1.14 I 23
grm 4.658 1
grn 1.17 V 7, 1.19 I 30, 1.71 11, 1.85 16, 4.296 16

grn 1.116 2 lg. śrdm
gr[n 1.85 13
g[rn 1.97 3
grnm 1.14 IV 52 lg. grnt
gr.nn 1.14 III 6
grnn 1.14 IV 49
grnt 1.14 III 8, 1.14 IV 52(!), 1.20 II 6, 1.20 II 9, 2.61 8
grʿ 4.635 34
grp 4.63 I 23
grš 1.2 IV 12, 1.2 IV 12, 1.17 I 29, 1.17 II 18
gr[š 1.17 II 3
gr]š 1.17 I 47
gršh 1.3 IV 2
g]ršh 1.6 VI 2
gršm 1.16 V 12, 1.16 V 21
grš[m 1.16 V 15
g[ršm 1.16 V 18
gršnn 1.1 IV 24
gršt 1.16 V 27
gšl 4.309 16
gšm 2.38 14
]gšr 1.148 33
]gštn 4.69 II 7
gt 1.48 19, 1.79 4, 1.79 5, 1.79 6, 1.79 7, 1.80 1, 1.105 11, 2.21 8, 2.58 4, 4.89 4, 4.96 1, 4.96 11, 4.96 12, 4.97 6, 4.99 5, 4.103 45, 4.105 5, 4.110 3, 4.110 4, 4.110 5, 4.110 6, 4.110 7, 4.110 8, 4.110 9, 4.110 10, 4.110 11, 4.110 14, 4.110 16, 4.110 18, 4.110 19, 4.110 20, 4.110 22, 4.111 9, 4.118 8, 4.118 10, 4.120 1, 4.122 1, 4.125 2, 4.125 3, 4.125 6, 4.125 11, 4.125 16, 4.126 19, 4.139 2, 4.139 4, 4.139 6, 4.139 7, 4.139 8, 4.139 9, 4.141 III 11, 4.141 III 15, 4.143 1, 4.175 9, 4.200 8, 4.213 3, 4.213 5, 4.213 8, 4.213 12, 4.213 15, 4.213 18, 4.213 19, 4.213 20, 4.213 21, 4.243 12, 4.243 14, 4.243 16, 4.243 18, 4.243 20, 4.243 22, 4.269 19, 4.271 1, 4.271 7, 4.296 9, 4.296 10, 4.296 10, 4.297 2, 4.297 3, 4.297 4, 4.297 7, 4.307 1, 4.307 3, 4.307 21, 4.320 2, 4.345 7, 4.358 4, 4.358 5, 4.358 6, 4.382 27, 4.382 32, 4.397 5, 4.397 7, 4.397 13, 4.400 2, 4.400 5, 4.400 15, 4.409 7, 4.409 8, 4.424 3, 4.574 2, 4.618 1, 4.618 4, 4.618 7, 4.625 13, 4.625 17, 4.636 2, 4.636 5, 4.636 10, 4.636 15, 4.643 9, 4.696 6, 4.696 9, 4.707 21, 4.750 13, 4.788 6
gt[4.733 3
g[t 4.271 2, 4.696 5
]gt 1.79 1, 4.110 12, 4.110 13
g]t 4.125 15, 4.200 10, 4.271 9, 4.296 13, 4.618 23, 4.618 24, 4.625 15
g]t[4.696 4
gtxx 4.405 5
gth 3.5 7
gtn 4.63 I 28
]xgṯ 4.635 28
gṯḫp 1.42 61
gṯy 4.764 6
gṯpbn 4.106 13
gṯprg 4.106 12
gṯr 1.43 11, 1.43 14, 1.108 6, 2.4 15, 2.4 17, 2.4 21, 7.38 9
]gṯr 1.108 2
gṯrm 1.43 9, 1.43 17, 1.109 26, 1.112 18, 1.112 19, 1.112 20
g]ṯrm 1.43 19
gṯrn 1.166 25, 4.7 5, 4.25 5, 4.63 III 7, 4.103 52, 4.232 28
gṯtn 4.35 II 18, 4.41 9

D

d 1.1 III 5, 1.1 III 22, 1.1 IV 7, 1.1 IV 13, 1.2 I 18(*bis*), 1.2 I 34(*bis*), 1.2 III 12, 1.3 III 26, 1.3 III 42, 1.3 IV 18, 1.3 IV 45, 1.3 V 33, 1.3 V 36, 1.3 VI 23, 1.4 I 35, 1.4 I 36, 1.4 I 38, 1.4 I 39, 1.4 I 43, 1.4 II 10, 1.4 III 8, 1.4 III 9, 1.4 III 31, 1.4 IV 44, 1.4 IV 48, 1.4 IV 58, 1.4 VII 49, 1.4 VII 50(!), 1.4 VII 51, 1.5 I 3, 1.5 II 12, 1.5 II 20, 1.5 VI 12, 1.6 I 49, 1.6 III 4, 1.6 III 10, 1.6 III 14, 1.6 V 21, 1.6 VI 39, 1.7 30, 1.10 I 3, 1.10 II 32, 1.10 II 33, 1.10 III 6, 1.12 I 3, 1.13 25, 1.14 I 8, 1.14 II 30, 1.14 II 37, 1.14 II 38, 1.14 III 38, 1.14 III 41, 1.14 III 43, 1.14 III 46, 1.14 III 58, 1.14 IV 11, 1.14 VI 22, 1.14 VI 26, 1.14 VI 29, 1.14 VI 31, 1.15 V 26, 1.16 IV 9, 1.17 I 18, 1.17 I 29, 1.17 I 47, 1.17 II 19, 1.17 V 7, 1.17 V 18, 1.17 V 24, 1.18 I 15, 1.18 I 18(*bis*), 1.18 I 31, 1.19 III 46, 1.19 III 52, 1.19 IV 4, 1.19 IV 41, 1.19 IV 43, 1.19 IV 58, 1.20 I 8, 1.20 II 10, 1.23 74, 1.24 4, 1.24 38, 1.41 20, 1.80 2, 1.86 8, 1.86 13, 1.91 1, 1.92 1, 1.100 62, 1.104 2, 1.104 3, 1.108 3, 1.109 27, 1.111 19, 1.114 6, 1.114 7, 1.114 29, 1.123 21, 1.142 3, 1.144 2, 1.169 1, 1.169 14, 1.175 3, 2.10 17, 2.14 7, 2.19 3, 2.19 10, 2.31 46, 2.33 10, 2.34 32, 2.36 4, 2.36 7, 2.37 8, 2.41 17, 2.45 5, 2.45 13, 2.45 25, 2.47 8, 2.47 12, 2.47 15, 2.49 5, 2.50 14, 2.50 19, 2.57 5, 2.62 3, 2.77 7, 2.77 10, 2.81 9, 2.81 24, 2.81 26, 2.81 28(*bis*), 3.1 25, 3.2 7, 3.5 6, 3.7 1, 3.9 2, 3.9 16, 4.43 1, 4.44 26(!), 4.44 28, 4.53 1, 4.53 16, 4.54 1, 4.95 1, 4.103 45, 4.123 22, 4.123 23, 4.127 10, 4.132 4, 4.141 II 26, 4.141 III 8, 4.144 2, 4.145 10, 4.158 19, 4.163 15, 4.166 1, 4.166 6, 4.167 2, 4.167 6, 4.167 13, 4.167 16, 4.168 1, 4.169 6, 4.172 5, 4.195 4, 4.195 9, 4.195 11, 4.199 2, 4.203 9, 4.203 10, 4.203 11, 4.203 13, 4.207 3, 4.210 1, 4.213 2, 4.213 5, 4.213 7, 4.213 10, 4.213 12, 4.213 13, 4.213 15, 4.213 17, 4.213 19, 4.213 23, 4.213 24, 4.213 27, 4.219 1, 4.230 15, 4.248 2, 4.264 2, 4.272 1, 4.272 7, 4.274 3(!), 4.279 1, 4.280 6, 4.280 14, 4.282 2, 4.282 3, 4.282 6, 4.282 9, 4.282 11, 4.282 13, 4.282 15, 4.290 2, 4.294 2, 4.296 11, 4.296 12, 4.296 15, 4.296 16, 4.300 1, 4.313 27, 4.317 15, 4.318 4, 4.328 1, 4.328 2, 4.328 9, 4.333 12, 4.337 12, 4.337 16, 4.338 1, 4.338 12, 4.341 21, 4.348 1, 4.348 20, 4.361 1, 4.362 1, 4.362 4, 4.362 5, 4.363 2, 4.363 8, 4.367 1, 4.369 2, 4.369 4, 4.369 5, 4.369 8, 4.369 10, 4.369 11, 4.369 13, 4.370 2, 4.382 14, 4.382 25, 4.382 26, 4.382 27, 4.382 29, 4.382 33, 4.389 10, 4.389 11, 4.390 2, 4.393 13, 4.395 1, 4.396 19, 4.398 13, 4.415 1, 4.415 2, 4.415 3, 4.415 4, 4.415 5, 4.429 2, 4.429 3, 4.429 4, 4.429 5, 4.430 1, 4.430 2, 4.430 3, 4.470 1, 4.492 1, 4.548 3, 4.585 1, 4.619 1, 4.647 7, 4.659 1, 4.709 6, 4.721 8, 4.747 7, 4.747 8, 4.747 9, 4.752 1, 4.755 1, 4.766 12, 4.771 4, 4.771 9, 4.779 6, 4.779 7, 4.779 10, 4.779 13, 5.2 5, 5.2 6, 5.4 1, 5.6 1, 5.8 1, 5.9 I 17, 5.9 I 18, 5.9 II 2(*ter*), 5.9 II 3(*ter*), 5.11 18, 5.11 20, 5.11 21, 5.12 1, 5.13 1, 5.13 2, 5.13 3, 5.13 4, 5.13 7, 5.14 5, 5.16 1, 5.16 2, 5.16 8, 5.17 4, 5.19 1, 5.20 1, 5.20 4, 5.21 1, 5.24 1, 6.2 1, 6.13 1, 6.14 1, 6.27 2, 6.31 1, 6.47 2, 6.62 2, 6.66 6(!), 7.91 1, 7.217 3

d 4.274 3 lg. b

d[1.4 II 35, 1.5 IV 7, 1.14 II 7, 1.45 11, 1.70 28, 1.98 4, 1.114 25, 2.7 5, 2.83 1, 3.1 18, 4.157 8, 4.214 III 4,

4.235 1, 4.396 3, 4.404 3, 4.421 3, 4.424 22, 4.425 8, 4.463 1, 4.673 2, 4.673 3, 7.37 3, 7.109 4, 7.133 2, 7.207 2

]d 1.14 I 6, 1.14 II 16, 1.15 II 14, 1.52 19, 1.68 11, 1.86 11, 1.86 20, 1.113 5, 1.139 19, 1.153 11, 2.22 8, 2.22 14, 2.49 15, 2.50 17, 2.59 3, 4.104 2, 4.117 5, 4.227 IV 6, 4.234 3, 4.243 36, 4.243 39, 4.262 7, 4.285 4, 4.328 10, 4.411 2, 4.417 1, 4.562 1, 4.562 2, 4.562 3, 4.562 4, 4.636 20, 4.669 4, 4.673 6, 4.785 25, 6.41 1, 7.97 1, 7.108 4, 7.126 3, 7.177 1

]d[3.7 10, 4.1 4, 4.590 6, 4.747 1, 4.747 6, 7.35 2

xd 4.60 4, 4.200 5

xd/b 1.42 61, 1.70 10

dx[1.2 III 13, 1.67 14, 1.68 29, 4.182 54, 4.317 13

]dx[7.87 2

]dxx 4.788 1

]xd 1.22 I 3, 1.26 1, 1.108 12, 1.109 33, 1.125 12, 2.31 20, 4.424 18, 4.666 7, 6.45 1, 7.114 3

]xd 1.116 28 lg.]nd

]xd[4.11 8, 4.197 31

xdx 4.723 16

]xdx[4.590 5, 7.144 1

]xxxxd 2.32 2

dxṣ[4.24 3

]dxᶜrx[7.131 2

]dxġ[7.16 2

d/u[1.69 8

]d/u[7.114 7

d/ux[4.396 7

]d/b/l 4.769 5

d/u/l[4.389 13

d/b 7.220 1

d/b[1.22 IV 2, 1.53 8, 1.58 4, 2.57 5, 4.254 1, 4.256 2, 4.312 3, 4.357 12, 4.446 2, 4.746 11, 4.769 20, 6.55 2, 7.210 1

]d/b 1.42 11, 1.139 17, 2.31 35, 4.60 2, 4.180 1, 4.275 6, 4.398 9, 6.46 1, 7.82 2

]d/b[4.427 8

]xd/b[7.19 1

d/b/u[4.654 2

xd/b[4.34 1

d/u/l[4.44 16

]d/u/l 1.35 7, 1.42 22, 1.117 13

]xd/u/l[7.116 4

d/l[1.166 29

]d/l 1.42 54, 2.73 20, 4.104 9

]d/l[1.2 III 25, 4.490 4

]d/lx 4.410 12

]xl/d[4.306 10, 4.533 3

]xdt/ašm 4.755 13

]d/bat 1.172 3

di 1.16 V 48, 1.108 8

diy 1.18 IV 18, 1.18 IV 28, 1.19 III 9, 1.19 III 13, 1.19 III 17, 1.19 III 23, 1.19 III 27, 1.19 III 31, 1.19 III 37, 1.19 III 43

diym 1.19 I 33

d]\iym 1.18 IV 20f

diy[m 1.18 IV 31

]dir 7.52 4

dit 1.108 8

du 1.19 III 14, 1.19 III 28

db 1.164 4

db[4.334 7

db/d[1.77 1, 4.423 6

]d/bb/d[1.53 2, 7.195 2

dbatk 1.10 II 21, 1.10 II 22

dbb 4.611 7, 4.727 17

dbb[4.633 12

db]b 4.69 VI 34

dbbm 1.4 I 39, 1.169 1, 1.169 9

{dbḥ} 1.4 III 19

<dbḥ> 1.114 1(!)

dbḥ 1.4 III 18, 1.4 III 19, 1.4 III 20, 1.14 II 18, 1.14 II 23, 1.14 III 56, 1.14 IV 5, 1.16 I 39, 1.16 I 40, 1.16 I 61, 1.19 IV 23, 1.19 IV 29, 1.23 27, 1.41 20, 1.48 13, 1.79 7, 1.87 22, 1.87 43, 1.91 2, 1.91 3, 1.91 14, 1.114 1, 1.116 1, 1.127 1, 1.127 3, 1.127 7, 1.127 9, 1.127 12, 1.136 4, 1.136 5, 1.148 1, 1.161 1, 1.162 1, 1.176 9, 4.744 4

dbḥ[1.127 24, 4.213 24, 4.316 5

db[ḥ 1.14 III 59, 1.15 VI 5, 1.41 39

d[bḥ 1.14 II 14

]dbḥ 1.16 I 61

d]bḥ 1.14 V 28, 1.153 3, 1.170 1

db]ḥ 1.127 13, 1.139 15

d\bḥ 4.149 14f
dbḥh 1.14 IV 7
dbḥk 1.14 II 25
<d>bḥm 1.40 23
dbḥm 1.4 III 17, 1.39 17, 1.75 11
d[b]ḥm 1.40 32
dbḥn 1.40 32, 1.40 40
db[ḥn 1.40 23
]dbḥn 2.31 25
dbḥt 1.142 1
dbṭx[1.12 II 41
dby 4.64 IV 10
dbl 5.11 13
dblt 1.71 27, 1.72 37, 1.85 31, 4.14 17, 4.60 5, 4.60 9, 4.751 9
]dbʿ/š[7.16 11
dbr 1.5 V 18, 1.5 VI 6, 1.5 VI 29, 1.6 II 20, 2.71 14
]dbrh 1.76 9, 1.76 10
dbrm 2.32 8
]dbʿ/š[7.16 11
xxdb/ṣt 4.318 3
dg 1.23 63, 1.91 12, 1.92 38, 1.106 22, 1.124 15
]xdg 4.721 1
d/u/lg 4.86 18
]dgd[4.438 1
dgy 1.3 VI 10, 1.4 II 31
dgm 5.23 14
dgn 1.2 I 19, 1.2 I 35, 1.2 I 37, 1.5 VI 24, 1.6 I 6, 1.6 I 52, 1.10 III 12, 1.10 III 14, 1.10 III 34, 1.12 I 39, 1.14 II 25, 1.14 IV 7, 1.16 III 13, 1.24 14, 1.46 3, 1.47 4, 1.48 5, 1.100 15, 1.107 39, 1.109 21, 1.118 3, 1.123 4, 1.148 10, 1.148 26, 1.162 9, 1.166 9, 1.173 4, 6.13 2, 6.14 2
dgn[1.12 II 25, 1.127 22, 1.160 2
]dgn 7.168 4
dg]n 1.46 2 lg. [sp]n, [ʿ]n<t>?
xdgr 4.317 2
dgt 1.19 III 41(?)
dd 1.3 III 5, 1.3 III 7, 1.41 44, 1.87 7, 1.87 48, 1.101 17, 1.172 20, 2.71 18, 4.4 9, 4.14 1, 4.14 1, 4.14 7, 4.14 13, 4.42 4, 4.55 1, 4.55 2, 4.55 3, 4.55 4, 4.55 6, 4.55 7, 4.55 31, 4.55 32, 4.55 33, 4.128 5, 4.128 7, 4.128 8, 4.128 9, 4.128 10, 4.128 11, 4.128 12, 4.175 3, 4.175 4, 4.175 5, 4.175 6, 4.175 8, 4.175 12, 4.175 13, 4.175 14, 4.243 4, 4.243 5, 4.243 8, 4.243 8, 4.243 10, 4.243 11, 4.243 13, 4.243 15, 4.243 16, 4.243 18, 4.243 21, 4.243 23, 4.243 25, 4.243 27, 4.243 29, 4.243 31, 4.243 41, 4.243 43, 4.243 44, 4.243 45, 4.243 46, 4.269 2, 4.269 4, 4.269 24, 4.269 25, 4.269 31, 4.269 33, 4.284 4, 4.333 4, 4.333 5, 4.362 3, 4.387 9, 4.387 9, 4.387 19, 4.387 19, 4.387 26, 4.400 1, 4.400 3, 4.400 4, 4.400 12, 4.400 16, 4.402 1, 4.402 7, 4.558 4, 4.608 1, 4.608 2, 4.608 3, 4.691 4, 4.746 2, 4.746 3, 4.746 4, 4.746 5, 4.746 6, 4.746 7, 4.746 8, 4.746 9, 4.746 10, 4.746 11, 4.746 12, 4.746 13, 4.747 4, 4.786 1, 4.786 2, 4.786 4, 4.788 7, 4.790 16, 6.21 1, 6.61 2
dd[4.83 7, 4.387 8, 4.400 13, 4.423 4
d[d 1.41 6, 4.83 5, 4.83 6, 4.83 8, 4.83 9, 4.83 10, 4.83 11, 4.243 33, 4.243 36, 4.400 13, 4.400 17, 4.523 1
]dd 4.183 II 9, 4.426 4
]dd[7.181 2
d]d 4.60 3, 4.60 7, 4.243 6, 4.400 9, 4.426 3, 4.608 4, 4.746 1
d]\d 1.87 49f(!)
ddx[4.243 34
]d/bd 1.63 9, 4.120 3
]d/bd[4.306 9, 4.702 2
]d/bb/d[1.53 2, 7.195 2
]d/bl/d[7.166 2
db/d[1.77 1, 4.423 6
ddh 1.24 23
ddy 4.16 3, 4.635 44, 4.659 4
ddym 1.3 III 15, 1.3 IV 9, 1.3 IV 24, 1.3 IV 29
ddl 4.423 24
ddm 1.101 9, 4.60 1, 4.128 1, 4.128 2, 4.128 3, 4.128 4, 4.128 6, 4.175 9, 4.175 11, 4.225 11, 4.243 47, 4.269 3, 4.269 20, 4.269 21, 4.269 22, 4.269 23, 4.269 26, 4.269 32, 4.361 3, 4.387 18, 4.397 4, 4.397 11, 4.397 12, 4.609 38, 4.609 39, 4.688 4, 4.790 1, 4.790 17, 6.19 1(!)
dd[m 4.175 7

d[dm 4.60 3
]ddm 4.609 50, 4.788 3, 4.788 5
]dd[m 4.387 17
d]dm 1.148 43, 4.14 18, 4.387 25
ddm 4.377 31 lg. ṣmdm
d/k]dm{m} 6.18 2(?)
ddmy 1.40 20, 1.40 37, 1.84 4
ddm]y 1.40 11, 1.40 28
d/k]dmm 6.18 2 lg. [d/k]dm{m}?
ddmš 1.47 28, 1.109 18, 1.118 27, 1.120 3, 1.130 29, 1.148 8
ddmš[1.42 17
]ddmš 1.42 21
d]dmš[1.58 3
ddn 1.161 10, 4.760 5
d[dn 1.161 3
]ddn 1.170 2
ddt 6.19 1 lg. ddm
dḏy 4.769 18
]dḏn 4.83 8
]dh 4.733 3
]xdh 1.114 27 lg. lmdh
]d/bh[7.195 1
dw 1.16 II 20, 1.16 II 23, 4.767 3
dk/w[1.176 6
dwx[7.55 13
dwn 4.309 5, 4.354 7
]dy 1.172 27, 2.31 37, 4.31 7, 4.155 8, 4.238 1, 4.631 22
dyx 4.724 7
]xdy 2.20 5
]d/by 4.339 8
]d/by[4.427 5
]dyk[4.497 3
]dym 4.3 2, 4.55 17
]d/bymktmẓ$_2$k[1.77 5
dymrrs[1.70 1
]d/lyn 4.643 18
]dyt 4.247 15
]dytx[7.35 4
dk 1.5 III 8, 1.175 4
dk[7.206 6
]dk 1.147 9, 1.175 12
]dk[7.46 9
]d/bk 1.167 2
dk/w[1.176 6
]d/bkḫkyt[1.68 19
dkym 1.6 V 3
]dkm 1.84 32
dkr 1.86 2, 1.119 31
dkrm 1.43 19
dkr<t> 1.4 VI 54
dkt[7.206 7
dl 1.16 VI 48
dl[4.403 13
]dl 4.102 15
]dl[7.78 2
dlx 7.184 6
dlx[4.562 4
d]\l 1.87 49f lg. d]\d
]d/bl/d[7.166 2
]d/b/uṣ/l[7.79 4
dli 4.63 III 28
dld 1.148 15
]d/blḏ 1.42 27
dlhẓ[1.9 11
dlḥt 1.85 3
dly 4.75 V 15, 4.389 11, 4.724 2
]dly 4.396 9
dll 1.4 VII 45, 4.232 31, 4.374 13, 4.617 37
dll[1.70 26
dllp[1.70 25
dlm 4.618 9
dlq[4.98 4
]dlq 4.82 4
dlt 1.82 22, 1.82 24, 4.351 3, 5.7 5, 6.66 10
]dlt 4.351 4
dlthm[1.23 25
xḏ/ġltn 4.787 8
dm 1.1 III 12, 1.3 II 14, 1.3 II 27, 1.3 II 31, 1.3 II 34, 1.3 III 20, 1.4 I 32, 1.4 III 17, 1.4 IV 38, 1.5 III 9, 1.5 III 18, 1.5 III 25, 1.7 9, 1.12 II 46, 1.12 II 47, 1.14 III 10, 1.14 V 3, 1.16 I 32, 1.16 VI 1, 1.16 VI 13, 1.16 VI 14, 1.17 VI 34, 1.18 IV 24, 1.24 9, 1.64 22, 1.107 46, 1.114 31, 1.176 4, 2.8 2, 2.50 18, 2.78 6
dm[2.66 4, 4.423 5
d[m 1.2 III 18, 1.4 VI 59
]dm 1.2 I 44, 1.168 17, 4.75 I 5, 4.197 26, 4.610 48, 7.77 2
]dm[1.137 9, 7.34 3
d]m 1.4 III 44
]d/bm 1.147 22, 1.172 29
]d/bmx[7.61 4

d/u/lm[4.252 5
dmgy 1.12 I 16
dmd 4.377 34 lg. ṣmd
dmh 1.18 IV 35, 1.96 4
dmyn 7.61 15
dml 1.81 20, 2.26 6
dml[4.182 34
]dmlt 1.170 4
dmm 1.3 V 2
xdmm 4.191 11
xxxd/bmn[4.200 7
dmˤ 1.14 II 8
dmˤh 1.14 I 32
dmˤt 1.19 II 33
dmqt 1.24 50
dmr 4.377 32
]d/bmr[7.89 1
dmrn 1.4 VII 39, 1.92 30
d]mrn 1.81 23
dmt 2.31 46, 4.49 6, 4.68 13, 4.113 1, 4.244 15, 4.643 6, 4.643 7
dmt[4.762 9
dm[t 4.308 14, 4.610 41
d[mt 4.686 12
]dmt 4.643 5, 4.652 3
d]mt 4.553 6
dmty[4.81 3
dmtn 4.50 11
dn 1.12 II 58, 1.16 VI 33, 1.16 VI 46, 1.17 V 8, 4.12 7
dn[1.123 15
]dn 4.30 11, 4.58 3, 4.64 II 8, 4.94 7, 4.350 13, 4.658 47
dn 4.75 III 7 lg. bn
xxdn 4.115 7
]xdn 4.69 IV 26, 4.386 9
]xdn[4.64 V 3
xxdn/tx 4.752 10
]d/bn 4.217 4, 4.715 9
]d/bn[4.725 8
<dn>il 1.21 II 8(?)
<dn>i<l> 1.19 II 19
dn{.}il 1.17 II 24
dnil 1.17 I 6, 1.17 I 9, 1.17 I 12, 1.17 I 36, 1.17 II 8(!), 1.17 II 25, 1.17 II 27, 1.17 II 43, 1.17 V 4, 1.17 V 13, 1.17 V 26, 1.17 V 33, 1.18 IV 19, 1.18 IV 30, 1.19 I 19, 1.19 I 36, 1.19 I 38, 1.19 I 47, 1.19 II 12, 1.19 II 37, 1.19 II 41, 1.19 IV 8, 1.19 IV 9, 1.19 IV 12, 1.19 IV 17, 1.20 II 7
dn\il 1.19 IV 35f
d[nil 1.19 IV 25
d]nil 1.17 I 17
dn]il 1.17 I 14, 1.17 VI 52
]dnd 1.116 29 lg. kl]dnd
dnh 2.45 16, 2.62 8
dnhm 2.38 18
]d/bnyn 4.57 8
dnn 1.16 I 30, 4.86 5, 4.124 14, 4.366 4, 4.366 5, 4.377 1, 4.595 4, 4.617 35, 4.623 10, 4.759 4
dnn[7.106 2
]xxdnn[7.55 9
dnt 1.4 III 20, 4.214 I 2
dnty 1.17 V 16, 1.17 V 22, 1.17 V 28
]dnṯtnn 1.68 19
d/usgr[1.64 3
dˤ 2.34 30, 2.61 13, 2.61 13
]dˤ[6.51 2
dˤm 3.7 8
dˤ]mm 1.13 15
]xdˤn 4.327 5
dˤt 1.16 VI 10
dˤthm 1.2 I 32
dˤtk 1.6 VI 50
dˤtkm 1.2 I 16
dˤtm 1.169 10
dġm 4.284 7
]dġ[m 7.99 3
dġṯ 1.19 IV 24, 1.19 IV 31
dġṯh 1.19 IV 30
dġṯhm 1.19 IV 23
dġṯt 1.23 15
dġ]ṯt 1.23 15
]dp 4.718 6
]dp[1.66 23
xdpm 4.618 13
dpr 1.22 I 16
d/bpr 4.750 15
dprn 4.158 20
dprn[1.72 28, 4.244 13
dprnm 4.175 9
]d/b/uṣ/l[7.79 4
dq 1.6 I 50, 2.57 5, 4.4 3, 4.63 III 13
dq[1.136 6
]xdq 2.37 11
]xxdq 7.132 6

dqm 5.23 17
dqn 1.5 VI 19, 1.6 I 3, 4.33 37, 4.54 3, 4.98 17, 4.141 II 9, 4.183 II 26, 4.370 4, 4.424 7, 4.424 18, 4.609 6, 4.609 23, 4.609 26, 4.787 10
dqn[4.609 29
]dqn 4.424 10
]d/bq/tn 4.769 29
dqnh 1.3 V 2
dqnk 1.3 V 25, 1.4 V 4
dq]nk 1.18 I 12
dqr 1.111 16, 4.275 17, 5.22 2
dqry 4.63 II 33, 4.108 4, 4.116 17
<dqt> 1.41 13
dqt 1.4 I 41, 1.39 1, 1.39 1, 1.39 3, 1.39 4, 1.39 15, 1.39 16, 1.39 16, 1.41 13, 1.41 28, 1.41 42, 1.41 42, 1.46 4, 1.46 7, 1.87 34, 1.102 8, 1.106 20, 1.109 10, 1.112 27, 1.132 8(cor.), 1.132 9, 1.132 10, 1.132 11, 1.132 12, 4.189 1, 4.765 4
dqt[1.56 7
d[q]t 1.41 34, 1.109 33
dq[t 4.411 3
d]qt 1.41 31
[[dqt]] 1.39 16(?)
dqtd 1.116 19, 1.132 7, 1.135 12
d]qt[d 1.60 15
dqtm 1.39 4, 1.39 18, 1.41 32, 1.87 35(!), 1.105 27, 1.106 31, 1.109 6, 1.119 7, 1.130 18
dq[t]m 1.87 11
dq[tm 1.87 32
d[q]tm 1.46 12
d[qtm 1.87 15
]d/bq/tn 4.769 29
dqtt 1.132 8 cor. dqt[[t]]
dr 1.4 III 7, 1.4 III 7, 1.6 IV 26, 1.15 III 19, 1.19 III 48, 1.19 III 48, 1.19 III 56, 1.19 III 56, 1.19 IV 6, 1.19 IV 6, 1.39 7, 1.40 25, 1.40 33, 1.65 2, 1.162 16, 4.120 3, 4.357 24
dr[1.30 1
d[r 1.40 42
]dr 1.10 I 5, 1.11 18, 4.734 11
d]r 1.40 7, 7.184 10
]dr[4.71 III 13, 7.19 3
]xdr[7.89 3
]d/brx[4.457 2
d/lrx[4.242 3
drb 4.346 10, 4.385 8
drd<r> 1.10 III 6
d[rd]r 1.6 VI 37
drdrk 1.2 IV 10
]drh 1.108 17
]d/brḥn 7.50 2
drḫm 1.82 37
dry 1.6 V 13
dr]y 1.6 V 16
drk 1.43 6, 4.765 7
drkm 4.688 5
drkt 1.2 IV 10, 1.4 VII 44, 1.16 VI 24, 1.108 7
drk[t 1.14 I 42
dr[kt 1.22 II 18
]dr[kt 1.6 VI 36
drkth 1.1 IV 25, 1.2 IV 13, 1.2 IV 20, 1.3 IV 3, 1.6 V 6
drkth[1.6 VI 35
drk{.}tk 1.2 I 5
drktk 1.16 VI 38, 1.16 VI 53
drm 1.123 32
dr\m 4.4 1f
]drn 4.460 3
drʿ 1.6 V 19, 1.72 29, 4.243 1, 4.243 5, 4.243 7, 4.243 10, 4.243 12, 4.243 14, 4.243 16, 4.243 18, 4.243 20, 4.243 22, 4.243 24, 4.243 26, 4.243 46, 4.636 4, 4.636 8, 4.636 17, 4.636 28
drʿ[4.243 28
dr[ʿ 1.97 12, 4.636 22
]drʿ 4.243 3
d]rʿ 1.85 24, 4.636 13
drṣy 4.350 6, 4.700 6
drt 3.10 7, 4.243 1, 4.243 3, 4.243 5, 4.243 7, 4.243 10, 4.243 12, 4.243 14, 4.243 16, 4.243 18, 4.243 20, 4.243 22, 4.243 24, 4.243 26, 4.636 4, 4.636 8, 4.636 13, 4.636 18, 4.636 34, 4.792 8
dr[t 4.636 29
]drt 4.755 11
d]rt 4.243 28
[[drt]] 4.131 4
]d/brt 4.103 56
dš[4.201 7
]dšxym[4.249 4

d/bš 4.627 2, 4.627 3, 4.627 4
]d/bš 4.627 8
d/b]š 4.627 11, 4.627 13
dšk 6.66 6 lg. d šk\n
dšn 1.19 IV 27, 1.108 5
]dšpš 4.82 7
xdšq 4.123 13
dt 1.2 IV 10, 1.3 III 35, 1.4 I 30, 1.4 II 20, 1.4 II 45, 1.4 IV 6, 1.4 IV 10, 1.4 IV 11, 1.4 V 5, 1.4 VI 37, 1.5 III 7, 1.10 I 5, 1.16 V 30, 1.16 VI 1, 1.19 II 4, 1.19 II 5, 1.20 I 9, 1.22 I 13, 1.24 43, 1.25 2, 1.25 4, 1.101 7(?), 1.127 4, 1.127 10, 1.127 18, 1.143 1, 1.151 5, 2.22 6, 2.23 22, 2.33 7, 2.36 4, 2.38 10, 2.49 12, 2.73 15, 3.3 2, 3.3 6, 4.11 7, 4.33 2(!), 4.86 29, 4.110 2, 4.141 III 6, 4.141 III 10, 4.145 1, 4.192 3, 4.192 4, 4.214 I 4, 4.257 3, 4.270 8, 4.289 8, 4.296 1, 4.296 8, 4.335 1, 4.339 1, 4.339 17, 4.347 1, 4.374 1, 4.379 1, 4.395 2, 4.395 4, 4.422 1, 4.542 1, 4.617 1, 4.624 1, 4.627 1, 4.645 1, 4.655 1, 4.728 2, 4.790 15, 6.29 2
dt[1.1 IV 21, 1.151 11, 4.86 21, 4.160 4, 4.729 1
d[t 1.4 VI 42, 1.19 II 47, 7.184 9
]dt 1.82 21, 4.222 8
d]t 4.557 1
]dt[1.75 7
dtx[1.151 6
]xdt 7.33 5, 7.178 3
]xdt[2.57 2
xxdn/tx 4.752 10
d/ut[4.631 22
]d/bt 1.82 3, 7.185 5
]d/bt[4.64 V 1
dtm 1.4 VI 37
dtn 1.15 III 4, 1.15 III 15, 1.124 2, 1.124 4, 1.124 11, 1.124 14, 4.69 VI 29
dt[n 4.633 6
]d/btn 4.69 II 9
]xdt/ašm 4.755 13
dtnwrxktnid 7.61 1
dtt 1.104 13
dṯ 1.18 I 19
]dṯ[1.112 32
dṯn 1.65 15
]d/bṯn 1.55 5
dṯt 1.39 9

Ḏ

ḏ 1.24 45, 5.4 3, 5.6 2, 5.12 3, 5.13 8, 5.15 3, 5.16 3, 5.16 6, 5.17 2, 5.17 5, 5.19 3, 5.20 1, 5.20 4, 5.21 1, 5.24 1
ḏ 1.52 8(*bis*) cor. ḏḏ
ḏ[1.42 33, 1.45 10, 7.198 4
]ḏ 1.127 27, 4.111 5, 4.111 6, 4.460 8, 7.147 4
]ḏ[7.61 9
ḏx[1.134 11, 4.623 10
xḏx[4.161 1, 4.680 5
]xḏx[4.357 4
ḏ/š[4.69 VI 35
ḏ/šxyn 4.86 33
]xḏi 7.130 2
ḏbb 1.3 III 46
]ḏb/ṣbxx 1.81 25
]ḏbn 4.122 20
ḏd 1.1 III 23, 1.2 III 5(!), 1.3 V 7, 1.4 IV 23, 1.6 I 34, 1.17 VI 48, 1.23 59
]ḏdyy 4.668 4
ḏdk 1.19 IV 51
ḏdm 1.3 V 9, 1.18 IV 15, 1.19 IV 58
ḏḏ 1.23 61, 1.52 8(cor.)
ḏḏyy 4.245 II 3
ḏḏyn 2.31 47
]ḏḏyn 2.31 47
ḏhrth 1.14 I 36
ḏyn 4.775 11
ḏkr 4.484 3, 4.609 37
ḏkr[4.748 13
ḏkry 4.261 5, 4.383 4
]ḏktḏ 1.64 5
ḏl 1.2 III 5 lg. ḏd
ḏldd 1.131 10
ḏlṯ 1.42 36
ḏmx[7.168 2
]ḏmu 4.295 1
]ḏmy 7.55 3
ḏmn 4.51 7, 5.9 IV 2
ḏmr 1.3 II 14, 1.3 II 28, 1.3 II 31, 1.3 II 34, 1.17 I 28, 1.17 II 17, 4.348 17, 4.647 1
ḏm[r 1.17 II 2
]ḏmr 2.31 55
ḏ]mr 1.17 I 46
ḏmrbˁl[4.75 II 5
]ḏmrb[ˁl 4.731 1
ḏ/amrbˁl 4.261 8
ḏmrd 4.682 10, 4.775 3
ḏmrh 1.108 22
ḏmry 4.347 3, 4.347 5, 4.347 9, 4.617 31
ḏmry[4.655 7, 6.46 1
ḏmrk 1.69 1, 1.108 24
ḏmrn 4.423 1
ḏn 1.64 9
]ḏn 4.180 2
ḏnb 1.114 20
ḏnbtm 1.83 7
]ḏnnk 1.42 25
]ḏb/ṣbxx 1.81 25
xḏprḏ 4.64 V 14
ḏqnt[4.422 40
]ḏr[1.33 1
ḏrd[n 4.657 3
ḏrm 2.3 19, 4.64 V 12
ḏrm[4.635 53
]ḏrm 4.69 IV 2
ḏrn 4.769 63
ḏrˁ 1.103 55, 2.38 17, 2.81 15, 2.81 17, 2.81 23, 4.721 16
ḏrˁ[1.103 43
ḏr[ˁ 1.13 8, 1.103 14
ḏ[rˁ 2.39 9
ḏrˁh 1.5 VI 20, 1.6 I 4
ḏrˁhm 2.38 19
ḏrqm 1.5 I 6
ḏr[qm 1.18 IV 3
ḏrr 4.354 8
ḏrt 1.6 III 5, 1.6 III 11
ḏrt[hm 1.15 VI 8
ḏrty 1.14 III 47, 1.14 VI 32
ḏt[4.281 2

H

h 5.4 1, 5.6 1, 5.8 1, 5.9 I 17, 5.9 I 18, 5.12 1, 5.13 1, 5.13 2, 5.13 3, 5.13 4, 5.13 7, 5.14 6, 5.16 1, 5.16 2, 5.16 8, 5.17 4, 5.19 1, 5.19 5, 5.20 1, 5.20 4, 5.21 1, 5.24 1
h 5.10 8 lg. p
h[1.2 III 13, 1.9 8, 1.12 II 29, 1.19 I 25, 2.6 9, 2.21 20, 2.21 22, 2.31 41, 2.83 11, 4.60 4, 4.317 8, 4.743 6, 7.45 2, 7.99 4
]h 1.7 12, 1.7 50, 1.14 V 19, 1.18 I 4, 1.62 1, 1.62 12, 1.62 22, 1.62 24, 1.75 4, 1.92 25, 1.107 20, 1.146 7, 2.18 5, 4.182 4, 4.382 35, 4.398 11, 4.412 I 5, 4.739 5, 7.91 3, 7.138 1, 7.173 2
]h[1.26b 4, 1.68 7, 4.386 9, 7.176 7
]h[1.26b 4 lg.]in[
]\h 1.9 12f, 1.22 I 1f
hx[2.31 60, 4.391 8
hxx 1.19 II 37
hxx[2.21 29
xh 1.70 38
xh[4.610 34
]xh 1.16 II 31, 2.77 2, 4.386 16, 4.542 3, 7.46 4, 7.47 5, 7.49 4
xhxry 4.350 4
h/i 7.218 6
h/i[2.9 3, 4.178 10, 4.374 10
]h/i 1.10 II 32, 1.25 7, 7.46 6
]h/i[1.73 18, 1.167 14
h/ixxx 2.36 19
h/ixm 4.401 2
h/i/p[1.51 10
h/w[1.26 1
h/p/t 7.218 5
had 2.42 25 lg. hnd
hayn[4.118 3
]h/iiḏ/šn 1.68 32
]hb 7.143 1
]xhb[4.570 1
hbṭ 2.61 5
]hbṭn 4.635 10
hbṭnm 4.137 6, 4.163 10, 4.173 9, 4.174 6, 4.179 11
hbm 4.313 1
hbn 4.402 6
]h/ibn 4.28 8
hbr 1.1 III 3, 1.3 III 9, 1.3 VI 19, 1.4 VIII 27
hbt 2.70 16
hg 1.14 II 38
h/p/ig[1.30 5
hd 1.1 V 17, 1.2 I 46, 1.4 VI 39, 1.4 VII 36, 1.5 I 23, 1.5 II 22, 1.5 IV 7, 1.9 18, 1.10 II 5, 1.10 III 8, 1.12 I 41, 1.12 II 6, 1.12 II 22, 1.12 II 54, 1.67 17, 1.101 1
h]d 1.1 V 4
]hd 1.10 II 33
hdxmt 4.191 13
hdd 1.9 13
hdm 1.4 I 34, 1.4 IV 29, 1.5 VI 13, 1.5 VI 13, 1.6 I 60, 1.6 III 15, 1.17 II 11, 1.161 14
hdmm 1.3 II 22, 1.3 II 37, 1.3 II 37
h\[dmm] 1.7 5f
hdrʿy 1.108 3
hdrt 1.14 III 51
hdt 1.4 VII 38
hw 1.2 I 37, 1.6 II 23, 1.12 II 40, 1.17 I 38, 1.23 70, 1.23 75, 1.40 24, 1.40 24, 1.40 32, 1.40 33, 1.40 41, 2.3 13, 2.15 6, 2.31 41, 2.31 52, 2.31 54, 2.39 7, 2.61 5, 2.61 6, 2.72 27, 2.72 29, 2.72 31, 2.81 26, 2.81 27, 2.81 28, 2.81 28, 2.81 29, 2.81 29
hw[2.3 4, 2.45 27, 2.72 35
hwil 4.110 7
hwt 1.1 III 6, 1.1 III 13, 1.2 I 46, 1.3 III 13, 1.3 III 22, 1.3 IV 7, 1.3 IV 13, 1.3 VI 20, 1.4 III 36, 1.4 VII 20, 1.4 VIII 29, 1.5 I 13, 1.5 II 10, 1.5 II 18, 1.6 IV 11, 1.7 30, 1.14 VI 41, 1.17 VI 53, 1.18 IV 13, 1.19 I 15, 1.19 II 38, 1.19 III 17, 1.19 III 23, 1.19 III 27, 1.19 IV 61, 1.93 4, 1.103 43, 1.107 17, 2.4 16, 2.41 14

hwt[1.7 26, 2.3 9
h[wt 1.3 VI 25
hw]t 1.4 VIII 34
hwth 1.2 IV 6, 1.19 III 22, 1.19 III 36
hwt[h 1.19 III 7
hwty 1.4 VI 15, 1.4 VII 25
]hz/ḫ 2.36 18
hz<p> 1.105 14
hzp 1.91 28, 4.68 55, 4.355 16, 4.365 31, 4.380 33, 4.770 4
hz[p 4.73 7, 4.629 2
h]zp[4.661 5
hzpḫ 1.87 58
hzpy 4.51 16, 4.753 18, 4.754 9
hzpym[4.50 8
]h/iṭ/ḥ[1.4 VI 11
]hz/ḫ 2.36 18
hy 1.19 IV 39, 1.111 22, 1.124 10, 2.31 44, 2.31 45, 2.81 17
]hy 1.7 3
]hy[4.490 3
h]y 1.103 42
<h>y 2.14 9(?)
]h/iy 2.31 34
hyabn 4.110 20
hyadt 4.170 22
hyb/d[4.503 II 2
hyn 1.4 I 23, 1.17 V 18, 1.17 V 24, 1.17 V 32
h\yn 1.3 VI 22f
hyrm 1.9 8
hyt 1.3 III 10, 1.19 III 32, 1.19 III 37, 1.103 45, 1.103 55, 1.103 56
hkl 1.2 III 7, 1.2 III 11, 1.2 III 21, 1.4 V 57, 1.16 VI 25, 1.53 9, 1.100 72
hk[l 1.2 III 9, 4.224 8, 4.224 9
h[kl 1.9 9
]hkl 1.25 8, 1.82 26
hklh 1.3 II 18, 1.4 V 37, 1.4 VI 17, 1.4 VI 40, 1.4 VI 45, 1.10 II 2, 1.10 II 5, 1.17 I 26, 1.17 I 43, 1.17 II 25, 1.19 IV 9, 1.19 IV 10, 1.19 IV 26, 1.114 2
hkl]h 1.24 10
hk]l[h 1.2 III 10
hkly 1.4 VI 37, 1.19 IV 21, 1.20 II 1, 1.21 II 8, 1.22 II 2, 1.22 II 10
hkly[1.17 V 39
hk[ly 1.22 II 20
h]kly 1.21 II 3
hk]ly 1.4 VIII 37, 1.21 II 11
hklk 1.4 V 14, 1.4 V 31
h]kl[k 1.3 V 21
hklm 1.4 V 62, 1.4 VI 23, 1.4 VI 26, 1.4 VI 28, 1.4 VI 33, 1.4 VII 27
hk[lm 1.4 V 52, 1.4 V 54, 1.4 V 65
h]klm 1.4 VI 9, 1.4 VI 31
hk]lm 1.4 VI 6
hkl\m 1.4 VII 18f
hkm 1.10 I 2
hl 1.17 V 12, 1.23 44, 1.23 47, 1.24 7
hl 1.162 7 lg. il?
hl[1.107 1, 2.6 1, 2.39 27, 2.63 15
hl[1.92 4 lg. hl[l
h[l 1.23 41
]h/il 4.439 2
hṣ/l[7.40 5
]h/ilh/it̠drn 7.23 4
hlh 1.23 32, 1.23 32, 1.23 32, 1.23 33, 4.666 3
]h/ilh/it̠drn 7.23 4
hlk 1.3 IV 39, 1.4 II 13, 1.4 II 14, 1.14 II 39, 1.14 II 41, 1.14 IV 17, 1.14 IV 19, 1.17 V 10, 1.17 V 12, 1.19 I 28, 1.19 II 3, 1.19 II 7, 1.19 II 28, 1.19 IV 38, 1.114 17, 1.166 27, 2.72 25, 4.33 2
]hlk 1.107 13
hlkm 1.23 27
hlkt 1.45 5, 1.62 4, 1.96 1
hll 1.17 II 27, 1.17 II 31, 1.17 II 36, 1.17 II 38, 1.17 II 40, 1.24 6, 1.24 41
hll[1.24 15
hl[l 1.17 II 33, 1.92 4(!)
h\ll 1.24 41f
hlm 1.2 I 21, 1.2 IV 14, 1.2 IV 21, 1.3 III 32, 1.4 IV 27, 1.16 I 53, 1.19 II 29, 1.100 6, 1.100 11, 1.100 17, 1.100 22, 1.100 28, 1.100 33, 1.100 38, 1.100 43, 1.100 48, 1.100 54
hlmn 1.18 IV 22, 1.18 IV 33
hln 1.3 II 5, 1.3 II 17, 2.36 12
hlny 2.1 3, 2.13 9, 2.21 7, 2.30 8, 2.30 12, 2.70 11, 2.73 8, 2.77 8, 2.78 4, 2.79 2, 2.83 2, 3.1 18
hln[y 2.36 5
hl[ny 2.36 2
h[ln]y 2.24 8

h]lny 2.67 4
hlnr 1.45 1
<hm> 1.19 III 33
hm 1.1 IV 26, 1.2 I 24, 1.2 IV 2, 1.4 II 24, 1.4 II 25, 1.4 III 31, 1.4 IV 34, 1.4 IV 35, 1.4 IV 38, 1.4 IV 61, 1.4 V 11, 1.5 I 15, 1.5 I 16, 1.5 I 18, 1.5 I 20, 1.5 I 21, 1.6 III 2, 1.6 III 3, 1.14 I 42, 1.14 IV 40, 1.15 III 23, 1.15 III 25, 1.15 VI 7, 1.19 II 35, 1.19 II 35, 1.19 III 4, 1.19 III 4, 1.19 III 19, 1.19 III 19, 1.19 III 33, 1.19 III 44, 1.22 II 16, 1.23 39, 1.23 42, 1.23 68, 1.23 69, 1.23 71, 1.23 71, 1.23 72, 1.23 73, 1.82 5, 1.85 3, 1.85 4, 1.86 7, 1.127 30, 1.127 30, 1.133 7, 1.133 9, 1.133 10, 1.163 10, 1.163 12, 1.166 10, 2.3 8, 2.3 18, 2.7 8, 2.9 4, 2.10 9, 2.10 14, 2.30 16, 2.30 18, 2.31 63, 2.31 66, 2.33 26, 2.33 30, 2.39 22, 2.42 24, 2.45 6, 2.45 21, 2.48 3, 2.54 3, 2.82 10, 2.82 18, 2.83 6, 3.8 13, 4.322 5, 5.11 14
hm[1.82 28
h[m 3.4 12
]hm 1.17 VI 43, 1.107 36, 1.167 9, 2.41 6
h]m 1.163 5
hmx[7.40 2
hm/t 2.14 15
{h}mhkm 2.71 14
hmlt 1.2 I 18, 1.3 III 28, 1.4 VII 52, 1.5 VI 24, 1.6 I 7, 1.6 II 18, 1.83 12
hml[t 1.6 V 25
hml]t 1.2 I 35
hmn[4.644 6
]h/imr 7.46 5
hmry 1.4 VIII 12, 1.5 II 15
hmt 1.2 IV 36, 1.17 V 20, 1.17 V 30, 1.19 III 9, 1.19 III 13, 1.19 III 44, 1.104 19, 1.146 7, 2.32 8, 2.42 24, 2.44 10, 4.659 6
hn 1.4 VI 20, 1.4 VI 24, 1.6 V 23, 1.6 VI 10, 1.6 VI 48, 1.14 III 14, 1.16 VI 21, 1.17 I 5, 1.17 II 32, 1.17 V 3, 1.17 V 38, 1.22 I 2, 1.22 I 2, 1.22 I 3, 1.22 I 17, 1.22 I 21, 1.23 46, 1.23 50, 1.23 55, 1.23 75(?), 1.24 45, 1.40 17, 1.40 25, 1.40 34, 1.40 43, 1.107 4, 1.107 22, 1.114 28, 1.119 24, 1.166 27, 1.169 16, 1.176 24, 2.25 5, 2.33 8, 2.33 9, 2.33 10, 2.33 17, 2.33 27, 2.33 31, 2.33 37, 2.34 32, 2.42 23, 2.49 4, 2.81 24, 4.132 3, 4.132 6, 4.373 7, 5.11 3
hn[1.6 VI 37, 2.36 20, 2.81 15, 3.1 40, 4.178 13
]hn 1.35 6, 2.31 7, 4.14 2
h]n 2.2 12
hn 1.16 V 22 lg. in
]h/in 1.52 24
]h/in[1.34 4
]h/pn 4.275 2
hnd 1.143 4, 2.19 9, 2.19 11, 2.19 13, 2.33 32, 2.33 35, 2.42 25(!), 2.79 1, 3.2 1, 3.2 14, 3.4 1, 3.5 1
hn[d 2.33 21
hndn 2.72 10
hndt 1.19 IV 62, 2.38 12, 2.45 7
hnh 4.721 16
hnhmt 3.3 8
]h/iny 4.34 3
hnk 2.33 23, 2.71 9
hnk[2.33 11
hnkt 2.21 10, 2.46 12
hnm 2.41 14
hnn 2.65 1
hnny 2.11 10, 2.38 6, 2.46 6, 2.71 5, 2.72 7
h]nny 2.56 4
hnn]y 2.68 11
]h/pġ 4.107 10
]hph 2.31 8
hṣ/l[7.40 5
hr 1.23 51, 1.23 56, 7.53 3
hr[4.546 1
]hr 1.63 4
hrg 1.13 5
hrgb 1.19 III 15, 1.19 III 22, 1.19 III 26, 1.19 III 27
hr[g]b 1.19 III 16
hrh 1.13 31
hry 1.11 5, 4.365 13
hrym 4.398 3
hrm 1.107 32, 1.107 44
hr[m 1.107 34, 1.107 37
]h/irn 1.12 I 7
hrnmy 1.17 I 18, 1.17 I 37, 1.17 II 29,

1.17 V 15, 1.17 V 35, 1.19 I 37, 1.19 IV 24, 1.19 IV 31
hrnmy[1.20 II 8
hr[nmy 1.19 I 48
hrnm[y 1.17 V 5
h]rnmy 1.17 I 36, 1.19 I 21
hrsn 4.711 6
hrr[1.12 II 9
hrš 4.207 3
hrt 1.17 II 41
hrtm 4.390 5
]xhrt̠t 1.116 25
h/p/iški/pr[4.53 16
ht 1.2 IV 8, 1.2 IV 9, 1.2 IV 9, 1.6 I 39, 1.17 VI 40, 1.19 IV 5, 1.21 II 6, 2.3 7, 2.3 20, 2.4 18, 2.10 8, 2.14 10, 2.17 4, 2.17 9, 2.30 14, 2.33 11, 2.33 30, 2.34 6, 2.35 10, 2.36 12, 2.39 11, 2.40 13, 2.42 22, 2.71 13, 2.72 20, 2.73 3, 2.73 10, 2.76 5, 2.81 21
ht[2.39 13, 2.76 6, 7.68 1
]ht 7.30 4
]ht[1.159 5
htx[2.73 9
xhtx 1.35 13
]h/it 4.22 6
hm/t 2.14 15
h/prtn 4.64 IV 8
htm 2.25 4
]htm 1.107 16
]h/itm 4.210 3
ht̠x[1.157 6
]ht̠h 1.62 23

W

{w} 1.4 III 19, 1.100 61

w 1.1 II 3, 1.1 II 16, 1.1 III 3, 1.1 III 4, 1.1 III 13, 1.1 III 16, 1.1 III 17, 1.1 III 17, 1.1 III 18, 1.1 IV 13, 1.1 IV 14(?), 1.1 IV 15, 1.1 IV 26, 1.1 IV 31, 1.1 V 12, 1.1 V 15, 1.2 I 16, 1.2 I 23, 1.2 I 25, 1.2 I 28, 1.2 I 35, 1.2 I 42, 1.2 II 5, 1.2 II 7, 1.2 III 5, 1.2 III 6, 1.2 III 6, 1.2 III 7, 1.2 III 13, 1.2 III 15, 1.2 III 18, 1.2 III 19, 1.2 III 24, 1.2 IV 3, 1.2 IV 5, 1.2 IV 6, 1.2 IV 7, 1.2 IV 7, 1.2 IV 11, 1.2 IV 18, 1.2 IV 23, 1.2 IV 23, 1.2 IV 26, 1.2 IV 27, 1.2 IV 30, 1.2 IV 33, 1.2 IV 35, 1.3 I 5, 1.3 I 9, 1.3 I 18, 1.3 I 27, 1.3 II 3, 1.3 II 4, 1.3 II 5, 1.3 II 17, 1.3 II 19, 1.3 II 23, 1.3 II 24, 1.3 II 38, 1.3 III 9, 1.3 III 10, 1.3 III 11, 1.3 III 21, 1.3 III 22, 1.3 III 23, 1.3 III 27, 1.3 III 28, 1.3 III 36, 1.3 III 36, 1.3 IV 13, 1.3 IV 14, 1.3 IV 21, 1.3 IV 33, 1.3 IV 41, 1.3 IV 42, 1.3 IV 53, 1.3 IV 55, 1.3 V 7, 1.3 V 19, 1.3 V 29, 1.3 V 37, 1.3 V 37, 1.3 VI 19, 1.3 VI 20, 1.3 VI 21, 1.3 VI 22, 1.4 I 29, 1.4 II 12, 1.4 II 21, 1.4 II 27, 1.4 II 40, 1.4 III 8, 1.4 III 12, 1.4 III 13, 1.4 III 19, 1.4 III 20, 1.4 III 22, 1.4 III 27, 1.4 III 32, 1.4 IV 3, 1.4 IV 8, 1.4 IV 13, 1.4 IV 19, 1.4 IV 23, 1.4 IV 25, 1.4 IV 26, 1.4 IV 28, 1.4 IV 29, 1.4 IV 30, 1.4 IV 33, 1.4 IV 34, 1.4 IV 40, 1.4 IV 44, 1.4 IV 49, 1.4 IV 49, 1.4 IV 51, 1.4 IV 58, 1.4 V 1, 1.4 V 2, 1.4 V 8, 1.4 V 18, 1.4 V 18, 1.4 V 21, 1.4 V 26, 1.4 V 28, 1.4 V 33, 1.4 V 34, 1.4 V 41, 1.4 V 42, 1.4 V 44, 1.4 V 46, 1.4 V 47, 1.4 V 58, 1.4 V 58, 1.4 V 63, 1.4 VI 1, 1.4 VI 3, 1.4 VI 7, 1.4 VI 18, 1.4 VI 20, 1.4 VI 24, 1.4 VI 56, 1.4 VII 14, 1.4 VII 19, 1.4 VII 20, 1.4 VII 21, 1.4 VII 22, 1.4 VII 37, 1.4 VII 51, 1.4 VII 54, 1.4 VIII 7, 1.4 VIII 14, 1.4 VIII 27, 1.4 VIII 28, 1.4 VIII 29, 1.5 I 9, 1.5 I 11, 1.5 I 12, 1.5 I 24, 1.5 I 25, 1.5 II 5, 1.5 II 12, 1.5 II 13, 1.5 II 17, 1.5 II 20, 1.5 II 21, 1.5 III 13, 1.5 III 14, 1.5 III 20, 1.5 III 21, 1.5 III 27, 1.5 IV 2, 1.5 IV 13, 1.5 IV 19, 1.5 V 6, 1.5 V 14, 1.5 V 16, 1.5 V 22, 1.5 V 22, 1.5 VI 13, 1.5 VI 19, 1.5 VI 22, 1.5 VI 26, 1.6 I 3, 1.6 I 17, 1.6 I 35, 1.6 I 37, 1.6 I 38, 1.6 I 39, 1.6 I 40, 1.6 I 40, 1.6 I 47, 1.6 I 49, 1.6 I 53, 1.6 I 61, 1.6 I 65, 1.6 II 2, 1.6 II 5, 1.6 II 11, 1.6 II 13, 1.6 II 15, 1.6 III 2, 1.6 III 3, 1.6 III 8, 1.6 III 16, 1.6 III 16, 1.6 III 17, 1.6 III 18, 1.6 III 19, 1.6 IV 9, 1.6 IV 17, 1.6 IV 20, 1.6 IV 21, 1.6 V 11, 1.6 V 20, 1.6 V 23, 1.6 V 26, 1.6 VI 13, 1.6 VI 50, 1.6 VI 51, 1.6 VI 52, 1.6 VI 53, 1.7 16, 1.7 31, 1.7 33, 1.8 II 3, 1.8 II 4, 1.8 II 7, 1.9 18, 1.9 19, 1.10 II 3, 1.10 II 7, 1.10 II 11, 1.10 II 13, 1.10 II 14, 1.10 II 14, 1.10 II 15, 1.10 II 17, 1.10 II 18, 1.10 II 19, 1.10 II 19, 1.10 II 20, 1.10 II 25, 1.10 II 26, 1.10 II 27, 1.10 II 27, 1.10 II 28, 1.10 II 28, 1.10 II 29, 1.10 III 3, 1.10 III 4, 1.10 III 10, 1.10 III 12, 1.10 III 17, 1.10 III 21, 1.10 III 24, 1.10 III 25, 1.10 III 29, 1.10 III 30, 1.10 III 34, 1.10 III 36, 1.11 1, 1.11 2, 1.11 5, 1.12 I 13, 1.12 I 19, 1.12 I 31, 1.12 I 33, 1.12 I 34, 1.12 I 37, 1.12 I 41, 1.12 II 3, 1.12 II 20, 1.12 II 34, 1.12 II 45, 1.12 II 49, 1.12 II 51, 1.12 II 54, 1.12 II 61, 1.13 8, 1.13 9, 1.13 16, 1.13 20, 1.13 22, 1.14 I 14, 1.14 I 24, 1.14 I 25, 1.14 I 27, 1.14 I 31, 1.14 I 34, 1.14 I 35, 1.14 I 35, 1.14 I 37, 1.14 II 9, 1.14 II 21, 1.14 II 26, 1.14 II 32, 1.14 II 34, 1.14 II 40, 1.14 II 47, 1.14 III 2, 1.14 III 4, 1.14 III 5, 1.14 III 6, 1.14 III 10, 1.14 III 14, 1.14 III 15, 1.14 III

19, 1.14 III 22, 1.14 III 23, 1.14 III 27, 1.14 III 30, 1.14 III 31, 1.14 III 32, 1.14 III 34, 1.14 III 35, 1.14 III 49, 1.14 III 50, 1.14 III 51, 1.14 III 52, 1.14 IV 2, 1.14 IV 18, 1.14 IV 26, 1.14 IV 28, 1.14 IV 32, 1.14 IV 35, 1.14 IV 39, 1.14 IV 43, 1.14 IV 44, 1.14 IV 48, 1.14 IV 52, 1.14 V 1, 1.14 V 3, 1.14 V 7, 1.14 V 32, 1.14 VI 6, 1.14 VI 11, 1.14 VI 16, 1.14 VI 18, 1.14 VI 19, 1.14 VI 34, 1.14 VI 39, 1.15 I 8, 1.15 II 5, 1.15 II 10, 1.15 II 24, 1.15 III 20, 1.15 III 21, 1.15 III 25, 1.15 III 26, 1.15 III 27, 1.15 III 27, 1.15 IV 10, 1.15 IV 11, 1.15 IV 23, 1.15 V 15, 1.15 V 20, 1.15 V 21, 1.15 VI 3, 1.16 I 11, 1.16 I 13, 1.16 I 22, 1.16 I 24, 1.16 I 30, 1.16 I 37, 1.16 I 38, 1.16 I 45, 1.16 I 50, 1.16 II 4, 1.16 II 8, 1.16 II 13, 1.16 II 16, 1.16 II 21, 1.16 II 25, 1.16 II 35, 1.16 III 1, 1.16 III 2, 1.16 III 6, 1.16 III 8, 1.16 IV 4, 1.16 IV 8, 1.16 IV 12, 1.16 V 4, 1.16 V 23, 1.16 V 26, 1.16 VI 2, 1.16 VI 4, 1.16 VI 10, 1.16 VI 14, 1.16 VI 16, 1.16 VI 18, 1.16 VI 18, 1.16 VI 20, 1.16 VI 21, 1.16 VI 22, 1.16 VI 26, 1.16 VI 28, 1.16 VI 30, 1.16 VI 41, 1.16 VI 42, 1.16 VI 44, 1.16 VI 54, 1.16 VI 58, 1.17 I 14, 1.17 I 19, 1.17 I 20, 1.17 I 25, 1.17 I 42, 1.17 II 9, 1.17 II 10, 1.17 II 12, 1.17 II 13, 1.17 II 13, 1.17 II 15, 1.17 II 21, 1.17 II 30, 1.17 II 32, 1.17 II 33, 1.17 II 35, 1.17 II 38, 1.17 V 3, 1.17 V 9, 1.17 V 11, 1.17 V 18, 1.17 V 23, 1.17 V 26, 1.17 VI 7, 1.17 VI 10, 1.17 VI 17, 1.17 VI 18, 1.17 VI 20, 1.17 VI 24, 1.17 VI 25, 1.17 VI 27, 1.17 VI 28, 1.17 VI 31, 1.17 VI 31, 1.17 VI 33, 1.17 VI 38, 1.17 VI 41, 1.17 VI 42, 1.17 VI 46, 1.17 VI 50, 1.17 VI 52, 1.17 VI 53, 1.18 I 6, 1.18 I 13, 1.18 I 14, 1.18 I 15, 1.18 I 16, 1.18 I 22, 1.18 I 23, 1.18 I 24, 1.18 IV 7, 1.18 IV 11, 1.18 IV 15, 1.18 IV 16, 1.18 IV 19, 1.18 IV 39, 1.18 IV 40, 1.18 IV 42, 1.19 I 9, 1.19 I 11, 1.19 I 17, 1.19 I 29, 1.19 II 15, 1.19 II 22, 1.19 II 27, 1.19 II 29, 1.19 II 33, 1.19 II 48, 1.19 III 5, 1.19 III 12, 1.19 III 14, 1.19 III 14, 1.19 III 16, 1.19 III 18, 1.19 III 19, 1.19 III 20, 1.19 III 23, 1.19 III 24, 1.19 III 26, 1.19 III 28, 1.19 III 29, 1.19 III 30, 1.19 III 33, 1.19 III 34, 1.19 III 38, 1.19 III 39, 1.19 III 40, 1.19 III 42, 1.19 III 42, 1.19 III 51, 1.19 IV 3, 1.19 IV 6, 1.19 IV 18, 1.19 IV 20, 1.19 IV 22, 1.19 IV 28, 1.19 IV 35, 1.19 IV 42, 1.19 IV 46, 1.19 IV 52, 1.19 IV 53, 1.19 IV 55, 1.19 IV 56, 1.19 IV 62, 1.20 II 5, 1.20 II 7, 1.21 II 8, 1.22 I 9, 1.22 I 13, 1.22 I 21, 1.23 2, 1.23 5, 1.23 6, 1.23 7, 1.23 8, 1.23 12, 1.23 13, 1.23 13, 1.23 15, 1.23 16, 1.23 18, 1.23 26, 1.23 28, 1.23 30, 1.23 33, 1.23 34, 1.23 35, 1.23 42, 1.23 42, 1.23 45, 1.23 46, 1.23 46, 1.23 48, 1.23 49, 1.23 51, 1.23 52, 1.23 53, 1.23 54, 1.23 56, 1.23 56, 1.23 57, 1.23 58, 1.23 62, 1.23 63, 1.23 63, 1.23 64, 1.23 66, 1.23 68, 1.23 69, 1.23 70, 1.23 71, 1.23 71, 1.23 72, 1.23 72, 1.23 73, 1.23 76, 1.24 1, 1.24 19, 1.24 20, 1.24 23, 1.24 30, 1.24 37, 1.24 38, 1.24 47, 1.25 1, 1.25 2, 1.27 5, 1.27 7, 1.27 9, 1.27 13, 1.39 2, 1.39 3, 1.39 4, 1.39 5, 1.39 6, 1.39 7, 1.39 8, 1.39 9, 1.39 12, 1.39 12, 1.39 19, 1.39 20, 1.39 20, 1.40 9, 1.40 19, 1.40 23, 1.40 26, 1.40 26, 1.40 27, 1.40 27, 1.40 27, 1.40 28, 1.40 32, 1.40 35, 1.40 35, 1.40 40, 1.41 5, 1.41 6, 1.41 9, 1.41 10, 1.41 11, 1.41 11, 1.41 13, 1.41 14, 1.41 22, 1.41 22, 1.41 25, 1.41 29, 1.41 31, 1.41 36, 1.41 37, 1.41 39, 1.41 42, 1.41 44, 1.41 47, 1.41 48, 1.41 48, 1.41 52, 1.41 53, 1.41 54, 1.41 54, 1.41 55, 1.43 4, 1.43 6, 1.43 11, 1.43 12, 1.43 15, 1.43 16, 1.46 2, 1.46 4, 1.46 7, 1.46 8, 1.46 9, 1.46 12, 1.46 13, 1.46 14, 1.46 15, 1.46 16, 1.47 12, 1.49 8, 1.50 7, 1.50 8, 1.50 9, 1.50 10, 1.50 10, 1.50 11, 1.53 5, 1.53 6,

1.56 2, 1.63 11, 1.65 4, 1.65 5, 1.67 3, 1.67 5, 1.69 15, 1.71 4, 1.71 5, 1.71 6, 1.71 7, 1.71 8, 1.71 9, 1.71 10, 1.71 25, 1.71 26, 1.71 27, 1.72 7, 1.72 10, 1.72 11, 1.72 15, 1.72 18, 1.72 19, 1.72 20, 1.72 24, 1.72 32, 1.72 33, 1.73 10, 1.73 11, 1.73 12, 1.73 13, 1.73 15, 1.79 2, 1.82 1, 1.82 1, 1.82 3, 1.82 15, 1.82 34, 1.82 35, 1.82 36, 1.82 37, 1.82 42, 1.84 12, 1.84 13, 1.85 3, 1.85 4, 1.85 5, 1.85 6, 1.85 7, 1.85 7, 1.85 8, 1.85 9, 1.85 9, 1.85 10, 1.85 11, 1.85 13, 1.85 14, 1.85 14, 1.85 15, 1.85 16, 1.85 16, 1.85 17, 1.85 18, 1.85 19, 1.85 20, 1.85 21, 1.85 23, 1.85 26, 1.85 26, 1.85 27, 1.85 29, 1.85 30, 1.85 32, 1.86 2, 1.86 4, 1.86 6, 1.86 7, 1.86 9, 1.86 10, 1.86 11, 1.86 11, 1.86 13, 1.86 14, 1.86 24, 1.86 32, 1.87 6, 1.87 8, 1.87 8, 1.87 11, 1.87 14, 1.87 15, 1.87 17, 1.87 18, 1.87 19, 1.87 20, 1.87 21, 1.87 23, 1.87 24, 1.87 34, 1.87 39, 1.87 40, 1.87 41, 1.87 43, 1.87 46, 1.87 57, 1.87 58, 1.88 1, 1.88 3, 1.88 3, 1.89 3, 1.90 3, 1.90 4, 1.90 5, 1.90 6, 1.90 7, 1.90 21, 1.91 33, 1.91 36, 1.92 4, 1.92 5, 1.92 10, 1.92 32, 1.92 38, 1.94 22, 1.94 28, 1.94 29, 1.94 30, 1.94 33, 1.96 1, 1.96 2, 1.97 3, 1.97 5, 1.98 4, 1.100 1, 1.100 7, 1.100 13, 1.100 18, 1.100 20, 1.100 24, 1.100 29, 1.100 34, 1.100 36, 1.100 39, 1.100 44, 1.100 46, 1.100 50, 1.100 52, 1.100 56, 1.100 61, 1.100 64, 1.100 65, 1.100 67, 1.100 72, 1.100 72, 1.100 74, 1.103 4, 1.103 5, 1.103 6, 1.103 9, 1.103 10, 1.103 11, 1.103 14, 1.103 15, 1.103 19, 1.103 26, 1.103 27, 1.103 28, 1.103 30, 1.103 31, 1.103 35, 1.103 37, 1.103 38, 1.103 39, 1.103 39, 1.103 41, 1.103 42, 1.103 49, 1.103 52, 1.103 53, 1.103 55, 1.103 56, 1.103 57, 1.103 58, 1.103 58, 1.103 59, 1.104 6, 1.104 8, 1.104 9, 1.104 10, 1.104 11, 1.104 13, 1.104 14, 1.104 15, 1.104 17, 1.104 18, 1.104 20, 1.104 24, 1.105 2, 1.105 8, 1.105 10, 1.105 10, 1.105 16, 1.105 22, 1.105 23, 1.105 25, 1.106 6, 1.106 15, 1.106 19, 1.106 21, 1.106 21, 1.106 23, 1.106 27, 1.106 29, 1.106 30, 1.106 31, 1.106 33, 1.107 7, 1.107 11, 1.107 39, 1.107 39, 1.107 40, 1.107 41, 1.107 41, 1.107 43, 1.107 43, 1.108 1, 1.108 2, 1.108 3, 1.108 4, 1.108 4, 1.108 6, 1.108 8, 1.108 10, 1.108 26, 1.108 27, 1.109 6, 1.109 7, 1.109 8, 1.109 8, 1.109 9, 1.109 10, 1.109 11, 1.109 12, 1.109 14, 1.109 15, 1.109 18, 1.109 19, 1.109 20, 1.109 24, 1.109 27, 1.109 27, 1.109 28, 1.110 11, 1.111 21, 1.112 3, 1.112 4, 1.112 6, 1.112 6, 1.112 9, 1.112 12, 1.112 14, 1.112 20, 1.112 21, 1.112 25, 1.112 26, 1.112 26, 1.112 28, 1.113 1, 1.113 5, 1.114 3, 1.114 7, 1.114 9, 1.114 11, 1.114 14(!), 1.114 19, 1.114 19, 1.114 20, 1.114 21, 1.114 23, 1.114 26, 1.114 27, 1.114 30, 1.114 30, 1.115 5, 1.115 6, 1.115 8, 1.115 11, 1.115 13, 1.116 8, 1.116 10, 1.117 11, 1.118 11, 1.119 3, 1.119 4, 1.119 7, 1.119 9, 1.119 10, 1.119 16, 1.119 21, 1.119 21, 1.119 24, 1.119 34, 1.121 3, 1.121 8, 1.123 1, 1.123 4, 1.123 5, 1.123 6, 1.123 8, 1.123 9, 1.123 11, 1.123 12, 1.123 13, 1.123 16, 1.123 25, 1.123 26, 1.123 27, 1.124 3, 1.124 4, 1.124 6, 1.124 7, 1.124 9, 1.124 9, 1.124 10, 1.124 13, 1.124 15, 1.124 16, 1.126 18, 1.126 22, 1.127 5, 1.127 6, 1.127 11, 1.127 17, 1.127 20, 1.127 24, 1.127 32, 1.130 8, 1.130 14, 1.130 18, 1.130 20, 1.130 21, 1.130 24, 1.130 25, 1.132 14, 1.132 28, 1.133 1, 1.133 4, 1.133 18, 1.134 2, 1.136 3, 1.136 4, 1.136 5, 1.136 6, 1.139 4, 1.139 12, 1.139 16, 1.139 19, 1.146 3, 1.148 2, 1.148 3, 1.148 4, 1.148 5, 1.148 6, 1.148 10, 1.148 22, 1.148 24, 1.148 26, 1.148 27, 1.148 28, 1.148 31, 1.148 41, 1.148 44, 1.151 11, 1.151 14, 1.156 2, 1.157 5, 1.161 6, 1.161 14, 1.161 16, 1.161 17, 1.161 18,

1.161 22, 1.161 23, 1.161 27, 1.161 28, 1.161 28, 1.161 29, 1.161 30, 1.161 32, 1.162 3, 1.162 4, 1.162 17, 1.162 20, 1.163 10, 1.163 11, 1.163 12, 1.163 16, 1.164 2, 1.164 4, 1.164 5, 1.164 5, 1.164 6, 1.164 8, 1.164 10, 1.164 14, 1.164 16, 1.164 19, 1.164 20, 1.165 2, 1.165 3, 1.166 14, 1.166 27, 1.168 2, 1.168 3, 1.168 4, 1.168 6, 1.168 9, 1.168 11, 1.168 12, 1.169 2, 1.169 6, 1.169 10, 1.169 14, 1.170 3, 1.170 3, 1.170 9, 1.171 2, 1.171 4, 1.172 22, 1.172 27, 1.173 3, 1.173 4, 1.173 5, 1.173 14, 1.173 16, 1.173 17, 1.175 3, 1.175 5, 1.175 6, 1.175 6, 1.175 7, 1.175 8, 1.175 9, 1.175 11, 1.175 12, 1.175 13, 1.175 14, 1.175 16, 1.176 24, 2.1 4, 2.1 6, 2.2 9, 2.3 3, 2.3 4, 2.3 7, 2.3 8, 2.3 9, 2.3 10, 2.3 13, 2.3 14, 2.3 15, 2.3 18, 2.3 20, 2.3 21, 2.4 7, 2.4 19, 2.4 20, 2.4 22, 2.6 3, 2.7 4, 2.7 7, 2.7 9, 2.7 10, 2.7 10, 2.8 6, 2.9 4, 2.10 6, 2.10 10, 2.10 11, 2.10 16, 2.10 18, 2.11 4, 2.11 13, 2.12 9, 2.13 13, 2.13 16, 2.13 17, 2.14 10, 2.14 14, 2.14 15, 2.14 17, 2.15 10, 2.16 9, 2.16 10, 2.16 12, 2.16 16, 2.17 4, 2.17 6, 2.17 8, 2.17 9, 2.17 14, 2.18 5, 2.19 12, 2.21 13, 2.21 17, 2.21 18, 2.21 29, 2.23 1, 2.23 15, 2.23 20, 2.23 21, 2.24 6, 2.25 6, 2.26 11, 2.26 13, 2.26 15, 2.26 17, 2.27 3, 2.30 9, 2.30 11, 2.30 14, 2.30 16, 2.30 17, 2.30 18, 2.30 19, 2.30 20, 2.30 22, 2.31 15, 2.31 26, 2.31 37, 2.31 40, 2.31 41, 2.31 45, 2.31 47, 2.31 50, 2.31 51, 2.31 52, 2.31 56, 2.31 56, 2.31 60, 2.31 60, 2.31 65, 2.32 9, 2.33 11, 2.33 12, 2.33 15, 2.33 20, 2.33 22, 2.33 27, 2.33 33, 2.33 37, 2.33 39, 2.34 9, 2.34 10, 2.34 12, 2.34 24, 2.35 10, 2.35 15, 2.35 19, 2.36 3, 2.36 4, 2.36 8, 2.36 10, 2.36 17, 2.37 6, 2.37 10, 2.37 11, 2.38 15, 2.38 18, 2.38 23, 2.38 24, 2.38 26, 2.39 8, 2.39 9, 2.39 10, 2.39 17, 2.39 25, 2.39 32, 2.39 35, 2.40 11, 2.40 13, 2.40 15, 2.40 18, 2.41 7, 2.41 17, 2.41 19, 2.41 20, 2.41 22, 2.42 5, 2.42 11, 2.42 13, 2.42 14, 2.42 18, 2.42 19, 2.42 23, 2.42 24, 2.42 25, 2.42 26, 2.42 27, 2.42 27, 2.44 8, 2.44 9, 2.44 15, 2.45 15, 2.45 17, 2.45 19, 2.45 20, 2.45 21, 2.45 22, 2.45 24, 2.45 26, 2.45 27, 2.45 28, 2.45 29, 2.45 29, 2.46 11, 2.46 12, 2.46 15, 2.46 23, 2.47 3, 2.47 6, 2.47 6, 2.47 7, 2.47 8, 2.47 12, 2.47 20, 2.47 22, 2.47 24, 2.49 9, 2.49 13, 2.50 9, 2.50 16, 2.51 3, 2.57 13, 2.61 6, 2.61 13, 2.62 5, 2.62 6, 2.62 11, 2.62 12, 2.62 14, 2.62 16, 2.63 15, 2.68 6, 2.69 3, 2.70 4, 2.70 13, 2.70 13, 2.70 14, 2.70 15, 2.70 16, 2.70 18, 2.70 20, 2.70 23, 2.70 25, 2.72 15, 2.72 16, 2.72 17, 2.72 27, 2.72 28, 2.72 29, 2.72 31, 2.72 44, 2.73 5, 2.73 6, 2.73 7, 2.73 9, 2.73 10, 2.73 12, 2.73 13, 2.73 16, 2.73 17, 2.73 18, 2.73 21, 2.75 7, 2.75 9, 2.77 6, 2.77 14, 2.77 15, 2.79 3, 2.79 4, 2.80 6, 2.80 7, 2.80 8, 2.80 11, 2.81 18, 2.81 21, 2.81 30, 2.82 6, 2.82 8, 2.82 10, 2.82 13, 2.82 20, 3.1 6, 3.1 9, 3.1 10, 3.1 16, 3.1 21, 3.2 17, 3.3 5, 3.4 4, 3.4 5, 3.4 6, 3.4 7, 3.4 8, 3.4 10, 3.4 12, 3.4 19, 3.5 11, 3.5 13, 3.5 19, 3.5 20, 3.8 7, 3.8 13, 3.9 5, 3.9 11, 3.9 14, 3.9 20, 4.4 3, 4.4 5(!), 4.4 6, 4.12 4, 4.14 2, 4.16 2, 4.16 12, 4.23 12, 4.29 2, 4.29 4, 4.31 8, 4.34 2(!), 4.34 3, 4.34 4, 4.34 4, 4.34 5, 4.34 6, 4.34 7, 4.35 II 6, 4.49 1, 4.49 4, 4.53 15, 4.55 5, 4.55 8, 4.55 10, 4.55 11, 4.55 12, 4.55 14, 4.55 16, 4.55 20, 4.55 22, 4.55 25, 4.55 27, 4.55 28, 4.63 I 2, 4.63 I 4, 4.63 I 5, 4.63 I 8, 4.63 I 9, 4.63 I 12, 4.63 I 26, 4.63 I 27, 4.63 I 29, 4.63 I 30, 4.63 I 31, 4.63 II 5, 4.63 II 6, 4.63 II 7, 4.63 II 9, 4.63 II 10, 4.63 II 14, 4.63 II 15, 4.63 II 16, 4.63 II 17, 4.63 II 18, 4.63 II 19, 4.63 II 22, 4.63 II 23, 4.63 II 24, 4.63 II 25, 4.63 II 28, 4.63 II 38, 4.63 II 41, 4.63 II 42, 4.63 II 43, 4.63 II 45, 4.63 II 46, 4.63 II 47, 4.63 III 2, 4.63 III 3, 4.63 III 4, 4.63 III 5,

4.63 III 6, 4.63 III 8, 4.63 III 10, 4.63 III 11, 4.63 III 12, 4.63 III 13, 4.63 III 14, 4.63 III 15, 4.63 III 16, 4.63 III 20, 4.63 III 21, 4.63 III 22(cor.), 4.63 III 23, 4.63 III 25, 4.63 III 26, 4.63 III 28, 4.63 III 29, 4.63 III 33, 4.63 III 34, 4.63 III 35, 4.63 III 36, 4.63 III 39, 4.63 III 40, 4.63 III 41, 4.63 III 44, 4.63 III 45, 4.63 III 46, 4.63 IV 1, 4.63 IV 4, 4.63 IV 5, 4.63 IV 7, 4.63 IV 8, 4.63 IV 9, 4.63 IV 12, 4.63 IV 13, 4.63 IV 16, 4.63 IV 17, 4.65 11, 4.66 3, 4.66 4, 4.66 10, 4.66 11, 4.68 15, 4.68 19, 4.68 49, 4.69 I 4, 4.69 I 7, 4.69 I 8, 4.69 I 11, 4.69 II 10, 4.69 II 11, 4.69 II 17, 4.69 II 21, 4.69 II 22, 4.69 II 23, 4.69 III 18, 4.69 V 3, 4.69 VI 24, 4.69 VI 25, 4.77 3, 4.80 7, 4.80 7, 4.80 10, 4.80 13, 4.80 20, 4.86 2, 4.86 3, 4.86 4, 4.86 14, 4.86 15, 4.86 16, 4.86 17, 4.86 18, 4.95 4, 4.95 5, 4.95 6, 4.95 8, 4.95 10, 4.97 4, 4.102 2, 4.102 5, 4.102 6, 4.102 7, 4.102 8, 4.102 11, 4.102 16, 4.102 17, 4.102 18, 4.102 18, 4.102 19, 4.102 19, 4.102 20(*bis*), 4.102 21, 4.102 21, 4.102 22, 4.102 23, 4.102 25, 4.102 28, 4.118 2, 4.122 3, 4.123 2, 4.123 3, 4.123 4, 4.123 7, 4.123 8, 4.123 9, 4.123 10, 4.123 16, 4.123 17, 4.123 18, 4.123 19, 4.123 20, 4.123 20, 4.123 21, 4.123 21, 4.123 22, 4.123 23, 4.127 13, 4.131 3, 4.131 13, 4.132 2, 4.132 3, 4.132 4, 4.132 6, 4.132 6, 4.136 4, 4.141 III 5, 4.141 III 7, 4.143 3, 4.145 6, 4.145 8, 4.145 8, 4.146 3, 4.150 5, 4.157 2, 4.158 13, 4.160 2, 4.160 4, 4.160 11, 4.163 2, 4.163 4, 4.163 13, 4.166 3, 4.166 6, 4.167 3, 4.167 12, 4.167 15, 4.168 1, 4.168 6, 4.169 2, 4.169 4, 4.169 8, 4.172 4, 4.172 5, 4.173 1, 4.173 6, 4.175 12, 4.182 57, 4.189 2, 4.191 7, 4.191 8, 4.191 10, 4.191 11, 4.194 2, 4.194 4, 4.195 4, 4.195 5, 4.195 14, 4.199 3, 4.199 4, 4.200 11, 4.204 3, 4.204 5, 4.205 4, 4.213 2, 4.213 3, 4.213 4, 4.213 7, 4.213 9, 4.213 11, 4.213 14, 4.213 17, 4.213 22, 4.227 I 4, 4.227 I 6, 4.227 I 8, 4.227 I 10, 4.227 II 10, 4.230 10, 4.232 11, 4.232 12, 4.237 1, 4.237 2, 4.243 1, 4.243 2, 4.243 3, 4.243 3, 4.243 4, 4.243 5, 4.243 7, 4.243 10, 4.243 11, 4.243 12, 4.243 13, 4.243 14, 4.243 15, 4.243 16, 4.243 16, 4.243 18, 4.243 20, 4.243 21, 4.243 22, 4.243 23, 4.243 24, 4.243 25, 4.243 26, 4.243 27, 4.243 29, 4.243 31, 4.243 32, 4.244 10, 4.246 5, 4.248 3, 4.262 8, 4.266 4, 4.268 5, 4.268 6, 4.268 7, 4.269 10, 4.269 12, 4.269 14, 4.269 16, 4.269 18, 4.269 27, 4.269 27, 4.269 28, 4.279 1, 4.279 2, 4.279 3, 4.279 3, 4.279 4, 4.279 5, 4.280 2, 4.280 5, 4.281 9, 4.282 2, 4.282 6, 4.282 8, 4.282 17, 4.288 7, 4.290 3, 4.295 2, 4.295 2, 4.295 2, 4.295 2, 4.295 3, 4.295 4, 4.295 5, 4.295 6, 4.295 6, 4.295 7, 4.295 8, 4.295 8, 4.295 8, 4.295 10, 4.295 11, 4.295 12, 4.295 13, 4.295 16, 4.295 16, 4.295 17, 4.295 17, 4.296 10, 4.311 3, 4.311 4, 4.311 5, 4.311 15, 4.313 4, 4.317 14, 4.323 6, 4.332 7, 4.337 4, 4.337 13, 4.337 14, 4.337 26, 4.338 3, 4.338 14, 4.339 3, 4.339 3, 4.339 4, 4.339 6, 4.339 6, 4.339 7, 4.339 8, 4.339 9, 4.339 12, 4.339 15, 4.339 19, 4.339 19, 4.339 23, 4.339 25, 4.339 26, 4.339 27, 4.341 9, 4.341 10, 4.341 20, 4.343 9, 4.347 3, 4.347 5, 4.347 8, 4.349 4, 4.356 10, 4.360 3, 4.360 3, 4.360 5, 4.360 8, 4.360 9, 4.360 11, 4.360 13, 4.362 5, 4.362 6, 4.363 3, 4.363 6, 4.363 8, 4.363 9, 4.364 8, 4.367 9, 4.367 10, 4.368 2, 4.368 5, 4.368 7, 4.368 8, 4.368 15, 4.369 18, 4.374 2, 4.374 4, 4.374 6, 4.374 8, 4.374 9, 4.374 10, 4.374 14, 4.374 15(!), 4.377 5, 4.377 6, 4.377 25, 4.380 5, 4.380 6, 4.380 14, 4.380 15, 4.380 16, 4.380 18, 4.380 19, 4.380 20, 4.380 23, 4.380 24, 4.380 26, 4.382 30, 4.384 11, 4.385 3, 4.385 4, 4.385 5, 4.386 4, 4.387 15, 4.387 26, 4.388 8,

4.391 1, 4.391 2, 4.391 3, 4.391 4, 4.391 5, 4.391 6, 4.391 7, 4.391 8, 4.391 11, 4.391 12, 4.391 13, 4.391 14, 4.391 15, 4.392 2, 4.398 2, 4.398 5, 4.398 10, 4.399 13, 4.400 4, 4.400 9, 4.400 14, 4.400 18, 4.411 6, 4.412 I 26, 4.412 I 28, 4.412 II 2, 4.412 II 15, 4.412 II 32, 4.412 III 12, 4.417 3, 4.417 5, 4.417 6, 4.417 6, 4.417 7(*bis*), 4.417 8, 4.417 8, 4.417 9, 4.417 10, 4.417 13, 4.417 13, 4.417 14, 4.417 15, 4.417 16, 4.417 18, 4.421 3, 4.435 4, 4.436 7, 4.437 4, 4.448 3, 4.513 3, 4.519 2, 4.519 4, 4.521 3, 4.540 3, 4.548 6, 4.558 1, 4.558 2, 4.558 3, 4.558 4, 4.561 4, 4.571 1, 4.571 6, 4.571 8, 4.575 3, 4.578 1, 4.578 4, 4.581 8, 4.593 3, 4.605 1, 4.609 20, 4.609 31, 4.611 8, 4.611 27, 4.618 2, 4.618 5, 4.618 11, 4.618 12, 4.624 2, 4.624 3, 4.624 4, 4.624 5, 4.624 6, 4.624 7, 4.624 8, 4.624 10, 4.624 11, 4.624 12, 4.625 20, 4.625 21, 4.632 3, 4.632 3, 4.632 4, 4.632 7, 4.632 7, 4.632 8, 4.632 11, 4.632 12, 4.632 13, 4.632 16, 4.632 17, 4.632 21, 4.644 7, 4.647 3, 4.658 46, 4.658 48, 4.688 4, 4.689 4, 4.689 5, 4.689 5, 4.689 6, 4.690 16, 4.691 5, 4.691 6, 4.692 6, 4.693 29, 4.698 5, 4.704 7, 4.704 8, 4.707 8, 4.707 12, 4.707 20, 4.707 23, 4.709 3, 4.710 13, 4.715 3, 4.715 10, 4.715 11, 4.721 6, 4.721 8, 4.724 8, 4.729 2, 4.729 3, 4.729 5, 4.729 8, 4.729 9, 4.734 5, 4.734 6, 4.742 11, 4.744 2, 4.750 4, 4.759 7, 4.759 10, 4.771 3, 4.771 8, 4.778 13, 4.778 17, 4.779 2, 4.779 9, 4.779 11, 4.782 2, 4.782 20, 4.782 26, 4.788 3, 4.788 5, 4.788 7, 5.2 7, 5.3 6, 5.4 1, 5.6 1, 5.8 1, 5.9 I 5, 5.9 I 9, 5.9 I 12, 5.9 I 13, 5.9 I 14, 5.9 I 16, 5.9 I 17, 5.9 I 18, 5.9 II 3, 5.10 2, 5.10 5, 5.11 7, 5.11 12, 5.11 17, 5.11 18, 5.11 20, 5.12 1, 5.13 1, 5.13 2, 5.13 3, 5.13 4, 5.13 7, 5.14 7, 5.16 1, 5.16 2, 5.16 8, 5.17 4, 5.19 1, 5.20 1, 5.20 4, 5.21 1, 5.24 1, 6.13 3, 6.20 3, 6.30 1, 6.39 1, 6.40 2, 6.42 1, 6.42 2, 6.45 1, 6.47 1, 6.48 3, 6.54 1, 6.54 2, 6.66 9, 7.41 1, 7.47 5, 7.51 19, 7.53 2, 7.53 5, 7.93 3, 7.133 3, 7.135 4, 7.140 4, 7.142 4, 7.142 6, 7.184 2, 7.197 7

w[1.2 II 13, 1.2 III 8, 1.2 IV 31, 1.5 III 23, 1.13 23, 1.14 II 6, 1.14 IV 13, 1.16 II 31, 1.16 VI 31, 1.18 I 12, 1.18 IV 14, 1.18 IV 16, 1.19 I 4, 1.19 II 40, 1.19 III 10, 1.40 36, 1.41 7, 1.41 15, 1.46 1, 1.50 7, 1.69 4, 1.72 38, 1.72 39, 1.85 26, 1.85 27, 1.86 1, 1.90 9, 1.90 12, 1.90 13, 1.90 14, 1.90 17, 1.104 25, 1.118 18, 1.121 6, 1.134 1, 1.136 8, 1.137 3, 1.137 4, 1.138 4, 1.148 45, 1.164 12, 1.176 14, 2.1 7, 2.2 10, 2.3 5, 2.6 11, 2.6 12, 2.6 13, 2.9 5, 2.31 8, 2.45 10, 2.59 3, 2.77 12, 3.1 12, 4.4 6, 4.123 8, 4.191 3, 4.191 6, 4.243 8, 4.302 2, 4.302 3, 4.387 23, 4.417 2, 4.421 5, 4.422 15, 4.422 26, 4.461 1, 4.560 1, 4.644 4, 4.672 1, 4.736 5, 4.743 13, 4.764 2, 6.33 3, 7.9 1, 7.28 2, 7.45 5, 7.91 2, 7.117 4, 7.167 3

]w 1.4 III 7, 1.4 VI 14, 1.4 VIII 47, 1.5 VI 1, 1.17 I 4, 1.17 VI 16, 1.19 III 1, 1.40 1, 1.46 18, 1.48 38, 1.53 7, 1.71 2, 1.82 5, 1.82 43, 1.84 18, 1.89 6, 1.94 33, 1.97 14, 1.107 1, 1.113 3, 1.117 4, 1.139 5, 1.151 10, 1.161 27, 1.163 17, 1.171 3, 1.172 6, 1.172 8, 2.8 3, 2.22 2, 2.31 61, 4.34 4, 4.102 30, 4.162 1, 4.162 2, 4.205 14, 4.384 8, 4.384 11, 4.391 10, 4.419 4, 4.420 5, 4.420 11, 4.459 3, 4.483 1, 4.489 1, 4.581 3, 4.581 4, 4.647 1, 4.657 4, 4.740 4, 6.47 2, 7.1 1, 7.7 2, 7.19 5, 7.51 19, 7.140 3

]w[1.38 1, 1.64 24, 1.136 7, 1.151 7, 4.521 1, 7.35 3, 7.36 2

[[w]] 1.148 25, 4.709 10

w 1.1 II 9 lg. k

wx[4.619 2

]xw[7.140 5

w/h[1.26 1

w/k 4.744 6, 7.63 8

w/k[1.12 II 35, 4.69 III 21, 4.521 4, 4.737 2, 4.743 7

xw/k[1.37 5
w/k/p/r[4.393 24
w/k/r[1.176 17, 4.73 6
]w/k/r 7.51 12
]w/n 7.51 13
]w/r[7.184 8
]w/kxxnth 1.157 10
]wz/ḫ[7.39 6
]xwrṯt 1.116 33 lg. ḫwrṯt
wi[1.166 21
wḏny 4.763 10
]wy 1.62 15, 4.460 6
]wyn 4.648 1
wk 1.37 3
wl[1.67 7
wld 1.12 I 27, 1.13 30, 1.14 III 48, 1.14 VI 33, 1.15 III 5, 1.15 III 20, 1.15 III 21
]wldm 1.25 4
]xwlm[1.35 7
w/klt 4.34 5
wm 1.67 20, 1.104 21
wm 1.17 I 20 lg. km
w/kmtmtm 1.20 I 3
wn 1.2 III 22, 1.3 V 38, 1.4 IV 50, 1.4 V 6, 1.12 I 36, 1.24 31, 1.82 17
]wn 4.666 3, 7.56 4
]wn[4.331 2
wspm 1.14 IV 42 lg. kspm
]xw/rˁn 4.557 3
xw/kˁr 1.70 11
wpṯm 1.4 VI 13
wql 4.147 8
wrx[2.63 3
wrḫ 1.70 29
wry 4.81 7
wrk 1.6 V 9
wrmp[4.364 12
wrt 4.369 18
]wrṯt 1.135 13 lg. ḫ]wrṯt
wt[1.67 19
]wt 7.85 5
wtb[ḏ/ṯr 4.382 19
]wth 1.107 12
wṯ[7.15 1

Z

z 5.6 1, 5.9 I 17, 5.9 I 18, 5.12 1, 5.13 1, 5.13 2(!), 5.13 3, 5.13 4, 5.13 7, 5.14 8, 5.16 2, 5.16 5, 5.16 8, 5.17 1, 5.17 4, 5.19 2, 5.20 1, 5.21 1, 5.24 1, 6.70 1, 6.70 2
z[7.184 1
]z 1.103 54, 1.151 9, 1.153 9, 4.237 1
]z[1.68 6
zx 2.45 19
z/g/ḫ[1.176 13, 4.422 51
]xz/ḫ 4.98 1
zbl 1.2 I 38, 1.2 I 43, 1.2 III 8, 1.2 III 16, 1.2 IV 7, 1.2 IV 8, 1.2 IV 14, 1.2 IV 16, 1.2 IV 22, 1.2 IV 24, 1.3 I 3, 1.5 VI 10, 1.6 I 42, 1.6 III 3, 1.6 III 9, 1.6 III 21, 1.6 IV 5, 1.6 IV 16, 1.9 17, 1.13 26, 1.13 28, 1.14 II 45, 1.14 IV 23, 1.15 II 4, 1.15 II 6, 1.19 IV 2, 1.22 I 10, 1.133 19, 4.213 13, 5.22 9
zbl[1.129 3
zb[l 1.2 IV 29, 1.6 III 1
z]bl 1.2 III 21
]zbl 1.2 III 23, 4.75 III 13
zblhm 1.2 I 24, 1.2 I 29
zblkm 1.2 I 25, 1.2 I 28
zblk[m 1.16 V 25
zbln 1.16 V 21, 1.16 V 28, 1.16 VI 9, 1.16 VI 36, 1.16 VI 52
zb[ln 1.16 V 50
z[bln 1.16 V 12
zblnm 1.14 I 17
zbrm 1.23 9
zg 1.44 10
zd 1.23 24
zd 1.1 V 25 lg. atzd
zzb[4.679 6
]zy 4.371 5, 4.430 3
]zk 4.425 15
zl 4.244 13
zlbn 4.7 9, 4.616 16, 4.753 8
zlbn[4.611 20
zlb[n 4.362 2
zlyy 4.85 2, 4.85 4, 4.85 11, 4.113 3, 4.686 17
zmyy 4.412 III 5
]zn 4.75 I 5, 4.183 I 23
xzn 4.199 2
]xzn 7.2 5
znxxn 4.42 5
znan 4.63 II 44
z/ḫnan 4.52 14
]xznl/ṣ[1.73 17
znm 4.230 2
]xznl/ṣ[1.73 17
zntn 1.1 IV 16
z/g/ḫslrš 4.63 II 15
zġt 1.14 III 18, 1.14 V 11
zql 4.617 3
zr 4.609 52
zr[4.15 12
zry 4.63 I 30, 4.628 1
zrm 1.169 14
zt 1.5 II 5, 1.22 I 15, 1.24 43, 1.114 31, 4.91 14, 4.143 2, 4.164 3, 4.386 13, 4.399 7, 4.764 6, 4.764 7, 4.786 13
[[zt]] 4.764 11
zth 3.5 8
ztm 4.284 8, 4.429 2, 4.429 3, 4.429 4, 4.429 5, 4.710 11
z[t]m 4.429 1
ztr 1.17 I 27, 1.17 II 17
z[tr 1.17 II 1

Ḥ

ḥ 5.2 4, 5.4 2, 5.6 1, 5.9 I 17, 5.9 I 18, 5.9 II 2, 5.12 2, 5.13 1, 5.13 2, 5.13 3, 5.13 4, 5.13 6, 5.13 7, 5.14 9, 5.16 1, 5.16 2, 5.16 5, 5.16 8, 5.17 1, 5.17 4, 5.19 2, 5.20 1, 5.21 1, 5.24 1
ḥ[1.8 II 12, 1.12 II 18, 1.82 13, 1.126 11, 1.155 1, 1.174 1, 1.176 15, 2.17 10, 2.31 61, 2.47 8, 2.53 3, 2.82 12, 4.4 10, 4.41 7, 4.65 5, 4.157 3, 4.161 7, 4.195 4, 4.243 30, 4.313 11, 4.340 14, 4.372 8, 4.400 5, 4.569 3, 4.617 14, 4.644 1, 4.711 1, 4.743 3, 6.39 1, 7.47 3, 7.82 2, 7.207 3
]ḥ 1.3 V 47, 1.5 VI 4, 1.7 45, 1.10 I 3, 1.103 17, 1.103 44, 1.113 10, 2.31 24, 2.31 31, 4.75 IV 13, 4.186 7, 4.224 2, 4.522 2, 4.676 6
]ḥ[1.82 18, 4.11 1, 4.386 7, 4.608 19, 7.16 12, 7.47 1, 7.153 1
ḥx[1.107 30, 1.136 9, 4.586 3, 4.743 5, 4.748 14
]xḥ[1.35 4, 4.599 4, 7.172 3
xxḥ[1.94 26
xxḥxx 4.213 30
]xḥx[4.473 2, 7.124 1
ḥ/ṭ[1.5 III 12, 1.174 4, 4.61 5, 4.515 2
]ḥ/ṭ 1.17 I 38, 4.428 9, 7.139 3
]ḥ/ṭ[7.146 2, 7.160 1
]ḥ/ṭx 1.172 31
]xḥ/ṭ[4.732 3
ḥ/ṭxmi 4.345 7
ḥxxy 4.214 I 14
ḥb[1.82 11
]ḥb 1.113 6
ḥbḫ 1.80 4 lg. ṭbḫ?
ḥby 1.114 19, 4.775 20
ḥbl 1.10 II 30, 1.11 6, 1.18 IV 31, 1.19 I 33, 4.779 3
ḥ]bl 1.10 II 40
ḥblx 1.8 II 10
ḥblm 4.247 30, 4.247 31
ḥbq 1.23 51, 1.23 56
]ḥbq 4.201 6
ḥbqh 1.17 I 40
ḥbr 1.108 5
ḥbrh 1.23 76
ḥbrk 1.6 VI 49
ḥbrm 1.169 10
ḥbš 1.5 IV 22, 1.17 VI 8, 4.48 10
ḥ]bš 4.610 28
ḥbšh 1.3 II 13, 1.18 IV 28
ḥb[šy 1.18 IV 17
ḥbšk 1.13 6
]ḥg 1.151 7
ḥgb 1.90 2, 1.106 1, 1.168 2
ḥgb[1.134 3
ḥgbḏr 4.724 3
ḥgby 4.93 II 5, 4.226 8, 4.348 29
]ḥgby[4.498 10
ḥgbn 4.69 I 19, 4.77 28, 4.141 I 18, 4.183 I 26, 4.263 9, 4.319 3, 4.343 10, 4.609 11, 4.609 27, 4.769 8, 4.769 16, 4.769 69
ḥgbn[4.383 2
]ḥgbn 4.682 9
ḥgbt 4.55 28
ḥ]gbt 4.408 2
ḥgln 4.7 6
ḥd 2.77 8, 2.77 15, 2.77 18
ḥd[4.432 22
ḥdgk 1.12 I 18
ḥdy 2.83 4
ḥdn 4.720 2, 4.785 21
ḥdn[4.322 10
]ḥdn[4.498 9
ḥdr 4.195 6
ḥ[d]r 4.195 14
ḥd[r 1.16 II 51
]ḥdr 7.178 6
ḥdrh 1.14 I 26
ḥdrm 1.3 V 26, 4.195 3
ḥ[d]rm 1.3 V 11
ḥdṯ 1.14 II 48, 1.14 IV 26, 1.41 48, 1.78 1, 1.87 1, 1.87 53, 1.105 15, 1.112 2, 1.112 10, 1.124 7, 1.163 2, 1.163 10, 4.172 1, 4.182 50, 4.205 19, 4.266 1, 4.281 17, 4.336 1, 4.689

3

ḥd]ṯ 1.46 1

ḥdṯh 1.104 18

ḥdṯm 1.91 13

ḥdṯn 4.63 II 3, 4.116 11, 4.153 10, 4.609 18, 4.609 19, 7.221 2

ḥd[ṯ]n 4.63 IV 8

ḥ]dṯn 7.221 3

]ḥdṯn 4.243 34

ḥdṯt 1.146 2, 4.213 12, 4.243 22, 4.707 21

ḥḏm 4.609 25

ḥḏrt 1.71 12, 1.85 14, 1.85 27

ḥḏr[t 1.72 19

]ḥh 4.359 7

]xḥhm[1.36 3

ḥw 1.82 6

]ḥw[7.70 1

ḥwgn[7.53 2

ḥwy 1.17 VI 30, 1.176 17

ḥwyh 4.145 10

ḥwt 1.4 I 42, 1.10 II 20, 1.103 1, 1.103 3, 1.103 5, 1.103 16, 1.103 35, 1.103 37, 1.103 41, 1.103 45, 1.103 50, 1.103 51, 1.103 55, 1.103 56, 1.103 59, 1.140 6, 2.36 16, 2.47 13, 2.70 15, 2.73 4, 2.73 5, 2.73 6, 2.81 3, 2.81 18, 3.3 4, 3.8 10, 4.779 12, 6.26 3

ḥwt[2.18 4, 2.42 10, 2.49 10, 2.73 2

ḥw[t 1.103 7, 1.140 2, 2.36 17, 2.47 9, 2.78 7

ḥ[wt 1.103 8, 2.36 17

ḥ]wt 2.76 10

ḥwth 2.33 9

ḥwtk 2.36 4, 2.39 20, 2.47 2, 2.81 7

]ḥwtm 2.36 18

ḥ]wtm 2.36 19

ḥwtn 1.103 4, 1.103 6, 1.103 53

ḥḥbm 4.609 20 lg. ḥṭbm

]ḥḥḥ[7.197 2

ḥḫ 1.80 5 lg. ṭbḫ?

ḥṭb 4.269 24, 4.611 2

ḥṭbh 1.14 III 8 lg. ḥṭbt

ḥṭbm 4.609 20(!)

ḥṭbt 1.14 III 8(!)

ḥṭb<t> 1.14 IV 51

ḥṭm 4.211 5, 4.225 9, 4.269 25, 4.269 32, 4.345 5, 4.400 9, 4.400 17, 4.608 4

ḥṭ[m 4.400 4, 6.61 2

ḥ[ṭm 4.225 11

ḥ]ṭm 4.400 13

ẖṭm 4.710 4, 4.710 7, 5.22 24

ḥṭt 1.14 II 29, 1.14 IV 10, 1.16 III 9

ḥẓ 1.82 3, 1.90 5

ḥẓhn 4.145 4

ḥẓk 1.14 III 12

ḥẓm 4.141 III 19, 4.169 2, 4.180 1, 4.204 1, 4.204 2, 4.204 4, 4.630 14

ḥẓr 1.1 II 14, 1.2 III 19, 1.3 V 39, 1.4 IV 51, 1.4 V 1, 1.4 V 28, 1.8 II 4, 1.13 21

ḥẓ]r 1.3 V 4

ḥẓrh 1.19 IV 10, 1.100 68, 1.114 18, 7.35 1

ḥẓry 1.14 III 29, 1.14 IV 42, 1.14 V 45, 1.19 IV 22

ḥẓr[y 1.14 VI 15

ḥẓrk 1.15 II 23

ḥẓt 1.3 V 31, 1.4 IV 42

ḥy 1.6 III 2, 1.6 III 8, 1.6 III 20, 2.23 18, 2.82 17, 4.366 4, 5.10 2, 5.11 4

]ḥy 1.2 IV 2

]xḥy 4.71 II 7

ḥyil 2.26 3

ḥyi[l 4.427 14, 4.554 4

ḥ]yil 4.497 2

ḥyk 1.16 I 14, 1.16 II 36

]ḥyk 1.4 III 8

ḥyl 4.200 8, 4.214 II 1

ḥy[ly 1.22 II 12

ḥyl\y 1.22 I 9f

ḥym 1.17 VI 26, 1.17 VI 27

]xḥym 3.6 6

ḥyn 4.51 6, 4.55 24, 4.64 II 4, 4.214 II 3, 4.232 35, 4.763 2

ḥyn[4.746 4

ḥypx[7.67 1

ḥyt 1.3 V 31, 1.4 IV 42

ḥ[ytk 1.18 IV 41

]ḥkx[4.57 6

]ḥ/tkl[4.191 10

ḥkm 1.3 V 30, 1.4 IV 41

]ḥkm 1.19 IV 60

ḥkmk 1.3 V 30

ḥkmt 1.4 IV 41, 1.4 V 3, 1.16 IV 2

]ḥkmt 1.129 4

ḥkpt 1.3 VI 15, 1.17 V 21, 1.17 V 31, 4.247 26
ḥkp[t 1.1 III 19
ḥkr 1.93 6
ḥl 1.13 27, 1.16 I 8, 1.16 II 47, 1.41 47, 1.41 53, 1.46 9, 1.106 23, 1.106 33, 1.112 9, 1.119 4, 1.119 24, 1.132 28, 1.173 17, 4.68 40, 4.186 6, 4.320 8, 4.424 22, 4.610 23, 4.618 32
ḥl[1.87 57, 4.234 4
]ḥl 1.81 15, 2.31 51, 7.177 3
]ḥl[4.490 1
ḥ]l 4.610 31
ḥ\l 1.112 14f
]ḥlx[7.76 1
]xḥl 1.168 22
ḥlb 1.15 II 26, 1.23 14, 4.272 2, 4.272 5, 4.707 20
ḥlbt 4.617 12
]ḥly 4.658 24
ḥll 1.115 6
ḥlm 1.6 III 4, 1.6 III 10, 1.14 III 50, 1.16 I 7, 1.16 I 8, 1.16 II 45, 1.86 28
ḥ[l]m 1.16 II 46
ḥlmh 1.14 I 35
ḥlmy 1.14 III 46, 1.14 VI 31
ḥlmm 1.86 1
ḥln 1.4 V 62, 1.4 VI 6, 1.4 VI 9, 1.4 VII 17, 2.31 46
]ḥln 4.307 12
ḥ\ln 1.4 VII 25f
ḫln 5.22 27
ḥl]n 1.4 V 65
ḥlnm 4.195 15
ḥlqm 1.3 II 14, 1.3 II 28
ḥlš 1.109 25
ḥlt 1.164 20, 4.219 13
ḥlt[4.220 4
ḥm 1.2 IV 33, 1.19 I 40
]ḥm[7.121 3
]xḥm 4.296 15, 4.744 9
ḥmdm 1.12 I 38, 1.12 II 8
ḥmdrt 1.19 II 21
ḥ]mdrt 1.19 II 23
ḥmḥmt 1.17 I 40, 1.17 I 41, 1.23 51
ḥ[m]ḥmt 1.23 56
ḥmḥ<mt>h 1.16 I 29
ḥmyt 1.40 36
ḥmytkm 1.119 27
ḥmytkm[1.119 36
]ḥmytny 1.119 29
]ḥmk 1.1 V 18 lg. ḥmr?
]xḥmm 4.734 9
]ḥmn 4.69 I 25
ḥmny 4.108 3
ḫmš 4.31 4, 4.31 5, 4.31 11
ḫ[mš 4.31 6
ḥmṣ 1.19 I 17, 1.175 6, 4.269 27, 4.269 28, 4.269 35(!)
ḥmr 1.1 V 18(?), 1.5 I 19, 1.85 17, 1.85 28, 1.86 9, 1.97 4, 4.14 18, 4.29 2, 4.29 4, 4.269 24, 4.380 5, 4.380 6, 4.380 14, 4.380 15, 4.380 23, 4.380 24, 4.380 26, 4.426 2, 4.691 5, 4.698 5, 5.3 1, 5.3 2, 5.3 3, 5.3 3, 5.3 4, 5.3 4, 5.3 5, 5.3 5, 5.3 6
ḥmr[1.72 23, 1.86 9
ḥm[r 1.71 15, 1.86 12, 4.20 5, 4.380 12, 4.380 17, 4.698 1
ḥ[m]r 4.14 12, 4.380 16, 5.3 2
ḥ[mr 1.111 16, 4.23 5, 4.380 9, 4.380 10, 4.380 13
ḥ]mr 5.3 1
ḥm]r 1.97 17, 4.14 6
ḥmrh 1.14 III 17
ḥmr[h 1.14 V 10
ḥmrm 4.377 30, 4.380 7, 4.380 20, 4.618 3, 4.691 7, 4.790 1, 6.19 1
ḥmr[m 4.268 1, 4.268 4, 4.380 4, 4.698 3
ḥm[r]m 4.380 21
ḥm[rm 4.380 3
ḥ[mrm 4.377 25
]ḥmrm 3.6 3
ḥmr]m 4.380 8
ḥ<m>t 1.100 68
ḥmt 1.14 II 22, 1.14 IV 4, 1.100 6, 1.100 11, 1.100 17, 1.100 22, 1.100 28, 1.100 33, 1.100 38, 1.100 43, 1.100 48, 1.100 54, 1.100 60, 1.107 6, 1.107 7, 1.107 35, 1.107 36, 1.107 38, 1.107 39, 1.107 40, 1.107 40, 1.107 41, 1.107 42, 1.107 42, 1.107 43, 1.107 44, 1.107 45
ḥmt[1.107 24, 1.107 36
ḫmt 4.710 4
]ḥmt 1.82 32
ḥ]mt 1.107 33, 1.107 38

ḥmthm 1.16 III 15

ḥmṯ 1.82 7, 1.172 28

]ḥn 4.35 II 22

]ḥ/ṭn 4.628 2, 4.769 20

ḥnil 4.332 8

ḥnbn 1.123 15

]ḥnḏr[1.35 3

ḥnn 1.65 6, 3.8 22, 4.75 IV 5, 4.214 III 9, 4.298 2, 4.356 7, 4.729 3, 5.18 6

ḥnn[4.422 46

ḥn[n 4.586 1

]ḥnn 2.55 1

ḥnny 2.15 3

ḥnth 1.17 I 16

ḥswn 4.4 9 cor. ḫswn

ḥsk 4.230 1

ḥsm 1.176 15

ḥsn 1.14 III 1, 1.14 IV 30

ḥsp 4.213 24, 4.213 25, 4.213 26, 4.213 27

ḥs[p 1.91 36

ḥspt 1.19 II 2, 1.19 II 6, 1.19 IV 37

ḥġ[1.19 II 32

ḥġmn 4.682 10

]ḥp 4.25 2

ḥpnk 1.16 VI 58

ḥpr 2.71 17, 4.243 6, 4.243 8, 4.243 15, 4.243 17, 4.243 19, 4.243 21, 4.243 23, 4.269 1, 4.609 1, 4.636 7, 4.636 12, 4.688 3

ḥp[r 4.243 13, 4.243 27, 4.609 51, 4.636 27

ḥ[p]r 4.636 3

ḥ]pr 4.243 25, 4.636 23

ḥpšt 1.14 III 8, 1.14 IV 52

ḥṣ 1.1 IV 11, 1.16 IV 5

ḥṣb 4.409 7

ḥṣbn 4.33 14

]xxḥṣm 4.304 1

ḥṣn 4.63 III 11, 4.232 19

ḥṣqt 4.428 7

ḥṣqtn[4.692 9

ḥ{q}kpt 1.3 VI 13

]xḥq[7.95 3

ḥqr 4.557 1

ḥr 1.82 13, 1.82 13, 1.103 58, 1.174 7, 4.41 5, 4.110 8, 4.139 5, 4.781 5

ḥr[1.176 23, 1.176 28

]ḥr[4.122 16, 6.56 1

ḥrx 4.197 19

ẖr 5.22 1

ḥrb 1.2 I 32, 1.3 I 7, 1.4 VI 57, 1.5 IV 14, 1.6 II 31, 1.6 V 13, 1.15 IV 25, 1.19 IV 45, 1.96 4

ḥ]rb 1.17 VI 4

ḥrbm 1.2 IV 4

ḥrh 1.103 54

]ḥrḥrtm 1.2 III 13

ḥrẓn 4.63 II 23, 4.69 V 10, 4.93 I 5, 4.93 I 8, 4.711 3, 4.759 1

ḥrẓn[4.422 39

]ḥrẓn 4.260 3

ḥry 1.14 III 39, 1.14 IV 40, 1.14 VI 24, 1.15 III 24, 1.15 IV 26, 1.15 V 9, 1.15 VI 3, 1.16 VI 17, 1.16 VI 19, 4.281 14

ḥ]ry 1.15 IV 14

ḥryth 1.100 36

ḥrk[4.315 3

ḥrm 4.69 I 9, 4.75 I 1, 4.775 14

ḥrn 1.16 VI 55, 1.16 VI 55, 1.82 27, 1.82 41, 1.100 58, 1.100 61, 1.100 67, 1.107 31, 1.124 6, 1.169 9, 1.176 20

]ḥrn 1.107 29, 1.107 38

ḥr<n> 1.100 73(?)

ḥr[nm 1.82 27

ḥrnqm 1.24 23

]ḥrġ[1.82 30

ḥrp[4.64 II 6

ḥrṣ 1.17 VI 37, 1.19 I 8, 1.19 I 10, 4.145 8, 4.169 4, 4.169 8, 4.363 9, 4.368 2, 4.368 5, 4.368 7, 4.368 8, 4.368 15, 4.377 5, 4.377 6, 4.384 11

ḥrṣ[4.323 2

]ḥrṣ 4.577 2, 4.577 3

ḥrṣbʿ 4.770 3

ḥrr 1.5 II 5, 4.214 I 11

ḥrrx[1.12 II 40

ḥrš 1.1 III 5, 1.3 VI 23, 1.12 II 61, 1.17 V 19, 1.17 V 24, 1.92 17, 2.70 14, 4.35 I 16, 4.38 6, 4.47 8, 4.47 9, 4.47 10, 4.98 6, 4.98 8, 4.98 9, 4.103 3, 4.103 58, 4.125 1, 4.141 III 7, 4.183 II 12, 4.214 II 15, 4.215 1, 4.243 2, 4.277 9, 4.321 1, 4.339 16, 4.370 14, 4.545 II 6, 4.547 1, 4.609

18, 4.609 23, 4.609 28, 4.610 19, 4.618 12, 4.630 8, 4.630 12, 4.745 8, 4.745 9
ḥr[š 4.207 1, 4.618 11
ḥr]š 4.742 12
ḥr\š 4.46 13f
ḥršm 1.19 IV 60, 4.141 III 5, 4.141 III 12, 4.141 III 14, 4.145 9, 4.155 1, 4.705 2
ḥršm[4.201 6
ḥr[šm 4.216 2
ḥr]šm[1.1 II 10
ḥrt 4.371 14, 4.711 4
]ḥrt 2.36 9
]ḥrth 1.61 2
ḥrtn 4.658 21
ḥrṯ 1.14 III 18, 1.14 V 11, 4.296 15, 4.296 17
ḥrṯh 4.296 9
ḥrṯm 1.16 III 12, 2.45 22, 4.141 III 1, 4.141 III 11, 4.175 10, 4.609 27, 4.625 17, 4.630 6
ḥrṯm[4.65 1
ḥr]ṯm 4.618 21
ḥš 1.1 III 27, 1.1 IV 7, 1.4 V 51, 1.4 V 52, 1.4 V 53, 1.4 V 54
]ḥš 1.82 15
ḥ]š 1.2 III 10
ḥšbn 4.309 7
ḥšk 1.1 II 21, 1.1 III 10, 1.3 III 18, 1.3 IV 11
ḥšn[1.5 III 4
ḥš[n 1.5 III 3
]ḥ/ṭšr[4.325 6
ḥt 4.396 17
ḥt[4.247 11
]ḥt 7.222 6
]ḥt[7.13 3
ḥtk 1.10 III 34, 7.53 4
ḥtk[1.81 9
ḥtkh 1.14 I 21, 1.14 I 22, 1.108 23
ḥtkk 1.1 II 18, 1.6 IV 11, 1.108 25
ḥt[kk 1.16 II 15
ḥ[tkk 1.16 II 12
ḥtkn 1.14 I 10
ḥtlk 1.12 I 19
ḥtp 1.119 32
ḥtt 1.82 23, 1.82 23
ḥtṯ 1.14 II 18, 1.14 IV 1
ḥṯn 3.4 6, 4.141 I 19, 4.141 II 10, 4.277 11
ḥṯb 4.779 12
ḥṯbn 4.158 2, 4.337 1, 4.771 7
ḥṯm 1.41 22

Ḫ

ḫ 5.4 1, 5.6 1, 5.8 1, 5.9 I 17, 5.9 I 18, 5.12 1, 5.13 1, 5.13 2, 5.13 3, 5.13 4, 5.13 6, 5.13 7, 5.14 4, 5.15 3, 5.16 1, 5.16 2, 5.16 8, 5.17 4, 5.19 1, 5.20 1, 5.20 4, 5.21 1, 5.24 1, 5.25 15
ḫ[1.26a 4, 1.64 13, 1.107 32, 4.237 2, 4.335 35, 4.408 3, 4.608 24, 7.176 3
]ḫ 1.42 33, 4.30 12, 4.609 52, 4.769 20, 7.114 8
]ḫ[1.7 49, 4.427 11
ḫx 1.42 51, 1.148 13, 2.34 27
ḫx[1.2 II 15, 1.66 1, 1.104 28, 1.126 24, 4.673 4, 4.743 4
]ḫx[4.324 1
xḫ 1.90 18, 4.772 6
]xḫ 1.11 17
]xḫ[1.75 6, 4.566 5, 7.25 3
]xḫ/z 4.98 1
ḫ/g/z[1.176 13, 4.422 51
ḫ/y[4.458 3, 4.524 2, 4.742 12
]ḫ/y 1.10 II 37, 4.197 8, 4.306 6, 4.531 2, 4.769 45, 7.23 1
]ḫ/y[4.37 7, 7.209 1
xḫ/y[4.359 1
ḫxn 1.42 51
ḫ/sxxry 4.245 I 5
ḫpxxxn 4.278 3
ḫisp 1.107 40 lg. yisp
ḫiṯ[7.15 3
ḫup 1.128 20
ḫurl 1.149 5
ḫurn 1.128 2
ḫuṯtr 1.66 13
ḫb[4.161 8
ḫbb 1.75 10
ḫbd[4.39 2
ḫbd{.}ṯr 4.46 11
ḫby 4.103 22, 4.339 4
ḫbl 1.1 IV 8, 4.689 5
ḫbly 1.39 17, 1.102 11, 1.162 14
ḫbsn 4.307 15
ḫbr 1.14 II 29, 1.14 IV 10, 1.15 IV 8, 1.15 IV 9, 1.15 IV 19, 1.15 IV 20
]ḫbr 1.15 V 25
]ḫbr[7.144 3
ḫbrtn[r 3.1 34
ḫbrtn]r 3.1 36
ḫbrṯ 1.4 II 9
ḫbrṯḫnd 1.125 15
ḫb]šh 1.7 2
ḫbt 1.32 3, 1.35 9, 1.35 11, 1.35 12, 1.42 60, 1.42 60, 1.42 62, 1.52 9, 1.52 13, 4.382 15
ḫbt[1.32 5
]ḫbt 4.119 6
ḫbtd 1.60 11, 1.64 32, 1.116 19, 1.132 5, 1.132 14, 1.132 20
ḫ]btd 1.135 10
ḫb\t]d 1.26 5f
ḫbty 3.10 3, 4.33 39, 4.53 3, 4.792 4
ḫbtkm 1.40 30
ḫbtkn 1.40 21, 1.84 5
ḫ[btk]n 1.40 38
ḫbtm[1.42 56
ḫbtṯ[1.59 4
ḫbṯ 4.360 8, 4.430 3
ḫbṯh 3.3 4
ḫbṯm 2.17 1
ḫgbt 4.214 II 11
ḫd[4.10 3, 4.452 1
]ḫd[7.64 6
]xxxxxxxḫd[4.196 1
ḫdi 4.63 III 8
ḫdbṯ 4.320 7
ḫdd 4.80 2
ḫdḏnnk 1.42 21, 1.42 46, 1.42 59, 1.42 62
ḫd[ḏ]nnk 1.42 37
ṯxxṯbxḫdḏnnk 1.42 14
]ḫdḫd[1.64 2
ḫdy 4.635 55
ḫdyn 4.33 8, 4.69 VI 11, 4.98 18, 4.214 III 20, 4.724 6
ḫdlr 1.42 32, 1.42 33, 1.132 8, 1.135 11
ḫdlrṯt 1.116 20
ḫdlrṯ[t 1.60 14, 1.60 16(!)

ḫdmn 4.103 43, 4.624 9, 4.681 5
ḫdn 1.42 32, 1.42 33, 1.64 25, 1.64 29, 1.132 8
]ḫdn 1.63 5
ḫ]dn 1.135 11
ḫd]n 1.64 33
ḫdnṯt 1.60 14
ḫ]dnṯt 1.116 20
ḫdś 1.171 7
ḫdpḏṯr 4.63 III 18
ḫdpṯr 4.64 II 7
ḫdr 1.64 6
ḫdš$_2$bˁl[? 6.70 2
ḫḏ 1.13 34, 1.30 2
ḫḏ[4.729 7
ḫḏḏ 1.14 II 39, 1.14 IV 17, 1.66 20, 1.66 34
ḫḏl 4.611 4
ḫḏlḏ 1.42 1, 1.42 6, 1.42 10, 1.42 32, 1.42 35, 1.42 38, 1.42 41, 1.42 44, 1.42 47, 1.42 50, 1.42 54, 1.42 60
ḫ[ḏlḏ 1.42 29
ḫ]ḏlḏ 1.42 15
ḫḏ]lḏ 1.42 17
ḫḏl]ḏ 1.42 22
ḫḏm 1.149 4, 7.53 7
ḫḏm[4.178 6
ḫḏmḏr 4.643 25
ḫḏmḏr[4.748 15
ḫ[ḏm]ḏr 4.190 2
ḫḏmyn 4.748 14
ḫḏmrd 4.102 22
ḫḏmtn 4.417 4
ḫḏnr[4.56 5
ḫḏġb 4.269 25, 4.269 28, 4.690 2(cor.)
ḫḏġlm 4.138 2, 4.609 16
ḫḏġl[m 4.188 1
]ḫḏġlm 4.154 5
ḫḏprš[p 4.760 3
ḫḏr 1.42 1, 1.42 6, 1.42 10, 1.42 29, 1.42 38, 1.42 41, 1.42 44, 1.42 47, 1.42 50, 1.42 54, 1.42 60
ḫḏr[1.66 16
ḫḏ[r 1.42 32, 1.42 35
ḫ[ḏr 1.42 17, 1.42 26
ḫḏrw[1.30 2
ḫḏrġl 1.112 2
ḫwrn 1.120 4, 1.125 2
ḫwrṯt 1.116 33(!)
ḫ]wrṯt 1.135 13(!)
ḫwt[4.161 9
ḫwṯtr 1.66 28, 1.66 35
ḫzzdm 1.125 11
ḫzḫz 1.42 24
ḫzḫ[z 1.42 16
ḫz[ḫz 1.42 20
ḫzzy 1.116 5(!)
ḫzli 4.75 III 6
ḫzmyn 4.356 15, 4.374 12
ḫzn 4.425 7
ḫzr 1.149 11, 4.141 III 4, 4.141 III 7, 4.141 III 9, 4.609 51, 4.630 2
ḫzry 4.763 6
ḫzrm 4.216 6
ḫzrn 4.69 II 15
ḫ[z]rn 4.632 6
]ḫḫyi[4.32 2
ḫḫ 1.4 VIII 13, 1.5 II 16
ḫḫm 1.17 VI 35
ḫṭ 1.2 III 18, 1.6 VI 29, 1.23 8, 1.23 9, 1.95 4, 1.169 5, 1.169 5
ḫṭ[at 2.72 33
ḫṭh 1.19 I 14, 1.23 37
ḫṭk 1.23 40, 1.23 43, 1.23 47
ḫṭm 1.16 VI 8, 1.114 8, 1.169 14
ḫẓ 1.172 21
]ḫ/yy 4.701 14
ḫym 1.4 I 29, 1.44 10
ḫyml 4.165 3
ḫyr 1.78 2, 1.105 3, 1.105 15, 1.148 23, 4.219 11, 4.220 3, 4.258 3, 4.688 1
ḫy[r 1.112 1
ḫyrḫ[1.149 5
ḫyrn 4.75 III 11, 4.75 IV 11, 4.148 2, 4.214 I 17, 4.307 5, 4.343 8, 4.374 2, 4.378 7, 4.609 4, 4.729 5
ḫyrn[4.332 20
ḫl 1.10 II 29, 1.12 I 25, 1.44 4, 1.128 2
ḫl[4.235 9, 4.567 4, 4.683 13
]xḫl 1.172 24
]xḫl[7.5 2
ḫlan 4.222 20, 4.350 2, 4.715 5
ḫlan[4.413 4
ḫla[n 4.391 17
]ḫlan[4.526 2

ḫli 4.282 6

ḫlu 1.91 12

ḫluy 4.75 V 13

ḫlb 1.4 VIII 6, 1.5 V 14, 1.82 4, 1.85 20, 1.91 22, 1.109 16, 1.109 33, 1.130 11, 1.148 26, 4.6 2, 4.48 1, 4.48 2, 4.48 7, 4.63 II 30, 4.68 3, 4.68 50, 4.73 12, 4.100 5, 4.108 1, 4.267 2, 4.303 4, 4.346 7, 4.365 12, 4.365 17, 4.380 13, 4.380 16, 4.621 14, 4.685 5, 4.693 14, 4.693 29, 4.693 46, 4.728 2, 4.784 19

ḫl[b 3.7 14

ḫ[lb 1.134 8

ḫ]lb 4.382 18, 4.676 4

ḫl]b 4.94 16, 4.119 7, 4.610 26, 4.610 27, 4.693 28

ḫlby 4.274 4, 4.337 6, 4.348 25, 4.610 24, 4.621 6, 4.770 8

ḫ]lby 4.784 23

ḫlbym 4.7 7, 4.93 I 2

ḫlbn 4.77 27

ḫlbġ 1.42 10, 1.148 13

ḫld 1.44 1, 1.54 1, 1.128 1, 1.131 1

ḫldy 4.636 10

ḫldp 1.128 4, 1.128 5

ḫlṯ/ḏ[4.196 10

ḫlh 1.124 10

ḫly 4.244 12

ḫlyn 4.692 10

]ḫlyn 4.64 II 9

ḫlly/ḫ 4.391 12

]xḫlly[1.35 19

ḫlly/ḫ 4.391 12

ḫlln 4.53 12, 4.335 23

ḫllt 1.17 II 42

ḫlm 1.131 13, 4.348 16

ḫlmẓ 1.115 2, 1.115 4, 1.115 12

ḫln 1.64 17, 1.128 18

]ḫln[4.242 1

ḫl/sġl 4.396 18

ḫlp 4.172 4, 4.266 4, 4.611 11

ḫlpn 4.782 2, 5.10 5

ḫ[lpn 1.19 IV 44

ḫlpnm 4.117 1, 4.385 6

ḫlpnt 4.630 5

ḫlpn[t 4.192 2

ḫlṣ 1.169 7

ḫlq 1.5 VI 10, 1.6 I 42, 1.6 III 1, 1.18 IV 42, 2.61 11, 4.213 3, 4.611 2, 4.611 4, 4.611 8, 4.611 9, 4.611 12, 4.611 14, 4.611 18, 4.613 6, 4.613 9

ḫl]q 4.613 1

ḫ]lq[4.613 5

ḫlqt 2.61 12

ḫlt 1.172 11

ḫlṯ/ḏ[4.196 10

ḫm 1.15 IV 23

ḫm[1.48 12, 2.80 5, 7.5 3

ḫmx[1.86 16

]xḫm 4.55 19

]xxḫm 1.5 II 1

]ḫ/ym 4.71 IV 2, 4.125 12

ḫmat 1.23 14

ḫm]nd 1.135 7

ḫmn 1.112 8, 1.128 10, 1.128 18, 1.164 1, 4.54 5, 4.332 12

ḫ[mn 1.53 5

]ḫmn 4.69 IV 24

ḫmnd 1.116 6, 1.116 16

ḫmnh 1.106 13, 1.106 14, 1.112 3

ḫm[n]h 1.104 16

ḫmnnd 1.60 6

ḫmr 1.3 I 16, 1.23 6, 1.42 60, 4.564 3

ḫ[mr 4.420 4

]ḫmr[7.136 6

]ḫmrbn 7.43 6

ḫmrm 4.244 22

ḫmrn 4.683 30

ḫmš 1.4 VI 29, 1.14 II 30, 1.14 III 3, 1.14 III 11(!), 1.14 IV 11, 1.14 V 5, 1.17 II 36, 1.22 I 22, 1.23 57, 1.39 9, 1.41 38, 1.106 25, 1.112 21, 1.119 20, 1.161 29, 1.164 17, 2.80 4, 4.20 4, 4.27 13, 4.27 18, 4.27 19, 4.27 21, 4.40 13, 4.41 6, 4.44 12, 4.44 27, 4.92 5, 4.95 6, 4.95 7, 4.95 8, 4.95 10, 4.102 17, 4.123 6, 4.123 14, 4.132 1, 4.137 1, 4.137 3, 4.138 1, 4.141 IV 1, 4.149 14, 4.150 2, 4.150 4, 4.150 5, 4.152 7, 4.152 10, 4.158 10, 4.158 12, 4.158 19, 4.160 5, 4.165 12, 4.165 13, 4.166 2, 4.166 4, 4.169 4, 4.173 4, 4.173 5, 4.174 1, 4.174 7, 4.174 9, 4.179 4, 4.179 5, 4.181 2, 4.182 36, 4.203 4, 4.203 6, 4.203 7, 4.203 8, 4.203 9, 4.203 9, 4.203 10, 4.203 11, 4.213 1, 4.213 4,

4.213 9, 4.213 14, 4.213 21, 4.218 5, 4.226 3, 4.226 8, 4.230 13, 4.247 2, 4.247 29, 4.261 7, 4.261 21, 4.261 22, 4.269 3, 4.269 33, 4.272 2, 4.272 3, 4.272 4, 4.279 5, 4.284 3, 4.285 12, 4.296 3, 4.310 9, 4.337 2, 4.337 6, 4.338 10, 4.341 7, 4.341 12, 4.344 1, 4.344 2, 4.345 6, 4.358 3, 4.380 4, 4.380 21, 4.381 18, 4.381 19, 4.381 20, 4.381 21, 4.381 22, 4.387 12, 4.390 3, 4.390 9, 4.392 1, 4.392 1, 4.399 4, 4.400 6, 4.402 4, 4.402 5, 4.407 3, 4.550 1, 4.609 38, 4.609 39, 4.616 5, 4.616 6, 4.616 7, 4.618 17, 4.618 21, 4.618 29, 4.625 7, 4.625 9, 4.626 9, 4.691 1, 4.697 8, 4.709 4, 4.721 8, 4.721 11, 4.721 11, 4.721 12, 4.775 4, 4.775 8, 4.777 8, 4.786 1, 4.786 2, 4.786 3, 4.786 6, 4.786 7, 4.790 16, 4.790 17, 6.12 3

ḫmš[1.164 13, 2.80 8, 4.18 2, 4.18 3, 4.23 6, 4.182 39, 4.195 3, 4.247 3, 4.299 5, 4.305 3, 4.558 6, 4.558 7, 4.639 4

ḫm[š 4.56 4, 4.95 4, 4.95 5, 4.157 5, 4.285 10, 4.291 4, 4.387 3, 4.625 17

ḫ[mš 4.270 5, 4.285 11, 4.627 5

]ḫmš 1.17 I 11, 4.466 4, 4.719 1

]ḫmš[4.640 5

ḫ]mš 3.1 22, 4.301 1, 4.618 15, 6.18 1

ḫm]š 3.1 23, 4.141 III 22, 4.228 5, 4.271 4, 4.380 4

ḫ]mš[1.126 16, 4.525 3

ḫ]m[š 4.399 14

ḫmšm 1.148 20, 2.47 4, 3.9 9, 4.4 8, 4.14 6, 4.14 12, 4.14 18, 4.91 9, 4.123 23, 4.141 II 24, 4.143 2, 4.143 4, 4.158 22, 4.163 14, 4.174 13, 4.182 2, 4.182 16, 4.201 5, 4.213 17, 4.226 1, 4.230 13, 4.243 16, 4.262 7, 4.273 3, 4.273 4, 4.273 5, 4.273 6, 4.273 7, 4.273 8, 4.280 13, 4.284 2, 4.333 10, 4.337 25, 4.338 14, 4.340 18, 4.341 23, 4.344 1, 4.344 3, 4.344 4, 4.344 7, 4.344 17, 4.369 9, 4.387 11, 4.400 4, 4.400 6, 4.402 1, 4.402 3, 4.550 2, 4.625 3, 4.627 2, 4.658 10, 4.658 24, 4.690 16, 4.691 5, 4.721 11, 4.749 1, 4.755 3, 4.779 8, 4.782 28

ḫ[mšm 4.400 9

ḫ]mšm 4.258 4, 4.523 1

]ḫmšm 4.340 15

ḫm]šm 4.683 3

ḫmšt 1.87 59, 4.113 4, 4.113 5, 4.132 6, 4.146 3, 4.158 22, 4.182 17, 4.203 17, 4.267 2, 4.280 7, 4.281 4, 4.281 8, 4.281 11, 4.281 13, 4.281 14, 4.281 15, 4.281 16, 4.281 19, 4.281 20, 4.281 24, 4.281 25, 4.281 26, 4.281 27, 4.281 28, 4.290 8, 4.290 12, 4.290 14, 4.333 8, 4.337 7, 4.337 17, 4.341 5, 4.341 6, 4.632 1, 4.658 7, 4.658 17, 4.658 32, 4.658 42, 4.658 44, 4.658 45, 4.707 14, 4.771 3, 4.778 10, 4.779 5, 4.782 16

ḫmšt[4.317 3

ḫmš[t 4.281 6

ḫm[št 4.276 4, 4.276 6, 4.281 30

ḫ[mšt 4.281 31

]ḫmšt 4.640 3

ḫm]št 4.281 29, 4.386 19, 4.658 34

ḫm<š>t 4.281 9

<ḫ>mšt 4.123 1

ḫmt 1.14 III 55

ḫn[4.393 20, 7.39 1

]ḫn 4.75 III 12

]ḫ/yn 4.611 20, 4.613 11, 4.654 2, 4.654 3

ḫ/znan 4.52 14

ḫndlt 4.182 17

ḫndrṯ 1.71 7, 1.85 7, 4.34 5

ḫndrṯm 4.34 6

ḫnzn[1.148 17

ḫnzr 4.64 II 2, 4.69 I 14, 4.98 16, 7.218 3

ḫnzrk 1.5 V 9

ḫny 4.170 17

ḫnyn 4.69 VI 19, 4.93 III 2

ḫnn 1.148 16, 4.170 19, 4.611 18

ḫnnġd 1.132 9

ḫnp 1.18 I 17

ḫnpm 1.9 15

ḫnq 4.232 25

ḫnqn 4.98 20, 4.233 6

ḫnqtm 1.39 18, 1.102 13

ḫnt[4.178 7

ḫnṯ 1.66 14
ḫ[n]ṯ 1.66 36
ḫsw<n> 4.60 2
ḫswn 4.4 9(cor.), 4.14 3, 4.44 26, 4.232 32, 4.786 9
ḫśwn 4.14 11(cor.)
ḫs[yn 4.19 2
ḫ/g/zslrš 4.63 II 15
ḫsn 1.79 2, 1.79 3, 1.79 5, 4.35 I 23
ḫsnm 4.137 1, 4.137 8, 4.137 10, 4.162 1, 4.162 2, 4.163 2, 4.163 4, 4.163 13, 4.173 1, 4.173 6, 4.173 8, 4.174 2, 4.179 2, 4.179 7
ḫ]snm 4.542 1
ḫss 1.1 III 17, 1.2 IV 7, 1.3 VI 22, 1.4 I 24, 1.4 V 41, 1.4 V 44, 1.4 V 58, 1.4 VI 3, 1.4 VII 20, 1.4 VII 21, 1.6 VI 50, 1.6 VI 52, 1.6 VI 53, 1.15 II 5, 1.17 V 11, 1.17 V 18, 1.17 V 23, 1.17 V 26, 1.17 VI 24, 1.100 46, 1.107 43, 1.123 9, 1.123 28, 2.31 18
ḫ[ss 1.2 III 7
ḫ]ss 1.4 VI 1
ḫssm[1.92 17
ḫl/sġl 4.396 18
ḫsr 4.361 3, 4.721 5, 4.778 5, 4.778 8, 4.782 8, 6.48 4
ḫ[sr 4.782 12
ḫsrt 1.6 II 17, 2.41 17, 2.41 20
ḫp 1.3 II 7, 1.7 38
]ḫp 1.82 6
ḫph 1.107 32
ḫpn 2.70 28, 4.156 5, 4.166 2, 4.168 1, 4.182 57, 4.188 9, 4.188 10, 4.188 13, 4.188 16, 4.190 4, 4.609 17
ḫp[n 4.188 4
ḫ]pn 4.156 3
ḫpnm 4.4 4, 5.11 16
ḫpn[m 4.182 35
ḫpnt 1.148 19, 4.152 5, 4.152 9, 4.152 10, 4.188 18, 4.188 20, 4.270 7, 4.363 3, 4.363 7
]ḫpnt 4.765 4
ḫpśry 4.124 2
ḫpsry 4.129 2
ḫprt 1.4 VI 48
ḫpš[1.149 3
ḫpt[4.686 3
ḫpty 1.91 30, 4.68 49, 4.346 8, 4.355 12, 4.610 4
ḫptr 1.4 II 8
ḫpṯ 1.14 II 37, 1.15 I 6, 1.144 3, 2.72 10, 4.351 6, 4.382 25
ḫpṯh 1.103 57
ḫpṯml 1.149 4
ḫpṯt 1.4 VIII 7, 1.5 V 15
ḫṣ 4.131 5 lg. ḫṣt
ḫṣu 1.164 19
ḫṣt 4.131 5(!)
ḫṣth 1.39 10
ḫqn 4.658 41
ḫqrn 1.48 10
ḫr 1.2 I 41, 1.13 17, 1.43 1, 1.85 5, 1.85 7, 1.103 6, 1.103 30, 1.112 13, 4.278 6
ḫr[1.24 5, 1.151 9, 4.235 10, 4.244 33, 4.441 6, 4.629 3
]ḫr 1.54 6, 4.35 II 9, 4.106 6
ḫrx[4.50 12
ḫr[a 1.72 12
ḫr]a 1.71 9
ḫran 4.33 30, 4.51 10, 4.55 8, 4.90 1
ḫri 4.125 5
ḫrih 1.114 21
ḫrbġlm 4.625 19, 4.644 8
]ḫrg 4.682 5
ḫrd 2.16 13, 2.47 17, 2.61 6, 4.179 15, 4.230 12, 4.683 1, 4.777 12, 4.784 1
ḫr[d 4.777 1
ḫ]rd 1.103 39
]ḫrd[4.656 2
]ḫ/yrd[4.627 11
ḫrdh 1.103 46, 2.47 15
ḫrdk 2.47 19
ḫrdn 1.103 52
ḫrḫb 1.24 2, 1.24 2, 1.24 24
ḫr[ḫ]b 1.24 17
ḫrẓʿh 1.12 I 41 lg. ḫrẓph
ḫrẓph 1.12 I 41(!)
ḫry 1.40 29, 1.84 4
]ḫry 1.43 22
ḫ]ry 1.40 37
ḫr[ym 4.11 6
ḫrk 4.689 4
]ḫrm 1.13 3
ḫrmln 4.35 I 12, 4.103 42, 4.103 43
ḫrmṯn 1.64 27
ḫrmṯt 1.86 23, 4.625 1, 4.625 4, 4.625

7, 4.625 9, 4.625 11, 4.632 4, 4.632 17
ḫrmṯ[t 4.625 13
ḫr[mṯt 4.632 13
ḫ[r]mṯ[t 4.632 8
ḫr]mṯt 4.670 4
ḫrn 1.4 V 13, 1.4 V 29, 1.4 V 36, 1.64 30, 4.33 39
ḫrny 4.391 1
ḫrnk 2.61 3
ḫrs 4.695 5
ḫrġd 1.42 16
ḫrġḏġ 4.631 16
ḫrp 1.82 18
ḫrpn 4.75 IV 6
ḫrpnt 1.114 31
ḫrṣ 1.3 III 47, 1.4 I 26, 1.4 I 27, 1.4 I 32, 1.4 I 37, 1.4 II 28, 1.4 IV 37, 1.4 V 16, 1.4 V 18, 1.4 V 33, 1.4 V 34, 1.4 V 39, 1.4 VI 34, 1.4 VI 38, 1.4 VI 59, 1.14 III 22, 1.14 III 34, 1.14 IV 2, 1.14 VI 5, 1.14 VI 18, 1.16 I 45, 1.17 VI 5, 1.22 I 15, 1.43 5, 1.43 10, 1.43 13, 1.90 4, 1.105 22, 1.164 5, 1.164 16, 1.168 3, 1.168 10, 2.36 12, 2.72 28, 2.79 10, 3.1 20, 3.1 27, 3.1 29, 4.167 2, 4.172 8, 4.265 6, 4.266 7, 4.336 10, 4.337 20, 4.341 1, 4.341 5, 4.341 16, 4.341 18, 4.550 3, 7.135 4
ḫrṣ[1.14 V 35, 4.23 3, 4.738 1
ḫr[ṣ 1.5 IV 16, 2.83 9, 4.388 12, 4.738 7
ḫ]rṣ 1.14 II 19, 2.36 6
ḫ\rṣ 1.24 20f
ḫrṣbʿ 4.73 8, 4.288 5, 4.346 9, 4.355 15, 4.610 6, 4.693 56(!), 4.712 1
ḫrṣbq 4.693 56 lg. ḫrṣbʿ
ḫrṣm 1.14 IV 43
ḫrṣn 4.278 4, 6.10 1
ḫrṣp 1.103 27
ḫ]rš 4.141 III 20
ḫr]š 4.183 II 6
ḫršḫ 1.105 2, 4.341 19
ḫršn 1.1 II 23, 4.63 III 40, 4.222 13, 4.715 17
ḫrš[n 1.1 III 22
ḫrt 1.5 V 5, 1.6 I 17, 1.19 III 6, 1.19 III 20, 1.19 III 35, 1.175 11
ḫr[t 4.224 6
ḫš 1.65 9, 1.100 22, 1.114 29(!)
ḫšm 1.123 30
ḫštk 1.16 I 3, 1.16 I 4, 1.16 I 17, 1.16 I 18, 1.16 II 39, 1.16 II 41
ḫt 1.16 VI 1, 1.16 VI 13, 1.83 12, 2.21 22, 2.30 16
ḫt[4.325 4
]ḫtx[7.118 2
]xḫt 4.75 V 4
ḫti 2.10 7
ḫtb 4.356 2
ḫty 1.40 20, 1.40 29, 1.40 37, 4.149 4, 4.216 9, 4.343 5
ḫtym 4.687 4
ḫtyn 4.57 10, 4.281 18, 4.643 11
ḫtyn[4.611 26
ḫ]tyn 4.659 2
ḫtyt 4.269 3
ḫtm 2.25 7
ḫtn 4.269 20, 4.269 23, 4.269 27
ḫtnh 4.80 17
ḫtny 1.24 32
ḫtn\m 1.24 25f
ḫtt 1.2 IV 1, 1.176 26
ḫttk 1.176 27
ḫṯpy 4.130 2, 4.635 20
ḫṯr 1.6 II 32
ḫṯr[4.66 7
ḫṯrhm 6.39 2
ḫṯrm 4.385 2
ḫṯtx[4.436 3

Ṭ

ṭ 5.4 2, 5.6 1, 5.9 I 17, 5.9 I 18, 5.12 2, 5.13 1, 5.13 2, 5.13 3, 5.13 4, 5.13 5, 5.13 6, 5.13 7, 5.14 10, 5.16 1, 5.16 2, 5.16 5, 5.16 8, 5.17 1, 5.17 4, 5.19 2, 5.20 1, 5.21 1, 5.24 1
ṭ[1.4 II 46, 4.610 37
]ṭ 1.107 49
]ṭ[2.7 1, 4.697 1
]ṭx 1.172 9
ṭ/ḥ[1.5 III 12, 1.174 4, 4.61 5, 4.515 2
]ṭ/ḥ 1.17 I 38, 4.428 9, 7.139 3
]ṭ/ḥ[7.146 2, 7.160 1
]ṭ/ḥx 1.172 31
]xṭ/ḥṭ[4.732 3
ṭ/ḥxmi 4.345 7
ṭb 1.3 I 20, 1.23 14, 1.43 12, 1.43 15, 4.213 1, 4.213 2, 4.213 4, 4.213 5, 4.213 6, 4.213 7, 4.213 9, 4.213 10, 4.213 11, 4.213 12, 4.213 13, 4.213 14, 4.213 15, 4.213 16, 4.213 17, 4.213 20, 4.213 22, 4.213 23, 4.780 8, 4.780 13, 4.780 14
ṭ[b 4.738 4
ṭ]b 4.213 19
ṭbḫ 1.1 IV 30, 1.4 VI 40, 1.15 IV 4, 1.16 VI 17, 1.22 I 12, 1.80 3, 1.80 4(?), 1.80 5(?)
ṭbn 1.19 I 46
ṭbq 1.17 I 28, 1.17 II 18, 4.27 22, 4.68 54, 4.213 5, 4.243 10, 4.365 23, 4.369 5, 4.380 29, 4.685 11, 4.693 21, 4.698 3, 4.770 2
ṭb[q 4.198 3
ṭ[bq 4.27 11
]ṭbq 4.119 3, 4.198 6
ṭb]q 4.223 6
]ṭbq[4.414 2, 4.477 2, 4.661 4
ṭbqym[4.40 18
ṭbrn 4.103 16, 4.356 1, 4.432 12
ṭbr[n 4.356 14
ṭbt 1.82 34, 2.37 6
]ṭbt 4.736 2
]xṭbt 1.107 5
ṭgd 4.69 VI 28
ṭhrm 1.4 V 19, 1.4 V 34, 2.39 33
ṭḥl 1.103 12
ṭḥ]n 1.6 V 15
ṭḫ 1.17 I 32, 1.17 II 6, 1.17 II 22
ṭḫṣʿṯ 5.23 7
]xṭy 4.592 6
]ṭyk 4.722 3, 4.722 4
ṭ]yk 4.722 5
]ṭ/ḥkl[4.191 10
ṭl 1.3 II 39, 1.3 II 40, 1.3 IV 43, 1.3 IV 43, 1.19 I 41, 1.19 I 44, 1.19 II 2, 1.19 II 6, 1.19 IV 38, 1.22 I 20(!)
ṭlb 1.5 IV 2
ṭly 1.3 I 24, 1.3 III 7, 1.3 IV 51, 1.3 V 42, 1.4 I 17, 1.4 IV 56, 1.101 5
ṭl]y 1.4 VI 11
ṭlm 1.117 9
ṭlmyn 4.277 7
ṭmrn 4.69 VI 31
ṭmṯ 1.82 7
]xṭn 4.438 5
]ṭ/ḥn 4.628 2, 4.769 20
]xṭnn[7.71 3
ṭ]ʿn 1.5 I 26
ṭṣ 1.22 I 20 lg. ṭl
ṭrd 1.3 III 47
xṭrd 1.151 3
]ṭrd 4.428 3
ṭ]rdh 1.6 VI 1
ṭry 1.6 VI 43, 1.142 2
]ṭ/ḥšr[4.325 6
]ṭtb[1.26b 2
ṭtm 1.1 IV 8

Ẓ

ẓ 5.4 3, 5.6 2, 5.12 3, 5.13 8, 5.16 3, 5.16 6, 5.17 2, 5.17 5, 5.19 3, 5.19 6, 5.20 1, 5.20 4, 5.21 1, 5.24 1
ẓ[1.15 V 4, 4.201 4
]ẓ 4.313 23
ẓx[1.10 III 15
]xẓ[4.122 13
ẓ/k[7.222 4
ẓi 1.12 I 14, 1.12 I 19
ẓiẓ[7.55 4
ẓuh 1.3 III 2, 1.3 IV 46, 1.19 IV 43
ẓbx[1.152 3
]ẓb/ṣx[4.461 4
ẓbyh 1.15 IV 18
ẓbyy 1.15 IV 7
ẓbm 1.108 5, 1.133 14, 7.184 5
ẓbr 4.93 II 11
ẓhrm 1.24 21
ẓẓ 1.82 42, 1.100 36, 1.107 41
ẓẓn 4.63 II 32, 4.108 2
]xẓk 1.94 29
ẓl 1.4 II 27, 1.14 III 55, 1.92 27, 4.611 12
ẓll 4.631 6
ẓlm 1.161 1, 1.169 8
ẓlmt 1.4 VII 55
ẓlm[t 1.8 II 8
ẓm 1.169 7
ẓmn 4.617 24
]ẓn 1.82 20
]ẓb/ṣx[4.461 4
ẓq 4.55 8
ẓr 1.1 II 4, 1.2 I 23, 1.2 I 25, 1.2 I 27, 1.2 I 29, 1.4 I 34, 1.4 II 9, 1.4 VII 4, 1.4 VIII 6, 1.5 V 14, 1.14 II 20, 1.14 II 21, 1.14 IV 3, 1.16 III 13, 1.17 VI 37, 1.101 12, 7.137 7
ẓr[4.69 V 4, 4.545 II 3
ẓrh 1.3 III 35, 1.12 II 32, 1.169 4
ẓr[h 1.4 II 20
ẓrw 1.148 22, 4.402 11
ẓrl 4.93 IV 23
ẓrm 4.283 7
ẓrn 4.68 9, 4.95 6, 4.629 13(cor.)

Y

y 1.2 I 36, 1.3 V 20, 1.6 IV 1, 1.6 IV 12, 1.6 IV 22, 1.15 II 21, 1.16 VI 55, 1.17 V 37, 1.17 VI 34, 1.18 I 7, 1.19 III 46, 1.19 III 51, 1.19 IV 3, 1.19 IV 57, 1.23 40, 1.23 43, 1.23 46, 1.23 64, 1.23 65, 1.23 69, 1.35 13, 1.67 7, 1.100 73(?), 1.119 28, 1.119 29, 1.129 5, 5.2 5, 5.2 7, 5.4 2, 5.6 1, 5.9 I 17, 5.9 I 18, 5.12 2, 5.13 7, 5.16 1, 5.16 2, 5.17 5, 5.19 2, 5.20 1, 5.21 1, 5.24 1

y[1.2 I 42, 1.4 II 36, 1.4 VII 6, 1.16 II 8, 1.31 1, 1.49 14, 1.50 9, 1.101 4, 1.103 9, 1.104 6, 1.106 11, 1.107 29, 1.121 5, 1.140 12, 1.163 8, 2.31 42, 2.44 6, 2.45 26, 2.49 14, 4.24 6, 4.68 40, 4.141 I 21, 4.182 53, 4.254 3, 4.327 5, 4.335 19, 4.405 8, 4.417 1, 4.426 2, 4.455 5, 4.502 4, 4.608 14, 4.608 17, 4.655 2, 4.694 5, 5.10 7, 7.9 2, 7.162 2, 7.174 3

]y 1.2 III 14, 1.4 I 2, 1.4 III 9, 1.21 II 9, 1.40 3, 1.62 10, 1.82 1, 1.82 13, 1.82 34, 1.84 39, 1.153 8, 2.9 5, 2.21 27, 2.31 41, 2.31 44, 2.31 49, 2.31 59, 2.44 21, 2.58 4, 2.65 1, 2.81 27, 2.81 29, 2.83 5, 4.3 3, 4.18 5, 4.28 1, 4.33 17, 4.55 34, 4.69 IV 1, 4.69 IV 3, 4.69 IV 4, 4.106 7, 4.122 21, 4.172 5, 4.186 2, 4.205 12, 4.214 III 18, 4.258 5, 4.259 5, 4.295 7, 4.326 2, 4.357 12, 4.368 16, 4.370 40, 4.382 1, 4.447 3, 4.476 4, 4.559 1, 4.559 5, 4.559 8, 4.584 2, 4.597 4, 4.609 29, 4.643 23, 4.645 6, 4.645 10, 4.648 4, 4.648 5, 4.682 7, 4.693 47, 4.701 15, 4.754 4, 4.756 1, 4.756 3, 4.763 5, 4.784 22, 7.16 7, 7.49 5, 7.50 15, 7.62 1, 7.69 1, 7.69 3, 7.88 2, 7.135 5, 7.149 5

]y[1.64 8, 1.119 3, 2.41 6, 2.45 27, 4.197 29, 4.488 5, 4.498 1, 4.621 17, 4.651 9, 7.120 1, 7.196 1

y\[7.51 10f

]\y 1.5 III 3f, 1.16 V 5f

yx[1.4 II 48, 1.9 13, 1.16 II 55, 1.107 10, 1.129 4, 1.137 6, 1.139 19, 1.163 11, 4.17 22, 4.66 13, 4.326 9, 4.398 10, 4.496 5, 4.607 31, 4.608 15, 7.64 4, 7.158 4, 7.165 1

]yx[4.434 1, 4.617 13, 7.188 1

yxx[1.86 22

]yxx 4.194 16

]yxx[2.57 8, 4.401 16

]yxxx[1.20 I 11

yxxxx[4.748 6

yxxxxxxxx 2.44 7

xy 1.70 37, 2.44 13

]xy 1.10 I 22, 1.30 3, 1.63 13, 1.76 7, 1.82 2, 1.107 19, 1.126 17 2.31 61, 2.32 8, 2.41 4, 2.50 9, 2.50 15, 2.50 22, 4.12 1, 4.222 4, 4.234 8, 4.368 3, 4.408 3, 4.409 3, 4.410 17, 4.443 4, 4.443 6, 4.484 2, 4.589 2, 4.635 14, 4.693 30, 4.707 4, 4.744 7, 7.30 1, 7.88 1

]xy[4.160 8, 4.619 6, 6.53 3, 7.14 3, 7.120 3

]xxxxy 4.197 4

]xyx[4.540 2, 7.221 1

y/ḫ[4.458 3, 4.524 2, 4.742 12

]y/ḫ 1.10 II 37, 4.197 8, 4.306 6, 4.531 2, 4.769 45, 7.23 1

]y/ḫ[4.37 7, 7.209 1

xy/ḫ[4.359 1

yxxxy[4.214 II 18

yxw 4.750 4

]xyxzx[7.169 2

yxkn 1.70 6

yx]n 5.1 1

ya 1.106 3

yabd 1.11 3

yadm 1.14 III 52

yazr 1.82 13

yaḫd 4.44 28

y'kl 4.767 2

yamr 1.172 22

yasp 1.107 36

yark 1.24 39
yarš 1.14 I 42, 4.44 26
yaršil 1.102 18, 1.102 24
yaṯr 1.103 2
yiḫd 1.6 V 1, 1.11 1, 1.15 II 16, 1.16 I 47, 1.72 21, 1.97 2, 1.103 7, 2.19 1
yiḫd[1.72 16
]yiḫd 1.17 I 34
y]iḫd 1.85 12
y[i]ḫd/ibh 1.163 7
yikl[1.12 II 13
]yiṣ/l[7.14 1
yisp 1.107 38, 1.107 40(!), 1.107 41, 1.107 42, 1.107 43
y[i]sp 1.107 39
yi]sp 1.107 42
yis]p 1.107 44
yisphm 1.12 II 24
yip 1.14 II 30, 1.14 IV 11
]yiṣ/l[7.14 1
]yirš 2.81 26
]yišr 7.51 16
yitbd 1.14 I 24
yitmr 1.2 I 32
yitsp 1.14 I 18
yitṯm 4.398 5
]xyu[1.49 12
yuhb 1.5 V 18
yu\[h]b 1.92 31f
yuḫd 1.103 17
yuḫ[d 1.22 II 17
yuḫ]d 1.2 I 39
yuḫdm 1.4 IV 16
yukl 4.244 16
yb 1.100 66
yb[1.16 V 4, 1.62 1, 2.31 49, 4.213 26
]yb[7.148 1
yb/d[4.376 1
yb/ṣxxkx 7.197 7
ybu 1.2 III 5
ybd 1.3 I 18, 1.17 VI 31
ybdn 4.75 I 3
ybk 1.19 IV 11, 1.19 IV 15
yb<ky> 1.19 III 40
ybky 1.14 I 26, 1.14 I 39, 1.16 I 12, 1.19 III 40, 1.107 8, 1.129 2, 1.161 15
ybl 1.2 I 37, 1.5 II 5, 1.14 IV 26, 1.19 IV 61, 1.23 52, 1.23 59, 1.131 7, 2.34 29, 2.72 27, 3.1 25, 4.272 7, 4.337 12, 7.50 4
]ybl 1.2 I 38
y]\bl 1.19 IV 50f
yblhm 1.4 I 37
yblk 1.4 V 17
yblmm 1.2 III 14
ybln 1.17 V 12
yblnh 1.100 67
yblnn 1.4 V 38, 1.4 V 40
yblʿ 1.161 16
yblt 1.4 V 27, 2.17 1, 2.17 3
ybm 1.6 I 31
ybmh 1.16 II 32
ybmt 1.3 II 33, 1.4 II 15, 1.10 III 3, 1.17 VI 19, 1.17 VI 25
y[bmt 1.3 IV 22
ybn 1.4 IV 62, 1.19 III 12, 1.19 III 13, 1.19 III 26, 1.19 III 27, 4.226 5
ybnil 4.141 I 8, 4.148 3
ybnil[4.160 2
ybni[l 4.84 5
ybnmlk 1.144 2
ybnn 2.64 1, 2.72 25, 4.91 1, 4.158 2, 4.260 5, 4.277 3
ybnn[4.680 3
ybn[n 2.64 9
]ybnn 4.57 1
y]bnn 4.384 9
ybnt 1.3 IV 40
ybśr 4.617 10
ybʿ 4.224 6, 6.47 3
ybʿl 1.17 VI 24
ybʿlhm 4.182 56
ybʿlnn 4.182 59
ybʿr 1.3 IV 26, 1.14 II 48, 1.14 IV 27, 1.103 58
ybʿrn 2.41 22
ybġ 1.172 20
ybṣr 1.18 IV 20, 1.18 IV 31, 1.19 I 33
ybqʿ 1.19 III 10, 1.19 III 24, 1.19 III 38
ybqṯ 2.42 26
ybrd 1.3 I 6
ybrdmy 1.24 29
ybrk 1.15 II 18, 1.15 II 19, 1.17 I 34, 4.336 6
ybr[k 4.377 31

]ybrk 1.77 3
yb]\rk 1.17 V 35f
]ybrkn 1.77 2
ybšl 1.147 7
ybšr 1.94 1, 1.94 23
ybt 2.33 14
ybṯ.nn 1.2 IV 31
ygx[1.9 2
ygb 4.247 23
ygz 1.80 5
ygl 1.82 1
ygly 1.1 III 23
ygmḏ 1.12 I 13
ygmr 4.134 5
ygʿr 1.2 I 24, 1.72 27, 1.85 2, 1.114 11
yg[ʿr 1.85 23
ygʿ]r 1.97 11
ygry 4.682 12
ygrm 4.635 42
ygrš 1.2 IV 12, 1.2 IV 12, 1.169 9
ygršk 1.82 12, 1.82 40, 1.82 40
yd 1.1 IV 10, 1.2 I 39, 1.3 III 6, 1.4 IV 38, 1.4 VIII 23, 1.4 VIII 45, 1.6 II 25, 1.6 VI 52, 1.12 I 24, 1.14 III 23, 1.14 III 35, 1.14 VI 19, 1.15 I 1, 1.15 I 2, 1.15 IV 24, 1.15 V 7, 1.16 I 41, 1.16 I 47, 1.17 I 3, 1.17 I 4, 1.17 I 13, 1.17 I 14, 1.17 V 19, 1.18 I 14, 1.19 II 17, 1.19 II 24, 1.19 II 35, 1.19 IV 25, 1.19 IV 26, 1.19 IV 58, 1.23 33, 1.23 34, 1.23 34, 1.23 35, 1.103 46, 1.103 59, 1.106 17, 1.107 19, 1.166 24, 2.10 11, 2.19 14, 3.4 14, 3.5 8, 3.5 8, 3.5 9, 4.80 15, 4.80 16, 4.80 19, 4.125 8, 4.125 9, 4.145 3, 4.145 4, 4.145 5, 4.243 35, 4.243 41, 4.243 42, 4.358 8, 4.360 4, 4.363 2, 4.363 5, 4.398 1, 4.618 3, 4.618 3, 4.618 6, 4.618 6, 4.639 6, 4.659 2, 4.659 7
yd[1.23 4, 1.82 14, 4.66 8, 4.80 15, 4.80 18, 7.58 2
yd[? 6.70 1
y[d 1.3 V 18, 4.80 5, 4.618 8
]yd 1.10 I 11, 1.14 II 1, 1.15 II 17, 4.107 1, 4.107 2, 4.107 3, 4.243 43
y]d 3.5 7, 4.107 4, 4.644 4, 4.644 9
ydx[6.52 1
yb/d[4.376 1
ydu 1.103 42
ydbil 1.102 17, 1.102 21, 1.106 3
ydbbʿl 1.102 25
ydbhd 1.102 28
ydbḥ 1.115 1, 1.119 8, 1.119 13, 1.164 1, 1.164 3, 2.40 16
yd]bḥ 1.41 50
ydbʿl 4.64 II 3, 4.704 10
]ydbr 1.82 8
yd<d> 1.5 III 19
ydd 1.4 III 12, 1.4 VII 46, 1.4 VII 48, 1.4 VIII 31, 1.5 I 8, 1.5 I 13, 1.5 II 9, 1.5 III 10, 1.5 III 26, 1.10 II 17, 1.133 16, 3.9 12, 4.277 12
ydd[4.647 6, 4.706 13
]ydd 1.152 4
y\dd 1.6 VI 30f
yddll 1.103 46
yddn 4.63 II 38, 4.313 6, 4.379 8
yddt 4.79 2
ydh 1.3 I 11, 1.3 II 32, 1.3 II 34, 1.4 VII 40, 1.10 II 6, 1.13 33, 1.14 III 53, 1.14 III 56, 1.14 IV 5, 1.14 V 20, 1.17 I 30, 1.19 I 7, 1.19 III 49, 1.19 III 56, 1.19 IV 7, 1.23 37, 1.24 8, 1.24 12, 1.25 10, 1.101 15, 1.103 15, 1.103 28, 1.103 48, 1.172 21
ydh[1.101 16
yd[h 1.7 20, 1.41 55
]ydh 1.137 6
ydy 1.5 I 20, 1.5 VI 18, 1.16 V 18, 1.16 V 21, 1.17 II 19, 1.100 5, 1.100 11, 1.100 17, 1.100 22, 1.100 27, 1.100 32, 1.100 38, 1.100 42, 1.100 48, 1.100 54, 1.100 60, 1.100 64, 1.119 35, 1.169 1, 4.245 I 2, 4.611 13
ydy[5.1 6
]ydy 1.10 I 21
]yd[y 1.2 IV 1
yd[y]n 4.690 10
ydyt 4.348 1
ydy[t 4.348 20
ydk 1.14 II 22, 1.14 III 13, 1.16 VI 32, 1.16 VI 45, 1.17 II 5, 1.22 I 4, 1.23 40, 1.23 44, 1.23 47, 1.71 10, 1.71 17, 1.82 14, 1.85 3, 1.85 6, 1.85 8, 1.85 14, 1.85 17, 1.85 19, 1.85 28, 1.86 22, 1.97 7, 1.176 23

ydk[1.85 22
y]dk 1.14 II 10
yd]k 1.14 II 13, 1.85 11
ydll 5.11 22
ydlm 5.1 7
ydl[m 4.506 2
ydln 4.103 9, 4.103 38, 4.183 II 24, 4.188 8, 4.224 10, 4.229 9, 4.264 7, 4.364 9, 4.581 6, 4.609 34, 4.638 4, 5.1 12
ydln[4.81 4
ydlp 1.2 IV 17, 1.2 IV 26
ydm 1.1 IV 19, 1.2 IV 14, 1.2 IV 16, 1.3 VI 23, 1.4 VIII 5, 1.5 V 13, 1.16 II 56, 1.17 V 25, 1.73 9, 1.75 1, 1.115 6, 4.275 1
ydm[1.4 II 33
y[dm 1.1 III 5
]ydm 1.75 2
]ydm[1.53 4
ydmʿ 1.14 I 27, 1.14 I 40, 1.19 IV 12, 1.19 IV 16, 1.161 14
y<dn> 1.19 II 12
ydn 1.17 V 7, 1.19 I 23, 1.19 II 19, 2.31 65, 2.47 1, 2.47 14, 4.16 11, 4.219 9, 4.347 7, 4.617 42, 4.617 45, 4.647 5, 5.1 3
]ydn[7.159 2
ydnm 1.166 23, 4.407 2
ydʿ 1.1 V 21, 1.3 I 25, 1.6 I 48, 1.10 I 3, 1.13 31, 1.107 6, 2.17 8, 2.33 21, 2.40 19, 2.75 12, 4.617 26
ydʿ[2.8 6, 4.161 5
y]dʿ 2.39 10
ydʿm 2.39 14
ydʿn 4.748 5
ydʿnn 1.114 6, 1.114 7
ydʿt 1.1 V 21, 1.13 10, 1.16 I 33, 1.19 II 7, 1.19 IV 38, 2.3 24, 2.9 3, 2.23 9, 2.39 10, 2.39 14
ydʿ[t 1.19 II 2
]ydʿt 1.1 V 8
yd]ʿt 1.3 I 26
ydʿtk 1.18 I 16
ydʿ[tk 1.3 V 27
ydr 1.14 IV 37, 1.22 II 16
]ydr 2.33 15
]ydr[7.64 5
ydrm 1.107 3, 2.70 1, 4.102 6
ydrmt 5.1 5
ydt 1.16 V 27, 4.158 9
ydty 1.5 I 21, 1.133 11
ydṯ 1.18 I 19
yḏmr 1.108 3
yḏrd 4.344 12
yh 1.163 4
]yh 1.63 11, 2.47 5
]\yh 1.1 III 6f
yhbṭ 2.4 19
yhbr 1.23 49, 1.23 55
yhg/mb/ṣ 1.176 11
yhdy 1.5 VI 19
yhg/mb/ṣ 1.176 11
yhpk 1.6 VI 28, 1.86 7, 1.103 52
y[hpk 1.2 III 17
]yhpk 1.13 35
yhrrm 1.12 I 39
yw 1.1 IV 14 lg. y<m> w ?
ywl[7.50 15
ywsrnn 1.16 VI 26
ywpṯn 1.4 III 13
yzbrnn 1.23 9
yzg 4.93 IV 6
yzn 2.81 22
yḥ 1.12 I 35, 1.16 I 23, 1.16 II 44, 1.17 I 36, 1.19 I 18, 2.7 9, 6.30 1
yḥ[4.608 16
yḥbq 1.4 IV 13, 1.19 II 14, 1.24 4
yḥb[q 1.2 I 41
yḥ[bq 1.19 II 21
yḥd 1.14 II 43, 1.19 III 15, 1.19 III 24, 1.19 III 29, 1.19 III 38, 4.224 7, 4.750 5, 4.750 6, 4.750 7
yḥdh 1.175 12
yḥdy 1.127 32
yḥdṯ 1.18 IV 9
yḥwy 1.17 VI 30
y]ḥ\wyn 1.24 9f lg. t]ḥ\wyn
yḥmdm 1.12 I 38
yḥmdnh 1.92 29
yḥmn 4.41 2, 4.609 19, 4.609 33, 4.647 3
y]ḥmrm 1.6 I 28
yḥn 4.138 5
yḥnn 4.635 16
yḥnnn 1.10 I 12
yḥsl 1.103 14, 1.103 55
yḥslnn 1.103 38

y]ḥslnn 1.103 36
yḥpn 1.22 I 9, 1.22 II 12
yḥṣdq 4.332 17
yḥr 1.151 4
yḥr 1.100 73 lg. y ḥr<n>?
y]ḥrkn 1.175 7
yḥr[r 1.12 II 37
yḥrṯ 1.5 VI 20, 1.22 I 20
yḥšr 4.243 11
yḥš[r 4.746 6
yḫṯ 1.14 III 50
yḫlm 4.118 9
yḫlq 1.103 15, 1.103 16
]yḫlq 1.103 18
]yḫms[6.48 2
yḫmš 1.16 V 17
yḫnpk[1.82 15
yḫssk 1.4 IV 39
yḫsp 1.19 I 31
yḫsr 1.163 13, 2.39 9
yḫpn 2.23 4
yḫru 1.85 9
yḫrb[1.19 I 30
yḫrṭ 1.23 38
yṭb 1.6 I 58, 1.13 21
yṭbḫ 1.17 II 29
yṭll 1.19 I 41
yṭp 1.18 IV 7, 1.18 IV 16
yṭpn 1.18 IV 6, 1.18 IV 11, 1.18 IV 27, 1.19 IV 52
yṯ[pn 1.19 IV 50
yṯ[p]n[1.19 IV 56
yẓḥq 1.12 I 12
yy 4.63 IV 14
yy[4.744 6
]yy 4.236 4, 4.244 19
]yy[7.74 2
]xxxyy 4.69 IV 29
]y/ḫy 4.701 14
yyn 4.55 25, 4.269 5, 4.635 18, 4.658 15, 4.715 20, 4.739 11, 5.1 10
yyn[4.739 3
yk[7.50 10
]yk 7.51 8
yr/k[4.529 2
]y/ṣk[1.69 14
]ykxh/i 7.51 25
ykbd 1.171 4
ykb[d 1.119 19
ykb[dnh 1.2 III 6
y\[kbdnh] 1.1 II 16f
ykhp 1.71 26, 1.85 30
yky 4.35 I 7, 4.52 6, 4.226 7, 4.785 7
ykl 1.91 1, 1.104 3
ykly 1.2 IV 27, 1.103 40, 1.127 8
ykllnh 1.4 V 10
ykn 1.17 I 25, 1.17 I 42, 1.103 3, 1.103 5, 1.163 10, 2.75 7, 4.51 12, 4.55 20, 4.141 I 15, 4.232 11, 4.263 8, 4.283 4, 4.635 46, 4.780 5
ykn[4.381 20, 4.427 20
y[kn 1.103 12
yk]n 1.103 12
]ykn[2.43 5
yknil 4.86 15, 4.165 12
ykny 4.635 22
yknn[1.10 III 6
yknnh 1.3 V 36, 1.4 IV 48
yknʿ 1.143 2, 4.101 2
yknʿm 4.49 7, 4.68 17, 4.113 5, 4.244 11, 4.307 21, 4.365 37, 4.610 32, 4.619 11
yk[n]ʿm 4.308 8
ykn[ʿm 4.686 16
yk]nʿm[4.553 10
yknʿmy 4.295 5, 4.295 15
yks 1.5 VI 16
ykr 1.100 62, 4.116 8
ykrkr 1.4 IV 29
ykrʿ 1.10 II 18
ykš[7.54 2
yl[4.93 I 18
]xyl 4.643 9
]xyl[7.182 2
yṣ/l[1.174 8
y<l>ak 1.4 V 41
ylak 1.2 I 11, 1.14 III 19, 1.24 16, 2.33 36
ylbš 1.43 22
yld 1.10 III 35, 1.11 5, 1.17 II 14, 1.103 2, 1.124 3
yl[d 1.18 IV 39
yldhnaxx 1.172 30
yldy 1.23 53
<y>lḥm 1.16 VI 20
ylḥm 1.17 I 2, 1.17 I 7, 1.17 I 12, 1.17 I 21, 1.115 10, 1.176 21
y]lḥm 1.17 I 10

ylḥn 1.5 II 21, 1.6 I 48, 4.35 I 8
yly 4.204 11, 4.382 26, 4.723 3
yly[4.427 19
ylyh 1.12 II 51
ylk 1.14 IV 44, 1.43 23, 1.43 24, 1.163 6, 1.175 14
ylk[1.166 25
yl[k 1.43 25
ylkn 1.1 IV 7
y/ṣlkn 4.77 14
ylm 1.2 IV 16, 1.2 IV 24, 1.82 16
y{.}lmn 1.114 8
yln 1.17 I 5, 1.17 I 15
ylq[ḥ 4.548 5
ylšn 1.114 20
ylt 1.17 I 41, 1.23 53, 1.23 53, 1.23 60, 1.23 60
[[ym]] 1.17 I 11
ym 1.1 V 15, 1.2 I 11, 1.2 I 17, 1.2 I 22, 1.2 I 26, 1.2 I 28, 1.2 I 30, 1.2 I 33, 1.2 I 44, 1.2 I 45, 1.2 III 7, 1.2 III 8, 1.2 III 12, 1.2 III 12, 1.2 III 16, 1.2 III 23, 1.2 IV 3, 1.2 IV 3, 1.2 IV 7, 1.2 IV 12, 1.2 IV 12, 1.2 IV 14, 1.2 IV 16, 1.2 IV 17, 1.2 IV 19, 1.2 IV 19, 1.2 IV 22, 1.2 IV 22, 1.2 IV 25, 1.2 IV 25, 1.2 IV 27, 1.2 IV 32, 1.2 IV 34, 1.3 III 39, 1.3 V 41, 1.3 VI 5, 1.4 I 14, 1.4 I 21, 1.4 II 6, 1.4 II 29, 1.4 II 35, 1.4 III 25, 1.4 III 27, 1.4 III 29, 1.4 III 34, 1.4 III 38, 1.4 IV 40, 1.4 IV 53, 1.4 V 2, 1.4 VI 12, 1.4 VI 24, 1.4 VI 26, 1.4 VI 29, 1.4 VII 16, 1.4 VII 55, 1.5 I 16, 1.6 I 44, 1.6 I 45, 1.6 I 47, 1.6 I 53, 1.6 II 26, 1.6 V 19, 1.6 VI 51, 1.8 II 8, 1.9 14, 1.12 II 11, 1.14 I 20, 1.14 III 2, 1.14 III 2, 1.14 III 3, 1.14 III 10, 1.14 III 11, 1.14 III 12, 1.14 IV 32, 1.14 IV 44, 1.14 IV 45, 1.14 V 3, 1.14 V 4, 1.14 V 5, 1.16 VI 21, 1.17 I 5, 1.17 I 8, 1.17 I 11, 1.17 I 32, 1.17 I 33, 1.17 II 7, 1.17 II 8, 1.17 II 22, 1.17 II 23, 1.17 II 32, 1.17 II 34, 1.17 II 37, 1.19 IV 8, 1.19 IV 41, 1.19 IV 42, 1.19 IV 43, 1.20 I 5, 1.20 II 5, 1.22 I 17, 1.22 I 21, 1.22 I 22, 1.22 I 23, 1.23 30, 1.23 33, 1.23 34, 1.23 59, 1.23 61, 1.23 63, 1.25 6, 1.39 13, 1.41 8, 1.41 47, 1.41 48, 1.46 6, 1.47 30, 1.48 13, 1.67 9, 1.75 1, 1.78 1, 1.83 4, 1.83 7, 1.87 1, 1.87 9, 1.87 52(!), 1.102 3, 1.104 7, 1.104 15, 1.105 15, 1.107 49, 1.109 3, 1.112 10, 1.115 14, 1.118 29, 1.119 1, 1.126 22, 1.130 16, 1.133 5, 1.133 9, 1.148 9, 1.151 9, 1.155 3, 1.163 4, 1.163 7, 2.23 20, 2.33 14, 2.45 23, 2.46 14, 2.47 24, 2.47 24, 2.81 26, 2.81 28, 3.2 1, 3.4 1, 3.5 1, 4.172 1, 4.266 1, 4.279 1, 4.279 2, 4.336 1
ym 1.22 II 14 lg. [iln]\ym
ym[1.1 IV 15, 1.2 I 46, 1.3 III 2, 1.4 IV 4, 1.4 VII 4, 1.9 14, 1.22 II 16, 2.46 19, 2.48 2, 4.445 5, 4.610 70
y[m 1.2 III 21, 1.3 II 7, 1.3 IV 46, 1.4 II 34
]ym 1.2 III 21, 1.20 I 6, 1.23 23, 4.234 1, 4.443 11
]ym[4.570 4, 7.192 2
y]m 1.4 IV 31, 1.8 II 2, 4.70 1
y]\m 1.87 52f
y<m> 1.1 IV 14(?)
]y/ḫm 4.71 IV 2, 4.125 12
ymx 4.401 16
yman 1.4 I 42, 1.40 27, 1.84 2
ymid[6.43 1
ymil 4.75 V 14, 4.183 II 2
y]mil 4.588 2
ymgn 1.25 6
ymd 4.609 31
ymz 2.83 3, 4.103 35
ymzl 1.14 II 47, 1.14 IV 25
ymḥ 1.3 II 30
ymḫṣ 1.6 V 2, 1.6 V 3
ymḫṣk 1.1 IV 27
ymp/ẓ[1.45 4
ymẓa 1.12 I 37
ymy 1.103 34, 4.75 V 22, 4.214 IV 12
]ymy[1.147 2
ymk 1.2 IV 17
ymlu 1.3 II 25, 1.7 7, 1.16 V 28
ymlu]n 1.17 VI 6
ymlk 1.6 I 55, 1.6 I 65, 1.15 V 20, 1.157 9, 4.635 15
yml[k 1.2 IV 32, 4.505 4
yml]k 1.15 V 23
ym\lk 1.4 VII 49f

ymm 1.1 V 15, 1.2 I 36, 1.2 III 11, 1.6 II 26, 1.6 II 26, 1.17 I 15, 1.17 II 39, 1.17 V 4, 1.19 IV 13, 1.111 2, 1.155 2, 2.47 20, 2.82 8, 4.95 7, 4.95 8, 4.95 10, 5.9 I 4

y[m]m 4.95 6

y[mm 1.4 VI 32

]ymm 1.13 4, 1.13 5, 7.133 6

y]mm 1.1 V 2, 1.6 V 7

ym]m 4.95 4

ym\m 1.13 3f

ymmt 1.3 III 12

ymn 1.2 I 39, 1.4 V 47, 1.14 II 14, 1.16 I 42, 1.16 I 48, 1.23 63, 1.92 13, 1.103 26, 1.103 35, 4.64 IV 9, 4.69 II 3, 4.123 4, 4.227 I 5, 4.607 31, 4.617 19, 4.785 9, 5.1 13, 6.67 1

y[mn 1.103 28

]ymn 4.331 4

ym]n 1.15 II 18

ymnh 1.4 II 4, 1.4 VII 41, 1.10 II 7, 1.18 IV 10, 1.19 IV 56

ym[nh 1.5 V 25

ymny 1.3 V 22, 1.19 IV 54

]ymnk 1.5 V 3

ymnn 1.23 37

ymsk 1.3 I 17, 1.5 I 21

ymsś 1.85 3

ymġ 1.15 V 18, 1.19 III 50, 1.19 IV 1, 1.124 10

ymġy 1.1 V 16, 1.6 I 60, 1.12 I 36, 1.14 IV 47, 1.17 V 25, 1.86 8, 1.114 9, 1.124 1, 2.70 25

ymġy[1.17 II 46

ym[ġy 1.14 IV 34

]ymġy 1.113 7

ym[ġyh 1.12 II 48

ymġyk 2.2 8

ymġyn 1.17 II 24

ymp/ẓ[1.45 4

ymṣḫ 1.6 V 4

ymṣḫn 1.6 VI 20

ymr 1.17 I 35

ymru 1.4 VII 50

ym]ru 1.4 VIII 45

ymrm 4.547 5

ym]rm 1.15 II 20

ymrn 4.417 9

ymš 1.14 III 11 lg. ḫmš

ymšḥ 1.10 II 22

ymšḥ.hm 1.10 II 23

ymt 1.2 III 12, 1.108 26, 2.82 19, 6.30 1, 7.51 18

ymtḏr 4.727 23

ymtm 1.1 II 8, 1.25 4

ymtn[1.8 II 15

ymtšr 4.313 3

{yn} 4.279 1

<yn> 1.4 VI 54, 4.279 2

y<n> 1.114 3

yn 1.4 III 43, 1.4 IV 37, 1.4 VI 47, 1.4 VI 51, 1.4 VI 53, 1.5 I 25, 1.6 I 10, 1.6 IV 18(!), 1.6 VI 45, 1.14 II 19, 1.14 IV 1, 1.15 IV 5, 1.15 IV 16, 1.16 III 15, 1.17 I 31, 1.17 II 6, 1.17 II 20, 1.17 VI 5, 1.17 VI 8, 1.19 IV 53, 1.19 IV 57, 1.22 I 17, 1.22 I 18, 1.22 I 18, 1.22 I 19, 1.23 6, 1.23 74, 1.23 76, 1.41 23, 1.45 1, 1.87 1, 1.91 1, 1.91 21, 1.91 23, 1.91 24, 1.91 25, 1.91 26, 1.91 27, 1.91 28, 1.91 35, 1.101 9, 1.112 13, 2.31 66, 4.123 8, 4.123 14, 4.123 22, 4.123 23, 4.149 10, 4.149 14, 4.160 2, 4.182 32, 4.213 1, 4.213 2, 4.213 3, 4.213 4, 4.213 5, 4.213 6, 4.213 7, 4.213 9, 4.213 10, 4.213 11, 4.213 12, 4.213 13, 4.213 14, 4.213 15, 4.213 16, 4.213 17, 4.213 20, 4.213 21, 4.213 22, 4.213 23, 4.213 24, 4.213 25, 4.213 26, 4.213 27, 4.213 28, 4.213 30, 4.216 1, 4.221 5, 4.230 1, 4.230 11, 4.230 15, 4.246 4, 4.246 6, 4.269 27, 4.269 28, 4.269 34, 4.274 1, 4.279 3, 4.279 4, 4.279 5, 4.284 5, 4.285 1, 4.285 2, 4.285 3, 4.285 4, 4.285 5, 4.285 6, 4.285 7, 4.285 8, 4.285 9, 4.387 21, 4.400 5, 4.400 10, 4.691 3, 4.691 6, 4.786 7, 4.786 10, 5.1 11, 5.9 I 15, 6.11 1

yn[1.19 IV 61, 1.93 9, 4.8 2, 4.221 6, 4.246 2, 4.388 8, 4.397 1, 4.400 1, 4.715 2

y[n 1.4 VI 49, 1.91 22, 4.41 6, 4.400 14

]yn 1.92 38, 4.62 1, 4.69 I 28, 4.69 IV 16, 4.75 V 2, 4.187 4, 4.219 12, 4.225 3, 4.243 41, 4.243 42, 4.422 6,

4.424 16, 4.424 17, 4.444 4, 4.560 7, 4.573 1, 4.717 2, 4.747 5, 4.769 62, 4.772 2

y]n 1.4 VI 58, 1.17 VI 3, 1.114 16, 4.213 19, 4.219 1

]yn[1.3 V 16, 7.56 2

xxyn 4.290 16

]xyn 4.5 2, 4.176 1, 4.260 12, 4.320 12, 4.368 8, 4.410 15, 4.718 4

ynx 4.610 20

]y/ẖn 4.611 20, 4.613 11, 4.654 2, 4.654 3

ynaṣn[1.1 IV 23

ynghn 1.6 VI 17

ynh[1.23 75

ynḥm 3.4 4, 4.41 10, 4.52 7, 4.63 I 37, 4.130 7, 4.130 9, 4.170 3, 4.188 16, 4.214 IV 6, 4.282 15, 4.283 9, 4.339 5, 4.609 27, 4.635 21, 4.635 30, 4.635 47, 4.645 8

ynḥ[m 4.258 13

y]nḥm 4.141 I 3, 4.194 7

yn]ḥm 4.350 15

ynḥn 4.51 15, 4.775 12

ynḥt 1.2 IV 11, 1.2 IV 18

y]nḥtn 1.17 VI 9

ynṭm 4.75 V 16

yny 4.44 22, 4.52 4, 4.55 30, 4.320 2, 4.355 20, 4.379 6, 4.379 7, 4.693 43, 4.696 9, 4.770 11, 4.784 18, 5.1 2

yn[y 4.765 9

yny 5.11 7 lg. ṯyny

yns 1.4 III 5

ynsk 1.82 1

ynˤrah 1.100 65 lg. ynˤrnh?

ynphy 1.163 5

y{n}pˤ 1.19 II 16

ynpˤ 1.5 IV 8

ynṣl 1.90 22

ynq 1.15 II 26

ynqm 1.23 24, 1.23 59, 1.23 61

ynšq 1.19 II 15, 1.19 II 22

ynt 1.39 1, 1.87 23, 1.109 6, 1.119 10, 1.130 18

yn[t 1.41 10

y[nt 1.87 11

yn]t 1.46 12

ynṯkn 1.6 VI 19

yś[4.178 9

ysb 1.19 II 12, 1.19 II 19

ysgr 1.14 IV 21

yśd 4.106 10, 4.139 7

ysd 4.63 I 32, 4.93 IV 2, 4.377 12

ysdk 1.4 III 6

ysy 1.9 14

ysynh 1.100 66

ysk 1.17 VI 36

ysmm 1.10 II 30, 1.23 2

ys[mm 1.10 III 18

ysmsm 1.19 II 11, 1.96 3

ysmsmt 1.4 IV 15, 1.17 II 42

ysmt 1.5 VI 7, 1.5 VI 29, 1.6 II 20

ysny 2.30 15

ysˤ 1.2 III 17, 1.6 VI 27, 3.9 17

yspi 1.20 II 10

yspu 1.103 51

yspr 1.23 57

ys]pr 1.17 II 43

ysr 4.281 29

ystrn 1.4 VII 48

yˤx[7.18 1

]yˤ[7.157 3

yˤbd 4.370 37

yˤbdr 1.3 III 8, 1.3 IV 52, 1.4 I 18, 1.4 IV 57

y[ˤbdr 1.7 24

yˤby 4.100 8

yˤbš 1.22 I 6, 1.22 I 7

yˤdb 1.4 VI 39, 1.6 I 51, 1.17 V 27, 1.23 63, 1.50 11, 1.100 7, 1.100 18, 1.100 23, 1.100 29, 1.100 34, 1.100 39, 1.100 44, 1.100 49, 1.100 55, 1.114 4, 1.114 7, 1.176 10

yˤdb[4.383 6

yˤd[b 1.41 10

y<ˤ>db 1.100 12

yˤdbkm 1.4 VIII 17

yˤdd 4.133 1, 4.424 4

yˤdynh 1.100 66

yˤdn 1.4 V 7

yˤḏrd 1.113 17, 4.165 9, 4.338 7, 4.356 2, 5.1 8

yˤḏrk 1.18 I 14

yˤḏrn 4.227 I 7, 4.759 2

yˤḏrn[4.39 4, 4.75 II 10

yˤzz 1.103 57, 1.140 4

yˤl 1.6 I 57, 1.10 III 11, 1.10 III 25, 1.17 I 14, 1.17 I 38, 1.127 30, 4.96 7

yʿlm 1.6 I 26, 1.17 VI 22, 1.169 4
yʿmdn 1.7 34
yʿm[d]n 1.2 III 12
yʿmsn 2.41 21
yʿmsnh 1.4 V 11
yʿmsn.nn 1.114 18
yʿn 1.1 III 17, 1.1 IV 13, 1.1 V 7, 1.1 V 20, 1.2 III 18, 1.2 III 24, 1.2 IV 34, 1.3 I 23, 1.3 IV 5, 1.3 IV 39, 1.4 IV 58, 1.4 V 58, 1.4 V 63, 1.4 VI 1, 1.4 VI 14, 1.4 VII 14, 1.4 VII 37, 1.5 I 11, 1.6 I 49, 1.6 I 61, 1.10 II 14, 1.10 II 15, 1.14 I 21, 1.14 I 22, 1.16 IV 9, 1.16 V 23, 1.17 V 11, 1.17 V 11, 1.17 VI 20, 1.17 VI 33, 1.18 I 15, 1.18 IV 11, 1.19 I 12, 1.19 IV 35, 1.19 IV 52, 1.19 IV 56, 1.20 II 7, 1.21 II 8, 1.24 24, 1.24 30
yʿn[1.19 IV 18
y[ʿ]n 1.3 V 10
y[ʿn 1.2 IV 33
]yʿn 1.4 V 49, 1.15 II 12
yʿ]n 1.2 I 36
y\ʿn 1.16 III 1f
yʿny 1.3 V 25, 1.10 III 4, 1.14 VI 16, 1.15 I 8, 1.16 I 24, 1.16 II 21, 1.16 VI 54, 1.107 12, 1.133 1, 4.243 26, 4.296 14, 4.348 12
y[ʿ]ny 1.15 V 21
y]ʿnyh 1.92 33
yʿnyn 1.3 IV 5
y]ʿnynn 1.17 VI 32
yʿny.nn 1.124 4, 1.124 13
yʿr 1.5 VI 18, 1.6 VI 31, 4.609 18
yʿrb 1.5 II 3, 1.14 I 26, 1.16 I 12(!), 1.16 VI 40, 1.23 62, 1.111 2
yʿ[rb 1.41 8
y[ʿrb 1.87 9
yʿrm 1.4 VII 36
yʿrn 4.63 II 18, 4.63 III 10
yʿrṣ 1.16 I 12 lg. yʿrb
yʿrr 1.24 30
yʿrt 4.355 35, 4.365 18, 4.643 13
yʿr[t 4.68 42, 4.770 12
yʿrty 4.33 7, 4.379 4
yʿr[ty 4.54 10
yʿrtym 4.25 4, 4.55 9
]yʿšn 7.61 7
yʿšr 1.3 I 9, 1.17 VI 30
yʿš\r 1.17 VI 30f
yʿtqn 1.6 II 5, 1.6 II 26
yġḏ 1.17 VI 12
yġly 1.19 I 31
yġlm 1.19 II 14, 1.19 II 16
yġr 1.2 IV 6
yġr[k 1.6 IV 23
]yġš 1.10 I 8
yġtr 1.24 28, 1.103 39
yp 1.84 10
ypx[4.244 32
]ypdx[4.619 12
ypdd 4.182 61, 4.182 63
<yph> 1.19 II 20(?)
yph 1.19 II 13, 1.19 II 14, 1.19 II 19, 1.19 II 20(!), 1.90 1, 1.168 1, 1.168 8
yp<h>n 1.19 III 14
yphn 1.17 V 9, 1.19 III 29
yphnh 1.4 IV 27
ypḥ 3.6 2, 3.8 17, 3.8 19, 3.8 21, 3.9 18, 4.258 5, 4.632 22, 4.778 3, 4.778 11, 4.782 5, 4.782 18, 4.782 27
ypḥ[4.248 10, 4.754 4
yp]ḥ 4.778 19
ypḥm 4.659 6
ypẖ 4.31 9
ypḫ[1.127 19
ypy 4.33 28, 4.51 5
ypkm 1.40 28, 1.40 30, 1.40 32
ypkn 1.40 36, 1.40 39
yp[kn 1.40 40
y]pkn 1.84 6
ypl 1.2 IV 5
ypltႉ 4.214 IV 4
ypltk 1.18 I 13
ypltn 4.215 5
ypln 4.35 I 8, 4.364 8
ypltn 4.277 4
]ypn 2.77 13
ypʿ 1.3 III 37, 1.3 IV 4, 1.3 IV 5, 1.19 II 16, 1.19 II 20, 1.19 III 54, 4.134 14, 4.261 14, 4.366 14, 4.424 4, 4.635 24, 4.655 3
ypʿ[4.37 5
ypʿ 1.19 II 20 lg. yph
ypʿbʿl 4.116 19
ypʿmlk 4.609 12
ypʿn 4.63 I 6, 4.339 23, 4.609 8, 4.658 16, 4.775 8

ypʿr 1.2 IV 11, 1.2 IV 18, 1.12 I 28
ypʿt 1.2 I 3
ypġdmrx 1.68 21
ypġdmrzaṯmky 1.68 25
ypq 1.14 I 12, 1.103 13, 1.103 29, 4.617 26
yp[q 1.140 11
ypqd 1.16 VI 14
ypr 4.68 7, 4.69 III 10, 4.73 9, 4.95 10, 4.214 IV 11, 4.355 22, 4.365 30, 4.610 5, 4.629 15, 4.693 53, 4.770 5
ypr[4.489 1
yprḫ 4.278 9
ypry[4.417 17
yprsḥ 1.2 IV 22, 1.2 IV 25
yprq 1.4 IV 28, 1.6 III 16, 1.17 II 10
ypš 1.93 5
ypt 1.10 III 3, 1.23 39, 1.143 1, 2.5 2
ypṯḥ 1.4 VII 17, 1.4 VII 25, 1.4 VII 27, 1.143 3
y]ptḥ 1.4 VII 19
ypṯḥd 6.68 1
yṣ 4.43 1 cor. yṣa
yṣ[1.126 22, 4.227 II 6
]yṣ[7.188 2
]xyṣ[4.566 2
yṣ/l[1.174 8
yṣ/bxxkx 7.197 7
yṣ{.}a 4.166 1
yṣa 1.2 IV 6, 1.2 IV 30, 1.19 II 26, 1.19 II 28, 1.19 II 29, 1.19 II 29, 1.19 III 7, 4.43 1(cor.), 4.341 21
yṣa[4.193 3, 4.193 8
y[ṣ]a 1.19 III 35
yṣan[1.165 3
yṣat 1.16 I 51, 1.18 IV 36
yṣi 1.14 II 32, 1.14 II 34, 1.14 II 47, 1.17 II 44, 1.92 6, 1.166 21, 4.75 VI 6
yṣi[1.126 6
]yṣix[7.20 1
yṣih[m 3.8 9
yṣin 2.54 2
yṣu 1.15 II 10, 1.16 I 53, 1.103 45, 1.103 51, 2.31 36, 4.192 2
yṣb 1.15 II 25, 1.16 I 52, 1.16 VI 25, 1.16 VI 27, 1.16 VI 39
y]ṣb 1.15 V 21
yṣbt 1.17 VI 9
yṣd 1.12 I 34
yṣh 1.10 II 19
yṣhl 1.17 II 9
yṣḥ 1.3 V 35, 1.3 V 36, 1.4 IV 47, 1.4 IV 48, 1.4 VII 22, 1.4 VII 53, 1.5 VI 22, 1.6 I 43, 1.6 II 37, 1.6 III 17, 1.6 III 22, 1.6 V 11, 1.6 VI 13, 1.8 II 6, 1.14 V 23, 1.16 IV 6, 1.16 VI 16, 1.16 VI 41, 1.17 II 12, 1.17 V 15, 1.19 III 1, 1.19 III 12, 1.19 III 16, 1.19 III 26, 1.19 III 30, 1.19 III 42, 1.19 III 51, 1.19 IV 3, 1.19 IV 20, 4.7 5
yṣ[ḥ 1.4 IV 30, 1.14 V 14, 1.19 II 48
y]ṣḥ 1.1 II 17
yṣ]ḥ 1.4 I 4, 1.4 I 6
yṣḥm 4.47 7, 4.68 67, 4.99 19, 4.126 10, 4.147 5, 4.151 II 2, 4.207 5, 4.609 9, 4.626 1, 4.692 1, 4.692 8
yṣḥm[4.105 2
yṣḥn[4.692 13
yṣḥq 1.4 IV 28, 1.6 III 16, 1.17 II 10
yṣly 1.19 I 39
yṣm 1.19 III 46
yṣmdnn 1.23 10
yṣmḫ 4.12 4
yṣmḫ[4.545 II 5
yṣġd 1.10 III 7, 1.23 30, 1.174 1
yṣq 1.3 II 31, 1.4 I 25, 1.4 I 26, 1.4 I 29, 1.5 VI 14, 1.14 IV 1, 1.16 III 1, 1.22 I 17, 1.71 4, 1.71 6, 1.71 8, 1.71 10, 1.71 25, 1.72 24, 1.72 26, 1.85 4, 1.85 6, 1.85 8, 1.85 11, 1.85 14, 1.85 17, 1.85 29, 1.85 32, 1.97 5, 1.97 7, 2.72 31
yṣq[1.72 15, 1.72 20
y[ṣ]q 1.85 19
y[ṣq 1.72 11
]yṣq 1.7 21, 1.101 14
yṣ]q 1.71 25
y]ṣq[1.85 22
yṣq\m 1.4 I 27f
yṣr 4.46 11, 4.46 12, 4.90 10, 4.339 24, 4.367 8, 4.609 37
yṣr[4.86 5, 4.86 12
y]ṣr 4.382 27
yṣ]r 4.382 26
yṣrk 1.19 I 43
yṣrm 4.99 11, 4.126 28, 4.358 10

y]ṣrm 4.87 3
yq[7.108 4
yqb 1.17 V 35
yq[bh 1.17 V 36
yqbr 1.19 III 40
yqbr.nn 1.19 III 41
yqdm 1.89 7
yqḥ 1.3 I 16, 1.17 VI 35, 1.17 VI 36, 1.19 III 39, 1.23 35, 1.23 36, 1.41 20, 1.127 26, 1.127 31, 2.19 12, 2.71 11, 3.2 13, 6.26 2
yqḥ[2.7 3, 2.45 5, 2.62 15
y]qḥ 1.2 III 19, 2.33 9
yqḥnn 3.5 17
{l}<y>qẓ 1.19 III 40(!)
yql 1.2 IV 23, 1.2 IV 25, 1.6 V 26, 1.10 II 18, 1.19 II 38, 1.19 III 18, 1.19 III 23, 1.163 7
yql[1.2 III 6
yq[ln 1.46 11
yqlṣn 1.4 III 12
yqm 1.4 III 13, 1.10 II 17
yqmṣ 1.14 I 35
yqny 1.19 IV 58, 1.141 1
yqr 1.17 VI 14, 1.108 2, 1.113 26, 1.166 13
yqra 1.4 VII 47
yqr.un 1.5 II 22
yqrb 1.5 IV 10, 1.14 I 37, 1.16 I 49
]yqrb 1.17 I 16
yqr[y 1.19 IV 22
yqrṣ 1.16 V 29
yqš 4.114 8
]yqš 1.48 7
yqšm 4.99 6, 4.126 25
yqṯ 1.2 IV 27
yqṯqṯ 1.114 5
yr 1.14 II 40, 1.14 IV 18, 1.19 I 40, 1.23 38, 1.23 38, 1.82 3, 1.105 19
yr[1.23 18, 4.372 2, 4.412 II 4, 6.42 2
]yr[1.157 8, 7.192 3
yrx[4.178 16, 7.67 3
yr/k[4.529 2
yraun 1.5 II 6
yraš 1.71 26, 1.72 25, 1.85 18, 1.85 30, 1.97 6
yr[a]š 1.72 36
yritn 2.31 45
yru 1.6 VI 30
yrb 4.95 5
]yrb[4.563 4
yrbˁm 4.123 7, 4.232 38
yrbˁm[4.764 10
yrgb 1.6 VI 58
yrgbbˁl 1.102 16
y<r>gbhd 1.102 15
yrgblim 1.102 22
yrgm 1.4 V 12, 1.16 I 20, 1.23 12, 2.15 8, 2.33 30, 3.9 14
yr[gm 1.41 53
yrd 1.5 II 4, 1.5 VI 12, 1.6 I 63, 1.6 I 63, 1.14 I 36, 1.14 II 26, 1.14 IV 8, 1.92 30
yrd[1.2 III 14
]y/ḫrd[4.627 11
yrdm 1.114 22, 1.151 13
y\rdm 1.4 VIII 8f, 1.5 V 15f
yrdn 1.112 18
yrdnn 2.3 15
yrdt 1.24 42, 1.39 20
yrḥṣ 1.14 III 53
yrḫ 1.12 I 15, 1.15 II 4, 1.16 II 19, 1.17 II 44, 1.17 II 44, 1.18 I 31, 1.18 IV 9, 1.19 IV 2, 1.24 4, 1.24 16, 1.24 31, 1.24 33, 1.24 38, 1.39 14, 1.41 1, 1.43 11, 1.43 14, 1.46 11, 1.87 28, 1.87 54, 1.92 16, 1.100 26, 1.102 4, 1.102 14, 1.105 15, 1.107 40, 1.108 26, 1.109 5, 1.109 17, 1.111 7, 1.112 1, 1.114 4, 1.118 13, 1.119 1, 1.123 6, 1.127 1, 1.130 12, 1.130 17, 1.138 1, 1.148 29, 1.162 10, 1.163 2, 1.163 4, 1.163 5, 1.163 5, 1.163 10, 1.163 12, 4.95 4, 4.95 6, 4.95 8, 4.95 9, 4.95 10, 4.172 2, 4.192 1, 4.220 4, 4.220 5, 4.221 2, 4.221 3, 4.221 4, 4.246 1, 4.269 30, 4.336 2, 4.387 13, 4.387 21, 4.609 1, 4.688 1, 4.786 5
yrḫ[1.148 5
yr[ḫ 1.106 12, 4.193 1, 4.193 6
y[rḫ 4.387 1
]yrḫ 1.163 14, 4.220 3, 4.220 6, 6.59 1
y]rḫ 1.39 19, 1.58 5, 1.87 1, 4.219 11, 4.316 1, 4.316 3, 4.316 5
yr]ḫ 1.1 V 16, 4.182 32, 4.182 35, 4.182 38, 4.182 40, 4.258 3
y]r[ḫ 1.17 II 45

yr<ḫ> 4.266 2
y\rḫ 1.24 17f, 1.24 38f
yrḫh 1.17 II 43
yrḫm 1.6 II 27, 1.6 V 7, 1.6 V 7, 1.14 II 31, 1.16 II 22, 1.17 II 46, 1.17 VI 29, 1.19 IV 13, 1.19 IV 14, 1.123 7, 4.95 3, 4.360 4
yrḫ[m 1.14 IV 12
yry 5.1 14
yry[4.647 4
yryt 4.411 3, 4.411 6
yrk 1.10 III 27, 1.82 10, 1.82 38, 1.143 3
]yrk[7.52 3
yrkt 1.13 14
yrm 3.10 14, 4.124 4, 4.214 III 19, 4.321 3, 4.347 4, 4.347 9, 4.791 8, 5.1 15
yrmhd 2.70 4
yrmy 1.92 32
yrml 4.648 17, 4.648 18, 4.648 19, 4.648 20, 4.648 21, 4.648 22, 4.648 23, 4.693 48
y]rml 4.648 9
yr]ml 4.648 6, 4.648 8
yrmly 4.648 16
yrmm 1.9 9
yrmn 4.35 II 19, 4.159 2, 4.282 13, 4.755 2, 5.1 9
yr[m]n 4.232 8
yrmˁl 4.338 4
yrġmil 1.102 19
yrġmbˁl 1.102 26
yrpi 4.344 18
yrpu 4.617 22
yrp\[u 1.21 II 5f
y]rps 1.103 50
yrq 1.4 IV 11, 1.6 I 50, 1.14 III 22, 1.14 III 34, 1.14 VI 18, 1.19 II 5, 1.163 14
yrq[1.4 IV 6
yr]q 1.14 V 34
yrš 2.41 15
yrt 1.5 I 6, 4.138 4
yrtx[4.677 3
yrtḥṣ 1.14 III 52, 1.46 10, 1.87 3, 1.106 26, 1.109 2, 1.112 10, 1.119 5
yr[tḥṣ 1.87 55
yrt{.}ḥṣ 1.112 16
yrtqṣ 1.2 IV 15, 1.2 IV 23
yrṯ 1.14 I 25, 4.154 6, 4.188 15
yrṯy 1.92 29
yš[1.23 5, 1.107 13
]yš[7.124 2
yšal 1.124 3, 2.14 11, 2.14 16
yš\al 2.47 24f
yši[2.57 11
yšiḫr 2.42 11
y]šil 1.101 8
yšu 1.4 IV 30, 1.4 VII 22, 1.5 IV 5, 1.5 VI 22, 1.6 III 17, 1.6 V 10, 1.6 VI 13(!), 1.10 II 13, 1.10 II 14, 1.10 II 19, 1.14 II 46, 1.14 IV 24, 1.16 VI 15, 1.16 VI 40, 1.17 II 11, 1.19 III 11, 1.19 III 16, 1.19 III 25, 1.19 III 30, 1.19 III 42, 1.19 III 51, 1.19 IV 2, 1.23 37
yš[u 1.2 I 39, 1.6 VI 32
y[šu 1.41 55
]yšu 1.167 8
y]šu 1.1 II 6, 1.19 IV 19
yšul 5.11 2
yšb 5.22 28
yšbˁ 1.16 V 20
yšb\[ˁ] 1.4 VII 51f
yšbˁl 2.70 27
yšdd 1.103 37
y]šdd 1.103 35
yšk/w[7.57 3
yšḥx[1.12 II 12
yšḥmm 1.175 7
yšḫn 1.12 II 38
yšk/w[7.57 3
yškb 1.14 I 34, 1.17 I 4, 1.17 I 14, 4.163 16
yšk]b 1.17 I 39
yškn 2.46 13
yšl 1.6 VI 13 lg. yšu
yšl\ḥ 1.4 I 25f
yšlḥm 1.17 II 30, 1.17 II 32, 1.17 II 37, 1.100 6, 1.100 12, 1.100 17, 1.100 23, 1.100 28, 1.100 33, 1.100 38, 1.100 43, 1.100 49, 1.100 55
yšl\ḥm 1.17 II 34f
yšlḥmnh 1.3 I 5
]yšlḥn 1.2 III 24
yšlm 1.103 54, 2.1 1, 2.4 4, 2.6 4, 2.10 4, 2.13 7, 2.16 4, 2.20 2, 2.30 6, 2.33

4, 2.34 3, 2.38 4, 2.44 4, 2.46 4, 2.63 4, 2.68 8, 2.71 3, 2.75 4, 2.81 6, 4.398 6
yšl[m 2.2 2
yš[lm 2.2 1, 2.23 34, 2.41 1, 4.398 7
y]šlm 2.21 4
]yšl[m 2.52 1
<y>šlm 2.72 5
yšmḫ 1.10 III 37
yšm[ḫ 1.17 VI 54
yšmʿ 1.3 V 10, 1.4 IV 8, 1.5 V 17, 2.4 18, 4.69 VI 16, 4.245 I 8, 4.280 10, 4.682 2, 4.715 21
yšmʿk 1.2 III 17, 1.6 VI 26
yšn 1.14 I 31, 1.14 III 15, 1.14 V 7, 4.98 6, 4.103 3, 4.103 58, 4.425 16, 4.753 10
yšnn 1.16 I 13
yšʿly 1.19 IV 23
yšṣi 1.15 V 24
yšq 1.23 49, 1.23 55
yšqy 1.17 I 10, 1.17 I 13, 1.17 I 22
yšqynh 1.3 I 9, 1.17 VI 31
yšql 1.23 10, 1.107 4
yšqp 2.82 7
yšr 1.3 I 18, 1.3 I 20, 1.17 VI 31, 1.23 57, 1.106 15, 1.108 3, 1.112 21, 4.780 16
yšr[4.50 6
yšril 4.623 3
yš\rbʿ 1.17 V 12f
yšrh 1.14 I 13
yšrn[2.46 14
yššil[2.18 5
yššq 1.17 II 33, 1.17 II 35, 1.17 II 38
y\ššq 1.17 II 30f
yš<t> 1.23 36
yšt 1.2 IV 27, 1.3 IV 25, 1.15 II 9, 1.23 38, 1.24 34, 1.108 1, 1.108 1, 1.108 10, 1.108 13, 1.114 16, 1.114 29, 1.114 31, 1.139 13, 1.164 2, 1.175 8, 1.175 13, 2.38 27, 2.42 16, 4.736 4
]yšt 7.51 24
yštal 2.42 23, 2.70 12, 2.71 10
yštd 1.6 IV 25
yštḥwy[1.1 III 25
y]štḥw[y 1.2 III 6
yšt]ḥwyn 1.1 II 16
yštk 1.6 IV 2, 1.6 IV 13, 1.19 IV 5, 1.169 13, 1.169 13, 2.66 3
yštkn 1.4 VII 44
yštn 1.4 IV 14
]yštn 7.81 3
yštql 1.17 II 25, 1.100 68, 1.114 17
yšt\ql 1.19 IV 8f
yt 1.176 3, 1.176 8, 4.339 28, 4.786 3
yt[4.308 4, 4.422 11, 4.424 15, 7.91 1
]yt 1.87 60, 2.31 60, 4.206 3, 4.363 1, 4.785 2
]yt[4.200 1
yt 1.87 52 lg. ym
]ytx[4.510 2
]xyt 4.270 13
]xyt[4.17 5
ytbʿ 1.16 VI 39
ytbʿ[2.18 3
]ytd 7.169 3
ytḥm 4.63 I 22
yty 4.7 18
ytk 1.19 II 33, 1.41 12, 1.107 17
ytkxx 1.84 31
ytlk 1.12 I 34
y[tl]k 1.4 VI 18
ytm 1.16 VI 49, 1.17 V 8, 4.618 3
ytmr 1.3 I 22
ytmt 1.82 22
ytn 1.2 I 20, 1.2 III 4, 1.3 I 10, 1.3 V 3, 1.4 V 27, 1.4 VII 29, 1.5 I 10, 1.5 II 14, 1.6 VI 10, 1.9 12, 1.10 I 13, 1.10 II 8, 1.14 III 46, 1.14 VI 31, 1.14 VI 37, 1.15 II 10, 1.15 II 10, 1.16 I 13, 1.79 2, 1.79 5, 1.80 2, 1.100 63, 1.104 12, 1.173 16, 2.3 14, 2.4 20, 2.33 26, 2.45 13, 2.45 18, 2.45 21, 2.69 3, 2.83 6, 3.2 5, 3.5 4, 4.168 8, 4.182 62, 4.182 64, 4.548 3, 4.573 5, 4.609 35, 4.637 6, 4.728 2, 4.779 4, 6.17 2
ytn[1.1 IV 9
yt[n 1.1 III 21
]ytn 2.31 39, 4.635 6
ytna 1.14 III 31 lg. ytnt
ytnk[2.2 9
ytnm 1.23 3, 4.93 I 1
ytnn 1.17 V 26
y]tnn 3.2 8
ytn.nn 3.5 11

ytnnn 5.9 I 9
ytnt 1.6 VI 14, 1.14 III 31(!), 1.127 5, 2.39 23
ytn[t 1.14 VI 12
ytˁdd 1.4 III 11
ytˁn 1.6 VI 16
ytr 1.6 VI 53, 4.611 15, 4.710 6
ytr[6.38 1
ytrhd 2.4 22
ytrḫ 1.24 18, 1.24 33
ytrm 4.63 III 25, 4.214 II 10
ytrˁm 4.628 3
ytrš 4.281 11
ytršn 4.424 19
ytršp 4.93 I 11, 4.141 II 23, 5.1 4
ytrt 1.87 59
ytši 1.40 24, 1.40 25, 1.40 33, 1.40 41, 1.40 42
yt[ši 1.40 16
y[t]ši 1.40 33
]ytši 1.122 2
ytšu 1.17 V 6, 1.19 I 21
]ytšp[7.47 8
ytt 1.100 75, 4.710 6
yṯ 5.11 13
yṯ[2.39 30, 4.406 2, 4.406 5
]\yṯ 1.67 7f, 1.67 19f
yṯx[2.57 3
yṯil 4.269 11
yṯir 1.2 III 21
yṯ]ir 1.2 III 16
yṯb 1.1 IV 4, 1.2 I 19, 1.2 I 21, 1.3 IV 54, 1.3 IV 55, 1.4 VII 42, 1.5 I 9, 1.5 II 13, 1.5 VI 12, 1.5 VI 13, 1.6 V 20, 1.6 VI 12, 1.10 I 9, 1.10 III 13, 1.14 VI 36, 1.16 VI 22, 1.16 VI 23, 1.16 VI 25, 1.17 II 43, 1.17 V 6, 1.18 IV 7, 1.18 IV 29, 1.19 IV 19, 1.19 IV 62, 1.20 II 8, 1.23 8, 1.23 29, 1.41 7, 1.87 7, 1.100 7, 1.100 13, 1.100 18, 1.100 24, 1.100 29, 1.100 34, 1.100 39, 1.100 44, 1.100 50, 1.100 56, 1.101 1, 1.108 2, 1.114 14, 1.114 15, 1.171 6, 2.31 40, 4.86 29, 4.149 12, 4.382 24, 4.382 26, 4.382 27, 4.382 28, 4.382 32, 4.382 33, 4.557 1, 5.11 5
yṯb[4.430 2
yṯ[b 4.382 29, 4.627 1
y[ṯ]b 1.4 III 10
y[ṯb 1.6 V 5
]yṯb 4.769 48
]yṯb[4.650 2
yṯ]b 1.2 III 20, 1.10 I 17, 1.14 II 6, 1.21 V 1, 4.382 23, 4.382 34
yṯbn 1.23 56
yṯb<r> 1.19 III 2, 1.19 III 17
yṯbr 1.2 III 18, 1.6 VI 29, 1.16 VI 54, 1.16 VI 55, 1.19 I 4, 1.19 III 2, 1.19 III 8, 1.19 III 17, 1.19 III 31, 1.19 III 31, 1.19 III 43, 1.19 III 43
yṯbr[1.18 IV 2
yṯb[r 1.2 I 7
yṯ[br 1.19 II 46
yṯbt 2.72 21
yṯdṯ 1.16 V 19
yṯk[1.107 4
yṯkḥ 1.11 1, 1.24 4
yṯlṯ 1.5 VI 20, 1.5 VI 21
yṯn 4.168 6
]yṯn 4.734 2
yṯny 1.4 VII 30
yṯ[ny 1.16 V 13
yṯnm 1.72 38
yṯn[m 1.71 27
yṯ[nm 1.85 31
yṯnt 1.71 27, 1.85 31
yṯ[nt 1.72 37
yṯˁd 4.377 21
y]ṯˁd 4.322 2
yṯˁk 1.94 27
yṯˁn 4.371 9
yṯˁr 1.3 I 4, 1.24 35
yṯpd 1.4 IV 29, 1.6 III 15, 1.17 II 11
yṯpṭ 1.17 V 8, 4.63 II 4
y]ṯpṭ 1.19 I 24
yṯprx[4.357 21
yṯq 1.100 6, 1.100 11, 1.100 17, 1.100 22, 1.100 28, 1.100 33, 1.100 38, 1.100 43, 1.100 48, 1.100 54
yṯrm 1.16 VI 21
yṯtn 1.71 9, 1.85 9
y\ṯtqt 1.24 47f(!)
yṯṯb 1.4 V 47, 1.41 45, 1.112 20, 1.126 21, 2.57 12
yṯṯ[b 1.41 46
yṯ[ṯb 1.2 III 23
yṯṯbn 1.6 VI 33

K

<k> 1.6 II 22

k 1.1 II 9(!), 1.1 IV 11(*bis*), 1.2 I 37, 1.2 I 38, 1.2 IV 29, 1.3 II 9, 1.3 II 10(*bis*), 1.3 II 27, 1.3 IV 1, 1.3 IV 48, 1.3 V 1, 1.3 V 3, 1.3 V 4, 1.3 V 27, 1.3 V 28, 1.3 V 39, 1.4 I 41, 1.4 I 42, 1.4 II 14, 1.4 II 27, 1.4 II 29, 1.4 III 21, 1.4 IV 17, 1.4 IV 27, 1.4 IV 51, 1.4 V 1, 1.4 V 42, 1.4 VII 41, 1.4 VII 53, 1.4 VIII 18, 1.4 VIII 19, 1.5 I 1, 1.5 I 4(?), 1.5 I 27, 1.5 II 5, 1.5 III 8, 1.5 V 17, 1.5 VI 21(*bis*), 1.6 I 5, 1.6 I 10, 1.6 I 15, 1.6 I 19, 1.6 I 41, 1.6 I 42, 1.6 II 6, 1.6 II 7, 1.6 II 23, 1.6 II 28(*bis*), 1.6 III 1, 1.6 III 8, 1.6 III 9, 1.6 III 20, 1.6 III 21, 1.6 VI 16, 1.6 VI 18, 1.6 VI 19, 1.6 VI 21, 1.7 14, 1.8 II 4, 1.10 III 5, 1.10 III 6, 1.10 III 35, 1.12 I 10, 1.12 II 46, 1.12 II 48, 1.13 13, 1.13 14, 1.13 24, 1.13 25, 1.13 28, 1.14 I 30, 1.14 I 39, 1.14 I 43, 1.14 II 50, 1.14 III 41, 1.14 IV 30, 1.14 VI 26, 1.15 I 7, 1.16 I 2(*bis*), 1.16 I 3, 1.16 I 15, 1.16 I 16, 1.16 I 17, 1.16 I 33, 1.16 II 7, 1.16 II 19, 1.16 II 20, 1.16 II 22, 1.16 II 23, 1.16 II 38, 1.16 II 39, 1.16 II 40, 1.16 III 10, 1.16 III 11, 1.16 IV 2(*bis*), 1.16 IV 5(*bis*), 1.16 IV 9, 1.16 VI 43, 1.17 II 6, 1.17 II 14, 1.17 II 20, 1.17 V 11, 1.17 V 15, 1.17 V 36, 1.17 VI 11, 1.17 VI 30(*bis*), 1.18 I 16, 1.18 IV 28, 1.19 I 7(*bis*), 1.19 I 8, 1.19 I 12(*bis*), 1.19 I 13, 1.19 I 46, 1.19 II 38, 1.19 II 39, 1.19 II 43, 1.19 II 44, 1.20 I 3(?), 1.20 I 4, 1.22 I 14, 1.23 33, 1.23 34(*bis*), 1.23 35, 1.23 39, 1.23 50, 1.24 10, 1.41 9, 1.41 52, 1.43 1, 1.64 16, 1.70 9, 1.70 30, 1.71 26, 1.72 6, 1.72 9, 1.72 12, 1.72 16, 1.72 21, 1.72 25, 1.72 27, 1.72 36, 1.82 4, 1.82 43(*bis*), 1.85 2, 1.85 5, 1.85 7, 1.85 9, 1.85 15, 1.85 18, 1.85 23, 1.85 30, 1.87 10, 1.91 10, 1.91 11, 1.91 14, 1.92 27, 1.96 3, 1.97 2, 1.97 6, 1.101 1, 1.101 2, 1.101 9, 1.103 41, 1.107 18, 1.114 22, 1.117 5, 1.117 10, 1.119 26, 1.124 1, 1.127 9, 1.127 12, 1.133 7, 1.140 1, 1.140 3, 1.140 5, 1.140 7, 1.140 9, 1.140 14, 1.141 1, 1.143 3, 1.148 18, 1.155 2, 1.157 9, 1.169 3(*bis*), 1.169 4(*bis*), 1.175 8, 2.3 20, 2.8 3, 2.8 5, 2.9 3, 2.10 12, 2.23 1, 2.23 4, 2.23 6, 2.31 66, 2.32 4, 2.33 14, 2.33 21, 2.34 5, 2.34 10, 2.34 12, 2.34 30, 2.36 21, 2.39 7, 2.45 23, 2.45 28, 2.70 23, 2.70 25, 2.73 7, 2.76 15, 4.168 6, 4.182 61, 4.182 63, 4.362 1, 4.690 18, 4.734 7, 4.770 21, 5.2 5, 5.2 6(*bis*), 5.2 8, 5.4 2, 5.6 1, 5.12 2, 5.13 7, 5.16 1, 5.16 2, 5.17 5, 5.19 2, 5.20 1, 5.21 1, 5.24 1, 6.54 1, 6.55 1, 6.68 1, 7.42 5, 7.55 8, 7.163 4

k 4.4 5 lg. w

k 1.19 I 8 lg. knr

k 2.70 22 lg. klt?

k 1.19 I 10 lg. klb?

k[1.5 III 6, 1.5 III 7, 1.7 44, 1.9 1, 1.13 15, 1.14 I 3, 1.15 III 31, 1.42 28, 1.42 54, 1.49 11, 1.85 20, 1.87 43, 1.89 5, 1.90 10, 1.104 9, 1.125 5, 1.126 10, 1.136 13, 1.166 4, 2.8 2, 2.31 4, 2.36 7, 2.39 29, 2.44 9, 4.23 8, 4.35 I 3, 4.66 12, 4.111 16, 4.242 2, 4.247 2, 4.269 1, 4.300 5, 4.325 3, 4.328 10, 4.335 37, 4.401 2, 4.405 2, 4.746 12, 6.33 1, 7.1 1, 7.98 3, 7.116 1, 7.129 1

k[1.125 5 lg. atnd

]k 1.1 V 9, 1.1 V 10, 1.5 I 27, 1.5 V 4, 1.14 II 7, 1.17 VI 12, 1.61 1, 1.82 21, 1.82 41, 1.94 28, 1.108 20, 1.139 13, 1.152 2, 2.20 6, 2.21 14, 2.31 48, 2.58 9, 2.77 10, 4.109 2, 4.176 10, 4.182 58, 4.199 6, 4.243 42, 4.258 9, 4.382 12, 4.435 22, 4.439 1, 4.566 4,

4.619 2, 4.647 5, 4.744 6, 7.61 9, 7.164 5, 7.164 7, 7.175 4
]k[4.308 1, 4.523 2, 7.110 1, 7.114 1
k\[1.168 18f
kx 2.44 6, 2.46 21
kx[1.1 IV 27, 1.2 II 2, 1.2 III 18, 1.4 II 39, 1.27 14, 1.94 34, 1.169 20, 2.36 1, 2.77 16, 2.80 9, 4.114 1, 4.198 5, 4.335 31, 4.399 18, 4.469 1, 4.739 2
]kx 3.6 2
]kx[2.37 1, 7.90 3, 7.128 1, 7.132 1
]kxxx[7.92 2
xxxk 1.45 2
]xk 1.2 III 14, 1.7 11, 1.82 10, 1.94 30, 1.129 6, 2.37 7, 2.44 12, 2.79 4, 4.703 3
]xxk 1.23 30, 2.7 6
]xxxxk 2.35 6
xkx[4.496 1
]xkx[7.206 2
xxkx[2.45 8
]xxkx 4.396 22
]kxxxb/d 4.744 8
k/w 4.744 6, 7.63 8
k/w[1.12 II 35, 4.69 III 21, 4.521 4, 4.737 2, 4.743 7
xk/w[1.37 5
k/w/p/r[4.393 24
k/w/r[1.176 17, 4.73 6
]k/w/r 7.51 12
]k/wxxnth 1.157 10
k/ẓ[7.222 4
k/p/r[4.737 3
k/r[1.174 5, 4.160 7, 4.422 32, 4.529 1, 7.45 3, 7.45 4
]k/r 1.42 24, 1.75 1, 2.31 33, 2.31 36, 2.57 11, 4.104 11, 4.224 1, 4.275 20, 4.438 7, 4.628 8, 4.770 21, 7.20 2, 7.109 2
]k/r[1.7 52, 4.64 V 6, 4.627 4
]k/rx[7.187 2
]k/rxxx[1.86 10
]xk/r[4.219 16
]k/t 4.64 IV 1
k/aa[1.70 3
kaddm 1.70 5
kat 4.402 10 lg. kṯt?
ki[1.149 7
]k/ri 7.190 2
kh/idn 4.715 8
]kim 4.357 13
kin 1.66 31
kuḏnx[1.42 25
kb 1.4 III 4
kb 4.313 6 lg. kd
kb[1.12 II 10, 1.94 25, 1.157 8, 4.329 2
kbx[2.41 7
]xkb 7.185 2
kb/d[4.743 9
]kb/ṣ 2.37 13
]k/rb 1.63 7
kbb 1.81 10
kbbd 1.116 23
kbby 4.659 7
k{b}d 1.112 12
kbd 1.1 II 20, 1.3 II 26, 1.3 III 10, 1.3 III 16, 1.3 III 17, 1.3 IV 10, 1.3 IV 10, 1.3 IV 24, 1.3 IV 30, 1.3 IV 31, 1.3 VI 20, 1.5 VI 27, 1.5 VI 28, 1.6 II 16, 1.6 II 17, 1.7 28, 1.12 I 10, 1.12 I 13, 1.17 V 20, 1.19 I 35, 1.27 10, 1.39 2, 1.41 39, 1.46 13, 1.109 8, 1.109 8, 1.119 21, 1.123 16, 1.123 21, 1.143 1, 1.155 1, 2.77 16, 2.79 8, 2.83 8, 3.1 20, 3.10 13, 4.43 6, 4.43 7, 4.44 12, 4.48 6, 4.75 VI 4, 4.92 6, 4.123 22, 4.127 7, 4.127 9, 4.128 1, 4.132 1, 4.137 9, 4.137 10, 4.137 13, 4.139 10, 4.141 II 24, 4.143 5, 4.151 II 5, 4.156 7, 4.162 12, 4.163 11, 4.164 2, 4.166 3, 4.169 10, 4.171 2, 4.173 10, 4.174 10, 4.174 11, 4.174 14, 4.179 14, 4.179 17, 4.182 2, 4.182 6(!), 4.197 21, 4.198 10, 4.201 4, 4.201 4, 4.203 4, 4.203 6, 4.203 7, 4.211 5, 4.212 3, 4.213 2, 4.213 4, 4.213 6, 4.213 7, 4.213 11, 4.213 14, 4.213 16, 4.213 17, 4.213 22, 4.213 23, 4.213 25, 4.213 26, 4.213 28, 4.226 3, 4.226 8, 4.230 14, 4.243 8, 4.243 19, 4.243 21, 4.243 23, 4.243 27, 4.243 46, 4.243 47, 4.243 49, 4.243 50, 4.244 18, 4.262 5, 4.265 3, 4.269 31, 4.270 3, 4.270 4, 4.270 6, 4.270 9, 4.270 10, 4.272 4, 4.272 5, 4.273 3, 4.273 4, 4.273 5, 4.273 6,

4.273 8, 4.280 7, 4.280 9, 4.280 11, 4.280 13, 4.284 3, 4.290 19, 4.296 2, 4.296 4, 4.296 7, 4.304 4, 4.313 28, 4.333 11, 4.336 10, 4.337 2, 4.337 5, 4.337 8, 4.337 17, 4.338 11, 4.340 22, 4.341 1, 4.341 17, 4.341 23, 4.344 1, 4.344 9, 4.344 11, 4.344 22, 4.345 1, 4.345 3, 4.345 5, 4.352 1, 4.352 3, 4.352 5, 4.353 2, 4.369 7, 4.377 24, 4.378 9, 4.387 12, 4.387 14, 4.387 19, 4.387 22, 4.392 4, 4.394 2(!), 4.396 12, 4.397 6, 4.397 8, 4.399 11, 4.400 5, 4.400 10, 4.407 3, 4.411 5, 4.595 1, 4.618 30, 4.626 3, 4.626 5, 4.626 9, 4.630 1, 4.632 19, 4.636 6, 4.636 7, 4.636 11, 4.636 12, 4.636 19, 4.658 6, 4.690 13, 4.690 14, 4.709 5, 4.721 2, 4.721 3, 4.721 8(!), 4.721 9(!), 4.721 10, 4.743 16, 4.749 4, 4.755 3, 4.755 5, 4.755 10, 4.777 2, 4.777 5, 4.777 10, 4.777 13, 4.778 10, 4.779 2, 4.779 9, 4.782 16, 4.791 6

kbd[1.91 36, 4.142 7, 4.211 3, 4.227 IV 7, 4.243 47, 4.244 21, 4.258 6, 4.432 19, 4.572 1

kb[d 1.3 IV 25, 4.201 7, 4.213 19, 4.237 3, 4.243 50, 4.299 3, 4.333 1, 4.333 8, 4.352 11, 4.387 11, 4.396 5, 4.407 1, 4.400 11, 4.411 8, 4.508 2, 4.683 3, 4.697 6

k[b]d 4.721 7

k[bd 4.317 12, 4.333 6, 4.333 7, 4.345 8, 4.397 5, 4.397 11, 4.400 6, 4.729 12(!)

]kbd 4.139 1, 4.240 3, 4.240 5, 4.397 10, 4.683 4, 4.683 5, 4.683 6, 4.707 2

k]bd 1.14 V 24, 1.92 28, 4.162 9, 4.197 25, 4.201 3, 4.213 21, 4.271 8, 4.274 2, 4.397 2, 4.533 2, 4.636 27, 4.683 11, 4.721 15

kb]d 4.197 17, 4.212 5, 4.397 12, 4.636 16, 4.636 21, 4.683 10, 4.683 12

]kbd[4.201 11

k]bd[4.541 2

]kb[d] 4.683 7

]k[bd] 4.273 7

k\bd 1.4 VIII 28f

[[kbd]] 4.709 8

kbdh 1.3 II 25, 1.5 II 4, 1.13 31, 1.19 III 24, 1.19 III 33, 1.19 III 38

kbd[h] 1.19 III 18

kbdy 4.611 11

kbdk 1.18 I 18

kbdm 1.78 5, 1.109 12(!), 1.130 20

kb[d]m 1.46 16

]kbdm 1.46 1

kbdn 1.12 I 9

kbdt 1.73 12, 1.86 26

kbdthm 1.19 III 10

kby 1.131 3

]k/rby 4.756 5

kbkb 1.4 IV 17, 1.84 25, 7.50 7

]kbkb 1.163 7

kbkbm 1.3 II 41, 1.3 III 25, 1.3 IV 44, 1.5 II 3, 1.13 17, 1.19 II 3, 1.19 II 7, 1.19 IV 31, 1.23 54, 1.43 3, 1.92 27, 1.164 15

kbkbm[1.7 32

kbkb[m 1.5 III 8

[k]bkbm 1.13 13

[k]\bkbm 1.19 IV 24f

kbkbt 1.92 28

kbkm 1.19 IV 38

kbl 4.232 40

kbl 4.182 6 lg. kbd

kblx[4.669 3

]x/kbl 4.182 23

kblbn 4.149 6, 4.635 57

kblbn[4.335 12

kbln 4.55 5, 4.76 5, 4.112 III 1, 4.277 2, 4.377 17, 4.571 7, 4.705 7, 4.707 13, 4.788 6

kbln[4.317 4

kbm 1.103 55, 4.205 8

kbm 4.313 5 lg. kdm

kbmh 1.106 15

kbn 4.785 14

kbny 1.131 4

kbnṯ 1.66 17

kbś 4.332 13

kbs 4.128 6, 4.682 9

kbśm 4.71 III 5, 4.99 7

kbsm 4.125 19, 4.610 47

kbʿ 1.4 VI 26 lg. rbʿ

kbr 2.50 14, 4.309 20, 4.425 14

xxkbr[1.70 13
kbrt 1.6 V 16
]xkbt[7.50 13
]k/rg[7.84 2
]kgm 6.34 1
]k/rgn 4.183 I 13
kgr 4.218 4
kd 1.1 IV 23, 1.3 I 16, 1.6 II 3, 1.6 II 4, 1.19 I 14, 1.91 27, 4.14 2(*bis*), 4.14 8, 4.14 8, 4.41 4, 4.41 7, 4.41 12, 4.42 3, 4.131 3, 4.149 1, 4.149 3, 4.149 4, 4.149 6, 4.149 9, 4.149 19, 4.216 5, 4.216 6, 4.216 7, 4.216 11, 4.216 12, 4.219 7, 4.219 8, 4.219 9, 4.230 3, 4.230 5, 4.230 7, 4.230 8, 4.230 9, 4.244 25, 4.246 4, 4.269 27, 4.269 27, 4.269 28, 4.269 28, 4.279 1, 4.279 1, 4.279 3, 4.279 5, 4.283 5, 4.283 7, 4.283 8, 4.283 9, 4.284 6, 4.290 3, 4.313 1, 4.313 2, 4.313 3, 4.313 6(!), 4.313 7, 4.313 8, 4.313 17, 4.313 19, 4.313 20, 4.313 23, 4.313 24, 4.313 25, 4.373 7, 4.454 2, 4.558 8, 4.710 3, 4.710 11, 4.716 5, 4.716 7, 4.716 9, 4.716 11, 4.716 13, 4.716 15, 4.761 9, 4.778 5, 4.778 7, 4.780 13, 4.780 16, 4.782 7, 4.782 11, 4.786 8, 6.11 1
kd[1.51 7, 4.448 2, 4.558 3, 4.715 6, 4.715 8, 4.715 24, 4.715 26, 4.726 2, 4.726 3, 4.726 4, 7.163 3
k[d 4.14 15
]kd 1.3 V 3, 4.160 2, 4.221 5, 4.716 3, 4.717 1
k]d 4.283 4, 4.283 11, 4.313 9, 4.313 15, 4.313 16, 4.429 2, 4.429 3, 4.429 4, 4.716 1, 4.716 2
]kd[4.275 11, 7.93 1
]xkd 1.151 1
kb/d[4.743 9
kdb 4.721 8, 4.721 9 lg. kbd
kdgdl 4.69 VI 7, 4.93 I 13, 4.412 III 4, 4.681 7
]kdgdl 4.769 51
kdd 1.19 IV 12, 1.19 IV 16
kdh 1.16 I 54
kdw/r 4.123 11
kdwṯ 4.205 19, 4.270 3, 4.337 24
kdwṯm 4.152 6, 4.152 11, 4.341 10
kdy 4.743 15
]xkdy 2.44 15
kdkdy 4.696 7
kdl[4.624 11
kdld 1.128 11
kdln 4.307 22, 4.368 21
kdm 1.41 23, 1.91 26, 1.91 30, 1.136 9, 4.41 3, 4.41 8, 4.41 9, 4.41 11, 4.149 7, 4.149 13, 4.213 2, 4.213 16, 4.216 9, 4.216 10, 4.219 5, 4.219 6, 4.230 2, 4.230 4, 4.230 6, 4.269 34, 4.269 35, 4.274 7, 4.279 2, 4.279 4, 4.284 7, 4.284 8, 4.285 5, 4.285 7, 4.285 8, 4.313 5(!), 4.400 5, 4.710 12, 4.717 4, 4.761 8, 4.761 10, 4.761 11, 4.780 5, 4.780 8, 4.780 10, 4.780 13
k[d]m 4.213 17
kdm[4.715 3, 4.715 9, 4.715 25
kd[m 4.225 15, 4.715 10, 4.715 11
kd]m 4.313 10
kd]m[4.313 11
k/d]dm{m} 6.18 2(?)
k]dmḥsp 1.91 29
kdml 4.276 12
k/d]dmm 6.18 2 lg. [k/d]dm{m}?
kdn 4.75 III 3, 4.85 2, 4.354 6, 4.432 8, 4.617 23
]kdnm 1.32 2
kdnt 5.23 8
kdġbr 4.71 III 11 cor. kḏġbr
kdr 1.50 10, 4.275 8, 5.22 3, 5.22 10
kdw/r 4.123 11
kdrl 4.147 7, 4.264 3
kdrn 4.33 22, 4.55 26, 4.350 1
kdrš 4.391 5
kdrt 1.3 II 9
]kdrt 1.7 8
kdt 1.174 3
]k/rḏ[1.52 17
kḏd 1.5 I 17, 1.133 8
kḏyn 4.635 28, 4.727 16
kḏmr 1.148 14
kḏġ 1.128 13
kḏġ[4.725 5
kḏġbr 4.71 III 11(cor.)
kḏġd 1.110 4, 1.111 5, 1.111 10, 1.125 9
kḏ]ġd 1.135 4

kd̲ġdl 3.5 5, 4.183 II 3
kh 4.710 5
kh/idn 4.715 8
khn 4.282 5
khn[1.107 18
k]hn 4.481 5
khnm 1.6 VI 56, 2.4 1, 4.29 1, 4.36 1, 4.38 1, 4.68 72, 4.69 VI 22, 4.99 9, 4.126 6, 4.357 24, 4.745 5, 4.752 6, 6.6 1, 6.7 1, 6.8 1, 6.9 1, 6.10 1
khnm[4.633 4, 4.761 1
kh[nm 4.416 6
]khnm 4.410 50
kw 2.47 17
kwy 4.313 27
kwyn 4.53 6
kwn 4.307 10, 4.692 7, 4.692 12
]kwn 4.5 1
kwrt 1.148 16
kwt 4.93 IV 8, 4.691 6
]kz[1.68 2
kzbn 4.631 17
kzym 4.68 62, 4.99 10, 4.126 14, 4.222 3
kzmm 5.22 25
kzn 4.69 II 20, 4.340 2, 5.18 2
kzn[4.445 4
]kzn 4.424 15
]kzn[4.160 13
]kzġ 1.68 6
kzġb 4.147 17
kzġd 1.116 6, 1.116 14
]kzt̲r 1.68 31
]k/rḥ[7.100 1
]k/rḥxb[4.247 12
]kḥb/d[7.177 5
kḥdnn 2.70 13
kḥt̲ 1.2 I 23, 1.2 I 25, 1.2 I 27, 1.2 I 29, 1.2 IV 13, 1.2 IV 20, 1.3 IV 3, 1.4 I 33, 1.6 I 58, 1.6 I 64, 1.6 V 6, 1.16 V 25, 1.16 VI 24, 1.22 II 18
kḥ[t̲ 1.10 III 14
kḥt̲m 1.4 VI 51
]kḫ[1.35 5
ky 1.123 7, 2.16 7, 2.17 13, 2.36 5, 2.36 14, 2.39 17, 2.39 19, 2.46 9, 2.72 18, 2.72 34, 4.110 6
ky[4.355 1
]ky 4.75 IV 15, 4.702 4
]xky 2.31 61
]k/ryx[4.619 12
]r/ky 4.433 3
]k/rym 4.72 2
kyd̲d 1.125 12
kyy 4.764 5
kyn 4.141 II 21, 4.341 13, 4.424 20, 4.611 6
]kyt 4.32 3
]kk[7.96 3
xkk[4.426 5
kk/r[4.434 4
kkb 4.767 1
kkbm 1.10 I 4
kkbn 4.734 2
]kkd[1.68 3
kkdm 1.109 12 lg. kbdm
kky 4.321 3
kkln 4.148 4, 4.352 10, 4.609 5
kkn 4.645 4
kkn[4.610 69
kknt 1.6 I 67
kkr 2.32 5, 2.32 6, 2.32 11, 4.91 9, 4.91 11, 4.123 2, 4.131 5, 4.131 6, 4.131 8, 4.131 10, 4.131 11, 4.131 13, 4.158 12, 4.158 14, 4.158 17, 4.181 4, 4.201 3, 4.201 5, 4.203 1, 4.203 2, 4.203 16, 4.203 17, 4.206 3, 4.225 13, 4.247 32, 4.272 2, 4.272 3, 4.272 4, 4.272 6, 4.280 5, 4.304 5, 4.337 26, 4.341 3, 4.341 12, 4.341 14, 4.342 4, 4.353 1, 4.390 4, 4.396 1, 4.396 15, 4.396 16, 4.608 5, 4.608 6, 4.707 15, 4.707 19, 4.709 1, 4.709 2, 4.709 3, 4.721 4, 4.721 9
kkr[4.342 3, 4.548 1, 4.608 7, 4.608 8, 4.608 9, 4.742 3
kk[r 4.218 8, 4.288 8, 4.342 1, 4.540 3, 4.608 10, 4.608 11, 4.608 12, 4.742 8
k[kr 4.548 2, 4.608 13
]kkr 4.721 14
k]kr 4.98 31, 4.98 34, 4.396 17, 4.608 2, 4.707 17
kk]r 4.198 9, 4.608 3
kk]r[4.608 4
[[kkr]] 4.131 4
kkrdnm 4.126 27
kkrm 4.43 5, 4.91 6, 4.131 2, 4.158

10, 4.280 2, 4.337 2, 4.337 9, 4.353 1, 4.396 10, 4.626 4, 4.626 8, 4.709 4, 4.721 5
kk[rm 4.23 4
]kkrm 4.304 3
kkr]m 4.396 11
kl 1.5 I 22, 1.5 VI 26, 1.5 VI 27, 1.6 II 15, 1.6 II 16, 1.16 I 45, 1.17 VI 38, 1.18 IV 4, 1.80 5, 1.82 26, 1.107 14, 1.115 10, 1.117 2, 1.127 1, 1.127 7, 1.127 8, 2.3 4, 2.3 26, 2.32 8, 2.32 9, 2.35 15, 2.38 17, 2.38 19, 2.38 20, 2.42 8, 2.81 3, 2.81 9, 2.82 9, 4.191 12, 4.639 6, 7.50 3
kl[1.87 60, 1.103 30, 4.178 8, 4.609 29
]kl 1.1 V 14, 1.84 25, 1.146 4, 7.138 4
k\l 1.106 21f
klx 2.44 7
klx[4.405 3
klxpt 4.197 7
kxn 4.12 15, 4.389 5
kxt 4.351 2
]xk/rl 7.52 7
klat 1.1 IV 10, 1.3 I 11, 1.3 II 3, 1.5 I 19, 1.23 57
kla[t 1.7 36
klatnm 1.14 III 57
kl[atn]m 1.14 II 15
kli 3.8 3
klb 1.14 III 19, 1.14 V 11, 1.16 I 2, 1.16 I 15, 1.16 II 38, 1.19 I 10(?), 1.19 I 13, 1.114 12(!), 1.124 15, 4.75 III 5, 4.232 44
klb 1.114 29 lg. ʿrk lb
k[l]b 1.114 5
]klb 4.69 II 8
klby 2.10 6, 4.63 II 19, 4.69 I 24, 4.75 V 18, 4.76 8, 4.103 36, 4.277 5, 4.357 17, 4.364 1, 4.366 7, 4.609 26, 4.609 29, 4.690 2
klbyn 4.370 20
klbm 4.54 4
klbr 4.391 2
k{.}lbt 1.3 III 45
kld 1.66 8, 1.128 11, 1.128 20, 4.277 1
]kld 1.52 10
k]ld 1.52 14
k\ld 1.44 10f
]xkld[4.459 2
kldn 1.42 2
kldnd 1.125 16, 1.132 12
kl]dnd 1.116 29(!)
klh 1.3 VI 14, 1.6 I 65, 1.17 V 21, 1.17 V 31, 2.31 52, 4.230 1, 7.141 11
klhm 1.9 11, 1.14 II 42, 1.14 IV 20, 1.43 26, 4.278 12
klhn 1.14 I 24, 1.111 7
kly 1.16 III 13, 1.16 III 14, 2.72 43, 4.214 III 6, 4.361 1, 4.362 1, 6.43 2
kly[1.67 8, 4.390 8
k[l]y 1.16 III 15
]xklyx[1.36 4
klyy 1.6 VI 11
kl\yy 1.6 VI 15f
klyn 4.80 11, 4.141 I 17, 4.148 4, 4.214 III 7, 4.609 13, 4.609 25
klyn[1.7 18
]klyn 4.615 5
klyth 1.82 3
]klkl 4.275 21
k]lklh 3.5 10
klklhm 2.38 21
kll 1.173 14, 2.11 11, 2.13 10, 2.16 15, 2.34 7, 2.36 3, 2.39 3
kll[7.20 2
k[ll 2.1 3, 2.78 5
]kll 2.41 5, 2.68 12
kl]l 2.72 7
klm 1.42 2, 1.98 5, 2.81 17
klm[1.67 18
]klm 7.43 2
kln 4.309 23
klnyy 1.3 V 33, 1.3 V 34
klnyn 1.4 IV 45, 1.4 IV 46
klnmw 4.44 25
]klnmw 4.44 21
]kls 1.68 30
klġd 1.128 11
klt 1.3 I 26, 1.3 III 39, 1.3 III 46, 1.4 I 15, 1.4 IV 54, 1.14 II 16, 1.14 III 58, 1.60 16(!), 1.69 2, 1.69 6, 1.135 11, 2.70 22(?), 4.370 38, 4.786 5, 6.24 2
klt[1.69 5, 4.257 3
]klt 7.36 1

k/wlt 4.34 5
kltd 1.116 7, 1.116 23
k]ltd 1.116 34
klth 4.80 4, 4.80 13
kl[th 4.80 19
kltn 3.5 13, 3.5 18
klṯb 4.103 46, 4.357 27, 4.616 12, 4.638 7
km 1.1 V 7, 1.2 IV 13, 1.2 IV 15, 1.2 IV 21, 1.2 IV 24, 1.3 III 8, 1.3 V 38, 1.4 III 34, 1.4 IV 51, 1.4 V 1, 1.4 V 28, 1.4 V 29, 1.4 VII 6, 1.6 I 4, 1.6 II 8, 1.6 II 29, 1.8 II 3, 1.12 I 7, 1.12 I 8, 1.12 I 11, 1.12 I 31, 1.12 I 32, 1.12 II 14, 1.12 II 39, 1.12 II 40, 1.12 II 46, 1.12 II 47, 1.12 II 54, 1.12 II 55, 1.14 I 29, 1.14 II 40, 1.14 III 1, 1.14 III 42, 1.14 IV 18, 1.14 IV 29, 1.14 VI 27, 1.15 III 23, 1.15 III 25, 1.15 VI 6, 1.16 I 20, 1.16 II 27, 1.16 II 28, 1.16 VI 8, 1.16 VI 35, 1.16 VI 50, 1.17 I 19, 1.17 I 19, 1.17 I 20(!), 1.17 I 21, 1.17 II 14, 1.17 II 15, 1.17 VI 14, 1.18 IV 17, 1.18 IV 18, 1.18 IV 23, 1.18 IV 24, 1.18 IV 24, 1.18 IV 25, 1.18 IV 25, 1.18 IV 28, 1.18 IV 29, 1.18 IV 35, 1.18 IV 36, 1.18 IV 37, 1.19 II 33, 1.19 IV 61, 1.20 I 3(?), 1.22 I 10, 1.23 11, 1.41 55, 1.44 1, 1.69 5, 1.70 5, 1.82 3, 1.82 11, 1.82 24, 1.82 24, 1.82 25, 1.92 28, 1.95 2, 1.100 68, 1.100 69, 1.100 73, 1.100 73, 1.107 8, 1.107 9, 1.107 11, 1.114 5, 1.114 21, 1.114 28, 1.147 9, 2.19 2, 2.36 12, 3.9 6, 7.114 4
km[2.31 35, 4.56 6, 4.122 11
k[m 1.2 III 22, 1.107 11
]km 1.21 II 6, 1.94 36, 1.146 3, 2.9 1, 4.627 1
]km[1.5 III 30, 1.126 15
]k/rm 2.4 14, 2.62 10, 4.734 3, 7.145 4
kmy 4.63 III 43
kmkty 4.648 10, 4.648 11, 4.648 15
kmk]ty 4.648 7
kmlt 1.111 19
kmm 1.16 IV 15, 1.27 3, 1.41 33, 1.46 15, 1.50 8, 1.87 36, 1.90 4, 1.107 14, 1.109 11, 1.109 28, 1.132 16, 1.132 21, 1.132 24, 1.146 3, 1.146 4, 1.148 11, 1.148 11, 1.148 11, 1.148 11, 1.148 12, 1.164 5, 1.164 7, 1.164 8, 1.168 3, 1.168 10, 1.168 13
kmm[1.49 7
km[m] 1.148 12
k[mm] 1.50 6
]kmm 4.609 29
k]mm 1.24 11(!)
kmn 1.2 III 11, 1.3 IV 38, 1.3 VI 18, 1.4 V 24, 1.4 V 57, 1.17 V 10, 1.18 I 22, 1.44 2, 4.14 9, 4.377 3, 4.704 2
kmn[4.445 3
]kmn 1.18 I 32
km]n 1.3 VI 6, 1.19 I 26
]kmn[4.414 7
k\mn 1.4 VIII 25f
kmnt 4.778 11, 4.782 17
kmsk 4.282 2, 4.282 4, 4.341 9, 4.707 20, 4.707 23
km]sk 4.707 7
kmġ 1.82 42 lg. kmṯ
kmr[4.178 17
kmrb 1.42 6, 1.42 7, 1.44 7, 1.125 4, 1.128 14
kmrbnd 1.42 7, 1.111 4, 1.116 14
km[rbnd 1.26 3, 1.111 9
[kmr]bnd 1.135 3
[kmrbn]d 1.60 3
k\mrbnr 1.44 8f
kmrbnṯ 1.42 8
kmrwnd 1.110 5
kmrn 4.631 8
kmrṯn 4.63 I 3, 4.322 6
kmt 2.19 3
k/wmtmtm 1.20 I 3 lg. km tmtm or k mtmtm?
kmṯ 1.82 42(!), 1.100 36, 1.107 41(!)
km⊕ 1.123 5
kn 1.12 II 53, 1.169 21, 2.7 10, 2.31 45, 4.624 1, 6.71 1
kn[4.746 9
]kn 1.12 I 6, 2.77 12, 4.270 1, 4.382 7
xkn 4.424 5
]xkn[7.156 1
]k/rn 4.151 IV 3, 4.350 7, 4.769 22
]k/rn[2.25 1

kndwm 4.4 2
kndpnṯ 4.4 3
knḫ 4.176 2
kny 4.171 3
]kny 4.697 10, 4.762 4
]knys 4.431 4
knyt 1.3 IV 53, 1.4 I 15, 1.4 IV 54
kny]t 1.3 I 27
knkny 1.5 V 13
knm 1.23 54
knn 3.7 14, 4.63 I 15, 4.63 II 36, 4.69 VI 20, 4.307 18, 4.350 12, 4.617 8, 4.631 19, 4.635 36, 4.723 9
knn[4.635 14
knʿm 4.96 9, 4.232 41, 4.245 I 7, 4.309 19, 4.356 4, 4.366 2, 4.370 6, 4.370 42
knʿm[4.31 9
knʿny 4.96 7
knp 1.10 II 10, 1.10 II 11, 1.19 III 8, 1.19 III 12, 1.19 III 16, 1.19 III 22, 1.19 III 26, 1.19 III 30, 1.19 III 36, 1.19 III 42, 1.46 6
kn[p 1.19 III 1
knpy 4.243 18, 4.271 1, 4.296 10
knr 1.19 I 8(!), 1.47 32, 1.108 4, 1.118 31, 1.148 9
]knr[1.148 38
knrh 1.101 16
knrt 1.19 III 41
knt 1.65 17
k<s> 1.4 IV 37(!)
ks 1.1 III 12, 1.3 I 10, 1.3 I 13, 1.4 III 16, 1.5 I 21, 1.5 IV 16, 1.5 IV 17, 1.15 II 16, 1.16 V 39, 1.17 VI 5, 1.19 IV 54, 1.96 5, 1.133 9, 3.1 27, 3.1 29, 3.1 31, 4.280 14, 5.9 I 15
ks[2.31 34, 4.142 6, 4.178 14, 7.68 5
]ks 1.4 VI 59, 4.189 1
k]s 3.1 20
]xks 7.50 14
ksa 1.6 VI 28, 1.100 7, 1.100 12, 1.100 18, 1.100 23, 1.100 29, 1.100 34, 1.100 39, 1.100 44, 1.100 49, 1.100 56, 1.123 6
ksa[1.57 5, 4.496 4
ksank 1.12 I 18
ksat 1.3 II 21, 1.3 II 36, 1.3 II 36, 1.4 VI 52, 1.151 3
ksi 1.2 IV 7, 1.3 IV 2, 1.5 VI 12, 1.6 V 5, 1.16 VI 23, 1.161 13
ksi[1.10 III 13
k[si 1.1 IV 24
ks<i>h 1.161 20
ksih 1.2 IV 12, 1.2 IV 20
k]sih 7.69 2
ksiy 2.31 15
kśu 1.53 7
k]śu 1.57 4
ksu 1.3 VI 15, 1.4 V 46, 1.4 VIII 12, 1.5 II 15, 1.106 28
ksu[1.1 III 1
k]su 1.50 2
ksb/d/u[4.297 7
ksd 4.69 II 18, 4.286 9
ksd[4.332 18
ksb/d/u[4.297 7
ksdm 4.99 16, 4.125 8, 4.126 15, 4.286 1
ksh 1.3 V 34, 1.4 IV 46, 1.12 II 28, 1.17 VI 15
ksyn 4.70 9
ksl 1.3 II 16, 1.3 III 33, 1.4 II 17, 1.19 II 46
]ksl 4.182 26
]ksl/ṣ[7.50 9
kslh 1.3 III 35, 1.17 VI 11
ks]lh 1.4 II 19
kslk 1.16 VI 50
kslm 1.163 4, 4.182 9
ksln 4.12 3, 4.122 5
kśm 1.39 9
ksm 1.5 VI 5, 1.16 III 4, 1.41 19, 4.385 2
ksmh 1.17 I 31
ksmy 1.17 II 21
ksmk 1.17 II 4
kśmm 4.345 2, 4.345 4, 4.400 7, 4.400 16, 4.269 20(cor.), 4.269 30(cor.), 4.691 4, 4.691 5
ksmm 4.608 2, 4.747 2
kśmn 4.269 4
kśmn 4.269 20, 4.269 30 cor. kśmm
k]śmm 4.225 17, 4.345 9, 4.400 12
ksn 4.10 5, 4.704 1
]ksn 4.368 7
ksp 1.3 III 46, 1.4 I 25, 1.4 I 26, 1.4 I 31, 1.4 II 26, 1.4 II 27, 1.4 IV 6, 1.4

IV 10, 1.4 V 15, 1.4 V 18, 1.4 V 32, 1.4 V 33, 1.4 V 38, 1.4 VI 34, 1.4 VI 37, 1.14 III 22, 1.14 III 34, 1.14 VI 17, 1.16 I 44, 1.17 VI 17, 1.19 II 4, 1.22 I 14, 1.24 20, 1.43 12, 1.50 11, 1.90 3, 1.105 22, 1.112 4, 1.112 12, 1.164 4, 1.168 3, 1.168 9, 1.172 21, 2.26 21, 2.49 8, 2.70 19, 2.81 24, 3.1 31, 3.4 14, 3.4 18, 3.9 9, 3.9 16, 3.10 2, 3.10 3, 3.10 4, 3.10 6, 3.10 13, 3.10 15, 3.10 17, 3.10 19, 3.10 21, 4.47 6, 4.68 74, 4.99 14, 4.123 1, 4.123 4, 4.123 6, 4.123 7, 4.123 11, 4.123 12, 4.132 3, 4.132 6, 4.135 1, 4.156 2, 4.156 6, 4.158 1, 4.183 II 22, 4.197 9, 4.197 18, 4.197 19, 4.199 4, 4.219 1, 4.225 12, 4.226 1, 4.235 2, 4.240 3, 4.240 5, 4.258 4, 4.258 8, 4.258 11, 4.265 3, 4.265 4, 4.274 3, 4.276 14, 4.280 1, 4.280 3, 4.280 6, 4.290 6, 4.290 15, 4.290 17, 4.337 5, 4.337 8, 4.337 10, 4.337 11, 4.337 13, 4.337 15, 4.337 17, 4.337 19, 4.337 20, 4.337 21, 4.337 22, 4.337 23, 4.337 27, 4.338 11, 4.338 14, 4.338 17, 4.341 2, 4.341 6, 4.341 8, 4.341 11, 4.341 22, 4.369 2, 4.369 4, 4.369 5, 4.369 7, 4.369 10, 4.369 11, 4.369 13, 4.369 15, 4.369 17, 4.373 1, 4.373 7, 4.386 1, 4.386 5, 4.386 14, 4.386 19, 4.389 5, 4.609 32, 4.632 2, 4.632 5, 4.632 19, 4.658 2, 4.682 6, 4.682 7, 4.682 9, 4.682 10, 4.682 11, 4.682 12, 4.721 8, 4.738 2, 4.745 7, 4.751 2, 4.755 1, 4.771 2, 4.778 2, 4.778 9, 4.778 13, 4.778 16, 4.779 3, 4.779 10, 4.781 7, 4.782 1, 4.782 19, 4.782 23, 4.782 28, 4.791 1, 4.791 6, 4.791 9, 4.791 12, 4.791 15, 4.791 17, 4.792 1, 4.792 3, 4.792 5, 4.792 7, 5.11 7

ksp[1.5 IV 17, 1.139 18, 4.23 7, 4.262 3, 4.262 7

ks[p 2.42 20, 4.262 5, 4.398 7, 4.488 1, 4.598 1

k[sp 1.14 VI 4, 2.25 6, 3.8 11, 4.121 2, 4.268 6, 4.268 7, 4.333 9, 4.337 28, 4.597 1, 6.20 1

]ksp 4.111 16, 4.176 9, 4.249 2, 4.258 10, 4.594 1, 4.608 1, 4.758 2

k]sp 4.197 12, 4.197 23, 4.197 27, 4.262 4, 4.262 6, 4.262 9, 4.699 5, 4.735 2, 4.758 4, 4.781 4

ks]p 4.699 2, 7.135 4

]ksp[4.197 30

[[ksp]] 4.709 8, 4.709 10

ksph 4.132 5, 4.158 11, 4.158 13, 4.158 16, 4.158 18, 4.333 3, 4.341 4, 4.376 1

]ksph 4.376 2

ksphm 2.17 2, 4.158 5, 4.779 4

k]sphn 4.707 23

kspy 1.1 IV 21, 2.21 15

kspm 1.14 IV 42(!), 4.212 1

]ksl/ṣ[7.50 9

kśt 1.86 24

kst 1.19 I 36, 1.19 I 47, 1.151 6, 2.3 12, 4.206 5

kst[1.168 7, 2.27 2

kʿy[4.694 1

]kʿsp 4.197 6

xk/wʿr 1.70 11

kp 1.3 II 10, 1.3 II 11, 1.13 6, 1.24 35, 1.157 10

kp[4.126 32

k/rpil 4.194 12

kpḫ 4.387 18

kpyn 4.759 3

kpln 4.412 II 12

kpltn 4.71 III 7

kpsln 4.786 7

kpslnm 4.274 6

kp]slnm 4.274 1

kpr 1.3 II 2, 1.7 15, 1.7 35, 2.72 43

kprm 4.611 8

kprt 4.767 2

kpt 1.3 II 13, 1.70 18, 1.82 17, 1.128 18

kptr 1.3 VI 14

kp]tr 1.1 III 1

kpt]r 1.2 III 2

kptrh 1.100 46

kpṯ 1.108 8, 4.689 6

]kṣ 4.9 2

]kṣḥṯ[1.75 8

]kb/ṣ 2.37 13

]kṣn 3.6 8

kr 1.123 9, 1.175 3

kr 1.114 14 lg. w l
kr[1.103 25, 4.8 3, 6.64 1
]kr 4.234 4, 7.152 3
]kr[4.741 1
krx[4.64 IV 12
kk/r[4.434 4
kran 4.41 6
kri/hl 1.42 8
krb 4.357 22
krb/d[7.189 2
krd 4.48 2, 4.68 3, 4.143 3, 4.365 17, 4.380 13, 4.610 26, 4.693 29
krd[4.119 7
kr[d 4.685 5
k[rd 4.6 2, 4.693 14, 4.693 46
k]rd 3.7 14
krb/d[7.189 2
kri/hl 1.42 8
krw 4.188 4, 4.261 16, 4.385 1
krwn 3.10 18, 4.35 II 20, 4.69 III 14, 4.77 15, 4.85 3, 4.97 2, 4.128 10, 4.141 I 11, 4.175 3, 4.269 19, 4.281 12, 4.282 9, 4.340 4, 4.356 5, 4.356 11, 4.370 19, 4.374 11, 4.379 6, 4.609 3, 4.609 9, 4.609 36, 4.754 12, 4.791 14
krwn[1.87 60
k]rwn 4.183 II 11
kr]wn 4.367 4
krws 4.655 2
krwt 4.147 14
krzn 4.102 1, 4.391 11, 4.616 6
krz[n] 4.357 28
kry 1.12 I 23, 4.371 11, 4.647 5
kryn 4.110 5
krk 4.390 8, 4.611 12, 4.625 2, 4.625 6, 4.625 8, 4.625 10, 4.625 16, 4.625 18
krk[4.390 13
k]rk 4.625 12, 4.625 14
krkm 4.184 3
krlnm 4.780 14
krm 1.4 VI 47, 1.92 23, 1.92 24, 4.141 III 17, 4.244 5, 4.244 6, 4.244 7, 4.244 8, 4.244 9, 4.244 11, 4.244 12, 4.244 12, 4.244 13, 4.244 14, 4.244 14, 4.244 15, 4.244 16, 4.244 17, 4.244 17, 4.244 20, 4.244 23, 4.244 24, 4.244 26, 4.244 27, 4.244 28, 4.244 29*, 4.282 6, 4.282 8, 4.282 12, 4.292 1, 4.424 2, 4.424 4, 4.424 5, 4.424 23, 4.609 12
krm[4.254 5
kr[m 4.244 15, 4.244 30, 4.424 21, 4.642 3
krt/m[4.391 15
k]rmh 3.5 9
krmm 1.19 I 31, 1.24 22, 2.61 10, 4.244 10, 4.244 11, 4.244 19, 4.244 25
krm[m 4.244 22
k[rmm 4.244 4
krmn 4.35 I 5, 4.232 10, 4.631 12
krmn[4.635 50
krmpy 4.408 4
krmt 4.687 1, 4.692 2, 4.692 4
krn[4.611 25
krny[4.335 14
krs 1.67 3, 4.631 13
krs 1.5 I 4 lg. k r<k>s?
krsi 4.225 17
krśu 4.225 16
krśnm 5.22 23
krsnm 4.279 3
krsnm[4.123 13
krʿ 1.103 15, 1.103 28
kr[ʿ 1.103 27
krpn 1.1 IV 10, 1.3 I 14, 1.5 IV 18, 1.15 II 17, 1.17 VI 6, 1.17 VI 6
kr[pn 1.16 V 40
krpnm 1.3 I 11, 1.4 III 43, 1.4 IV 37
krp[nm 1.4 VI 58
kr[pnm 1.5 IV 15
krr 4.139 9
krr[4.75 I 7
kr{k}\t 1.14 VI 33f
krt 1.14 I 1, 1.14 I 10, 1.14 I 11, 1.14 I 22, 1.14 I 38, 1.14 I 39, 1.14 II 7, 1.14 II 27, 1.14 III 20, 1.14 III 26, 1.14 III 28, 1.14 III 48, 1.14 III 50, 1.14 IV 8, 1.14 IV 37, 1.14 VI 9, 1.14 VI 15, 1.14 VI 16, 1.14 VI 40, 1.15 I 4, 1.15 I 8, 1.15 II 8, 1.15 II 19, 1.15 II 21, 1.15 III 2, 1.15 III 23, 1.15 IV 21, 1.15 V 12, 1.15 V 19, 1.15 VI 5, 1.15 VI 6, 1.15 VI 8, 1.16 I 1, 1.16 I 10, 1.16 I 21, 1.16 I 24, 1.16 I 57, 1.16 II 24, 1.16 II 48, 1.16

III 17, 1.16 VI 3, 1.16 VI 15, 1.16 VI 22, 1.16 VI 41, 1.16 VI 54
kr[t 1.16 II 20, 1.103 32
k[rt 1.14 V 31, 1.15 III 28, 1.16 II 23
]krt 1.15 IV 28
k]rt 1.14 V 17, 1.15 V 17, 1.16 I 60
kr]t 1.14 V 45, 1.15 V 22
k]\rt 1.16 V 42f
krt/m[4.391 15
krty 4.371 18, 4.617 20, 4.617 39, 4.760 1
krtn 1.16 I 39
kš 1.22 I 15, 1.151 9
kš[4.258 8, 7.42 3
kšpm 1.169 9
kšt 4.707 15
kt 1.4 I 30, 1.4 I 31, 1.13 10, 1.13 12, 4.141 II 1, 4.230 9, 4.425 5, 4.710 13, 4.734 12, 4.786 13, 4.786 14, 7.142 8
kt[2.47 5, 7.46 7, 7.142 1, 7.142 2
]kt 1.147 8, 1.153 4, 4.113 7, 4.463 2
]kt[4.118 11, 4.196 4, 4.386 17
]ktx[6.32 1
]xkt 2.35 11, 7.222 9
]xktx[7.57 4
]k/rt 1.92 23, 2.31 5, 2.76 6, 4.182 34, 4.382 13
ktb 2.19 9
kt[y] 1.131 4
ktkt 4.33 16
ktl 4.394 6
k]tl 4.56 3
ktln 4.69 VI 14, 4.93 I 15
ktm 7.222 11
ktmn 4.15 8, 4.93 IV 14, 4.224 8, 4.224 11, 4.571 5
ktmsm 1.6 I 52
ktn 1.43 4, 2.79 10, 3.1 27, 3.1 29, 3.1 31, 4.132 4, 4.284 1, 4.607 30, 4.779 7
kt[n 3.1 21
kt]n 3.1 33
ktnm 4.132 6
ktnt 3.1 21, 4.132 2, 4.203 7, 4.206 1, 4.337 18, 4.363 1, 4.402 4, 4.738 3, 4.771 2
ktġ[4.335 18
ktp 1.2 IV 14, 1.2 IV 16, 1.6 I 14, 1.6 V 2, 1.114 11, 1.114 13
ktpm 1.2 I 42
ktr 4.141 II 7
ktry 4.638 6
ktrm 4.126 29
ktš 4.778 15, 4.782 22
ktt 4.203 14, 4.288 9, 4.382 28, 4.721 4
]xktt 2.33 17
ktṯ 1.107 41 lg. kmṯ
kṯ 1.101 8, 1.148 22, 1.148 22, 4.61 4, 4.635 58
kṯ[1.130 20, 4.116 22, 4.754 1
]kṯ 1.5 III 29, 4.236 6
]xkṯ 4.82 8
kṯan 4.40 8
kṯwn 4.339 2
kṯḫd 1.128 8
kṯy 1.39 19, 1.102 14, 4.7 2, 4.63 III 39, 4.170 16, 4.617 23
k⊕y 1.123 7
kṯkym 4.319 2, 6.3 2
kṯkn 4.336 5
kṯkn[4.245 I 12
k]ṯkn[4.574 4
kṯl 4.309 9
kṯly 4.55 10, 4.611 5
kṯm 4.60 6, 4.707 8
k[ṯm 4.60 8
]kṯm 4.60 8
kṯ]m 4.707 6
kṯn 1.92 28, 4.335 24, 4.694 4, 4.785 15
kṯpm 1.107 48
kṯ<r> 1.3 VI 18
kṯr 1.1 III 7, 1.1 III 17, 1.2 III 8, 1.2 IV 7, 1.2 IV 11, 1.2 IV 18, 1.3 VI 21, 1.4 V 41, 1.4 V 44, 1.4 V 58, 1.4 VI 14, 1.4 VII 15, 1.4 VII 16, 1.4 VII 20, 1.4 VII 21, 1.6 VI 52, 1.6 VI 53, 1.17 V 10, 1.17 V 17, 1.17 V 23, 1.17 V 25, 1.17 V 31, 1.17 VI 24, 1.43 8, 1.87 59, 1.100 46, 1.102 5, 1.105 12, 1.108 5, 1.118 15, 1.123 28, 1.136 8, 1.148 6, 1.148 30
kṯ[r 1.1 III 4
k[ṯ]r 1.92 17
k[ṯr 1.4 V 50, 1.4 VI 1, 1.4 VI 3
]kṯr 1.2 III 7

k]ṯr 1.15 II 5
kṯ]r 1.17 VI 10, 1.107 43
k\[ṯr] 1.17 VI 13f
[[kṯr]] 1.39 14(?)
k⊖r 1.123 9
kṯrm 1.6 VI 49, 1.14 I 16
kṯrm[1.2 III 20
kṯrmlk 4.86 24, 4.188 9, 4.609 32
k]ṯrmlk 4.658 49
kṯrn 4.313 10
kṯrt 1.10 II 30, 1.10 II 40, 1.11 6, 1.17 II 26, 1.17 II 30, 1.17 II 33, 1.17 II 35, 1.17 II 37, 1.17 II 40, 1.24 15, 1.24 50, 1.118 12, 1.148 25, 4.412 II 5
kṯr[t 1.24 11, 1.24 40, 1.148 5
kṯr]t 1.47 13
kṯ\rt 1.17 II 29f
k]\ṯrt 1.24 5f(!)
kṯt 4.60 4, 4.161 7, 4.402 10(?), 6.12 2
kṯt[4.594 4
]kṯtx 1.35 8
kṯ<t>ġlm 4.643 25
kṯtġlm 4.310 2, 4.643 26

L

{l} 4.44 24, 4.163 15

<l> 1.40 34, 4.143 2, 4.636 4

l 1.1 II 10, 1.1 II 20, 1.1 III 4, 1.1 III 8, 1.1 III 15, 1.1 III 19, 1.1 III 21, 1.1 III 24, 1.1 IV 2, 1.1 IV 3, 1.1 IV 7, 1.1 IV 16, 1.1 IV 24, 1.1 V 21, 1.1 V 27(*bis*), 1.1 V 28, 1.2 I 16, 1.2 I 19, 1.2 I 20, 1.2 I 20(?), 1.2 I 21, 1.2 I 23(*bis*), 1.2 I 25, 1.2 I 27, 1.2 I 29, 1.2 I 30, 1.2 I 31(*bis*), 1.2 I 33, 1.2 I 45, 1.2 III 2, 1.2 III 4, 1.2 III 11, 1.2 III 16(*bis*), 1.2 III 17(*bis*), 1.2 III 18, 1.2 III 21, 1.2 III 22, 1.2 IV 2, 1.2 IV 3, 1.2 IV 5(*bis*), 1.2 IV 6, 1.2 IV 7, 1.2 IV 8(*bis*), 1.2 IV 12, 1.2 IV 13, 1.2 IV 17(*ter*), 1.2 IV 20(*bis*), 1.2 IV 23, 1.2 IV 26, 1.2 IV 28, 1.2 IV 29, 1.2 IV 32, 1.2 IV 33, 1.2 IV 34, 1.2 IV 35, 1.2 IV 37, 1.3 I 6, 1.3 I 14, 1.3 I 15, 1.3 II 12, 1.3 II 17, 1.3 II 18, 1.3 II 19, 1.3 II 21, 1.3 II 22(*bis*), 1.3 II 36, 1.3 II 37(*bis*), 1.3 III 5(*bis*), 1.3 III 9, 1.3 III 11, 1.3 III 12, 1.3 III 16, 1.3 III 17, 1.3 III 26, 1.3 III 27(*bis*), 1.3 III 37, 1.3 III 38(*bis*), 1.3 III 39, 1.3 III 40, 1.3 IV 2, 1.3 IV 3(*bis*), 1.3 IV 4(*bis*), 1.3 IV 5, 1.3 IV 6(*bis*), 1.3 IV 10(*bis*), 1.3 IV 18, 1.3 IV 24, 1.3 IV 25, 1.3 IV 30, 1.3 IV 31, 1.3 IV 34, 1.3 IV 35, 1.3 IV 37, 1.3 IV 40, 1.3 IV 47, 1.3 V 1, 1.3 V 3(*bis*), 1.3 V 15, 1.3 V 29, 1.3 V 35, 1.3 V 38, 1.3 VI 10, 1.3 VI 11, 1.3 VI 18, 1.3 VI 21, 1.3 VI 22, 1.4 I 23, 1.4 I 27, 1.4 I 28, 1.4 I 43, 1.4 II 2, 1.4 II 8, 1.4 II 9, 1.4 II 29, 1.4 III 21, 1.4 IV 14, 1.4 IV 15, 1.4 IV 17, 1.4 IV 20, 1.4 IV 25, 1.4 IV 29, 1.4 IV 47, 1.4 IV 50, 1.4 IV 62, 1.4 V 3, 1.4 V 4, 1.4 V 5, 1.4 V 9, 1.4 V 12(*bis*), 1.4 V 22, 1.4 V 41, 1.4 V 42, 1.4 V 47, 1.4 V 59, 1.4 V 60, 1.4 VI 2, 1.4 VI 4, 1.4 VI 15, 1.4 VI 18, 1.4 VI 19, 1.4 VI 34, 1.4 VI 35, 1.4 VII 4, 1.4 VII 7, 1.4 VII 8, 1.4 VII 9, 1.4 VII 23(*bis*), 1.4 VII 25, 1.4 VII 42, 1.4 VII 45, 1.4 VII 46, 1.4 VII 52, 1.4 VIII 6, 1.4 VIII 16, 1.4 VIII 26, 1.4 VIII 30, 1.4 VIII 31, 1.5 I 6, 1.5 I 9, 1.5 I 10, 1.5 II 2, 1.5 II 3, 1.5 II 8, 1.5 II 9, 1.5 II 11, 1.5 II 13, 1.5 II 14, 1.5 III 6, 1.5 III 7, 1.5 III 12, 1.5 III 21, 1.5 IV 2, 1.5 V 14, 1.5 V 20, 1.5 V 21, 1.5 V 25, 1.5 VI 6, 1.5 VI 7, 1.5 VI 8(*bis*), 1.5 VI 12, 1.5 VI 13(*bis*), 1.5 VI 14, 1.5 VI 15, 1.5 VI 16, 1.5 VI 27, 1.5 VI 28(*bis*), 1.5 VI 30, 1.6 I 1, 1.6 I 11, 1.6 I 14, 1.6 I 31, 1.6 I 32, 1.6 I 36, 1.6 I 44, 1.6 I 45, 1.6 I 50, 1.6 I 51, 1.6 I 58, 1.6 I 59, 1.6 I 60, 1.6 I 62, 1.6 I 64, 1.6 II 7, 1.6 II 8, 1.6 II 14, 1.6 II 16, 1.6 II 17, 1.6 II 19, 1.6 II 26, 1.6 II 27, 1.6 II 28, 1.6 II 29, 1.6 II 35, 1.6 II 36, 1.6 II 37, 1.6 III 15, 1.6 III 22, 1.6 III 23, 1.6 III 24, 1.6 IV 7, 1.6 IV 22, 1.6 IV 23, 1.6 V 4, 1.6 V 5, 1.6 V 6(*bis*), 1.6 V 7(*ter*), 1.6 V 8, 1.6 V 22, 1.6 VI 23, 1.6 VI 24, 1.6 VI 27, 1.6 VI 28, 1.6 VI 29, 1.6 VI 34, 1.6 VI 42, 1.6 VI 43, 1.6 VI 44, 1.7 5, 1.7 25, 1.7 28, 1.7 34, 1.8 II 3, 1.8 II 5, 1.9 12, 1.9 19, 1.10 I 3, 1.10 I 8, 1.10 I 9, 1.10 I 17, 1.10 I 18, 1.10 II 8, 1.10 II 17, 1.10 II 18, 1.10 II 31, 1.10 III 2, 1.10 III 3, 1.10 III 13, 1.10 III 14, 1.10 III 15, 1.10 III 16, 1.10 III 21, 1.10 III 32, 1.10 III 35, 1.10 III 36, 1.11 3, 1.12 I 14, 1.12 I 16, 1.12 II 27, 1.12 II 48, 1.12 II 49, 1.12 II 56, 1.13 6, 1.13 7, 1.13 8, 1.13 9, 1.13 15, 1.13 22, 1.13 31, 1.14 I 1, 1.14 I 12, 1.14 II 20, 1.14 II 21, 1.14 II 23, 1.14 II 27, 1.14 II 28, 1.14 II 29, 1.14 II 39, 1.14 II 40, 1.14 II 48, 1.14 III 4, 1.14 III 5, 1.14 III 15, 1.14 III 16, 1.14 III 17, 1.14 III 18, 1.14

III 28, 1.14 III 29, 1.14 III 48, 1.14 III 49, 1.14 IV 3, 1.14 IV 6, 1.14 IV 9(*bis*), 1.14 IV 10, 1.14 IV 17, 1.14 IV 18, 1.14 IV 27, 1.14 IV 28, 1.14 IV 34, 1.14 IV 35, 1.14 IV 47, 1.14 V 7, 1.14 V 8, 1.14 V 9, 1.14 V 13, 1.14 V 19, 1.14 V 45, 1.14 VI 14, 1.14 VI 15, 1.14 VI 33, 1.14 VI 34, 1.14 VI 36, 1.14 VI 37, 1.15 I 5, 1.15 I 6, 1.15 II 10, 1.15 II 13, 1.15 II 14, 1.15 II 15, 1.15 III 18, 1.15 III 19, 1.15 IV 2, 1.15 IV 23, 1.15 IV 27, 1.15 V 6, 1.15 V 10, 1.15 V 18, 1.15 VI 1, 1.15 VI 4(*bis*), 1.15 VI 5, 1.16 I 1, 1.16 I 4, 1.16 I 18, 1.16 I 23, 1.16 I 31, 1.16 I 38, 1.16 I 45, 1.16 I 52, 1.16 I 54, 1.16 II 29, 1.16 II 31, 1.16 II 41, 1.16 II 44, 1.16 III 3, 1.16 III 4, 1.16 III 5, 1.16 III 6, 1.16 III 7, 1.16 III 8, 1.16 III 9, 1.16 III 13, 1.16 IV 10, 1.16 IV 13, 1.16 IV 14, 1.16 IV 16, 1.16 V 24, 1.16 V 25, 1.16 VI 11, 1.16 VI 12, 1.16 VI 16, 1.16 VI 22, 1.16 VI 23, 1.16 VI 24(*bis*), 1.16 VI 27, 1.16 VI 33, 1.16 VI 34, 1.16 VI 37, 1.16 VI 38, 1.16 VI 41, 1.16 VI 45, 1.16 VI 46, 1.16 VI 47, 1.16 VI 48, 1.16 VI 49, 1.16 VI 52, 1.16 VI 53, 1.17 I 23(*bis*), 1.17 I 24, 1.17 I 27, 1.17 I 28, 1.17 I 38, 1.17 II 2, 1.17 II 11, 1.17 II 17, 1.17 II 25, 1.17 II 29, 1.17 V 15, 1.17 V 17, 1.17 V 18, 1.17 V 23, 1.17 V 24, 1.17 V 27, 1.17 V 32(*bis*), 1.17 VI 8, 1.17 VI 15, 1.17 VI 24(*bis*), 1.17 VI 25, 1.17 VI 26, 1.17 VI 34, 1.17 VI 37, 1.17 VI 42, 1.17 VI 43, 1.18 I 20, 1.18 IV 4, 1.18 IV 12, 1.18 IV 13, 1.18 IV 19(*bis*), 1.18 IV 24, 1.18 IV 27, 1.18 IV 29, 1.18 IV 30, 1.18 IV 41, 1.19 I 2, 1.19 I 13, 1.19 I 16(*bis*), 1.19 I 42, 1.19 I 49, 1.19 II 2, 1.19 II 6, 1.19 II 10, 1.19 II 11, 1.19 II 26, 1.19 II 29, 1.19 II 32, 1.19 II 33, 1.19 II 38, 1.19 II 41, 1.19 III 7, 1.19 III 35, 1.19 III 40, 1.19 III 50, 1.19 IV 1, 1.19 IV 5, 1.19 IV 6, 1.19 IV 9, 1.19 IV 11, 1.19 IV 12, 1.19 IV 13(*bis*), 1.19 IV 14(*bis*), 1.19 IV 15, 1.19 IV 16, 1.19 IV 26, 1.19 IV 27, 1.19 IV 29, 1.19 IV 32, 1.19 IV 37, 1.19 IV 48, 1.19 IV 50(*bis*), 1.19 IV 60, 1.19 IV 62, 1.20 II 4, 1.20 II 6, 1.21 II 4, 1.21 II 7, 1.21 II 12, 1.21 V 1, 1.22 I 15(*bis*), 1.22 II 6, 1.22 II 11, 1.22 II 23, 1.23 3, 1.23 5, 1.23 30, 1.23 31, 1.23 36, 1.23 39, 1.23 41(*bis*), 1.23 44, 1.23 45, 1.23 48(*bis*), 1.23 52, 1.23 54(*bis*), 1.23 57(*bis*), 1.23 59, 1.23 62, 1.23 62, 1.23 63, 1.23 64, 1.23 66(*bis*), 1.23 75(?), 1.24 6, 1.24 8, 1.24 9, 1.24 12, 1.24 13, 1.24 15, 1.24 19, 1.24 24, 1.24 25, 1.24 36, 1.25 3, 1.27 3, 1.27 8, 1.27 11, 1.27 12, 1.39 2, 1.39 12, 1.39 19, 1.39 21, 1.39 22, 1.40 23(*bis*), 1.40 25(*bis*), 1.40 32(*bis*), 1.40 33(*bis*), 1.40 34, 1.40 35, 1.40 40, 1.40 41, 1.40 42, 1.40 43, 1.41 5, 1.41 25(*bis*), 1.41 26, 1.41 27, 1.41 33, 1.41 34(*bis*), 1.41 35, 1.41 36, 1.41 40, 1.41 42, 1.41 43, 1.41 49, 1.41 50, 1.43 8(*bis*), 1.43 11(*bis*), 1.43 13, 1.43 14(*bis*), 1.43 17, 1.43 18, 1.43 20, 1.43 21, 1.43 26, 1.46 2, 1.46 8(*bis*), 1.46 9, 1.46 13, 1.48 5, 1.48 15, 1.48 16, 1.48 17, 1.49 2, 1.49 3, 1.49 4, 1.49 6, 1.49 9, 1.50 3, 1.50 4(*bis*), 1.50 5, 1.50 7, 1.67 19, 1.69 10, 1.71 9, 1.72 12, 1.73 2, 1.73 4, 1.76 8, 1.76 9, 1.76 10, 1.76 11, 1.79 2, 1.79 5, 1.79 6, 1.79 7, 1.81 1, 1.81 2, 1.81 3, 1.81 4, 1.81 5, 1.81 6, 1.81 7, 1.81 8, 1.81 9, 1.81 10, 1.81 18, 1.81 19, 1.81 20, 1.81 21, 1.81 22, 1.82 2(*bis*), 1.82 5(*bis*), 1.82 7, 1.82 10, 1.82 26(*bis*), 1.82 27, 1.82 32, 1.82 37, 1.82 39, 1.82 43(*bis*), 1.83 8, 1.83 10, 1.83 13, 1.84 35, 1.85 9(*bis*), 1.86 12, 1.86 13, 1.87 2, 1.87 5, 1.87 27, 1.87 28(*bis*), 1.87 29, 1.87 36, 1.87 37(*bis*), 1.87 38, 1.87 39, 1.87 44, 1.87 56, 1.88 3(*bis*), 1.89 4, 1.90 6, 1.90 7, 1.90 19, 1.90 21, 1.90 22, 1.92 7, 1.92 9, 1.92 13, 1.92 14, 1.92 30, 1.92 34, 1.92 35, 1.92 39, 1.94 31, 1.96 4, 1.96 5, 1.96 9,

1.96 10, 1.96 11, 1.96 12, 1.96 13, 1.100 2, 1.100 8, 1.100 14, 1.100 19, 1.100 25, 1.100 30, 1.100 35, 1.100 40, 1.100 45, 1.100 51, 1.100 57, 1.100 63, 1.100 67, 1.100 68, 1.101 17, 1.103 13, 1.103 24, 1.103 25, 1.103 29, 1.103 43, 1.103 49, 1.103 52, 1.103 54, 1.104 24, 1.105 4, 1.105 7, 1.105 8, 1.105 12, 1.105 16, 1.105 22, 1.105 24(*bis*), 1.105 25, 1.105 26, 1.106 1, 1.106 2, 1.106 6, 1.106 11, 1.106 16, 1.106 24, 1.106 26, 1.106 27, 1.106 32, 1.107 6(*ter*), 1.107 14, 1.107 19, 1.107 32, 1.107 34, 1.107 35(*bis*), 1.107 37, 1.107 44, 1.107 45(*bis*), 1.108 18, 1.108 20(*bis*), 1.108 23, 1.108 26, 1.109 5, 1.109 7, 1.109 8, 1.109 9, 1.109 10, 1.109 25, 1.109 26, 1.109 29, 1.109 30, 1.109 32, 1.109 34, 1.109 35, 1.111 7, 1.111 17, 1.111 18, 1.111 21, 1.111 23, 1.112 4, 1.112 5, 1.112 13, 1.112 15, 1.112 19, 1.112 24(*bis*), 1.112 28, 1.112 32, 1.113 2, 1.113 4, 1.113 6, 1.114 2, 1.114 7, 1.114 13, 1.114 14(!), 1.114 17, 1.114 18, 1.114 29, 1.115 2, 1.115 3, 1.115 4, 1.115 5, 1.115 9, 1.115 10, 1.115 11, 1.115 12, 1.115 13, 1.116 8, 1.119 2, 1.119 6, 1.119 7, 1.119 8, 1.119 11, 1.119 12, 1.119 13, 1.119 14, 1.119 15, 1.119 16, 1.119 17, 1.119 21, 1.119 27, 1.119 28, 1.119 34, 1.119 35, 1.119 36, 1.122 2, 1.124 15(*bis*), 1.127 12, 1.127 24, 1.130 3, 1.130 4, 1.130 5, 1.130 7, 1.130 9, 1.130 10, 1.130 11, 1.130 12, 1.130 13, 1.130 15, 1.130 17, 1.130 19(*bis*), 1.130 20, 1.130 22, 1.130 23, 1.130 24, 1.130 25, 1.130 29, 1.132 16, 1.134 8, 1.134 9, 1.134 11, 1.136 3, 1.136 8, 1.136 11, 1.139 11, 1.140 11, 1.141 1, 1.142 2, 1.144 3, 1.151 10, 1.151 10, 1.151 11(*bis*), 1.151 12, 1.151 13, 1.161 15, 1.161 20, 1.162 6, 1.162 7, 1.162 8, 1.162 9, 1.162 10, 1.162 11, 1.162 12, 1.162 14, 1.162 15, 1.162 16, 1.162 19, 1.162 21, 1.163 1, 1.163 7, 1.163 11, 1.164 2, 1.164 3, 1.164 6, 1.164 7, 1.164 9, 1.165 2, 1.166 12, 1.166 24, 1.168 11, 1.168 13, 1.169 5, 1.169 6, 1.169 14, 1.169 14, 1.169 15, 1.169 16, 1.169 17, 1.170 9, 1.170 10, 1.171 3, 1.171 5, 1.172 18, 1.172 22, 1.172 26, 1.173 2, 1.174 2, 1.176 7, 1.176 22, 1.176 23, 1.176 25, 1.176 28, 2.2 3, 2.2 5, 2.2 6(*bis*), 2.3 5, 2.3 14, 2.4 1, 2.4 19, 2.5 1, 2.6 2, 2.6 3, 2.10 2, 2.10 5, 2.10 6, 2.11 1, 2.11 5, 2.11 18, 2.12 1, 2.12 6, 2.12 15, 2.13 1, 2.13 5, 2.13 6, 2.13 16, 2.14 2, 2.14 13, 2.14 14, 2.14 18, 2.14 19, 2.15 2, 2.15 3, 2.15 6, 2.16 2, 2.16 8, 2.17 1, 2.17 3, 2.19 1, 2.19 12, 2.21 8, 2.21 11, 2.21 17, 2.21 18, 2.23 4, 2.23 17, 2.23 19, 2.23 21(*bis*), 2.24 1, 2.24 5, 2.26 3, 2.26 6, 2.26 17, 2.28 2(?), 2.30 1, 2.30 4, 2.30 19, 2.31 42, 2.31 47, 2.31 49, 2.31 53, 2.31 63, 2.31 66, 2.33 9, 2.33 16, 2.33 24, 2.33 26, 2.33 28, 2.33 29, 2.33 39, 2.34 2, 2.35 11, 2.35 15, 2.36 10, 2.36 11, 2.38 1, 2.39 2, 2.39 5, 2.39 9, 2.39 10, 2.39 11, 2.39 14, 2.39 16, 2.40 1, 2.41 18, 2.42 1, 2.42 4, 2.42 6, 2.42 7(*bis*), 2.42 8(*bis*), 2.44 1, 2.45 11, 2.45 14, 2.45 18, 2.45 26(*bis*), 2.45 29, 2.46 2, 2.47 3, 2.47 4, 2.47 14, 2.49 2, 2.50 16, 2.50 19, 2.61 1, 2.61 9, 2.63 7, 2.63 10, 2.64 1, 2.64 6, 2.64 9, 2.64 13, 2.68 1, 2.68 4, 2.68 17, 2.70 1, 2.70 6, 2.70 8, 2.70 26, 2.70 27, 2.70 28, 2.70 29, 2.71 2, 2.72 19, 2.72 20, 2.72 28, 2.72 31, 2.73 6, 2.73 13, 2.75 1, 2.75 5, 2.77 14, 2.78 2, 2.81 5, 2.81 7(*bis*), 2.81 8, 2.81 9, 2.82 1, 2.82 2, 2.82 7, 3.1 9, 3.1 17, 3.1 19, 3.1 25, 3.1 28, 3.1 30, 3.1 32, 3.1 38, 3.1 39, 3.2 1, 3.2 13, 3.4 1, 3.4 19, 3.5 1, 3.5 12, 3.5 13, 3.5 17, 3.8 14, 3.9 14, 4.4 7, 4.7 2, 4.7 3, 4.7 4, 4.7 5, 4.7 6, 4.7 7, 4.7 8, 4.7 9, 4.7 10, 4.7 11, 4.7 12, 4.7 13, 4.7 14, 4.7 15, 4.7 16, 4.7 17, 4.7 18, 4.7 19, 4.7 20, 4.11 6, 4.28 7, 4.34 5, 4.34 6, 4.34 7, 4.34 8, 4.43 3, 4.43 4, 4.44 2, 4.44 3,

4.44 4, 4.44 5, 4.44 6, 4.44 7, 4.44 8, 4.44 9, 4.44 11, 4.44 13, 4.44 16, 4.44 17, 4.44 22, 4.44 23, 4.44 24, 4.44 25, 4.44 28, 4.44 28, 4.44 29, 4.44 30, 4.44 31, 4.44 32, 4.52 10, 4.56 5, 4.88 3, 4.88 4, 4.88 5, 4.88 6, 4.88 7, 4.88 8, 4.91 3, 4.110 14, 4.110 16, 4.110 18, 4.110 19, 4.110 20, 4.110 22, 4.120 2, 4.123 6, 4.128 1, 4.128 2, 4.128 3, 4.128 4, 4.128 5, 4.128 6, 4.128 7, 4.128 8, 4.128 9, 4.128 10, 4.128 11, 4.128 12, 4.137 14, 4.139 9, 4.143 4, 4.144 3, 4.144 5, 4.145 6, 4.149 3, 4.149 4, 4.149 6, 4.149 8, 4.149 9, 4.149 11, 4.158 3, 4.158 4, 4.158 5, 4.161 8, 4.163 14, 4.163 16, 4.167 6, 4.168 2, 4.168 3, 4.168 4, 4.168 10, 4.168 12, 4.171 3, 4.173 8, 4.173 10, 4.174 13, 4.175 2, 4.175 3, 4.175 4, 4.175 5, 4.175 6, 4.175 7, 4.175 8, 4.175 10, 4.175 11, 4.175 12(*bis*), 4.175 13, 4.175 14, 4.178 15, 4.179 16, 4.182 3, 4.182 11, 4.182 15, 4.182 18, 4.182 25, 4.182 31, 4.182 34, 4.182 57, 4.182 58, 4.182 60, 4.188 2, 4.188 3, 4.188 4, 4.188 5, 4.188 6, 4.188 7, 4.188 8, 4.188 9, 4.188 10, 4.188 18, 4.188 19, 4.188 20, 4.195 5, 4.195 16, 4.198 5, 4.198 6, 4.201 6, 4.208 6, 4.208 7, 4.208 8, 4.212 2, 4.212 5, 4.213 2, 4.213 5, 4.213 7, 4.213 9, 4.213 10, 4.213 12, 4.213 13, 4.213 15, 4.213 17, 4.213 19, 4.213 23, 4.213 25, 4.213 26, 4.213 27, 4.213 29, 4.213 30, 4.216 1, 4.216 2, 4.216 4, 4.216 5, 4.216 6, 4.216 7, 4.216 8, 4.216 9, 4.216 10, 4.216 11, 4.216 12, 4.219 2, 4.219 5, 4.219 6, 4.219 7, 4.219 8, 4.219 9, 4.219 12, 4.222 18, 4.222 19, 4.222 20, 4.222 21, 4.223 2, 4.223 6, 4.223 7, 4.223 8, 4.226 8, 4.230 1, 4.230 2, 4.230 3, 4.230 6, 4.230 7, 4.230 12, 4.242 3, 4.243 1, 4.243 2, 4.243 3, 4.243 4, 4.243 7, 4.243 8, 4.243 9, 4.243 11(*bis*), 4.243 12, 4.243 13, 4.243 14, 4.243 15, 4.243 24, 4.243 25, 4.243 45(*bis*), 4.243 49, 4.244 9, 4.246 4, 4.246 7, 4.256 2, 4.257 5, 4.259 3, 4.259 4, 4.259 5, 4.259 6, 4.259 7, 4.267 2, 4.268 2, 4.268 3, 4.268 5, 4.268 6, 4.268 7, 4.269 2, 4.269 3, 4.269 4, 4.269 20, 4.269 21, 4.269 22, 4.269 23, 4.269 24, 4.269 25, 4.269 26, 4.269 27, 4.269 28, 4.269 29, 4.272 6, 4.274 1, 4.274 4, 4.274 5, 4.274 6, 4.276 11, 4.276 12, 4.276 13, 4.280 8, 4.280 10, 4.280 12, 4.280 14, 4.284 6, 4.290 18, 4.291 3, 4.337 3, 4.337 6, 4.337 12, 4.337 15, 4.337 24, 4.338 3, 4.338 13, 4.339 1, 4.339 17, 4.341 21, 4.342 5, 4.344 6, 4.348 1, 4.352 2, 4.352 7, 4.352 8, 4.352 9, 4.352 10, 4.356 1, 4.356 2, 4.356 3, 4.356 4, 4.356 5, 4.356 6, 4.356 7, 4.356 8, 4.356 9, 4.356 10, 4.356 11, 4.356 12, 4.356 13, 4.356 14, 4.356 15, 4.361 2, 4.363 6, 4.369 9, 4.369 15, 4.373 1, 4.377 31, 4.377 32, 4.377 33, 4.387 7, 4.387 10, 4.387 12, 4.387 17, 4.387 18, 4.387 20, 4.387 24, 4.387 26, 4.392 1, 4.392 2, 4.392 3, 4.394 5, 4.394 6, 4.396 14, 4.396 17, 4.396 18, 4.396 20, 4.396 21, 4.404 2, 4.405 2, 4.405 3, 4.405 4, 4.405 5, 4.405 6, 4.405 7, 4.405 8, 4.405 9, 4.410 23, 4.410 28, 4.410 29, 4.410 30, 4.410 31, 4.410 32, 4.410 33, 4.410 37, 4.410 38, 4.410 39, 4.411 4, 4.417 7, 4.424 3, 4.424 4, 4.424 5, 4.424 7(!), 4.424 16, 4.424 17, 4.424 18, 4.424 19, 4.424 20, 4.424 21, 4.424 23, 4.425 10, 4.425 11, 4.425 12, 4.425 13, 4.425 14, 4.425 15, 4.425 16, 4.467 2, 4.521 2, 4.534 2, 4.550 3, 4.570 2, 4.579 1, 4.580 1, 4.580 2, 4.595 2, 4.609 51, 4.631 5, 4.631 9, 4.631 12, 4.631 16, 4.631 17, 4.631 20, 4.631 21, 4.631 23, 4.636 3, 4.636 4, 4.636 9, 4.636 18, 4.636 24, 4.636 31, 4.638 3, 4.638 4, 4.638 5, 4.638 6, 4.638 7, 4.658 3, 4.658 7, 4.658 17, 4.658 42, 4.658 45, 4.688 5, 4.692 2, 4.692 3, 4.692 4, 4.692 5, 4.692 6, 4.692 7, 4.705 2, 4.705 4, 4.705 6,

4.705 9, 4.706 1, 4.706 4, 4.706 11, 4.706 12, 4.706 13, 4.710 6, 4.710 10, 4.721 9, 4.728 2, 4.732 2, 4.734 2, 4.734 3, 4.734 4, 4.734 7, 4.746 1, 4.746 2, 4.746 3, 4.746 4, 4.746 5, 4.746 6, 4.746 7, 4.746 8, 4.746 9, 4.746 10, 4.746 11, 4.746 12, 4.746 13, 4.747 7, 4.747 8, 4.747 9, 4.755 4, 4.755 6, 4.755 7, 4.755 8, 4.755 9, 4.755 11, 4.775 2, 4.775 5, 4.775 9, 4.777 6, 4.777 9, 4.779 4, 4.779 5, 4.779 12, 4.781 1, 4.786 3, 4.786 4, 4.786 5, 4.788 4, 4.788 7, 4.790 1, 4.790 16, 4.790 17, 5.2 3, 5.2 5, 5.2 7(*quater*), 5.6 1, 5.7 1, 5.9 I 2, 5.9 I 8(*bis*), 5.9 I 10(*bis*), 5.9 I 13, 5.9 II 2, 5.9 IV 3, 5.10 1, 5.10 3, 5.11 4, 5.11 6, 5.11 7(!), 5.11 8, 5.11 12, 5.11 14, 5.11 17, 5.12 2, 5.13 7, 5.15 1(*bis*), 5.15 3, 5.16 1, 5.17 2, 5.17 5, 5.19 2, 5.20 1, 5.20 4, 5.21 1, 5.24 1, 6.1 1, 6.3 1, 6.11 2, 6.13 2, 6.13 3, 6.14 2, 6.18 1, 6.19 1, 6.29 4, 6.30 1, 6.44 1, 6.49 2, 6.54 2, 6.62 2, 6.70 2, 6.71 1, 7.130 3, 7.135 1, 7.135 2, 7.154 1, 7.184 3, 7.207 5, 7.218 6, 9.530 1

l[1.1 IV 26, 1.5 IV 23, 1.15 VI 1, 1.19 II 31, 1.22 IV 1, 1.73 9, 1.77 4, 1.92 7, 1.104 27, 1.104 29, 1.152 5, 1.152 6, 2.3 2, 2.21 19, 2.34 13, 2.73 7, 2.76 13, 2.77 13, 4.34 3, 4.34 4, 4.139 7, 4.201 8, 4.235 7, 4.256 1, 4.289 8, 4.396 12, 4.400 7, 4.412 II 3, 4.464 1, 4.534 1, 4.555 1, 4.589 3, 4.755 8, 5.11 10, 7.21 3, 7.117 3, 7.120 4, 7.204 2, 7.208 1

]l 1.1 II 4, 1.1 V 12, 1.3 III 3, 1.6 II 1, 1.6 II 2, 1.10 I 16, 1.11 1, 1.18 I 25, 1.28 1, 1.38 2, 1.48 11, 1.62 7, 1.69 10, 1.82 14, 1.82 15, 1.84 8, 1.84 9, 1.94 32, 1.101 12, 1.107 17, 1.107 28, 1.107 53, 1.119 18, 1.137 1, 1.147 12, 1.157 6, 1.168 7, 1.172 5, 1.173 9, 1.175 11, 2.3 12, 2.8 2, 2.18 4, 2.21 12, 2.31 15, 2.32 1, 2.50 20, 2.53 3, 2.54 2, 2.66 3, 2.81 15, 4.14 12, 4.18 2, 4.105 5, 4.111 4, 4.176 7, 4.182 29, 4.182 33, 4.222 3, 4.251 1, 4.262 3, 4.329 6, 4.405 11, 4.482 1, 4.547 3, 4.552 11, 4.557 2, 4.580 3, 4.584 3, 4.603 1, 4.607 9, 4.638 8, 4.642 4, 4.642 5, 4.697 4, 4.706 15, 4.742 10, 4.758 3, 4.764 2, 4.776 3, 5.11 22, 7.16 9, 7.37 3(cor.), 7.47 9, 7.66 2, 7.84 4, 7.86 2, 7.92 1, 7.115 1, 7.137 9, 7.138 7, 7.176 2, 7.194 2, 7.194 3

]l[1.64 23, 1.68 5, 1.156 2, 4.71 IV 1, 4.200 3, 4.214 IV 15, 4.410 3, 4.424 13, 4.432 4, 4.460 1, 4.607 15, 4.661 8, 4.746 14, 7.13 1, 7.117 2, 7.140 13, 7.170 1, 7.180 2

l 1.4 VII 50, 4.44 26 lg. d

l 1.40 39 lg. u

l 2.70 22 lg. klt?

lx[1.16 VI 29

]lx[1.126 13, 4.222 1, 4.335 21, 7.140 6

xl 1.24 13, 1.42 31, 1.70 9, 1.70 33, 1.88 1, 4.763 7

]xl 1.17 VI 11, 1.144 1, 1.157 3, 1.168 23, 2.2 10, 2.32 9, 2.76 15, 4.11 6, 4.75 IV 3, 4.142 5, 4.293 1, 4.302 2, 4.545 I 4, 7.208 1

]xl[1.36 1, 2.23 37, 4.725 7, 7.87 1, 7.96 1, 7.119 1, 7.187 1

]xxl 4.641 3, 4.788 2

]xxxxxxl 4.197 3

xxl[4.198 3

xlxxxx 4.196 3

]xlx[1.147 4, 4.398 11, 7.188 3

]xlxx 4.410 4

]xlxx[1.86 4, 2.57 6, 4.675 7

]l/b/d 4.769 5

]l/d 4.104 9

l/u/d[4.44 16, 4.389 13

]l/u/d 1.35 7, 1.42 22

l/d[1.166 29

]l/d 1.42 54, 2.73 20

]l/d[1.2 III 25, 4.490 4

]l/u/d 1.117 13

]xl/u/d[7.116 4

]l/dx 4.410 12

]xl/d[4.306 10, 4.533 3

]l/ṣ 1.6 V 23

l/ṣ 5.2 3

l/ṣ[7.47 5

]l/ṣ 4.397 1, 4.744 2
l/ṣxx 1.70 2
]lxz[7.161 3
]lxxxmḥy 1.151 2
xxxxlxḫ 4.123 1
lxḫmxkl 1.35 15
la 1.3 V 18, 1.4 VIII 22, 1.6 II 25
]la 4.44 19
lak 1.176 25, 2.10 10, 2.42 27, 2.70 13
lakm 2.30 19
lakt 1.2 II 10
lan 1.16 VI 14, 1.107 37
l\[anh] 1.108 22f
la\nk 1.108 24f
li 1.16 VI 2, 1.128 4
li[1.5 IV 21
]li 1.157 5
]li[7.190 1
]xli[7.191 2
liy 4.35 II 15, 4.155 2, 4.155 14, 4.244 5, 4.280 12, 4.309 25, 4.377 22, 4.617 25, 4.754 17, 4.785 19
li[y] 4.645 5
]liy 4.431 1
lik 1.5 IV 23, 1.5 IV 24, 2.46 9, 4.777 3, 4.777 5, 4.777 6, 4.777 8, 4.777 9
lik[2.42 22
l[ik] 4.777 2
]lik 2.44 13, 2.53 1
likt 2.14 7, 2.30 17, 2.32 3, 2.34 5, 2.36 5, 2.36 11, 2.36 14, 2.38 11, 2.39 18, 2.50 20, 2.63 7, 2.63 10, 2.72 23, 2.82 3
likt[2.42 12
li[kt 2.63 13, 2.73 7
l{.}ikt 2.45 25
lim 1.3 II 7, 1.5 VI 23, 1.6 I 6, 1.7 38, 1.84 35
xlim 4.350 5
limm 1.3 II 33, 1.3 III 12, 1.3 IV 22, 1.6 VI 6, 1.10 I 8, 1.10 I 15, 1.10 I 16, 1.13 20, 1.13 23, 1.17 VI 19, 1.17 VI 25, 1.101 16
limm[1.27 8
lim[m 1.10 III 3
]lir 7.52 6
luk 2.17 4
]lumm 1.113 2
lb 1.5 VI 21, 1.6 I 5, 1.6 II 6, 1.6 II 7, 1.6 II 8, 1.6 II 28, 1.6 II 28, 1.6 II 29, 1.12 I 13, 1.15 V 15, 1.17 VI 41, 1.19 I 3, 1.19 I 34, 1.114 29(!), 1.39 8, 2.25 3, 2.82 6, 5.11 21, 7.63 8
lb 1.19 I 10 lg. klb?
lb[5.11 11
l[b 1.87 19
]lb 7.95 2
]lb[4.227 IV 1
xlb[4.75 I 9, 4.693 47
]xlb 4.736 3
lb/d[1.166 8
]lba 6.31 1
lbiy 4.376 2, 4.780 1
lbim 1.5 I 14, 1.133 3, 1.169 4
lbu 1.24 30
lbdm 1.2 III 20
lbh 1.3 II 26, 1.7 7, 1.19 IV 61, 1.41 52, 1.82 3, 2.38 27
lbh[1.101 9
l]bh 1.103 51
lbw[4.643 13
lby 2.72 16
]lby 4.311 4, 4.766 6
]xlby 4.443 3
l<b>k 2.71 15
lbk 2.8 4, 2.30 23
lb[k 1.18 I 17
xlbmxtm 4.721 6
lbn 4.61 5, 4.412 III 6, 4.609 3, 4.624 2, 4.632 23, 4.727 11, 4.787 12
lbn[4.60 10, 7.55 7
lb[n 1.167 11
]lbn[7.14 2
lbny 4.103 15
lbnym 4.50 13, 4.261 19
lbnm 1.91 21, 4.68 2, 4.182 4, 4.348 10, 4.355 21, 4.693 39, 4.770 14
lbnm[4.610 16
l[b]nm[4.621 1
lb[nm/n 4.686 19
lbnn 1.4 VI 18, 1.17 VI 21, 1.22 I 20, 1.22 I 25, 4.65 4
lb[n]n 1.148 43
l]bnn 1.4 VI 20
lbn[n/m 4.684 3
lbnt 1.4 IV 62, 1.4 V 11, 1.4 VI 35, 1.13 13, 1.83 10

lbš 1.12 II 46, 1.43 4, 1.169 12, 4.17 15, 4.146 1, 4.146 8, 4.156 4, 4.182 4, 4.182 21, 4.182 64, 4.205 5, 4.337 16, 4.338 16, 4.721 1

lbš[4.182 22, 4.193 9

]lbš 4.101 1, 4.182 16, 4.182 20, 4.185 9

l]bš 4.101 2, 4.101 3

lb]š 4.101 4

lbšk 2.50 17

lbšm 4.146 6, 4.168 9, 4.337 14, 4.721 2, 4.721 3, 4.721 13

l[bš]n 1.41 54

lbšt 1.13 25

lbtġḏ[1.42 36

lbṯ 1.73 5

lg 1.23 75, 1.148 21, 1.174 8, 4.360 10, 5.10 7, 5.10 8, 6.12 4

lg[1.82 31

]lg 4.609 22, 4.673 2

l/d/ug 4.86 18

]xl/ugx[4.315 7

lgm 4.34 3, 4.34 4, 4.34 6

l]gm 4.34 9

lgn 4.33 23, 4.53 7, 4.700 8, 5.22 29

]lgn 4.151 I 9

]lgn[4.444 6

lgrt 1.119 10 lg. ugrt

ld 1.12 I 25

]ld 4.82 9, 7.51 18

]xld 1.173 3

lb/d[1.166 8

]ldk 2.21 19

ldn 4.222 14, 4.264 8

ldtk 2.34 33 lg. ṣdtk?

]lḏ[7.147 3

lḏmrky[1.69 7

lh 1.3 III 40, 1.3 IV 55, 1.14 I 9, 1.14 I 15, 1.14 III 33, 1.15 III 20, 1.15 III 21, 1.17 I 18, 1.17 I 20, 1.62 6, 1.114 7, 1.114 10, 1.163 13, 2.3 26, 2.31 66, 2.70 13, 2.71 19, 4.182 64, 4.627 2, 4.627 3, 4.627 4, 4.627 8, 4.627 9, 4.627 11, 4.627 13

lh[4.86 4

]lh 4.627 6, 4.627 7, 7.141 5

l]h 4.627 5, 4.627 10

]l[h] 4.627 12

lhm 1.9 12, 2.26 20, 2.38 23, 2.69 7, 2.70 22, 3.4 17, 4.53 2, 4.168 8, 4.180 1, 4.422 1

lhm[4.298 1

]lhm 1.82 28, 4.609 41

lhn 1.23 75 lg. l hn?

lht 4.214 I 5

]lw 4.12 2

]l/ṣwd 4.734 8

lwn 1.2 I 46, 4.360 6

lwsnd 2.40 10

lz[7.1 2

lzy 4.75 III 6

lzn 4.611 14

lḥ[7.37 4, 7.56 1, 7.132 8

]xlḥ 1.146 1

lḥx[2.17 12

lḥk 1.176 8

lḥm 1.4 IV 35, 1.4 IV 36, 1.4 V 48, 1.4 VI 55, 1.5 I 24, 1.5 IV 11, 1.5 VI 19, 1.6 I 3, 1.6 VI 44, 1.14 II 30, 1.14 IV 11, 1.16 III 14, 1.16 VI 11, 1.18 IV 19, 1.23 6, 1.23 6, 1.114 7, 1.169 6, 4.247 15, 5.23 13, 6.47 2, 6.55 2

lḥm[1.5 IV 12

lḥ[m] 1.4 IV 35, 1.18 IV 29

lḥ[m] 1.2 I 20 lg. l <l>ḥ[m] or lḥ[mm]?

l[ḥ]m 1.15 VI 4

l]ḥm 1.15 IV 27, 1.23 71

l]ḥm[1.17 VI 2

lḥ]m 1.15 V 10

lḥmd 1.4 V 39 lg. mḥmd

lḥmh 1.14 III 58

l[ḥmk 1.14 II 16

lḥmm 1.5 I 24

lḥ[mm] 1.2 I 20(?)

lḥmt 2.82 9

l[ḥ]n[4.229 1

lḥr 4.69 III 20

lḥt 1.2 I 26, 1.17 I 28, 1.17 II 3, 1.17 II 18, 2.14 6, 2.31 43, 2.34 5, 2.39 17, 2.45 22, 2.46 10, 2.72 17, 2.72 23, 2.73 7, 2.73 12

lẖt 4.710 2

xxlḫ[1.64 20

]lḫx[6.35 2

lḫsn 4.70 9, 4.83 10, 4.244 15

lḫšt 1.3 III 23, 1.3 IV 14, 1.7 31

lṭpn 1.1 IV 13, 1.1 IV 18, 1.4 IV 58, 1.5 VI 11, 1.6 I 49, 1.6 III 4, 1.6 III 10, 1.6 III 14, 1.6 IV 11, 1.15 II 13, 1.16 I 11, 1.16 I 21, 1.16 I 23, 1.16 II 44, 1.16 II 49, 1.16 IV 9, 1.16 V 10, 1.16 V 23
lṭpn[1.1 III 6
lṭp[n] 1.16 IV 2
l]ṭpn 1.1 II 18
lṭšt 1.2 I 32
lẓb 1.70 30
lẓpn 1.24 44, 1.25 5
lẓtm 1.169 11
l.y 1.117 5
ly 1.3 III 21, 1.3 IV 54, 1.3 IV 55, 1.6 I 12, 1.14 III 39, 1.14 VI 24, 1.16 I 26, 1.16 I 30, 1.17 II 14, 1.17 VI 42, 1.17 VI 42, 1.19 I 17, 1.82 2, 1.93 5, 2.3 17, 2.8 5, 2.13 13, 2.15 5, 2.30 5, 2.30 11, 2.33 27, 2.34 9, 2.35 7, 2.36 12, 2.39 35, 2.45 23, 2.45 24, 2.68 7, 2.71 8, 2.72 9, 2.77 7, 2.81 23, 5.10 9, 5.11 15, 5.11 18, 7.2 3
ly[2.31 44, 2.48 3, 4.30 7
]ly 1.2 III 19, 2.3 27, 2.33 4, 2.39 32, 2.50 7, 2.63 10, 2.72 5, 4.769 25, 4.784 24, 5.10 7
]xly 4.260 11, 4.311 7, 4.313 22
xxly 4.68 47
]l/ṣyd 4.766 7
lyḏ 1.44 5
lym 1.162 11
]l/ṣym 1.84 24
]lyn 4.368 1
]l/dyn 4.643 18
lyt 1.6 IV 19
]lyt 1.101 10
lyṯr 4.153 5
lk 1.2 IV 8, 1.3 IV 32, 1.3 IV 32, 1.4 V 28, 1.4 VII 23, 1.5 III 14, 1.5 III 20, 1.5 III 27, 1.13 4, 1.13 12, 1.14 III 2, 1.14 III 20, 1.15 II 23, 1.15 II 25, 1.15 III 6, 1.16 I 43, 1.16 VI 27, 1.16 VI 27, 1.17 VI 42, 1.18 I 27, 1.18 IV 17, 1.19 III 51, 1.19 IV 3, 1.21 II 1, 1.21 II 9, 1.22 II 3, 1.22 II 8, 1.24 29, 1.82 10, 1.82 38, 1.169 10, 2.10 4, 2.16 4, 2.21 4, 2.26 8, 2.31 35, 2.32 7, 2.34 3, 2.38 4, 2.44 4, 2.45 20, 2.45 21, 2.45 24, 2.46 4, 2.63 4, 2.71 3, 2.79 3, 2.79 5, 4.710 5
lk 4.205 18 lg. m{.}lk?
lk[1.5 III 13, 1.5 III 28, 1.16 II 6, 1.67 1, 2.39 26, 2.67 3, 7.198 7
l[k] 2.32 10
]lk 1.82 37, 2.31 45, 2.35 15, 4.5 3, 4.499 2, 5.10 5, 7.41 4
]lk[2.31 9, 2.48 1, 4.508 4, 4.508 5
l]k 1.2 III 22
]xlk 1.173 1, 2.55 5, 2.57 4
]xlk[4.450 1
]lkxlm 2.50 14
lkd[7.53 5
lky 4.63 III 27
]lkynt 4.222 10
lkm 1.19 III 46, 3.9 6
lkm[2.3 16
lk[m 2.6 4
]xlkm 7.222 3
lkn 4.141 II 6, 4.609 8, 4.780 6
]lkn 2.73 3
lkt 1.10 II 28, 1.10 II 29
ll 1.2 I 20, 1.39 12, 1.49 9, 1.50 7, 1.69 3, 1.106 27, 1.132 17, 1.132 25
ll[1.165 2
l[l 1.90 6
]ll 4.355 42
xṣ/ll 4.63 II 28
ll[[x]]m 1.111 2 lg. llym
lla 1.14 II 15, 1.14 III 57
llay 1.24 44
lli 1.4 VIII 19, 1.6 II 23, 1.7 14
llim 1.22 I 14
l[l]im 1.4 VI 43
llit 4.123 6
llu 1.86 15
]llb 4.769 53
llwn 4.264 6, 4.307 7
llḫhm 4.363 5
llym 1.111 2(!)
]l/ṣly 7.50 10
]llm 1.16 I 32, 1.82 33
]llt[4.71 III 2
llṯ 1.66 16
lm 1.2 I 24, 1.4 VII 38, 1.4 VII 39, 1.10 III 5, 1.12 II 57, 1.14 II 49, 1.14 III 33, 1.14 VI 17, 1.15 IV 22, 1.16 II 18, 1.22 II 14, 1.114 12, 2.4 14, 2.21

13, 2.26 4, 2.32 3, 2.33 23, 2.33 25, 2.39 16, 2.63 7, 2.70 16, 2.72 10, 2.73 8, 4.223 9, 7.1 2

lm[2.50 9

]lm 1.10 I 23, 1.147 13, 1.159 3, 2.31 23, 2.76 14, 4.11 5, 4.607 4, 7.3 1, 7.51 3, 7.177 7

]lm[4.733 1

l]m 2.63 13

l/d/um[4.252 5

lmx 2.31 34

]xxxxxxxlmxktxd 4.196 2

lmd 1.6 VI 55, 1.111 1, 4.138 4, 4.138 5, 4.138 7, 4.188 12, 4.188 17, 4.277 10

[lm]d 4.188 15

lmdh 1.114 27(!), 4.194 2, 4.194 4, 4.194 6, 4.194 8, 4.194 10, 4.227 I 2, 4.227 I 4, 4.227 I 6, 4.227 I 8, 4.227 I 10, 4.269 10, 4.269 12, 4.269 14, 4.269 16, 4.269 18

lm[dh 4.227 II 10

l]mdh 4.227 I 12

lmdhm 4.125 8, 4.125 9

lmdm 4.138 3, 4.138 6, 4.138 8, 4.138 9, 4.154 1

]lmdm 4.154 3

lm]dm 4.154 4

lmdth 4.175 12

]lmy 1.14 V 26

]lmy[7.115 2

]xlmy 4.634 4

]xlmy[4.589 4

lmn 4.571 4

]lmn 4.262 8

lmt 1.73 2

]lmṯym[7.47 4

ln 1.2 I 25, 1.2 I 27, 1.2 I 29, 1.17 II 19, 1.70 23, 2.75 7, 2.81 6, 2.81 26, 4.131 2

ln[1.64 10

]ln 1.4 III 53, 1.64 28, 4.64 V 13, 4.69 IV 25, 4.433 2, 4.718 1, 7.163 5

]ln[4.401 13

]xln 1.12 I 4, 4.59 1, 4.75 I 4

]xlnb 4.609 28

lnh 1.17 I 29, 1.100 5, 1.100 5, 1.100 10, 1.100 11, 1.100 16, 1.100 16, 1.100 21, 1.100 22, 1.100 27, 1.100 27, 1.100 32, 1.100 32, 1.100 37, 1.100 37, 1.100 42, 1.100 42, 1.100 47, 1.100 48, 1.100 53, 1.100 54, 1.100 59, 1.100 60, 1.111 21

lnl 1.67 5

lnṯ 4.209 19 lg. unṯ

ls[2.17 11

lsḫ[1.67 10

lsk[1.70 6

lsmm 1.6 VI 21

lsmt 1.22 I 6(?)

lsn 4.83 11

]lġ 7.136 2

]xxlġ[4.191 9

]l(?)ġn 4.682 11

lp 1.172 14

lp[1.1 IV 3

]lp 1.123 18, 4.701 6

]lp[7.166 1, 7.199 1

]xlp 4.588 3

]xlp[2.18 6

lpwt 4.690 17

]lpl 4.233 2

lpn 1.169 2

]lpn 1.68 34

lpš 1.5 VI 16, 1.6 II 10, 1.12 II 46, 2.66 2, 4.166 3, 4.166 6, 4.205 2

]lpš 2.79 2

]lpt[4.675 4

]l/ṣġ 7.151 1

]lṣ 4.93 III 5

lṣb 1.4 IV 28, 1.6 III 16, 1.17 II 10

lṣbh 1.103 49, 1.114 29

l]ṣbh 1.103 57

lṣn 4.33 5, 4.51 13

]xlq 7.9 4

lqḥ 1.14 III 55, 1.14 III 59, 1.43 23, 1.79 4, 1.79 6, 1.124 12, 2.38 17, 2.45 15, 2.70 18, 2.72 29, 4.41 1, 4.125 8, 4.131 1, 4.131 6, 4.144 4, 4.144 6, 4.172 3, 4.266 3, 4.336 3, 4.338 15, 4.378 2, 4.378 11, 4.609 51, 4.630 3, 4.630 4, 4.630 7, 4.630 9, 4.630 13, 4.630 15, 4.779 10

lqḥ[4.721 8

lq[ḥ 4.199 2, 4.388 4

lqḥt 2.38 22, 2.70 15, 4.290 2

l[q]ḥt 2.62 9

lq<ḥ>t 2.13 17

lqẓ 1.19 III 40 lg. {l}<y>qẓ
]lr[1.147 3
l/drx[4.242 3
lrgth 1.100 26
]xlrm 4.721 4
lrmnm 4.751 11
lrmn[m] 1.23 50
lrn 4.298 3
lšxr 7.198 8
lšn 1.103 31, 1.174 8, 1.175 5, 1.176 4
lšn[1.93 2
]lšn 1.5 II 3
lšnh 1.103 53
lš]nhm 1.2 I 33
lšnk 1.169 12
lšnm 1.83 5
]xlšrx[7.20 3
lt 1.98 1, 4.33 2, 4.710 5, 4.710 11, 4.710 13, 4.765 6
lt 4.33 2 lg. dt
lt[1.82 37, 1.98 5
]lt 1.5 II 24, 4.170 23, 7.38 9
]xlt[7.79 3, 7.101 1
]xltx[4.526 5
]ltgm 7.137 6
ltd 1.64 16
]lth[4.675 3
ltḥ 4.14 3, 4.14 4, 4.14 4, 4.14 9, 4.14 10, 4.14 16, 4.14 17, 4.263 3, 4.263 4, 4.263 6, 4.263 7, 4.263 8, 4.263 9, 4.269 27, 4.361 3, 4.611 14, 4.747 3, 4.751 4, 4.751 7
l]tḥ 4.14 16, 4.14 17
]ltḥ[4.569 1
xxltḫ 1.70 42
ltẖ 5.22 20
lty 1.20 I 9
]ltybt[4.675 6
]xltl 4.189 2
ltlkn 1.67 19
ltm 1.100 67
]xltm 4.231 10
]l/ṣtm 1.57 1
ltn 1.5 I 1
]ltn[4.708 8
]xltn 1.12 I 8
lṯ 5.11 7 lg. l
lṯ[1.16 V 38
lṯlm 1.73 7
lṯpn 1.18 I 15

M

m 1.6 V 16, 1.19 II 37, 1.70 40, 3.5 7, 5.2 1, 5.2 7, 5.4 3, 5.6 2, 5.9 II 2, 5.12 2, 5.13 8, 5.15 2, 5.15 3, 5.16 1, 5.16 3, 5.17 2, 5.17 5, 5.19 3, 5.20 1, 5.20 4, 5.21 1, 5.24 1, 5.25 16
m 4.205 18 lg. m{.}lk?
m 1.23 43 cor. attm
m[1.13 35, 1.58 1, 1.166 11, 2.23 28, 2.31 50, 2.36 7, 2.45 30, 2.49 12, 2.57 3, 2.75 1, 4.60 5, 4.102 21, 4.127 2, 4.160 3, 4.182 26, 4.193 5, 4.193 10, 4.213 25, 4.227 II 5, 4.316 2, 4.322 13, 4.332 25, 4.337 21, 4.386 4, 4.396 11, 4.423 16, 4.424 16, 4.424 17, 4.449 1, 4.455 3, 4.462 3, 4.477 3, 4.524 1, 4.575 5, 4.580 1, 4.633 2, 4.635 11, 4.640 2, 4.693 51, 5.2 2, 7.37 2, 7.68 7, 7.171 1
]m 1.2 III 9, 1.2 IV 4, 1.4 VII 59, 1.5 III 1, 1.13 34, 1.14 I 3, 1.14 I 5, 1.15 IV 10, 1.42 49, 1.48 36, 1.64 8, 1.82 21, 1.101 9, 1.122 7, 1.129 2, 1.133 14, 1.147 16, 1.151 7, 1.163 9, 1.164 17, 1.167 7, 1.169 21, 2.20 3, 2.21 25, 2.22 1, 2.31 30, 2.31 57, 2.31 66, 2.36 22, 2.41 9, 2.44 17, 2.48 3, 2.48 9, 2.73 21, 2.81 30, 2.83 2, 2.83 8, 4.11 7, 4.11 9, 4.11 11, 4.30 7, 4.30 8, 4.34 8, 4.62 3, 4.64 II 5, 4.75 VI 5, 4.94 2, 4.94 3, 4.94 11, 4.125 13, 4.126 16, 4.176 6, 4.177 1, 4.182 37, 4.182 53, 4.184 1, 4.185 8, 4.196 10, 4.200 3, 4.225 5, 4.227 IV 7, 4.243 9, 4.247 3, 4.258 8, 4.296 2, 4.297 5, 4.299 4, 4.352 11, 4.362 5, 4.396 17, 4.397 6, 4.397 8, 4.400 11, 4.420 6, 4.424 17, 4.430 2, 4.446 2, 4.470 1, 4.484 1, 4.546 1, 4.608 24, 4.610 45, 4.610 52, 4.610 72, 4.610 73, 4.613 15, 4.618 9, 4.618 11, 4.619 1, 4.627 5, 4.634 1, 4.707 1, 4.721 8, 4.721 12, 4.734 12, 4.735 3, 4.744 1, 4.752 15, 4.769 59, 4.786 9, 5.2 1, 5.2 2, 5.11 22, 7.1 3, 7.3 4, 7.41 6, 7.58 3, 7.59 2, 7.91 1, 7.164 2, 7.164 9, 7.165 2, 7.176 4, 7.203 3
]m[1.67 14, 1.68 17, 1.158 4, 2.20 7, 2.37 4, 4.125 14, 4.420 1, 4.635 54, 4.765 11, 7.8 1, 7.120 2, 7.140 14, 7.206 5
]\m 1.8 II 11f, 1.8 II 13f
mx 2.34 26, 2.46 23, 4.42 5, 4.273 11
mx[1.2 II 16, 1.13 16, 1.69 2, 1.103 8, 1.148 40, 2.17 13, 2.83 3, 4.75 IV 2, 4.157 6, 4.244 24, 4.318 6, 4.388 5, 4.601 2, 4.683 21, 7.132 6, 7.132 9, 7.145 3
]mx[2.37 11, 2.58 1, 4.410 3, 4.427 6, 7.149 4
mxx[4.702 7
]mxx 7.16 8
mxxx[1.70 35
xm 4.723 16
xxm 1.15 VI 1, 1.70 36, 4.340 13, 6.48 5
xm[1.168 24
]xm 1.11 6, 1.12 I 1, 1.15 II 1, 1.23 5, 1.66 1, 1.139 18, 1.146 9, 1.147 14, 1.159 2, 2.21 20, 2.23 34, 2.50 19, 2.74 3, 2.83 6, 4.28 9, 4.30 13, 4.77 1, 4.94 9, 4.185 1, 4.357 3, 4.396 8, 4.467 1, 4.492 1, 4.518 2, 4.555 1, 4.568 3, 4.618 6, 4.658 41, 4.697 7, 4.707 25, 7.3 3, 7.44 1, 7.55 12, 7.114 2, 7.135 3, 7.203 2
]xm 1.116 30 lg. b]tm
]xm[4.30 1, 4.227 IV 1, 4.410 2, 4.444 7, 4.498 2, 4.721 14
xmx[1.87 61, 4.6 1
]xmx 4.368 10
]xmx[4.432 13, 4.652 4
]xxm 1.10 III 1, 4.227 IV 2, 4.366 15
]xxmx[7.132 4
xxxxmx[4.401 1
]m/g 1.13 35, 4.234 2
m/t[4.178 15
]mxxg[2.57 1
]mxxxd 4.275 4

mxxy 1.116 32(!)
]xxmxxk 4.721 11
mxl/d/ux[6.52 2
]xmšxdt[2.57 9
maxt 4.786 10
mab 2.16 11 lg. mad?
mad 1.14 II 35, 2.16 11(?), 4.723 6
[m]ad 2.3 23
madt 4.704 9
madtn 1.103 1
maḫbt 4.16 7
maḫdh 4.149 5
maḫdy 4.181 3, 4.782 4
]maḫdy[4.742 2
maḫdym 4.263 5
maḫr[1.166 7
]mar[7.57 1 cor.]mlar[
mašmx[4.318 1
mašmn 6.17 1
mat 1.14 II 36, 1.14 IV 16, 1.148 20, 2.21 16, 2.34 26, 2.34 27, 3.1 22, 4.14 3, 4.14 5, 4.14 11, 4.14 14, 4.91 2, 4.91 4, 4.123 14, 4.123 16, 4.123 17, 4.127 1, 4.132 1, 4.158 1, 4.158 7, 4.164 1, 4.168 11, 4.171 1, 4.172 7, 4.182 2, 4.182 10, 4.182 19, 4.201 4, 4.203 4, 4.203 6, 4.203 9, 4.203 12, 4.247 26, 4.247 31, 4.261 3, 4.261 4, 4.261 5, 4.261 6, 4.261 7, 4.261 8, 4.261 10, 4.261 11, 4.261 12, 4.261 22, 4.261 24, 4.266 7, 4.271 4, 4.272 4, 4.274 2, 4.296 3, 4.296 5, 4.296 6, 4.299 3, 4.310 9, 4.337 4, 4.337 28, 4.338 10, 4.340 22, 4.341 7, 4.352 1, 4.353 2, 4.369 4, 4.387 11, 4.388 12, 4.402 7, 4.407 1, 4.407 3, 4.626 5, 4.626 7, 4.626 9, 4.636 6, 4.636 16, 4.664 3, 4.664 5, 4.709 5, 4.721 11, 4.721 12, 4.776 1, 4.777 13, 4.779 8, 4.780 9
mat[2.80 4, 4.23 2, 4.121 1, 4.247 30, 4.299 4, 4.397 10
ma[t 4.550 1, 4.636 11, 4.636 21, 4.636 26
m[at 4.201 3, 4.261 9, 4.261 21, 4.396 1
]mat 4.664 1
m]at 2.47 7, 3.1 23, 4.182 30, 4.531 3
matm 4.721 8

m\aṯr 6.66 7f(!)
mi[2.42 3 lg. mi[ḫd] or mi[dḫ]?
mid 1.3 II 23, 1.3 V 16, 1.4 V 15, 1.4 V 32, 1.4 V 38, 1.14 I 23, 1.15 III 13, 1.71 26, 1.72 37, 1.85 30, 2.10 13, 2.11 11, 2.16 10, 2.76 5
]mid 2.41 8
mi]d 2.56 5, 2.68 13
midḫ 4.166 1(cor.,!), 4.610 22, 4.643 16
midḫ[4.621 12
mid[ḫ 4.68 37, 4.622 3
mi[dḫ] 2.42 3(?)
]midḫ 4.302 7
]mid[ḫ/ḫy 4.589 5
mid[ḫy 4.33 4
m]idḫy 4.645 9
midy 2.46 11
midm 2.39 3
midpt 4.166 4 cor. mispt
mizrth 1.17 I 15
mizrtm 1.5 VI 17
miz[rtm] 1.5 VI 31
miḫd 4.172 6, 4.266 5, 4.355 26
miḫd 4.166 1(!) cor. midḫ
miḫd[4.81 1
mi[ḫd] 2.42 3(?)
miḫdy 4.778 3
miḫdym 4.611 1
miḫdy[m 4.383 1
miḫ[dy]m 4.124 12
miyt 1.169 8
milx[4.23 14
milḫ 4.166 1 lg. midḫ(cor.)
minš 1.19 IV 48
mispt 4.166 4(cor.)
mišmn 2.19 6, 6.23 1, 6.75 1
mit 1.5 IV 3, 1.49 10, 1.50 9, 2.72 27, 3.1 27, 3.1 28, 3.1 29, 3.1 30, 3.1 31, 3.1 32, 3.1 33, 3.4 13, 3.10 2, 4.60 2, 4.91 7, 4.137 12, 4.143 4, 4.158 3, 4.158 4, 4.158 8, 4.163 14, 4.168 3, 4.173 10, 4.174 13, 4.179 16, 4.182 8, 4.203 10, 4.211 4, 4.213 6, 4.213 11, 4.213 25, 4.213 26, 4.213 28, 4.243 1, 4.243 3, 4.243 3, 4.243 5, 4.243 7, 4.243 7, 4.243 8, 4.243 12, 4.243 13, 4.243 14, 4.243 15, 4.243 18, 4.243 24, 4.243 25, 4.247 15,

4.247 23, 4.247 27, 4.262 3, 4.270 4, 4.272 1, 4.280 3, 4.280 7, 4.280 9, 4.280 11, 4.280 13, 4.290 18, 4.291 4, 4.310 1, 4.337 17, 4.341 19, 4.344 9, 4.344 11, 4.345 3, 4.352 8, 4.369 5, 4.369 9, 4.369 13, 4.369 15, 4.386 12, 4.394 1, 4.397 12, 4.400 3, 4.400 11, 4.402 9, 4.407 2, 4.625 2, 4.625 2, 4.636 3, 4.658 30, 4.720 2, 4.721 1, 4.721 5, 4.775 2, 4.777 3, 4.778 13, 4.782 20
mit[4.18 6, 4.139 1, 4.344 16, 4.344 18, 4.636 13
mi[t 4.30 9, 4.212 5, 4.300 3, 4.397 4, 4.411 4, 4.721 9, 6.26 2
m[i]t 2.47 4, 4.352 7
m[it 4.120 2, 4.720 1
]mit 3.1 39
m]it 4.352 3, 4.636 22
mi]t 4.386 5
]mit[4.18 7
mitm 2.77 4, 4.132 5, 4.143 2, 4.182 9, 4.206 4, 4.213 24, 4.243 45, 4.247 28, 4.261 20, 4.265 2, 4.272 5, 4.280 1, 4.336 8, 4.341 22, 4.345 1, 4.373 1, 4.396 18, 4.400 6, 4.548 2, 4.626 3, 4.636 4, 4.636 22, 4.690 13, 4.721 12, 4.721 12, 4.755 3, 4.777 5, 4.778 17, 4.782 26
mitm[4.30 12
m[i]tm 4.397 2
m]itm 4.43 7
mi]tm 4.60 6, 4.60 10, 4.352 5, 4.548 1
muid[1.5 III 24
mud 1.5 III 22, 1.5 III 23
mud[1.5 III 17
mu[d 1.5 III 16
muṣl[7.41 5
]mb 4.185 6, 7.51 6
mbk 1.2 III 4, 1.3 V 6, 1.4 IV 21, 1.6 I 33, 1.17 VI 47(!), 1.82 17, 1.100 3
mbkm 1.1 V 20
mbġl 6.71 1
mbr 1.17 VI 47 lg. mbk
mbtx[4.74 3
mgxx 4.7 18
mg[4.684 8
mgx[1.57 9
]mgxxx[4.747 10
mgdl 1.14 II 21, 1.14 IV 3, 1.18 I 31, 1.39 11, 1.112 25
m[g]dl 1.14 II 20
]mgdl 7.47 3
mgdly 4.244 10
mgdly[4.417 11
mgdlm 4.410 27
mglb 4.69 VI 33, 4.76 2, 4.77 30
mglb[4.761 4
mgl[b 4.633 11
mgmr 4.168 12, 4.182 38
mgm[r 4.192 1, 4.316 3
m[gmr 4.316 1
]mgmr 1.81 16
mgn 1.4 I 21, 1.8 II 1, 4.127 3, 4.617 6
xmgn[4.175 4
mgnk 1.16 I 45
mgntm 1.4 III 30
m/ˁgš 4.769 60
mgšḫ 2.33 10
mgṯ 1.16 VI 18, 1.16 VI 21
md 1.4 VIII 23, 1.148 14, 4.188 7, 4.188 19, 4.245 I 1, 4.245 I 11, 4.245 II 1
md[1.15 IV 13, 4.106 17, 7.147 4
mdxxṯ 4.713 6
mdx[1.95 1
]xmdx 1.84 36
md/l[1.86 15
mdb 1.23 34, 1.23 35, 1.101 2, 1.107 19
]mdb 1.82 27
mdbḥ 1.41 41
md]\bḥ 1.87 44f
mdbḥt 1.13 16, 1.39 20, 1.41 24, 1.87 26
m]dbḥt 1.41 38
mdbm 1.82 27
mdbr 1.12 I 21(!), 1.12 I 35(!), 1.14 III 1, 1.14 IV 31, 1.23 4, 1.23 65, 1.23 68
mdbr[1.92 3
mdgl 1.119 12
mdgt 1.19 III 41 lg. dgt?
mdd 1.1 IV 20, 1.3 III 38, 1.3 III 43, 1.4 II 34, 1.4 VII 3, 4.692 5
m]dd 1.4 III 3, 1.4 VI 12

md\d 1.4 VIII 23f
mddbˤl 4.70 1, 4.85 1
mddt 1.14 IV 28, 1.17 II 41, 1.157 4
mddth 1.14 II 50
mdh 1.4 II 6, 4.385 4
mdw 1.16 VI 35, 1.16 VI 51
mdḫ 4.783 7
mdḫl 4.371 20
]mdy 4.325 4
mdym 2.62 4 lg. m<n>dym?
mdkn 1.131 6
mdl 1.4 IV 9, 1.19 II 3, 1.86 13, 4.75 VI 1
m]dl 1.86 12
mdlh 1.3 IV 26
mdlk 1.5 V 7
mdllkn 1.40 38
m[dl]lkm 1.40 30
md[llk]n 1.40 21
mdm 1.131 4, 4.38 4, 4.47 4, 4.54 13, 4.99 4, 4.103 1, 4.387 25, 4.690 1
]mdn 4.769 33
ml/dn 4.245 I 4
mdnt 1.3 II 16
mdˤ 1.107 10, 4.387 12, 4.609 4
mdpt 5.22 11
]mdrg 4.646 3
mdrˤ 1.23 69, 1.23 69, 1.23 73, 4.141 III 16, 4.149 16, 4.618 6
mdrˤh 1.146 6
mdth[4.182 55
mdṯbn 4.275 3
mḏ 4.772 6
]mḏ 4.697 11, 7.132 5
mḏgd 1.42 39
mḏl 4.289 5, 4.643 26
mḏlġ 5.22 22
mḏnt 5.22 7
mḏr 1.119 30
mḏrn 4.167 12
mḏrnm 4.167 11
mḏrġl 3.7 2, 3.7 3, 3.7 4, 4.635 18
mḏrġlm 4.53 1, 4.54 1, 4.68 61, 4.69 VI 17, 4.99 17, 4.137 9, 4.162 9, 4.163 12, 4.173 7, 4.174 12, 4.179 13, 4.183 II 15, 4.213 29, 4.230 6, 4.379 1, 4.387 10, 4.387 20, 4.387 24, 4.751 1
mḏrġl[m 4.216 11
mḏr[ġ]lm 4.174 10
mḏr[ġlm 4.33 1, 4.216 4
]mḏrġlm 4.102 14
mḏ]rġlm 4.69 VI 6, 4.103 54
m<h> 1.14 I 38 lg. mn
mh 1.3 II 38, 1.3 IV 42, 1.3 V 28, 1.4 II 39, 1.6 II 13, 1.17 VI 35, 1.17 VI 36, 1.23 53, 1.23 60, 2.14 9(?)
mh 6.66 2 lg. ilrˈmh
mh 1.16 VI 6 lg. m<nt>h?
]mh 7.51 17
mhbn 1.105 1
mhb[n] 1.106 6
mhy 2.14 9 lg. mh <h>y(?)
mhyt 1.5 VI 5, 1.16 III 4
mhk 2.38 26
mhkm 2.30 22
mh\mrt 1.5 I 7f
mhr 1.3 II 11, 1.3 II 21, 1.10 I 11, 1.18 IV 6, 1.18 IV 27, 1.22 I 8, 1.22 I 9, 1.22 II 7, 4.176 7, 4.214 I 5
m[hr 1.18 IV 11, 1.19 IV 52
mh]r 1.19 IV 56
mhrh 1.24 19
mhrh 1.18 IV 38 lg. mprh
<mhry> 1.100 73
mhry 1.100 74
mhrk 1.13 7, 1.100 75
mhrm 1.3 II 15, 1.3 II 28, 1.3 II 35
]mhrm 1.17 VI 40
mhrn 4.727 8
mwx 4.17 1
mzx[4.324 6
mzgn 1.66 7
mzy 1.48 15, 4.272 1
mzyn 4.297 3
mzl 1.14 II 46, 1.14 IV 25
mzl[1.9 15
mzln 4.110 16, 4.110 18, 4.110 20, 4.110 22, 4.307 1
mz[l]n 4.110 19
mzn 1.43 5, 1.137 7, 2.79 7
mznh 2.81 25, 4.341 1
mznm 1.24 34, 1.24 35, 1.24 37, 4.385 5
mznt 4.692 5
]mznth 4.291 2
mzt 4.412 II 13, 4.778 6, 4.782 9
mztn 4.69 II 5, 4.374 6, 4.378 6, 4.724

9
mḥ[1.41 54, 4.152 4, 7.142 5
mḥy 1.124 14
mḥ[y 1.87 8
mḥllm 1.119 23
mḥmd 1.4 V 16, 1.4 V 32, 1.4 V 39(!), 1.4 VI 19, 1.4 VI 21
xmḥn 4.748 6
mḥs[4.324 4
mḥrṯt 1.6 IV 3, 6.14 3
mḥrṯth 1.6 IV 14
mḥtrt 1.92 25
mḫ 1.17 I 38, 1.19 IV 39
mḫ 1.16 I 27 lg. my?
mḫ[4.359 2
]mḫ 4.756 4
]mḫ[2.43 2
]xmḫ 4.69 IV 23
mḫdy 4.635 17
mḫlpt 1.19 II 33
mḫlpt[1.107 20
]mḫm 4.55 18
mḫmšt 1.14 I 18, 1.14 I 30
mḫnm 1.83 4
mḫsrn 4.300 1, 4.310 1, 4.310 3
mḫṣ 1.2 I 39, 1.19 III 47, 1.19 III 52, 1.19 IV 4, 1.19 IV 34, 4.182 56, 4.332 14, 4.332 15, 4.332 16, 4.332 17, 4.635 7
mḫṣ[1.19 II 49, 1.19 IV 39
m[ḫṣ] 1.4 VII 11
]mḫṣ 1.82 1
m]ḫṣ 1.4 II 24
mḫṣy 1.4 II 24
m[ḫṣk 1.18 IV 42
mḫṣm 4.99 15, 4.103 57, 4.124 1, 4.125 9, 4.128 5, 4.187 1, 4.269 8(!), 6.48 4
mḫṣt 1.19 IV 58
mḫ[ṣt] 1.2 I 40
mḫr 1.96 7, 1.96 10, 1.96 11, 4.100 9
mḫrhn 4.338 18, 4.625 2
mḫrk 2.32 9
mḫšt 1.3 III 38, 1.3 III 41, 1.3 III 43, 1.3 III 45
mḫt 1.16 V 30
]xmḫt 1.103 8
mḫtn 4.214 II 13
mṭ 1.2 I 9, 1.2 I 41, 1.19 III 49, 1.19 III 56, 1.19 IV 7, 1.23 37, 1.23 40, 1.23 44, 1.23 47
mṭḫ 4.149 7
mṭm 1.3 II 15
mṭnt 1.82 34
mṭʿt 1.20 II 7
m[ṭʿt 1.20 II 9
mṭr 1.16 III 5, 1.16 III 6, 1.16 III 7, 1.16 III 8
mṭrh 1.4 V 6
mṭrtk 1.5 V 8
]mṭt 1.175 16
mṭth 1.14 I 30
mẓah 1.12 II 50, 1.12 II 51
mẓll 1.3 V 40, 1.4 I 12, 1.4 I 17, 1.4 IV 52, 1.4 IV 56, 1.117 6
mẓma 1.15 I 2
mẓrn 1.163 6
my 1.5 VI 23, 1.5 VI 24, 1.6 I 6, 1.6 I 7, 1.16 I 27(?), 1.16 V 14, 1.19 II 1, 1.19 II 6
my[1.16 II 9
m[y 1.16 V 17
]my 2.31 59, 2.41 13, 4.318 11, 4.319 5, 4.371 4, 4.430 4, 4.460 7, 4.721 10
]my[7.84 5
xxmy 4.748 7
]xmy 4.64 IV 3, 6.58 1, 6.60 1
]xxmy 4.389 1
myy[4.243 39
]myy 4.785 23
mym 1.19 III 46, 1.19 IV 28, 1.19 IV 37
my[m] 1.19 III 45
]mym 1.19 I 2
myn 4.617 50
]myn 4.460 4
myṣm 4.269 8 lg. mḫṣm
]mytxxxx 1.157 9
mk 1.4 VI 31, 1.4 VIII 12, 1.5 II 15, 1.14 III 3, 1.14 V 6, 1.15 III 22, 1.17 I 15, 1.17 II 39, 1.22 I 25, 2.73 14
mk[4.617 10
m[k] 1.6 V 8
m]k 1.19 IV 17
m]kḫd 2.4 17
mk]ḥd 2.4 16
mkkm 5.23 16
mkktm[1.69 6

mkl 4.147 16
]mkl 6.50 1
mkly 1.19 IV 40
mkly[4.299 4
m\kly 1.19 IV 34f
mknpt 1.16 I 9
mk[n]pt 1.16 II 47
mknt 1.14 I 11
mks 1.4 II 5
mkr 2.42 25, 4.369 2, 4.369 10, 4.369 11, 4.369 13
]mkr 4.217 1, 4.430 1
mkry 2.21 8
mkrm 4.27 12(!), 4.36 4, 4.38 3, 4.68 75, 4.126 9, 4.163 7, 4.173 3, 4.174 4, 4.179 8, 4.207 6, 4.214 IV 2, 4.217 1, 4.263 1, 4.745 6, 6.16 3
m]krm 4.137 5
mkrn 2.42 27
mkšr 1.71 11, 1.85 12, 1.85 16, 1.97 3
mkš[r 1.72 17
mk[šr 1.72 22
mkt 1.48 16
]mkt 1.3 I 28
mkṯr 1.4 II 30
ml 1.100 21, 5.10 4, 5.10 4
ml[4.19 3, 4.423 14, 4.423 18, 4.679 4
]ml 4.75 V 7
]ml[7.167 4
mlx[2.77 18, 4.276 11, 4.396 6
]xml 6.71 1
md/l[1.86 15
ml/ṣ[2.36 7, 4.570 2, 4.607 29
mla 1.4 I 38, 1.10 III 8, 1.12 II 44, 1.23 76, 1.45 10
mlak 1.2 I 22, 1.2 I 26, 1.2 I 28, 1.2 I 30, 1.2 I 41, 1.2 I 42, 1.2 I 44, 1.13 25, 2.76 3
mlakk 1.124 11
mlakm 1.2 I 11, 1.14 III 20, 1.14 III 33, 1.14 VI 35
m]lakm 1.62 6
mlakt 2.23 3, 2.23 7, 2.31 50, 2.75 10
ml[akt] 2.17 4
mlakth 2.17 7
mlakty 2.23 5, 2.33 35
mla[k]tk 2.36 11
]mlar[7.57 1(cor.)
<mlat> 1.130 16
mla<t> 1.10 II 9
mlat 1.10 II 12, 1.109 3
ml]at 1.46 11
mli 7.51 17
mli[1.10 III 7
mlix[2.1 6
mlit 2.2 7
mlu 1.87 20
]mlu 1.15 V 28
mlun 1.39 10
mlbr 1.12 I 21, 1.12 I 35 lg. mdbr
mlbš 2.79 10, 4.168 5, 4.168 7, 4.182 3, 4.182 61, 4.182 62
mlbš[4.257 5
mlbšh 4.182 63
mlgh 1.24 47(!)
mlghy 1.24 47 lg. mlgh y\ṯtqt
mlgy 1.116 31
mld 4.114 7, 4.346 5, 4.364 11
mldy 4.379 10
mlḥ 4.17 17
mlḥmy 1.5 II 23
mlḥmt 1.3 III 15, 1.3 IV 8, 1.3 IV 23, 1.3 IV 28
mlḥ]mt 1.1 II 19
mlḥt 1.3 I 7, 1.4 VI 57, 1.175 6, 4.247 20, 4.344 22, 4.720 1, 6.48 5
mlḥ[t 1.17 VI 4
m]lḥt 1.4 III 42
]mlḫ 4.197 24
mlḫš 1.100 5, 1.100 11, 1.100 16, 1.100 27, 1.100 32, 1.100 37, 1.100 42, 1.100 47, 1.100 53, 1.100 59
mly 2.50 12, 2.73 11, 4.412 III 8
mlk 1.2 II 9, 1.2 III 5, 1.2 IV 10, 1.3 V 36, 1.4 I 5, 1.4 III 9, 1.4 IV 24, 1.4 IV 38, 1.4 IV 48, 1.4 VII 43, 1.4 VII 43, 1.4 VIII 49, 1.6 I 36, 1.6 VI 57, 1.9 10, 1.9 16, 1.12 II 58, 1.13 26, 1.14 I 41, 1.14 III 16, 1.14 III 21, 1.14 III 27, 1.14 V 8, 1.14 VI 14, 1.14 VI 38, 1.16 I 40, 1.16 I 56, 1.16 I 59, 1.16 VI 23, 1.16 VI 37, 1.16 VI 52, 1.17 VI 49, 1.19 III 46, 1.22 I 10, 1.23 7, 1.24 2, 1.24 17, 1.24 24, 1.39 12, 1.41 50, 1.41 53, 1.43 2, 1.43 10, 1.43 23, 1.43 25, 1.46 10, 1.87 3,

1.87 7, 1.90 1, 1.90 21, 1.91 2, 1.91 7, 1.91 10, 1.91 11, 1.100 41, 1.103 7, 1.103 17, 1.103 47, 1.103 52, 1.105 7, 1.105 11, 1.105 20, 1.106 10, 1.106 12, 1.106 17, 1.106 17, 1.106 24, 1.106 26, 1.106 33, 1.107 42, 1.108 1, 1.108 6, 1.108 12, 1.108 19, 1.108 21, 1.109 2, 1.111 3, 1.111 18, 1.112 6, 1.112 7, 1.112 9, 1.112 15, 1.115 1, 1.119 4, 1.119 5, 1.119 14, 1.119 24, 1.123 20, 1.132 3, 1.132 28, 1.139 14, 1.157 10, 1.161 11, 1.161 12, 1.161 15, 1.161 25, 1.161 26, 1.164 1, 1.164 3, 1.168 1, 1.168 8, 1.171 4, 1.171 6, 1.173 13, 2.7 9, 2.13 3, 2.13 18, 2.14 13, 2.15 3, 2.19 7, 2.19 8, 2.19 13, 2.23 2, 2.23 17, 2.23 23, 2.26 2, 2.26 14, 2.30 3, 2.30 13, 2.31 39, 2.31 56, 2.33 8, 2.33 14, 2.33 18, 2.33 20, 2.33 22, 2.33 26, 2.33 30, 2.33 33, 2.34 1, 2.36 5, 2.36 14, 2.36 21, 2.38 1, 2.38 3, 2.40 1, 2.40 12, 2.40 14, 2.40 18, 2.42 1, 2.42 9, 2.42 23, 2.42 27, 2.44 1, 2.44 19, 2.45 13, 2.45 14, 2.45 17, 2.45 19, 2.46 2, 2.47 1, 2.47 8, 2.47 12, 2.47 12, 2.47 14, 2.49 2, 2.62 10, 2.69 4, 2.72 11, 2.72 14, 2.72 17, 2.72 24, 2.72 26, 2.72 29, 2.72 32, 2.75 5, 2.76 1, 2.76 4, 2.76 8, 2.76 9, 2.76 10, 2.77 3, 2.77 6, 2.81 1, 2.81 2, 2.81 10, 2.81 16, 2.81 19, 2.81 19, 2.81 20, 2.81 30, 2.81 30, 2.81 31, 2.81 31, 3.1 6, 3.1 13, 3.1 14, 3.1 16, 3.1 24, 3.1 26, 3.2 4, 3.5 3, 4.17 18, 4.27 17, 4.28 7, 4.54 1, 4.68 5, 4.93 II 8, 4.117 2, 4.122 9, 4.137 14, 4.141 II 25, 4.144 1, 4.145 2, 4.149 12, 4.151 II 6, 4.163 16, 4.164 4, 4.167 5, 4.167 14, 4.168 7, 4.182 13, 4.182 56, 4.182 61, 4.182 62, 4.205 18(?), 4.230 8, 4.270 11, 4.274 7, 4.337 16, 4.338 2, 4.338 13, 4.338 15, 4.339 17, 4.341 21, 4.344 10, 4.344 16, 4.348 22, 4.355 38, 4.365 3, 4.367 1, 4.369 3, 4.370 1, 4.375 6, 4.380 3, 4.384 2, 4.421 2, 4.548 3, 4.609 1, 4.635 1, 4.635 3, 4.635 57, 4.721 7, 4.750 1, 4.750 13, 4.766 12, 4.779 11, 4.790 17, 6.23 3, 6.29 4, 6.75 3, 7.63 6, 7.63 7, 7.63 8, 9.530 1(*bis*), 9.530 9(*bis*)

mlk[1.4 II 44, 1.14 I 2, 1.126 18, 1.148 18, 1.164 11, 1.166 16, 1.166 24, 1.171 1, 2.23 33, 2.44 3, 2.48 8, 2.49 1, 2.57 4, 2.69 2, 4.27 6, 4.105 5, 4.219 13, 4.245 II 1, 4.259 5, 4.396 17

ml[k 1.43 22, 1.49 13, 1.87 59, 1.106 10, 2.42 17, 2.73 10, 4.141 I 1, 4.683 5

m[l]k 1.3 V 8

m[lk 1.106 9, 2.4 3, 2.72 3, 3.1 17, 4.182 29

]mlk 1.41 48, 1.41 53, 1.103 43, 1.107 30, 1.108 22, 2.23 9, 2.35 9, 2.81 1, 2.81 11, 2.81 20, 4.182 64, 4.190 1, 4.197 22, 4.318 6, 4.350 2, 7.85 4

]mlk[4.75 II 12, 4.260 1, 4.382 10

m]lk 1.14 I 8, 1.87 55, 2.20 2, 2.43 4, 2.81 10, 4.627 1, 4.784 4

m]lk[1.168 23

ml]k 1.41 20, 1.87 57, 1.112 11, 2.23 7, 2.35 17, 2.63 1, 2.73 7, 2.76 9, 3.2 7

m\lk 1.24 2f, 1.112 16f

m\[lk] 1.117 3f

mlk\i 6.66 5f

mlkbn 4.611 3

mlkh 1.3 IV 2, 1.6 V 5, 1.6 VI 34

mlky 4.96 5, 4.625 21, 4.706 11

mlk[y 4.80 14

m[l]ky 4.693 50

mlkyy 4.93 II 1, 4.282 3, 4.412 III 13

mlkym 4.99 5, 4.126 19

]mlkym 4.666 6

mlkytn 2.15 2, 2.15 8, 4.264 2

mlkk 1.2 III 18, 1.6 VI 28

mlkm 1.22 I 17, 1.47 33, 1.118 32, 1.119 25, 1.163 4, 2.21 18, 2.81 20

mlk[m 2.76 9, 2.76 10

ml[km 2.76 1, 9.530 1, 9.530 9

m]lkm 2.81 3

mlkn 1.3 V 32, 1.4 IV 43, 1.103 7, 1.103 9, 1.103 13, 1.103 37, 1.103 46, 1.103 54, 1.103 57, 1.103 58, 1.163 7, 2.42 10, 2.42 26

mlk[n 1.103 10

]mlkn 2.33 5
]mlkn[2.28 1
mlkn/t[2.36 8
mlknʿm 4.165 5, 4.344 15, 4.616 3
]mlknʿm 4.57 2
ml]knʿ[m 4.460 2
]mlkrpi 4.682 3
mlkrš[p 4.635 45
mlkt 1.2 III 22, 1.23 7, 2.12 1, 2.13 1, 2.13 15, 2.21 9, 2.24 1, 2.30 1, 2.36 1, 2.36 3, 2.68 1, 2.73 15, 2.82 1, 3.1 28, 4.22 4, 4.143 1, 4.149 15, 4.219 12, 4.244 9, 4.246 3, 4.265 1, 4.382 1, 4.382 2, 4.635 2, 4.635 6, 7.122 3
mlkt[4.259 6
m[l]kt 1.170 1
]mlkt 1.2 III 22, 2.21 2
m]lkt 4.230 5
ml]kt 4.230 4
mlkn/t[2.36 8
mll 1.1 IV 11, 4.35 I 9
mll[4.44 30
mlm[4.216 5
mln[1.82 21
ml/dn 4.245 I 4
mlsm 1.162 22
mlʿn 4.63 III 35, 4.785 13
mlġt 2.40 17
mlṣ 4.422 6, 4.624 7
m]lṣ 4.526 4
m]lṣ[4.590 1
mlt 2.75 8
mlṭḥ 4.282 14, 4.304 5, 4.337 26, 4.707 9
mlṭḥm 4.778 7, 4.782 12
]mltm 4.127 2
mltn 4.769 45
]xmltn 4.260 8
mm 1.22 I 1, 1.119 21, 1.166 28, 4.91 14, 4.786 13
mm 2.10 9 lg. m<n>m?
]mm 1.62 4, 1.91 16, 1.139 11, 2.45 30, 4.568 2
]mm 1.24 11 lg. k]mm
]mm[4.389 2
mmh 1.16 I 34
mmṭr 4.195 11
mmy 4.69 VI 18, 4.715 16
mmlat 1.14 III 10, 1.14 V 2
mmnnm 1.23 40, 1.23 44, 1.23 47
mmskn 4.123 18
mmʿ 1.3 II 14, 1.3 II 28, 1.3 II 35
mmʿm 1.3 V 25, 1.18 I 12
mmrtn 1.128 10
mn 1.3 III 37, 1.5 IV 23, 1.14 I 38(!), 1.16 II 19, 1.16 II 20, 1.19 I 11, 2.45 25, 2.72 22, 3.1 20, 4.350 3, 4.710 3
mn[1.9 7, 1.92 32, 2.42 13
]mn 1.15 II 4, 1.52 20, 2.37 6, 3.1 19, 4.182 47, 4.183 II 4, 4.225 4, 4.370 36, 4.481 4, 4.618 30, 4.703 2, 4.785 22, 7.116 3
xmn 4.207 2
xmn[1.17 V 2
]xmn 4.75 V 8, 4.116 2
]xxmn 4.744 4
xmnxx 1.86 19
mnipʿl 4.116 15
mnu 1.92 38
mndym 2.62 7
m<n>dym 2.62 4(?)
mndʿ 1.16 II 24, 2.34 10, 2.34 11
m]ndʿ[2.45 31
mndġ 1.85 4
mnḥ 3.10 1, 4.91 1, 4.771 9
mnḥyk 1.2 I 38
mnḥm 3.8 21, 4.55 5, 4.75 III 11, 4.123 9, 4.139 4, 4.183 II 13, 4.232 45, 4.609 7, 4.609 9, 4.609 13, 4.635 49, 4.728 4
mnḥ[m 4.178 5
m<nḥm> 3.8 18(?)
mnḥt 4.709 6
[[mnḥt]] 4.709 9
mnḫ 1.2 IV 3
mny 4.617 38, 4.635 23
]mny 4.82 6
mnyy 4.96 2
mnyn 4.77 26
mnk 3.2 12
]mnk 1.1 II 25
xmnkb[1.35 17
]mnkl[4.706 10
mnkm 2.19 12, 3.2 13
mnm 1.2 IV 3, 1.3 IV 4, 1.4 I 39, 2.10 16, 2.11 16, 2.12 13, 2.13 12, 2.16 16, 2.24 11, 2.30 10, 2.34 8, 2.38 8, 2.41 16, 2.41 19, 2.46 8, 2.50 4, 2.64

17, 2.68 15, 2.70 29, 2.72 8, 2.72 33, 3.3 5
mn[m] 3.2 18
]mnm 2.65 4
m<n>m 2.10 9(?)
<mnm> 2.71 7(?)
mnmn 1.123 22
mnmnm 1.67 4
mn{.}n 4.46 7
mnn 4.16 12, 4.35 I 5, 4.35 II 13, 4.35 II 16, 4.41 9, 4.64 V 9, 4.339 15, 4.609 37, 4.658 14, 5.9 I 2
]mnn 1.55 7, 4.706 7
mnny 3.10 1, 4.791 2
mnny[4.401 3
]mnʿrt 4.275 9
mnqt 2.45 16
mnrt 5.22 5
mnt 1.4 VII 56, 1.100 4, 1.100 15, 1.100 20, 1.100 26, 1.100 31, 1.100 36, 1.100 41, 1.100 46, 1.100 52, 1.100 58, 1.100 70, 1.100 71, 1.100 79, 4.355 33, 4.710 7
]mnt 1.82 20
mnth 1.6 II 36
m<nt>h 1.16 VI 6(?)
]mnth 1.17 I 32
mn\thn 1.24 46f
mnty 1.100 9
]mnty[1.75 9
mn[t]\y 1.17 II 21f
mnt̠ 4.134 6
msg 4.52 6, 4.52 7, 4.52 8, 4.52 9, 4.52 13, 4.52 14, 4.52 15, 4.52 16, 4.52 17, 4.167 15
ms[g] 4.52 11
m[sg] 4.52 5
]msg 4.52 18
]ms[g] 4.52 19
m]sg 4.52 12
msgm 4.53 2
msgr 2.2 11
msdt 1.4 I 40
ms]wn 1.14 V 31
mswnh 1.14 III 21, 1.15 I 4
msk 1.16 II 16, 1.19 IV 61
mskh 1.3 I 17
mskt 1.85 3
mslmt 1.10 III 28
mss 1.71 9, 1.72 13
ms]s 1.85 10
mspr 1.4 V 42, 1.19 IV 62, 1.40 35
msp[r 1.107 14
msrr 1.14 III 59
ms[rr 1.14 II 17
mʿ 1.2 III 15, 1.4 I 20, 1.4 VI 4, 1.6 I 12, 1.6 VI 23, 1.7 40, 1.14 II 34, 1.14 IV 15, 1.14 V 14, 1.15 III 28, 1.16 VI 41, 1.17 VI 16
mʿ[1.19 II 36, 6.40 1
m[ʿ 1.18 I 23
mʿx[4.97 3
]mʿx[4.504 4
]xmʿ 7.185 4
mʿbd 1.86 23
mʿbr 4.243 12
mʿd 1.2 I 14, 1.2 I 17, 1.2 I 20, 1.2 I 31
mʿdbh 4.573 2, 4.573 3
mʿdbhm 4.573 1
mʿ[lt] 1.87 25
m[ʿlt] 1.41 23
mʿmsh 1.17 I 30
mʿmsy 1.17 II 20
mʿmsk 1.17 II 6
mʿmʿ 1.82 41
mʿn 5.7 2
mʿn[4.412 I 10, 4.583 4
]mʿn 1.11 9, 1.35 4
mʿnh 1.67 5, 1.67 20, 1.69 4, 1.70 3
mʿnk 2.10 15
mʿnt 1.73 10, 4.281 27, 4.412 I 12, 4.611 10, 4.632 22
mʿṣd 4.625 3, 4.625 8, 4.625 10, 4.625 12, 4.625 14, 4.625 18, 4.632 3
mʿṣ[d 4.625 16
mʿ[ṣd] 4.632 12
m]ʿṣd 3.6 7
mʿṣdm 4.625 5, 5.23 12
mʿqb 4.68 31, 4.73 10, 4.348 7, 4.365 27, 4.380 34, 4.610 2, 4.629 14
mʿq[b 4.686 4
m]ʿqb 4.750 14
mʿqby 4.33 16, 4.295 11, 4.417 10
mʿq[bym 4.40 4
mʿqbk[1.18 I 19
mʿr 1.16 IV 5, 4.63 II 13, 4.68 26, 4.100 3, 4.348 9, 4.355 32, 4.365 9,

4.380 9, 4.610 10, 4.621 5, 4.629 11, 4.693 37, 4.770 7
mʿr[4.683 15, 4.693 10
mʿrb 4.307 3
mʿrb[1.87 21
mʿr[b] 1.19 IV 48
]mʿr[b] 1.41 19
mʿrby 4.27 21, 4.33 26, 4.63 I 25, 4.68 57, 4.213 8, 4.365 8, 4.375 8, 4.380 8, 4.384 5, 4.777 9
mʿrby[4.693 8
m[ʿ]rby 4.377 26
mʿrb[y] 3.7 7
m[ʿrby 4.27 10
[mʿr]by 4.784 9
mʿrbym 4.45 6
mʿrḥp 4.365 33
mʿry 4.420 9
mʿt 1.172 18
mġ 1.3 VI 11, 1.23 75, 2.73 19
mġd 1.14 II 31
m[ġ]d 1.14 IV 12
mġẓ 1.4 I 22, 1.5 V 24, 1.8 II 2
mġy 1.3 III 36, 1.4 II 22, 1.4 III 23, 1.4 V 44, 1.15 II 11, 1.20 II 6, 1.100 67, 2.31 45, 2.34 11, 2.61 4, 2.76 3, 2.80 10
mġy[1.16 II 24, 1.22 II 25, 1.157 7, 2.1 8
mġ[y 3.1 3
]mġy 1.108 16
mġyh 1.16 I 50
mġyy 2.71 16
mġyt 1.4 II 23, 1.4 III 24, 1.4 IV 31
mġy[t] 1.19 IV 49
]mġk 1.108 19
mġln 4.129 12
mġmġ 1.71 5, 1.85 5, 1.85 27
mġmġ[1.72 31
mġm]ġ 1.97 15
mġny 1.5 VI 5, 1.5 VI 8
mġrt 4.125 18
mġt 1.6 II 19, 2.36 8, 2.36 10
]mpx[2.22 7
mpḫm 1.4 I 23
<mpḫrt> 1.40 34
mpḫrt 1.40 25, 1.40 34, 1.65 3, 4.17 2
]mpḫrt 1.40 42
mpḫ]rt 1.40 17
mpḫr]t 1.122 3
mpr 6.40 1
mprh 1.18 IV 26, 1.18 IV 38(!)
mptẖ 5.22 12
]mptm 7.16 6
ml/ṣ[2.36 7, 4.570 2, 4.607 29
mṣb 1.24 34, 1.91 32, 1.91 33, 1.91 35, 4.213 28, 4.213 30
mṣb[1.91 34
mṣ[b 1.91 29, 1.91 30, 1.91 31
mṣbx[4.61 3
mṣbm[4.664 4
mṣbtm 1.4 I 24
mṣbt 4.345 2
mṣb[t 4.68 39
m]ṣbt 4.302 5
mṣbty 4.85 9
mṣd 1.114 1
mṣdh 1.100 58, 1.112 19
m]ṣdh 1.14 IV 8(!)
mṣ[dy 1.5 IV 11
mṣdk 1.14 II 26(!)
mṣl 4.225 5
mṣlm 4.126 30
mṣlt 1.12 II 61
mṣltm 1.3 I 19, 1.108 4
mṣ\ltm 1.19 IV 26f
mṣmt 3.1 17, 6.27 1
mṣprt 1.23 25
mṣpt 4.689 4
mṣṣ 1.15 II 27
mṣqt 1.103 19, 2.72 21
mṣr 1.3 V 8, 4.775 13
mṣry 3.7 1, 4.53 13, 4.63 I 47, 4.96 6, 4.644 2, 4.753 15
mṣrym 4.230 10
mṣrm 2.23 22, 2.36 15, 2.36 16, 2.38 11, 2.81 1, 2.81 19, 3.8 15, 4.213 27, 4.230 7, 4.352 4
mṣrm[2.48 4
mṣr[m] 2.81 10
mṣ]rm 2.81 31
mṣr]m 2.81 4
mṣrn 4.35 II 3, 4.52 5, 4.71 III 12, 4.88 10, 4.93 II 15, 4.98 8, 4.183 II 14
mṣrn[4.574 3
mṣrpk 1.82 33

msrrt 4.270 9
mṣrt 4.721 14
mṣt 1.12 II 28
mq[4.42 6
mqb 4.625 3, 4.625 8, 4.625 10, 4.625 12, 4.625 14
mqbm 4.625 5, 4.780 8
mqdm 4.158 19
mqdšt 4.609 15
mq[dšt] 6.25 3
mqwṭ 4.229 2
mqḥ 4.127 4
mqḥm 4.123 21, 4.127 4, 4.385 3
mql[7.55 15
mqmh 1.14 II 1, 1.14 III 23, 1.14 III 35, 1.14 VI 19
mqm]h 1.14 V 35
mqp 4.127 2
mqp[m] 4.390 6
]mqpm 3.6 5
mqr 1.14 III 9(!), 1.14 V 2
mqrtm 4.123 19
mr 1.2 III 11, 1.2 IV 19, 1.2 IV 19, 1.15 IV 23, 1.19 I 7, 1.19 I 12, 1.73 5, 1.85 7, 1.87 22, 1.123 22, 1.124 5, 1.124 16, 4.14 2, 4.14 8, 4.14 15, 4.91 16, 4.786 14, 5.23 1, 6.31 1, 6.45 2, 7.51 19
mr[1.53 3, 1.53 4, 1.157 10, 1.167 2, 4.303 1, 4.322 4, 4.432 5, 4.622 1, 4.743 12, 7.132 7, 7.222 1
m[r 1.124 7
]mr 1.62 3, 1.107 2, 1.108 10, 4.28 4, 4.187 6, 4.707 24
m]r 1.71 7
mrxxx 1.79 5
mrx[1.30 4, 4.641 2
xmr 1.64 22
]xmr 1.148 42
xxxxxxxmr[1.70 36
mra 1.4 V 45
mradn 4.666 5
mrat 4.95 7, 4.128 2, 4.247 20, 4.247 21, 4.348 30
[mr]at 4.693 26
mri 1.3 I 8, 1.22 I 13, 4.92 2, 4.103 37, 4.212 2, 4.247 16, 4.247 17
mri[4.651 5
m[ri 1.1 IV 31
m]r\i 1.4 VI 57f
mria 1.3 IV 41
]m\ria 1.4 VI 41f
m]rih 1.15 IV 15
mrik 1.15 IV 4
mril 4.68 51, 4.267 3, 4.345 9
mril[4.621 13
mrily 4.625 22, 4.750 1
mrim 4.103 20, 4.128 1
mru 1.175 1, 4.47 2, 4.47 3, 4.68 63, 4.68 64, 4.69 V 6, 4.99 12, 4.99 13, 4.105 1, 4.126 23, 4.126 24, 4.332 9, 4.610 45, 4.752 7
mr[u 4.69 V 17, 4.610 44
m[r]u 4.36 3
mr\u 6.66 4f
mrum 4.68 69, 4.69 III 11, 4.126 2, 4.137 7, 4.163 3, 4.173 6, 4.174 3, 4.179 6, 4.207 4, 4.382 30, 4.416 2, 4.745 1
mr[um] 4.752 2
mrbd 4.385 9, 4.780 3
m]rbd 4.127 7
mrbdt 4.270 11
mrbᶜ 4.751 8, 4.751 9, 4.751 10
mrbᶜt 1.14 I 17
mrbᶜ[t 4.362 6
mrd 4.575 4
mrd[1.123 19
mrl/d[4.60 9
mrdml 1.131 2
mrdt 4.205 4, 4.205 6
mrdt{t} 2.72 28
mrh 1.100 78
mrzḥ 3.9 1, 3.9 13, 4.399 8, 4.642 4, 4.642 5, 4.642 6
m[rzḥ 1.1 IV 4
mr]zḥ 4.642 2, 4.642 7
mrzḥh 1.114 15
]mrzᶜy 1.21 II 1, 1.21 II 5
mrḥ 1.6 I 51, 1.65 12, 4.169 9
mr[ḥ 4.65 7, 4.65 8, 4.65 10, 4.65 11
m[rḥ 4.65 6
]mr[ḥ 4.670 5
mrḥh 1.16 I 51, 1.92 7, 1.92 12
m]rḥh 1.16 I 47
mrḥy 1.103 7, 1.103 47, 1.140 10
mrḥm 4.385 7, 4.624 5, 4.624 8
mrḥm[4.624 19

mr[ḥ]m 4.624 3
mrḥ[m 4.624 20
mr[ḥm] 4.390 9
mrḥ]m 4.624 22
]mrḥ[m 4.624 15
m]r[ḥm] 4.624 6
mrḥqm 1.127 32
mrḥqm 2.33 3 lg. mrḥq<t>m(cor.,?)
mrḥq[t 2.69 6
mrḥqtm 2.11 6, 2.12 10, 2.64 15, 2.68 5, 2.70 10
mrḥqt[m 2.24 7, 2.50 3
m[r]ḥqtm 2.40 7
m[rḥ]qtm 2.45 11
]mrḥ[qtm] 2.52 3
mrḥq<t>m 2.33 3(cor.,?)
mrḫm 4.624 10
mrḫq<t>m? 2.33 3 cor. mrḥq<t>m?
mrḫt 1.172 27
mrṭn 4.141 II 15, 4.609 15
mrṭn[4.695 4
]mrṭn 4.646 5
mry[4.56 1, 4.56 10
mr[y 4.56 2
m[ry 4.56 8, 4.56 9, 4.56 11
mrym 1.3 IV 1, 1.3 IV 38, 1.4 IV 19, 1.4 V 23, 1.5 I 11, 1.83 10, 1.100 9
mr]ym 1.1 IV 1
mryn 4.93 IV 21, 4.155 10, 4.244 16, 4.377 5, 4.609 2, 4.772 5
mry[n 4.528 3, 4.617 5
]mryn 4.260 5, 4.331 3
m]ryn 4.311 8
]mryn[4.457 1
mrynm 4.69 I 1, 4.69 III 6, 4.103 7, 4.126 1, 4.137 2, 4.137 4, 4.149 9, 4.149 11, 4.163 6, 4.163 8, 4.173 2, 4.173 5, 4.174 5, 4.174 8, 4.179 3, 4.179 9, 4.230 1, 4.232 33, 4.377 34, 4.416 1
mry[n]m 4.623 1
mryn[m 4.216 8, 4.216 12
mry[nm 4.322 1, 4.561 1
mr[ynm 4.485 2, 4.485 8
m]rynm 4.162 3
mr]ynm 4.162 5
mryt 1.131 2
mrkbt 1.14 II 3, 1.14 III 24, 1.14 III 36, 1.14 VI 21, 1.162 22, 2.31 31, 4.47 8, 4.98 6, 4.98 8, 4.141 III 20, 4.145 1, 4.167 5, 4.167 13, 4.180 3, 4.183 II 12, 4.339 16, 4.392 1, 4.392 2, 4.447 3, 4.609 28, 4.745 9
mrkb[t 4.167 1, 4.447 2
mrk[bt 4.551 2, 4.551 5, 4.551 6, 4.551 7
mr[k]b[t 4.547 1
mr[kbt 4.551 1, 4.551 3, 4.551 4, 4.551 8
m[rkbt] 1.14 VI 7, 4.618 12
]mrkbt 4.447 4
m]rkbt 4.447 5
mr]kbt 4.363 9, 4.447 6
]mrkbt[4.527 3
]mrk[bt 4.527 2, 4.602 2, 4.602 3
]mr[kbt 4.527 1
m]rkb[t 4.500 3, 4.500 4, 4.527 4
m]rk[bt] 4.602 4
m]r[kbt] 4.602 1
mr]kbt[4.500 2
mr]kb[t 4.500 1, 4.500 5
mrkbthm 1.20 II 4
mrk[bthm 1.22 II 22
mr[kbthm 1.22 II 23
mrkbtk 2.81 8
mrkbtm 4.145 6
]mrky[1.70 31
mrkm 4.217 9
mrkm 4.27 12 lg. mkrm
mrl 4.128 8
mrl[1.70 39
mrl/d[4.60 9
mrm 1.12 I 11, 1.19 I 12, 1.46 5
mrmt 1.169 7
]mrn 4.182 63, 4.408 5
mrnn 4.75 III 13, 4.75 IV 7, 4.278 11
mrʿm 4.165 6, 4.344 1
mrġt 1.13 24
mrġṯm 1.4 III 41, 1.4 VI 56
mr[ġṯm 1.5 IV 13
mrṣ 1.16 I 56, 1.16 V 15, 1.16 V 18, 1.16 V 21
mr[ṣ 1.16 V 49
m[rṣ] 1.16 II 19, 1.16 II 22
]mrṣ 1.16 I 59
m]rṣ 1.16 V 27
mrqdm 1.19 IV 27
m\rqdm 1.108 4f

mr[r] 1.4 VII 12
mrrt 1.19 III 50, 1.19 III 51, 1.175 2, 6.44 2
mršp 4.382 3
mrti[7.55 14
xxmrty 1.70 12
mrṯ 1.22 I 18, 1.22 I 20, 2.34 32
mrṯd 4.63 I 13
mš[1.2 IV 39, 1.81 4
]mš 2.83 12
mšx[4.182 38
]mšx[4.324 3
mšxx[4.755 11
mšu 4.130 1, 4.635 39, 4.769 58
mšbʿthn 1.14 I 20
mšbt 4.621 7
mšdpt 1.14 III 14
mšḥ[m 4.387 7
mšḥt 1.107 48
mšḫt 1.2 I 39, 4.167 12, 4.167 15
mškb 4.195 6
mškbt 4.275 4, 4.385 10
mškkm 5.23 18
mškn[4.335 28
mš\knth 1.17 V 32f
mšknthm 1.15 III 19
mškrt 4.781 5
mšl[1.2 I 5
mšlḥ 4.689 3
mšlm 4.778 4, 4.782 5
mšlt 1.148 19, 4.337 14, 4.337 23, 4.385 3
mš[lt 4.193 4
]mšm[4.734 1
mšmṭr 1.174 9
mšmn 6.66 1
mš\mn 6.69 1f
mšmʿt 2.72 11, 2.72 14
mšmš 1.12 II 55
mšmš[1.12 II 36
mšnqt 1.15 II 28
mšspdt 1.19 IV 10, 1.19 IV 21
mšpy 1.16 IV 14
mšṣu 1.17 I 27, 1.17 I 45
mšṣṣ 1.3 IV 1
mšq 4.265 1
mšr 1.3 III 5, 1.40 26, 1.40 26, 1.40 35, 1.123 14, 1.131 15
m[šr] 1.40 35
]mšr 1.148 39
m]šr 1.84 38
mšrn 4.30 13, 4.342 2, 4.425 13, 4.615 3, 4.753 4
mšrrm 1.24 36
mšt 1.108 9, 4.170 5
mštʿltm 1.23 31, 1.23 31, 1.23 35, 1.23 36
mštt 4.230 5, 4.230 8
mštt[4.216 3
<m>t 1.6 VI 30
mt 1.2 IV 32, 1.2 IV 34, 1.3 I 13, 1.4 VII 46, 1.4 VII 47, 1.4 VIII 17, 1.4 VIII 24, 1.4 VIII 26, 1.4 VIII 30, 1.5 I 7, 1.5 I 13, 1.5 II 8, 1.5 II 11, 1.5 II 14, 1.5 II 19, 1.5 II 20, 1.5 III 9, 1.5 III 18, 1.5 III 25, 1.5 VI 9, 1.5 VI 23, 1.6 I 6, 1.6 I 41, 1.6 II 9, 1.6 II 12, 1.6 II 13, 1.6 II 25, 1.6 II 31, 1.6 V 9, 1.6 VI 5, 1.6 VI 7, 1.6 VI 9, 1.6 VI 17, 1.6 VI 18, 1.6 VI 20, 1.6 VI 21, 1.6 VI 23, 1.6 VI 24, 1.6 VI 31, 1.16 VI 13, 1.17 I 17, 1.17 I 18, 1.17 I 35, 1.17 I 37, 1.17 II 28, 1.17 II 28, 1.17 V 4, 1.17 V 5, 1.17 V 14, 1.17 V 14, 1.17 V 34, 1.17 VI 27, 1.17 VI 35, 1.17 VI 36, 1.17 VI 52, 1.19 I 36, 1.19 I 37, 1.19 I 38, 1.19 I 47, 1.19 I 48, 1.19 II 41, 1.19 II 42, 1.19 IV 13, 1.19 IV 17, 1.19 IV 36, 1.20 II 8, 1.23 8, 1.23 40, 1.23 40, 1.23 46, 1.23 46, 1.82 5, 1.100 65, 1.113 5, 1.114 21, 1.127 30, 1.133 2, 1.133 9, 2.73 8, 3.9 13, 4.335 15, 4.785 12
mt[1.7 40, 1.86 11, 7.157 2
m[t 1.17 V 33, 1.19 IV 19, 1.133 16
]mt 1.4 VIII 43, 1.15 VI 1, 1.17 VI 38, 1.83 15, 4.104 6, 4.182 52, 7.47 2, 7.210 2
m]t 1.3 V 18, 1.15 VI 8, 1.16 VI 1, 1.19 I 20, 1.19 IV 18, 1.113 1
]mt[1.93 9, 1.107 52, 7.52 2
mtx[4.679 7
xmt 4.192 5
]xmt 1.18 I 28, 1.126 6, 1.137 3, 5.23 15
]xmt[2.7 2
mtb 4.310 4
mtbʿl 4.75 V 21, 4.130 10

mtdb[m 4.775 1
mth 1.111 23
mtḥ 1.3 IV 36
mty 4.86 26
mtk 1.16 I 15, 1.16 II 37, 1.119 25
mtm 1.6 VI 48, 1.10 I 10, 1.12 II 41, 1.15 V 14, 1.15 V 16, 1.16 I 3, 1.16 I 17, 1.16 II 40, 1.17 VI 38, 1.22 I 6, 1.117 8, 2.10 12, 4.195 16
mtmtm 1.20 I 3(?)
mtn 3.3 3, 3.3 10, 4.101 1, 4.114 3, 4.214 II 12, 4.214 IV 8, 4.227 I 3, 4.310 10, 4.342 5, 4.609 22, 4.609 34, 4.753 14, 4.754 14, 4.769 11, 4.778 12, 4.778 19, 4.782 18, 4.782 27, 6.61 1
mtn[4.86 9, 4.259 3
]mtn[4.653 2
mtnbʿl 4.115 11, 4.754 13
mtnh 1.1 V 14
mtny 1.1 V 12, 1.1 V 25, 4.369 18
mtnm 1.12 II 38, 1.17 VI 22
mtnn 4.309 15
mtnt 1.41 21, 1.87 23
mt<n>tm 1.130 19
mtntm 1.39 2, 1.109 7
mtqtkḏx[4.707 22
mtqtm 1.23 50, 1.23 50
mtqt[m 1.23 55
mtr 2.71 19
mtrḫt 1.14 I 13, 1.24 10
mtrn 1.162 23
mtrt 1.42 62, 4.180 3
mtt 1.2 IV 1, 1.5 V 17
mṯ 1.5 V 22, 1.69 2, 3.7 15
mṯ[1.69 10
mṯb 1.3 IV 50, 1.3 V 39, 1.3 V 41, 1.3 V 42, 1.3 V 43, 1.4 I 13, 1.4 I 14, 1.4 I 16, 1.4 I 18, 1.4 IV 52, 1.4 IV 53, 1.4 IV 54, 1.4 IV 55, 1.4 IV 57, 1.15 IV 22, 1.15 V 6
mṯ[b 1.3 IV 49
m[ṯ]b 1.4 I 12
m]ṯb 1.3 V 40
]mṯbh 1.82 36
mṯbk 1.13 11
mṯbt 1.23 19, 1.41 51
]mṯbt 1.53 5
]mṯbth[1.137 8
mṯ[bth 1.137 5
mṯbtkm 1.16 V 24
mṯdndy 1.116 4 lg. ndym ṯd ndy
mṯdṯt 1.14 I 19
mṯṯm 4.689 2
mṯy 1.116 5(!)
]mṯy[4.653 4
mṯyn 4.146 5
mṯkt 1.15 I 1, 1.15 I 2
mṯlṯt 1.14 I 16, 1.98 3
mṯmkadd[1.70 17
mṯmṯx[7.55 8
mṯ{.}n 1.103 6
mṯn 1.3 IV 31, 1.4 I 19, 1.103 18
mṯn[1.86 10, 2.60 1
m]ṯn 1.17 VI 39
mṯnn[2.3 21
mṯpit 4.103 40
mṯpdm 1.1 III 20, 1.3 IV 35
mṯpṭ 4.63 I 2
mṯpṭk 1.2 III 18, 1.6 VI 29
mṯpẓ 1.124 3, 1.124 12
mṯrm 4.127 8
mṯt 1.14 III 39, 1.14 VI 24, 1.15 IV 14, 1.15 IV 26, 1.15 V 9, 1.15 VI 3, 1.16 VI 16, 1.16 VI 19, 1.17 V 16, 1.17 V 22, 1.17 V 28, 1.69 5
]mṯt 7.50 3
mṯty 1.69 2, 1.69 6
mṯtnx 7.50 8

N

n 5.2 3, 5.2 4, 5.2 6(*bis*), 5.4 3, 5.6 2, 5.7 1, 5.9 II 1(*bis*), 5.9 II 2, 5.11 10, 5.12 3, 5.13 8, 5.15 1(*bis*), 5.15 2, 5.16 3, 5.16 6, 5.17 2, 5.17 5, 5.19 3, 5.20 1, 5.20 4, 5.21 1, 5.24 1

n[1.1 III 8, 1.3 II 1, 1.10 II 33, 1.12 II 5, 1.26a 5, 1.64 14, 1.64 18, 1.81 11, 1.82 29, 1.82 34, 1.94 35, 1.107 31, 1.136 3, 1.166 18, 2.45 2, 2.45 32, 2.62 16, 3.8 6, 4.41 5, 4.69 V 19, 4.191 10, 4.207 2, 4.232 5, 4.243 44, 4.294 1, 4.332 7, 4.340 16, 4.397 9, 4.422 33, 4.435 7, 4.520 5, 4.536 1, 4.575 2, 4.581 5, 4.609 22, 4.628 7, 4.635 10, 4.679 3, 4.769 1, 4.773 2, 6.49 2

n[1.173 9 cor. rn[

]n 1.2 III 13, 1.4 VI 60, 1.4 VI 63, 1.10 II 36, 1.14 V 18, 1.15 V 27, 1.17 VI 8, 1.17 VI 55, 1.20 I 5, 1.24 12, 1.40 5, 1.42 13, 1.52 11, 1.62 2, 1.62 8, 1.64 31, 1.69 15, 1.94 21, 1.107 16, 1.107 27, 1.108 1, 1.122 5, 1.139 12, 1.149 5, 1.151 6, 1.153 6, 1.163 3, 1.172 17, 2.31 65, 2.35 10, 2.35 14, 2.83 11, 4.13 29, 4.13 30, 4.35 II 7, 4.52 16, 4.52 17, 4.55 2, 4.55 32, 4.69 IV 22, 4.69 VI 36, 4.75 I 6, 4.103 31, 4.103 55, 4.103 61, 4.111 10, 4.111 11, 4.112 II 7, 4.112 II 8, 4.141 II 11, 4.151 IV 1, 4.151 IV 2, 4.155 10, 4.156 2, 4.162 12, 4.176 2, 4.182 60, 4.183 I 4, 4.183 I 18, 4.183 II 5, 4.185 5, 4.187 5, 4.191 10, 4.197 7, 4.217 7, 4.227 IV 3, 4.243 33, 4.244 1, 4.259 7, 4.290 9, 4.325 7, 4.335 6, 4.335 30, 4.351 1, 4.357 8, 4.359 4, 4.370 34, 4.374 10, 4.384 7, 4.384 12, 4.399 14, 4.401 10, 4.406 7, 4.412 I 1, 4.432 6, 4.454 1, 4.467 2, 4.487 2, 4.487 3, 4.553 1, 4.559 4, 4.573 2, 4.597 8, 4.606 3, 4.609 16, 4.610 9, 4.610 61, 4.611 9, 4.613 10, 4.613 17, 4.616 8, 4.635 9, 4.638 5, 4.640 4, 4.648 14, 4.648 22, 4.657 5, 4.658 29, 4.658 32, 4.658 41, 4.701 16, 4.718 5, 4.747 2, 4.769 8, 4.769 22, 4.769 27, 4.769 30, 4.769 37, 4.769 38, 4.769 40, 4.769 56, 4.769 64, 4.769 68, 4.769 69, 4.792 8, 7.17 2, 7.23 2, 7.43 10, 7.49 7, 7.58 1, 7.72 2, 7.72 3, 7.85 3, 7.99 2, 7.120 4, 7.135 1, 7.141 4, 7.145 1, 7.145 3, 7.162 2, 7.178 2, 7.189 2, 7.203 1

]n[1.2 III 1, 1.10 II 36, 1.64 11, 2.51 5, 2.54 5, 2.63 11, 4.194 13, 4.227 I 1, 4.233 1, 4.275 12, 4.295 9, 4.374 9, 4.432 2, 4.442 1, 4.511 3, 4.606 5, 4.608 20, 4.727 1, 4.769 21, 7.1 5, 7.37 6, 7.46 1, 7.133 1, 7.136 1, 7.164 3, 7.186 3, 7.199 2, 7.201 1

]n[1.116 29 lg. tg]n[d

]\n 1.69 2f, 4.412 I 24f

nx 1.42 18, 4.191 12, 4.748 12

nx[4.357 5, 4.372 3, 4.398 14, 4.434 7, 4.445 1

]nx[1.164 15, 4.397 4, 7.79 5

nxx[1.86 20, 4.332 8, 4.610 43

]nxx 4.744 5

xn 1.14 I 45, 1.86 18, 4.7 13, 4.273 4, 4.690 10

xn[4.412 II 30

]xn 1.4 III 4, 1.15 II 6, 1.107 4, 1.107 48, 1.108 11, 1.114 25, 1.136 1, 2.31 52, 2.31 58, 2.35 1, 2.46 20, 2.46 21, 2.46 22, 2.54 9, 4.13 31, 4.69 IV 18, 4.70 2, 4.102 14, 4.104 4, 4.224 3, 4.259 1, 4.259 2, 4.259 3, 4.320 9, 4.335 29, 4.359 9, 4.432 10, 4.444 3, 4.545 I 6, 4.559 6, 4.581 2, 4.591 2, 4.609 24, 4.609 39, 4.610 25, 4.612 4, 4.646 1, 4.658 2, 4.668 1, 4.733 2, 7.22 1, 7.22 4, 7.80 1, 7.162 5, 7.167 2

]xn[1.68 17, 1.159 1, 4.64 II 11, 4.327 1, 4.491 1, 4.497 4, 4.535 1, 4.661 1, 4.702 1, 7.25 4, 7.48 1, 7.74

4
]xnx[1.107 49, 4.624 12, 7.118 3
]xnxx[7.71 1
xxn[4.340 10, 4.393 15
]xxn 1.152 6, 4.75 V 10, 4.766 3
]xxxn[7.69 4
n/a[1.107 21, 4.2 5, 4.17 7, 4.24 2, 4.69 V 2, 4.258 3, 4.650 4, 4.743 14, 7.114 2
]n/a 1.53 4, 2.35 19, 4.188 13, 4.328 1, 4.769 18, 4.769 70, 7.3 2
]n/a 7.222 1 cor.]n/at
]n/a[1.64 11
n/a/t[4.629 17
]n/w 7.51 13
n/r[7.108 6
]n/r 1.172 15
]xxxn/txx 4.721 7
xn/a[4.97 8
]n/at 7.222 1(cor.)
]xn/t 4.676 5
nxbxxxx[1.86 27
]nxbnnḫmn 1.35 10
]xnxd 4.32 4
nxxḏḏ 1.148 13
]nxm[4.35 II 1
nxnḏ 7.197 5
nxprnprdpkṣṣ/l[1.68 20
]nxrx[4.650 6
nxt[1.70 33
]na 4.768 1
nad 1.124 5
nark 1.10 II 20
nat 1.127 4, 1.127 10
naṯt 1.175 3
]ni[7.121 2
niḫ/y[7.135 5
]nil 4.183 I 21
niṣ 1.5 IV 26
niṣh 1.17 I 29
niṣy 1.17 II 18
niṣk 1.17 II 3
niršn 4.422 2
nit 1.65 13, 4.625 2, 4.625 7, 4.625 11, 4.625 18, 4.632 3, 4.632 7, 4.632 16
nit[1.86 21
ni[t 4.625 9, 4.632 11
ni]t 4.625 16
]nitk 2.72 45
nitm 4.625 5
]nu 1.69 11
nd/u/llḥp 4.42 3
nb[1.56 8, 4.69 V 24
]nb 4.55 20
]nb[4.619 10
nb/dx[1.68 30
]n/aba/n 4.682 6
nbdg 1.125 5, 4.69 I 18
[n]bdg 1.42 50
nbdgd 1.60 9, 1.110 10, 1.116 8, 1.116 16, 1.132 10
nbdg[d 1.116 35
nb]dgd 1.135 9
]nbdgn 7.43 5(cor.)
]nbgdn 7.43 5 cor.]nbdgn
]nbhm 1.12 I 5
nbzn 4.631 9
nbk 1.87 35, 4.269 19
nbk[4.86 10
nbkm 1.105 10, 4.141 III 13
nbl 1.3 V 34, 1.4 IV 46, 1.117 2
nbl[1.101 13
nblat 1.4 VI 25, 1.4 VI 28, 1.4 VI 30
nb[l]at 1.4 VI 23
n[bl]at 1.4 VI 33
nbluh 1.45 4
nbln 1.3 V 34
nb[ln] 1.4 IV 45
]n/aba/n 4.682 6
n/rbˁl 6.70 2
nbˁm 4.425 12
nbq 4.93 III 3
nbšt 1.130 17
nbt 1.4 I 31, 1.14 II 19, 1.14 IV 2, 1.41 21, 1.148 22, 4.14 2, 4.14 8, 4.14 15, 4.751 6, 4.780 13
nbtm 1.6 III 7, 1.6 III 13
ng 1.14 III 27, 1.14 VI 15
ng[4.139 15
]ng 1.81 10
ngxn 4.75 I 1
ngb 1.14 II 32, 1.14 II 33, 1.14 IV 13
ngb[1.14 IV 14
ngh 1.123 12
ngẓḥn 4.103 23
ngḥt 4.643 18
ngln 1.16 I 15, 1.16 II 37

ngġln 4.180 5
ngr 1.16 IV 3, 1.16 IV 6, 1.16 IV 7, 1.16 IV 10, 1.16 IV 11, 4.125 3
ng/ˁr 7.221 4
ngršp 4.180 4
ngr[šp 4.382 23
ngrt 1.16 IV 4, 1.16 IV 8, 1.16 IV 12
ngš 1.6 II 21, 1.23 68
ngšnn 1.114 19
ngtḏriḏḫurn 1.68 27
ngṯhm 1.12 I 40
nd 1.10 III 16
]nd 1.116 28(!), 4.182 3, 4.481 6, 4.673 4
]nd[1.26a 2, 7.25 1
ndx[1.9 19
]ndx[7.48 4
]xnd 1.68 33
xndx[1.35 6
nb/dx[1.68 30
ndb 4.648 12, 4.648 13, 4.648 14
ndb[4.610 13
ndbd 4.15 9
nd[b]d 1.131 6
ndbḥ 1.40 32, 1.40 41
n[dbḥ 1.121 4
ndb]ḥ 1.40 15, 1.40 23
ndb[y] 4.33 38
ndbym 4.55 21
nd/u/llḥp 4.42 3
ndbn 4.424 23
ndd 1.3 I 8, 1.23 63
ndwd 4.704 5
ndy 1.116 4(!)
xxndy 4.200 6
ndym 1.116 4(!)
ndk 1.79 4
ndr 1.127 2
ndr 2.13 14, 2.30 13 lg. ṯyndr Dietrich-Loretz UF 26, 1994, 63-71.
nd]r 1.127 14
ndrg 1.81 18
ndrh 1.15 III 26
ndr[m 1.15 III 29
]ndrṯt 1.116 26
ndt 1.18 I 26
]nḏ 1.42 26
xnḏxx[4.34 8
nḏbn 4.311 11, 4.313 8, 4.609 16
nḏr 1.42 58
nḏrm 1.128 3
nh 1.24 12 cor. ˁnh
]nh 1.172 22, 2.53 2, 4.382 31
]xnh 1.107 7
]nhm 4.176 5
nhmmt 1.14 I 32, 1.14 I 34
nhqt 1.14 III 17, 1.14 V 9
nh<r> 1.2 I 26
nhr 1.2 I 7, 1.2 I 28, 1.2 I 30, 1.2 I 34, 1.2 I 41, 1.2 III 9, 1.2 III 16, 1.2 III 23, 1.2 IV 4, 1.2 IV 13, 1.2 IV 15, 1.2 IV 17, 1.2 IV 20, 1.2 IV 22, 1.2 IV 25, 1.2 IV 27, 1.2 IV 30, 1.3 III 39, 1.5 I 22, 1.9 16, 1.9 19, 1.14 I 6, 1.75 2, 1.133 10, 4.459 5
nh[r 1.2 I 44, 1.2 III 21
n[hr 1.2 III 7
n]hr 1.2 III 8
n]\hr 1.4 II 35f
]xnhr 4.443 5
nhrm 1.3 VI 6, 1.4 II 7, 1.4 IV 21, 1.6 I 33, 1.17 VI 47, 1.100 3
nhr[m 1.3 V 6
n[hrm 1.2 III 4
[nhr]m 1.2 I 37
]xnk/w[7.28 4
nwgn 3.4 3
]nwy 1.172 7
nwr[4.678 6
nwrḏ 4.102 3, 4.103 17
nwrḏr 4.286 3
nwrwnd 1.125 13
nz[4.366 3, 4.441 5
nzdt 2.49 11, 2.49 12
nzl 1.14 II 16, 1.14 III 58
]nzm 7.44 4
nzˁn[4.335 16
n]zˁn 4.588 4
nzt 1.22 II 18 lg. nḫt?
nḥ 4.91 4
nḥx 4.138 6
nḥbl 4.103 18
nḥl 4.7 13
n]ḥl 4.664 2
nḥlh 4.12 2, 4.12 4, 4.35 I 20, 4.35 I 22, 4.35 II 6, 4.35 II 20, 4.35 II 21, 4.57 11, 4.65 11, 4.66 3, 4.69 I 4, 4.69 I 7, 4.69 I 11, 4.69 II 10, 4.69 II

17, 4.69 II 21, 4.69 III 18, 4.69 VI 24, 4.86 14, 4.103 12, 4.122 3, 4.155 12, 4.215 6, 4.232 11, 4.281 9, 4.311 3, 4.311 4, 4.311 5, 4.311 15, 4.356 10, 4.382 30, 4.412 I 26, 4.412 I 28, 4.412 II 15, 4.412 II 32, 4.412 III 12, 4.571 6, 4.581 3, 4.611 8, 4.611 27, 4.631 2, 4.631 3, 4.631 7, 4.631 8, 4.631 10, 4.631 11, 4.631 15, 4.631 18, 4.631 20, 4.692 6, 4.704 7, 4.715 3, 4.724 8, 4.727 10, 4.759 7, 4.759 10

nḥlh[4.86 15, 4.86 16, 4.512 4, 4.635 61

n[ḥ]lh 4.715 10, 4.715 11

nḥl[h] 4.35 I 26

nḥ[lh 4.66 10, 4.69 V 3, 4.77 3, 4.86 3, 4.413 1, 4.435 4, 4.448 3, 4.571 8

n[ḥlh 4.513 3, 4.578 4, 4.581 8, 4.605 1

]nḥlh 4.155 9

n]ḥlh 4.59 2, 4.59 3, 4.59 4, 4.209 8, 4.223 9, 4.311 9, 4.315 4, 4.436 7, 4.561 4, 4.631 12, 4.668 5

nḥ]lh 4.69 IV 17, 4.71 IV 5, 4.209 7, 4.209 9, 4.209 18, 4.209 22, 4.315 5

nḥl]h 4.209 15, 4.209 17, 4.315 1, 4.437 3

]nḥlh[4.436 1, 4.498 5

nḥl]h[4.71 III 1

nḥlhm 4.66 4, 4.69 I 8, 4.69 II 11, 4.69 II 22, 4.69 II 23, 4.69 VI 25, 4.232 12, 4.581 4, 4.581 5, 4.704 8

nḥ[lhm 4.66 11

nḥ]lhm[4.71 IV 6

nḥl]hm 4.69 IV 19

nḥlth 1.3 VI 16, 1.4 VIII 14, 1.5 II 16

nḥlty 1.3 III 30

n]ḥlty 1.3 IV 20

nḥr 4.713 4

<nḥš> 1.100 6

nḥš 1.100 4, 1.100 4, 1.100 6, 1.100 10, 1.100 10, 1.100 12, 1.100 12, 1.100 15, 1.100 16, 1.100 17, 1.100 18, 1.100 21, 1.100 21, 1.100 23, 1.100 23, 1.100 27, 1.100 28, 1.100 28, 1.100 31, 1.100 32, 1.100 33, 1.100 33, 1.100 36, 1.100 37, 1.100 38, 1.100 38, 1.100 41, 1.100 42, 1.100 43, 1.100 43, 1.100 46, 1.100 47, 1.100 48, 1.100 49, 1.100 52, 1.100 53, 1.100 55, 1.100 55, 1.100 58, 1.100 59, 1.100 79, 1.107 5

nḥ[š 1.103 2

n[ḥ]š 1.100 26

nḥšm 1.100 73, 1.100 75

nḥt 1.23 37

nḥtm 1.23 40, 1.23 43, 1.23 47

n{.}ḫ 1.16 IV 14

]nḫḫ 1.61 5

nḫḫy 4.687 2

nḫl 1.100 68, 4.243 24, 4.296 9, 4.348 11

nḫlh 4.438 2

nḫlm 1.6 III 7, 1.6 III 13, 1.172 9

nḫry 4.89 2

]xnḫlt 1.35 9

nḫt 1.3 IV 3, 1.4 I 33, 1.16 VI 24, 1.22 II 18(?), 2.11 14

n[ḫt 1.6 VI 34

n]ḫ[t] 1.6 V 6

<n>ḫtu 1.6 II 23

nḫtu 2.10 8, 2.10 10

nṭṭt 1.82 9

nṭʿn 1.10 II 24

nẓril 4.12 16

]ny 2.31 57, 2.32 4, 4.69 IV 30, 4.93 III 1, 4.170 20, 4.327 6, 4.355 41, 4.370 41, 4.386 8, 4.410 44(cor.), 4.658 50

]ny[4.658 40

]nyx[4.326 3, 7.176 13

]xny 7.2 4

]xxnym 4.634 2

nyn 4.158 19

]nys 4.368 18

nyr 1.16 I 37, 1.24 16, 1.24 31, 1.161 19

]nyšx[1.157 2

nk 1.131 16

nk[4.315 9

]nk[1.156 1

nkx[2.31 2

]xxxnk 1.22 I 26

]xnk/w[7.28 4

nkyt 1.16 II 27

nkl 1.24 1, 1.24 17, 1.24 32, 1.24 33, 1.24 37, 1.41 26, 1.106 14, 4.63 I 40

n[kl 1.87 28
nklb 4.93 IV 20, 4.260 9, 4.708 4
]nklb 4.122 19, 4.769 52
n]klb 4.432 16
nkld 1.110 8, 1.111 6, 1.116 22, 1.135 12
nkly 4.213 24, 4.227 IV 6, 4.230 15, 4.279 1, 4.280 6
]nkly 4.243 45
nkn 4.611 19
nkr 1.14 II 49, 1.14 IV 28, 1.70 38
xnkš[4.666 2
nk\šy 6.66 3f
nkt 1.40 24, 1.40 33, 1.40 33
n[k]t 1.40 24
n]kt 1.40 41
nk]t 1.122 1
xnktxxxx[4.748 8
nktt[4.422 37
xnkṯiṣṯr 1.70 40
nl 1.63 11
]nl 4.673 3
nlx[1.159 3
nliym[1.19 II 35
nlbn 4.115 12
nlḥm 1.23 72
nd/u/llḥp 4.42 3
n/aln 1.42 51
nlqḥt 4.659 1
nm 6.66 7 lg. šk\n m\aṯr
nm[1.51 18, 1.70 11, 1.82 15, 6.49 1
]nm 1.42 55, 1.52 22, 1.151 4, 4.67 10, 4.107 9, 4.162 10, 4.162 11, 4.610 46, 4.706 13
]nm[4.17 6, 4.329 7, 7.34 1
]nmx[1.158 2
]xnm 1.14 II 4, 1.42 30, 1.147 23
]n/am 4.94 4, 4.94 5, 7.77 1
nˁ/m[1.166 19
nmgn 1.4 III 33, 1.4 III 36
nmy 2.76 3
nmkr[2.48 5
nmlu 1.119 31, 1.119 32
nmlk 1.6 I 48, 1.6 I 54
nmq 1.69 12, 4.7 4, 4.233 7, 4.339 6
nmq[4.422 42
nmqx[4.386 18
nmrx[1.70 19
nmry 2.42 9
nmrk 1.70 23, 1.70 24
nmrrt 1.19 IV 33
nmrth 1.108 23
nmrtk 1.108 25
nmš 4.63 IV 16
nn 2.80 12, 4.52 11, 4.769 60
nn[1.55 3, 1.57 8
]nn 1.2 III 15, 4.103 26, 4.574 5, 4.658 46, 4.718 2, 4.766 10, 7.62 2
nnx[4.393 5
nnxx[4.64 IV 13
xnn[4.86 34
]xnn 1.107 13, 4.701 4
]xnn[4.64 V 2, 6.53 2
]x.nn 1.129 3, 2.33 6
nni 1.72 22, 1.85 15, 1.85 26, 4.355 18
n[ni 1.97 14
nnu 1.91 24, 4.68 23, 4.621 2, 4.693 38, 4.770 9
nnu[4.684 5
nnbkzulġmtnn 1.68 22
nngy 1.116 31
nnd[4.408 1
nnḏ 4.147 15
nnw 1.42 40, 1.54 3
nny 1.16 I 8, 1.16 II 46
nnr 4.69 VI 2
nnr[4.607 29
nnt 1.135 11
n]n[t 1.60 16(!)
xxnnt 1.70 41
nntd 1.116 7
nnt[d 1.116 34(!)
nntdm 1.116 22
ns 2.40 15
ns[4.86 24, 7.30 1
nsb 1.4 VI 35
nsk 4.35 II 8, 4.47 6, 4.68 74, 4.98 17, 4.99 14, 4.126 18, 4.133 3, 4.183 II 22, 4.183 II 27, 4.222 8, 4.222 9, 4.222 10, 4.222 11, 4.310 2, 4.310 5, 4.310 8, 4.396 20, 4.609 25, 4.609 32, 4.630 14, 4.745 7, 6.20 1
ns]k 4.44 20
]nsk[2.8 1
nskh 1.3 II 41, 1.3 IV 44
nskm 4.43 4, 4.261 1, 4.337 3
nskn 4.261 15, 4.335 26

nskt 1.105 22, 1.162 2
n]skt 4.299 2, 4.299 5
nsʿk 1.19 III 54
nʿ[1.73 13, 1.86 12, 1.166 6, 4.503 II 3
n[ʿ] 1.119 32
]nʿ[1.167 13
nʿ/m[1.166 19
nʿkn[2.3 11
nʿl 1.4 I 36, 1.119 33
nʿl[1.107 2
nʿlm 1.107 21
nʿm 1.3 I 19, 1.3 III 31, 1.5 III 15, 1.10 III 31, 1.13 18, 1.14 III 41, 1.14 VI 26, 1.16 III 7, 1.16 III 9, 1.16 V 29, 1.23 17, 1.85 1, 1.96 2, 1.113 2, 1.113 4, 1.113 6, 1.113 10, 1.166 14, 2.50 17, 2.50 19, 2.76 6, 2.81 21, 2.81 22, 2.81 24, 2.81 29, 2.81 31, 4.247 29
nʿ]m 2.81 2
]nʿm 2.50 8, 4.568 1
n]ʿm 1.113 9
]nʿm[4.547 6
nʿmxy[1.86 29
nʿmh 1.14 III 41, 1.14 VI 27
n]ʿmh 1.92 27, 1.92 30
nʿmy 1.5 VI 6, 1.6 II 19, 1.17 II 41
nʿmy[4.436 4
nʿm[y] 1.5 VI 28
]nʿmy 4.75 V 6
nʿmyn 4.611 9
nʿmm 1.10 III 18, 1.23 23, 1.23 58, 1.23 60, 1.23 67, 2.45 17, 2.45 20, 2.79 10, 2.79 10, 2.79 10
nʿm[m 2.79 10
]nʿmm 1.10 II 30
nʿmn 1.14 I 40, 1.14 II 8, 1.14 VI 41, 1.15 II 15, 1.17 VI 45, 1.18 IV 14, 1.24 25, 1.101 13, 1.163 13, 4.35 I 21, 4.63 I 26, 4.63 IV 2, 4.96 6, 4.134 2, 4.232 39, 4.244 12, 4.298 4, 4.320 20, 4.366 10, 4.658 17, 4.754 15, 4.787 3
nʿm[n 1.15 II 20, 1.17 VI 32
n[ʿ]mn 7.218 1
nʿ[mm 1.23 1
nʿmt 1.10 II 16, 1.10 III 10, 1.14 III 40, 1.14 VI 25, 1.23 27, 1.108 27
n]ʿmt[1.14 V 15
nʿr 1.107 8, 1.107 11, 1.114 28, 1.175 16, 3.7 16, 4.60 3, 4.179 3, 4.362 3, 4.402 2, 4.786 1, 4.788 4, 4.788 7
nʿr[4.426 3
ng/ʿr 7.221 4
nʿrb 4.103 45
nʿrh 4.339 3, 4.339 25
nʿry 2.33 29
nʿrm 4.68 60, 4.102 8, 4.126 12, 4.367 7, 4.745 10
nʿr[m] 4.419 4
nʿrm.w.bt 4.360 5
nʿrs[1.18 IV 15
nʿrt 4.102 17
]xnʿt[4.444 5
nʿtq 1.16 I 2, 1.16 I 16, 1.16 II 38
nġ[1.64 11
n]ġẓ 1.4 III 35
nġsk 4.69 III 15
nġs[k 4.571 3
n]ġsk 4.769 46
nġr 1.4 VIII 14, 1.23 68, 1.23 69, 1.23 69, 1.23 70, 1.23 73, 1.92 23, 1.92 33, 2.39 8, 2.47 2, 4.141 III 17, 4.609 12, 4.618 6
]nġr 4.30 3, 4.141 III 16
n\[ġr] 1.92 34f
nġry 4.309 13
nġrnn 1.42 58
nġrn<nk> 1.42 53
nġrṯ[1.35 14
nġṯ 2.36 17, 2.45 21
nġṯ[2.45 4
n[ġṯ 2.36 18
nġṯy 4.85 10
np 1.3 VI 9
np[4.671 3
]np 1.175 1, 5.11 9
xnpx[1.86 28
npin 4.244 14
npṭry 1.76 11
npẓl 1.169 15
npy 1.40 2, 1.40 9, 1.40 27, 1.40 27, 1.40 27, 1.40 28, 1.40 35, 1.84 3, 1.84 12, 1.84 13, 1.84 18
npy[1.40 1
np[y 1.40 19, 1.40 26
n[py 1.121 8

n]py 1.40 18, 1.84 2, 1.84 40

np]y 1.40 10, 1.40 18, 1.40 36

npynh 1.4 II 5, 1.4 II 7

n<p>k 1.14 III 9

npk 1.14 V 1, 4.103 45

npl 1.5 VI 8, 1.12 II 36, 1.12 II 53, 4.130 8

np[l] 1.5 VI 30

nplṭ 2.82 4, 2.82 12

nplt 1.107 10

]nplt 1.107 10

]nps[1.18 IV 1

npṣ 1.19 IV 44, 1.19 IV 46, 4.123 16, 4.248 1, 4.385 1, 4.689 1, 4.706 4

]npṣ 4.9 1

npṣh 1.17 I 33, 1.173 16, 2.31 51, 4.107 1, 4.107 2, 4.107 3, 4.107 4

np]ṣh 4.107 5, 4.107 6, 4.107 7

npṣ]h 4.107 8

npṣhm 4.624 1

npṣy 1.17 II 23

npṣk 1.17 II 8

npṣm 1.104 16, 4.92 1, 4.166 1

npr 1.2 I 12, 4.343 4

npr[m] 1.6 II 37

npršn 4.340 18

npš 1.1 V 16, 1.5 I 7, 1.5 I 14, 1.5 I 18, 1.5 V 4, 1.6 II 17, 1.6 II 18, 1.6 III 19, 1.16 VI 34, 1.16 VI 47, 1.17 I 36, 1.17 II 14, 1.17 V 17, 1.17 V 23, 1.19 IV 36, 1.19 IV 39, 1.27 9, 1.43 15, 1.46 1, 1.46 16, 1.88 2, 1.90 3, 1.105 25, 1.106 5, 1.109 12, 1.119 14, 1.119 15, 1.133 3, 1.133 4, 1.164 4, 1.164 14, 1.168 2, 1.168 9, 1.169 16, 1.170 3, 1.171 8, 2.23 23, 2.38 20, 4.91 13, 4.102 29, 4.228 2, 4.228 3, 4.228 4, 4.228 5, 4.228 6, 4.228 7, 4.338 1, 7.51 20

npš[1.2 II 11, 1.48 38, 1.107 27, 1.134 12, 7.69 1

np[š 1.43 12, 1.46 18, 2.23 18

n[pš 1.2 IV 2

]npš 1.1 V 3, 4.228 1

n]pš 1.106 19, 7.51 15

np]š 1.43 18, 1.43 20

np{.}š 1.5 I 14

npšh 1.4 VII 48, 1.16 I 35, 1.16 VI 11, 1.18 IV 25

npš[h 1.18 IV 36

np]š[h 1.1 II 9

npšhm 1.19 II 38

npšy 1.93 3

n]pšy 2.31 65

npškm 1.40 31, 6.48 6

npškn 1.40 39

npš[kn 1.40 22

npšm 1.133 2

n]pšm 2.23 32

npšny 1.2 III 20

npt 1.16 IV 14, 1.50 10

npṯt 4.643 19

nṣ 1.117 10, 4.14 5, 4.14 11, 4.60 6, 4.60 10, 4.62 2, 4.112 II 1

nṣb 1.17 I 26, 1.17 II 16, 1.157 5

nṣbt 1.65 7

nṣd 4.182 60

nṣdn 4.229 8, 4.281 4, 4.356 8

nṣḥy 1.19 II 36

nṣp 2.25 6, 4.34 4, 4.49 1, 4.49 4, 4.49 5, 4.132 6, 4.337 13, 4.337 27, 4.779 2, 4.779 9

nṣ[p] 6.20 3

nṣṣn 4.63 II 11

nṣrt 1.16 VI 5

nq[4.448 1

]nq[6.53 1

nqum 4.745 4 lg. nqdm

nqbny 1.19 II 5

nqbnm 1.4 IV 11

nqḍ 1.42 38, 4.98 12

nqdm 1.6 VI 56, 4.68 71, 4.103 44, 4.126 5, 4.369 8, 4.681 1, 4.745 4(!)

nqd[m 4.416 5

n]qdm 4.624 1

nqh 1.169 5

nqṭn 4.309 26

nql 4.182 35

n[ql 1.138 1

nqly 4.15 4, 4.69 VI 26, 4.761 9

nql[y 4.633 8

nqmd 1.4 VIII 49, 1.6 VI 57, 1.40 28, 1.84 40, 1.113 25, 1.161 12, 1.161 13, 2.19 6, 2.19 8, 3.1 10, 3.1 14, 3.1 17, 3.1 24

nqmd[3.1 9

nq[md 1.121 9, 1.161 26

]nqmd 2.36 2

n]qmd 3.1 18
nq]md 1.113 23, 7.63 2
nqm]d 1.113 19
nqmpˁ 1.113 18, 1.113 21, 1.113 23, 3.2 3, 3.5 3
n]qmpˁ 1.113 14, 7.63 1
nq]mpˁ[1.113 21
nqpnt 1.12 II 45
nqpt 1.23 67
nqq 4.35 I 15, 4.422 48
]xn/aqr 4.198 3
nqt 1.73 3
nr 1.4 II 27, 1.51 18, 2.13 18, 2.16 9, 4.284 6, 4.786 8, 5.22 4, 5.22 18, 5.23 6
nr 1.19 I 8 lg. knr
nr[1.123 16, 4.8 7, 4.86 7
]nr 1.19 I 4
]nr[4.367 3
nrx 7.219 2
nrx[4.77 18
]nrx[4.609 30
]xnr[1.123 17
nrd 1.6 I 7
nryn 4.33 11, 4.75 VI 3
nrl 1.125 3
nrm 2.31 33
nrn 2.26 19, 4.35 I 22, 4.69 I 3, 4.75 VI 1, 4.80 6, 4.86 9, 4.103 8, 4.154 4, 4.753 3, 4.753 13, 4.759 1, 4.785 20, 6.62 2
]nrn 4.386 17, 4.420 9, 4.431 2
n{.}rn 4.188 12
nrġp 1.42 58
nrt 1.2 III 15, 1.3 V 17, 1.4 VIII 21, 1.6 I 8, 1.6 I 11, 1.6 I 13, 1.6 II 24, 1.6 III 24, 1.6 IV 8, 1.6 IV 17, 1.16 III 10, 1.19 IV 47, 1.19 IV 49
nrṯt 4.41 10
nš 1.107 52
nš[7.176 6
]nš 4.351 5, 7.132 9
]nš[7.176 14
xnš[2.35 14, 4.114 9
nša 1.14 IV 4
nšat 1.92 27
nši 1.4 II 12, 1.17 V 9, 1.17 VI 10, 1.19 II 27, 1.19 III 14, 1.19 III 28, 2.31 17, 2.82 16
nši[1.19 II 56
n]ši 1.19 I 28
nšu 1.16 III 12, 4.11 7
nšb 1.1 V 6, 1.114 10, 1.114 13
nšbm 4.247 18
nšgh 1.19 IV 45
nšdd 4.272 1
nšy 1.107 19
nšk 4.199 3
nškḥ 2.38 15
nšk[ḥ 2.73 19
nšlḥ 2.34 14
nšlm 4.328 1, 4.328 2, 4.328 9, 4.328 10
n]šlm 4.328 3, 4.328 4, 4.328 5, 4.328 6
nšm 1.3 III 27, 1.4 VII 51, 1.6 II 18, 1.17 VI 45
nš[m 1.1 III 15, 1.3 IV 15
nšmḫ 1.16 I 14(!), 1.16 II 37
nšˁr 7.55 5
nšq 1.17 I 39, 1.23 51, 1.23 56
nšqdš 1.119 30
nš[q]dš 1.119 31
nšr 1.2 IV 15, 1.2 IV 21, 1.2 IV 24, 1.18 IV 17, 1.18 IV 28
nš\r 1.2 IV 13f
nšrk 1.13 8
nšrm 1.18 IV 20, 1.18 IV 21, 1.18 IV 30, 1.18 IV 32, 1.19 I 32, 1.19 III 8, 1.19 III 12, 1.19 III 13, 1.19 III 15, 1.19 III 29, 1.19 III 42
nšt 1.5 I 26, 1.23 72
nt[1.149 2, 4.393 18
]nt 1.63 14, 1.120 1, 2.81 25, 4.251 3, 7.121 1
]nt 2.33 13 lg. ˁ]nt?
]nt[7.11 3, 7.73 2, 7.107 2
]ntx[7.170 3
xnt 4.396 8, 7.64 3
]xnt 1.168 14, 2.79 5
]xnt[1.82 17, 4.528 2
]ntil 4.658 45
ntb 1.17 VI 43, 1.17 VI 44
ntbt 1.119 33, 2.36 15, 4.336 7
ntb[t 4.388 10
[nt]bt 2.36 16
ntbtk 1.82 37
ntbtš 4.288 6

]xnty 2.36 14
ntk 4.278 12
ntlk 1.119 34
ntmx[1.94 22
ntn 1.16 I 4, 1.16 I 18, 4.219 1, 4.274 3, 5.10 4
ntn[4.669 4
]xntn 4.436 9, 4.609 30
n/t/atn 4.63 IV 3
ntp 4.65 3, 4.76 3, 4.106 21, 4.122 8
]n/atṯ[1.107 53
]xnṯ[7.24 4
]nṯb 7.43 3
]xnṯb 2.36 9
xnṯdn[1.35 18
nṯk 1.100 4, 1.100 9, 1.100 15, 1.100 20, 1.100 26, 1.100 31, 1.100 36, 1.100 41, 1.100 46, 1.100 52, 1.100 58, 1.100 79, 1.107 6, 4.682 3, 4.682 12
n]ṯk 1.107 35, 1.107 45
nṯkh 4.225 14, 4.225 16
nṯkp 2.10 14
nṯʿy 1.40 24, 1.40 32
n[ṯʿy 1.40 41
nṯʿ]y 1.40 6
nṯġx[4.69 V 12
nṯp[1.116 34 lg. nnt[d
nṯq 1.4 VII 39, 4.169 3
nṯt 1.67 22
nṯtrbn 1.131 7
nṯṯ 1.79 1, 1.79 5, 4.409 8

S / Ś

ś 5.4 6, 5.5 1, 5.6 3, 5.12 4, 5.13 9, 5.14 20, 5.16 4, 5.17 3, 5.17 6, 5.19 4, 5.20 2, 5.20 3, 5.21 2, 5.25 17
ś[4.372 9, 4.415 2, 4.645 6
]ś[1.164 2
s 5.2 8, 5.6 2, 5.12 3, 5.13 8, 5.15 1(*bis*), 5.16 3, 5.17 6, 5.19 3, 5.20 1, 5.20 4, 5.21 2, 5.21 3, 5.24 1
s 7.53 5 cor.]\ṣ
s[1.22 IV 3, 1.127 23, 1.164 18, 2.45 29, 4.69 V 1, 4.93 I 26, 4.124 5, 4.138 3, 4.157 7, 4.255 5, 4.357 10, 4.359 6, 4.672 4, 7.133 3
]s 4.196 1, 4.730 3
]s[4.427 7
sx[1.127 20, 2.49 5, 4.406 8, 4.434 2
xs[4.505 2
]xs 1.41 9
xxs[4.651 2
]xs/b 1.74 2
sxpx[4.214 I 12
s/ḫxxry 4.245 I 5
]xsxš[4.198 7
sad 1.17 V 20
si[4.429 2
sigyn 4.93 II 7
sid 1.3 I 3
sin 1.6 II 10
sip 1.2 II 4, 2.3 9
]su 2.83 10
]śuxxx[7.16 10
su/d/lsg 4.205 14(?)
sb 1.4 VI 34, 1.16 III 3
sb[1.64 8
sbx[6.26 1
sbbyn 4.14 4, 4.14 9, 4.707 8
sbb[y]n 4.14 16
sbd 4.609 16
śbl 4.69 I 13
]śbl 4.122 17
sbn\[y 1.5 VI 3f
sbsg 4.205 14 lg. su/d/lsg?
sbrdnm 4.337 1, 4.352 6
sgld 3.9 21, 4.98 13, 4.309 3
sgld[4.678 7
]sglth 2.39 7, 2.39 12
śgn 4.382 33
sǧsr 1.66 12 cor. sġsr
sgr 1.14 II 43, 4.69 VI 12, 4.166 6, 4.205 2
śgryn 4.379 7
sgryn 4.101 4, 4.384 1
sgrm 4.195 4
sgrt 1.3 V 12, 1.3 V 27, 1.100 70
sgṯtn 4.131 9
]śd 1.171 7
sd 1.20 I 4
]sd 4.236 3
s]dwn 4.658 48
śdy 4.33 15
sdy 4.55 23
śdmy 4.244 13
śdn 4.332 13
sdn 1.161 6, 1.161 23
sdnt 4.595 2
su/d/lsg 4.205 14(?)
sdrn 4.374 8, 4.378 5
]sh 1.69 16
shrxx[1.20 II 11
św 4.342 3
sw 4.635 32
swy 4.628 3
śwn 4.631 3, 4.648 24, 4.782 14
swn 4.80 9, 4.281 15, 4.295 12, 4.417 6
]swn 4.433 5
swr 4.39 5
śz 4.283 8
śzn 3.10 3, 4.432 9
szn 4.77 29, 4.93 I 12
sḫlm 2.73 16
sḫl[m] 2.73 18
sḫr 4.422 4, 4.609 7
]sḫr 4.331 6
sḫrn 4.348 6, 4.631 10, 4.631 20
]sḫrn 4.650 5
sy 4.700 9
]sy 7.76 2

syxx 1.139 11
]xsy[4.382 31
syn 4.382 34
sy[n 4.430 3
syny 4.135 2
synym 6.28 2
synn 4.7 15, 4.103 50, 4.309 19
sy[n]n 4.371 21
syr 2.40 14
sk 1.3 III 16, 1.3 IV 9, 1.16 II 31, 1.133 10, 4.182 18
]sk[4.525 1
skh 1.169 4
skm 1.148 19, 4.270 6
śkn 4.36 3
skn 1.12 II 52, 1.17 I 26, 1.17 II 16, 1.78 6, 2.17 8, 2.21 8, 2.54 4, 3.1 38, 4.64 V 10, 4.68 63, 4.69 V 6, 4.92 3, 4.99 13, 4.102 17, 4.110 2, 4.126 23, 4.132 5, 4.160 6, 4.165 1, 4.184 4, 4.288 2, 4.288 3, 4.288 4, 4.288 5, 4.342 1, 4.357 30, 4.361 1, 4.373 2, 4.410 33, 4.592 3, 4.609 10, 4.609 11, 4.610 45, 4.635 8, 4.635 11, 4.635 12, 4.635 15, 4.635 37, 4.635 75, 4.707 4, 6.13 1, 7.63 5
skn[4.160 9
s[kn 4.47 2
sk]n 4.555 4
sknm 1.12 II 52, 4.213 3
s]knm 4.243 7
śknt 4.135 2
sknt 1.4 I 42
sk[r 1.148 42
skt 1.1 III 8
]skt 1.101 13
sktndm 1.125 1
sl[4.21 1
slbˁl 6.1 1
slg 1.66 11, 1.66 33
ślgyn 4.69 II 6
]ślgy[n 4.450 2
śld 4.303 3, 4.621 15
sld 4.783 6
slḫ 1.46 1, 1.168 9, 4.68 16, 4.355 19, 4.365 34, 4.693 42, 4.770 10
slḫu 1.48 20
slḫy 4.44 31
sly 4.617 11
slyn 4.35 I 7, 4.760 10
sll 4.114 6, 4.610 29
slm 1.43 21
]slm 2.31 40
slmu 4.339 16
slmz[4.335 17
sln 4.311 14, 4.425 1
s/gln 4.86 6
su/d/lsg 4.205 14(?)
slˁy 4.321 2
slˁn 4.263 2, 4.714 7, 4.769 15
slpd 4.93 IV 12
slṯmg 4.147 6, 4.264 4
]sm 4.104 5
]sm[7.140 1
smx[2.73 11
smd 1.22 I 19
smdn 1.66 5
smwn 4.696 8
st/mḫ 4.769 61
smyy 4.624 4
smy[y] 4.318 7
smkt 1.16 I 35
smm 1.16 III 10
]smm 4.664 4
s̄mn 4.31 2
s̄mn[4.31 11
smr[4.68 33
sn 1.70 4, 4.723 15
sn[4.77 5, 4.623 9, 4.635 12, 7.52 4
]sn 4.93 II 19, 4.311 6
]sn[7.94 1
snb 4.311 3
śnd 4.628 7
śn[d 4.415 3
sndrn 4.129 7
sny 4.412 I 29
snnt 1.17 II 27, 1.17 II 31, 1.17 II 34, 1.17 II 36, 1.17 II 38, 1.17 II 40, 1.24 41
sn]nt 1.24 15
snp 2.81 26
snr 4.273 2, 4.355 26, 4.365 35, 4.432 7, 4.610 21, 4.621 8, 4.693 52
snr[4.622 4
s]nr 4.302 6
snry 4.33 36, 4.55 22, 4.278 10
snrym 4.40 14, 4.645 1
snrn 4.69 VI 27, 4.93 III 4, 4.154 3,

4.425 14, 4.548 4
snr[n 4.633 9
sn[rn 4.761 2
śnrn[4.619 5
snt 3.4 10
sntrxmm 1.70 6
]śś[1.71 3
ss 4.75 III 9
s̄s̄ 4.31 2
ssg 4.63 I 36
śśw 1.71 7, 1.72 25, 1.85 2, 1.85 5, 1.85 7, 1.85 9, 1.85 12, 1.85 15, 1.85 18, 1.85 20, 1.86 6, 1.86 6, 1.86 7, 4.427 22, 4.427 23, 4.790 16, 4.790 17
śśw[1.72 36, 1.97 6, 1.97 11, 4.391 14
śś[w 1.97 8
ś[św 1.72 21, 1.97 2
]śśw 1.71 11, 4.470 2
ś]św 1.71 5, 4.384 1
śś]w 1.71 14
ś]św[4.650 1
śśw]k 2.81 8
śśwm 1.85 1, 2.33 24, 2.33 32, 2.45 17, 2.45 19, 4.169 5, 4.363 4, 4.363 7, 4.595 2
śśwm[4.323 5, 4.582 3
śś[wm 4.398 4
ś[śwm 4.589 1
]śśwm 2.33 38
ś]śwm[4.528 1
sswm 1.14 III 24, 1.14 III 36, 1.14 VI 7, 1.14 VI 20, 1.20 II 3
ss[wm 1.14 V 37
ssw]m 1.14 II 3
sswt 6.63 3
ssl 4.15 6
ssm 4.170 18
ssn 4.153 11
ssnm 1.100 66
sst 4.63 I 14
śstm 4.158 6
]sˁ 7.1 4
sˁ/t[1.13 36
sˁt 1.14 III 7, 1.14 III 9, 1.14 IV 51, 1.14 V 1, 2.47 18
sġy 4.213 15, 4.625 7
sġsr 1.66 12(cor.), 1.66 34
sġ]sr 1.66 27
śġr 4.277 13, 4.374 3, 4.374 7, 4.374 12, 4.374 13, 4.729 4, 4.729 6, 4.729 7
śġr[4.359 4
ś]ġr 4.374 11
sġr 4.129 2, 4.129 3, 4.129 4, 4.129 5, 4.129 6, 4.129 7, 4.129 8, 4.129 9, 4.129 10, 4.129 11, 4.129 12, 4.343 2, 4.343 4, 4.343 8
s]ġr 4.343 1
śġrh 4.374 2, 4.374 4, 4.374 6, 4.374 8, 4.374 9, 4.374 10
ś[ġr(h) 4.729 2, 4.729 9
śġ]rh 4.359 2
ś]ġrh[4.359 1
sġrh 4.243 43, 4.343 9, 4.374 15
sġr[h 4.243 35
sġ[rh 4.243 42
s]ġrh 4.243 38, 4.243 44
sġ]rh 4.243 40
śġrm 4.378 10
ś[ġrm] 4.729 12 lg. k[bd]
ś]ġrm 4.359 8
sp 1.14 III 44, 1.14 VI 30, 1.54 14, 4.44 23, 4.44 27, 4.56 2, 4.56 6, 4.56 8, 4.56 9, 4.56 10, 4.56 11
sp[1.12 II 14, 4.56 3, 4.56 7, 4.56 12
]sp 1.107 32, 1.151 8, 2.79 10, 4.545 I 5
s]p 4.56 1
spu 1.17 I 31, 1.17 II 4, 1.17 II 21, 1.20 II 10
spuy 1.6 VI 11, 1.6 VI 15
spḥy 4.393 14
spy 4.167 6
spyy 4.754 19
spl 1.104 8, 4.123 17, 4.385 3
spm 4.34 2, 4.34 3, 4.34 4, 4.34 5, 4.34 6, 4.34 7, 4.34 8, 4.44 22, 4.44 24, 4.44 25, 4.44 29, 4.44 30, 4.44 31, 4.44 32
sp[m 4.34 9
sps[1.59 2
ś]pśg 4.182 8
spsg 1.17 VI 36
spsgm 4.459 4
spr 1.1 II 24, 1.6 VI 54, 1.14 II 37, 1.16 VI 59, 1.45 2, 1.75 10, 1.85 1,

1.161 1, 2.10 19, 2.14 7, 2.19 9, 2.19 13, 2.39 32, 3.3 1, 3.8 23, 4.33 1, 4.74 1, 4.93 I 1, 4.120 1, 4.124 1, 4.134 1, 4.144 1, 4.155 1, 4.160 3, 4.160 4, 4.166 1, 4.181 1, 4.183 II 29, 4.207 1, 4.215 1, 4.261 1, 4.263 1, 4.264 1, 4.269 1, 4.288 1, 4.322 1, 4.338 1, 4.338 3, 4.348 1, 4.369 1, 4.370 1, 4.378 1, 4.385 1, 4.424 1, 4.554 1, 4.561 1, 4.609 1, 4.631 1, 4.680 1, 4.683 1, 4.689 1, 4.690 1, 4.714 1, 4.775 1, 4.777 1, 4.784 1, 4.791 1, 5.11 19, 6.24 1, 6.25 1, 6.28 1, 6.29 1

spr[4.160 1, 4.247 1, 4.427 1

s[p]r 1.86 1, 4.245 I 1, 4.337 1

sp[r 4.485 1, 4.515 1, 4.574 1

]spr 2.32 3

s]pr 4.273 1, 4.367 1

sp]r 4.141 I 1, 4.355 1, 4.636 1

]spr[4.627 10, 4.656 1

s]p[r] 4.335 1

sprhm 4.690 18

sp\rhn 1.24 45f

sprm 2.62 13

sprn 2.39 33, 3.10 1

sprt 1.127 9

]sr 1.107 31

]srx[4.575 1

srd 4.12 5

śrdm 1.116 2(!)

srdnnm 4.204 3, 4.204 5, 4.204 6, 4.204 7, 4.204 8, 4.204 9, 4.204 10, 4.204 11, 4.204 12

]srh 1.62 9

srwd 4.309 14

s̀rn 4.629 13 cor. ẓrn

śrn 4.75 III 2, 4.225 11, 4.366 12, 4.371 22

srn 1.66 10, 4.39 3, 4.63 I 42, 4.263 7

srnm 1.22 I 18, 1.147 10

srp 4.283 6

srr 1.24 3, 1.123 12

srt 4.75 VI 7, 4.90 2, 4.197 18

srty 4.611 13

sšm 4.785 30

sˁ/t[1.13 36

st/mḫ 4.769 61

str[1.164 14, 4.86 20

stry 4.778 14, 4.782 21

ʿ

ʿ 4.734 7, 5.2 1, 5.2 3, 5.2 6, 5.4 4, 5.6 2, 5.12 3, 5.13 8, 5.16 3, 5.17 6, 5.19 3, 5.20 1, 5.20 4, 5.21 2, 5.24 1

ʿ[1.16 II 1, 1.58 2, 1.82 14, 1.93 7, 1.176 7, 2.7 4, 2.23 27, 4.66 9, 4.93 I 22, 4.139 3, 4.208 6, 4.227 III 1, 4.243 43, 4.260 3, 4.313 17, 4.335 20, 4.371 3, 4.393 23, 4.404 4, 4.436 6, 4.471 1, 4.491 2, 4.545 II 1, 4.599 5, 4.736 3, 4.743 8, 4.755 13, 4.755 14, 7.38 3, 7.45 6, 7.55 3, 7.136 2, 7.163 6, 7.167 2, 7.218 2

]ʿ 1.63 1, 4.24 2, 4.154 1, 4.186 6, 4.228 2, 4.228 4, 4.693 29

]ʿ[4.122 14, 7.86 1

]\ʿ 1.5 IV (0-)1

ʿxx 4.399 7

ʿx[2.63 11, 4.2 4, 4.196 6, 4.248 1, 4.424 2, 4.637 6, 4.755 15, 7.186 1

]ʿx[1.67 14, 7.176 1

xʿ[2.44 11, 4.191 1

]xʿ[4.730 1, 7.51 21

xʿx[4.619 3

]xʿxxxxx 4.721 10

ʿ/t 6.73 1

]ʿxy[4.619 5

]xʿxm 4.785 27

xʿxn 4.86 32

ʿxrt 1.15 IV 11

ʿb[2.23 35, 4.258 15

]ʿb 1.147 5

]ʿb[7.82 1

ʿb/d[2.23 26

ʿd/b[4.178 2, 4.372 6

ʿbb 1.92 14

ʿbd 1.3 I 2, 1.4 IV 59, 1.4 IV 60, 1.14 III 23, 1.14 III 35, 1.14 III 49, 1.14 III 51, 1.14 VI 6, 1.14 VI 19, 1.14 VI 34, 1.15 IV 10, 1.16 III 13, 1.79 3, 1.82 41, 2.7 10, 2.47 14, 2.57 2, 2.76 12, 4.35 I 24, 4.35 II 5, 4.63 I 18, 4.75 VI 3, 4.98 19, 4.116 6, 4.155 13, 4.183 II 19, 4.214 I 16, 4.269 7, 4.281 11, 4.286 8, 4.311 2, 4.313 19, 4.318 2, 4.332 10, 4.332 11, 4.332 12, 4.340 21, 4.424 20, 4.609 5, 4.609 24, 4.617 27, 4.635 35, 4.754 18, 5.9 I 19

ʿbd[1.14 V 36, 2.41 3, 4.77 4, 4.227 II 7, 4.432 18, 4.529 3, 4.554 5, 4.570 3, 4.746 8, 4.760 8

ʿb[d 4.536 2, 4.746 2

ʿ[bd 4.635 28

]ʿbd 2.50 21, 4.658 51

ʿb]d 1.14 II 2

ʿbdx[4.114 2

ʿbdadt 3.3 12, 4.183 II 28, 4.281 24, 4.609 12

[ʿ]bdadt 4.214 IV 14

ʿbdil 4.35 I 3, 4.133 2(cor.), 4.147 11, 4.283 5, 4.659 5, 4.720 3, 4.723 12, 4.730 7

ʿb]dil 1.9 20, 4.754 9

ʿbdilm 4.33 41, 4.51 16, 4.183 II 25, 4.188 10, 4.261 11, 4.285 9

ʿ]bdilm 4.223 8

ʿbdilt 3.8 17, 4.35 II 14, 4.609 25

ʿ]bdilt 4.151 I 8

[ʿbd]ilt 4.311 5, 4.730 4

ʿbdbʿl 4.75 III 3, 4.110 21, 4.183 II 18, 4.222 18, 4.750 4

ʿbdbʿl[4.742 4

ʿb]dbʿl 4.766 5

ʿbdby[2.67 2

ʿbdg̱r 4.214 I 10

ʿ]bdg̱r 4.151 I 4

ʿbdh 1.17 I 34, 2.12 15, 2.19 11, 2.23 3, 2.33 24, 4.362 5

ʿ]bdh 2.39 6

ʿbdḥ 4.687 3

ʿbdḥgb 4.69 I 23, 4.769 10, 4.769 12

ʿbdḥy 4.93 IV 10

ʿbdḥr 4.318 5, 4.611 7

ʿbdḫmn 4.75 I 3, 4.170 14, 4.177 3, 4.617 17, 4.787 2

[ʿb]dḫmn 4.93 II 18

ʿbdy 4.50 10, 4.232 48, 4.628 6, 4.754 15, 4.769 64, 4.775 16, 4.785 10

ʿbdym 3.3 10, 4.7 7, 4.103 18, 4.103 47

[ʿb]dym 4.341 3

ʿbd{.}yrḫ 4.46 10

ʿbdyrḫ 2.45 14, 2.45 18, 4.63 III 26, 4.98 12, 4.148 1, 4.226 6, 4.339 10, 4.339 18, 4.609 18, 4.727 19, 4.727 22, 4.775 7

ʿbdyr[ḫ 4.75 II 11, 4.35 II 18, 4.141 I 5, 4.658 24

ʿ]bdyrḫ 4.364 3, 4.424 22

ʿb]dyrḫ 4.357 31

ʿbd]yrḫ 4.584 4

ʿbdyrġ 4.277 2

ʿbdk 1.2 I 36, 1.2 I 36, 1.5 II 12, 1.5 II 19, 2.11 4, 2.11 18, 2.12 5, 2.23 6, 2.24 4, 2.33 2, 2.40 9, 2.41 14, 2.64 12, 2.64 20, 2.68 3, 2.68 17, 2.70 5, 2.70 20, 2.70 24, 2.70 26, 2.70 29, 2.75 4, 2.76 5, 2.81 5

ʿbd[k 2.25 3, 2.64 11

]ʿbdk 2.35 3

ʿ]bdk 2.40 4

ʿb]dk 2.50 6

ʿbdkb 3.3 12

ʿbdkṯr 4.175 6, 4.177 8, 4.183 II 19

ʿb[d]kṯr 4.194 21

ʿ]bdkṯr 4.151 I 3

ʿbdlbit 4.63 III 38

ʿbdll 4.133 2 cor. ʿbdil

ʿbdm 4.71 III 10, 4.126 13, 4.195 9, 4.320 1, 4.636 3, 4.636 7, 4.636 12, 4.636 23

ʿb[dm 2.39 12

ʿ[bdm 2.39 7

ʿ]bdm 4.35 II 2, 4.87 2, 4.362 6

[ʿ]b[dm 4.99 1

ʿ]bd[m] 4.636 33

ʿb]dm 4.636 19

ʿbdmhr 4.769 14

ʿb<d>mlk 4.609 15

ʿbdml[4.81 6

ʿbdmlk 2.82 5, 2.82 11, 2.82 18, 3.2 15, 3.4 9, 4.75 III 2, 4.75 IV 8, 4.103 2, 4.103 16, 4.141 I 20, 4.214 IV 5, 4.244 6, 4.412 III 25

ʿbdmlk[4.644 3

ʿb]dmlk 3.2 9

[ʿb]dmlk 4.69 I 27

ʿbdn 1.15 I 3, 3.9 20, 4.313 4, 4.339 19

ʿbdnkl 4.63 II 43

ʿbdnt 4.277 4, 4.277 8

ʿbdssm 1.75 12

ʿbdʿn 4.75 V 23

ʿbdʿnt 4.609 7

ʿ]bdʿnt 4.151 I 6

ʿbdʿṯtr 4.232 49

ʿbdʿṯ[tr 4.75 II 1

ʿbdpr 4.222 17

ʿbdr[4.105 3

ʿbd{.}r[4.288 7

ʿbdrš 4.31 1

ʿbdrpu 4.269 15, 4.609 33

ʿbdršp 4.258 5, 4.298 5, 4.754 16

[ʿb]dršp 4.222 9

ʿbdš[ḫr 4.383 8

ʿbdṯrm 4.283 4

ʿby 4.371 16

ʿby[4.604 3

ʿbk 1.85 26

ʿbl 4.63 III 15, 4.90 8, 4.93 IV 17, 4.311 12, 4.412 II 33

ʿbl 1.148 10 lg. bʿl

]ʿbl 4.155 6

ʿbldmlk 4.714 6

ʿbs 6.27 1

ʿbṣ 4.617 40

ʿbṣk 1.3 III 18, 1.3 IV 11

ʿb[ṣk 1.1 III 10

ʿbr 1.3 VI 7, 1.3 VI 8, 1.4 VII 7(!), 4.69 III 12, 4.116 14

[ʿ]br 1.3 VI 7

ʿbrm 1.22 I 15, 1.22 I 15

ʿg[4.520 2

ʿgx[4.632 15

ʿgw 4.63 III 20, 4.90 4, 4.670 3

ʿg[w 4.63 IV 7

ʿgwn 4.69 VI 15

ʿgy 4.611 19

ʿ]gy 4.769 65

ʿgl 1.3 III 44, 1.5 V 4, 1.108 9, 1.108 11, 4.658 8, 4.783 4

ʿglh 1.6 II 7, 1.6 II 28, 1.15 I 5

ʿglm 1.4 VI 42, 1.22 I 13, 4.783 2, 4.783 6, 4.783 8

ʿg[l]m 7.184 9

ʿglt 1.5 V 18, 4.340 20

ʿgltn 4.131 12, 4.410 36, 4.410 37, 4.410 38, 4.410 39
ʿ]gltn 4.410 23
ʿgml[. 1.41 9
ʿgmm 1.14 I 27
ʿgrn 4.106 22
ʿ/mgš 4.769 60
ʿd 1.3 II 29, 1.4 V 48, 1.4 VI 55, 1.5 IV 12, 1.5 VI 4, 1.6 I 9, 1.12 II 45, 1.14 II 11, 1.14 III 54, 1.19 IV 14, 1.19 IV 26, 1.23 12, 1.23 67, 1.114 3, 1.114 4, 1.114 16, 1.114 16, 1.123 13, 2.1 8, 2.19 5, 2.19 15, 2.63 9, 2.71 16, 3.2 11, 3.2 17, 3.4 17, 3.5 14, 3.5 19, 5.9 I 6
ʿd[1.82 1, 4.114 13, 4.332 22
ʿ[d 1.17 VI 3
]ʿd 1.117 8
ʿ]d 1.7 17
ʿb/d[2.23 26
ʿd/b[4.178 2, 4.372 6
]ʿdxm 1.151 8
ʿdb 1.1 II 11, 1.1 III 9, 1.4 IV 7, 1.4 IV 12, 1.4 VI 39, 1.14 II 27, 1.14 IV 9, 1.14 V 19, 1.17 V 16, 1.19 III 49, 1.19 III 56, 1.19 IV 7, 1.23 54, 1.23 65, 4.631 13, 4.631 19
]ʿdb 1.1 II 10
ʿdbk 1.18 IV 22
ʿdbnn 1.6 II 22
ʿdbʿl 4.723 4
ʿdbt 1.4 VI 38, 1.100 71
ʿd]bt 1.4 VI 39
ʿdd 1.4 VII 46, 4.734 6
ʿdh 1.16 VI 22, 1.62 8
]ʿdḫin 4.608 23
ʿdy 4.55 27, 4.93 II 16, 4.124 15, 4.188 6, 4.229 10, 4.273 8, 4.321 2, 4.352 8, 4.364 5, 4.366 9, 4.609 26, 4.617 28, 4.617 48, 4.706 12
ʿdyn 4.63 II 14, 4.86 13, 4.159 6, 4.183 II 17, 4.417 12, 4.748 4, 4.775 4
ʿdk 1.6 VI 48, 1.6 VI 49
ʿdm 1.15 VI 2
]ʿdm 7.48 2
ʿdmlk 4.148 5, 4.214 I 7
ʿdmn 4.645 8
ʿdmt 1.161 17, 1.161 17, 1.161 17

ʿdn 1.4 V 6, 1.4 V 7, 1.12 II 52, 1.14 II 32, 1.14 II 34, 1.14 IV 13, 2.71 10, 2.71 18, 4.7 6, 4.46 6, 4.63 I 8, 4.86 22, 4.129 4, 4.141 II 5, 4.227 I 9, 4.261 7, 4.261 22, 4.332 4, 4.343 9, 4.378 4, 4.398 12, 4.609 3, 4.609 20, 4.609 27, 4.617 7, 4.617 34, 4.635 36, 4.658 19, 4.690 6, 4.729 8, 4.739 8, 7.61 14
ʿdn[4.40 2
ʿ[d]n 4.347 8
ʿdnhm 1.16 III 14
ʿdnm 1.12 II 53
ʿdnm 4.358 8 lg. adn<h>m?
ʿdr 1.4 VII 7 lg. ʿbr
ʿdr[4.227 II 9, 4.381 17, 4.388 9
ʿdrš/ḏ 4.106 19
ʿdršp 4.52 3, 4.134 8, 4.153 7, 4.269 17, 4.286 5, 4.307 17, 4.609 13, 4.690 4, 4.783 5
ʿd[rš]p 4.147 1
ʿdš 4.261 12
ʿdt 1.4 VII 16, 1.15 II 7, 1.15 II 11, 1.100 3
ʿdt[1.16 V 5
ʿdtm 1.100 66
ʿdṯ 4.170 15
ʿḏbm 1.12 II 26
ʿḏbt 1.4 V 14, 1.4 V 30, 1.4 V 37
]ʿḏl/ṣam[7.16 4
ʿḏr 4.86 18
ʿḏrt 1.140 8
]ʿ/ṯh 7.57 3
ʿwr 1.14 II 46, 1.14 IV 24
ʿwrt 1.19 IV 5
ʿ{.}z 1.133 18
ʿz 1.2 IV 17, 1.6 VI 17, 1.6 VI 17, 1.6 VI 18, 1.6 VI 19, 1.6 VI 20, 1.6 VI 20, 1.86 14, 1.103 17, 1.108 21, 1.119 26, 1.119 28, 1.119 35, 1.127 26, 1.127 31, 2.10 13
ʿzbʿl 1.102 27
ʿzk 1.108 24
ʿ̲zʾl 4.31 8
ʿzm 1.80 4
ʿzn 4.35 I 9, 4.69 II 13, 4.76 1, 4.93 II 8, 4.148 6, 4.214 IV 3, 4.232 34, 4.281 26, 4.281 31, 4.320 11, 4.609 7, 4.609 22, 4.609 28, 4.609 31,

4.773 3, 4.780 11, 4.785 16, 5.11 1, 6.14 2
ʿzn[4.562 3
ʿ]zn 4.319 4
ʿḫdbʿ[l 4.75 II 7
ʿṭ 4.247 24, 4.765 8
ʿṭr[1.16 V 44
ʿṭrṭrt 1.16 III 11
ʿṭtr 1.6 I 54
ʿẓ[1.73 14
ʿẓm 1.3 I 12, 1.12 I 24, 1.19 III 5, 1.19 III 11, 1.19 III 25, 1.19 III 34, 1.19 III 39
ʿẓmny 1.2 IV 5
ʿẓmt 4.352 7
ʿẓrn 1.166 15
]ʿẓrn 1.167 10
ʿẓrnm 1.166 11
]ʿy 4.693 25
ʿyy 4.356 12
ʿyn 2.70 11, 2.70 17, 4.273 5, 4.348 18, 4.357 26, 4.366 10, 4.371 7, 4.617 6
ʿyn[4.422 52, 4.692 15
ʿky 2.38 25, 2.82 4, 4.63 III 37
ʿl 1.1 IV 19, 1.2 I 21, 1.3 I 21, 1.4 II 33, 1.4 VII 20, 1.4 VII 50, 1.4 VIII 5, 1.5 IV 22, 1.5 V 13, 1.6 IV 19, 1.13 17, 1.14 II 20, 1.14 II 21, 1.15 V 23, 1.15 VI 6, 1.16 I 11, 1.16 I 43, 1.16 III 11, 1.16 IV 13, 1.16 VI 9, 1.16 VI 39, 1.16 VI 48, 1.17 II 9, 1.17 V 36, 1.17 VI 6, 1.18 IV 23, 1.18 IV 34, 1.18 IV 40, 1.19 I 14, 1.19 I 15, 1.19 I 32, 1.19 II 30, 1.19 II 32, 1.19 III 44, 1.19 IV 40, 1.19 IV 46, 1.20 I 9, 1.22 II 17(?), 1.23 12, 1.23 14, 1.23 15, 1.82 35, 1.85 21, 1.103 57, 1.107 33, 1.107 34, 1.107 37, 1.107 44, 1.140 4, 2.26 10, 2.26 12, 2.26 13, 2.26 16, 2.30 17, 2.30 19, 2.42 18, 2.47 15, 2.73 18, 3.3 7, 3.10 2, 3.10 3, 3.10 4, 3.10 6, 3.10 13, 3.10 15, 3.10 17, 3.10 19, 3.10 21, 4.123 2, 4.123 4, 4.123 4, 4.123 5, 4.123 6, 4.123 7, 4.123 8, 4.123 9, 4.123 10, 4.123 11, 4.123 12, 4.135 2, 4.197 6, 4.197 9, 4.197 12, 4.197 19, 4.197 27, 4.201 3, 4.225 11, 4.225 12, 4.225 15, 4.240 3, 4.258 2, 4.258 4, 4.258 8, 4.258 10, 4.258 13, 4.262 4, 4.262 6, 4.262 8, 4.262 9, 4.279 2, 4.283 6, 4.283 7, 4.283 8, 4.283 9, 4.290 6, 4.290 16, 4.310 2, 4.310 4, 4.310 5, 4.310 7, 4.310 10, 4.313 1, 4.313 4, 4.313 5, 4.313 6, 4.313 7, 4.313 8, 4.313 9, 4.313 16, 4.313 17, 4.313 18, 4.313 19, 4.313 20, 4.313 21, 4.313 22, 4.313 28, 4.369 16, 4.369 17, 4.369 18, 4.381 18, 4.381 20, 4.381 21, 4.381 22, 4.381 23, 4.386 10, 4.386 19, 4.398 1, 4.398 2, 4.398 11, 4.632 2, 4.632 6, 4.632 10, 4.632 20, 4.632 21, 4.640 2, 4.690 16, 4.699 2, 4.699 4, 4.749 1, 4.749 2, 4.755 2, 4.778 2, 4.778 6, 4.778 8, 4.778 10, 4.778 14, 4.778 18, 4.779 11, 4.780 1, 4.780 2, 4.780 3, 4.780 4, 4.780 5, 4.780 7, 4.780 16, 4.781 6, 4.781 7, 4.782 3, 4.782 9, 4.782 13, 4.782 17, 4.782 21, 4.782 24, 4.782 28, 4.791 7, 4.791 10, 4.791 13, 4.791 16, 4.791 18, 7.140 3
ʿl[1.18 IV 32, 1.92 5, 4.24 4, 4.258 16, 4.313 13, 4.313 15, 4.381 19, 4.699 5, 4.743 10, 4.747 8, 4.747 9
ʿ[l 1.18 IV 12, 4.313 14, 4.313 24, 4.386 1, 4.640 3, 4.747 7
]ʿl 1.18 IV 21, 1.167 6, 2.37 5, 4.258 14, 4.258 15, 4.581 8, 4.592 4, 4.769 41, 7.9 2, 7.137 7
ʿ]l 1.19 IV 35, 4.262 1, 4.386 6, 4.632 15
]ʿl[7.48 3, 7.183 1
ʿlx[1.10 III 5
ʿṣ/l[7.52 6
ʿlby 4.277 6
ʿlh 1.3 II 10, 1.15 IV 17, 1.15 IV 18, 1.15 V 3, 1.17 VI 31, 1.18 IV 30, 1.19 IV 25, 1.19 IV 26, 1.101 7, 1.103 2
ʿl[h 1.15 V 4
]ʿlh 7.51 2
ʿ]lh 1.92 26
ʿly 1.4 I 23, 1.14 IV 2, 1.16 III 6, 1.16 III 8, 2.22 8, 2.33 25
ʿly[1.23 3, 1.87 41

]ˁly 2.31 4
ˁlyh 1.41 46, 1.106 14, 1.126 20, 1.163 14
ˁl[yh 1.87 50, 1.163 12
ˁ]lyh 1.163 16
ˁlyqm 1.172 19
ˁlyt 1.176 6
ˁlk 1.6 V 11, 1.6 V 12, 1.6 V 13, 1.6 V 15, 1.6 V 17, 1.6 V 18, 1.19 III 52, 1.19 IV 4
ˁ[lk 1.6 V 16, 1.19 III 46
]ˁlk 7.163 6
ˁllmy 1.22 I 10
ˁl{.}lmn 1.161 24
ˁllmn 1.1 IV 5, 1.161 7
ˁlln 4.309 24
ˁlm 1.2 IV 32, 1.3 V 31, 1.4 IV 42, 1.14 II 2, 1.14 III 23, 1.14 III 36, 1.14 VI 20, 1.43 9, 1.49 7, 1.50 6, 1.87 9, 1.87 56, 1.105 3, 1.105 7, 1.105 11, 1.105 12, 1.105 21, 1.106 28, 1.108 1, 1.108 21, 1.108 22, 1.109 32, 1.109 32, 1.111 14, 1.132 13, 1.136 13, 1.164 10, 1.175 14, 2.19 5, 2.19 15, 2.42 7, 2.42 9, 3.2 17, 3.5 14, 3.5 20, 4.190 3, 5.9 I 6, 5.9 I 11, 6.48 4
ˁlm[4.637 4
ˁ]lm 1.41 8
ˁl]m 3.2 12
ˁlm.h 1.19 III 48
ˁlmh 1.19 III 55, 1.19 IV 6, 1.23 42, 1.23 46, 1.23 49
ˁlmk 1.2 IV 10, 1.5 II 12, 1.5 II 20
ˁlmt 3.5 15
ˁln 1.3 III 34, 1.3 V 14, 1.4 I 37, 1.6 VI 22, 1.15 V 21, 1.15 V 22, 1.111 24, 1.161 19
ˁl[n 1.19 II 45
]ˁln 1.4 III 52, 4.154 2
ˁlnh 1.3 V 33, 1.4 IV 44
ˁlpy 4.205 20, 4.225 12, 4.617 22
ˁlṣ 1.2 I 12
ˁlṣm 1.2 I 12
ˁlr 4.15 5, 4.635 19
{t}ˁlt 1.4 II 4(?)
ˁlt 1.82 9, 1.82 10, 4.271 9
]ˁlt 4.209 14
ˁltn 2.39 31
ˁm 1.2 I 14, 1.2 I 20, 1.2 III 4, 1.3 III 24, 1.3 IV 37, 1.3 V 31, 1.4 IV 21, 1.4 IV 42, 1.4 V 23, 1.4 VIII 2, 1.4 VIII 3, 1.4 VIII 4, 1.5 I 10, 1.5 I 22, 1.5 I 23, 1.5 I 24, 1.5 I 25, 1.5 II 14, 1.6 I 32, 1.6 I 51, 1.6 I 52, 1.6 IV 8, 1.6 V 10, 1.6 VI 12, 1.6 VI 25, 1.7 32, 1.9 14, 1.13 20, 1.14 III 20, 1.14 V 31, 1.15 I 4, 1.17 VI 18, 1.17 VI 28, 1.17 VI 29, 1.17 VI 47, 1.18 IV 6, 1.23 69, 1.24 16, 1.24 44, 1.24 49, 1.100 2, 1.100 9, 1.100 14, 1.100 19(!), 1.100 25, 1.100 30, 1.100 35, 1.100 40, 1.100 45, 1.100 51, 1.100 58, 1.100 78, 1.124 2, 1.124 11, 1.176 21, 2.11 15, 2.12 12, 2.13 11, 2.14 8, 2.16 17, 2.17 4, 2.17 7, 2.30 9, 2.34 8, 2.34 13, 2.36 3, 2.36 6, 2.36 13, 2.39 3, 2.39 18, 2.39 29, 2.40 12, 2.42 11, 2.42 27, 2.47 1, 2.62 10, 2.62 14, 2.64 16, 2.68 14, 2.70 12, 2.72 26, 2.75 8, 2.81 19, 4.41 4, 4.230 4, 4.290 3, 4.792 1, 4.792 3, 4.792 5, 4.792 7
ˁm[1.1 III 14, 2.23 8, 2.41 8, 2.43 4, 2.49 8, 2.50 7, 3.1 2, 4.563 3, 4.662 4, 4.748 9
ˁ[m 2.46 7
]ˁm 2.37 12, 4.243 8
ˁ]m 1.14 VI 1, 2.77 3, 4.197 23
ˁmx 2.34 22, 2.62 12
]xˁm 2.31 60, 4.111 15, 4.243 49
ˁmdm 1.169 3
ˁmḏl 4.165 8
ˁmh 1.6 I 8, 1.17 I 27, 1.24 48, 2.23 5
ˁmy 1.1 III 11, 1.3 III 19, 1.3 III 19, 1.3 IV 11, 1.3 IV 12, 1.7 29, 1.17 II 17, 2.10 11, 2.10 19, 2.16 19, 2.21 12, 2.26 4, 2.32 2, 2.33 36, 2.34 6, 2.36 10, 2.36 11, 2.36 13, 2.39 15, 2.41 15, 2.46 10, 2.50 20, 2.72 16, 4.16 4, 4.63 III 36, 4.98 14, 4.117 6, 4.197 26, 4.357 25, 4.399 8, 4.592 4
ˁmy[2.41 4, 2.60 2
ˁm[y 2.63 14, 2.76 4
ˁ]my 1.1 II 1
ˁmyd 4.344 3
ˁmyḏtmr 6.23 2(cor.), 6.75 2
ˁ(?)myḏtmr 6.23 2 cor. ˁmyḏtmr

ʿmyn 4.69 III 5, 4.75 IV 8, 4.75 V 20, 4.76 4, 4.77 11, 4.232 36, 4.280 12, 4.290 11, 4.315 10, 4.356 5, 4.677 5, 4.727 5, 4.728 7, 4.755 9, 4.785 19
ʿmk 1.5 V 8, 1.5 V 10, 1.5 V 11, 2.21 14, 2.30 18, 2.34 29, 2.36 4, 2.38 8, 2.50 15, 2.51 4, 2.65 3, 2.70 27, 2.71 7, 2.72 8, 2.75 11
ʿm[k] 2.45 25
ʿml 5.11 8
ʿmlbi 4.344 6, 4.356 8, 4.432 6
]ʿmlbi 4.260 10
]ʿmlb[i 4.498 8
ʿmlbu 4.165 7
ʿmm 1.8 II 8, 1.14 VI 37
ʿmn 1.3 III 25, 1.24 32, 2.13 15, 2.17 16, 2.30 12, 2.33 34, 2.38 6, 2.46 6, 2.71 6, 2.72 7, 2.77 17, 3.1 7, 3.1 11, 4.33 41, 4.280 1, 4.280 3, 4.290 5, 4.317 6, 4.399 5
ʿmn[2.79 1, 4.178 4, 4.445 2
ʿ[mn 1.3 IV 17
]ʿmn 2.65 2
ʿmnh 1.5 V 20
ʿmny 2.11 10, 2.13 9, 2.16 14, 2.30 8, 2.34 6
ʿm]ny 2.24 8
ʿ/ṯmny 4.34 7
ʿmnk 2.3 21, 2.70 21, 2.71 11, 3.9 16
ʿmnkm 2.21 16, 2.36 9
ʿmnr 4.222 21, 4.356 3, 4.356 4, 4.377 2, 4.432 10
ʿms 1.6 I 12, 4.335 3
ʿmsn 4.370 2
ʿmph 1.113 15 lg. ʿmrpi?
ʿmq 1.3 II 6, 1.3 II 19, 1.5 VI 21, 1.6 I 5, 1.7 4, 1.17 VI 45, 2.36 18, 4.625 9
ʿ]mq 1.151 14
ʿm[q]t 1.148 6 lg. thmt
ʿmr 1.5 VI 14
ʿmrbi 5.22 21
ʿmrpi 1.113 15(?), 1.113 20, 2.39 2, 2.76 2, 9.530 2
ʿmrp[i 2.76 11
ʿmr[pi 1.161 31, 4.707 22
ʿ[mrpi] 2.78 2
ʿmrpu 4.775 19
ʿmt[7.81 2
]ʿmt 2.79 3
ʿmḏl 4.77 10, 4.344 5
ʿmtr 1.102 20, 1.102 23, 1.106 5
ʿmṯdy[4.748 10
ʿmṯtmr 1.161 11, 1.161 25, 3.2 2, 3.5 2
ʿm]ṯtmr 1.113 13
ʿmṯ]tmr 1.113 22
ʿmṯtm]r 1.113 18, 2.81 5
]ʿmṯtmrw 1.125 7
ʿn 1.1 V 6, 1.2 IV 7, 1.3 V 13, 1.4 II 30, 1.4 VI 7, 1.4 VII 40, 1.4 VII 53, 1.5 I 17, 1.6 I 53, 1.6 II 13, 1.6 IV 18, 1.8 II 6, 1.12 II 31, 1.12 II 59, 1.16 III 4, 1.16 III 9, 1.23 73, 1.24 31, 1.96 5, 1.96 6, 1.96 7, 1.96 7, 1.96 8, 1.96 8, 1.96 9, 1.96 10, 1.96 11, 1.96 12, 1.98 2, 1.100 1, 1.133 8, 4.33 32, 4.35 II 19, 4.232 47, 4.753 14, 5.22 8
ʿn[1.12 II 3, 1.92 11, 2.3 13, 4.178 12, 4.435 3, 4.505 3, 4.529 4
]ʿn 4.70 4, 4.75 IV 1, 4.613 21, 4.785 1
ʿ]n 1.6 VI 9
ʿnx[4.393 19
ʿnxx[4.635 60
ʿn/txx[4.64 V 15
ʿnil 4.159 3
ʿnbr 4.617 29
ʿnh 1.4 II 12, 1.10 II 13, 1.10 II 14, 1.10 II 26, 1.10 II 27, 1.14 III 45, 1.17 V 9, 1.17 VI 10, 1.19 I 29, 1.19 II 27, 1.19 III 14, 1.24 12(cor.), 1.92 10, 1.101 5, 1.103 49, 1.103 49
ʿnh[1.2 IV 40, 1.103 57, 1.167 7
ʿ]nh 1.103 8
ʿnha 1.24 8 lg. ʿnhn
ʿnhn 1.24 8(!)
ʿnḫ 1.19 III 28
ʿny 1.2 I 28
ʿnyh 1.16 V 13, 1.16 V 22
ʿn[yh 1.16 V 19
ʿ[nyh 1.16 V 16
ʿnk 1.16 I 27, 1.82 16, 1.82 42
]xʿnk 1.172 13
ʿnkm 1.3 VI 3, 1.119 27
]ʿ/ṯnlbm 4.721 5

ʿnm 1.2 IV 22, 1.2 IV 25, 7.218 4
ʿnm[] 4.247 29
]ʿnm 3.6 4
ʿnmk 4.95 9
ʿnm[k 4.686 18
ʿn[m]k[4.308 7
ʿnmky 4.68 52, 4.113 6, 4.243 28, 4.244 3, 4.303 5, 4.365 38, 4.380 26, 4.693 54, 4.770 6
ʿnmky[4.244 9
ʿnn 1.3 IV 32, 1.4 IV 59, 1.4 VIII 15, 1.10 II 33, 1.96 1, 2.8 4
ʿnnh 1.2 I 35
ʿnnm 7.135 3
ʿnnn 4.405 6
ʿnq 1.22 I 19
ʿnqpat 4.68 53, 4.296 11, 4.348 26, 4.365 20, 4.380 19, 4.693 18, 4.698 4
ʿnqpat[4.683 20
ʿnqpa[t 4.685 7
ʿnqpaty[4.86 27
ʿnqp[aty 4.86 30
ʿnqpt 4.610 12
ʿnqt 4.175 11
ʿnt 1.1 II 15, 1.3 II 4, 1.3 II 5, 1.3 II 17, 1.3 II 24, 1.3 II 26, 1.3 II 33, 1.3 III 9, 1.3 III 11, 1.3 III 32, 1.3 IV 36, 1.3 V 29, 1.3 V 29, 1.4 II 15, 1.4 II 24, 1.4 III 24, 1.4 III 33, 1.4 III 39, 1.4 IV 18, 1.4 V 20, 1.4 V 25, 1.5 VI 26, 1.6 I 15, 1.6 II 14, 1.6 II 27, 1.6 II 30, 1.6 III 23, 1.6 III 23, 1.6 IV 1, 1.6 IV 2, 1.6 IV 3, 1.6 IV 6, 1.6 IV 12, 1.6 IV 13, 1.6 IV 14, 1.6 IV 21, 1.7 37, 1.10 I 1, 1.10 I 14, 1.10 II 10, 1.10 II 15, 1.10 II 21, 1.10 II 26, 1.10 II 31, 1.10 II 35, 1.10 III 2, 1.11 4, 1.11 7, 1.13 19, 1.13 30, 1.14 III 41, 1.14 VI 26, 1.17 VI 24, 1.17 VI 26, 1.17 VI 41, 1.18 I 20, 1.18 IV 4, 1.18 IV 5, 1.18 IV 12, 1.18 IV 16, 1.18 IV 32, 1.18 IV 38, 1.19 I 5, 1.19 II 38, 1.19 II 43, 1.19 III 48, 1.19 III 48, 1.19 III 55, 1.19 III 56, 1.19 IV 6, 1.22 I 9, 1.22 I 11, 1.22 II 8, 1.39 7, 1.39 17, 1.41 16, 1.42 44, 1.42 45, 1.46 5, 1.46 17, 1.82 11, 1.82 39, 1.82 39, 1.100 20, 1.101 15, 1.102 11, 1.107 39, 1.108 6, 1.108 8, 1.109 13, 1.109 17, 1.109 22, 1.109 25, 1.114 9, 1.114 11, 1.114 22, 1.118 20, 1.130 13, 1.148 7, 1.151 12, 1.162 14, 1.168 8, 1.168 11, 1.168 13, 1.173 12, 2.42 8, 4.307 6, 6.74 1
ʿnt[1.27 2, 1.61 1, 1.114 26
ʿ[n]t 1.13 29
ʿn[t 1.3 V 19, 1.6 II 8, 1.10 III 9, 1.17 VI 19, 4.642 2, 4.642 4, 4.642 5, 4.642 7
ʿ[nt 1.6 I 30, 1.19 I 3, 1.130 5, 4.642 6
ʿ]nt 1.2 I 40, 1.3 IV 21, 1.109 36, 2.33 13(?)
ʿ]nt 1.46 2(?) cor. ʿ]n<t>
ʿ]n[t 1.87 12
ʿ]n<t> 1.46 2(cor.,?)
ʿntd 1.60 7, 1.110 7, 1.116 17
ʿn]td 1.135 8
ʿnth 1.43 13
ʿntm 1.43 18, 1.43 20
ʿnt]m 1.43 17
ʿntn 4.37 1, 4.610 26
ʿs̱ 4.767 1
]ʿsb 1.94 26
ʿsl 4.658 6
ʿsn 4.141 II 13
ʿs̄r 4.31 2, 4.31 4, 4.31 11
ʿs̄r[4.31 5
ʿs[t] 1.4 IV 34
ʿp 1.10 II 11, 1.10 II 23, 1.13 8
ʿp[1.167 8
]ʿp[1.18 I 34
ʿps 2.47 17, 2.47 19
ʿpsm 6.29 1
ʿpsn 4.170 6
ʿpʿph 1.14 VI 30
ʿp[ʿp]h 1.14 III 43
ʿpṣpn 4.366 9
ʿpr 1.1 IV 8, 1.2 IV 5, 1.5 VI 15, 1.10 II 25, 1.12 I 24, 1.17 I 28, 1.17 II 2, 1.17 II 17, 1.82 12, 1.161 22
ʿpr[1.7 27, 1.167 6
ʿprm 1.3 III 15, 1.3 IV 9, 1.3 IV 23, 2.47 7, 4.48 1, 4.73 12, 4.346 7, 4.380 16, 4.610 27, 4.693 28, 4.752 1
ʿ]prm 4.784 21

]ʿp[r]m 1.3 IV 29

ʿp\[rm] 1.1 II 19f

ʿprt 4.780 9

ʿpt 1.18 IV 42, 1.22 I 11

ʿpṯb 4.617 17

ʿpṯn 4.35 I 4, 4.46 9, 4.98 9, 4.366 11, 4.370 44

ʿpṯrm 4.116 5, 4.350 10, 4.609 10, 4.628 6

ʿṣ 1.3 III 23, 1.3 IV 14, 1.100 65, 1.101 4

ʿṣ 1.22 II 17 lg. ʿl?

ʿṣ[2.5 2, 7.126 2

ʿṣ/l[7.52 6

ʿṣh 1.4 VI 18, 1.4 VI 20

]ʿṣh 7.138 2

ʿṣy 4.367 6

]ʿṣy[4.98 25

ʿṣk 1.1 III 10, 1.3 III 18, 1.3 IV 11

ʿṣm 1.4 III 44, 1.4 IV 38, 1.5 II 6, 1.23 66, 1.82 37, 1.82 43, 1.82 43, 1.100 64, 2.26 6, 2.26 8, 2.26 9, 2.26 17

ʿṣp 1.93 7

ʿṣr 1.3 IV 1, 1.14 III 59, 1.23 38, 1.23 41, 1.23 44, 1.23 47, 1.23 62, 1.103 41, 1.105 24, 1.119 20, 1.130 23, 1.161 30, 4.14 5, 4.112 II 2

ʿṣr[1.50 8

]ʿṣr 1.14 II 17

ʿ]ṣr 1.49 4, 1.50 5

ʿṣ]r 1.6 VI 3

ʿṣrxxx[4.635 56

ʿṣrm 1.6 II 36, 1.8 II 12, 1.39 21, 1.41 40, 1.46 8, 1.48 1, 1.48 3, 1.48 18, 1.50 7, 1.87 29, 1.87 39, 1.105 26, 1.106 1, 1.111 6, 1.112 5, 1.136 12, 1.148 9, 1.164 8, 1.171 5, 4.751 5

ʿṣrm[1.27 5, 1.106 7

ʿṣr[m 1.41 24, 1.171 3

ʿṣ[rm 1.41 27, 1.87 6

ʿ]ṣrm 1.41 36

ʿṣrmm 1.119 20, 1.132 17

ʿṣrt 1.109 5

ʿqb 4.645 1

ʿqbt 1.17 VI 23

ʿqh 1.14 III 43, 1.14 VI 29

ʿqy 4.124 5, 4.711 5

ʿq[l] 1.103 56

ʿqltn 1.3 III 41, 1.5 I 2

ʿqqm 1.12 I 27, 1.12 I 37

ʿq]rb 1.71 22

ʿqrbn 1.85 2

ʿqšr 1.100 5, 1.100 6, 1.100 10, 1.100 12, 1.100 16, 1.100 18, 1.100 21, 1.100 23, 1.100 27, 1.100 29, 1.100 32, 1.100 37, 1.100 42, 1.100 44, 1.100 47, 1.100 49, 1.100 53, 1.100 55, 1.100 59

ʿq{.}šr 1.100 39

ʿq\š<r> 1.100 33f

ʿr 1.4 IV 9, 1.4 IV 14, 1.4 VII 9, 1.14 V 24, 1.19 II 3, 1.19 II 8, 1.19 II 10, 1.40 26, 1.40 34, 1.62 5, 1.100 62, 1.119 16

ʿr[4.435 5, 4.436 5, 4.629 21, 4.686 20, 7.83 1

ʿ[r] 1.40 43

]ʿr 4.697 8

]ʿr[7.123 2

ʿrxx 4.610 25

]xʿr 2.44 20

ʿrb 1.1 V 24, 1.14 II 12, 1.14 III 55, 1.15 II 9, 1.15 V 18, 1.17 II 26, 1.19 IV 9, 1.23 71, 1.23 74, 1.46 9, 1.87 52, 1.87 56, 1.119 4, 1.119 23, 1.132 27, 3.3 2, 3.7 1, 3.8 6, 4.145 2, 4.337 16, 4.338 2, 4.338 12, 4.347 1, 4.347 3, 4.347 5, 4.347 8, 4.347 10, 4.634 1, 4.634 2, 4.634 3, 4.634 4, 4.634 5

ʿrb[1.16 V 3, 1.126 23

ʿr[b 1.16 V 1, 1.16 V 2

ʿ[r]b 1.41 47

ʿ]rb 1.4 VII 13, 1.112 9

]ʿrb[7.217 2

ʿrb/d 4.214 IV 13

ʿrbm 1.23 7, 1.23 12, 1.23 18, 1.23 26

ʿrbn 1.3 III 9

ʿrbn[4.699 3

ʿrbnm 3.3 1, 3.3 7

ʿrbt 1.78 2, 2.16 7

ʿrbt[4.18 4

ʿr[bt] 1.19 IV 47

ʿrgz 1.85 5, 1.85 10, 4.158 22, 4.365 36, 4.621 16, 4.750 2

ʿrgz[1.72 14, 4.693 45

ʿrg[z 4.68 41, 4.684 4

ʿ]rgz 4.302 4
ʿ]rg[z] 4.94 15
ʿrgzy 4.55 27
ʿrgzm 1.20 I 8, 1.24 43
ʿrb/d 4.214 IV 13
ʿrhm 1.22 II 24
ʿrhm[1.18 I 32
]ʿrwt 1.14 I 7
ʿrẓ 1.6 I 54, 1.6 I 55, 1.6 I 56, 1.6 I 61, 1.6 I 63, 1.12 II 30
ʿrym 1.16 II 29
ʿrym[2.8 3
ʿryt 2.38 25
ʿrk 1.114 29(!), 4.728 1
ʿrkm 1.105 18
ʿrkt 1.119 2(?)
ʿrm 1.4 VII 7, 1.14 III 6, 1.14 IV 49, 1.16 V 47, 1.16 VI 6, 1.169 13, 2.71 17(?), 4.68 22, 4.348 28, 4.621 3, 4.693 40, 4.770 13
ʿrmy 4.51 13
ʿrm[y] 4.33 5
ʿ]rmy 4.55 22
ʿrmn 4.93 II 13
ʿrmt 1.40 27, 4.355 36
ʿ]rmt 1.84 13
ʿrʿr 1.109 29
ʿr{.}ʿr 1.100 64
ʿrʿrm 1.100 65
ʿrp 1.83 4 lg. ṯrp?
ʿrpm 4.721 2, 4.721 13
ʿrpt 1.2 IV 8, 1.2 IV 29, 1.3 II 40, 1.3 III 38, 1.3 IV 4, 1.3 IV 6, 1.4 III 11, 1.4 III 18, 1.4 V 8, 1.4 V 60, 1.4 VII 19, 1.4 VII 28, 1.4 VII 57, 1.5 II 7, 1.8 II 11, 1.10 I 7, 1.10 III 36, 1.13 34, 1.19 I 39, 1.19 I 40, 1.19 I 44, 1.92 37, 1.92 40
ʿrpt[1.19 II 57
ʿr]pt 1.3 IV 27
ʿrptk 1.5 V 7
ʿrq 1.107 46, 1.107 47, 4.46 14, 4.186 1, 4.186 2, 4.186 3, 4.243 2
ʿrš 1.16 VI 35, 1.16 VI 36, 1.16 VI 51, 1.16 VI 52, 1.17 II 41, 1.17 II 42, 1.132 2, 1.132 26, 2.22 2
ʿrš[4.248 5
ʿršh 1.17 I 38
ʿršm 1.14 II 45, 1.14 IV 23
]ʿrt 1.107 2
xʿrt[4.494 1
ʿš[4.65 9, 4.241 2, 4.241 4, 4.769 18, 4.775 5
ʿšdm 4.269 27, 4.786 11
ʿšy 1.17 I 29, 1.17 I 47, 1.17 II 19, 1.17 VI 8, 4.282 7, 4.282 10, 4.282 14
ʿšq 4.124 4
ʿšr 1.15 II 8, 1.16 I 40, 1.43 2, 1.43 2, 1.91 21, 1.91 23, 1.91 29, 1.104 15, 2.76 15, 4.34 3, 4.44 1, 4.44 27, 4.48 2, 4.48 3, 4.48 4, 4.48 7, 4.48 9, 4.48 11, 4.48 12, 4.53 15, 4.56 8, 4.56 9, 4.56 11, 4.73 1, 4.73 10, 4.73 15, 4.95 7, 4.123 5, 4.125 8, 4.125 9, 4.127 5, 4.128 3, 4.128 4, 4.137 1, 4.137 2, 4.137 5, 4.137 7, 4.139 6, 4.141 III 7, 4.150 1, 4.152 11, 4.156 5, 4.158 9, 4.163 3, 4.163 5, 4.163 7, 4.163 13, 4.165 14, 4.165 15, 4.167 2, 4.173 3, 4.173 6, 4.173 9, 4.174 3, 4.174 4, 4.174 5, 4.174 6, 4.174 8, 4.179 2, 4.179 6, 4.179 10, 4.206 1, 4.206 2, 4.213 1, 4.213 4, 4.213 6, 4.218 2, 4.239 1, 4.243 10, 4.243 34, 4.244 3, 4.244 4, 4.244 18, 4.244 21, 4.247 17, 4.247 29, 4.247 32, 4.270 10, 4.270 12, 4.274 1, 4.275 19, 4.275 20, 4.295 17, 4.312 5, 4.312 6, 4.312 8, 4.341 9, 4.341 14, 4.341 20, 4.342 2, 4.344 11, 4.345 1, 4.345 6, 4.349 1, 4.355 4, 4.355 6, 4.355 7, 4.358 2, 4.358 4, 4.358 5, 4.358 7, 4.377 29, 4.380 18, 4.381 19, 4.381 23, 4.387 8, 4.387 26, 4.394 6, 4.399 9, 4.400 3, 4.400 13, 4.400 16, 4.400 17, 4.402 10, 4.594 2, 4.616 2, 4.616 3, 4.616 4, 4.618 1, 4.618 2, 4.618 5, 4.618 8, 4.618 10, 4.618 19, 4.630 8, 4.636 11, 4.688 2, 4.691 2, 4.691 4, 4.697 3, 4.697 7, 4.697 10, 4.721 4, 4.721 9, 4.749 2, 4.769 58, 4.780 12, 4.780 15, 4.786 2, 4.786 6, 4.790 16, 5.10 7, 6.12 1, 6.12 3
ʿšr[1.104 5, 2.69 1, 4.23 11, 4.34 5, 4.34 7 4.80 10, 4.152 2, 4.218 3, 4.247 12, 4.247 13, 4.317 9, 4.558 5, 4.618 11, 4.618 25, 4.769 4, 4.769 19

ʿš[r 4.67 11, 4.182 24, 4.218 5, 4.243 38, 4.244 1, 4.247 4, 4.247 9, 4.247 10, 4.326 1, 4.362 3, 4.381 16, 4.387 2, 4.390 3, 4.394 1, 4.400 8, 4.400 12 4.439 3, 4.478 1, 4.478 2, 4.501 2, 4.507 2, 4.538 2, 4.558 2, 4.594 1, 4.625 15, 4.683 30
ʿ[š]r 4.270 8
ʿ[šr 4.40 5, 4.139 16, 4.218 1, 4.270 6, 4.323 4, 4.618 29, 4.764 4
]ʿšr 1.16 I 62, 4.442 5, 4.582 5
ʿ]šr 2.48 2, 4.123 12, 4.195 7, 4.218 8, 4.355 43
ʿš]r 1.17 II 45, 4.582 2, 4.586 2, 4.589 1
]ʿš[r 4.475 2, 4.538 1
ʿ]šr[4.323 1, 4.479 3
ʿš]r[4.390 11
[[ʿš[r]]] 4.764 12
ʿšrid 2.42 12
ʿšrh 1.39 10, 1.106 20, 1.112 14, 1.112 27, 1.132 1, 1.164 18, 4.27 16, 4.141 IV 1, 4.173 2, 4.174 2, 4.182 14, 4.219 3, 4.243 2, 4.243 4, 4.243 29, 4.243 33, 4.269 2, 4.282 1, 4.284 5, 4.290 1, 4.290 4, 4.344 2, 4.363 3, 4.392 1, 4.399 6, 4.609 52, 4.625 4, 4.630 4, 4.771 6, 4.777 5, 4.777 8, 4.783 4
ʿšrh[2.69 5, 4.141 III 22
ʿšr[h 4.27 19, 4.363 1
]ʿšrh 4.312 9, 4.742 5
ʿ]šrh 4.249 1
ʿš]rh 1.164 14
]ʿšrh[4.141 III 21
ʿ\šrh 1.112 21f
ʿšrm 1.41 43, 1.87 44, 1.106 24, 1.106 26, 1.148 21(!), 1.162 21, 3.1 20, 3.10 4, 4.22 5, 4.34 4, 4.48 6, 4.56 7, 4.68 68, 4.91 11, 4.91 13, 4.91 14, 4.92 4, 4.99 2, 4.103 30, 4.120 2, 4.126 3, 4.128 1, 4.128 5, 4.135 1, 4.137 10, 4.139 10, 4.142 1, 4.142 2, 4.144 3, 4.150 3, 4.158 5, 4.165 5, 4.165 6, 4.165 7, 4.165 8, 4.165 9, 4.165 10, 4.165 11, 4.166 2, 4.173 8, 4.182 7, 4.213 9, 4.213 14, 4.213 26, 4.213 27, 4.213 30, 4.219 2, 4.226 2, 4.226 2, 4.226 8, 4.243 3, 4.243 11, 4.243 13, 4.243 14, 4.243 20, 4.243 24, 4.243 25, 4.243 26, 4.243 28, 4.243 44, 4.243 44, 4.244 20, 4.267 2, 4.272 6, 4.291 3, 4.336 9, 4.337 7, 4.340 3, 4.340 4, 4.340 21, 4.342 1, 4.344 6, 4.344 10, 4.344 12, 4.345 3, 4.345 5, 4.353 1, 4.355 10, 4.363 6, 4.367 10, 4.369 2, 4.369 15, 4.369 17, 4.377 23, 4.377 33, 4.392 3, 4.394 5, 4.396 1, 4.398 7, 4.402 6, 4.416 3, 4.609 51, 4.625 3, 4.636 3, 4.636 16, 4.636 34, 4.658 6, 4.658 9, 4.658 12, 4.658 16, 4.658 17, 4.658 18, 4.658 25, 4.658 29, 4.658 42, 4.658 45, 4.658 47, 4.658 49, 4.682 5, 4.697 4, 4.697 9, 4.707 14, 4.721 2, 4.729 12, 4.745 2, 4.755 9, 4.769 7, 4.769 8, 4.769 9, 4.769 15, 4.769 16, 4.769 22, 4.769 24, 4.769 34, 4.769 42, 4.769 46, 4.769 47, 4.769 49, 4.769 52, 4.769 53, 4.769 56, 4.769 59, 4.769 61, 4.769 62, 4.769 64, 4.769 65, 4.769 67, 4.769 68, 4.769 69, 4.769 71, 4.771 1, 4.774 2, 4.775 2, 4.775 9, 4.775 11, 4.777 4, 4.777 13, 4.779 5, 4.781 1, 4.781 4, 4.782 19, 4.786 3, 6.18 1
ʿšrm[4.243 40, 4.775 12
ʿšr[m 2.42 15, 4.387 17
ʿš[r]m 4.281 5
ʿš[rm 4.30 3, 4.30 4, 4.329 6
ʿš[rm/t] 4.658 21
ʿšr[t/m] 4.769 10, 4.769 19, 4.769 37, 4.769 38, 4.769 41
ʿ[šrm] 4.344 19, 4.752 4
]ʿšrm 4.552 2, 4.552 3, 4.552 13, 4.658 27, 4.658 33, 4.769 23
ʿ]šrm 2.32 5, 4.102 29, 4.142 4, 4.243 36, 4.412 III 15, 4.427 23, 4.658 28, 4.712 1, 4.769 14, 4.769 21, 4.769 39, 4.769 43
ʿš]rm 4.274 2, 4.340 13, 4.378 9, 4.552 12, 4.658 39, 4.742 3, 4.765 1
ʿš]\rm 1.87 46f
ʿšr]m 4.552 5, 4.552 8, 4.658 35, 4.769 36, 4.792 5
ʿ]šrm[4.30 2
ʿ]š[rm 4.386 5
[[ʿšrm]] 4.709 11

ʿšrt 1.16 I 41, 1.16 I 62, 1.46 11, 1.87 3, 1.87 4, 1.105 17, 1.105 19, 1.112 16, 1.112 18, 1.119 5, 1.119 11, 1.119 32, 3.10 3, 3.10 6, 4.113 7, 4.146 2, 4.146 6, 4.146 8, 4.158 7, 4.158 8, 4.158 9, 4.158 11, 4.170 25, 4.225 12, 4.226 3, 4.226 4, 4.226 4, 4.226 5, 4.226 5, 4.226 6, 4.226 6, 4.226 7, 4.226 7, 4.226 8, 4.258 6, 4.267 3, 4.267 5, 4.281 7, 4.281 12, 4.281 17, 4.281 18, 4.281 21, 4.281 22, 4.281 23, 4.290 8, 4.290 14, 4.337 10, 4.337 11, 4.337 15, 4.337 19, 4.337 21, 4.341 1, 4.341 4, 4.341 6, 4.341 8, 4.341 11, 4.341 13, 4.341 16, 4.341 18, 4.552 4, 4.552 7, 4.609 2, 4.609 5, 4.609 7, 4.609 8, 4.632 5, 4.658 2, 4.658 4, 4.658 5, 4.658 7, 4.658 8, 4.658 13, 4.658 15, 4.658 19, 4.658 32, 4.658 34, 4.658 44, 4.658 50, 4.682 8, 4.682 10, 4.714 1, 4.755 10, 4.769 6, 4.769 11, 4.769 13, 4.769 14, 4.769 18, 4.769 20, 4.769 25, 4.769 27, 4.769 28, 4.769 30, 4.769 31, 4.769 32, 4.769 33, 4.769 35, 4.769 44, 4.769 45, 4.769 48, 4.769 50, 4.769 51, 4.769 54, 4.769 60, 4.769 63, 4.769 70, 4.774 3, 4.778 13, 4.781 7, 6.20 2, 6.22 1

ʿš\rt 1.87 54f

ʿšr[t 1.109 1, 1.112 29, 4.290 10, 4.632 1, 4.632 9, 4.682 7

ʿ[š]rt 1.46 10, 4.769 40

ʿ[šrt 1.41 3

]ʿšrt 4.376 1, 4.658 37, 4.769 15

ʿ]šrt 4.267 1, 4.552 6, 4.682 9, 4.769 26

ʿš]rt 4.552 10

ʿš]\rt 1.112 27f

ʿšr]t 4.552 20, 4.658 31

]ʿšrt[4.640 1

ʿ]šr[t 4.632 14

ʿšr[t/m] 4.769 10, 4.769 19, 4.769 37, 4.769 38, 4.769 41

ʿš[rm/t] 4.658 21

ʿšt 1.112 13, 2.27 1, 4.141 III 7, 4.290 4, 4.323 4, 4.358 7, 4.609 52

ʿšt[4.390 11

ʿ]št 4.127 5, 4.552 4, 4.552 7

ʿšty 1.161 27

ʿt 4.68 24

ʿt 1.100 19 lg. ʿm

]ʿt 4.250 6

]ʿtx[4.466 1

]xʿt 1.170 10, 4.14 10, 7.58 2

ʿn/txx[4.64 V 15

ʿtgrm 4.420 7, 4.420 12

ʿtk 1.3 III 44, 1.13 7, 4.421 5

ʿtkm 4.421 4

ʿtkt 1.3 II 11, 1.7 2

ʿtn 2.16 13

]xʿtnx 4.401 14

ʿtq 1.16 I 5, 1.16 I 19, 1.16 II 41

]xʿtq[7.136 3

ʿṯ[1.81 3, 7.185 2

ʿṯb 1.166 14

ʿṯlṯ[4.37 3

ʿṯqbm 1.13 14

ʿṯqbt 4.63 II 27

ʿṯrb 1.97 12

ʿṯ[rb 1.85 24

ʿṯṯ 2.23 3

ʿṯṯ[4.86 6, 4.252 3

ʿṯty 5.10 1 lg. ʿṯt<r>y(cor.)?

ʿṯtpl 1.46 4

ʿṯtpr 1.107 41, 1.123 10

ʿṯtr 1.2 III 12, 1.2 III 24, 1.6 I 55, 1.6 I 56, 1.6 I 61, 1.6 I 63, 1.24 28, 1.86 30, 1.111 19, 1.118 17, 1.123 10, 1.148 30, 4.696 6, 4.778 6

ʿṯtr[1.142 2, 1.159 4, 4.188 19, 4.216 10, 4.427 17

ʿṯ[t]r 1.2 III 18

ʿṯ]tr 1.46 4

ʿṯt]r 1.107 41

ʿ]ṯtr[4.391 7

ʿṯtrab 4.232 12

ʿ]ṯtrab 4.260 4, 4.432 17

ʿṯtrum 4.410 31

ʿṯt[rum 4.485 4

]ʿṯtrum[4.504 2

ʿ]ṯtrum[4.426 1

ʿṯt<r>y 5.10 1(cor.,?)

ʿṯtry 4.7 13, 4.93 I 4, 4.782 10

ʿṯtry 5.10 1(?) cor. ʿṯt<r>y

ʿ]ṯtry 4.225 2

ʿṯtrn 4.86 31

ʿṯtrn[4.75 II 4

ʿṯt[rn] 4.769 41
ʿṯtrt 1.2 I 8, 1.2 I 40, 1.2 IV 28, 1.14 III 42, 1.14 VI 28, 1.16 VI 56, 1.43 1, 1.48 17, 1.81 18, 1.81 19, 1.86 6, 1.91 10, 1.92 2, 1.92 8, 1.100 77, 1.100 78, 1.107 39, 1.107 42, 1.108 2, 1.112 13, 1.114 9, 1.114 10, 1.114 23, 1.116 1, 1.118 24, 1.148 7, 1.148 18, 2.42 7, 4.125 6, 4.168 4, 4.182 58(cor.), 4.219 2, 4.790 17
ʿṯtrt[1.49 6, 1.50 3
ʿṯtr[t 1.92 18, 4.245 I 11
ʿṯ[trt 1.50 4
ʿ[ṯt]rt 4.245 I 1
]ʿṯtrt 4.182 55
ʿ]ṯtrt 1.47 25
ʿṯ]trt 1.114 26
ʿṯtr]t 1.41 49
]ʿṯ[trt 1.50 1
ʿ{.}ṯtrt 1.100 20
ʿṯtrth 1.100 41

Ġ

ġ 5.2 5, 5.2 7, 5.4 5, 5.6 3, 5.12 4, 5.13 8, 5.14 16, 5.17 3, 5.17 6, 5.19 4, 5.20 2, 5.20 3, 5.21 2, 5.24 1
ġ[1.14 I 45, 1.41 35, 1.42 49, 2.5 7, 4.422 34, 4.486 1
]ġ 4.67 9, 4.645 7
]ġ[2.17 12
ġx[4.126 33, 7.135 2
]xġ 2.58 5, 4.82 1, 7.132 3
]ġx[4.244 28
ġx[xxxt 2.25 8
ġxbxxxx[4.748 12
]xġxbt 7.107 4
ġb 1.91 15, 1.105 3, 1.105 21, 4.63 III 24, 4.149 13
ġb[1.2 II 6, 1.12 II 39, 1.146 1, 7.88 2
]ġb 1.105 1, 4.399 1
]ġb[1.93 7
]ġby 4.312 3
ġbl 4.27 18, 4.177 7, 4.348 21, 4.355 31
ġbl[4.27 7, 4.683 4
ġbny 2.46 11
ġbr 1.40 20, 1.40 38
]ġbr 1.40 4
ġb]r 1.40 12
ġbt 1.101 8
]ġddn[4.646 6
ġdyn 1.65 18, 4.63 I 4
ġdm[1.173 2
ġdmh[1.173 1
ġdˁ 4.371 6
ġdġd 4.635 31
ġdrg 4.42 1
ġw 4.700 5
ġw[4.695 6
ġz 1.16 VI 43
]ġz 4.419 1
ġzl 4.617 7
ġzly 4.769 54
ġzlm 4.358 9
ġzm 1.16 VI 43
ġzr 1.3 I 20, 1.4 VII 47, 1.4 VIII 32, 1.5 I 8, 1.5 I 14, 1.5 II 9, 1.6 VI 31, 1.16 I 46, 1.16 I 58, 1.16 II 21, 1.16 II 33, 1.17 I 1, 1.17 I 17, 1.17 I 35, 1.17 I 37, 1.17 II 28, 1.17 V 5, 1.17 V 14, 1.17 V 34, 1.17 VI 20, 1.17 VI 26, 1.17 VI 33, 1.17 VI 34, 1.17 VI 42, 1.17 VI 51, 1.18 I 21, 1.18 IV 14, 1.19 I 20, 1.19 I 37, 1.19 I 48, 1.19 II 18, 1.19 II 42, 1.19 III 47, 1.19 III 53, 1.19 IV 4, 1.19 IV 12, 1.19 IV 16, 1.19 IV 19, 1.19 IV 44, 1.20 II 8, 1.23 17, 1.73 11, 1.133 17, 1.141 1, 1.169 1, 1.175 14, 4.102 18, 4.102 19, 4.102 20
ġz[r] 1.19 II 24
ġ]zr 1.17 VI 33, 1.18 I 24
ġz]r 1.4 VIII 46, 4.102 3
ġ\zr 1.19 IV 58f
ġ]zrh 1.6 I 31
ġzrm 1.3 II 22, 1.22 I 7, 1.23 14, 4.102 23, 4.349 1
ġzr[m] 4.102 16
]ġḥ 2.31 3
ġḥpn 4.76 4
ġẓtm 1.4 III 31
]ġyx[6.38 3
]xġy[4.446 4
ġyk[2.5 5
ġyn 1.19 IV 8
]ġyn 4.97 1
ġyrm 1.1 III 21, 1.3 IV 36
ġyrn 4.277 3
ġp/k[4.244 7
ġl 1.17 VI 23, 1.92 8, 4.141 III 15, 4.200 8, 4.243 14, 4.356 9, 4.636 15
ġl[7.47 9
]ġl 4.766 4
]xġl 4.103 63
]ġlb[4.590 3
ġlbx[4.760 7
ġlh 1.92 6
]ġlhm 2.62 11
ġlwš 4.391 4
ġly 1.6 V 17, 1.19 III 54, 4.16 8, 4.617

34, 4.778 18, 4.782 25
ġlyn 4.214 II 19
ġlyn[4.649 2
ġlkz 4.165 4, 4.244 23, 4.333 12
ġll 1.22 I 19
ġllm[1.12 II 34
ġlm 1.2 III 11, 1.9 17, 1.10 II 3, 1.14 I 19, 1.14 I 40, 1.14 II 8, 1.14 III 49, 1.14 VI 34, 1.15 II 20, 1.15 II 25, 1.16 I 50, 1.16 VI 39, 1.119 7, 1.169 10, 4.55 6, 7.137 4
ġlmh 1.4 II 29, 1.6 VI 8, 1.8 II 5
ġ\[l]mh 1.4 VII 52f
ġlmy 4.617 33
ġlmk 1.5 V 9, 1.176 18
ġlmm 1.2 I 19, 1.2 I 39, 1.3 II 4, 1.3 III 8, 1.3 IV 5, 1.4 V 43, 1.19 II 28
ġlm[m 1.2 I 13
ġl[m]m[1.3 V 15
ġlmn 4.33 13, 4.51 1, 4.55 24, 4.214 II 9, 4.232 22, 4.309 2, 4.609 13
ġlm[n] 4.625 19
ġlmt 1.4 VII 54, 1.8 II 7, 1.14 IV 41, 1.24 7, 1.39 19, 1.41 25
ġlm[t 1.87 27
ġ]lmt 1.15 II 22, 1.123 19
ġl]mt 1.139 10, 1.148 34
ġlmtm 1.119 8
ġlp 1.19 IV 42
ġlph 1.19 I 19
ġlpṯr 4.244 10
ġlṣ 4.52 9
ġlt 1.16 VI 32, 1.16 VI 45
ġltm 1.2 I 24
ġltn 4.609 24
xḏ/ġltn 4.787 8
ġlṯlp 1.42 36
ġm[4.126 34
ġmit 1.4 IV 34
ġmu 1.4 IV 34
ġmr 4.214 IV 1
ġmrm 4.63 I 11, 4.63 I 33, 4.63 III 32, 4.111 11
ġmšd 4.93 IV 9
ġn 4.346 3
]ġt/n 4.607 29
ġnbm 1.19 I 42, 1.23 26
ġnbn[4.393 2
ġnṯ 1.108 11
ġs 4.321 1
ġsb[1.167 3
]ġsb 1.167 3
ġp/k[4.244 7
ġprt 4.182 7
]ġprt 4.182 24
ġṣb 1.109 26
ġṣmn 4.75 I 4
ġṣr 1.4 VIII 4
ġr 1.1 III 12, 1.1 V 12, 1.2 I 20, 1.3 II 5, 1.3 III 30, 1.3 IV 20, 1.4 VII 5, 1.4 VII 37, 1.4 VIII 2, 1.4 VIII 3, 1.4 VIII 5, 1.5 V 12, 1.5 V 13, 1.5 VI 17, 1.5 VI 26, 1.6 I 2, 1.6 II 16, 1.10 III 27, 1.10 III 28, 1.10 III 31, 1.16 I 6, 1.16 II 45, 1.16 II 55, 1.16 IV 16, 1.19 IV 11, 1.19 IV 22, 1.41 22, 1.82 4, 1.87 24, 1.93 3, 1.101 1, 1.101 3, 1.117 9, 2.33 16, 4.27 12, 4.40 6, 4.40 9, 4.365 39, 4.380 22, 4.693 57, 4.777 12
ġr 1.93 1 lg. bġr?
ġr[1.48 16, 4.123 12
ġ[r 1.10 III 11, 7.136 4
]ġr 1.25 5, 1.52 21
ġ]r 1.1 V 25
]ġr[7.56 5, 7.65 3, 7.128 2, 7.181 1
]ġrbtym 4.55 15
ġrgn 4.69 V 8, 4.69 VI 9, 4.93 I 16
ġrg[n 4.413 5, 4.422 36
]ġrgn[4.564 4
ġrdn 2.61 1
ġrh 1.101 2
ġry 1.3 III 29
ġ]ry 1.3 IV 19
ġrk 1.13 9, 1.13 10
ġrm 1.4 V 15, 1.4 V 31, 1.4 V 38, 1.4 VII 32, 1.16 VI 44, 1.118 18, 1.148 6
]ġrm 1.107 29
ġ]rm 1.16 VI 31
ġr]m 1.148 41(!)
ġrmn 1.3 II 11
ġrn 4.33 34, 4.50 15, 4.296 5, 4.609 14
ġrpd 4.214 I 13
ġrpl 1.107 34, 1.107 44
ġr[pl] 1.107 37
ġrp]lt 1.163 6
ġrt 1.1 III 9, 4.278 5
]ġt 1.107 28, 4.607 10
]ġt/n 4.607 29
ġtr 4.754 16
]ġṯ 1.30 4

P

p 1.4 IV 59, 1.4 IV 60, 1.5 I 14, 1.5 I 19, 1.5 I 26, 1.6 V 5, 1.6 VI 10, 1.10 III 9, 1.10 III 10, 1.14 III 38, 1.14 VI 22, 1.16 V 45, 1.17 I 15, 1.19 III 48(*bis*), 1.19 III 55, 1.19 III 56, 1.19 IV 6, 1.19 IV 60, 1.107 5, 1.107 35, 1.107 45(*bis*), 1.133 16, 2.2 4(*bis*), 2.3 19, 2.5 3, 2.10 12, 2.14 12, 2.15 7, 2.23 17, 2.26 7, 2.33 28, 2.44 9, 2.45 9, 2.70 5, 2.70 27, 2.72 11, 2.72 22, 2.72 42, 2.73 14, 5.4 4, 5.6 2, 5.9 II 1, 5.10 8(!), 5.11 4, 5.12 3, 5.13 8, 5.15 1, 5.15 4, 5.16 3, 5.17 6, 5.19 3, 5.20 1, 5.20 4, 5.21 2
p[1.22 IV 4, 1.64 22, 1.69 12, 1.73 3, 1.77 3, 1.81 2, 1.98 7, 1.104 24, 1.107 35, 2.37 7, 2.60 6, 4.75 V 23, 4.106 15, 4.201 3, 4.205 9, 4.214 III 14, 4.214 IV 16, 4.227 III 2, 4.244 23, 4.333 5, 4.412 III 24, 4.427 18, 4.464 2, 4.473 3, 4.482 3, 4.569 2, 4.683 22, 5.2 3, 5.2 5, 5.10 4, 7.30 3, 7.38 7, 7.40 1, 7.98 2, 7.165 2, 7.175 3, 7.176 2, 7.184 4, 7.184 11, 7.187 3
]p 1.14 V 27, 1.17 I 5, 1.64 28, 1.66 26, 1.68 10, 1.82 24, 1.84 31, 1.91 17, 1.122 6, 1.122 8, 1.173 5, 2.29 2, 2.33 10, 2.47 20, 2.58 7, 2.81 28, 4.141 III 21, 4.769 67, 7.56 3, 7.141 3, 7.147 1
]p[4.517 3, 7.21 1
f 5.24 1
px 3.8 7, 4.111 9
px[1.5 IV 26, 1.136 10, 2.77 5, 2.77 8, 4.421 1, 4.469 2
px[1.116 33 lg. ptg[nt]t
]px[4.386 8
pxx[4.401 14
]pxx[4.675 2
xxxxp 1.86 30
]xp 1.5 II 23, 4.673 1, 7.134 2
]xp[7.187 4
]xxp[1.93 8
p/h/i[1.51 10
p/h/t 7.218 5
p/k/w/r[4.393 24
p/k/r[4.737 3
]pxn 4.708 7
]pa[7.106 1
]xpaz 4.176 4
palt 1.19 II 13, 1.19 II 16
palth 1.19 II 12
pam 1.162 20 cor. pamt
pamt 1.23 20, 1.39 20, 1.41 43, 1.41 52, 1.43 7, 1.43 26, 1.87 40, 1.109 30, 1.110 11, 1.112 7, 1.162 20(cor.), 1.173 15
pam[t 1.87 47
pat 1.12 I 35, 1.14 III 1, 1.14 IV 30, 1.23 68, 1.176 16, 2.75 7, 4.136 4
pixxn 1.48 6
pid 1.1 III 22, 1.4 II 10, 1.4 III 31, 1.4 IV 58, 1.5 VI 12, 1.6 III 4, 1.6 III 10, 1.6 III 14, 1.6 VI 39, 1.15 II 14, 1.16 V 23, 1.24 45
pi[d] 1.16 IV 9
p[id 1.1 IV 13, 1.18 I 15
pi\d 1.6 I 49f
pil 4.751 7
pil[4.747 4
piln 4.278 7
pit 1.13 15, 1.17 II 9, 1.107 3
pith 1.103 11, 1.103 54
pity 4.69 III 17, 4.93 II 6, 4.93 IV 15
pi[ty 4.77 2
[p]itm 1.2 IV 5
pu/d/l[1.28 3
pb[4.93 I 17, 4.334 6*
pb/d[1.70 14, 1.104 2, 7.53 9
]pb/d[7.147 8
]xpb/d[4.324 2
pbyn 4.63 II 37
pbl 1.14 III 15, 1.14 III 21, 1.14 V 7, 1.14 VI 37, 1.107 4
[p]bl 1.14 V 13
pblnk[1.73 1
pbn 1.42 60, 4.31 3, 4.609 16, 4.611

30, 4.715 25
pbnḏx[1.42 30
pbnḫwn 1.128 9
pbṯr 4.775 9, 4.775 15
pg 1.42 61
pgx[4.192 3, 7.189 3
p/h/ig[1.30 5
pgam 4.117 1
pgi 4.721 1
pglu[4.393 8
p[gl]t 1.4 III 15
pgm 1.82 26, 1.82 26
pgn 2.46 1
pgn[2.47 21
pgr 1.39 12, 1.39 17, 1.102 12, 6.13 2, 6.14 1
pḫ/gr 1.73 8
pgrm 4.172 2, 4.182 40, 4.193 7, 4.266 2, 4.336 2
pgr[m] 4.193 2
]pgš 4.718 3
pd 1.19 II 32, 1.132 2, 1.148 15, 4.365 2, 4.380 2, 4.683 3, 4.693 2, 4.750 10, 4.784 3
pd[1.16 V 46, 4.101 7, 4.245 I 9
pdx[4.2 3
pd/b[1.70 14, 1.104 2, 7.53 9
]pd/b[7.147 8
]xpd/b[4.324 2
pd/u/l[1.28 3
pdu 4.85 5
pdgl 1.42 48, 1.42 48
pddm 1.42 43
pddm 4.363 8 lg. pldm
pdḏn 1.64 4*, 4.748 11
pdy 3.4 2, 3.4 12, 4.15 3, 4.46 12, 4.86 7, 4.98 23, 4.112 III 2, 4.424 8, 4.425 6
pdy[4.178 3, 4.376 2
]pdy 4.299 3
pdym 4.40 12
pdyn 4.307 19, 4.393 12, 4.696 2
pdk[4.196 9
pdm 1.19 II 31, 4.643 13, 4.748 3
pdn 4.75 IV 14, 4.780 17
pdn[4.393 3, 4.649 8
pdnx[1.67 23
pdġb 2.36 1
pdġy 4.635 17
pdġy[1.91 18
pdr 1.3 I 25, 1.4 VII 10, 1.50 5, 1.92 33, 1.106 11, 4.19 3, 4.269 7, 4.655 8
pdr[1.49 4, 2.1 4
pd[r 1.4 VII 8
pd]r 4.19 2
pdr<y> 1.130 15
pdry 1.3 I 23, 1.3 III 6, 1.4 I 16, 1.4 IV 55, 1.5 V 10, 1.24 26, 1.39 15, 1.42 62, 1.102 7, 1.109 14, 1.109 18, 1.117 11, 1.118 16, 1.139 15, 1.148 6, 1.173 6
pdr[y 1.3 IV 50, 1.7 23, 1.134 9
p[dry 1.130 7
p]dry 1.91 7, 1.117 7, 1.139 14
pdr]y 1.3 V 41, 1.4 VI 10
pdrm 1.14 III 7, 1.14 IV 50, 1.16 VI 7, 1.44 11, 1.52 10, 1.52 12, 1.128 20
pd[rm 1.52 14
p]drm 1.4 VII 8
pdrn 4.56 4, 4.63 III 46, 4.98 22, 4.658 9
pdrn[4.635 59
pdṯn 4.764 4
pḏ[4.116 21
pḏḏpḫ 1.42 35
pḏḏpḫnd 1.60 10, 1.116 18, 1.135 9
pḏh 1.2 I 19, 1.2 I 35
pḏy 1.42 8
pḏp 1.148 13
pḏp[1.66 9
ph 1.4 VIII 18, 1.5 II 4, 1.15 III 28, 1.19 I 9, 1.19 II 26, 1.19 III 7, 1.19 III 35, 1.45 3, 1.62 3, 1.101 8, 1.103 51, 7.141 1
]ph 1.2 IV 6, 1.10 II 35, 1.164 11
phy 3.1 15
phy[7.75 1
phm 1.23 62, 1.23 64
]phn[7.37 1
phnn 2.62 6
phr 1.2 I 20 lg. pḫr
pht 1.6 V 12, 1.6 V 12, 1.6 V 14, 1.6 V 16, 1.6 V 17, 1.6 V 18
pwn 4.70 8
pwnx[4.97 7
pw/rn 1.64 9
pwt 4.182 10, 4.626 6, 4.771 4
pzdp 1.42 36

pzy 2.71 2
pz[n 4.495 2
pzny 4.69 VI 32, 4.761 10
pzn[y 4.633 10
]xpzq[7.132 2
pzry 2.6 2
pḥ 4.90 7
]pḥ 4.386 3
pḥẓ[4.323 3
pḥl 1.4 IV 5, 1.4 IV 9, 1.4 IV 15, 1.19 II 4, 1.19 II 9, 1.19 II 11, 1.100 1
pḥlt 1.100 1
pḥm 1.23 39, 1.163 12, 1.163 16, 2.73 9, 3.1 22, 3.1 27, 3.1 29, 3.1 31, 3.1 39, 4.132 1, 4.132 4, 4.132 5, 4.203 3, 4.268 5
pḥm[4.738 6
pḥ[m] 3.1 33
p]ḥm[2.73 8
pḥ]m 3.1 35
pḥmm 1.4 II 9, 1.23 41, 1.23 45, 1.23 48
pḫd 1.17 V 17, 1.17 V 23
pḫyrh 1.14 I 25
pḫn 4.141 III 6
pḫr 1.2 I 14, 1.2 I 15, 1.2 I 20(!), 1.2 I 31, 1.4 III 14, 1.15 III 15, 1.23 57, 1.47 29, 1.84 41, 1.87 18, 1.96 7, 1.96 9, 1.96 10, 1.118 28, 1.148 9, 1.162 17
pḫr[1.16 V 30
p[ḫ]r 1.39 7
]pḫr 1.10 I 4
pḫ/gr 1.73 8
pḫrk 1.82 39
p]ḫrk 1.82 40
pḫtinmx[1.70 21, 1.70 22
]pṭ 4.431 3
pṭḏ 4.357 23
pṭḏn 4.69 I 17, 4.340 7
pṭr 1.16 VI 8
pṭry 4.724 10, 4.755 4
pẓġm 1.19 IV 11, 1.19 IV 22
pẓr 1.107 5, 1.107 5
py 1.6 II 22, 1.24 45, 1.93 2, 4.617 9
]py 4.127 13, 4.708 2, 4.769 19
]\py 1.138 2f
]py[4.657 1
pyx[4.382 32
]xpy 4.766 11
pyn 4.52 4, 4.244 8, 4.696 8
pynq 4.86 27
pyġ[1.64 12
pk 1.82 4, 1.82 4
pk[4.760 9
]pk 2.31 21
pkdy 5.11 14
pr/ky 4.55 11
pkly 4.780 7
pl 1.6 IV 1, 1.6 IV 2, 1.6 IV 12, 1.6 IV 13, 1.66 12, 1.66 13, 1.66 14, 1.66 28, 1.66 29, 1.66 34, 1.66 35, 1.66 36, 1.83 11, 4.356 10, 4.377 13, 4.425 4
pl[1.70 38, 1.82 24, 4.114 14, 4.513 1
p[l 1.66 19, 1.66 20, 1.66 27, 1.66 33, 1.66 34
]pl 7.108 5
p]l 1.66 20
]xpl 4.186 1
pl/u/d[1.28 3
pl/ṣ[1.73 4
plg 1.100 69, 1.176 3, 1.176 5
pld 4.146 7, 4.152 4, 4.152 7, 4.152 8, 4.205 1, 4.205 7, 4.270 12
pl[d 1.148 21
pldm 4.4 4, 4.4 5, 4.270 8, 4.363 8(!), 5.23 4
plwn 4.41 11
plzn 4.80 12
p]lḫt 1.70 39
plḫtṯ 1.73 4
xplḫtṯ 1.70 38
plṭ 4.222 2, 4.374 7, 4.727 18
ply 4.658 17
plk 1.4 II 4
plkh 1.4 II 3
pll 4.103 24
pll[4.545 II 4
]pll 4.103 25
]xplm[4.315 12
pln 4.295 9, 4.417 8, 4.631 15, 4.631 18
]pln 2.22 6
]xplnt 1.82 31
plś 4.617 15
pls 2.44 17, 4.63 III 31, 4.75 IV 5,

4.283 8, 4.769 11
plśbʿl 4.366 3
plsbʿl 6.1 1
plsy 2.10 2, 4.134 4, 4.214 I 19, 4.214 II 14, 4.214 IV 9, 4.261 6, 4.262 6, 4.635 40
plġn 3.8 4
plšn 4.63 III 34
plṯt 1.5 VI 15
pm 2.71 11
pm[2.23 30
pmlk 4.159 4
pmn 4.63 I 29, 4.170 8, 4.232 27
pn 1.2 III 12, 1.2 III 16, 1.2 III 16, 1.9 13, 1.12 I 33, 1.86 29, 1.103 33, 1.106 16, 1.114 12, 1.132 16, 1.132 25, 2.13 17, 2.15 3, 2.16 8, 2.16 9, 2.23 19, 2.23 21, 2.23 21, 2.33 29, 2.72 19, 6.62 2, 7.37 3
pn[2.80 1, 7.184 3
p[n 1.2 III 21, 2.39 5
]pn 1.25 6, 4.78 2, 4.151 I 5, 4.316 6, 4.319 6, 7.46 2
pnxx[4.340 9
]xpn 1.81 21
]p/hn 4.275 2
pn/t 4.396 19
pni 4.350 8
]xpnil[7.55 16
pndḏn 4.79 5
pndyn 4.658 44, 4.658 53
pndyn[4.118 6
pndn 4.33 38, 4.35 I 14
pndr 4.617 32, 4.714 3, 4.715 19
pndr[4.322 8
pnḏnn 1.42 62
pnh 1.3 III 34, 1.3 IV 42, 1.4 V 46, 1.16 I 52, 1.82 38, 1.92 30, 1.103 33, 1.152 5, 1.161 15
p]nh 1.4 II 18
pn]h 1.41 54
pnwh 1.3 I 6
pnḥṯ 2.70 3
pny 1.82 10
pny[2.31 62
pnk 1.5 V 12, 1.16 VI 48
pn<m> 1.5 II 14
pnm 1.2 III 4, 1.3 IV 37, 1.3 VI 13, 1.4 IV 17, 1.4 IV 20, 1.4 V 22, 1.4 VIII 1, 1.4 VIII 11, 1.5 I 10, 1.6 I 32, 1.6 IV 7, 1.10 II 8, 1.14 VI 36, 1.16 VI 5, 1.17 II 9, 1.100 61, 1.100 63, 1.116 9
pnm 1.12 II 37 lg. a{n}pnm
pnm[1.12 II 4, 1.14 V 30
]pnm 4.275 16
p]nm 1.3 V 5, 1.17 VI 47
pnmn 4.131 7, 4.281 23
pnnh 1.3 IV 40, 1.10 II 17
pnġnṯt 1.116 24
]pnpḫmxxḫ 1.42 19
pnt 1.3 III 34
pnt[1.4 II 19
pnth 1.2 IV 17, 1.2 IV 26
pnṯbl 4.127 12
pnṯḫb[1.148 14
]xps 1.147 15
]pszyn 4.592 2
psḥn 4.63 III 42, 4.96 12, 4.343 2
psl 4.103 36, 4.141 III 19
psl[7.47 7
]psl 4.141 III 18
pslm 4.68 65, 4.99 18, 4.126 8, 4.370 45, 4.412 III 9
pslm[4.207 7
psltm 1.5 VI 18, 1.6 I 2
psm 1.42 53, 4.205 5
psś 4.366 8, 4.371 12
pʿ 1.147 15
]pʿ 1.113 26
pʿl 6.70 1
pʿlk 1.13 21
pʿn 1.2 I 30, 1.3 III 9, 1.3 V 15, 1.3 VI 18, 1.4 IV 25, 1.4 VIII 26, 1.6 I 36, 1.12 II 33, 1.17 II 11, 1.107 18, 2.11 5, 2.12 6, 2.13 5, 2.24 5, 2.30 4, 2.42 4, 2.45 11, 2.64 13, 2.68 4, 2.70 8, 2.81 5
pʿ[n 2.64 6
]pʿn 2.40 5, 2.51 2
p]ʿn 1.1 II 15, 1.3 V 4, 2.72 4
pʿnh 1.4 IV 29, 1.6 I 59, 1.6 III 15, 1.10 II 18, 1.12 I 40, 1.19 III 10, 1.19 III 24, 1.19 III 38, 1.103 39, 1.161 14
pʿnh[1.166 26
pʿn[h 1.174 2
pʿny 1.19 III 3, 1.19 III 18, 1.19 III 32

pʿnk 1.1 II 1, 1.3 III 19, 1.3 IV 11, 2.82 2
pʿ]nk 1.1 II 22
pʿnm 1.3 III 32, 1.4 II 16, 1.4 V 21, 1.43 24, 1.43 25
pʿ]nm 1.17 VI 46
pʿnt 1.103 52
pʿṣ 4.53 3, 4.64 V 11, 4.98 7, 4.103 29, 4.170 25, 4.617 24
pʿr 1.1 IV 15, 1.1 IV 29, 1.13 32
pʿrt[1.1 IV 19
]p/hġ 4.107 10
]xpġdd[7.24 2
pġdm 1.42 3
pġdrm 4.270 10
pġḏn 4.98 10, 4.141 II 2, 4.148 6, 4.183 I 24, 4.609 3
pġy 4.349 4
pġyn 4.63 III 29, 4.631 12, 4.643 14
pġm[4.63 IV 1
pġn 4.4 1
pġsdb 2.17 5
pġrḏ[1.149 1
pġrḏnṯ[1.149 11
pġt 1.15 III 7, 1.15 III 8, 1.19 I 34, 1.19 II 1, 1.19 II 6, 1.19 IV 28, 1.19 IV 48, 1.19 IV 50, 1.19 IV 55, 4.102 2, 4.102 6, 4.102 7, 4.102 11, 4.102 18, 4.102 20, 4.102 21, 4.102 26, 4.102 28, 4.102 30, 4.349 3
pġ[t 1.15 III 9, 1.16 II 5, 1.19 IV 36
p[ġt 1.15 III 10, 1.15 III 11, 1.15 III 12
]pġt 2.3 23
pġtm 4.102 19
]pp 1.10 I 2
ppn[4.39 6
pprn 4.63 I 38
ppšr 1.82 36
ppšrt 1.82 36
ppṯ 3.7 9, 4.54 7
pl/ṣ[1.73 4
pṣn 4.335 4
pṣn[4.715 14
pq 1.4 VI 56, 1.5 IV 13, 1.107 6
pqq 1.114 30
pqr 4.147 2, 4.224 7, 4.286 6
pr 1.5 II 5, 1.66 15, 1.66 22, 1.66 37, 1.72 19, 1.85 14, 1.85 24, 1.85 26, 1.85 27, 1.86 3, 1.105 13, 2.83 11
pr[1.49 9, 1.51 5, 1.66 15, 1.66 30, 1.72 33, 1.97 15, 1.166 17, 2.17 14, 2.77 17, 4.323 8, 4.434 5
]pr 1.73 14, 1.113 4, 4.236 5
p]r 1.71 12, 1.97 12
]pr[7.105 2
prx[4.227 II 8, 4.382 29
xpr 4.326 8
xpr[4.412 II 11
]xpr 7.137 8
prxprṣṣd 1.68 24
pxxxrt 1.48 10
pri 4.297 2
prbḫṯ 1.24 49
prgl 1.41 50
prgn 4.115 13
prd 4.295 11, 4.337 12, 4.417 10
prdm 4.786 4
prdmn 1.3 I 2
prdnḏ 1.149 3
prdny 4.369 19
]prḏ 4.58 2
prwsdy 4.44 24
prz 1.111 1
przndd 1.110 4, 1.111 5
prẖ 5.22 19
prḫ 4.88 2, 4.134 7
prḫn[2.77 19
prṭl 1.82 7, 1.82 19
prẓ 1.13 12
pry 4.350 7
pr/ky 4.55 11
prk 1.5 V 2 lg. pr<ʿ>k?
prkb/d[7.47 6
prkl 4.12 10, 4.647 7
prl 1.149 4
prln 1.6 VI 55
]prln 1.17 VI 56, 6.47 1
prm 4.142 1, 4.710 4, 4.710 5, 4.710 7
prmn 4.188 2, 4.356 6
prn 4.71 III 8, 4.85 10, 4.110 3, 4.110 4, 4.110 5, 4.110 6, 4.110 7, 4.110 8, 4.110 9, 4.110 10, 4.110 11, 4.110 12, 4.110 13, 4.147 10, 4.631 2, 4.715 15, 4.780 10
pr[n] 4.110 14
]prn 4.484 4
pr/wn 1.64 9

prś 4.225 9, 4.269 29, 4.275 16, 4.328 1, 4.677 4, 4.788 3, 4.788 5, 4.789 2
]prś 4.275 14, 4.328 2, 4.387 5
pr]ś 4.328 9
prs 1.41 23, 1.87 25, 1.139 12, 4.263 2, 4.377 32, 4.392 1, 4.715 6, 4.786 11, 4.786 12
pr[s 4.558 9
prsg 4.727 21
prsn 4.69 I 21, 4.374 3, 4.377 6, 4.425 10
prst[1.22 II 15
prˁ 1.19 I 18, 1.22 I 24, 1.124 9, 2.31 16, 2.31 37, 4.279 1
pr[ˁ 2.31 15
pr<ˁ>k 1.5 V 2(?)
prˁm 1.17 V 37, 1.17 V 38
p[rˁm] 1.17 V 38
prˁt 1.8 II 9
prˁ]t 1.4 VII 56
prġṯ 4.128 7, 4.317 1
prpr 4.63 I 44
prṣ 1.23 70
prṣm 1.157 3
prqdš 3.8 20
prqt 4.205 3, 4.205 4
pr[r 4.218 4
]prr 4.608 20
prš[1.73 15
prša 1.4 I 35
pršwn 1.149 9
pršm 1.149 7
pršt 1.149 8
prt 1.5 V 18, 1.86 4, 4.142 2, 4.739 7
]prt 4.399 12
prt{.}wn 4.46 4
prtn 4.69 III 9, 4.122 19, 4.611 17, 4.720 1
p/hrtn 4.64 IV 8
prtṯr[4.547 4
prṯ 4.144 2, 4.165 14, 4.417 11, 5.9 III 1, 6.11 2
]prṯ[4.569 4
pr⊕ 1.66 37
pr⊕[1.66 15, 1.66 30
prṯy 1.116 32(!)
]prṯy 1.116 32 lg. prṯy
prṯn 1.64 23
pr⊕⊕ 1.66 30, 1.66 36
p[r⊕⊕ 1.66 14
pr⊕]⊕ 1.66 22
pš[1.57 4, 4.441 4
]pš 1.129 1, 4.106 3, 7.179 1, 7.193 1
]pš[1.147 29
p/h/iški/pr[4.53 16
]pšm 4.103 64
]pšmtkm 1.84 30
pšˁ 1.17 VI 43
pšt 1.6 I 30 lg. tšt
pt[1.83 12
]pt 1.7 46, 7.33 3
]xpt 4.17 4
pn/t 4.396 19
]ptg 4.215 7
ptg[nt]t 1.116 33(!)
ptḥ 1.15 IV 5, 1.23 70, 1.23 70, 1.100 71, 1.100 72, 1.103 5, 1.106 17, 4.195 14
ptḥ[1.157 3
p[tḥ 4.195 5
p]tḥ 4.195 1
pt]ḥ 4.195 7, 4.195 9
ptḥy 1.82 21
ptḥm 4.195 10, 4.195 11
ptḥ[m 4.195 13
pt[ḥm 4.195 12
ptm 4.153 6, 5.11 22
]ptm 2.31 43
ptn 2.45 29
ptr 1.49 11, 5.22 6
ptr[4.248 9
]ptr 4.190 3
pṯ 5.9 III 2
pṯ[1.94 31, 4.334 6
pṯmn 4.7 19
]pṯn 7.61 3
]pṯn[7.61 5
pṯpṯ 4.347 3
pṯrty 4.297 3
pṯt 4.152 8, 4.152 9, 4.205 1, 4.205 4, 4.247 22, 4.270 7
p[ṯt 4.270 9
]pṯt[7.84 3
pṯtm 1.92 25, 4.156 5, 4.168 11, 4.182 8, 4.190 4, 4.626 7, 5.10 5
p]ṯtm 4.182 25, 4.206 4
pṯtn 1.67 17

Ṣ

ṣ 5.2 7, 5.4 4, 5.6 2, 5.9 II 1(*quinquies*), 5.12 3, 5.13 8, 5.14 12, 5.16 3, 5.17 3, 5.17 6, 5.19 3, 5.20 1, 5.20 4, 5.21 2, 5.24 1
ṣ[4.93 IV 26, 4.188 5, 7.142 4, 7.156 2, 7.185 5, 7.185 6
]ṣ 1.175 15, 4.11 3, 7.117 3, 7.140 4
]\ṣ 7.53 5(cor.)
]ṣ[1.16 II 60, 4.32 1, 4.584 1
ṣ 4.424 7 lg. l
ṣxx 2.40 17
ṣx[4.788 1, 7.67 4, 7.159 3
ṣxx[1.17 VI 55
]ṣxx[7.150 1
]xṣ 1.97 8, 2.33 39, 4.483 2
xṣxxlk 1.16 II 30
xxṣxm[7.140 4
ṣ/b[4.267 5, 4.434 9, 4.686 21, 7.98 4
]ṣ/b 4.258 16, 4.573 5, 4.717 4
]ṣ/b[7.84 6
ṣ/l 5.2 3
ṣ/l[7.47 5
]ṣ/l 1.6 V 23, 4.397 1, 4.744 2
l/ṣxx 1.70 2
ṣat 1.3 II 8, 1.4 VII 32, 1.16 I 35
ṣ[at 1.4 VII 30
ṣin 1.4 VI 41, 1.5 III 23, 1.6 I 22, 1.22 I 12, 1.43 7, 1.49 5, 1.86 14, 1.103 1, 1.105 4, 1.106 13, 1.106 29, 4.127 9, 4.128 2, 4.275 19, 4.275 20, 4.295 2, 4.295 14, 4.295 17, 4.337 22, 4.341 9, 4.389 10, 4.616 2, 4.691 2, 4.775 6, 4.775 7, 4.775 8, 4.786 6
ṣin[1.5 III 22
ṣi[n 4.80 20
ṣ[in 1.49 8
[[ṣin]] 4.709 11
ṣinh[4.417 18
ṣink 2.82 7
ṣb[2.78 8, 7.149 5
]ṣb 4.106 2, 4.765 9
ṣb/d[4.773 4
ṣba 1.14 IV 14, 1.16 I 36, 1.112 14
ṣbi 1.14 II 33, 1.19 IV 47, 1.91 15
ṣbia 1.15 V 19
ṣbim 1.3 II 22, 1.7 5
ṣbu 1.14 II 33, 1.41 47, 1.41 53, 4.40 7, 4.40 10
ṣb[u 4.40 1
ṣbuh 1.14 IV 15
ṣbuk 1.14 II 35
ṣbṭ[4.413 3
]ṣbm 4.420 8
]ṣ/gbn 4.57 7
ṣbr 4.375 3, 4.375 5, 4.375 7, 4.375 9, 4.375 11
ṣbr[1.82 25, 4.400 2
ṣbrm 4.375 1
ṣbrt 1.3 V 37, 1.4 IV 49
ṣ]brt 1.4 II 25
ṣb\rt 1.6 I 40f
ṣgx[1.94 32
ṣd 1.17 V 39, 1.22 I 11, 1.108 12, 1.114 1, 4.408 5
ṣd[1.18 I 27, 4.262 2
ṣ[d 1.18 I 29
ṣ]d 1.65 19
ṣd/b[4.773 4
ṣdx[4.30 8
ṣdh 1.14 IV 8 lg. m]ṣdh
ṣdynm 1.14 IV 36, 1.14 IV 39
ṣdk 1.17 V 37, 1.17 V 38
ṣdk 1.14 II 26 lg. mṣdk
]ṣdmn 4.122 18
ṣdkn 4.277 6
ṣdġn 4.715 18 lg. ṣdqn
ṣdq 1.123 14, 2.81 2, 2.81 20, 2.81 31, 4.129 8, 4.232 6, 7.63 4
ṣdq[4.754 2
ṣ[dq 2.81 11
]ṣdq 2.8 5, 4.151 I 13, 4.432 15
ṣdqil 4.63 III 4
ṣdqh 1.14 I 12
ṣdqy 4.432 19
ṣdqm 4.63 II 6
ṣdqn 4.33 27, 4.75 III 8, 4.75 III 10, 4.79 4, 4.124 13, 4.260 3, 4.269 6, 4.280 1, 4.286 2, 4.611 5, 4.659 5,

4.690 19, 4.715 18(!), 6.5 1
ṣdqn[4.607 32
ṣ[d]qn 4.609 25
ṣdq[n 4.383 9
]ṣdkn 4.742 6
ṣ]dqn 4.188 14
ṣdqšlm 4.103 28, 4.165 11, 5.7 4
ṣdqš[lm] 4.102 23
[ṣ]dqšlm 4.616 5
ṣdtk 2.34 33(?)
]ṣ/lwd 4.734 8
ṣwd[t 1.92 2
ṣwy 4.232 23
ṣḥ 1.1 IV 2, 1.1 IV 4, 1.4 V 13, 1.4 V 29, 1.4 V 36, 1.4 VI 44, 1.4 VI 45, 1.15 IV 6, 1.16 I 28, 1.16 IV 3, 1.16 IV 16, 1.23 69, 1.114 2, 4.362 1
ṣḥ[1.129 1
]ṣḥ 4.635 4
]ṣḥ[7.85 2
ṣḥn 1.5 I 22
ṣḥq 1.3 II 25, 1.4 V 25, 1.4 VII 21, 1.18 I 22
ṣḥ]q 1.7 7
]ṣḥr 1.172 4
ṣḥrn 4.628 4
ṣḥrrm 1.8 II 10
ṣḥr<r>t 1.23 48
ṣḥrrt 1.4 VIII 22, 1.6 II 24, 1.23 41, 1.23 45
ṣḥr[rt] 1.12 II 43
ṣḥr]rt 1.3 V 17
ṣḥt 1.4 VIII 42
ṣḥtkm 1.15 IV 27, 1.15 VI 4
ṣḥtk[m] 1.15 V 10
ṣṭqšlm 2.19 1, 2.19 4, 2.19 10, 2.19 14
]ṣ/lyd 4.766 7
]ṣ/lym 1.84 24
]ṣ/yk[1.69 14
ṣl[4.635 54, 7.185 3
xṣ/ll 4.63 II 28
]ṣ/lly 7.50 10
ṣlyh 1.27 6
ṣ/ylkn 4.77 14
ṣlm 1.13 18
]ṣlm 2.31 62
ṣlmm 1.23 57
ṣlʿt 4.247 16
ṣlpn 4.309 29
ṣlt[km] 1.119 34
]xṣm 4.424 7
ṣ/bm[4.65 14, 4.413 6
ṣmd 1.2 IV 15, 1.2 IV 23, 1.4 IV 5, 1.4 IV 9, 1.6 V 3, 1.19 II 4, 1.65 14, 4.367 10, 4.368 2, 4.368 5, 4.368 7, 4.368 8, 4.368 15, 4.377 5, 4.377 6, 4.377 21, 4.377 34(!), 4.427 23, 4.586 2, 4.618 15, 4.618 17, 4.618 19
ṣmd[4.302 7, 4.306 6, 4.535 3, 4.582 2, 4.582 5
ṣm[d 4.377 17, 4.377 19, 4.487 3, 4.576 4
ṣ[m]d 4.618 10
ṣ[md 4.377 23, 4.517 2
ṣm]d 4.582 6, 4.586 1, 4.586 3
]ṣmd 4.576 2
]ṣm[d 4.535 4
ṣm]d[4.576 1
ṣmdx 1.91 18
ṣmd{.}m 4.377 27
ṣmdm 1.2 IV 11, 1.2 IV 18, 1.23 10, 1.82 16, 1.170 7, 4.88 1, 4.89 1, 4.89 3, 4.136 1, 4.145 8, 4.167 2, 4.169 4, 4.169 7, 4.302 5, 4.368 21, 4.368 22, 4.377 1, 4.377 31(!), 4.384 9, 4.384 10, 4.585 2, 4.618 1, 4.618 4, 4.618 7, 4.618 21, 4.691 8
ṣmdm[4.88 9, 4.208 3, 4.208 4, 4.306 4
ṣm[d]m 4.208 8
ṣmd[m 4.302 4, 4.585 3
ṣ[m]dm 4.384 11
]ṣmdm 4.384 3
ṣ]mdm 4.368 1, 4.384 2
]ṣmdm[4.576 3
]ṣm[dm 4.585 4
ṣ]mdm[4.208 2, 4.302 1, 4.306 1
ṣ/aḥ/m]dm 4.384 4, 4.384 6
]ṣmḫ 7.63 9
ṣmy 4.617 4, 4.617 8
ṣml 1.19 III 29, 1.19 III 30, 1.19 III 36, 1.169 7, 4.158 10, 4.341 12
ṣmṣ 4.269 35 lg. ḥmṣ
ṣmq[4.77 8
ṣmqm 1.71 27, 1.72 38, 1.85 31, 4.14 17, 4.751 10
]ṣmqm 4.14 5

ṣmrt 4.75 VI 5
ṣmt 1.3 III 44, 1.12 II 34, 1.18 IV 38
]ṣn 4.183 II 7, 4.769 32
ṣnr 4.15 10, 4.35 II 16, 4.281 30, 4.370 45, 4.749 2
]ṣnr 4.769 35
ṣnrn 4.103 8
ṣʿ 1.3 II 32, 1.4 I 41, 1.5 I 21, 1.15 IV 24, 1.15 V 7, 1.16 III 1, 1.112 4, 1.133 11, 1.170 8, 4.48 5, 4.68 4, 4.346 4, 4.380 14
ṣʿ[1.101 14, 4.685 3
]ṣʿ 1.139 1
]ṣʿ[1.22 I 28
ṣʿṣ 1.82 18, 1.82 41
ṣʿq 4.6 4, 4.48 4, 4.365 15, 4.380 15, 4.693 15, 4.770 19
ṣʿq[4.685 4
ṣ]ʿq 4.68 58
]ṣ/lġ 7.151 1
ṣġr 1.9 18, 1.13 33, 1.22 I 4, 1.107 9, 4.232 43
ṣġr[7.163 1
ṣ]ġr 1.107 12
ṣġrm 1.6 V 4
ṣġrt 1.24 50
ṣġrth 1.10 III 26
ṣġrthn 1.15 III 16
ṣp 1.14 III 45, 1.105 2
ṣp[7.66 2
]xṣp 1.87 61
ṣ/bp/tx[1.20 II 12
ṣ]py 4.167 2
]ṣpy 2.79 10
]xṣpy 2.83 9
ṣpym 4.167 4
ṣpyt 4.167 2
ṣpm 1.41 54
ṣpn 1.1 V 5, 1.1 V 18, 1.3 I 22, 1.3 III 29, 1.3 IV 1, 1.3 IV 19, 1.3 IV 38, 1.4 IV 19, 1.4 V 23, 1.4 V 55, 1.4 VII 6, 1.5 I 11, 1.6 I 57, 1.6 I 62, 1.6 VI 13, 1.10 III 30, 1.16 I 7, 1.16 II 45, 1.19 II 35, 1.39 10, 1.41 34, 1.41 42, 1.46 4, 1.46 7, 1.46 14, 1.46 17, 1.47 1, 1.47 5, 1.65 10, 1.87 27, 1.87 37, 1.87 46, 1.91 3, 1.100 9, 1.101 2, 1.105 21, 1.105 24, 1.109 9, 1.109 10, 1.109 14, 1.109 17, 1.109 29, 1.109 33, 1.118 4, 1.118 14, 1.130 13, 1.130 22, 1.130 23, 1.148 1, 1.148 6, 1.148 10, 1.148 27, 1.148 29, 1.162 19, 1.170 10, 1.173 5, 1.173 6, 2.44 10, 4.68 50, 4.94 16, 4.303 4, 4.610 28, 4.676 4
ṣpn[1.1 IV 1, 1.109 34, 1.109 36
ṣp[n 1.27 11, 1.130 25, 2.42 6
]ṣpn 2.23 19, 4.117 3
ṣ]pn 1.19 II 35, 1.46 12
ṣ]p[n] 1.130 5
ṣp{ʿ}n 1.6 I 16
ṣ\pn 1.112 22f
ṣp]n 1.46 2(?)
ṣpṣ 4.194 18
ṣpr 1.14 III 19, 4.170 7, 4.296 8, 4.332 18
ṣ]pr 1.14 V 12
ṣprn 4.232 20, 4.261 4
ṣṣ 4.340 1, 4.340 2, 4.340 3, 4.340 4, 4.340 5, 4.340 7, 4.340 8, 4.340 9, 4.340 10, 4.340 11, 4.340 12, 4.340 13, 4.340 14, 4.340 15, 4.340 16, 4.340 19, 4.340 20, 4.340 21, 4.344 1, 4.344 2, 4.344 3, 4.344 4, 4.344 6, 4.344 7, 4.344 8, 4.344 9, 4.344 10, 4.344 11, 4.344 12, 4.344 13, 4.344 14, 4.344 15, 4.344 16, 4.344 17, 4.344 18, 4.344 19, 4.720 4
ṣ[ṣ] 4.340 18
ṣ]ṣ 4.340 6, 4.340 17, 4.344 5
]xṣṣ 4.275 18
ṣṣb 4.611 1
ṣṣn 4.609 14
ṣṣr 1.64 13
ṣṣt 1.83 11
ṣq 1.22 I 25, 1.82 25
ṣq[1.14 II 18
ṣqm 4.635 51
ṣqn 4.69 III 7, 4.398 4
ṣ]qn[4.567 1
ṣqrn 1.41 50
ṣr 1.13 5, 1.176 19, 2.38 3, 2.38 12, 2.40 11, 4.132 4, 5.22 9
ṣr[4.102 11
]xṣr 4.436 8, 7.163 3
ṣrbn 1.131 3, 1.131 5
ṣrṭn 4.311 1, 4.412 II 34
ṣry 4.69 II 4, 4.338 5, 4.778 4, 4.782 6

]ṣry 4.124 11
]xṣry 4.708 6
ṣrym 4.122 6
ṣrm 1.14 IV 35, 1.14 IV 38
ṣrp 4.182 10, 4.626 10, 4.776 2
ṣr[p 4.182 27
ṣ]rp 4.206 6
ṣrptn 4.63 I 46
ṣrr 1.19 I 17
ṣrry 1.16 I 5, 1.16 I 19, 1.16 II 42
ṣrrt 1.3 I 21, 1.4 V 55, 1.6 I 16, 1.6 I 57, 1.6 I 62, 1.6 VI 12, 1.16 I 43
ṣrt 1.3 III 37, 1.3 IV 4, 1.3 IV 6
ṣrtk 1.2 IV 9
ṣrṯ[4.609 22
ṣrṯd 1.131 6
ṣt[1.136 11
]ṣt 4.591 3, 1.5 VI 4
]xṣt 7.153 2
ṣ/bt 4.769 42
ṣ/bp/tx[1.20 II 12
ṣth 1.17 I 13, 1.17 I 14
]ṣ/ltm 1.57 1
ṣtqn 1.79 4, 1.79 6, 1.79 7, 1.80 2, 1.80 3
ṣtry 4.690 15

Q

q 5.2 5(*bis*), 5.4 4, 5.6 2, 5.9 II 1, 5.12 3, 5.13 8, 5.14 13, 5.16 3, 5.16 7, 5.17 3, 5.17 6, 5.19 4, 5.19 5, 5.20 2, 5.20 3, 5.21 2, 5.24 1
q 4.63 III 22 cor. w
q[1.22 I 3, 1.166 1, 4.44 5, 4.335 11, 4.393 12, 4.593 6, 4.610 36
]q 1.11 5, 1.53 3, 1.107 6, 1.153 1, 2.73 21, 4.122 14, 4.170 1
]\q 1.67 20f, 4.227 I 1f
qx[4.693 44
]qx[1.16 V 31
]xq 2.33 18, 2.66 2
q/t[1.4 II 32, 4.513 4
]qa 1.5 I 27
]qa/n 4.382 21
xxqixb/d 4.4 8
]qb[1.168 19
qbat 1.6 VI 40
qbitm 1.161 3, 1.161 10
qbd[7.163 4
qbṭ[4.86 31
qbẓ 1.133 13
qby 1.73 6
qb[l 1.81 12
qblbl 1.4 I 36
qbʿl[y 4.254 2
qbʿt 1.6 IV 18, 1.19 IV 54, 1.19 IV 56
q[bʿthm] 1.16 III 16
qbṣ 1.15 III 4, 1.15 III 15, 1.79 7, 1.161 3, 1.161 10
qbṣt 1.163 17
qbr 1.16 II 25, 1.19 III 44, 6.44 2
qd[4.32 3
]qd 1.172 16
qdḥm 5.23 19
qdm 1.4 VII 40, 1.12 I 8, 1.100 62, 2.81 25, 4.538 3
qdmh 1.3 IV 41, 1.4 V 45
qdmym 1.4 VII 34, 1.161 8, 1.161 24
qd[mym 1.20 II 10
qdmn 4.33 40
qdm[n 4.50 3
q]dmn[4.498 3
qdmt 6.39 1
qdnt 2.7 7
qdqd 1.2 IV 24, 1.18 IV 22
[q]dqd 1.19 II 30
qdq\d 1.2 IV 21f
qdqdh 1.4 VII 4, 1.5 VI 16, 1.18 IV 11
qdqdy 1.17 VI 37
qdqdk 1.3 V 24, 1.16 VI 57(!)
qdq]dk 1.18 I 11
qdqdr 1.16 VI 57 lg. qdqdk
[q]dr 1.163 10
qdš 1.2 I 21, 1.2 I 38, 1.3 I 13, 1.3 III 30, 1.3 VI 11, 1.4 IV 13, 1.4 IV 16, 1.4 VII 29, 1.14 IV 34, 1.16 I 7, 1.16 I 11, 1.16 I 22, 1.16 II 46, 1.17 I 3, 1.17 I 8, 1.17 I 13, 1.17 I 22, 1.17 I 26, 1.17 I 44, 1.17 II 16, 1.23 65, 1.94 23, 1.94 24, 1.94 25, 1.112 21, 1.114 24, 1.115 7, 1.119 6, 1.119 33, 1.123 20, 1.123 26, 1.166 12, 1.169 8, 2.73 5, 4.643 5, 4.643 6, 4.643 7
qdš[1.104 12
qd[š 1.3 IV 20
q[dš 1.4 VII 31, 1.94 1, 4.652 3
]qdš 4.643 4
qd]š 1.2 III 20
]qdš[1.57 3
qd<š> 1.4 IV 8
qdšh 1.106 13
qdšm 4.29 3, 4.36 2, 4.38 2, 4.68 73, 4.126 7, 4.412 II 8, 4.752 5
qd[šm 4.47 1
q[dšm 4.416 7
qdšt 4.69 V 11, 4.412 I 11
]qdšt 1.81 17
qdt[1.22 II 14
qhm 4.240 4
qr/wd[1.73 8
qwḥn 4.754 8
qk/wqp[4.607 30
qḥ 1.4 II 32, 1.5 V 6, 1.12 I 17, 1.14 II 13, 1.14 II 17, 1.14 III 22, 1.14 III

26, 1.14 V 34, 1.14 VI 4, 1.14 VI 9, 1.16 I 41, 1.124 5, 1.124 7, 1.124 8, 4.188 18, 4.188 20
]qḥ 4.401 16
]qḥ[7.140 2
qḥn 1.19 IV 53
qḥn 4.183 II 6 lg. qṭn
qḥny 1.82 8, 1.82 8
qṭ 1.72 26, 1.85 18, 2.36 17, 4.166 5
q]ṭ 1.71 17
qṭx 4.787 9
qṭḫ 4.103 19 lg. qṭy
qṭy 1.40 36, 1.84 14, 4.103 19(!)
qṭy[4.37 4
q[ṭy 1.40 28
q]ṭy 1.84 19, 4.236 2
qṭn 3.7 6, 4.44 20, 4.47 9, 4.63 I 12, 4.69 VI 8, 4.83 9, 4.98 9, 4.183 II 6(!), 4.214 IV 10, 4.370 35, 4.617 46, 4.630 12, 4.742 12, 4.745 8
qṭn[4.609 23, 4.695 1
qṭnn 4.232 22*
qṭr 1.18 IV 26, 1.18 IV 37, 1.169 3
q]ṭr 1.167 11
qṭrh 1.17 I 27
qṭt 1.40 31, 1.40 39, 1.84 22
q[ṭt 1.121 1
q]ṭt 1.84 7
qṭ]t 1.40 14
qẓ 1.19 I 18, 1.19 I 41, 1.20 I 5, 1.24 2, 1.24 17, 1.24 24
qẓb 1.5 II 24
qẓrt 1.109 30
qym 1.22 I 5
]qym 1.17 VI 7
]qk 1.11 13
qk/wqp[4.607 30
ql 1.1 III 3, 1.3 I 20, 1.3 III 10, 1.3 VI 19, 1.4 VIII 27, 1.6 VI 21, 1.6 VI 22, 1.10 III 15, 1.10 III 16, 1.10 III 32, 1.13 23, 1.14 III 17, 1.14 V 9, 1.19 I 46, 1.44 4, 1.82 6, 1.82 28, 1.82 32, 1.100 2, 1.100 8, 1.100 14, 1.100 19, 1.100 30, 1.100 35, 1.100 40, 1.100 45, 1.100 51, 1.100 57, 1.107 28, 1.114 21, 1.151 11, 1.169 2, 3.1 5, 4.213 27, 4.337 12, 4.710 5
q[l 1.16 II 25
]ql 4.67 4
q]l 1.16 II 33, 1.100 25, 1.107 46
]ql[7.100 2
qlx 2.72 12
]qlx 4.17 1
qldn 4.7 2, 4.7 11, 4.75 III 4
qlh 1.3 V 10, 1.4 V 8, 1.4 VII 29, 1.4 VII 31, 1.6 VI 32
qlḥ 1.115 5, 1.115 13
qlẖt 5.22 16
qly 4.780 4
qlm[4.468 2, 4.468 3
]xqlm[4.94 10
qln 4.609 34, 4.612 7
qlny 2.11 7, 2.70 10
qlˤ 1.162 2, 4.63 I 4, 4.63 I 5, 4.63 I 8, 4.63 I 9, 4.63 I 12, 4.63 I 26, 4.63 I 27, 4.63 I 29, 4.63 I 30, 4.63 I 31, 4.63 II 3, 4.63 II 5, 4.63 II 6, 4.63 II 7, 4.63 II 9, 4.63 II 10, 4.63 II 14, 4.63 II 15, 4.63 II 16, 4.63 II 17, 4.63 II 18, 4.63 II 19, 4.63 II 22, 4.63 II 23, 4.63 II 24, 4.63 II 25, 4.63 II 28, 4.63 II 38, 4.63 II 41, 4.63 II 42, 4.63 II 43, 4.63 II 46, 4.63 II 47, 4.63 II 48, 4.63 III 6, 4.63 III 10, 4.63 III 11, 4.63 III 12, 4.63 III 13, 4.63 III 14, 4.63 III 16, 4.63 III 18, 4.63 III 20, 4.63 III 23, 4.63 III 25, 4.63 III 29, 4.63 III 34, 4.63 III 35, 4.63 III 36, 4.63 III 39, 4.63 III 40, 4.63 III 41, 4.63 III 45, 4.63 III 46, 4.63 IV 1, 4.63 IV 2, 4.63 IV 4, 4.63 IV 5, 4.63 IV 7, 4.63 IV 8, 4.63 IV 12, 4.63 IV 13, 4.63 IV 16, 4.63 IV 17, 4.624 3, 4.624 5, 4.624 6
qlˤ[4.624 13
ql[ˤ] 4.63 III 28
q[lˤ] 4.63 III 22, 4.63 III 26, 4.63 III 44
]qlˤ 4.624 8
q]lˤ 4.63 II 26
ql]ˤ 4.63 IV 9
<qlˤm> 4.624 9
qlˤm 4.63 II 45, 4.63 III 2, 4.63 III 3, 4.63 III 4, 4.63 III 5, 4.63 III 8, 4.63 III 15, 4.63 III 19, 4.63 III 21, 4.63 III 33, 4.167 10, 4.169 3
q[l]ˤm 4.63 I 2
]qlˤm[4.624 17

q]lʿm 4.63 I 3
qlṣk 1.18 I 17
ql[ṣ]k 1.3 V 28
qlṣn 1.4 VI 13
qlql 1.71 9, 1.85 10
qlt 1.4 II 4(?), 1.4 III 15, 1.6 V 12, 2.8 3, 2.12 11, 2.13 6, 2.30 5, 2.40 8, 2.45 12, 2.64 16, 2.68 7, 2.82 3
ql[t] 2.24 7
q[l]t 2.64 7
]qlt 1.18 I 27
ql]t 2.81 6
qlṯ[4.672 5
qm 1.2 I 21, 1.3 I 4, 1.3 I 18, 1.4 III 12, 1.10 II 25, 1.16 I 30
qm[6.40 2
]qm 7.132 7
]qm[4.313 26
xxxxqm 1.15 IV 11
qmḥ 1.41 23, 1.71 25, 1.85 32, 1.87 25, 4.328 1, 4.361 1, 4.362 1, 4.608 1, 4.751 4, 4.789 1
qmẖ 5.22 17
qmy 3.7 15, 4.48 3, 4.52 16, 4.365 16, 4.380 24, 4.382 16, 4.382 17, 4.770 20
qmm 1.2 I 31, 1.19 I 9
qmnz 4.68 15, 4.95 8, 4.113 2, 4.244 11, 4.308 9
qm[nz 4.686 9
qm]nz 4.553 3
qmnzy 4.85 5, 4.85 8, 4.295 3
qmṣ 1.4 VI 43, 1.22 I 14, 4.182 37, 4.365 14
qmṣ[4.693 16
q[mṣ 1.1 IV 32
]qmṣ 1.15 V 16
qn 1.5 VI 20, 1.6 I 4, 1.17 VI 9, 4.247 29
qn[4.422 7
]qn 2.36 19, 4.35 II 23, 4.217 2, 4.424 6, 4.424 9, 4.438 6, 4.609 18
]qa/n 4.382 21
qnim 2.73 7
qnuym 2.73 17
qnum 4.371 1
qnḏ 4.69 III 16, 4.77 7, 4.727 2
qnh 1.4 VIII 20
]qnh 1.17 VI 13
q<n>y 1.6 II 23
qny 3.9 2
qny[1.3 V 9
]qny 4.648 23
qnyn 1.10 III 5
qnyt 1.4 I 22, 1.4 III 26, 1.4 III 30, 1.4 III 35, 1.4 IV 32, 1.8 II 2
qnm 1.17 VI 23, 4.91 10, 4.158 12
qnmlk 4.63 I 21
]qns 4.706 14
qʿl 1.3 VI 8, 1.22 I 16, 1.22 I 16
qʿmr 4.734 4
]xqp 1.82 23
]qpḥn 4.428 4
qpt 4.123 21
qptm 4.42 2
qṣ 1.3 I 8, 1.4 III 42, 1.4 VI 57, 1.6 II 11, 1.114 2, 1.147 12
q]ṣ 1.17 VI 4
qṣḥm 4.751 8
qṣḫ 1.64 14, 1.64 15
qṣy 4.350 9
qṣm 1.3 II 10, 1.16 III 3
qṣn 4.63 III 6, 4.122 4, 4.204 10, 4.285 10, 4.617 21
qṣʿt 1.17 V 3, 1.17 V 13, 1.17 V 28, 1.17 VI 25
qṣʿth 1.10 II 7, 1.18 IV 13, 1.19 I 15
qṣʿtk 1.17 VI 19, 1.18 IV 41
qṣṣ 1.167 5
qṣr 1.16 VI 34, 1.16 VI 47, 1.103 10
qṣrt 1.103 39
q[ṣ]rt 1.40 31
q]ṣrt 1.40 22
qṣ]rt 1.40 39
qqln 4.35 II 12, 4.35 II 13, 4.35 II 14, 4.35 II 15, 4.66 2, 4.155 2
qr 1.12 II 60, 1.14 III 16, 1.16 I 27, 1.19 III 45, 1.19 III 46, 1.82 40
qr[1.1 IV 2, 1.164 10, 4.686 6
]qr[7.191 1
]xqr[4.540 1
qra 1.161 4, 1.161 5, 1.161 6, 1.161 7, 1.161 11, 1.161 12
q[ra] 1.87 8
qran 1.5 I 23
qrat 1.116 2
qrit 1.100 2
qritm 1.161 2, 1.161 9

qru 1.161 8
qrb 1.1 II 6, 1.4 IV 22, 1.4 V 14, 1.4 V 30, 1.4 V 37, 1.4 V 62, 1.4 V 65, 1.4 VI 45, 1.4 VII 13, 1.4 VII 18, 1.4 VII 27, 1.5 III 19, 1.6 I 33, 1.10 II 5, 1.17 I 25, 1.17 I 43, 1.20 I 4, 1.20 II 1, 1.20 II 9, 1.22 II 20, 1.62 5, 1.114 1, 1.169 5, 2.36 9
qrb[1.4 VI 6, 1.11 1, 1.19 I 2
qr[b 1.5 III 10, 1.5 III 26
q[rb 1.4 VI 9
q]rb 1.4 VIII 41
qr]b 1.3 V 6, 1.10 II 2, 1.18 I 25, 1.21 II 8
qr]\b 1.22 II 1f
qrbm 1.19 II 18, 1.19 II 25
qrd 1.119 26, 1.119 29, 4.159 8, 4.159 9
qr/wd[1.73 8
qrdy 4.617 31
qrdm 1.3 III 14, 1.3 IV 8, 1.5 II 11, 1.5 II 18
q\[rdm] 1.4 VIII 34f
qrdmn 4.658 20
qrht 4.95 1, 4.235 1
qr\ht 6.27 2f
qrwn 1.127 11, 4.13 36, 4.277 3
[[qrwn]] 4.277 14
qrzbl 1.40 30, 1.40 38
q[rzbl] 1.40 21
]qrzbl 1.84 21
qrḥ[4.617 28
qrṭy 4.85 6
qrṭym 4.85 1
qrẓ 1.92 9
qry 4.788 4
qryy 1.3 III 14, 1.3 IV 8
qrym 1.19 IV 29
qryt 1.14 II 28, 1.14 IV 9
qrytm 1.3 II 7
]qrmṯ[1.35 8
qrn 1.10 II 21, 1.10 II 22, 1.18 IV 10, 1.103 11, 4.17 17, 4.113 8, 5.23 2
qrn[4.17 13, 4.17 14
qr[n 4.17 9, 4.17 10, 4.17 11, 4.17 12
q[rn 1.18 IV 9
qrnh 1.12 II 39, 1.92 32, 2.72 30
q]rnh 1.3 IV 27
qr]nh 1.17 VI 14
qrnm 1.12 I 30, 1.114 20
qrn[m] 1.101 6
qrnt 1.17 VI 22
qrsam 4.705 3
qrsi 4.705 8
qrq 5.9 I 20
qrr 4.214 I 20
qrrn 3.7 2, 4.214 I 1
qrš 1.4 IV 24, 1.6 I 35
q]rš 1.2 III 5, 1.17 VI 49
qr]š 1.3 V 8
qrt 1.18 IV 8, 1.19 IV 1, 1.19 IV 2, 1.19 IV 3, 1.23 3, 1.46 12, 1.119 10, 1.127 30, 2.42 17, 2.61 7, 2.72 19, 2.72 22, 4.49 1, 4.68 21, 4.141 III 3, 4.182 15, 4.290 3, 4.290 6, 4.332 5, 4.555 4, 4.609 10, 4.609 11, 4.631 5, 4.631 6, 4.631 9, 4.631 14, 4.631 16, 4.631 21, 4.631 23, 4.691 6, 6.49 1
qrt[2.49 11
qr[t 1.109 6, 1.130 18, 4.308 12, 4.631 17
q[rt 1.87 23, 4.686 13
]qrt 1.18 I 30, 2.33 7, 4.419 2
q]rt 1.41 10, 4.553 7
qrth 1.4 VIII 11, 1.5 II 15, 1.14 III 13
qrty 4.295 12, 4.417 6, 4.648 24
qrty[4.80 9
qrtym 4.648 16
qrtm 1.3 II 20
qrtmt 4.628 4
qrtn 2.61 12
qšh 1.3 V 33
q[š]h 1.4 IV 45
qšm 1.16 VI 48
qšt 1.9 13, 1.17 V 2, 1.17 V 12, 1.17 V 27, 1.17 V 35, 1.17 VI 13, 1.17 VI 24, 1.19 I 4, 4.53 14, 4.63 I 4, 4.63 I 5, 4.63 I 6, 4.63 I 7, 4.63 I 8, 4.63 I 9, 4.63 I 10, 4.63 I 12, 4.63 I 13, 4.63 I 14, 4.63 I 15, 4.63 I 16, 4.63 I 17, 4.63 I 18, 4.63 I 19, 4.63 I 20, 4.63 I 21, 4.63 I 22, 4.63 I 23, 4.63 I 28, 4.63 I 30, 4.63 I 32, 4.63 I 34, 4.63 I 35, 4.63 I 36, 4.63 I 37, 4.63 I 38, 4.63 I 39, 4.63 I 40, 4.63 I 41, 4.63 I 42, 4.63 I 43, 4.63 I 44, 4.63 I 45, 4.63 I 46, 4.63 I 47, 4.63 II 2, 4.63 II 4, 4.63 II 5, 4.63 II 6, 4.63 II

7, 4.63 II 8, 4.63 II 9, 4.63 II 10, 4.63 II 11, 4.63 II 15, 4.63 II 16, 4.63 II 17, 4.63 II 18, 4.63 II 19, 4.63 II 22, 4.63 II 23, 4.63 II 24, 4.63 II 25, 4.63 II 27, 4.63 II 28, 4.63 II 31, 4.63 II 32, 4.63 II 36, 4.63 II 37, 4.63 II 38, 4.63 II 41, 4.63 II 42, 4.63 II 43, 4.63 II 44, 4.63 II 45, 4.63 II 47, 4.63 III 2, 4.63 III 5, 4.63 III 9, 4.63 III 11, 4.63 III 13, 4.63 III 14, 4.63 III 17, 4.63 III 20, 4.63 III 21, 4.63 III 23, 4.63 III 24, 4.63 III 25, 4.63 III 26, 4.63 III 27, 4.63 III 28, 4.63 III 29, 4.63 III 30, 4.63 III 31, 4.63 III 35, 4.63 III 36, 4.63 III 37, 4.63 III 38, 4.63 III 39, 4.63 III 40, 4.63 III 41, 4.63 III 42, 4.63 III 43, 4.63 III 44, 4.63 III 45, 4.63 III 46, 4.63 IV 5, 4.63 IV 6, 4.63 IV 7, 4.63 IV 8, 4.63 IV 9, 4.63 IV 10, 4.63 IV 11, 4.63 IV 12, 4.63 IV 13, 4.63 IV 14, 4.63 IV 15, 4.63 IV 17, 4.141 III 18, 4.169 1, 4.215 2, 4.624 2, 4.624 4, 4.624 7, 4.624 9, 7.222 4

qš[t 1.12 II 32, 4.63 II 26, 4.63 II 33, 4.63 IV 3

q[š]t 4.63 II 46, 4.63 III 7

q[št 4.63 IV 2

qšth 1.3 II 16, 1.19 I 14, 1.19 I 16

qšthn 1.10 II 6

qštk 1.17 VI 18

q[štk 1.18 IV 40

qš<t>m 4.63 III 34

qšt<m> 4.63 I 29, 4.63 IV 16

qštm 1.17 VI 39, 4.63 I 2, 4.63 I 3, 4.63 I 26, 4.63 I 27, 4.63 I 31, 4.63 II 14, 4.63 III 3, 4.63 III 4, 4.63 III 6, 4.63 III 8, 4.63 III 10, 4.63 III 12, 4.63 III 15, 4.63 III 16, 4.63 III 18, 4.63 III 19, 4.63 III 22, 4.63 III 33

qt 4.275 10

]qt 1.37 5, 4.182 11

]qt[4.459 1

]xxqt 7.51 23

]qtm 4.734 1

xqtn 4.350 6

R

r 5.2 4(*bis*), 5.2 5, 5.2 6, 5.2 7, 5.2 8, 5.4 4, 5.6 2, 5.7 1, 5.12 4, 5.13 8, 5.14 14, 5.15 2, 5.15 3, 5.17 3, 5.17 6, 5.19 4, 5.20 2, 5.20 3, 5.21 2, 5.24 1
r 4.34 2, 4.374 15 lg. w
r 1.173 9 cor. rn[
r 7.198 6 cor. xr
r[1.6 IV 27, 1.9 18, 1.24 13, 1.42 24, 1.57 1, 1.73 7, 1.86 13, 1.89 4, 1.91 1, 1.91 18, 1.95 2, 1.98 11, 1.101 1, 1.103 31, 1.129 6, 1.166 3, 2.3 23, 2.23 12, 2.83 4, 4.10 2, 4.41 4, 4.120 1, 4.329 3, 4.401 9, 4.412 I 24, 4.483 1, 4.575 4, 4.593 4, 4.618 9, 4.647 1, 4.647 3, 4.679 8, 4.683 23, 4.763 5, 6.57 1, 7.54 3, 7.58 1, 7.95 2, 7.103 2, 7.127 3, 7.149 2, 7.149 3
r[1.169 1 lg. r[gmm
]r 1.1 II 3, 1.15 III 8, 1.16 V 30, 1.18 I 29, 1.23 4, 1.33 2, 1.42 23, 1.64 20, 1.68 8, 1.68 13, 1.70 43, 1.83 1, 1.94 1, 1.94 20, 1.137 2, 1.153 10, 2.36 10, 2.44 9, 2.47 19, 2.54 12, 4.11 2, 4.28 5, 4.64 IV 5, 4.69 VI 35, 4.75 IV 16, 4.122 15, 4.141 I 21, 4.159 10, 4.183 I 15, 4.201 10, 4.205 9, 4.247 14, 4.283 3, 4.304 2, 4.339 9, 4.350 3, 4.351 3, 4.420 10, 4.534 1, 4.534 2, 4.545 I 7, 4.582 4, 4.592 7, 4.638 6, 4.701 9, 4.762 1, 4.762 5, 4.769 31, 4.785 26, 7.50 4, 7.51 5, 7.118 1, 7.130 1, 7.130 6, 7.133 3, 7.222 4
]r[1.11 21, 1.13 23, 1.64 31, 1.147 28, 1.167 12, 1.169 22, 4.77 5, 4.93 III 16, 4.304 6, 4.517 1, 4.769 28, 7.12 1, 7.19 6, 7.85 7, 7.103 1, 7.105 1, 7.123 3, 7.175 5, 7.176 3, 7.197 3, 7.211 1, 7.217 1
rxx 4.123 4, 4.401 8
rx[2.27 4, 2.36 20, 4.252 2
]rx[4.122 15, 7.102 1
rxx[4.401 10, 4.776 3
xr 1.22 II 1, 1.70 35, 2.34 20, 4.42 4, 7.198 6(cor.), 7.198 9
xr[4.86 2, 4.393 1
]xr 1.84 17, 1.147 20, 2.3 29, 2.31 41, 2.43 3, 2.74 2, 4.239 2, 4.239 4, 4.613 22, 7.41 2, 7.50 16, 7.185 3
]xr[1.16 VI 29, 1.42 23, 4.479 2, 4.526 6, 4.673 9, 7.150 5, 7.186 2
xrx 2.35 8, 4.191 15, 4.748 9
xrx[4.178 1
]xrx[4.103 32, 4.325 1, 4.467 3, 4.661 7, 7.39 2
xxrxx[1.70 43
]r/w[7.184 8
r/w/k[1.176 17, 4.73 6
r/w/k/p[4.393 24
r/k[1.174 5, 4.160 7, 4.422 32, 4.529 1, 7.45 3, 7.45 4
]r/k 1.42 24, 1.75 1, 2.31 33, 2.31 36, 2.57 11, 4.104 11, 4.224 1, 4.275 20, 4.438 7, 4.628 8, 4.770 21, 7.20 2, 7.109 2
]r/k[1.7 52, 4.64 V 6, 4.627 4
r/k/p[4.737 3
]r/kx[7.187 2
]r/kxxx[1.86 10
]xr/k[4.219 16
]r/k/w 7.51 12
r/n[7.108 6
]r/n 1.172 15
rxb/ḏdr[1.70 42
rxxxd 2.46 22
]rxwm 1.147 6
]xrkb/d[2.7 4
]rxm 1.13 14
ra 1.176 24
]xrab 4.151 I 1
ray 4.705 5
rašm 1.3 III 42, 1.5 I 3
rašthm 1.2 I 29
raštkm 1.2 I 27
]r/ki 7.190 2
rib 4.386 13
]ribẖ/y[7.217 4

ridn 1.3 I 12
ridn[1.41 36
riw 1.42 38
rimt 1.3 III 4, 1.7 22, 1.101 17
riʿbd 4.690 15
riš 1.3 II 9, 1.7 8, 1.16 III 12, 1.17 VI 37, 1.19 II 38, 1.19 III 54, 1.23 31, 1.23 36, 1.87 4, 1.114 30, 1.164 17, 1.169 19, 1.175 11, 2.72 31, 3.2 7, 4.182 32, 4.189 7, 4.387 21, 4.618 29
riš[4.141 I 2
r[i]š 4.387 27
ri[š 2.5 1
]riš 2.2 1
r]iš 1.87 1
]riš[4.491 3
rišh 1.2 IV 38, 1.5 VI 15, 1.6 I 60, 1.16 VI 9, 1.82 7, 1.101 5, 1.101 7, 1.103 43
rišhm 1.23 5
rišh[m] 1.19 II 31
rišy 4.310 4, 4.310 10, 4.352 7
rišym 4.347 1, 4.371 1, 4.779 3
ri[šym 4.424 1
rišyt 1.119 25
rišk 1.2 I 6, 1.2 I 8, 1.16 I 27, 1.16 VI 56
r]išk 1.3 VI 2
rišn 4.50 9
rišt 1.3 II 12
riš[t 1.13 7
r[išt] 1.7 2
rišthm 1.2 I 23
rišt\km 1.2 I 24f
rum 1.10 III 21, 1.10 III 36
]rum 1.16 IV 17
rumm 1.4 I 43, 1.5 I 17, 1.6 I 19, 1.6 VI 18, 1.10 II 9, 1.10 II 12, 1.17 VI 21, 1.133 7
r]umm 1.10 I 24
ruš 2.63 9
rb 1.3 I 12, 1.3 III 7, 1.3 V 42, 1.4 I 17, 1.4 IV 56, 1.4 VI 11, 1.5 V 11, 1.6 VI 55, 1.6 VI 56, 1.44 2, 2.4 1, 2.23 2, 2.23 7, 2.23 10, 2.23 24, 2.38 16, 2.38 22, 2.42 3, 2.76 1, 2.76 4, 2.76 8, 2.76 9, 2.78 2, 2.78 5, 2.81 1, 2.81 10, 2.81 16, 2.81 19, 2.81 30, 3.1 13, 3.1 26, 3.9 12, 4.90 8, 4.141 III 3, 4.145 9, 4.160 12, 4.222 3, 4.233 1, 4.288 6, 4.382 5, 4.410 27, 4.609 2, 4.609 5, 4.609 7, 4.609 8, 4.714 1, 4.721 9, 4.725 4, 4.752 1, 4.759 8, 6.2 1, 6.3 1, 6.6 1, 6.7 1, 6.8 1, 6.9 1, 6.10 1, 6.66 3, 7.69 3, 9.530 1, 9.530 9
rb[1.86 3, 2.23 14, 2.25 7
r[b 1.3 IV 51, 2.23 17, 3.1 16
]rb 1.3 I 25, 1.75 10, 2.81 22
r]b 3.1 21
rbx[1.9 3, 1.70 9
]r/kb 1.63 7
rbil 4.134 3, 4.635 27, 4.744 5
[r]bil 4.401 7
rbb 1.3 II 39, 1.3 IV 44, 1.19 I 44, 1.88 1
[r]bb 1.3 II 41
rbbt 1.4 I 28, 1.4 I 43
rbd 1.92 35
]rby 4.355 43
]r/kby 4.756 5
rbm 1.3 III 39, 1.6 V 2, 1.107 2, 1.124 2, 4.149 2
rbm[1.107 51
rbm 1.14 III 5 lg. rbt
]rbm 7.33 4
xrbn 4.787 11
rbʿ 1.4 VI 26(!), 1.14 III 2, 1.14 III 11, 1.14 IV 45, 1.14 IV 46, 1.14 V 4, 1.17 I 8, 1.17 II 34, 1.22 I 22, 1.119 20, 4.279 4
rbʿ[1.17 II 45
r/nbʿl 6.70 2
rbʿt 1.19 II 34, 4.707 9, 4.707 12
]rbʿt 4.707 3
rbṣ 1.13 9, 4.382 4
]rbṣ 4.788 8
]xrbš[6.38 2
rbt 1.3 I 17, 1.3 IV 38, 1.3 V 40, 1.3 VI 5, 1.3 VI 17, 1.4 I 13, 1.4 I 21, 1.4 II 28, 1.4 II 31, 1.4 II 33, 1.4 III 25, 1.4 III 27, 1.4 III 28, 1.4 III 34, 1.4 IV 31, 1.4 IV 40, 1.4 IV 53, 1.4 V 2, 1.4 V 3, 1.4 V 24, 1.4 V 57, 1.4 VIII 25, 1.5 III 3, 1.6 I 44, 1.6 I 45, 1.6 I 47, 1.6 I 53, 1.8 II 1, 1.14 II 36, 1.14 II 40, 1.14 III 5(!), 1.14 III 30,

1.14 IV 16, 1.14 IV 18, 1.14 IV 47, 1.14 VI 11, 1.15 IV 19, 1.15 V 25, 1.16 I 36, 1.16 I 38, 1.17 V 10, 1.23 54, 1.24 20, 1.100 63, 1.133 12, 1.161 19, 1.169 16, 5.9 I 5, 7.47 5

rbt[4.125 16

r[bt 1.1 III 2

]rbt 1.4 III 38

r]bt 1.15 IV 8

]rbt[7.34 2

rbtm 1.4 I 30

]rg 7.61 6

]rg[4.401 6

]xrg 4.217 5

]r/kg[7.84 2

rgbt 1.92 31, 1.112 4, 1.133 19

rgḥ/ṭ[4.561 2

rgln[4.619 7

{rgm} 2.26 1

<rgm> 2.26 3

rgm 1.1 III 4, 1.1 III 15, 1.2 I 16, 1.2 I 33, 1.2 I 42, 1.2 IV 6, 1.3 III 11, 1.3 III 20, 1.3 III 22, 1.3 III 27, 1.3 VI 21, 1.4 VI 3, 1.4 VIII 29, 1.5 II 8, 1.5 III 21, 1.6 III 24, 1.7 25, 1.15 VI 7, 1.15 VI 7, 1.16 I 38, 1.16 V 14, 1.16 V 17, 1.16 V 20, 1.16 VI 28, 1.19 II 26, 1.19 III 7, 1.19 III 35, 1.19 IV 50, 1.23 52, 1.23 59, 1.41 45, 1.41 46, 1.86 7, 1.93 1, 1.103 6, 1.103 18, 1.106 23, 1.106 32, 1.112 20, 2.4 2, 2.8 6, 2.10 3, 2.10 17, 2.11 2, 2.11 17, 2.12 3, 2.12 14, 2.13 2, 2.13 13, 2.14 3, 2.14 12, 2.14 17, 2.16 3, 2.16 20, 2.20 2, 2.20 3, 2.21 3, 2.21 8, 2.23 1, 2.24 2, 2.24 12, 2.30 2, 2.30 11, 2.31 41, 2.31 52, 2.34 2, 2.34 9, 2.36 2, 2.36 14, 2.36 20, 2.38 2, 2.38 9, 2.39 2, 2.40 2, 2.42 25, 2.44 2, 2.46 3, 2.46 8, 2.61 2, 2.63 2, 2.64 3, 2.64 19, 2.68 2, 2.68 16, 2.70 2, 2.71 2, 2.71 8, 2.72 9, 2.77 7, 2.78 3, 2.81 4, 4.332 12, 5.10 3, 9.530 2

rgm[2.3 14, 2.45 3, 2.73 12, 2.83 7, 7.36 1

rg[m 1.1 III 12, 1.14 V 32, 1.87 49, 1.93 3, 2.31 56, 2.42 2, 2.49 3, 2.64 10, 2.75 2

r[gm] 2.6 3

]rgm 1.15 V 13, 2.31 44, 2.76 2

r]gm 2.31 53, 2.65 5

rg]m 2.55 4, 2.56 2, 2.57 12, 2.58 2, 2.76 11

rgmh 2.17 8

rgmy 2.3 22, 2.13 16, 2.31 49

rgmm 1.3 IV 31, 1.4 I 19, 1.17 VI 39

r[gmm 1.169 1(!)

rgmt 1.2 I 45, 1.2 IV 7, 1.4 VII 23, 2.14 9, 2.21 10, 2.33 25, 2.42 6, 2.45 15, 2.45 23, 2.73 13

]r/kgn 4.183 I 13

rd 1.4 VIII 7, 1.5 V 14, 1.16 VI 37, 1.16 VI 52, 1.161 21, 1.161 22

rd[1.48 11, 4.84 1

]rd 1.69 9, 4.236 1, 4.409 6, 4.673 5, 4.730 2, 7.130 5

]xrd 4.706 4

rdyk 1.1 II 4

rdn 1.161 23

rd[n] 1.161 6

]xrḏx[7.147 5

]r/kḏ[1.52 17

]rh 4.359 5, 7.91 2

]rhd 4.443 10

]rw[7.74 3

rwy 4.69 III 4, 4.103 9

]rwtš 1.54 8

]rz 1.91 9

rznn 1.128 12

]rznnxx 1.68 29

rḥ 1.3 II 2, 1.4 III 8, 1.13 34, 1.18 IV 25, 1.18 IV 36, 1.19 II 38, 1.79 6, 1.166 22, 1.172 26

rḥ[4.739 4

r[ḥ 1.19 II 43

rḥxx[1.86 19

]r/kḥ[7.100 1

]r/kḥxb[4.247 12

rḥb 1.16 I 9, 1.16 II 47

rḥbn 4.143 1

]rḥbn 2.31 63

rḥbt 1.4 VI 53, 1.6 I 66, 1.15 IV 16

r[ḥ]bt 1.15 IV 5

r]ḥbt 1.5 III 2

rḥ]bt 1.15 V 2

rẖh 5.22 14

rḥk 1.5 V 7

rḥm 1.6 II 27, 1.6 II 34
rḥm[1.5 IV 3, 1.17 II 47
]rḥm 1.13 2
r[ḥm 1.6 II 5
rḥ\m 1.6 V 15f
rḥm<y> 1.23 13
rḥmy 1.15 II 6, 1.23 16, 1.23 28
rḥmt 1.16 I 33
rḥṣ 1.14 II 10, 1.17 I 33, 1.17 II 7, 1.17 II 23
]rḥṣnn 1.61 3
rḥq 1.1 III 19, 1.2 III 2, 1.3 IV 34, 1.3 IV 35, 1.14 III 28, 1.14 VI 14
]rḥq 1.4 VII 5
rḥqm 1.1 IV 3
rḥt[h] 1.16 V 28
rḥtm 1.4 VIII 6, 1.5 V 14
]rḫ 2.31 26, 4.615 2
]\rḫ 1.70 26f
]rḫx[1.81 14
rḫḏtx[1.70 34
]rḫy 4.197 14
rḫlxhx 1.35 11
xrḫlt[1.35 16
rḫnn[7.57 2
rḫn{n}t 1.4 V 5
rḫpt 1.108 8
rṭ 4.337 12
rṭd 4.131 3
rṭm 4.203 8, 4.206 2
ry 1.132 3
]ry 4.55 14, 5.11 23
]ry[4.401 4
]r/ky 4.433 3
]r/kyx[4.619 12
]r/kym 4.72 2
]ryn[4.603 2
ryb 1.69 3, 1.69 7
]ryt 1.117 10
]rk 1.107 30, 1.169 17
]\rk 1.70 14f
]rk[4.326 4
rkb 1.2 IV 8, 1.2 IV 29, 1.3 III 38, 1.3 IV 4, 1.3 IV 6, 1.4 III 11, 1.4 III 18, 1.4 V 60, 1.5 II 7, 1.10 I 7, 1.10 III 36, 1.14 II 21, 1.14 IV 3, 1.19 I 43, 1.92 40, 1.148 20, 5.22 15
r]kb 1.3 II 40
rk]b 1.92 37
rkby 4.63 II 35, 4.346 1, 4.379 8, 4.683 18
]rkl 4.769 7
r<k>s 1.5 I 4(?)
]rkṯ 4.63 III 16
]rl[4.733 4
]xr/kl 7.52 7
rlb 1.114 12 lg. klb
]rln 4.106 5
rm 1.3 V 21, 1.13 12, 1.15 III 13, 1.113 1, 1.113 3, 1.113 5, 4.710 10
rm[4.122 12, 4.682 8
]rm 1.20 I 7, 1.113 8, 1.171 4, 4.71 IV 3, 4.87 1, 4.199 1, 4.210 1, 4.610 47, 4.707 26, 7.132 10
]rm[4.401 5, 7.19 2
]xrm 4.368 2, 4.387 16
]r/km 2.4 14, 2.62 10, 4.734 3, 7.145 4
rmib 4.734 4
]xrmbt[l 7.222 2
rmy 4.170 12, 4.617 36
rmyy 4.69 I 5, 4.759 5
rmyy[4.623 2
rm<m> 1.108 9
rmm 1.4 V 52, 1.9 15, 1.87 41, 1.108 7
rm]m 1.2 III 7
rmmxxxxh/i 1.35 12
]rmn 4.64 IV 7, 4.755 6, 7.61 2
]xrmṣm 4.668 3
rmṣt 1.39 9, 1.41 18
rmš 1.109 7, 1.130 21
rm[š 1.46 13
rmt 1.8 II 9
r\[mt] 1.4 VII 55f
rmtrl/d/u[4.128 12
rmṯt 4.127 5
rn[1.173 9(cor.)
]rn 1.3 III 3, 1.5 V 22, 1.172 14, 4.18 4, 4.75 V 9, 4.82 3, 4.103 28, 4.106 1, 4.112 II 5, 4.138 3, 4.194 20, 4.214 II 7, 4.308 2, 4.412 III 16, 4.433 6, 4.658 30, 7.39 5
]rn[4.32 5
xrn 4.762 4
]xrn 1.42 18
]xrn[1.21 II 13
]r/kn 4.151 IV 3, 4.350 7, 4.769 22

]r/kn[2.25 1
rny 4.769 19
]xrny 2.31 53
xrs[4.77 25
]rsg 4.676 3
]rsd 4.54 6
]rsy[6.48 1
rˁ 5.9 I 11
]rˁx 4.732 3
]xrˁ 4.697 9
rˁh 1.22 I 27, 4.391 1, 4.391 2, 4.391 3, 4.391 4, 4.391 5, 4.740 4, 5.9 I 10
rˁ[h] 4.391 11, 4.391 12, 4.391 13, 4.391 14, 4.391 15, 4.391 16
r[ˁh] 4.391 8, 4.391 10
]rˁh 4.493 2, 4.493 3, 4.740 2, 4.740 3
r]ˁh 4.440 2, 4.440 3, 4.440 4, 4.493 1
rˁ]h 4.440 1, 4.440 5
rˁy 1.21 II 6, 2.2 1, 2.15 5, 4.75 IV 9, 4.129 1, 4.175 7, 4.618 3, 5.9 I 8
rˁ[y 4.153 1
rˁym 4.125 4, 4.243 45, 4.374 1, 4.378 1, 4.729 1, 4.768 8
rˁ[ym 4.243 49
r[ˁym 4.729 11
rˁkt 1.119 2 lg. ˁrkt or ugrt?
rˁm[1.9 6
]xr/wˁn 4.557 3
rˁt 1.101 4
]rˁtm 1.169 20
rġb 1.4 IV 33, 1.15 I 1
]rġb 1.103 19
r]ġb 1.7 10
rġbn 1.103 5
r]ġbn 1.103 12
rġ]bn 1.103 3
rġbt 1.4 IV 33
]rġrm 1.94 31
rp 6.63 2
rp[7.67 2
rpx[7.185 1
rp[a] 1.161 4, 1.161 5
rpan 4.45 7, 4.103 46, 4.116 4, 4.204 6, 4.269 13, 4.281 19, 4.339 26, 4.658 15, 4.753 9, 4.787 6
rpa[n 4.427 21, 4.506 3
rpi 1.15 III 14, 1.17 I 17, 1.17 I 35, 1.17 II 28, 1.17 V 5, 1.17 V 14, 1.17 V 34, 1.17 VI 52, 1.19 I 20, 1.19 I 37, 1.19 I 39, 1.19 I 47, 1.19 IV 13, 1.19 IV 18, 1.19 IV 36, 1.161 2, 1.161 9, 1.166 13
rpi[4.102 24
rp[i 1.19 IV 17
]rpi 1.108 21
r]pi 1.17 I 42
rp]i 1.17 I 1, 1.17 I 37
r\[p]i 1.108 23f
rpiy 4.141 II 14
rpiyn 4.232 8
r/kpil 4.194 12
rpim 1.6 VI 46, 1.21 II 9, 1.22 II 19, 1.161 8, 1.161 24
rpi[m 1.82 32
r[pim 1.22 II 3
rpu 1.22 I 8, 1.108 1, 1.108 19
]xrpu 4.398 10
rpum 1.20 II 6, 1.21 II 3, 1.21 II 11, 1.22 I 21, 1.22 I 23
r[pum 1.22 II 5
rp]um 1.20 I 1
]rpḫxxt 1.68 28
]rpl 7.46 3
rps 1.176 7
rpš 4.48 7, 4.63 II 30, 4.63 III 23, 4.100 5, 4.108 1, 4.243 4, 4.348 1, 4.348 20, 4.365 12, 4.784 19
rp[š 4.94 12
rpty 4.116 12
rṣ[4.632 10
]rṣ 1.107 3
]xrṣ 7.28 3
rṣmm 4.4 4
rṣn 4.370 16
rq 4.205 2, 4.205 5
rq[1.151 7
]rq 1.1 V 13, 7.55 4
]rq[4.769 21
rqd 1.91 33, 4.232 1, 4.348 24, 4.355 40, 4.365 24, 4.380 27, 4.610 18, 4.693 23, 4.698 5, 4.750 7, 4.777 6
rqd[4.629 9
rq[d 4.68 34
]rqd 4.119 4, 4.397 11
rq]d 4.770 1
]rqd[4.414 3

rqdy 4.33 32, 4.155 14, 4.339 21
rqdym 4.261 2
rqdn 3.10 2
r]qdn 4.792 2
rqḥ 1.41 21, 1.148 21, 4.91 5, 5.10 8
r[qḥ 4.60 6
r[qẖ] 4.31 2
rqm 1.4 VI 34
]xrqm[7.50 11
rqn 4.549 1
xxxxxrqšlxxṯl[4.198 2
rqth 1.19 II 38
]xrrsn[7.52 5
rš 1.14 I 10, 1.14 I 22
]rš 1.108 18, 7.51 20
]rš[2.41 13, 4.194 14, 4.762 2
ršil 1.106 4
]ršd 1.54 10
]ršn 4.432 11
ršp 1.14 I 19, 1.15 II 6, 1.39 4, 1.39 7, 1.41 13, 1.41 16, 1.47 27, 1.78 4, 1.79 8, 1.81 10, 1.81 11, 1.82 3, 1.90 2, 1.90 20, 1.91 15, 1.100 31, 1.100 77, 1.102 10, 1.103 40, 1.105 1, 1.105 7, 1.105 25, 1.106 1, 1.106 6, 1.107 40, 1.108 15, 1.109 22, 1.123 31, 1.126 5, 1.148 8, 1.148 32, 1.165 2, 1.165 3, 1.168 1, 1.171 3, 4.33 12, 4.155 15, 4.170 9, 4.219 3, 4.635 35, 4.790 16, 6.62 2
ršp[4.114 10
r[š]p 1.118 26
r[šp 1.87 31
]ršp 1.126 3, 1.134 3, 4.182 61, 4.262 2, 4.438 3, 4.627 2
[[ršp]] 1.39 16(?)
ršpab 4.63 III 45, 4.103 5, 4.129 10, 4.134 9, 4.141 I 16, 4.350 8, 4.370 15, 4.609 2
r]špab 4.148 8
ršpy 4.69 I 22, 4.93 II 17, 4.131 6, 4.339 12
ršpm 1.91 11
ršpn 4.86 11
rt 1.128 15, 4.69 III 19, 4.774 7, 7.142 7
rt[1.8 II 14
]rt 1.175 10, 2.81 21, 4.73 14, 4.182 56, 4.443 9, 4.769 66, 7.115 3
]rt[1.157 8, 4.762 5
rtxxx 4.374 14
]rtx[7.217 5
xrt 2.46 24, 4.421 5
]xrt 1.107 15, 6.45 2
]xrt[4.487 1
]xrtx[4.619 1
]r/kt 1.92 23, 2.31 5, 2.76 6, 4.182 34, 4.382 13
xxrtamixxlsk[1.70 7
]xrtḫ 4.273 10
]\rty 1.67 8f
]rtl 7.51 21
]rtm 2.56 3
]xrtm[7.19 4
rtn 1.148 20, 4.247 32
]xrtn 4.82 2
rtq 1.4 VII 33
rtqt 1.13 24
]rttx[4.497 1
rṯ 1.16 V 29, 1.17 I 33, 1.17 II 8, 1.17 II 23
]rṯ 4.581 7
]rṯdt 4.734 6
rṯn 1.1 IV 9
rṯt 1.4 II 32
]rṯt 7.141 6

Š

š 1.27 12, 1.39 2, 1.39 5, 1.39 6(*ter*), 1.39 7(*bis*), 1.39 10, 1.39 11(*ter*), 1.39 19, 1.40 17, 1.40 25, 1.41 6, 1.41 14, 1.41 15, 1.41 16(*bis*), 1.41 25, 1.41 35, 1.41 44, 1.41 51, 1.41 52, 1.43 6, 1.43 16, 1.46 3(*quater*), 1.46 6(*quater*), 1.46 13, 1.46 14, 1.46 17, 1.49 2, 1.49 3, 1.50 4, 1.58 4, 1.58 5, 1.87 6, 1.87 27, 1.87 38, 1.87 48, 1.87 56, 1.89 6, 1.90 6, 1.90 19, 1.90 20, 1.94 1, 1.104 12, 1.105 1, 1.105 8, 1.105 9, 1.105 10(*bis*), 1.105 11, 1.105 16, 1.105 23, 1.105 25, 1.106 6, 1.106 11, 1.106 13, 1.106 14, 1.106 15, 1.109 7, 1.109 8, 1.109 9, 1.109 13(*bis*), 1.109 14(*bis*), 1.109 15, 1.109 16(*bis*), 1.109 17, 1.109 18(*ter*), 1.109 19, 1.109 20, 1.109 21(*bis*), 1.109 22(*ter*), 1.109 24, 1.109 27, 1.109 30, 1.111 7, 1.111 10, 1.111 19, 1.111 21, 1.112 5, 1.112 22, 1.112 23(*bis*), 1.112 25, 1.112 28, 1.115 4, 1.115 6, 1.115 9, 1.115 12, 1.119 2, 1.127 16, 1.130 12, 1.130 14, 1.130 15, 1.130 18, 1.130 21(*bis*), 1.130 25, 1.130 29, 1.132 5, 1.134 2, 1.134 7, 1.139 5, 1.139 6, 1.139 8, 1.139 16, 1.148 2, 1.148 3, 1.148 4(*bis*), 1.148 5(*bis*), 1.148 6(*quater*), 1.148 7(*quinquies*), 1.148 8(*quater*), 1.148 9(*ter*), 1.148 10, 1.148 23, 1.148 24, 1.148 25(*bis*), 1.148 26(*bis*), 1.148 27, 1.148 28, 1.148 29(*bis*), 1.148 30(*bis*), 1.148 31(*bis*), 1.148 32(*bis*), 1.148 33, 1.148 34, 1.148 40, 1.148 42, 1.148 43, 1.148 43, 1.148 44, 1.162 3, 1.162 7, 1.162 8, 1.162 13, 1.162 15, 1.164 5, 1.164 7, 1.168 4, 1.168 11, 1.168 13, 1.168 15, 1.170 2, 1.170 3, 1.170 9, 1.171 2(*bis*), 1.171 3, 1.173 4(*bis*), 1.173 5, 1.173 12, 4.62 1, 4.160 2, 4.160 4, 4.160 11, 4.401 7, 4.716 1, 4.716 2, 4.716 3, 4.716 9, 4.716 13, 4.751 3, 5.2 4, 5.2 5, 5.2 6, 5.4 2, 5.6 1, 5.12 2, 5.13 7, 5.15 4, 5.16 1, 5.17 5, 5.19 2, 5.20 1, 5.21 1, 5.24 1, 7.177 2

š[1.5 V 26, 1.6 V 29, 1.10 III 12, 1.12 II 27, 1.15 IV 10, 1.16 V 41, 1.16 V 43, 1.16 V 45, 1.16 V 48, 1.18 I 31, 1.19 II 50, 1.41 43, 1.53 9, 1.58 5, 1.70 27, 1.73 10, 1.85 21, 1.87 7, 1.101 10, 1.119 3, 1.126 19, 1.127 25, 1.136 12, 1.148 20, 1.148 39, 1.151 5, 2.3 3, 2.7 7, 2.23 9, 2.31 18, 2.46 16, 2.53 2, 2.63 12, 2.73 20, 2.76 5, 3.1 39, 4.17 21, 4.69 VI 36, 4.77 23, 4.93 IV 27, 4.182 33, 4.194 22, 4.213 20, 4.244 34, 4.287 3, 4.315 4, 4.328 9, 4.332 23, 4.335 6, 4.335 30, 4.372 7, 4.424 8, 4.469 4, 4.533 1, 4.562 2, 4.608 6, 4.618 6, 4.629 19, 4.683 12, 4.683 24, 4.685 2, 4.715 27, 4.755 12, 6.76 1, 7.70 2, 7.134 2, 7.154 1, 7.184 8

]š 1.62 18, 1.83 17, 1.91 18, 1.107 19, 1.107 22, 1.107 54, 1.134 11, 1.160 2, 1.168 24, 2.23 31, 2.31 22, 2.36 20, 2.54 4, 2.79 10, 4.22 1, 4.62 2, 4.78 3, 4.78 6, 4.151 I 12, 4.160 7, 4.160 11, 4.182 50, 4.238 8, 4.240 6, 4.316 4, 4.618 29, 4.701 11, 4.734 7, 4.744 10, 7.46 8, 7.47 6, 7.51 10, 7.62 3, 7.133 7, 7.189 1, 7.204 2

]š[1.3 II 1, 1.58 6, 1.168 5, 2.41 12, 4.312 10, 4.399 3, 4.531 1, 7.55 1, 7.197 1

[[š]] 1.148 25

šx 1.157 4, 2.34 28, 7.222 8

šx[1.126 9, 4.33 3, 4.326 2, 7.198 5

]šx 1.148 32

]šx[1.107 51, 1.130 2, 4.105 6, 4.599 2

šxx[4.317 11, 4.618 8

]šxx[4.548 5

xš[4.340 12

]xš 1.29 2, 1.134 10, 4.78 5, 4.504 1,

4.772 1
]xš[1.61 2, 4.639 3, 7.214 1
xxš 4.399 4
xxš[2.6 7
]xxš 7.176 3
]xxš[1.86 13
]xšx[2.63 16, 6.38 5
]xxšxxx 1.15 VI 9
šxxd/lt 1.114 23
š/ḏ[4.69 VI 35
š/ḏxyn 4.86 33
šxxy 4.7 19
šxn 1.19 IV 57, 1.48 5
šxxr 4.412 II 9
ša 1.4 VIII 5, 1.5 V 13, 1.14 II 22, 4.68 76, 4.69 I 30, 5.15 2, 6.48 3
]ša 1.19 I 6, 7.136 4
xxša 4.318 4
šab 6.25 2
šal 1.14 I 38
šalm 3.3 5
šant 4.392 2
ši 1.1 V 26, 4.705 4
ši[1.8 II 16, 4.325 2(!), 4.325 5
]ši[2.37 3
]xxxšix[4.721 13
šib 1.16 I 51, 4.609 15
šibt 1.12 II 59, 1.14 III 9, 1.14 V 1
šiy 1.12 I 22, 1.18 IV 23, 1.18 IV 35
šil 2.63 8, 2.63 12
]šil 2.4 8, 2.50 10
]šilt 2.4 9
š]ilt 2.4 13
šim 4.181 7(cor.)
šink 2.15 4
šinm 1.86 27, 1.164 2
šir 1.6 II 37, 1.6 II 37, 1.10 I 18, 1.103 11, 4.282 6, 4.282 8, 4.282 10, 4.282 12, 4.282 14, 4.399 11
š[i]r 4.399 13
]šir 1.82 9, 4.642 3
š]ir 1.103 25
ši]r 1.6 VI 43
širh 1.6 II 35, 1.96 3
širm 4.282 5, 4.282 7
šu 1.2 I 27, 1.23 54, 1.23 65
šurt 4.44 1, 4.44 2, 4.44 4, 4.44 5, 4.44 6, 4.44 7, 4.44 9, 4.44 11, 4.44 13, 4.44 16
šurt[4.44 10, 4.44 14, 4.44 15
šurtm 4.44 3, 4.44 8, 4.44 17
šb 1.172 6
šb[7.58 3
]šb 1.1 II 13
]xšb 1.172 26
šb/d[4.318 8
šbxd 1.132 6 lg. šbrd
šbḥ 1.14 VI 25
šbḫ[1.59 6
šbyn 1.2 IV 29, 1.2 IV 30
šblt 1.19 I 18, 1.19 II 20, 1.19 II 20, 1.19 II 21, 1.19 II 23
š[blt] 1.19 II 22
šbm 1.3 II 16, 1.83 8
šbn 4.16 1, 4.124 2, 4.141 II 18, 4.177 5, 4.285 8, 4.288 3, 4.355 23, 4.365 22, 4.369 4, 4.380 28, 4.382 28, 4.424 5, 4.610 16, 4.629 9, 4.685 10, 4.693 20, 4.698 2
šbn[1.149 8
]šbn 4.119 2
]šbn[4.414 1
šbny 1.6 VI 54
šb[ny] 4.369 16
šbnt 4.147 12
šbʿ 1.3 II 2, 1.4 VI 32, 1.4 VII 10, 1.5 I 20, 1.5 V 20, 1.6 V 8, 1.7 35, 1.12 II 44, 1.14 I 8, 1.14 III 4, 1.14 III 15, 1.14 V 6, 1.15 II 23, 1.15 III 22, 1.16 II 32, 1.17 I 15, 1.17 II 39, 1.18 I 25, 1.19 I 42, 1.19 IV 17, 1.22 I 25, 1.23 20, 1.23 66, 1.41 52, 1.43 7, 1.43 8, 1.43 26, 1.73 10, 1.87 51, 1.91 32, 1.105 5, 1.106 21, 1.110 11, 1.111 17, 1.111 18, 1.112 7, 1.112 26, 1.114 3, 1.114 16, 1.119 1, 1.119 22, 1.133 11, 1.148 19, 1.152 2, 1.161 30, 1.171 7, 4.123 5, 4.123 22, 4.137 8, 4.138 3, 4.139 7, 4.139 16, 4.149 10, 4.162 2, 4.163 4, 4.163 13, 4.168 9, 4.173 1, 4.173 1, 4.173 6, 4.179 7, 4.182 14, 4.182 19, 4.188 1, 4.216 1, 4.219 13, 4.244 25, 4.246 2, 4.247 31, 4.247 31, 4.269 32, 4.272 6, 4.340 22, 4.341 20, 4.342 3, 4.345 8, 4.361 3, 4.395 4, 4.399 7, 4.400 12, 4.417 18, 4.658 48, 4.709 1, 4.712 1, 4.764 3, 4.775 7, 4.775 9, 4.775 19,

4.777 2, 4.777 6, 7.184 4
šbʿ[4.219 14, 4.747 3, 4.764 8
š[b]ʿ 1.41 47
šb[ʿ 1.17 V 3, 4.219 15, 4.387 22, 4.400 18
š[bʿ 1.91 35, 1.126 21, 4.247 11, 4.683 17
]šbʿ 1.17 I 31, 1.25 3, 1.112 10, 1.133 12, 1.164 15, 4.182 2, 4.456 2, 4.531 4
š]bʿ 1.106 12, 4.141 III 1, 4.221 1, 4.501 2
šb]ʿ 4.517 2
šbʿid 2.12 9
šbʿd 1.23 12, 1.23 14, 2.12 8, 2.24 6, 2.40 6, 2.42 5, 2.42 5, 2.51 3, 2.64 14, 2.68 6, 2.68 6, 2.70 9
šb[ʿd] 2.24 6, 2.50 2
šb]ʿd 2.40 6
šbʿdm 1.23 15
šbʿl 4.45 5, 4.55 16, 4.96 5, 4.366 6, 4.658 10
šbʿl[4.80 17
šbʿm 1.4 VI 46, 1.4 VII 10, 1.5 V 20, 1.6 I 18, 1.6 I 20, 1.6 I 22, 1.6 I 24, 1.12 II 48, 1.15 IV 6, 1.25 3, 3.10 13, 4.139 8, 4.158 6, 4.164 2, 4.243 1, 4.243 5, 4.243 18, 4.243 23, 4.243 24, 4.243 45, 4.243 46, 4.269 31, 4.296 4, 4.337 16, 4.636 8, 4.636 12, 4.636 19, 4.791 5
šbʿm[4.664 3
šbʿ[m 4.201 4, 4.337 27
]šbʿm 4.682 4
š]bʿm 1.6 I 26, 4.749 3
šbʿr 1.4 IV 16
šbʿt 1.3 II 19, 1.3 III 42, 1.3 V 11, 1.3 V 26, 1.5 I 3, 1.5 V 8, 1.6 VI 8, 1.12 II 48, 1.17 II 6, 1.17 II 20, 1.19 IV 15, 1.45 2, 1.101 3, 1.112 29, 1.119 4, 2.25 6, 4.113 8, 4.158 18, 4.226 4, 4.226 6, 4.226 9, 4.276 13, 4.333 6, 4.658 3, 4.658 4, 4.658 8, 4.779 9
š[bʿt 4.276 7
šbrd 1.132 6(!)
šbrh 1.92 13
š]brh 1.103 45
šbrm[4.574 7
šbšlt 1.106 22
šbšt 1.133 6
šbt 1.3 V 2, 1.3 V 25, 1.4 V 4
šb[t 1.18 I 12
šbth 1.3 V 2
šbtk 1.3 V 24
šbtm 2.36 15
šgbʿll 1.175 12
šgr 1.5 III 16, 1.5 III 17, 1.131 13, 1.148 31
šgty 4.321 1
šd 1.1 III 2, 1.2 III 11, 1.3 IV 38, 1.3 IV 45, 1.3 VI 17, 1.4 V 24, 1.4 V 56, 1.4 VIII 25, 1.5 V 19, 1.5 VI 7, 1.5 VI 29, 1.6 II 20, 1.6 II 34, 1.6 IV 18(!), 1.14 II 51, 1.14 IV 30, 1.16 III 6, 1.16 III 8, 1.17 V 10, 1.19 IV 43, 1.23 13, 1.23 13, 1.23 13, 1.23 28, 1.23 28, 1.23 68, 1.24 23, 1.91 10, 1.107 28, 1.148 18, 1.166 12, 2.4 16, 2.4 17, 3.5 5, 4.1 3, 4.7 2, 4.7 3, 4.7 4, 4.7 5, 4.7 6, 4.7 7, 4.7 8, 4.7 9, 4.7 10, 4.7 11, 4.7 12, 4.7 13, 4.7 14, 4.7 15, 4.7 16, 4.7 17, 4.7 18, 4.7 19, 4.7 20, 4.39 1, 4.39 2, 4.39 3, 4.39 4, 4.39 5, 4.39 6, 4.39 7, 4.103 2, 4.103 3, 4.103 4, 4.103 5, 4.103 6, 4.103 12, 4.110 1, 4.110 3, 4.110 4, 4.110 5, 4.110 6, 4.110 7, 4.110 8, 4.110 9, 4.110 10, 4.110 11, 4.110 14, 4.110 15, 4.110 17, 4.110 19, 4.110 20, 4.110 21, 4.120 3, 4.160 12, 4.182 55, 4.182 58, 4.183 I 1, 4.222 18, 4.222 19, 4.222 20, 4.222 21, 4.240 2, 4.240 3, 4.240 4, 4.280 6, 4.282 1, 4.282 3, 4.282 4, 4.282 5, 4.282 6, 4.282 7, 4.282 7, 4.282 8, 4.282 10, 4.282 10, 4.282 12, 4.282 14, 4.282 14, 4.282 16, 4.282 16, 4.290 7, 4.290 9, 4.298 1, 4.325 3, 4.356 1, 4.356 2, 4.356 3, 4.356 4, 4.356 5, 4.356 6, 4.356 7, 4.356 8, 4.356 9, 4.356 11, 4.356 12, 4.356 13, 4.356 14, 4.356 15, 4.357 12, 4.357 13, 4.357 14, 4.357 15, 4.357 16, 4.357 17, 4.357 18, 4.357 20, 4.357 21, 4.357 22, 4.357 23, 4.357 24, 4.357 25, 4.357 26, 4.357 28, 4.357 31, 4.357 32, 4.389 7, 4.399 3, 4.399 5,

4.399 6, 4.399 9, 4.399 10, 4.399 15, 4.399 19, 4.403 8, 4.403 9, 4.403 10, 4.403 11, 4.403 12, 4.403 13, 4.403 14, 4.423 3, 4.423 5, 4.423 7, 4.423 13, 4.423 15, 4.423 17, 4.423 19, 4.423 21, 4.423 23, 4.424 1, 4.425 3, 4.425 5, 4.544 3, 4.544 4, 4.544 5, 4.544 6, 4.547 2, 4.600 2, 4.600 3, 4.609 53, 4.631 2, 4.631 3, 4.631 4, 4.631 6, 4.631 7, 4.631 11, 4.631 12, 4.631 13, 4.631 14, 4.631 15, 4.631 16, 4.631 17, 4.631 18, 4.631 19, 4.631 20, 4.631 21, 4.631 22, 4.638 3, 4.642 3, 4.645 1, 4.645 3, 4.645 4, 4.645 5, 4.645 6, 4.645 7, 4.645 8, 4.645 9, 4.645 10, 4.692 2, 4.692 3, 4.692 4, 4.692 5, 4.692 6, 4.692 7

šd[4.240 5, 4.403 6, 4.403 7, 4.423 9, 4.423 11, 4.424 6, 4.424 7, 4.544 2, 4.638 4, 4.638 5, 4.641 3

š[d 1.18 I 21, 1.48 17, 4.290 11, 4.357 1, 4.357 2, 4.357 10, 4.357 11, 4.399 7, 4.403 5, 4.403 15, 4.403 16, 4.638 6

]šd 4.389 4, 4.389 6, 4.389 10, 4.399 2, 4.399 16, 4.425 7, 4.425 10, 4.425 11, 4.425 12, 4.516 2, 4.516 3, 4.547 4, 4.637 4, 4.637 5, 4.637 6

š]d 2.4 15, 4.103 8, 4.103 9, 4.103 10, 4.103 11, 4.103 13, 4.103 15, 4.103 16, 4.103 38, 4.103 40, 4.103 42, 4.103 43, 4.103 46, 4.103 47, 4.389 3, 4.389 8, 4.425 13, 4.516 1, 4.536 1, 4.536 2, 4.600 1, 4.631 8, 4.631 9, 4.631 10

šb/d[4.318 8

<š>d 4.356 10

šdh 1.24 22, 2.34 29

šdh[4.240 2

]šdh 4.493 4

šdy 1.108 12, 4.51 2

šd[y] 3.5 6

šdyn 4.46 3, 4.53 9, 4.63 IV 11, 4.83 7, 4.281 6, 4.285 6, 4.332 14, 4.382 36, 4.424 19, 4.609 6

šdyn 1.6 IV 18 lg. šd yn

šdyn[4.243 32

šdy[n 4.391 16

šdk[1.5 IV 1

]šdkm 1.89 5

š]d<m> 4.103 23

šdm 1.3 III 17, 1.3 IV 10, 1.5 VI 28, 1.6 II 17, 1.6 IV 1, 1.6 IV 2, 1.6 IV 12, 1.6 IV 13, 1.6 V 18, 1.12 II 43, 1.14 III 7, 1.14 IV 51, 1.16 I 34, 1.19 IV 48, 4.103 14, 4.103 45, 4.275 15, 4.320 18, 4.356 16, 4.357 19, 4.357 27, 4.357 29, 4.357 30, 4.424 2

š[dm 1.3 IV 31, 1.7 28

š]dm 1.1 II 21, 1.3 IV 25

šd]m 4.357 9

šdmt 1.2 I 43

šdmth 1.23 10

š]dn 4.769 58 lg. i[š]dn

šdq[4.340 17

šdqn 4.616 15

]šḏibt 7.178 4

šḏr 1.94 32

šḏrn 4.370 11

[š]ḏrn 4.748 2

šh 1.80 2, 1.80 4, 1.80 5

šh[4.325 2 lg. ši[

]xšh 1.79 2

šhr 1.23 53

]šhr[2.3 6

šwn 4.778 8

šzrm 1.82 11

šḥ[1.155 3, 4.93 IV 25

šḥlmmt 1.5 V 19, 1.5 VI 7, 1.6 II 20

šḥl]mmt 1.5 VI 30

šḥlt 4.14 4, 4.786 12

šḥl[t] 4.14 16

šḥq 4.48 6, 4.68 59, 4.100 7, 4.346 2, 4.683 17

šḥr 1.12 I 7, 1.23 52, 1.100 52, 1.107 43, 1.123 11, 2.18 2, 3.5 15, 4.373 5

]šḥr 4.373 4

šḥt 1.100 65, 2.2 10

]šḫ 3.1 6

šḫx[1.26b 3 lg.]ušḫr[d

šḫṭ 1.18 IV 24

šḫ[ṭ 1.18 IV 35

šḫyn 4.233 4, 4.690 4

šḫp 1.10 III 26

šḫph 1.10 III 25

šḫr 4.98 19

šṭpm 4.150 1

šy 1.82 8, 4.393 9

]šy 4.769 20
]šy[4.386 16
xšy 1.70 34
]xšy 1.172 20
šyy 4.64 II 1
šyn 4.63 I 17, 4.69 III 8, 4.214 III 2
šyn[4.583 3
]šyn 4.701 5
šk[2.41 5, 2.41 6
]šk 1.11 12
škb 1.5 V 19
]škb 2.31 50
škbḏ 4.408 3(cor.)
škl 1.44 10, 1.120 4, 1.128 16, 1.131 15
škllt 1.16 II 28
škm 4.14 6, 4.14 12, 4.14 18
škn 2.3 20, 2.33 23, 2.39 6, 4.245 I 3, 4.280 14
]škn 4.188 3
šk\n 6.66 6f(!)
škny 4.635 38
šknt 1.16 II 53, 1.117 8, 2.36 12
]šknt 2.20 4
škr 1.14 II 44, 1.14 IV 22, 1.114 4, 1.114 16
škrn 1.17 I 30
š[krn] 1.17 II 5
š\krn 1.17 II 19f
škt[4.251 1
šl 2.61 6
šl[1.168 6, 2.80 11, 4.244 19
]šl[7.109 3, 7.205 1
šlbšn 1.5 V 23
šlḥ 1.14 I 20
šlḥ[2.76 7
šlḥm 1.17 V 19
šlḥmt 1.106 25
šlḥm[t] 1.106 28
šlḥn 4.275 6
šlyṭ 1.3 III 42, 1.5 I 3, 1.5 I 29
<šlm> 2.71 7(?)
šlm 1.3 II 32, 1.3 III 16, 1.3 IV 9, 1.3 IV 30, 1.23 7(*bis*), 1.23 26, 1.23 52, 1.39 8, 1.41 17, 1.47 34, 1.65 8, 1.90 18, 1.90 21, 1.100 52, 1.101 14, 1.107 43, 1.109 8, 1.118 33, 1.119 24, 1.123 2, 1.123 11, 1.123 28, 1.123 29, 1.123 30, 1.123 33, 1.156 2, 1.161 31, 1.161 31, 1.161 32, 1.161 32, 1.161 33, 1.161 33, 1.161 34, 2.2 6, 2.5 3, 2.11 12, 2.11 16, 2.12 13, 2.13 10, 2.13 12, 2.16 14, 2.16 17, 2.34 5, 2.34 7, 2.34 8, 2.36 4, 2.38 7, 2.38 8, 2.39 4, 2.46 6, 2.46 8, 2.56 5, 2.64 18, 2.65 2, 2.65 4, 2.67 3, 2.68 13, 2.68 16, 2.70 5, 2.70 26, 2.71 6, 2.72 9, 3.1 12, 4.226 5, 4.226 6, 4.226 7, 4.226 9, 4.332 10, 4.667 2, 4.667 3, 4.667 4, 4.667 5, 4.755 1, 5.10 2, 5.10 3
šlm 4.181 7 cor. šim
šlm[1.6 IV 24, 2.2 4, 2.50 10, 2.72 7, 4.332 19, 4.342 5
šl[m 1.23 53, 1.130 21, 2.2 3, 2.30 10, 2.51 4, 2.56 6, 4.226 1, 4.226 3 4.439 2
š[lm] 1.19 II 27, 4.226 2
š]lm 1.123 3, 2.2 2, 2.4 6, 2.21 13, 2.30 8, 4.665 4, 4.665 6, 4.665 13, 4.667 6
]šlm 1.123 2, 2.21 15, 4.466 2, 4.665 7, 4.665 8, 4.665 9, 4.665 10, 4.665 11, 4.665 12
šl]m 4.665 14
šl<m>y 4.51 14
šlmy 2.63 8, 4.49 2, 4.68 18, 4.124 6, 4.261 16, 4.313 1, 4.382 29, 4.648 25, 4.750 12, 4.770 18
šlmy[4.308 10, 4.629 7
šl[my 4.686 10
šl]my 4.553 4
šlmym 4.41 1, 4.610 33, 4.748 13
šlmyn 4.313 28
šlmk 5.11 2
š]lmk 2.4 7
šlmm 1.14 III 26, 1.14 III 27, 1.39 4, 1.41 52, 1.43 7, 1.46 7, 1.46 15, 1.87 2, 1.87 15, 1.105 23, 1.109 10, 1.109 15, 1.109 23, 1.109 28, 1.115 9, 1.148 10, 1.162 4, 1.164 6, 1.164 8, 1.168 12, 1.170 4, 1.170 9, 1.173 12, 4.226 10
šlm[m] 1.109 37
šl[m]m 1.130 24
šl[mm 1.14 VI 10, 1.41 29, 1.138 6, 1.171 2
š[lmm 1.14 V 40, 1.14 VI 9, 1.41 13,

1.127 17, 1.130 8
šl]mm 1.46 2, 1.139 3
šlmn 4.33 37, 4.412 III 7, 4.624 6
šlmt 2.2 3, 2.2 4, 2.2 6
šlt[4.610 42
š{.}m 1.173 11
<šm> 1.105 13
šm 1.1 IV 14, 1.1 IV 15, 1.2 IV 28, 1.16 VI 56, 1.22 I 6, 1.22 I 7, 1.23 18, 1.41 5, 1.41 48, 1.46 2, 1.87 5, 1.105 6, 1.105 13, 1.105 22, 1.109 25, 1.112 3, 1.112 19, 1.112 24, 1.132 13, 1.132 23, 1.139 4, 1.162 6, 4.243 6, 4.258 7, 4.775 3, 4.775 14, 4.775 20
šm[1.87 53, 4.35 II 9, 4.240 6, 4.366 1, 4.593 7
š[m 1.2 I 8
]šm 4.94 6, 4.610 50, 4.624 11, 4.624 12, 4.766 9, 7.217 3
xxšm 4.318 4
šmx[3.7 12
xxxxxxxxxšmx[1.86 32
šmal 1.23 64, 1.103 37, 1.103 59, 1.109 26, 1.172 12, 7.137 9
šmal[1.92 9
šm[al 1.103 11
š[ma]l 1.103 9
š[mal 1.103 15
[šm]al 1.103 10
šmalh 1.2 I 40
šmbˁl 4.116 7, 4.682 8
šmgx[4.610 14
šmgy 1.91 27, 4.754 10, 4.770 17
šmḥ 1.133 16
šmḥy 1.5 II 25
šmḫ 1.4 II 28, 1.4 V 20, 1.4 V 35, 1.4 VI 35, 1.5 II 20, 1.6 III 14
šm[ḫ] 1.92 31
šmḫt 1.3 II 26
šmy 2.14 13
šmym 1.19 IV 24, 1.19 IV 30, 4.714 5
šmyn 4.122 2
šmk 1.1 IV 20, 1.2 IV 11, 1.2 IV 19, 1.10 II 9, 1.10 II 12
š]mk 4.693 3
šml 2.17 5, 4.66 5, 4.412 II 6
]šml 4.428 6
šmlbi 4.63 IV 13
šmlbu 4.366 13, 4.366 14
šm[lm 7.69 3
šmm 1.1 III 14, 1.3 I 13, 1.3 II 39, 1.3 II 40, 1.3 III 24, 1.3 III 26, 1.3 IV 43, 1.3 V 18, 1.3 VI 9, 1.4 VIII 23, 1.5 I 4, 1.5 II 2, 1.6 II 25, 1.6 III 6, 1.6 III 12, 1.10 I 5, 1.13 26, 1.13 27, 1.14 II 23, 1.16 III 2, 1.22 I 11, 1.23 38, 1.23 62, 1.23 62, 1.24 16, 1.24 31, 1.41 55, 1.47 12, 1.83 6, 1.100 1, 1.107 9, 1.107 15, 1.108 7, 1.111 8, 1.118 11, 1.148 5, 1.148 24, 4.232 9
šm[m 1.2 I 12, 1.3 IV 43, 1.101 7
š]m[m] 1.3 IV 26
š]mm 1.13 12
šm]m 1.3 IV 18, 1.108 9
šmmh 1.14 IV 5, 1.23 38, 1.100 52
šmmlk 4.75 V 19
šm{.}mn 3.9 11
šmmn 3.9 3, 3.9 15, 4.43 2, 4.170 11, 4.222 19, 4.261 12, 4.297 4, 4.344 19, 4.727 6, 4.782 29
š]mmn 4.350 14
š\mmn 5.18 7f
šmmny 4.770 16
šmn 1.3 II 31, 1.3 II 39, 1.3 IV 43, 1.6 III 6, 1.6 III 12, 1.15 IV 4, 1.15 IV 15, 1.16 III 1, 1.16 III 16, 1.22 II 15, 1.41 21, 1.41 44, 1.87 22, 1.87 48, 1.87 50, 1.101 14, 1.119 24, 1.148 21, 1.164 9, 2.15 6, 2.72 30, 4.14 2, 4.14 8, 4.14 15, 4.41 2, 4.91 3, 4.91 5, 4.91 16, 4.123 3, 4.123 5, 4.131 3, 4.150 2, 4.150 4, 4.158 3, 4.170 10, 4.171 2, 4.171 4, 4.198 5, 4.247 22, 4.272 1, 4.284 6, 4.290 1, 4.290 4, 4.313 1, 4.313 2, 4.313 3, 4.313 4, 4.313 5, 4.313 6, 4.313 27, 4.313 29, 4.341 20, 4.352 1, 4.352 3, 4.402 9, 4.432 11, 4.610 15, 4.617 27, 4.721 15, 4.728 3, 4.738 4, 4.771 7, 4.778 5, 4.778 7, 4.780 5, 4.780 8, 4.780 10, 4.780 11, 4.780 12, 4.780 13, 4.780 14, 4.780 16, 4.781 2, 4.782 7, 4.782 11, 4.786 8, 4.786 14, 5.10 7, 5.23 1, 5.23 6
šmn[4.717 1, 4.717 3, 7.140 2
šm[n 1.7 21, 4.272 4, 4.371 17

š[mn 4.123 9, 4.717 2
š]mn 4.225 15
šm]n 1.15 V 1
šmngy 4.355 25
šmny 1.91 26, 4.222 12, 4.355 24
šmʿ 1.4 V 59, 1.4 VI 4, 1.6 I 44, 1.6 III 23, 1.6 VI 23, 1.14 V 14, 1.15 IV 3, 1.15 VI 1, 1.16 IV 1, 1.16 IV 10, 1.16 VI 16, 1.16 VI 41, 1.17 V 16, 1.17 VI 16, 1.18 I 23, 1.18 IV 12, 1.19 II 1, 1.19 II 41, 1.22 II 13, 1.24 11, 1.93 5, 1.119 34, 4.332 12, 4.609 11(*del.*)
]šmʿ 1.2 I 46
šm]ʿ 1.2 III 15
šmʿh 2.17 7
šmʿy 4.247 33
šmʿk 1.13 22
šmʿn 4.609 5, 4.617 32
šmʿnt 4.75 IV 4
šmʿ<rgm> 4.609 11
šmʿrgm 4.128 3, 4.609 10
šmʿt 2.10 7, 2.49 10
šm[ʿt 1.87 54
]šmʿt 4.387 15, 4.387 23
]šmr[7.144 2
šmrḫt 1.4 I 32
šmrm 4.35 II 10, 4.63 II 48, 4.103 26, 4.170 24, 4.635 29
šmrm[4.655 4
šmrr 1.100 4, 1.100 10, 1.100 15, 1.100 21, 1.100 26, 1.100 31, 1.100 41, 1.100 47, 1.100 53, 1.100 59
šm\rr 1.100 36f
šmšr 1.3 VI 9
šmt 1.19 III 4, 1.19 III 11, 1.19 III 19, 1.19 III 25, 1.19 III 33, 1.19 III 39, 1.23 21, 4.168 1, 4.182 5, 4.182 17, 4.337 25, 4.341 7
šmt[4.50 5
šmthm 1.2 IV 11, 1.2 IV 18, 1.12 I 29
šmtr 1.41 2
šmt]r 1.87 2
šn 1.12 II 41, 1.40 28, 1.40 30, 1.40 32, 1.40 36, 1.40 39, 1.40 40, 2.17 5
šn[1.121 10, 2.8 5, 4.580 2
š[n 1.121 2
]šn 4.94 8, 4.151 I 7, 4.194 15
xxxšn 7.197 6
šnx[1.94 30
šna 1.4 III 17
šna[4.217 8
šnh/i 4.658 22
šnu 1.4 VII 36
šndrb 4.700 2
šnh/i 4.658 22
šnwt 1.96 1
šnl 4.398 4
šnm 1.1 III 24, 1.2 I 10, 1.4 IV 24, 1.6 I 36, 1.17 VI 49, 1.39 3, 1.39 6, 1.40 34, 1.65 4, 1.87 34, 1.114 19, 1.123 8
šn[m 1.87 17
š[nm 1.41 31, 1.87 14
]šnm 1.5 VI 2
š]nm 1.40 25
šn]m 1.40 17, 1.122 4
šnmyk 2.47 6
šnst 1.3 II 12
šnʿt[1.48 7
šnpt 1.39 10, 1.109 24, 1.112 22, 1.119 13
šnt 1.3 IV 33, 1.4 VI 43, 1.6 V 8, 1.6 V 9, 1.12 II 44, 1.14 I 33, 1.15 III 22, 1.17 VI 29, 1.19 I 42, 1.19 IV 14, 1.19 IV 15, 1.19 IV 18, 1.22 I 13, 1.23 66, 1.84 9, 1.86 1, 1.86 5, 1.108 27, 1.148 22, 2.2 7, 2.39 16, 4.168 13, 4.182 1, 4.182 60, 5.9 I 5
šn[t 1.86 6
]šnt 1.172 19, 7.46 7
]šnt[1.6 VI 38
šnth 1.19 I 9, 1.19 III 45
šntk 1.16 VI 58, 1.82 4
šntm 1.86 2, 2.39 16
šśb 4.167 8
šsk 1.13 6
šskn 1.4 I 20
šsʿn 2.81 24
šʿ[1.152 1
šʿx[1.126 4
šṯ/ʿ 1.88 2
šʿg[4.743 11
šʿd[1.16 V 42
šʿly 1.19 IV 30, 6.14 1, 6.62 2
šʿlyt 6.13 1
šʿr 1.19 II 2, 1.19 IV 37
šʿr 1.114 29 lg. ḫš ʿrk

šʿ]r 1.19 II 6

šʿrm 1.86 31, 4.14 1, 4.14 7, 4.14 13, 4.269 22, 4.269 23, 4.269 24, 4.269 33, 4.345 6, 4.400 8, 4.400 14, 4.402 8, 4.608 3, 4.786 4, 4.790 1, 6.19 1, 6.21 2

šʿr[m 4.60 1

š[ʿrm 4.60 7

šʿ<r>t 4.705 6

šʿ{.}rt 4.46 4

šʿr<t> 4.46 11

šʿrt 1.50 9, 4.46 5, 4.46 6, 4.46 7, 4.46 8, 4.46 9, 4.46 12, 4.46 14, 4.63 II 40, 4.100 4, 4.131 1, 4.144 6, 4.152 7, 4.152 10, 4.158 17, 4.168 3, 4.182 2, 4.182 19, 4.188 8, 4.188 11, 4.188 14, 4.205 7, 4.225 13, 4.270 5, 4.270 8, 4.270 12, 4.337 9, 4.341 3, 4.341 14, 4.378 2, 4.380 11, 4.382 25, 4.395 3, 4.610 13, 4.630 3, 4.630 7, 4.630 10, 4.630 13, 4.630 15, 4.705 1, 4.707 16, 4.707 18, 4.709 1, 4.721 9, 4.721 14, 4.750 17, 4.765 5

šʿrt[4.182 30

šʿr[t 4.693 12

šʿ[rt 1.49 10, 4.188 5, 4.355 8

š[ʿ]r[t] 4.188 6

š[ʿrt 4.152 3

]šʿrt 4.28 6, 4.182 14

šʿ]rt 4.182 28

š{.}ʿrt 4.46 10

[[šʿrt]] 4.709 9

šʿrty 4.33 25, 4.51 7, 4.96 2, 4.96 9

šʿtq 2.82 5

šʿtqt 1.16 VI 1, 1.16 VI 2, 1.16 VI 13

šp[1.23 2

]šp 1.168 16

]šp[4.251 4

št/p[4.86 32

špḥ 1.14 I 24, 1.14 III 40, 1.14 III 48, 1.14 VI 33, 1.16 I 10, 1.16 I 21, 1.16 I 23, 1.16 II 43, 1.16 II 49, 1.103 29, 2.47 13, 2.47 16

š[p]ḥ 1.103 13

]špḥx[1.73 16

š]pḥh 1.6 I 30

špk 1.7 19, 1.18 IV 23

špk[1.82 16

š[pk 1.18 IV 34

]špk[7.138 5

špl 1.161 22

šp[l 1.13 4

špm 1.1 II 11(!), 1.23 4

]xšpm 1.1 II 11 lg. špm

špq 1.4 VI 47, 1.4 VI 48, 1.4 VI 49, 1.4 VI 50, 1.4 VI 51, 1.4 VI 52, 1.4 VI 53, 1.4 VI 54

špqġhm 1.173 11

špr 1.108 10

špš 1.2 III 15, 1.3 II 8, 1.3 V 17, 1.4 VIII 21, 1.6 I 9, 1.6 I 11, 1.6 I 13, 1.6 II 24, 1.6 III 24, 1.6 IV 1, 1.6 IV 8, 1.6 IV 12, 1.6 IV 17, 1.6 IV 22, 1.6 VI 22, 1.6 VI 45, 1.6 VI 47, 1.15 V 18, 1.15 V 19, 1.16 I 37, 1.19 IV 47, 1.19 IV 49, 1.23 25, 1.23 54, 1.24 3, 1.39 12, 1.41 47, 1.41 53, 1.43 11, 1.43 14, 1.45 4, 1.45 6, 1.46 9, 1.62 10, 1.76 8, 1.76 9, 1.76 10, 1.78 3, 1.82 6, 1.87 52, 1.100 2, 1.100 2, 1.100 8, 1.100 8, 1.100 14, 1.100 14, 1.100 19, 1.100 19, 1.100 25, 1.100 25, 1.100 30, 1.100 30, 1.100 35, 1.100 35, 1.100 40, 1.100 40, 1.100 45, 1.100 45, 1.100 51, 1.100 51, 1.100 57, 1.100 57, 1.102 12, 1.107 9, 1.108 26, 1.112 9, 1.112 14, 1.118 21, 1.119 4, 1.119 23, 1.132 27, 1.146 8, 1.148 7, 1.161 18, 1.161 19, 2.16 8, 2.16 9, 2.19 2, 2.23 1, 2.23 7, 2.23 23, 2.34 13, 2.36 2, 2.36 6, 2.36 13, 2.39 1, 2.39 3, 2.39 5, 2.39 11, 2.39 13, 2.39 15, 2.39 18, 2.42 7, 2.44 6, 2.44 9, 2.76 7, 2.81 16, 2.81 19, 2.81 30, 3.1 19, 3.1 25, 4.63 IV 6, 4.227 I 11, 4.610 1, 4.628 5, 4.666 4, 5.11 4, 6.24 2

šp\š 1.87 56f

špš[1.38 2, 4.422 43, 4.746 7

š[p]š 1.39 17

šp[š 2.39 28, 2.28 2(?), 3.1 4, 3.1 11

š[pš 1.41 28, 2.78 1

]špš 4.238 2

š]pš 1.41 47, 1.107 34, 1.107 37, 1.107 47, 2.9 2

šp]š 1.47 22, 1.107 15, 1.107 32, 1.107 44, 2.23 16, 2.76 8

]špš[1.158 3
]šp[š 2.81 13
š]pš[2.47 10
špšy 4.785 10
špšyn 3.7 5, 4.35 I 20, 4.63 II 25, 4.115 5, 4.297 4, 4.297 6, 4.370 3, 4.382 24, 4.707 10
špšy[n] 4.35 I 11
špš[yn 4.75 I 8
š]pšyn 4.69 I 26, 4.741 2
špšm 1.14 III 3, 1.14 III 14, 1.14 IV 33, 1.14 IV 46, 1.14 V 6, 4.215 6, 4.261 3
š[pšm 1.20 II 5
špšmlk 4.177 1
špšn 1.103 45, 2.39 21, 3.10 4, 4.110 14, 4.233 9, 4.382 20
špš]n 4.792 6
špt 1.5 II 2, 1.23 61, 1.23 62
š\pt 1.24 8f
špth 1.2 IV 6, 1.4 VII 30, 1.19 II 26, 1.19 III 7, 1.19 III 36, 1.103 32
šp]\th 1.19 III 21f
[špt]h 1.4 VII 32
špthm 1.23 49, 1.23 50, 1.23 55, 1.23 55
špty 1.24 46
šptk 1.22 I 4, 1.82 5
šṣa 2.15 5, 4.145 10
š]ṣat 1.19 II 38
šṣu 2.34 31
šṣn/ty 4.115 10
šṣ[ṣ 1.1 IV 25
šṣq 2.33 27
šṣn/ty 4.115 10
šq 1.103 9, 1.103 26
šqy 1.1 IV 9
šqym 1.86 25, 1.115 11, 4.246 8
šqym[1.86 24
šqy[m 1.15 IV 13
šql 1.4 VI 41, 1.22 I 12, 1.91 25, 4.355 17, 4.365 32, 4.693 36, 4.770 15, 4.784 17
šq[l 4.684 6
]šql[4.661 6
šqln 4.723 10
šqlt 1.16 VI 32, 1.16 VI 44
šqrb 1.16 I 44, 1.40 26, 2.31 26
šr 1.12 II 50, 1.12 II 51, 1.16 I 43, 1.19 I 7, 1.19 I 11, 1.23 8, 1.103 58, 1.104 14, 1.106 15, 1.106 16, 1.107 10, 1.119 33, 1.123 3, 1.123 13, 1.147 11, 1.151 10, 1.151 12, 4.103 64, 4.123 6, 4.168 4, 4.199 3, 4.399 10, 4.430 2, 4.609 31, 4.609 37
šr[1.9 4, 4.567 2
š]r 1.107 8
]šr 4.617 2, 7.37 5
]šr[1.168 5, 7.201 2
šrx[7.53 3
šrbx 4.739 6
šrgk 1.17 VI 35
šrd 1.14 II 24, 1.14 IV 6
šrh 1.4 V 9, 1.10 III 25, 1.114 30
šrḥq 1.3 IV 40
]šry[1.93 6
šryn 1.4 VI 21
š]ryn 1.4 VI 19
šrk 1.15 V 17
šrm 1.23 22, 4.35 I 10, 4.68 66, 4.103 41, 4.126 11, 4.141 IV 2, 4.183 II 1, 4.399 1, 4.609 17, 4.610 46
]šrm 1.14 II 5, 4.769 57
]šrm[4.492 2
]xšrm 7.129 1
šrn 1.14 III 6
šrna 1.14 IV 50 lg. šrnn
šrny 4.658 43
šrnn 1.14 IV 50(!)
šrᶜ 1.19 I 45
šrᶜm 1.148 21 lg. ᶜšrm
šrġzz 1.107 8
š]rġzz 1.107 11
šrp 1.6 V 14, 1.39 4, 1.41 13, 1.46 7, 1.65 16, 1.105 2, 1.105 23, 1.106 2, 1.106 7, 1.109 10, 1.109 15, 1.109 28, 1.130 23, 1.138 4, 1.162 4, 1.164 6, 1.164 7, 1.168 11, 1.170 2, 1.171 2, 1.171 5
šr[p 1.27 6, 1.41 51, 1.134 2
š[r]p 1.87 56
š[rp 1.87 35, 1.127 16
]šrp 1.41 29
š]rp 1.39 17
šrpm 1.111 6
]xšrqt[4.637 3
šrr 1.2 IV 33, 1.2 IV 35, 1.2 IV 37, 1.16 VI 7, 1.19 II 36

šrš 1.17 I 19, 1.17 I 20, 1.17 I 25, 1.17 II 15, 1.91 32, 4.68 1, 4.355 37, 4.365 25, 4.380 30, 4.397 9, 4.643 15, 4.777 8
š]rš 4.693 24
]šrš[4.414 4
š[r]šy 4.75 I 2
šršk 1.19 III 53
šršn 4.45 10
šršˁm 4.344 14
šr<t> 4.410 16
]šr<t> 4.410 48
šrt 4.360 12, 4.410 3, 4.410 6, 4.410 10, 4.410 14, 4.410 18, 4.410 41, 4.410 43, 4.410 44, 4.410 45, 4.410 47, 4.774 1
šrt[4.410 20
šr[t 4.410 8, 4.410 17
š[rt 4.410 11, 4.410 15
]šrt 4.410 13, 4.410 26, 4.410 32, 4.410 40, 4.769 18, 4.769 58
š]rt 4.410 25, 4.410 51
šr]t 4.410 27, 4.410 35
šrtm 4.410 4, 4.410 5, 4.410 7, 4.410 9, 4.410 12, 4.410 19, 4.410 21, 4.410 49
šrt[m 4.410 22
]šrtm 4.410 2, 4.410 30, 4.410 34, 4.410 38, 4.410 53
š]rtm 4.410 52
šr]tm 4.410 33
šrt]m 4.410 23, 4.410 42
šš 4.658 19
šš[1.103 3, 4.283 3
ššy 4.313 7
šškrgy 4.175 8
ššl 4.229 7
ššlmt 4.46 3(cor.), 4.144 4, 4.153 6, 4.153 7, 4.153 8, 4.153 9, 4.153 10, 4.153 11, 4.378 11, 4.395 5, 4.786 5
ššlmt1 4.46 3 cor. ššlmt
š[šlmt] 4.46 1
š]šlmt 4.46 2
ššmḫt 2.73 10
ššmn 4.14 4, 4.14 10, 4.707 6
š[šm]n 4.60 8
š]šmn 4.594 4
ššqy 1.17 V 19
ššr 4.780 12
ššrt 1.5 V 3, 1.119 21, 4.341 1
<št> 1.23 59
št 1.1 II 3, 1.1 II 19, 1.1 III 8, 1.3 II 5, 1.3 III 15, 1.3 IV 9, 1.3 IV 41, 1.4 IV 10, 1.4 IV 36, 1.4 V 45, 1.18 IV 14, 1.18 IV 27, 1.19 II 4, 1.19 IV 53, 1.19 IV 57, 1.19 IV 57, 1.23 61, 1.71 9, 1.71 11, 1.72 17, 1.72 18, 1.72 22, 1.72 22, 1.72 23, 1.85 2, 1.85 10, 1.85 10, 1.85 12, 1.85 13, 1.85 15, 1.85 16, 1.85 16, 1.85 18, 1.85 26, 1.97 3, 1.97 14, 1.103 42, 1.124 6, 1.124 7, 1.124 9, 1.147 8, 1.172 13, 1.175 5, 2.10 18, 2.47 15, 3.1 17, 3.9 5, 4.338 3, 5.10 4, 6.29 2
št 1.132 3 lg. bt
št[1.2 IV 37, 1.19 IV 59, 1.48 9, 2.60 3
š[t 1.4 IV 5, 1.18 IV 6, 1.71 14, 1.72 13, 1.72 25, 1.72 32
]št 1.170 8, 1.175 17, 7.64 2
štx 1.54 15
štxx[1.6 V 27
xšt 1.148 15
]xšt 4.24 5, 7.185 1
št/p[4.86 32
šty 1.4 V 48, 1.4 VI 55, 1.5 IV 15, 1.15 IV 27, 1.15 V 10, 1.15 VI 4, 1.23 6, 1.175 9, 4.222 19, 4.356 1, 4.360 13, 4.412 III 3, 4.681 6
šty[4.667 1
štym 1.4 IV 35
štk 1.12 II 58, 1.12 II 59, 1.12 II 60, 4.232 16
štm 1.5 I 25
štm[1.151 5
štmn[1.151 8
štn 2.36 6, 2.39 35, 2.45 19, 4.12 11, 4.354 5, 4.727 14, 5.10 9
]štn 4.386 20, 4.701 8
štn[5.11 18
]štn[7.176 9
štnt 2.36 13, 2.50 16
štn[t] 2.36 13
štt 1.4 II 8, 1.4 III 14, 2.34 32, 2.36 7, 4.337 9
]štt[2.37 5
št/ˁ 1.88 2

T

t 5.2 3, 5.2 4, 5.2 4, 5.2 5, 5.2 6, 5.2 6, 5.2 7, 5.4 5, 5.6 3, 5.12 4, 5.13 9, 5.14 17, 5.15 2, 5.15 4, 5.15 4, 5.16 4, 5.17 3, 5.17 6, 5.19 4, 5.20 2, 5.20 3, 5.21 2, 5.24 1

t 7.127 1 cor.]t[

t 7.222 1 cor.]n/at

t[1.2 II 7, 1.2 II 14, 1.2 III 12, 1.3 I 1, 1.5 V 22, 1.7 42, 1.7 43, 1.8 II 17, 1.12 II 17, 1.14 V 29, 1.15 III 8, 1.16 II 30, 1.16 III 17, 1.16 V 51, 1.45 6, 1.50 10, 1.64 16, 1.73 11, 1.73 12, 1.92 10, 1.176 25, 2.2 7, 2.47 6, 4.1 2, 4.80 13, 4.80 22, 4.102 29, 4.157 9, 4.196 5, 4.205 10, 4.287 6, 4.287 8, 4.290 9, 4.332 24, 4.374 9, 4.382 22, 4.398 12, 4.425 9, 4.458 7, 4.482 1, 4.496 7, 4.578 3, 4.580 3, 4.605 2, 4.611 22, 4.623 4, 4.628 8, 4.673 7, 6.60 1, 7.38 6, 7.44 1

]t 1.1 V 17, 1.4 VI 61, 1.4 VII 60, 1.4 VIII 48, 1.10 I 12, 1.11 19, 1.13 36, 1.15 III 7, 1.15 V 5, 1.15 V 15, 1.16 V 31, 1.18 I 33, 1.42 20, 1.48 27, 1.48 34, 1.49 2, 1.64 3, 1.76 12, 1.84 1, 1.94 24, 1.107 52, 1.129 5, 1.157 8, 1.157 13, 1.160 1, 1.164 12, 1.172 2, 1.172 12, 1.175 8, 2.3 24, 2.7 3, 2.21 28, 2.35 7, 2.36 10, 2.36 15, 2.36 20, 2.47 8, 2.52 2, 2.58 8, 2.73 10, 4.13 4, 4.17 3, 4.18 1, 4.18 6, 4.24 4, 4.60 1, 4.71 II 8, 4.182 1, 4.182 57, 4.195 3, 4.196 6, 4.243 50, 4.316 7, 4.373 7, 4.408 1, 4.410 24, 4.439 3, 4.443 12, 4.459 5, 4.538 3, 4.555 2, 4.555 3, 4.597 7, 4.608 24, 4.613 16, 4.693 51, 4.755 12, 7.9 1, 7.51 7, 7.51 11, 7.55 2, 7.85 1, 7.111 2, 7.111 7, 7.172 2, 7.176 6, 7.176 12, 7.185 6, 7.208 3, 7.222 11

]t 1.135 13 lg. atnt]t

]t[1.7 53, 1.16 II 59, 1.16 V 33, 1.70 34, 1.130 28, 1.166 29, 2.57 2, 4.247 5, 7.12 2, 7.119 3, 7.127 1(cor.), 7.206 3, 7.209 2

]\t 1.69 3f, 1.73 5f, 1.87 9f

txx 1.15 V 11, 2.34 16, 4.7 14, 7.16 9

tx[1.2 II 9, 1.12 II 16, 1.12 II 28, 1.16 II 52, 1.73 5, 2.21 21, 2.49 6, 2.49 15, 4.325 7, 4.404 2, 4.658 39, 4.728 6, 7.55 2, 7.75 2

]tx[4.785 5, 7.41 8, 7.53 10

txx[1.168 4, 2.73 16

xt 2.45 13, 7.184 2

]xt 1.2 I 9, 1.4 VI 64, 1.5 V 25, 1.7 48, 1.12 II 2, 1.15 V 6, 1.23 73, 1.94 22, 1.107 23, 1.148 40, 1.157 6, 1.171 8, 1.173 8, 2.2 11, 2.22 13, 2.55 6, 2.83 3, 4.30 14, 4.105 1, 4.182 55, 4.183 I 3, 4.185 7, 4.225 7, 4.233 1, 4.238 4, 4.270 14, 4.318 8, 4.459 4, 4.540 4, 4.609 22, 7.41 1, 7.55 17, 7.70 2, 7.121 4, 7.141 9, 7.164 8, 7.167 3, 7.178 5

]xt[7.107 5, 7.110 3, 7.127 2

]xxt 1.87 53, 4.730 5

]xxt[7.33 6

xtx 1.15 IV 12

]xtxx[7.16 3

]x/t 4.275 15

]t/k 4.64 IV 1

t/a/n[4.629 17

t/ˁ 6.73 1

t/h/p 7.218 5

t/m[4.178 15

]xt/n 4.676 5

]xxxt/nxx 4.721 7

t/q[1.4 II 32, 4.513 4

txbk 1.94 33

txxg 2.58 5

txxḫzġ[1.42 11

txxl 1.19 IV 41

txxx]n 1.103 48

xxtxxp 4.752 9

]txplḫx[1.70 37

]txpn 7.137 1

]xtqb/dg/m 2.36 8

txx]rn 1.103 21

txt[1.7 39
ta 1.73 13
ta[2.2 8
ta/n[1.70 43
tadm 1.14 II 9, 1.19 IV 42
tan 4.232 4, 4.692 3
tan 1.83 8 lg. tnn?
t]an 4.368 20
tant 1.3 III 24
t[a/unt 1.3 IV 16
tasp 1.175 3
tasrn 1.1 V 9
]tasrn 1.1 V 22
tapq 1.169 12
tar 1.106 16
taršn 1.3 V 28, 1.6 II 14, 4.370 2
ti 1.52 23
ti[1.92 12, 1.175 2
tium 1.19 IV 42 lg. tidm
tiggn 1.82 43
tidm 1.19 IV 42(!)
tizr 1.116 9
tiḫd 1.4 VII 35, 1.6 II 9, 1.6 II 30, 1.11 2, 1.19 I 9, 1.101 16
ti]\ḫd 1.18 I 17f(!)
tiyn 4.631 18
tikl 1.4 VI 24, 1.4 VI 27, 1.4 VI 29, 1.6 II 35, 1.88 3
tikln 1.12 I 10
tilḏ 1.64 30
]th/in 4.82 10
tinm 1.42 8, 1.42 28
tinmkr 1.42 33
tinṯt 1.17 VI 40
ti]sp 1.107 40
tispk 1.19 II 17, 1.19 II 24
]xtir 2.32 10
tirkm 1.23 33
tišr 1.92 26, 4.158 4, 4.402 3
tišrm 4.91 7, 4.780 15
tit 1.20 II 10
tity 1.15 III 17, 1.15 III 18
ti[ty 1.20 II 4
titṯm 2.21 21
]titṯm 2.21 24
titṯmn 4.398 2, 4.398 3
tu 4.195 10
tubd 2.39 21
tud 2.26 19
tuzn 4.727 12
tuḫd 1.2 I 40, 1.2 I 40, 1.127 30
tunt 1.1 III 14
t[a/unt 1.3 IV 16
tusp[1.1 IV 11
tuṣl 1.106 25
tḅ 4.12 7
tb[1.16 II 3, 4.31 10, 4.763 3
t[b 4.31 1
]tb 1.158 1, 4.720 1
t]b 1.3 VI 1
tbx[4.31 3, 7.19 5
]tbx[4.620 5
tb/d[1.42 13, 2.37 4, 6.54 2
tba 1.5 VI 1
tbi 1.169 18
tbu 1.3 V 7, 1.4 IV 23, 1.6 I 35, 1.16 VI 3, 1.16 VI 4, 1.16 VI 5
[t]bu 1.3 V 9
tbun 1.15 IV 21, 1.15 VI 6
tbbr 4.103 11, 4.190 5
tbd 4.86 25
tbdn 4.354 4, 4.704 3
tbḥ 1.107 46
tbṭ 1.4 III 21
tby 4.159 5
tbk 1.18 IV 39, 4.167 16
tbk[1.16 II 33
tbky 1.16 I 55, 1.16 II 35, 1.19 I 34
tbkyk 1.16 I 6, 1.16 II 44
tbkynh 1.6 I 16
tbkn 1.15 V 12, 1.15 V 14, 1.16 I 25, 1.16 I 30
t\bl 1.6 IV 18f
tblk 1.4 V 15, 1.4 V 31
tblm 4.790 15
tbn 1.3 III 27
t]bn 1.2 III 8, 1.3 IV 15
tbnn 1.4 VI 16
tbn[n 1.2 III 10, 1.4 V 53
[t]b[nn] 1.4 V 51
tbˁ 1.2 I 13, 1.2 I 19, 1.2 III 7, 1.4 IV 19, 1.5 I 9, 1.5 II 8, 1.5 II 13, 1.17 II 39, 1.17 V 31, 1.17 V 32, 1.18 I 17, 2.17 6, 4.210 1, 4.213 27, 4.635 29
tbˁ[2.43 3
t[bˁ 1.19 IV 20
]tbˁ 1.2 III 8, 1.5 II 26, 1.146 6
t]bˁ 1.4 V 50

tbʿx[2.73 17
tbʿln 4.141 III 6, 4.141 III 8, 4.141 III 10
tbʿn 1.83 11
tbʿrn 1.16 II 18, 1.103 41, 1.103 56
tbʿt 1.14 I 14
tbṣʿ 1.147 13
tbṣr 6.24 1
tbṣrn 1.163 4
tbq 4.367 1, 4.610 17, 4.616 17, 4.629 8
tbqʿnn 1.6 II 32
tbqrn 1.78 5
tbr 1.142 3
tbrk{k} 1.12 I 26(?)
tbrk 1.15 II 14, 1.15 III 17
tbrkk 1.12 I 26 lg. tbrk{k}?
tbrkn 1.19 IV 32
tbrknn 1.17 I 23
tbrrt 2.19 10
tbšn 4.55 7, 4.63 III 21, 4.96 1
tbšr 1.4 V 26
tbtḫ 4.247 19
tbtṯb 4.103 15, 4.410 5, 4.753 2
tbṯḫ 1.4 I 29
tg 4.83 6
tg[4.195 16, 4.393 21
tgx[1.19 II 34
tgin 1.148 16
tgbry 4.271 9
tg]bry 4.271 7
tgḏn 4.33 9, 4.55 29, 4.69 VI 10
tgh 1.16 I 37
tghb 4.658 22
tgwln 1.82 4
tgḫṭk 1.169 1, 1.169 2
xxtgym 4.754 11
tgyn 4.33 10, 4.44 29, 4.97 3, 4.379 4, 4.410 11, 4.423 19, 4.632 20, 4.643 9, 4.696 6
tgy[n 4.44 13, 4.97 6
]tgyn 4.294 2
tgl 1.3 V 7
tgly 1.4 IV 23, 1.6 I 34, 1.16 VI 4, 1.17 VI 48
tglṯ 1.92 5
t[g]ml 1.87 10
tgmr 1.91 35, 4.67 10, 4.141 II 25, 4.151 II 1, 4.156 6, 4.173 11, 4.179 15, 4.230 14, 4.269 30, 4.269 32, 4.271 1, 4.271 2, 4.276 14, 4.282 16, 4.296 5, 4.296 6, 4.313 27(!), 4.333 9, 4.341 22, 4.636 5, 4.636 25, 4.777 12
tgmr[4.764 9
tgm[r 4.218 6, 4.636 10
tg[m]r 4.636 20
t[gm]r 4.636 15
t[gmr] 4.290 17
t]gmr 4.271 3, 4.636 2
tg]mr 4.137 13
tgm]r 4.337 28
tgm]r[4.636 30
tgn[4.64 V 7
tgnd 1.125 18, 1.132 11
tg]n[d 1.116 29(!)
tgʿrm 1.2 IV 28
tgġln 4.609 38
tgpḫ 4.658 43
tgr 1.1 IV 12, 7.135 2
tgrgr 1.23 66
tgrm 4.313 27 lg. tgmr
tgrš 1.3 II 15, 4.63 II 24
tgršp 4.728 8, 4.759 8
tgtn 4.69 V 9
td 1.4 VI 32, 1.6 I 2, 1.93 1
]td 4.619 9
]tdx[1.7 10
]xtd 1.30 1
tb/d[1.42 13, 2.37 4, 6.54 2
tl/d[2.17 9
tdu 1.16 VI 6, 1.16 VI 7
]tdbḥ 1.20 I 10
tdbḥn 1.20 I 1
tdbr 1.16 VI 31, 1.16 VI 43, 2.72 18
tdglym 4.125 7
tdgr 4.625 22
tdd 1.20 II 2, 1.20 II 2, 1.21 II 4, 1.21 II 12, 1.22 I 10, 1.22 II 6, 1.22 II 21, 1.70 5, 1.91 14, 1.151 12
td[d 1.4 VI 10
t[dd 1.22 II 11
tddn[1.166 10
tdḥln 2.16 12
tdḥl 2.30 21(?)
tdḥṣ 2.30 21 lg. tdḥl?
tdy 1.16 VI 47, 1.119 28
]tdy 4.608 22

tdyn 4.696 5
td[k 1.97 4
tdkn 1.72 39
tdlln 1.103 7
tdln 1.64 29, 4.295 3
tdm 1.16 I 26, 1.16 I 30
tdmm 1.4 III 20
tdmmt 1.4 III 22
tdmn[4.637 5
tdmʿ 1.19 I 35, 1.107 11
tdn 1.16 VI 33, 1.16 VI 45, 1.104 19, 1.119 22, 1.126 23, 1.128 12, 4.148 5, 4.609 22, 4.659 4
]tdn 1.4 III 2
tdʿ 1.1 III 15, 1.3 III 26, 1.3 III 27, 1.3 III 34, 1.4 II 18, 1.5 V 16, 1.98 4, 2.16 7, 2.33 19
t[dʿ 1.3 IV 18
td]ʿ 1.3 IV 15
tdʿṣ 1.4 V 20
tdġl 4.183 II 20, 4.264 9
tdġlm 4.609 21
tdr 1.15 III 23
tdry\nn 1.6 II 32f
]tdrk 1.82 38
tdrʿ.nn 1.6 II 35
tdrq 1.3 IV 39, 1.4 II 15, 1.17 V 11, 1.45 5
tdtt 4.609 35
tš/d̲[4.98 2
th 1.176 5
]th 1.14 V 22, 1.94 17, 1.101 11, 4.557 4
]thx[7.170 2
xxth 4.557 2
]xth[4.474 1
]thax[1.55 8
thbṭ 2.47 16
thbẓn 1.163 3
thbr 1.2 I 47, 1.4 IV 25, 1.6 I 37
t]hbr 1.17 VI 50
thdy 1.6 I 3
thw 1.5 I 15, 1.133 4
thwyn 1.92 36
thm 1.23 30, 1.100 1
]xxthm 1.157 7
thmt 1.3 III 25, 1.3 IV 17, 1.17 VI 12, 1.148 6(!), 1.92 5
thmt[1.148 41
thmtm 1.4 IV 22, 1.6 I 34, 1.17 VI 48, 1.19 I 45, 1.100 3
thm]tm 1.3 V 7
]th/in 4.82 10
]tw[4.93 III 17
twyn 4.52 2
twtḥ 1.1 III 11, 1.3 III 20, 1.3 IV 12
t[wtḥ 1.7 29
twt]ḥ 1.1 II 2
tzd 1.1 V 27, 1.107 46
tzdn 1.24 8, 1.24 12
tzn 5.10 1, 5.10 9
tznt 4.203 16, 4.721 6
tzġ 1.15 I 5, 1.105 21, 1.148 17, 1.149 10
tzġd 1.128 8
tzġm 1.91 4, 1.105 13
tḥ 1.19 IV 36, 1.82 34
tḥ[1.140 13
tḥbṭ 1.82 25
tḥbq 1.10 III 22, 1.10 III 23
tḥgrn 1.14 III 44, 1.23 17
tḥdy 1.3 II 24
tḥdṯn 1.92 4
tḥ[wy 1.18 IV 13
t]ḥ\wyn 1.24 9f(!)
tḥyt 1.103 32
tḥm 1.1 II 17, 1.2 I 17, 1.2 I 33, 1.3 III 13, 1.3 IV 7, 1.3 VI 24, 1.4 VIII 32, 1.5 I 12, 1.5 II 10, 1.5 II 17, 1.6 IV 10, 1.14 III 21, 1.14 V 16, 1.14 VI 3, 1.14 VI 40, 1.161 26, 2.2 12, 2.4 3, 2.6 1, 2.10 1, 2.11 3, 2.12 4, 2.13 3, 2.14 1, 2.16 1, 2.24 3, 2.26 1, 2.30 2, 2.34 1, 2.39 1, 2.40 3, 2.42 3, 2.44 3, 2.45 10, 2.46 1, 2.47 1, 2.49 1, 2.63 3, 2.64 4, 2.64 11, 2.70 3, 2.71 1, 2.76 2, 2.76 11, 2.78 1, 2.81 4, 2.81 17, 5.9 IV 1, 9.530 2
tḥm[1.14 V 33, 2.75 3
]tḥm 2.35 2
t]ḥm 2.67 1, 2.68 3, 5.9 I 1
tḥ]m 2.33 2, 2.36 1
tḥmxx[1.83 14
tḥmd[1.92 6
tḥmk 1.3 V 30, 1.3 V 31, 1.4 IV 41, 1.4 IV 43, 2.36 5, 2.77 5, 2.83 4
[t]ḥmk 1.1 II 3
tḥspn 1.3 II 38, 1.3 IV 42

tḥṣ 1.105 20
tḥrr 1.23 41, 1.23 44, 1.23 48
tḥrṯ 1.6 I 4
<tḥt> 1.114 7(!)
tḥ<t> 1.19 III 3
tḥt 1.1 III 20, 1.2 IV 7, 1.3 IV 36, 1.4 VII 58, 1.8 II 11, 1.9 12, 1.17 V 6, 1.17 VI 44, 1.19 II 38, 1.19 III 10, 1.19 III 18, 1.19 III 24, 1.19 III 32, 1.19 III 37, 1.84 10, 1.114 5, 1.114 8, 1.161 22, 1.161 23, 1.161 24, 1.161 25, 1.166 26, 4.133 1, 4.133 2, 4.133 3
t[ḥt] 1.19 IV 43
t]ḥt 1.19 I 22
tḥtx[2.80 3
tḥth 1.3 II 9
tḥt<yt> 4.271 7
tḥtk 1.6 VI 46, 1.6 VI 47
tḥtn 4.351 3
]tḫ 4.313 25
tḫṭa 1.169 5
tḫṭin 1.40 22, 1.40 23
tḫṭi[n 1.40 19
tḫlq 1.103 4, 1.103 59, 1.163 15, 2.73 6
t[ḫlq 1.140 6
]tḫlq 1.163 1
tḫl]q 1.103 8
tḫm 2.38 3
tḫss 1.15 III 25
tm\tḫṣ 1.3 II 5f
tḫš 1.4 VII 38, 1.4 VII 39
tḫtan 1.4 VIII 20
tḫtṣb 1.3 II 6, 1.3 II 20, 1.3 II 24, 1.3 II 30, 1.7 6
tṭbḫ 1.6 I 18, 1.6 I 20, 1.15 IV 15, 1.16 VI 20
tṭb[ḫ 1.15 V 1
[tṭ]bḫ 1.6 I 22, 1.6 I 24
tṭḥnn 1.6 II 34
tṭṭ 1.3 III 33, 1.19 II 45
tṭṭn 1.4 VII 35
tṭlb 1.5 IV 4
{t}ṭly 1.5 V 11
tẓpn 1.13 15
]ty 2.41 3, 4.51 4, 4.410 26, 4.443 7, 4.643 21
]xty 1.63 3, 2.3 2, 2.31 54
]tym 4.93 III 6
]xtym 4.634 5
tyn 1.42 57, 1.149 9, 4.631 11
ty[n 4.631 12
xtyn[4.424 3
typ 1.42 58
tyt 4.14 14, 4.203 17, 4.337 26
[[tk]] 1.10 III 27
tk 1.1 II 23, 1.1 III 22, 1.1 III 28, 1.2 I 20, 1.2 III 8, 1.2 III 9, 1.3 III 29, 1.3 IV 41, 1.3 VI 13, 1.4 III 13, 1.4 V 46, 1.4 V 55, 1.4 VII 3, 1.4 VIII 11, 1.5 II 15, 1.5 V 12, 1.10 II 9, 1.10 II 12, 1.12 I 21, 1.12 II 55, 1.14 V 17, 1.15 III 14, 1.23 65, 1.100 63, 1.101 2, 1.108 25, 4.195 8, 6.45 1
tk[1.2 II 3, 4.748 16
t[k 1.2 I 14
]tk 1.15 V 24, 1.18 I 7
]tk[7.120 5
]xtk 2.44 18
tr/k/p[4.227 III 3
tkbd 1.17 V 30
tkbdh 1.4 IV 26
tkbdnh 1.6 I 38
tkbd]nh 1.17 VI 51
tkwn 4.103 53
tkw[n 4.556 4
tky 4.683 31
tkyn 4.70 10, 4.690 12
tkyġ 4.363 4
tkl 1.5 III 5, 1.16 I 26, 1.19 IV 40
tkly 1.5 I 2, 1.5 I 28, 1.6 II 36
tkm 1.12 I 20
tkm[4.27 1
tk[[m]]ml 1.111 22
tkms 1.12 II 54
tkn 1.5 III 6, 1.14 I 15, 3.7 13, 4.355 27, 4.631 14
tk[n 1.140 8
tknm 4.126 31
tknn 3.3 6, 3.3 9
tks 1.5 VI 31
tksynn 1.10 III 24
tkpgʿ 6.15 1
tkrb 1.19 I 2
tkšd 1.5 I 16
tkt 1.86 4
tl 1.16 I 52

tl[1.42 27, 4.329 4
]tl 4.155 5, 4.635 7
]tl[7.119 2
tl/d[2.17 9
tlxy 4.739 10
tlak 1.13 27
tlakn 1.4 V 42
tliyt 1.3 III 31, 1.10 III 28, 1.10 III 31, 1.101 3
tlik 2.26 4
tlikn 2.72 10
tlu 1.100 68
tlun 1.14 I 33
tlb 4.357 16
]xxtlb 7.51 22
tlby[4.118 4, 4.161 3
t]lby[4.161 2
tlbr[4.83 2
tlbn 1.4 IV 61
tlbš 1.19 IV 44, 1.19 IV 46
tlgn 4.609 35
tld 1.13 2, 1.15 II 23, 1.15 II 25, 1.15 III 7, 1.15 III 8, 1.15 III 9, 1.15 III 10, 1.15 III 11, 1.15 III 12, 1.23 58, 1.24 5, 1.24 7, 1.107 49, 1.140 3, 1.140 5, 1.140 7, 1.140 9
tld[1.10 III 1, 1.10 III 20
t[]ld 1.140 1
t]ld 1.103 1
tldn 1.5 V 22, 1.23 52, 1.23 58, 3.8 1, 4.84 8
tlḥk 1.83 5
<t>lḥm 1.15 VI 2
tlḥm 1.6 VI 43, 1.22 I 21, 1.115 8, 1.169 6
tl]ḥm 1.4 III 40
tlḥmn 1.20 I 6, 1.22 I 23, 1.114 2
t\lḥn 1.15 IV 12f
tlḫty 1.64 7
tly 4.339 20
tly[4.4 7
tlyn 1.123 24
tlk 1.6 III 7, 1.6 III 13, 1.10 III 17, 1.18 I 27, 1.82 22, 1.82 24, 1.92 3, 2.39 16
tlk[1.95 5
]tlk 2.21 23
tlkm 1.23 16
tlkn 1.14 IV 31, 1.20 II 5, 2.72 15
tlk[n 1.22 II 24
tlkn[2.73 15
]tlkn[2.31 62
tlm 1.4 VIII 4, 1.16 III 11, 1.19 I 7, 1.172 15, 4.136 3
tlmi 4.337 7, 4.343 7
tlmin 1.42 2
tlmu 4.85 4, 4.678 4
tlmdm 4.384 8
tlmyn 2.11 3, 2.12 4, 2.71 1, 3.10 21, 4.63 I 31, 4.69 I 6, 4.226 4, 4.340 3, 4.352 8, 4.379 2, 4.791 18
tlmyn[4.84 7
tlmy[n 4.259 4
tlm[yn 4.383 5, 4.623 6
tlm[y]n 2.16 1
tl[m]yn 2.64 4
]tlmyn 4.330 1
]tlmš 4.643 20
tlsmn 1.1 II 22, 1.3 III 19
tls]mn 1.3 IV 12
tls]\[m]n 1.7 28f
]tl\ˁ 1.24 14f
tlˁm 1.2 IV 4
tlš 1.12 I 14, 4.214 III 22, 4.382 30
tlšx[1.5 IV 24
tlšn 1.17 VI 51, 4.311 13
tlšn[4.512 2
tltmṯk[1.70 41
tlṯ 4.197 18
tm 1.176 17
]tm 1.1 II 8, 1.13 16, 1.15 V 29, 1.37 4, 1.152 3, 2.23 29, 4.112 II 3, 4.275 5, 4.610 49, 7.138 3
]xtm 1.55 2, 1.147 21, 2.3 3, 7.133 4
]xxxxxtm 2.50 13
tml/u/d[4.84 10
tmgnn 1.4 III 25, 1.4 III 28
tml/u/d[4.84 10
tmdln 1.19 II 8
tmzˁ 1.19 I 36, 1.19 I 46
tmḫṣ 1.2 IV 9, 1.3 II 7, 1.5 I 1, 1.5 I 27, 1.19 IV 39, 1.19 IV 59
tmḫṣh 1.18 IV 13
tmṭr 1.19 I 41
tmṭrn 1.6 III 6, 1.6 III 12
tmy 4.724 11, 4.761 8
tmyn 4.41 12
tmk 1.169 11

tmkrn 3.8 16
tml/u/d[4.84 10
t]mlah 1.19 IV 61
tmll 1.101 6
tmn 4.344 4
]xtmn 4.436 6
tmnh 1.2 IV 18, 1.2 IV 26
tm]nym 4.777 2 cor. ṯm]nym
tmnn 4.734 12
tmntk 1.169 6
tmġ 1.5 VI 28
tm[ġ 1.5 VI 30
tmġy 1.14 III 4, 2.23 6
tmġyy 2.33 31
tmġyn 1.2 I 30, 1.3 II 17, 1.6 I 59, 1.19 II 40
tmġyn[2.1 5
tmr 1.13 26, 1.15 II 15, 1.69 5, 4.69 I 20, 4.724 1
tmr[4.651 3
tmrḏ[1.30 3
tmrym 4.126 20
tmrm 4.355 28
tmrn 1.19 IV 33
tmrnn 1.17 I 24
tmrnnk 1.42 5, 1.42 31
tmrtn 3.10 15, 4.45 4, 4.131 7, 4.188 11, 4.609 32, 4.791 10
tmt 1.14 I 16, 1.23 67
tmt[1.107 53
]tmt 1.25 11
tmtḫṣ 1.3 II 29
tm[tḫṣ 1.7 37
tm]tḫṣ 1.7 4
tmtḫ\ṣ 1.6 VI 24f
tmtḫṣh 1.3 II 19
tmtḫṣn 1.3 II 23
tmtm 1.20 I 3(?)
tmtn 1.16 I 4, 1.16 I 18, 1.16 I 22, 1.16 I 36, 1.16 II 40, 1.16 II 43
tmtn[1.94 28
tmtʿ 1.4 II 6
<t>mtt 2.38 13
tmtt 2.38 16, 2.38 22, 2.54 1, 4.231 9
]tmtṯb 4.608 21
tmṯl 1.85 25
tmṯl[1.72 30
]tmṯl 1.97 13
t]mṯl 1.85 25
tmṯ]l 1.71 23
tn 1.2 I 18, 1.2 I 18, 1.2 I 34, 1.2 I 35, 1.4 V 8, 1.6 I 45, 1.6 II 12, 1.6 V 19, 1.8 II 3, 1.14 III 39, 1.14 VI 23, 1.17 VI 18, 1.17 VI 24, 1.23 71, 1.24 17, 1.44 11, 1.100 73, 1.100 73, 1.128 20, 1.149 8, 2.46 23, 2.71 19, 3.9 15, 5.9 I 12, 5.9 I 15, 5.10 2, 5.10 2, 5.11 4, 5.11 5, 5.11 9, 5.11 15, 5.11 17
tn 2.70 22(?)
tn[1.52 10, 1.52 12, 4.80 21, 4.479 1, 4.496 6, 5.11 20
]tn 1.23 72, 1.37 2, 1.42 42, 4.64 IV 6, 4.370 21, 4.422 7, 4.476 3, 4.559 3, 4.609 45, 4.627 6, 4.772 3
]\tn 1.70 23f
t]n 4.399 6
]tn[4.468 1, 7.89 4
]xtn 1.17 I 41, 4.643 8
]xtn[4.71 II 10, 4.324 5, 4.590 2
ta/n[1.70 43
]xtna[4.414 6
tnabn 4.232 18
tngṯh 1.6 II 6, 1.6 II 27
tngṯnh 1.1 V 4, 1.1 V 17
]tnd 1.125 5 lg. atnd
tnḥn 1.15 I 7
tnḫ 1.6 III 19, 1.17 II 13
tny 4.114 5
]tny 4.438 4
]xtny 2.48 7
tnmy 1.1 IV 9
tnn 1.3 III 40, 1.6 VI 51, 1.16 V 31, 1.82 1, 1.83 8(?), 4.35 I 13, 4.103 42
tnnx 1.16 V 32
tnnb 1.131 8
]tnnm 1.5 II 27
tnʿr 1.132 25
tnġṣn 1.2 IV 17, 1.2 IV 26
tnqt 1.13 32, 1.16 II 34
tnq[th] 1.16 II 26
tnrr 1.119 9
tnšan 1.103 47
tnšq 1.22 I 4
tntkn 1.14 I 28
tnṯ 5.23 13
tsad 1.17 V 30
tsḫr 1.70 16
tskh 1.3 II 40

ts]kh 1.3 IV 43
tskn 1.73 9
tsm 1.14 III 42, 1.14 VI 27
tsmh 1.14 III 42, 1.14 VI 28
]tsˁ 2.33 8
tśˁn 3.8 12, 3.8 14
t]śˁm 4.142 8
tspi 1.96 3
tspr 1.4 VIII 8, 1.5 V 15, 1.17 VI 29, 2.26 18
tsrk 1.4 V 4
tˁ[1.176 12, 7.171 2
tˁbtnh 1.107 7
]tˁgd 4.275 17
<tˁdb> 1.114 11(!)
tˁdb 1.4 V 46, 1.17 V 22, 1.114 10
tˁdbn 1.114 12, 1.114 13
tˁdbnh 1.18 IV 33
tˁddn[1.5 IV 25
tˁdt 1.2 I 22, 1.2 I 26, 1.2 I 28, 1.2 I 30, 1.2 I 44
tˁ]dt 1.2 I 41
tˁḏr 1.47 26, 1.84 8, 1.109 21, 1.118 25, 1.148 8
t[ˁḏr] 1.162 12
t]ˁḏr 1.139 6
tˁḏ]r 1.84 47
tˁw[2.77 14
tˁzzk 5.9 I 4
tˁzz[k 2.4 6
]tˁzzn 1.103 20
tˁṭpn 1.103 2
tˁl 1.5 IV 20, 1.10 III 27, 1.10 III 29, 1.13 20, 1.17 VI 7, 2.33 37
tˁlg 1.169 11
tˁlgt 1.93 2
tˁln 1.20 II 4, 1.22 II 23, 1.112 7, 1.112 8
tˁlt 1.4 II 4 lg. {t}ˁlt or qlt?
]tˁm 4.509 2
tˁmt 1.16 VI 8
tˁn 1.3 I 15, 1.3 II 23, 1.3 IV 21, 1.3 V 19, 1.4 II 14, 1.4 II 27, 1.4 III 27, 1.4 III 32, 1.4 IV 40, 1.4 V 2, 1.6 I 47, 1.6 IV 17, 1.6 IV 21, 1.10 II 27, 1.10 II 28, 1.15 VI 3, 1.16 VI 58, 1.17 VI 25, 1.17 VI 52, 1.18 I 6, 1.18 IV 16, 1.19 IV 28, 1.117 11
tˁn[1.3 IV 53
tˁ[n 1.2 IV 35
t[ˁ]n 1.3 V 29
]tˁn 1.7 6, 1.15 IV 26
tˁny 1.2 I 26, 1.16 II 30, 1.124 5
tˁnyn 1.1 IV 16, 1.10 II 3, 1.23 12
tˁpn 1.19 III 44
tˁpp 1.4 II 10
tˁpr 2.71 12
tˁr 7.55 6
]tˁr[7.41 7
tˁrb 1.1 V 26, 1.7 3, 1.16 II 51, 1.43 1, 1.91 10, 1.148 18, 6.49 2
tˁrb[1.16 II 50, 1.94 36
tˁr[b 2.42 24
tˁr[b/k 1.56 6
tˁrbm 1.24 18
tˁrbn 1.43 9, 1.91 11
tˁr[k] 1.106 27
tˁrp 1.83 6
tˁr[rhm 1.12 II 30
tˁrrk 1.4 IV 39
]tˁrt 7.141 2
tˁrth 1.18 IV 29
tˁr[th] 1.19 IV 45
tˁrty 1.18 IV 18
tˁš 2.76 14
tˁtd 1.5 III 5
tˁtq 2.73 4
tˁtqn 1.1 II 12, 2.36 17
t/aġ/t[4.769 62
tġd 4.609 9
tġdd 1.3 II 25
tġḏ 1.4 VII 41
tġh 4.85 7
tġẓy 1.4 II 11
tġẓyn 1.4 III 26, 1.4 III 29
tġẓyt 1.6 VI 45
tġyn 4.98 5
tġl 1.3 I 1
tġly 1.2 I 23
tġll 1.3 II 27, 1.7 9, 1.19 III 50, 1.19 III 52
tġl[l] 1.3 II 13
tġln 1.19 III 9 lg. tqln
tġpy 1.92 11
tġpṯ 4.370 13
tġpṯm 4.183 II 10, 4.609 36
tġpṯn 1.42 49
]tġpṯn 4.57 3

tġṣ 1.3 III 34, 1.4 II 19
tġr 1.1 V 14, 7.164 4
tġrk 1.6 IV 24, 2.1 2, 2.11 8, 2.13 8, 2.14 4, 2.16 5, 2.30 7, 2.34 4, 2.38 5, 2.44 5, 2.46 5, 2.68 9, 2.70 7, 2.71 5, 2.75 6, 5.9 I 3
t[ġ]rk 2.63 5
tġ[rk 2.41 2
t]ġrk 2.21 6, 2.72 6
tġ]rk 2.4 5
tġrm 1.82 5
tġrn 2.23 22
[[trġt]] 1.75 3
tġt[r] 1.4 IV 33
tġṯyn 4.57 9
tġṯnnk 1.42 49
tp 1.96 2, 1.103 19, 1.108 4
tp[1.15 III 7, 1.83 13, 6.33 2
tp/k/r[4.227 III 3
tph 1.3 III 32, 1.16 I 53, 1.113 1, 1.113 5
tphhm 1.2 I 22
tphn 1.2 I 22, 1.4 II 12, 1.17 VI 10, 1.19 I 29, 1.19 II 27
tphnh 1.3 I 14
tpḥ 1.20 II 11, 4.643 14
tpḥ 1.19 IV 55 lg. tqḥ
]tpḥ/ṭ[7.18 2
tpky 1.107 11
tpl 1.2 I 15, 1.2 I 31, 1.13 13
tplg 1.100 69
tply 1.101 5
tpln 1.2 I 9
]tpn 4.608 5
tpnn 1.96 5, 1.96 6, 1.104 16
tpnr 3.1 32, 4.44 23, 4.44 28
tpʿ 1.19 II 23, 1.19 II 23
tpʿr[1.1 IV 17
tp]q 1.4 III 41
tpr 1.19 III 14, 1.19 III 28
tprš 1.103 53
tpš[1.103 23
tpšlt 1.103 45
tptḥ 1.15 IV 16, 1.16 VI 11
tpt[ḥ 1.15 V 2
tptq 1.1 V 27
tptrʿ 1.13 19
tṣi 1.18 IV 24, 2.8 2
tṣu 1.106 28, 1.164 19, 1.169 2
[tṣ]un 1.83 3
tṣb 1.17 VI 13
tṣd 1.5 VI 26
tṣd[1.23 16
tṣdn 1.17 VI 40, 1.23 68, 1.114 23
tṣḥ 1.3 III 36, 1.4 II 21, 1.4 V 26, 1.5 II 17, 1.6 I 11, 1.6 I 39, 1.6 IV 9, 1.6 VI 23, 1.17 VI 16, 1.17 VI 53, 1.18 I 23, 1.18 IV 7, 1.23 32, 1.23 33, 1.161 19
t[ṣḥ 1.2 III 15
tṣ]ḥ 1.5 VI 3
t[ṣ]\ḥ 1.6 II 11f
tṣḥn 1.14 VI 39, 1.23 39, 1.23 43, 1.23 46
tṣḥq 1.17 VI 41
tṣmd 1.19 II 9, 1.20 II 3
tṣmt 1.2 IV 9, 1.3 II 8
tṣq[1.16 II 13
tṣr 1.14 III 29, 1.16 II 25, 1.16 II 26, 1.16 II 34
t[ṣr] 1.14 VI 10
tq 6.47 1
tq[1.82 41
tqb[rn] 1.15 V 15
tqbrnh 1.6 I 17
tqdm 1.15 IV 23, 1.161 30
tqh 1.2 I 18, 1.2 I 34
tqḥ 1.2 IV 10, 1.15 II 22, 1.18 IV 27, 1.19 IV 55(!)
tq[ḥ 1.2 I 10
t[q]ḥ 1.19 IV 53
tq]ḥ 1.15 II 21
tq\ḥ 1.19 IV 54f
tqḥn 4.395 4
tqḥ[n] 4.395 2
tqṭṭ 1.40 31, 1.84 7
tqṭṭn 1.40 23, 1.40 40
tqyn 1.2 I 18
tqynh 1.2 I 34
tql 1.4 IV 25, 1.6 I 37, 1.17 VI 50, 1.19 I 3, 1.19 III 32, 1.19 III 37
tql[1.6 II 4
]tql 1.164 13
tqln 1.16 VI 57, 1.19 III 3, 1.19 III 9(!), 1.103 1, 1.109 4
tqm 1.82 39, 1.82 39
tqn 4.277 11
tqny 1.17 VI 41

tqnt 5.23 10
tqˁt 1.24 49
tqġ 1.16 VI 30, 1.16 VI 42
tqṣrn 1.103 33
tqr[1.7 16
tqru 1.100 8, 1.100 14, 1.100 19, 1.100 25, 1.100 30, 1.100 35, 1.100 40, 1.100 45, 1.100 51, 1.100 57, 1.107 9, 1.107 15
tqrb 1.4 VIII 16, 1.15 III 20, 1.15 III 21, 1.16 II 17
t]qrb 1.15 III 5
tqry 1.3 II 4
tqrṣn 1.12 I 11
tqtnṣn 1.23 58
tqt[nṣn 1.23 51
tr 1.4 V 21, 1.10 II 11, 1.10 II 28, 1.10 II 29, 1.10 II 29, 1.10 III 17, 1.16 II 12, 1.16 II 15, 1.16 III 2, 1.17 VI 46, 1.115 5, 1.115 13, 7.53 6
tr[1.16 II 16, 1.149 5, 2.9 1, 4.593 5, 4.671 2
trx[2.31 35
]xtr 2.37 7
tr/k/p[4.227 III 3
tral 4.370 10
tran 3.7 3
trb 4.348 27
trbd 1.132 2
trbyt 4.658 50
trbnn 4.269 21, 4.269 22
trbn[n 4.693 35
trbṣ{t} 1.14 III 37(?)
trbṣ 1.14 II 3, 1.14 III 25, 1.14 VI 8, 1.14 VI 21
t[rbṣ 1.14 V 38
trbṣt 1.14 III 37 lg. trbṣ{t}?
trgm 1.16 I 31, 1.86 22, 2.3 18
trgm[2.2 5, 2.3 8
trg[m 2.45 28
tr[gm 1.16 I 32
]trgm[7.30 2
trgn 4.85 7
trd 1.6 I 8
trd[1.168 22
trdn 4.617 25
trh 4.167 9
trhy 4.625 20
t]rhm 4.167 7
tr]hm 4.363 10
trhn 4.145 5
trzy 4.643 10
tr[zy 4.417 4
trḥ 1.124 6
trḥṣ 1.3 II 32, 1.3 II 38, 1.3 IV 42
t]rḥṣ 1.3 II 34, 1.7 20
trḥṣn 1.2 III 20
trḥṣ.nn 1.16 VI 10(cor.)
trḫ 1.14 I 14, 1.14 II 47, 1.14 IV 26, 1.24 26, 1.54 15
trḫn 1.42 55
trḫnḏr 1.42 57
t]rḫnm[1.64 32
trḫp 1.18 IV 32
trḫpn 1.18 IV 20, 1.18 IV 31, 1.19 I 32
trḫṣ.nn 1.16 VI 10 cor. trḥṣ.nn
trḫtt 1.111 20
trẓẓh 1.16 I 49
try 4.610 31
]t/aryn 1.52 7
trks 1.1 V 10, 1.83 9
]trks 1.1 V 23
trm 1.16 II 26, 1.16 II 34, 1.16 II 34, 1.23 32, 4.158 7, 4.167 2, 4.167 3
tr[my] 1.92 13
trmm 1.4 VI 17
trm[m 1.2 III 10
trmmn 1.4 V 54
trmmt 1.6 VI 44
trmn 1.161 5, 4.612 6
trmt 1.43 3
trn 4.55 11, 4.103 10, 4.350 13, 4.689 5
]trn 4.82 5
trnḏa 1.149 6
trnḏ.rm 1.128 5
trˁ 1.12 II 42
trˁn 1.12 II 42
xxxtrġ 4.752 8
trġds 2.10 5, 4.102 27, 4.425 2
trġzz 1.4 VIII 2
trġn 1.100 61
trġnds 4.400 15
trpa 1.114 28
trṣ 4.282 17
trqm 4.123 20
]trr 1.4 VII 31

trrm 4.7 1, 4.99 8, 4.103 48*, 4.126 26
tršwnḏ 1.149 2
tršʿ 1.169 6
trtbd[1.51 19
trtḥ[1.82 35
trtḥṣ 1.13 18, 1.14 II 9
trtḥ[ṣ] 1.19 IV 41
trtn 4.609 28, 5.11 5
trtqṣ 1.2 IV 13, 1.2 IV 20
trṯ 1.17 VI 7, 1.39 11, 1.39 16, 1.102 9, 1.114 4, 1.114 16
trṯ[1.5 IV 20
tš[1.12 II 15
]tš 7.47 7
tš/ḏ[4.98 2
tša 1.5 II 16, 1.19 II 40
]tšabn 1.6 I 66
t]šabn 1.6 I 67
tšal 2.70 23
tšan 1.14 VI 38
tša[n 1.14 VI 2
tšiḫrhm[2.79 4
tšu 1.2 I 29, 1.2 III 15, 1.3 III 35, 1.4 II 21, 1.4 V 25, 1.6 I 14, 1.6 I 39, 1.6 II 11, 1.6 IV 9, 1.10 II 10, 1.10 II 11, 1.10 II 26, 1.10 II 27, 1.15 III 27, 1.19 II 10, 1.92 10
tšun 1.119 27
tšbʿ 1.3 II 29, 1.6 I 9
tšbʿ[1.7 17
tšbʿn 1.23 64
tšḫṭa.nn 1.19 III 45
tšyt 1.3 II 27
tškḥ[2.73 14
tškn 1.14 II 51, 1.14 IV 29
tšknn 2.47 3
tšknn[2.47 5
tšknnnn 2.7 11
tškr 1.14 II 45, 1.14 IV 23
tškrġ 4.391 3
]tš[krġ 4.490 2
tšlḥ 1.15 IV 24
t[šl]ḥ 1.15 V 7
tšlḥm 1.16 VI 49, 1.17 V 29, 1.92 16
t]šlḥ[m] 1.92 15
tšlm 1.111 23
tšlmk 2.11 9, 2.13 8, 2.14 5, 2.16 6, 2.21 5, 2.34 4, 2.38 5, 2.44 5, 2.46 5, 2.63 6, 2.70 7, 2.71 4, 2.75 6, 5.9 I 3
tš[l]mk 2.30 7
tšlm[k 2.4 5, 2.72 6
tšl]mk 2.50 1, 2.68 10
tšlm]k 2.41 2
t]šl[mkm] 2.6 6
tš{š}lmn 4.95 1(?)
tšmḫ 1.3 V 21, 1.6 I 39, 1.17 II 9, 2.16 11
tš[mḫ 1.18 I 8
t]šmḫ 1.3 V 20
tšmʿ 1.6 I 13, 1.15 IV 14, 1.16 VI 19, 1.17 V 21, 2.10 17
tš[mʿ] 1.19 II 5
tšmʿm 2.71 9
tšnn 1.16 II 35
tšnpn 1.50 6
tšʿ 1.87 59, 1.91 28, 1.106 29, 1.132 1, 4.29 1, 4.29 3, 4.40 5, 4.40 15, 4.136 1, 4.137 6, 4.144 3, 4.163 1, 4.163 5, 4.163 10, 4.174 6, 4.213 19, 4.269 2, 4.270 6, 4.296 4, 4.337 22, 4.381 16, 4.395 2, 4.400 4, 4.400 7, 4.400 16, 4.618 11, 4.689 2, 4.707 11
tšʿ[1.104 11, 4.40 9, 4.161 10, 4.161 11, 4.237 1, 4.317 14
tš[ʿ 4.20 1, 4.20 2, 4.80 16, 4.174 8, 4.244 27, 4.729 10, 4.777 7
t[šʿ 4.558 1
]tšʿ 4.312 8, 4.777 10
t]šʿ 4.44 15, 4.285 3
tš]ʿ 4.775 13
tšʿxn 2.31 51
tšʿl 1.14 III 12
tšʿly 1.5 V 21, 1.19 II 38
tšʿlynh 1.6 I 15
tšʿm 1.4 VII 12, 4.56 12, 4.137 9, 4.169 9, 4.173 7, 4.174 11, 4.213 2, 4.213 13, 4.213 21, 4.243 14, 4.276 14, 4.397 12, 4.595 1, 4.779 1
tš[ʿm 4.56 13, 4.344 14
t]šʿm 1.76 6
tš]ʿm 1.76 5
tšʿrb 1.15 II 22, 1.15 IV 17, 1.15 IV 18
t[šʿ]rb 1.15 V 4
tšʿ]rb 1.15 V 3
tšʿt 4.333 7, 4.337 22
tš[t] 1.88 3

tšpkm 1.17 VI 15
tšpl 1.23 32, 1.92 14
tšṣḥq 2.25 5
tšṣqn[h] 1.6 II 10
tšqy 1.19 IV 61, 1.19 IV 61
tšqy[1.16 II 14
tšqyn 1.19 IV 53
tšqynh 1.19 IV 55
tšr 1.101 17, 2.44 11
]xtšr[4.451 1
tšrgn 1.17 VI 34
tšrpnn 1.6 II 33
tššy 1.82 5
tššlmn 4.95 1 lg. tš{š}lmn?
tššqy 1.17 V 29
tšt 1.4 V 64, 1.4 VI 8, 1.4 VI 22, 1.6 I 10, 1.6 I 30(!), 1.6 VI 44, 1.7 22, 1.16 I 34, 1.18 I 18, 1.19 I 10, 1.19 IV 44, 1.19 IV 45, 1.83 9, 1.92 9, 1.96 4, 1.108 6, 1.169 7, 2.7 7, 2.30 24, 2.71 15, 6.40 2
tšt[2.31 14
t]št 1.3 III 4, 1.19 IV 59
]t/ašt 2.31 19
tštil 2.17 15
tšth 1.6 I 15
tštḥwy 1.2 I 15, 1.2 I 31, 1.3 III 10, 1.4 IV 26, 1.4 VIII 28, 1.6 I 38
tštḥ\wy 1.3 VI 19f
tštḥ\[wy 1.17 VI 50f
t[štḥwy 1.1 III 3
tšty 1.4 III 40, 1.4 VI 58, 1.15 VI 2
tštyn 1.20 I 7, 1.22 I 22, 1.22 I 24
tštk 1.19 II 18, 1.19 II 25, 1.108 20
tštn 1.15 IV 25, 1.15 V 8, 1.18 IV 28, 1.104 20, 1.114 3, 1.114 3
]tštn 1.126 24
tštnn 1.6 I 17, 1.19 II 10
tštql 1.3 II 18, 1.6 VI 42
tštr 1.22 I 11
tštšḥ 1.82 11
tt 4.7 16, 4.102 26, 4.103 19, 4.132 2, 4.132 2, 4.160 5
tt[1.42 23, 7.142 6
]tt 1.10 I 13
]tt[7.107 7
xtt 4.16 10
]xtt 4.639 1
t/aġ/t[4.769 62
ttbʿ 1.6 IV 6, 1.14 VI 35, 1.16 VI 2
t]tbʿ 1.15 II 13, 1.18 IV 5
]ttwrb/d[1.167 4
ttḫ 4.153 3
ttyn 4.631 3
ttkn 1.12 II 57
ttl 1.24 14, 1.44 5, 1.131 3
tt\l 1.44 5f
ttlh 1.100 15
ttlk 1.5 VI 26
ttlkn 1.23 67
ttn 1.2 I 14, 1.2 IV 6, 1.3 IV 37, 1.3 VI 12, 1.4 IV 20, 1.4 V 22, 1.4 VIII 1, 1.4 VIII 10, 1.5 V 12, 1.6 I 32, 1.6 IV 7, 1.6 V 22, 1.14 III 38, 1.14 VI 23, 1.16 II 35, 1.18 I 20, 1.19 I 16, 1.82 43, 1.92 34, 1.92 35, 2.8 5, 2.42 20(?), 4.35 II 21, 4.63 II 16, 4.69 III 3, 4.245 I 10, 5.9 I 12, 5.9 I 13, 5.9 I 14, 5.11 18
ttn 2.70 22 lg. tn?
ttn[2.9 2
tt]n 1.14 V 30
t/n/atn 4.63 IV 3
ttnn 1.10 II 31, 1.10 III 32, 5.11 20
ttnt 5.11 13
ttġl 4.147 4
ttġr 1.92 33
ttpl 1.14 I 21
ttpp 1.3 III 1, 1.3 IV 45
tt\rḫ 1.24 28f
ttrp 1.5 I 4
]t/atṯtḫnm 1.64 32
tṯ[1.70 40
]tṯ 4.425 16
tṯx[7.46 5
tṯar 1.3 II 37
tṯibṯn 1.175 8
tṯb 1.3 IV 21, 1.4 VI 2, 1.16 VI 10, 1.19 I 6, 1.35 9, 1.42 10, 1.82 35, 1.92 8, 1.96 9, 1.96 10, 1.96 11, 1.96 12, 1.148 17, 1.169 19(cor.)
tṯ[b 1.66 31
t[ṯb 1.96 13
]tṯb 1.4 VI 15, 1.32 3, 1.52 9, 2.82 15, 4.357 32
t]ṯb 1.52 13
tṯ]b 1.92 14
tṯbb 1.169 19 cor. tṯb b

tṯbd 1.42 56, 1.110 3, 1.111 4, 1.111 9, 1.116 13, 1.125 8
]tṯbd 1.120 2
tṯ]bd 1.135 2
tṯbn 1.4 VII 24
tṯbr 1.3 III 33, 1.16 I 54, 1.19 I 3
t[ṯbr 1.6 II 3
tṯbrn 2.72 16
tṯbṯ 1.42 12, 1.42 13, 1.64 28, 1.64 29, 1.64 29
tṯwy 1.16 VI 44
tṯḥdṯn 1.104 17
t/aṯyx 1.86 28
tṯyn 4.631 4
tṯkḥ 1.5 I 4, 1.5 I 30
]tṯkḥ 1.11 2
tṯkl 1.100 61
tṯlṯ 1.6 I 5
t[ṯ]l[ṯ] 1.6 I 3
tṯmd 4.7 20, 4.103 12, 4.103 27
tṯn 4.46 5, 4.155 11, 4.281 22, 4.612 5
tṯnt[1.148 22
tṯtny[n 1.5 IV 19
tṯʿr 1.3 II 20
tṯp 1.149 10
tṯpṭ 1.16 VI 34, 1.16 VI 46
tṯpn 1.149 9
tṯrm 1.92 15
tṯ{t}mnm 1.15 II 24
]t/aṯt 1.64 6
tṯtg/ḫṯxt 1.64 31
tṯṯb 1.114 27, 2.12 14, 2.16 19, 2.35 7
tṯ[ṯb 2.4 7, 2.6 14
tṯṯbn 3.4 17
t[ṯ]ṯbn 1.41 54
]tṯṯbn 1.53 6
tṯṯkrn 1.15 I 3

Ṯ

ṯ 1.5 II 26, 1.69 5, 1.163 8, 4.203 12, 5.2 4, 5.2 5, 5.2 6, 5.6 2, 5.9 II 3, 5.12 4, 5.13 8, 5.14 15, 5.17 3, 5.17 6, 5.19 4, 5.20 2, 5.20 3, 5.21 2, 5.24 1
ṯ[1.2 III 14, 1.23 19, 1.27 10, 1.70 15, 1.107 28, 4.40 6, 4.69 II 1, 4.93 I 24, 4.240 4, 4.247 6, 4.247 7, 4.247 8, 4.399 2, 4.404 5, 4.449 3, 4.459 5, 4.537 2, 4.574 2, 4.609 8, 4.609 17, 4.609 33, 4.645 7, 7.37 5
]ṯ 1.4 VI 62, 1.42 28, 1.52 23, 1.64 4*, 1.66 4, 1.66 24, 2.36 7, 4.205 17, 4.228 6, 4.228 7, 4.401 4, 4.424 20, 4.475 1, 4.611 21, 4.624 16, 4.640 2, 7.5 3, 7.197 4
]ṯ[4.197 30
ṯx 4.139 5
ṯx[1.67 11, 4.74 5, 4.86 1, 4.287 2, 4.326 10, 4.434 3, 4.435 6, 7.41 2
]ṯx[4.620 1, 7.118 4
ṯxx[1.3 V 14, 4.322 5, 4.748 5
]ṯxx 4.399 17
ṯxxx[1.14 I 44
xṯ 4.34 6, 4.201 3
]xṯ 1.5 III 28, 1.94 34, 4.320 10, 7.135 6
]xṯ[1.67 9
xxṯ[4.201 2
xṯx 1.35 13, 4.198 1
]xṯx[1.76 1
xxxxxxṯxxlḫy 4.198 4
ṯxxṯbxḫdḏnnk 1.42 14
ṯar 1.14 I 15
ṯat 1.6 II 29, 1.111 18
ṯat[1.93 8
ṯa[t] 1.6 II 7
ṯi 1.64 22
ṯigt 1.14 III 16
ṯiṯ 1.17 II 7, 1.17 II 22
ṯ[iṯ] 1.16 V 29
ṯi]ṯ 1.17 I 33
ṯiy 4.245 II 6
ṯiyṯx[1.52 11
ṯip[1.51 2
ṯiqt 1.14 V 8
ṯirk 1.18 I 25
ṯu 1.149 3
ṯut 1.80 3
ṯuṯk 1.64 26, 1.116 9, 1.148 17
ṯuṯk[1.59 5
ṯu[ṯk 1.42 22, 1.59 1, 1.120 3
[ṯ]uṯk 1.149 10, 1.149 11, 4.673 7
ṯuṯkd 1.116 3, 1.116 13, 1.135 2
ṯ]uṯkd 1.116 31
ṯuṯ]kd 1.26 3, 1.60 2
ṯb 1.2 I 2, 1.4 V 42, 1.4 VII 8, 1.16 V 24, 1.17 VI 42, 1.17 VI 42, 1.18 IV 16, 1.40 35, 1.106 23, 2.33 39, 2.70 16, 3.4 19, 4.339 1
ṯb[1.67 17, 4.64 V 5, 4.609 28
]ṯb 2.8 3, 4.106 4, 4.267 5, 4.326 7, 4.701 3, 7.137 2
]ṯb[7.96 2
ṯbx[4.427 12
]xṯb 7.43 4
]ṯb/ṣ[4.678 8
ṯbil 1.92 1, 4.12 6, 4.229 5, 4.313 2, 4.380 25
ṯbil[4.322 11
ṯbg 4.339 21
ṯbh 2.62 12
ṯbṯ 4.123 22
ṯby 2.9 5, 4.222 11
]ṯby[4.431 6
]xṯbyy[7.39 4
]ṯbym[4.564 2
ṯbl 1.42 8, 1.42 27, 1.42 33
]ṯbl[4.450 3
ṯbln 4.322 7
xṯbndm 1.42 42
ṯbʿl 4.610 7
ṯbʿ[4.763 1
ṯbʿm 4.115 8, 4.116 10, 4.141 II 20, 4.204 7, 4.347 6, 4.347 8, 4.609 7, 4.645 10, 4.707 19
]ṯbʿm 4.461 3
]ṯbʿm[4.37 6

ṯbʿnq 4.377 14
]ṯbʿnq 4.260 6
ṯbġl 4.110 9
ṯbq 4.177 4
ṯbq[ym 4.40 3
<ṯbr> 1.19 III 36
ṯbr 1.2 I 13, 1.19 III 9, 1.19 III 22, 1.19 III 23, 1.19 III 37
ṯbr[4.761 5
]ṯbr 2.31 18
ṯbry 4.617 18
ṯbrn 1.4 VIII 19, 1.6 II 23, 4.93 II 4
ṯbt 1.5 III 2, 1.5 III 3, 1.101 1
ṯ[bt 1.1 III 9
]ṯbt 7.163 4
ṯbt<h> 1.5 II 16
ṯbth 1.3 VI 15, 1.4 VIII 13, 1.14 I 23
ṯbtk 1.2 III 17, 1.6 VI 28, 1.117 12
]ṯbtk 1.82 39
ṯbtnq 4.69 I 16
]xṯg[1.32 1
ṯgbr 4.224 9, 4.422 2
ṯgd 4.382 30, 4.761 11
ṯgdlḫ 1.42 61
ṯgmi 4.192 4
ṯgrb 4.611 28
ṯgr[b 4.633 5
ṯgrḫn 1.42 35
ṯgt 1.149 7, 4.269 9
ṯd 1.3 I 6, 1.4 VI 56, 1.13 19, 1.15 II 27, 1.116 4(!)
ṯd[1.64 21
]ṯd[4.386 20
ṯdx[4.239 1
ṯdh 1.10 III 24
]ṯdh 1.13 31
ṯdy 4.116 18
]ṯdy[4.650 3
ṯdyn 4.643 12
ṯdyn[4.649 4
]ṯdyn 4.650 4
ṯdl 1.149 5
[ṯ]dm 1.14 III 44
ṯdmn 1.128 8, 1.149 6
ṯdn 1.12 I 11, 1.44 3, 1.44 3, 4.290 13, 4.377 29
]ṯdn[7.9 3
ṯdny 3.10 20, 4.791 16
ṯdnyn 4.225 10, 4.611 29

ṯḏpṯn 4.631 21
ṯḏpṯn[4.114 4
ṯḏr 1.42 30, 4.275 2
ṯḏrṯḏ 1.131 8
ṯḏṯ 1.4 VI 29, 1.14 II 31, 1.14 III 3, 1.14 III 12, 1.14 IV 12, 1.14 V 5, 1.17 I 11, 1.17 II 37, 1.22 I 23, 1.41 45, 1.126 19, 1.171 6
ṯḏṯb 4.93 II 12
ṯš/ḏ[1.66 17
ṯḏyy 4.755 6
]tḏl[1.68 4
ṯh 2.33 25, 2.33 29, 2.33 37
]ṯ/ʿh 7.57 3
ṯp/k/w[1.67 6
ṯwyn 4.232 30
ṯwl 1.125 4
]ṯwly[1.81 24
ṯwrm 1.42 2
ṯwṯk 1.54 2, 1.54 12
ṯwṯkd 1.54 14
ṯḫr 1.123 27
ṯṭ 4.205 3
ṯy 1.44 8, 1.54 12
ṯy 2.13 14, 2.30 13 lg. ṯyndr Dietrich-Loretz UF 26, 1994, 63-71.
ṯy[4.334 5*
]ṯy[4.72 1
ṯyb 1.93 3
]ṯyb 4.93 III 18
ṯydr 6.21 2
ṯ]ydr[4.653 5
ṯydrd 1.131 9
ṯyl 4.155 11, 4.339 18
ṯylṯ 1.42 37
ṯyn 1.42 61, 1.125 3, 4.611 15
ṯyndr 2.13 14(!), 2.30 13(!) Dietrich-Loretz UF 26, 1994, 63-71.
ṯynḏr[4.97 5
ṯyny 5.11 7(!)
ṯynṯ]t 1.135 14(!)
ṯk 4.45 2
ṯk[1.23 74
]ṯk 1.82 22
ṯkx[1.3 V 13
ṯp/k/w[1.67 6
ṯk/r[4.333 2
ṯkl 1.23 8
ṯk[l 1.95 4

ṯkm 1.14 II 11, 1.14 III 54, 1.16 IV 13, 1.22 I 5, 1.22 I 5
ṯkmm 1.14 II 22, 1.14 IV 4
ṯkmn 1.39 3, 1.39 6, 1.40 34, 1.40 43, 1.41 31, 1.65 4(?), 1.87 14, 1.87 17, 1.114 18, 1.123 8
ṯ[kmn 1.41 12
ṯk]mn 1.41 15
ṯkm]\n 1.87 33f
ṯkmt 1.19 II 1, 1.19 II 6, 1.19 IV 28, 1.19 IV 37
ṯkn 4.16 13
ṯkn[4.506 4
ṯkṣṯxxx 4.52 10
ṯkt 1.4 V 7, 4.81 4, 4.81 5, 4.366 4, 4.366 5, 4.366 6, 4.366 7, 4.366 8, 4.366 9, 4.366 10, 4.366 11, 4.366 12, 4.366 13, 4.366 14
ṯkt[4.81 8
ṯk[t 4.81 9
ṯl 1.64 21, 5.11 14
ṯl[1.22 II 1, 1.64 7, 4.503 II 4, 4.610 38, 4.629 20
ṯlxxx 4.308 6
]xxxṯl[4.619 2
ṯlxʿx 4.308 5
ṯlb 1.108 4
ṯlbm 1.113 3, 1.113 8
ṯlr/wn 4.432 13
ṯlḥḫ 4.53 5
ṯlḥmy 5.11 6
ṯlḥn 1.4 I 38, 1.22 I 16, 1.109 31, 1.161 15, 4.13 4, 4.13 30, 4.13 31, 4.13 36
ṯlḥn 1.114 8 cor. ṯlḥnt
ṯlḥ[n 4.248 6
]ṯlḥn 4.13 2, 4.13 5, 4.13 6, 4.13 16, 4.13 17, 4.13 18, 4.13 19, 4.13 20, 4.13 21, 4.13 22, 4.13 23, 4.13 24, 4.13 25, 4.13 26, 4.13 27, 4.13 34, 4.13 35
ṯ]lḥn 4.13 1, 4.13 3, 4.13 8, 4.13 9, 4.13 10, 4.13 11, 4.13 12, 4.13 13, 4.13 14, 4.13 15, 4.13 29, 4.13 33
ṯl]ḥn 4.13 7, 4.13 28
ṯ]lḥ[n] 4.13 32
<ṯ>lḥn 4.13 36
ṯlḥny 1.4 III 15, 4.33 17, 4.68 11, 4.80 18, 4.95 5
ṯlḥn[y 4.629 16
ṯlḥ[ny 4.686 7
]ṯlḥnym 4.634 3
ṯlḥnm 1.3 II 30
<ṯlḥnt> 1.114 7(!)
ṯlḥn<t> 1.3 II 37
ṯlḥnt 1.3 II 21, 1.3 II 36, 1.4 IV 36, 1.114 6, 1.114 8(cor.)
]ṯlḥnt 4.594 3
ṯlḫh 1.24 47
ṯlṭ 4.63 III 5, 4.96 11
ṯlln 4.63 I 16, 4.711 2
ṯllt 1.107 18
ṯlmḥ[1.67 2
ṯlnd 1.110 1, 1.132 4, 1.132 18, 1.132 22
ṯ[l]nd 1.111 8
ṯ]lnd 1.26 2
ṯlnnṯtm 1.116 11
ṯlġḏy 4.290 2
ṯlġlḏ 1.148 13, 1.148 15
ṯlġmd 1.148 13
ṯlrbh 4.95 2
ṯlrby 4.68 12, 4.95 4, 4.244 21, 4.297 5, 4.762 8
ṯlr[by 4.619 3, 4.686 8
ṯ]lrby[4.610 9
ṯlr/wn 4.432 13
ṯlṯḫ 4.12 3
[[ṯlṯ]] 1.14 V 3
ṯlṯ 1.3 IV 36, 1.4 III 17, 1.4 VI 26, 1.14 II 2, 1.14 II 36, 1.14 II 42, 1.14 III 2, 1.14 III 11, 1.14 III 24, 1.14 III 36, 1.14 IV 16, 1.14 IV 20, 1.14 IV 33, 1.14 IV 45, 1.14 V 4, 1.14 VI 20, 1.16 II 22, 1.16 IV 15, 1.17 I 8, 1.17 II 34, 1.17 II 45, 1.22 I 22, 1.22 II 25, 1.43 6, 1.48 5, 1.49 8, 1.55 6, 1.91 22, 1.91 25, 1.91 33, 1.100 71, 1.104 29, 1.111 2, 1.111 16, 1.112 8, 1.132 22, 1.148 20, 1.148 20, 1.161 28, 1.163 5, 1.163 8, 1.175 17, 2.26 11, 2.32 5, 2.32 6, 4.4 10, 4.9 1, 4.23 4, 4.23 5, 4.27 15, 4.34 3, 4.34 4, 4.34 7, 4.34 8, 4.35 II 8, 4.41 2, 4.41 5, 4.41 10, 4.43 1, 4.44 6, 4.44 16, 4.44 32, 4.54 4, 4.60 3, 4.61 1, 4.63 III 3, 4.63 III 5, 4.63 III 21, 4.63 III 21, 4.73 2, 4.73 4, 4.73 11, 4.73 13,

4.80 19, 4.88 9, 4.89 1, 4.102 16, 4.113 1, 4.121 1, 4.123 3, 4.123 16, 4.123 17, 4.126 18, 4.127 6, 4.127 10, 4.132 2, 4.137 2, 4.137 4, 4.137 12, 4.138 6, 4.138 8, 4.138 9, 4.139 4, 4.145 8, 4.149 17, 4.152 5, 4.152 11, 4.158 7, 4.163 7, 4.163 8, 4.163 11, 4.164 1, 4.167 1, 4.167 5, 4.168 11, 4.168 12, 4.171 1, 4.179 10, 4.181 2, 4.181 4, 4.181 6, 4.182 10, 4.182 26, 4.182 60, 4.183 II 27, 4.188 7, 4.192 3, 4.203 1, 4.203 14, 4.205 7, 4.205 8, 4.216 2, 4.216 4, 4.219 3, 4.222 8, 4.222 9, 4.222 10, 4.222 11, 4.244 9, 4.244 10, 4.244 13, 4.247 22, 4.247 26, 4.268 2, 4.270 3, 4.270 9, 4.272 4, 4.272 5, 4.272 6, 4.274 5, 4.279 3, 4.280 2, 4.280 5, 4.282 3, 4.282 6, 4.283 6, 4.288 9, 4.296 2, 4.296 8, 4.299 4, 4.300 2, 4.302 4, 4.303 5, 4.310 1, 4.310 3, 4.310 5, 4.310 7, 4.310 9, 4.313 18, 4.313 21, 4.317 10, 4.326 9, 4.333 1, 4.333 5, 4.337 3, 4.337 6, 4.337 11, 4.337 18, 4.337 28, 4.339 25, 4.341 3, 4.342 2, 4.357 29, 4.360 2, 4.360 5, 4.363 6, 4.368 1, 4.369 4, 4.377 1, 4.387 11, 4.387 14, 4.390 7, 4.396 1, 4.396 11, 4.397 10, 4.399 6, 4.400 11, 4.402 7, 4.410 8, 4.410 15, 4.410 17, 4.417 5, 4.421 3, 4.585 3, 4.608 2, 4.616 1, 4.618 2, 4.618 12, 4.625 1, 4.626 3, 4.636 6, 4.636 11, 4.636 16, 4.636 26, 4.683 31, 4.691 2, 4.705 1, 4.715 2, 4.719 2, 4.719 3, 4.721 4, 4.722 3, 4.722 4, 4.722 5, 4.744 2, 4.750 12, 4.751 5, 4.752 4, 4.752 6, 4.775 15, 4.775 16, 4.775 18, 4.775 21, 4.776 1, 4.777 5, 4.783 4, 4.790 1, 5.10 8, 7.41 6

ṯlṯ[1.55 6, 4.195 7, 4.225 10, 4.268 8, 4.301 2, 4.303 4, 4.312 2, 4.396 4, 4.397 8, 4.627 4, 4.715 22, 4.715 23

ṯl[ṯ 1.27 15, 2.32 11, 4.247 5, 4.323 6, 4.465 1, 4.478 3, 4.540 4, 4.550 2, 4.683 19, 4.777 11

ṯ[l]ṯ 4.152 6

ṯ[lṯ 4.390 4, 4.396 17, 4.549 1

]ṯlṯ 4.60 4, 4.127 1, 4.127 9, 4.291 4, 4.300 2, 4.396 21, 4.410 20, 4.419 6, 4.446 3, 4.468 2, 4.579 1, 4.579 2, 4.598 1, 4.618 13, 4.722 2, 4.722 6

ṯ]lṯ 1.48 3, 1.163 4, 4.61 6, 4.102 16, 4.141 III 2, 4.363 1, 4.394 2, 4.400 10, 4.579 3, 4.594 2, 4.620 4, 4.664 3, 4.722 1, 4.752 11

ṯl]ṯ 4.63 III 19, 4.141 III 19, 4.213 22, 4.285 1, 4.664 5

]ṯlṯ[1.134 5, 4.541 1, 4.697 2

ṯl{.}ṯ 5.23 3

ṯl\ṯ 4.203 11f

ṯlṯid 1.18 IV 23, 1.18 IV 34, 1.19 II 30

ṯlṯh 1.15 II 7

ṯlṯm 1.27 7, 1.39 20, 1.41 19, 1.87 21, 1.104 4, 1.105 4, 1.109 30, 1.163 7, 2.80 5, 4.4 9, 4.10 4, 4.14 5, 4.34 6, 4.44 9, 4.44 23, 4.91 8, 4.123 22, 4.136 2, 4.139 9, 4.151 II 3, 4.156 6, 4.165 1, 4.165 2, 4.165 3, 4.165 4, 4.168 3, 4.171 1, 4.182 12, 4.182 37, 4.203 7, 4.206 5, 4.213 19, 4.226 1, 4.239 3, 4.243 21, 4.243 22, 4.243 27, 4.243 31, 4.269 4, 4.270 2, 4.270 9, 4.282 16, 4.284 1, 4.295 14, 4.310 5, 4.312 3, 4.317 12, 4.340 1, 4.340 2, 4.340 5, 4.340 6, 4.340 19, 4.340 20, 4.344 5, 4.344 9, 4.344 13, 4.352 3, 4.389 5, 4.392 4, 4.396 19, 4.398 9, 4.400 1, 4.411 4, 4.552 11, 4.632 18, 4.658 3, 4.658 11, 4.658 20, 4.658 48, 4.658 51, 4.658 52, 4.658 53, 4.659 1, 4.682 6, 4.682 12, 4.690 13, 4.691 3, 4.743 15, 4.743 16, 4.755 8, 4.777 6, 4.786 4

ṯlṯm[4.23 13, 4.182 28, 4.387 16, 4.397 2, 4.664 1

ṯlṯ[m 1.164 16, 4.30 11

]ṯlṯm 2.32 6, 2.32 11

ṯ]lṯm 1.173 15, 4.30 6, 4.340 12, 4.552 16

ṯl]ṯm 4.340 17, 4.386 1, 4.636 31, 4.658 36

]ṯlṯm[4.456 1, 4.620 2

ṯ]l[ṯm 4.552 1

[[ṯlṯm]] 4.709 10

ṯlṯt 1.41 3, 1.43 5, 1.46 5, 1.87 58, 1.112 15, 4.123 14, 4.146 4, 4.158 5,

4.158 13, 4.158 13, 4.226 9, 4.290 10, 4.337 5, 4.721 8, 4.721 8, 4.751 2, 4.779 1

t̲ltt[1.112 30

]t̲ltt   1.21 II 7

[t]ltt[1.87 61

tl\tt   5.11 7f

t̲ltth   1.14 IV 43

t̲ltth[1.16 V 9

t̲lttm   4.360 6, 4.360 7

t̲m   1.2 IV 4, 1.13 13, 1.14 IV 36, 1.22 I 4, 1.22 I 6, 1.22 I 8, 1.22 I 9, 1.23 66, 1.73 6, 2.80 2

t̲m[4.261 20, 4.323 7, 4.729 6

]t̲m   2.31 54, 4.122 1, 7.37 4

]t̲m[4.397 4, 7.55 10

t̲mx   4.424 3

t̲mg   1.42 38

t̲mg[4.785 6

]t̲mg[]   1.35 5

t̲mgxmxt̲hd   1.42 39

t̲mgdl   4.295 5

t̲mgn   4.753 5

t̲mgnd   1.60 8, 1.110 7, 1.111 12, 1.116 17, 1.135 8

t̲mgn[d   1.26 5

t̲md[4.621 9

t̲mdl   1.107 45

t̲myr   4.93 II 10

t̲mk   1.22 I 17

t̲mm   1.5 III 13, 1.5 III 27, 1.146 5

t̲mn   1.5 V 9, 1.5 V 21, 1.12 II 45, 1.15 II 24, 1.19 I 5, 1.19 I 43, 1.20 II 1, 1.23 19, 1.23 67, 1.64 24, 1.64 26, 1.104 22, 1.104 22, 1.104 23, 1.105 4, 1.106 18, 2.30 9, 2.41 21, 4.4 7, 4.27 16, 4.43 5, 4.44 1, 4.44 2, 4.48 5, 4.48 10, 4.53 14, 4.73 3, 4.141 II 24, 4.141 III 4, 4.144 5, 4.145 1, 4.173 2, 4.179 12, 4.179 14, 4.195 15, 4.203 1, 4.203 2, 4.212 3, 4.213 23, 4.243 50, 4.244 11, 4.247 31, 4.270 11, 4.273 8, 4.285 4, 4.285 9, 4.295 2, 4.313 28, 4.333 4, 4.337 14, 4.352 5, 4.377 27, 4.377 33, 4.411 8, 4.618 4, 4.625 11, 4.626 5, 4.626 7, 4.636 21, 4.688 2, 4.709 5, 4.717 2, 4.744 1, 4.744 3, 4.771 5, 4.783 2, 4.783 6, 6.19 1

t̲mn[1.64 10, 4.23 10, 4.157 4, 4.397 9

t̲m[n   1.104 21, 1.104 26, 4.18 1

]t̲mn   2.65 3, 4.30 9, 4.387 22, 4.525 2

t̲]mn   4.219 2

t̲m]n   4.206 5

]t̲mn[4.510 1

[[t̲mn]]   4.380 5

t̲mny   2.11 14, 2.13 11, 2.34 7, 2.34 22, 2.38 7, 2.40 15, 2.46 7, 2.68 14, 2.71 7, 2.72 8

t̲m[ny   2.24 10

t̲/ᶜmny   4.34 7

t̲mnym   1.4 VII 11, 1.5 V 21, 1.12 II 49, 1.15 IV 7, 4.123 1, 4.163 11, 4.171 4, 4.179 14, 4.213 20, 4.213 22, 4.243 8, 4.243 12, 4.243 15, 4.247 19, 4.265 5, 4.337 5, 4.369 6, 4.387 19, 4.636 4, 4.636 17, 4.636 27, 4.778 16, 4.782 23, 6.21 1

t̲mnym[4.18 5

t̲mny[m   1.76 8, 4.636 28, 4.664 5

t̲[mnym]   1.76 11

]t̲mnym   4.242 2

t̲m]nym   4.30 10, 4.777 2(cor.)

t̲mn]ym   4.127 3

[[t̲mnym]]   4.709 7

]t̲mnm[4.251 2

t̲mnr   4.315 11

t̲<m>nt   4.146 8

t̲mnt   1.3 V 26, 1.5 IV 9, 1.12 II 49, 1.14 I 9, 1.45 3, 1.87 60, 1.101 4, 1.105 19, 1.112 11, 1.119 11, 4.121 2, 4.226 5, 4.226 8, 4.337 15, 4.337 20

t̲]mn[t   1.3 V 11

t̲mnt   4.132 3

t̲mq   1.22 I 8, 4.93 IV 3, 4.106 20, 4.122 7, 4.226 10, 4.658 7

t̲mq[4.65 2

t̲mr[4.308 13

t̲m[r   4.622 5, 4.684 1, 4.686 14

t̲]mr   4.553 8

t̲mrg   1.85 25

t̲mry   4.49 4, 4.68 20, 4.70 8, 4.70 10, 4.244 4, 4.417 8

t̲mry[4.762 7

t̲m[ry   4.610 39

t̲mr[n   4.645 9

ṯmt 1.133 13, 2.10 18, 2.70 21

ṯn 1.1 III 20, 1.3 IV 35, 1.4 II 6, 1.4 III 17, 1.4 VI 3, 1.4 VI 24, 1.13 3, 1.14 I 27, 1.14 II 41, 1.14 II 41, 1.14 II 48, 1.14 III 2, 1.14 III 10, 1.14 IV 19, 1.14 IV 19, 1.14 IV 27, 1.14 IV 32, 1.14 IV 44, 1.14 V 3, 1.15 III 29, 1.16 VI 22, 1.17 II 32, 1.17 II 44, 1.19 I 11, 1.20 II 5, 1.22 I 21, 1.23 22, 1.41 5, 1.41 22, 1.41 43, 1.41 45, 1.41 48, 1.43 14, 1.46 2, 1.46 11, 1.48 12, 1.64 23, 1.79 3, 1.82 4, 1.87 53, 1.91 36, 1.105 6, 1.105 12, 1.105 13, 1.105 22, 1.106 24, 1.109 25, 1.111 15, 1.112 3, 1.112 19, 1.112 24, 1.119 18, 1.132 13, 1.132 23, 1.138 3, 1.139 4, 1.139 10, 1.148 19, 1.162 5, 1.162 5, 1.162 20, 2.26 13, 2.39 24, 2.45 6, 2.70 20, 2.72 15, 3.1 19, 3.1 36, 4.4 1, 4.4 2, 4.4 4, 4.4 4, 4.44 3, 4.44 8, 4.44 17, 4.44 22, 4.44 31, 4.48 2, 4.48 9, 4.54 13, 4.55 9, 4.63 I 2, 4.63 I 3, 4.63 III 2, 4.63 III 4, 4.63 III 5, 4.63 III 8, 4.63 III 15, 4.63 III 33, 4.73 6, 4.73 12, 4.80 7, 4.80 23, 4.95 3, 4.102 5, 4.102 8, 4.102 23, 4.103 43, 4.117 1, 4.118 7, 4.123 16, 4.123 20, 4.123 20, 4.129 1, 4.139 6, 4.139 9, 4.141 III 12, 4.141 III 14, 4.142 1, 4.146 3, 4.146 6, 4.146 8, 4.147 5, 4.152 4, 4.157 3, 4.169 3, 4.173 10, 4.179 17, 4.182 35, 4.185 5, 4.185 7, 4.195 13, 4.201 3, 4.205 1, 4.205 6, 4.231 4, 4.243 2, 4.243 4, 4.243 8, 4.243 23, 4.243 29, 4.243 33, 4.244 4, 4.244 10, 4.244 21, 4.244 26, 4.244 27, 4.244 28, 4.247 18, 4.247 30, 4.268 3, 4.269 31, 4.270 10, 4.274 1, 4.275 18, 4.295 4, 4.295 10, 4.295 13, 4.307 1, 4.307 2, 4.307 20, 4.307 21, 4.339 26, 4.339 27, 4.343 6, 4.345 3, 4.345 5, 4.355 8, 4.355 15, 4.355 19, 4.355 35, 4.355 36, 4.355 40, 4.355 41, 4.356 10, 4.356 16, 4.357 19, 4.357 27, 4.357 30, 4.358 5, 4.358 10, 4.360 4, 4.360 10, 4.363 3, 4.363 7, 4.364 1, 4.364 8, 4.367 7, 4.367 9, 4.374 8, 4.375 1, 4.378 9, 4.380 7, 4.380 11, 4.380 33, 4.385 2, 4.385 6, 4.390 6, 4.399 9, 4.400 17, 4.417 8, 4.417 13, 4.417 16, 4.420 11, 4.519 2, 4.595 1, 4.623 7, 4.625 5, 4.625 5, 4.636 19, 4.673 6, 4.716 5, 4.716 7, 4.716 11, 4.716 15, 4.716 17, 4.729 12, 4.742 11, 4.750 4, 4.750 13, 4.750 16, 4.750 17, 4.750 18, 4.752 2, 4.752 9, 4.752 10, 4.752 15, 4.775 3, 4.775 14, 4.777 9, 4.780 8, 4.780 14, 4.781 1, 5.11 16, 5.22 22, 5.23 17

[[ṯn]] 4.380 6, 4.380 12, 4.380 13

ṯn[1.48 11, 1.64 15, 1.112 23, 2.49 13, 4.3 2, 4.3 3, 4.3 4, 4.117 2, 4.157 1, 4.191 2, 4.248 8, 4.480 1, 4.629 18, 4.785 25, 7.85 3

ṯ[n 4.117 3, 4.117 4, 4.380 8, 4.380 8

]ṯn 1.75 11, 4.275 19, 4.296 16, 4.324 7, 4.350 11, 4.371 3, 4.442 4, 4.471 1, 4.491 2

ṯ]n 4.70 3, 4.103 14, 4.195 10, 4.195 11, 4.355 20, 4.468 3, 4.636 12, 4.775 20

]ṯn[1.89 8, 4.3 1, 4.35 I 1, 4.473 1

]xṯn 1.42 56, 1.103 12, 4.294 1

ṯn/t 4.401 2

ṯnid 2.50 18, 2.64 14, 2.70 9

ṯnbṯyġraṯṯpxxd 1.68 26

ṯndn 4.715 22

ṯnh 1.14 IV 42, 1.166 8

ṯnw 4.134 10

ṯnw[4.785 24

ṯny 1.2 I 16, 1.3 III 12, 1.3 VI 22, 1.4 VIII 31, 1.5 II 9, 1.16 VI 28, 4.339 14

ṯn]y 1.2 I 32

]ṯny[7.21 2

ṯnyx[4.258 2

]xṯny[4.651 8

ṯnyn 4.141 II 16

ṯnk[4.415 4

xṯnk 1.35 2

]ṯ/ʿnlbm 4.721 5

ṯnm 1.18 IV 22, 1.19 IV 61, 1.42 16, 1.42 46, 1.42 59, 1.42 62, 1.104 18, 1.104 20, 2.72 15

ṯnm[1.18 IV 33

ṯ[nm] 1.19 II 29

ṯnmxxx 4.127 7

ṯnn 1.14 II 38, 1.64 24, 1.103 17, 4.275 7, 4.727 20
ṯnn[4.556 1
ṯnnm 1.23 7, 1.23 26, 4.35 II 11, 4.66 1, 4.68 70, 4.126 4, 4.137 1, 4.163 1, 4.173 1, 4.174 1, 4.179 1, 4.382 5, 4.745 3
ṯnnm[4.416 4
ṯnn[m 4.485 7
ṯn[nm 4.752 3
ṯnnth[1.16 V 8
ṯnʿy 4.73 11
ṯnġly 4.128 9
ṯnġlyth 4.339 10
ṯnġrn 4.332 6
ṯnp 1.42 12, 1.42 53, 1.44 7, 1.52 7, 1.54 12, 1.64 28, 1.66 4, 1.128 17, 1.131 11
ṯ]np 1.52 6
ṯn]p 1.52 4, 1.52 5
ṯnq 4.355 29
ṯnqy 4.769 68
ṯnqym 4.126 21
ṯn]qym 4.87 4
ṯnt 1.2 IV 8, 1.175 16, 4.203 9, 4.203 10, 4.203 11, 4.203 13, 4.305 2, 4.402 5, 4.721 11, 4.721 12, 7.177 2
ṯnt[4.305 4
ṯ[nt] 4.4 10
ṯnth 1.114 21
ṯʿ 1.14 IV 37, 1.14 VI 16, 1.14 VI 40, 1.15 I 8, 1.15 II 8, 1.15 II 15, 1.15 V 22, 1.16 I 24, 1.16 VI 15, 1.16 VI 42, 1.16 VI 54, 1.39 1, 1.40 23, 1.40 24, 1.40 32, 1.40 32, 1.40 40, 1.40 41, 1.46 1, 1.119 11, 1.130 19, 1.130 19, 1.173 13
]ṯʿ 1.14 V 32
ṯʿdt 4.150 5
ṯʿh 1.173 17
ṯʿy 1.6 VI 57, 1.16 VI 59, 1.90 22, 1.119 8, 1.161 28, 1.161 29, 1.161 29, 1.161 30, 1.169 2, 4.69 VI 23, 4.76 7, 4.175 5, 4.354 2, 4.714 4, 4.715 7
ṯʿy[4.122 10
ṯʿ[y 1.161 27(*bis*), 1.161 28
]ṯʿy 4.610 30
ṯ]ʿy 1.4 VIII 49

ṯʿl 4.63 III 17
ṯʿl[4.359 3, 4.633 7
ṯʿlb 4.425 3
ṯʿly 4.133 3
ṯʿln 4.63 II 26, 4.214 I 3, 4.374 5, 4.378 8
ṯʿm 1.39 1, 1.39 1
ṯʿr 1.3 II 21, 1.3 II 36, 4.278 1
]ṯʿr 4.210 2
ṯʿrt 4.365 11
ṯʿt 4.751 6, 4.771 8, 4.778 5, 4.782 8
ṯġḏy 4.63 IV 4
ṯġr 1.16 I 52, 1.17 V 6, 1.96 8, 1.96 8, 1.96 9, 1.114 11, 1.128 17, 1.131 11, 1.136 3, 4.103 40, 4.128 11, 4.147 3, 4.195 14, 4.224 8, 4.224 9, 4.669 1, 7.63 6
ṯġr[1.16 II 27, 4.669 2
ṯ]ġr 1.19 I 22
]ṯġr[4.673 8
ṯġrh 1.78 3, 1.161 34
ṯġrkm 1.119 26, 1.119 35
ṯġrm 4.103 39, 4.126 22, 4.141 III 2, 4.609 13
ṯġrn 4.332 11
ṯġrn\y 1.119 28f
ṯġrt 1.3 II 3
ṯġ]r[t 1.7 36
ṯp 7.40 4
ṯp[1.67 16, 7.2 4
]ṯp[4.275 13
ṯp/k/w[1.67 6
ṯpdn 4.103 21, 4.112 III 3, 4.263 3
ṯpḥ 1.48 2
ṯpḥ[1.48 13
ṯpḫln 4.356 9
ṯpṭ 1.2 I 7, 1.2 I 26, 1.2 I 28, 1.2 I 30, 1.2 I 34, 1.2 I 41, 1.2 I 44, 1.2 III 7, 1.2 III 21, 1.2 IV 16, 1.2 IV 22, 1.2 IV 25, 1.2 IV 27, 1.2 IV 30, 1.16 VI 34, 1.16 VI 47, 1.17 V 8
ṯpṭ[1.2 I 17, 1.2 I 22
]ṯpṭ 1.2 III 23
ṯ]pṭ 1.2 III 16
ṯp]ṭ 1.2 IV 15
ṯpṭbʿl 2.40 3, 4.102 13, 4.103 34, 4.103 56, 4.384 10, 4.425 12, 4.775 13
ṯpṭbʿl[4.554 2

ṯpṭbˁ[l 4.81 2
ṯpṭb[ˁl 4.74 2
ṯpṭ[bˁl 4.746 5
ṯpṭy[4.140 2
ṯpṭn 1.3 V 32, 1.4 IV 44
ṯpẓ 1.108 3
]xṯpknt[7.133 5
ṯpllm 3.1 16
ṯpn 4.213 21, 4.348 8, 4.618 1, 4.618 23
ṯp[n 4.89 3
ṯpṣt 7.54 3
ṯprt 4.146 4
ṯprtm 4.341 10
ṯpš 1.48 7
ṯpt 1.67 8, 1.73 7
]ṯb/ṣ[4.678 8
]ṯṣn 1.66 2
ṯṣq[4.35 I 4
ṯṣr 1.20 II 11
ṯq 4.595 1, 4.595 3
ṯq[4.432 14
ṯqby 4.7 10
ṯqbm 1.17 VI 20
ṯqbn 4.63 I 20, 4.379 10, 4.700 3
ṯqd 1.85 7
ṯq[d 1.71 7
ṯ[qd 1.72 10
ṯ]qd[1.85 24
ṯqdy 4.103 48
ṯql 1.43 10, 1.43 12, 1.43 13, 1.43 15, 1.90 11, 1.112 3, 1.112 12, 3.1 20, 3.9 16, 4.49 2, 4.49 3, 4.49 4, 4.49 6, 4.49 7, 4.113 3, 4.139 10, 4.158 5, 4.158 20, 4.158 21, 4.337 13, 4.337 23, 4.707 18, 4.707 20, 4.707 23, 4.708 2, 4.708 3, 4.708 4, 4.717 6, 4.759 1, 4.759 2, 4.759 3
ṯq[l 1.87 42, 2.77 4, 4.708 5, 4.708 9
ṯql[4.287 1, 4.337 24, 4.337 25
ṯ[ql] 4.708 6, 4.708 7
]ṯql 4.250 1, 4.250 2
ṯqlm 1.14 I 29, 1.19 II 34, 2.70 18, 3.9 17, 3.10 13, 4.49 1, 4.98 7, 4.98 8, 4.98 9, 4.98 10, 4.98 11, 4.98 12, 4.98 13, 4.98 14, 4.98 15, 4.98 16, 4.98 18, 4.98 19, 4.98 21, 4.98 22, 4.101 3, 4.101 4, 4.113 2, 4.113 6, 4.123 8, 4.132 4, 4.156 3, 4.156 4, 4.156 5, 4.156 7, 4.202 3, 4.226 3, 4.226 10, 4.276 11, 4.276 12, 4.337 20, 4.341 1, 4.341 17, 4.341 19, 4.658 6, 4.690 3, 4.690 5, 4.690 7, 4.690 9, 4.690 11, 4.707 12, 4.707 16, 4.755 10, 4.791 5
ṯqlm[4.123 10
ṯql[m 4.98 5, 4.156 2, 4.276 9
ṯq[lm 4.98 6, 4.276 5, 4.276 8
ṯ[qlm] 4.98 23, 4.101 5
ṯq]lm 4.717 5
ṯqrn 4.103 22
ṯqt 4.595 4
ṯr 1.1 III 26, 1.1 IV 12, 1.1 V 22, 1.2 I 16, 1.2 I 33, 1.2 I 36, 1.2 III 16, 1.2 III 17, 1.2 III 19, 1.2 III 21, 1.3 IV 54, 1.3 V 10, 1.3 V 35, 1.4 I 4, 1.4 II 10, 1.4 III 31, 1.4 IV 39, 1.4 IV 47, 1.6 IV 10, 1.6 VI 26, 1.12 II 54, 1.14 I 41, 1.14 II 6, 1.14 II 23, 1.14 IV 6, 1.15 II 2, 1.15 IV 8, 1.15 IV 19, 1.16 IV 2, 1.17 I 23, 1.17 VI 23, 1.42 26, 1.42 48, 1.42 61, 1.48 8, 1.92 11, 1.92 13, 1.92 15, 1.101 8, 1.127 22, 1.128 7, 1.133 14, 1.149 6, 1.161 7, 1.161 23, 4.205 1, 4.360 3
ṯr[1.4 IV 1, 4.430 4
]ṯr 7.17 1
]ṯr[1.26a 3, 1.92 19
ṯrx[1.171 7
]ṯrx[7.25 2
ṯk/r[4.333 2
ṯrin 4.286 4
ṯrb/d[4.393 4
ṯrbn 1.54 3
ṯrb/d[4.393 4
ṯrdy 5.23 5
ṯrdm 5.23 9
ṯrdn[4.315 8
]ṯrdn 4.755 14
ṯrdnt 4.170 21
ṯrḏn 4.85 11
ṯrh 1.15 IV 17
ṯr[h 1.15 V 3
]ṯrw 4.327 4
ṯry 1.15 IV 6
ṯryl 1.161 32, 2.14 8, 2.14 12, 2.14 17, 2.16 2, 2.34 2, 6.13 2
ṯry[l 7.53 4

ṯryn 4.17 15, 4.123 5, 4.169 5, 4.169 6, 4.631 14, 4.636 1
ṯryn[4.81 5
ṯrk 4.98 21
ṯrkn 3.8 2
ṯrm 1.1 IV 31, 1.2 I 21, 1.4 VI 41, 1.12 I 31, 1.15 V 13, 1.15 VI 7, 1.16 VI 12, 1.18 IV 14, 1.18 IV 19, 1.18 IV 30, 1.22 I 12, 4.391 6, 4.610 17
]ṯrm[7.88 3
ṯr\m 1.44 9f
ṯrmg 1.4 VIII 3
ṯrml 1.14 III 44, 1.14 VI 30
ṯrmn 1.6 VI 58, 1.39 15, 1.48 19, 1.102 6, 1.127 6, 4.139 6, 4.182 15, 4.182 29, 4.243 20, 4.296 10
ṯrmn 1.65 4 lg. ṯkmn?
]ṯrmn 4.182 13
ṯrmnm 1.39 12, 4.168 5, 4.182 3, 4.182 11, 4.182 20
ṯr[mnm 4.182 31
ṯrmt 1.82 8
ṯrn 1.42 61, 1.175 4, 4.12 4, 4.15 7, 4.83 5, 4.320 6, 4.412 II 14, 4.696 1, 4.786 3
ṯrnd 1.125 5
ṯrnq 4.382 26
ṯrp 1.83 4(?)
ṯrptn 1.64 6
ṯrry 1.16 IV 15, 4.85 9
ṯrrt 1.14 III 5, 1.14 III 30, 1.15 IV 20, 1.100 64
ṯr[r]t 1.15 IV 9
ṯ]rrt 1.14 VI 12
ṯr]rt 1.14 IV 48
ṯrr]t 1.15 V 26
ṯrt 1.24 5
ṯrt 1.24 6 lg. k]\ṯrt
]ṯrt[1.36 5
ṯrtnm 4.163 9, 4.173 4(with syllabic A-sign placed under the end of r), 4.174 7, 4.179 5
ṯ[r]tnm 4.137 3
ṯrtn[m 4.216 7
ṯrtṯb 1.66 1
ṯrṯy 1.148 28
ṯrṯrdn 1.64 3
ṯš/ḏ[1.66 17
ṯt 1.27 9, 1.44 12, 1.66 4, 1.104 9, 1.105 22, 1.128 21, 1.132 9, 2.38 24, 4.63 I 2, 4.63 I 3, 4.63 I 26, 4.63 I 27, 4.63 I 29, 4.63 I 31, 4.63 II 14, 4.63 III 3, 4.63 III 4, 4.63 III 6, 4.63 III 8, 4.63 III 10, 4.63 III 12, 4.63 III 15, 4.63 III 16, 4.63 III 18, 4.63 III 19, 4.63 III 22, 4.63 III 33, 4.63 III 34, 4.63 IV 16, 4.102 7, 4.102 11, 4.102 18, 4.102 19, 4.102 20, 4.102 22, 4.123 19, 4.132 6, 4.145 6, 4.184 3, 4.195 16, 4.203 13, 4.239 4, 4.341 10, 4.385 2, 4.385 7, 4.390 5, 4.410 4, 4.410 5, 4.410 7, 4.410 9, 4.410 12, 4.531 2, 4.624 3, 4.624 5, 4.624 9, 4.624 20, 4.625 5, 4.691 6, 4.691 7, 4.780 2
ṯt[1.73 2, 1.86 30, 4.358 3
ṯ[t 4.355 31, 4.355 32, 4.624 6, 4.624 11, 4.624 12
]ṯt 4.410 19, 4.410 49, 4.594 5
ṯ]t 4.410 21, 4.410 22
]ṯt[1.55 1
]xṯt 4.262 5
]a/xṯt 4.205 13
ṯn/t 4.401 2
]xṯtb/d[1.34 2
ṯtgn 7.43 8
ṯth 3.3 4
ṯty 4.55 23, 4.80 5
ṯtyy 2.44 14
ṯtyn[4.432 20
ṯtm 1.16 II 52, 1.42 52, 1.169 17, 4.572 11, 4.658 11
]ṯtm 1.94 35
ṯtmnt 1.16 I 29, 1.16 I 39
]ṯtn 4.399 3
ṯtʿ 1.6 VI 30
ṯtʿ.nn 1.5 II 7
ṯtqt 1.24 48 lg. y\ṯtqt
ṯtrn 4.153 8
ṯtrt 4.182 58 cor. ʿṯtrt
ṯṯ 1.4 VII 9, 1.50 3, 1.50 5, 1.78 1(?), 1.91 34, 1.161 29, 2.17 9, 2.82 8, 4.4 10, 4.14 1, 4.14 7, 4.14 11, 4.14 13, 4.23 12, 4.34 6, 4.44 7, 4.44 11, 4.44 13, 4.44 25, 4.44 29, 4.48 1, 4.48 8, 4.48 12, 4.56 10, 4.61 2, 4.67 11, 4.73 7, 4.91 4, 4.128 2, 4.137 9, 4.152 8, 4.158 1, 4.158 5, 4.158 5,

4.162 1, 4.179 1, 4.182 22, 4.182 23, 4.188 17, 4.188 19, 4.195 12, 4.213 11, 4.216 3, 4.218 3, 4.243 21, 4.243 27, 4.244 11, 4.244 19, 4.244 22, 4.261 3, 4.261 4, 4.261 5, 4.261 6, 4.261 8, 4.261 9, 4.261 10, 4.261 11, 4.261 12, 4.261 24, 4.269 26, 4.284 5, 4.284 8, 4.312 6, 4.337 4, 4.344 6, 4.352 1, 4.353 2, 4.355 3, 4.355 6, 4.355 13, 4.355 14, 4.355 21, 4.355 38, 4.363 8, 4.377 24, 4.390 10, 4.392 2, 4.392 4, 4.397 11, 4.400 8, 4.609 51, 4.618 7, 4.618 10, 4.625 4, 4.625 13, 4.630 4, 4.630 6, 4.630 14, 4.636 7, 4.677 4, 4.764 5, 4.764 6, 4.775 6, 4.780 9, 4.780 11, 7.50 5

ṯṯ[4.56 14

ṯ[ṯ 4.27 20, 4.355 2

]ṯṯ 4.14 1, 4.291 3

ṯ]ṯ 2.21 16, 4.14 5, 4.123 11, 4.326 1, 4.442 3, 4.507 2

]xṯṯ 4.676 1

]ṯṯayy 4.103 27

ṯṯ<b> 2.72 9

ṯṯb 1.14 III 32, 1.106 32, 2.11 17, 2.13 13, 2.14 18, 2.34 9, 2.38 9, 2.38 23, 2.46 8, 2.50 5, 2.65 5, 2.68 17, 2.71 8

ṯṯb[2.58 2

ṯ]ṯb 1.41 41

ṯṯ]b 2.64 19

ṯṯd 7.130 6

ṯṯḫdm 1.42 52

ṯṯy 4.63 IV 5, 4.389 12

]ṯṯk 7.152 1

ṯṯm 1.4 VII 9, 2.26 21, 2.45 20, 3.10 19, 4.34 2, 4.56 3, 4.56 6, 4.80 20, 4.137 12, 4.142 4, 4.173 10, 4.213 7, 4.213 9, 4.213 11, 4.213 14, 4.218 6, 4.243 7, 4.243 16, 4.243 16, 4.243 18, 4.265 2, 4.280 9, 4.313 29, 4.333 1, 4.340 22, 4.344 21, 4.345 8, 4.352 1, 4.387 9, 4.411 8, 4.595 3, 4.625 1, 4.636 6, 4.636 7, 4.658 14, 4.658 43, 4.755 5, 4.791 15

ṯṯm[4.305 1, 4.404 1

ṯṯpḥ 4.141 I 6, 4.183 I 25, 4.609 15

ṯṯt 4.146 5, 4.226 7, 4.341 4, 4.341 9, 4.682 11, 4.755 5

ṯ[ṯt 1.112 27

ṯṯtm 4.141 III 7, 4.141 III 9

Θṭ 1.123 5

Θl 1.108 9

Θr 1.123 25

Appendices

1. Words in Syllabic Cuneiform

1.1 Syllables

A 4.173 4, placed under the end of r in ṯrtnm
a 5.14 1
be 5.14 2
ga 5.14 3
ḫa 5.14 4
di 5.14 5
ú 5.14 6
wa 5.14 7
zi 5.14 8
ku 5.14 9
ṭí 5.14 10
p]*u*[5.14 11
ṣa 5.14 12
qu 5.14 13
ra 5.14 14
ša 5.14 15
ḫa 5.14 16
tu 5.14 17
i 5.14 18
u 5.14 19
zu 5.14 20

1.2 Geographical Names

A-la-ši-ia[.KI] 4.102 31
ḫal-pí 4.768 4
ia-ku-SIG$_5$ 4.768 3
na-i-ni 4.768 1
na-ni-i 4.768 7
sú-a-li 4.768 2
ša-ḫa-qi 4.768 5
u-bur-a 4.768 6

1.3 Personal Names

^{m}*a-na-ni-ia-na* 4.768 3
^{m}*gu-ub-ru-na* 4.768 7
^{m}*lu-lu-wa-na* 4.768 5
^{m}*na-pa-ri* 4.768 4
^{m}*pu*]*r-ra-na* 4.768 7
^{m}[*p*]*u-us-ḫa-na* 4.768 6
^{m}*ta-mar-ti-nu* 4.768 2

1.4 Words

KUŠ.*ga-ba-bu* 4.63 I 24, 4.63 I 48, 4.63 II 12, 4.63 II 20, 4.63 II 29, 4.63 II 39, 4.63 II 49, 4.63 IV 18
]*ḫu-bu-la*$^?$ 5.15 3
ku-ub-šu 4.165 20
li-im 4.299 6, 4.610 56
]*li-im* 4.610 50
l]*i-im* 4.610 52
li-i]*m*[4.610 44
mar-ia-ne 4.69 I 29
me-at 4.48 13, 4.69 I 29, 4.69 III 22, 4.93 IV 42, 4.232 50, 4.340 23, 4.610 2, 4.610 14, 4.610 15, 4.610 18, 4.610 50, 4.610 52, 4.753 1, 4.753 2, 4.753 6, 4.753 14, 4.753 15, 4.753 16, 4.784 11
me-[*a*]*t* 4.610 21
me-[*at* 4.299 7
m]*e-at* 4.610 44
ù 4.381 12
ṭup-pu 4.68 76, 4.381 1
ta-pal 4.308 17
i-na 4.648 26
ia-na 4.648 26

1.5 Logograms

BAN.MEŠ 4.63 II 34
DUG 4.48 13, 4.381 2, 4.381 3, 4.381 4, 4.381 5, 4.381 6, 4.381 7, 4.381 8, 4.381 9, 4.381 10, 4.381 11
D[UG 4.381 12
DUG.G[IŠ.GEŠTIN 4.93 IV 42
DUMU 4.768 7
ÉRIN.MEŠ 4.68 76, 4.100 10, 4.704 11, 4.784 2(!)
GAL 4.165 16
GÁN.ME 4.416 1 lg. LÚ.MEŠ I. Márquez Rowe, NABU 1995 Nr. 63.
GEMÉ 5.15 2
GEŠTIN 4.48 13
GÍN 4.38 1, 4.90 11, 4.219 10
GIŠ.BA[N].MEŠ 4.68 77
GIŠ.[BAN.MEŠ] 4.63 II 29
GIŠ.BA[N.MEŠ] 4.63 II 49
GIŠ.BAN.MEŠ 4.63 I 24, 4.63 I 48, 4.63 II 12, 4.63 II 20, 4.63 II 39, 4.63 IV 18
GU$_4$ 4.308 17
GU$_4$.MEŠ 4.768 2, 4.768 3, 4.768 4, 4.768 5
G[U$_4$.MEŠ 4.768 1
GÚ.È.ME 4.165 19
GUR 4.38 1, 4.125 20
ḪI.MEŠ 4.340 23
Ì.MEŠ 4.381 1, 4.381 2, 4.381 3, 4.381 4, 4.381 5, 4.381 6, 4.381 7
Ì.MEŠ[4.381 8
Ì.M[EŠ 4.381 9
Ì[.MEŠ 4.381 10, 4.381 11
KÙ.BABBA[R] 4.219 10
KÙ.[BABBAR 4.38 1
KÙ.BABBAR.MEŠ 4.69 I 29, 4.69 III 22, 4.69 V 5, 4.69 V 26, 4.69 VI 5, 4.69 VI 21, 4.69 VI 37, 4.71 III 4, 4.71 III 9, 4.90 11, 4.610 51, 4.610 53, 4.610 57
KÙ.B]ABBAR.MEŠ 4.72 6
LÚ 4.768 1, 4.768 2, 4.768 3, 4.768 4, 4.768 5, 4.768 6, 4.768 7
LÚ.MEŠ 4.69 I 29, 4.416 1(!) I. Márquez Rowe in NABU 1995 Nr. 63.
PA 4.38 5
SAL.ME 4.165 18
[Š]ÁM.TI.LA 5.15 2
[Š]U 4.69 I 29
ŠU.NÍGIN 4.48 14, 4.63 I 48, 4.63 II 12, 4.63 II 20, 4.63 II 29, 4.63 II 34, 4.63 II 39, 4.63 IV 18, 4.69 I 29, 4.69 III 22, 4.69 V 5, 4.69 V 26, 4.69 VI 21, 4.69 VI 37, 4.71 III 4, 4.71 III 9, 4.90 12, 4.100 10, 4.308 17, 4.435 16, 4.610 53, 4.704 11, 4.754 20
ŠU.NÍGIN[4.299 6
ŠU.NÍ[GIN 4.69 V 16
[Š]U.NÍGIN 4.610 51
[ŠU.]NÍGIN 4.435 22
[ŠU.N]ÍGIN 4.610 57
TÚG 4.165 19
TÚG.ME 4.165 16, 4.165 17, 4.165 18, 4.165 20
TUR.ME 4.165 17
]UDU.ḪI.A 4.38 1
UGU 4.768 2, 4.768 3, 4.768 4, 4.768 5
URU 4.768 1, 4.768 2, 4.768 3, 4.768 4, 4.768 5, 4.768 6, 4.768 7
]URU. 4.102 31
URU.[MEŠ] 4.610 51
URU[.MEŠ] 4.610 53
ZÌ.KAL.KAL 4.38 1

2. Corrigenda to KTU[2]

1.3 VI 24 al[yn cor. al[iyn
1.10 III 8 uṣ[bʿh cor. uṣ[bʿth
1.16 VI 10 trḫṣ.nn cor. trḥṣ.nn
1.23 43 aṯt m cor. aṯtm
1.24 12 nh cor. ʿnh
1.46 2 ʿ]nt(?) cor. ʿ]n<t>(?)
1.52 8(*bis*) ḏ cor. ḏḏ
1.60 4 aṯṯbd cor. aṯtbd
1.66 12 sğsr cor. sġsr
1.114 8 ṯlḥn cor. ṯlḥnt
1.132 8 dqtt cor. dqt[[t]]
1.162 20 pam cor. pamt
1.169 19 tṯbb cor. tṯb b
1.173 9 r n[cor. rn[
2.33 3 mrḫq<t>m(?) cor. mrḥq<t>m(?)
4.4 9 ḥswn cor. ḫswn
4.14 11 bśwn cor. ḫśwn
4.43 1 yṣ cor. yṣa
4.46 3 ššlmt1 cor. ššlmt
4.62 1 aḫ<d>(?) cor. aḥ<d>(?)
4.63 III 22 q cor. w
4.71 III 11 kdġbr cor. kḏġbr
4.133 2 ʿbdll cor. ʿbdil
4.166 1 miḫd! cor. midḫ!
4.166 4 midpt cor. mispt
4.181 7 šlm cor. šim
4.182 58 ṯtrt cor. ʿṯtrt
4.269 20, 4.269 30 kśmn cor. kśmm
4.307 20 aṯṯl cor. aṯtl
4.334 5 byn[cor. gyn[
4.609 11 del. šmʿ
4.629 13 s̀rn cor. ẓrn
4.690 2 bḏġb cor. ḫḏġb
4.777 2 tm]nym cor. ṯm]nym
5.10 1 ʿṯtry(?) cor. ʿṯt<r>y(?)
6.23 2 ʿ(?)myḏtmr cor. ʿmyḏtmr
7.37 3]i cor.]l
7.43 5]nbgdn cor.]nbdgn
7.53 5 s cor.]\ṣ
7.57 1]mar[cor.]mlar[
7.127 1 t cor.]t[
7.198 6 r cor. xr
7.222 1]n/a t cor.]n/at

3. New Readings

1.1 II 11 špm M.S. Smith, SVT 55 (1994) 192.
1.1 V 25 atzd
1.4 IV 37 k<s>
1.6 IV 18 šd
1.6 IV 18 yn
1.12 I 41 ḫrẓph
1.12 II 37 a{n}pnm
1.14 I 38 mn
1.14 II 26 b
1.14 II 26 mṣdk
1.14 IV 8 b
1.14 IV 8 m]ṣdh
1.18 I 17f ti]\ḫd
1.19 I 8 knr
1.19 I 10 klb
1.19 III 40 {l}<y>qẓ
1.21 II 2 iqra\[km
1.22 II 13f [iln]\ym
1.24 5f k]\ṯrt
1.24 9f t]ḥ\wyn
1.24 11 k]mm
1.24 43 b
1.24 47 mlgh
1.24 47f y\ṯtqt
1.26 6 u[šḫrd M. Dietrich-W. Mayer, Subartu 4 (1996)
1.26b 3]ušḫr[d
1.26b 4]in[
1.60 1 il]d M. Dietrich-W. Mayer, Subartu 4 (1996)
1.60 16 ḫdlrṯ[t
1.60 16 klt
1.60 16 n]n[t
1.111 2 llym M. Dietrich-W. Mayer, ALASP 7/1 (1995) 17.
1.114 1 <dbḥ> M. Dietrich-O. Loretz, FS Gordon (1996)
1.114 7 <ṯlḥnt>
1.114 7 <tḥt>
1.114 11 <tʿdb>
1.114 14 w
1.114 14 l
1.114 15 ašk[r
1.114 27 lmdh
1.114 29 ḫš
1.114 29 ʿrk
1.114 29 lb
1.116 2 śrdm M. Dietrich-W. Mayer, Subartu 4 (1996)
1.116 4 ag
1.116 4 ndym
1.116 4 ṯd
1.116 4 ndy
1.116 5(*bis*) in
1.116 5 mṯy
1.116 5 ḫzzy
1.116 28 abn[d
1.116 28]nd
1.116 29 tg]n[d
1.116 29 kl]dnd
1.116 30 b]tm
1.116 32 mxxy
1.116 32 prṯy
1.116 33 ptg[nt]t
1.116 33 ḫwrṯt
1.116 34 nnt[d
1.125 5 atnd M. Dietrich-W. Mayer, ALASPM 14 (1996)
1.132 3 bt M. Dietrich-W. Mayer, UF 28 (1996)
1.132 6 šbrd
1.135 13 atnṯ]t M. Dietrich-W. Mayer, Subartu 4 (1996)
1.135 13 ḫ]wrṯt
1.135 14 ṯynṯ]t
1.135 14 abn[d
1.148 6 thmt B. Alster, DDD (1995) Sp. 1637.
1.148 41 ġr]m
1.169 1 r[gmm
1.169 18 u
1.169 18 bu
2.13 14 ṯyndr
2.30 13 ṯyndr
4.205 14 su/d/lsg
4.205 18 mlk
4.394 2 kbd
4.416 1 LÚ.MEŠ I. Márquez Rowe, NABU 1995 Nr. 63.

4.729 12 k[bd
4.769 58 i[š]dn
4.784 2 ÉRIN.MEŠ W.H. Van Soldt, UF 27 (1995)
5.11 7 l
5.11 7 ṯyny
6.66 2 ilr!mh J. Sanmartín in UF 27 (1995)
6.66 6 d
6.66 6f šk\n
6.66 7f m\aṯr

4. Supplemented Words

1.4 VI 54 <yn>
1.5 V 18 <arṣ>(?)
1.6 II 22 <k>
1.19 II 20 <yph>(?)
1.19 III 12 <bʿl>
1.19 III 33 <hm>
1.19 III 36 <ṯbr>
1.23 59 <št>
1.24 15 <bnt>
1.40 34 <il>
1.40 34 <bn>
1.40 34 <mpḫrt>
1.40 34 <l>
1.41 13 <dqt>
2.26 3 <rgm>
2.71 7 <mnm>(?)
2.71 7 <šlm>(?)
1.100 6 <nḥš>
1.100 73 <mhry>
1.105 13 <šm>
1.114 1 <dbḥ>
1.114 7 <tḥt>
1.114 7 <ṯlḥnt>
1.114 11 <tʿdb>
1.130 16 <mlat>
4.143 2 <l>
4.279 2 <yn>
4.609 11 šmʿ<rgm>
4.624 9 <qlʿm>
4.636 4 <alpm>
4.636 4 <l>

5. Words in Erasures

[[agzry]] 1.23 60
[[alp]] 1.148 25
[[arbʿt]] 4.709 7
[[b]] 4.131 4
[[bn]] 3.7 8, 4.281 28, 4.371 20, 4.617 15, 4.695 3
[[bt]] = bt<h> 1.19 IV 10
[[dqt]] 1.39 16(?)
[[drt]] 4.131 4
[[w]] 1.148 25, 4.709 10
[[zt]] 4.764 11
[[ym]] 1.17 I 11
[[kbd]] 4.709 8
[[kkr]] 4.131 4
[[ksp]] 4.709 8, 4.709 10
[[kṯr]] 1.39 14(?)
[[mnḥt]] 4.709 9
[[ʿš[r]]] 4.764 12
[[ʿšrm]] 4.709 11
[[ṣin]] 4.709 11
[[qrwn]] 4.277 14
[[ršp]] 1.39 16(?)
[[š]] 1.148 25
[[šʿrt]] 4.709 9
[[tk]] 1.10 III 27
[[trġt]] 1.75 3
[[ṯlṯ]] 1.14 V 3
[[ṯlṯm]] 4.709 10
[[ṯmnym]] 4.709 7
[[ṯmn]] 4.380 5
[[ṯn]] 4.380 6, 4.380 12, 4.380 13

6. Wrong Line Numbers

1.48 "15" = 14
1.54 "10" = 9
1.64 4 missing in KTU
1.71 "25" = 28
2.31 "35" = 36
2.79 rev. "10" = 12
4.103 after l. 47 left out: [ub]dy. trrm.
4.227 "II 5" = II 13
4.232 after l. 21 left out: [b]n . qṭnn 3.
4.244 after l. 28 left out: krm . [...]
4.255 "5" = 6
4.334 after l. 4 two lines left out: (5) bn. ṯy[...] / (6) bn . pb[...].
4.422 "50" = 49
4.692 "15" = 14
7.69 "1" = 2
7.150 "5" = 4
7.198 "5" = 6

7. Lines Left Out

1.64 4*]ṯ
1.64 4* pdḏn
4.103 48* trrm
4.103 49* bn
4.232 22* b]n
4.232 22* qṭnn
4.244 29* krm
4.334 5* ṯy[
4.334 5* bn
4.334 6* bn
4.334 6* pb[
4.692 13* birt[n
4.692 13* bn

8. Words Crossing the Line Boundary

1.1 II 16f y\[kbdnh]
1.1 II 19f ʿp\[rm]
1.1 III 6f]\yh
1.2 I 15f am]\r
1.2 I 24f rišt\km
1.2 IV 13f nš\r
1.2 IV 21f qdq\d
1.3 II 5f tm\tḫṣ
1.3 II 32f bt\lt
1.3 V 19f bht\k
1.3 VI 19f tštḥ\wy
1.3 VI 22f h\yn
1.4 I 25f yšl\ḥ
1.4 I 27f yṣq\m
1.4 II 35f n]\hr
1.4 VI 41f]m\ria
1.4 VI 57f m]r\i
1.4 VII 18f hkl\m
1.4 VII 23f ali\yn
1.4 VII 25f ḥ\ln
1.4 VII 49f ym\lk
1.4 VII 51f yšb\[ʿ]
1.4 VII 52f ġ\[l]mh
1.4 VII 55f r\[mt]
1.4 VIII 8f y\rdm
1.4 VIII 23f md\d
1.4 VIII 24f a\lp
1.4 VIII 25f k\mn
1.4 VIII 28f k\bd
1.4 VIII 34f q\[rdm]
1.5 I 7f mh\mrt
1.5 III 3f]\y
1.5 IV (0-1)]\ʿ
1.5 V 15f y\rdm
1.5 VI 3f sbn\[y
1.5 VI 8f a\rṣ
1.6 I 40f ṣb\rt
1.6 I 49f pi\d
1.6 II 11f t[ṣ]\ḥ
1.6 II 32f tdry\nn
1.6 IV 18f t\bl
1.6 V 15f rḥ\m
1.6 VI 3f u\[dnh]
1.6 VI 15f kl\yy
1.6 VI 24f tmtḫ\ṣ
1.6 VI 30f y\dd
1.7 5f h\[dmm]
1.7 28f tls]\[m]n
1.8 II 11f]\m
1.8 II 13f]\m
1.9 12f]\h
1.13 3f ym\m
1.13 28f am\rkm
1.14 V 13f aṯt\[h
1.14 VI 33f kr{k}\t
1.15 IV 12f t\lḥn
1.16 III 1f y\ʿn
1.16 V 5f]\y
1.16 V 42f k]\rt
1.17 II 19f š\krn
1.17 II 21f mn[t]\y
1.17 II 29f kṯ\rt
1.17 II 30f y\ššq
1.17 II 34f yšl\ḥm
1.17 V 12f yš\rbʿ
1.17 V 32f mš\knth
1.17 V 35f yb]\rk
1.17 VI 13f k\[ṯr]
1.17 VI 30f yʿš\r
1.17 VI 50f tštḥ\[wy
1.18 I 17f ti]\ḫd(!)
1.18 IV 20f d]\iym
1.19 III 21f šp]\th
1.19 IV 8f yšt\ql
1.19 IV 15f aq\ht
1.19 IV 24f [k]\bkbm
1.19 IV 26f mṣ\ltm
1.19 IV 34f m\kly
1.19 IV 35f dn\il
1.19 IV 50f y]\bl
1.19 IV 54f tq\ḥ
1.19 IV 58f ġ\zr
1.21 II 2 iqra\[km(!)
1.21 II 5f yrp\[u
1.21 II 7f bt\[y
1.22 I 1f]\h
1.22 I 9f ḥyl\y
1.22 II 1f qr]\b
1.22 II 3f aṣḥ]\km
1.22 II 13f [iln]\ym(!)

1.24 2f m\lk
1.24 5f k]\ṯrt(!)
1.24 8f š\pt
1.24 9f t]ḥ\wyn(!)
1.24 14f]tl\ʿ
1.24 17f y\rḫ
1.24 18f bh\th
1.24 19f a\bh
1.24 20f ḫ\rṣ
1.24 21f iq\nim
1.24 25f ḫtn\m
1.24 28f tt\rḫ
1.24 29f [a]\bh
1.24 36f a\bn
1.24 38f y\rḫ
1.24 40f [bn]\t
1.24 41f h\ll
1.24 44f i\l
1.24 45f sp\rhn
1.24 46f mn\thn
1.24 47f y\ṯtqt(!)
1.26 5f ḫb\t]d
1.44 5f tt\l
1.44 6f aṯ\m
1.44 8f k\mrbnr
1.44 9f ṯr\m
1.44 10f k\ld
1.46 6f g\[dlt
1.64 29f arḏln\ḫ
1.67 6f]\a
1.67 7f]\yṯ
1.67 8f]\rty
1.67 19f]\yṯ
1.67 20f]\q
1.69 2f]\n
1.69 3f]\t
1.69 6f]\bt
1.70 4f aṯb[šm]\y
1.70 14f]\rk
1.70 18f]\b
1.70 23f]\tn
1.70 26f]\rḫ
1.73 5f]\t
1.87 7f br\r
1.87 9f]\t
1.87 28f bʿ]\lt
1.87 33f ṯkm]\n
1.87 38f aṯ]\rt
1.87 44f md]\bḥ
1.87 46f ʿš]\rm
1.87 49f d]\d(!)
1.87 52f y]\m
1.87 54f ʿš\rt
1.87 56f šp\š
1.92 31f yu\[h]b
1.92 34f n\[ġr]
1.100 33f ʿq\š<r>
1.100 36f šm\rr
1.103 39f uḫr\y
1.106 21f k\l
1.108 4f m\rqdm
1.108 6f bʿ\lt
1.108 20f iršt\[k]
1.108 22f l\[anh]
1.108 23f r\[p]i
1.108 24f la\nk
1.112 14f ḥ\l
1.112 16f m\lk
1.112 21f ʿ\šrh
1.112 22f ṣ\pn
1.112 27f ʿš]\rt
1.117 3f m\[lk]
1.119 28f ṯġrn\y
1.128 17f ilwn\y
1.132 14f i\nš
1.138 2f]\py
1.168 18f k\[
2.47 24f yš\al
2.72 42f u\[my]
3.9 6f ag\rškm
4.4 1f dr\m
4.46 13f ḥr\š
4.149 14f d\bḥ
4.203 11f ṯl\ṯ
4.227 I 1f]\q
4.412 I 24f]\n
5.11 7f ṯl\ṯt
5.18 3f i\ly
5.18 7f š\mmn
6.27 2f qr\ht
6.66 3f nk\šy
6.66 4f mr\u
6.66 5f mlk\i
6.66 6f šk\n(!)
6.66 7f m\aṯr(!)
6.69 1f mš\mn
7.51 10f y\[
7.53 5]\ṣ(cor.)

9. A Supplementary Text

9.530

P. Bordreuil, Textes alphabétiques inédits de Ras-Shamra, in: AAAS 29/30 (1979/80) 11.

1 *l mlk rb . mlk . m*l[km]

2 *rgm . tḥm . ˁmrpi*

...

9 *mlk . rb . mlk* [.] *ml*[km]

Ugarit-Verlag Münster

Ricarda-Huch-Straße 6, D-48161 Münster

Abhandlungen zur Literatur Alt-Syrien-Palästinas und Mesopotamiens (ALASP)

Herausgeber: *Manfried* DIETRICH - *Oswald* LORETZ

Bd. 1 Manfried DIETRICH -Oswald LORETZ, *Die Keilalphabete.* 1988 (ISBN 3-927120-00-6), 376 S., DM 93,--; SFr 93,--; ÖS 650,--.

Bd. 2 Josef TROPPER, *Der ugaritische Kausativstamm und die Kausativbildungen des Semitischen.* 1990 (ISBN 3-927120-06-5), 252 S., DM 71,--; SFr 71,--; ÖS 493,--.

Bd. 3 Manfried DIETRICH - Oswald LORETZ, *Mantik in Ugarit.* Mit Beiträgen von Hilmar W. Duerbeck - Jan-Waalke Meyer - Waltraut C. Seitter. 1990 (ISBN 3-927120-05-7), 320 S., DM 98,--; SFr 98,--; ÖS 686,--.

Bd. 5 Fred RENFROE, *Arabic-Ugaritic Lexical Studies.* 1992 (ISBN 3-927120-09-X). 212 S., DM 77,--; SFr 77,--; ÖS 535,--.

Bd. 6 Josef TROPPER, *Die Inschriften von Zincirli.* 1993 (ISBN 3-927120-14-6). XII + 364 S., DM 108,--; SFr 108,--; ÖS 800,--.

Bd. 7 *UGARIT - ein ostmediterranes Kulturzentrum im Alten Orient. Ergebnisse und Perspektiven der Forschung.* Vorträge gehalten während des Europäischen Kolloquiums am 11.-12. Februar 1993, hrsg. von Manfried DIETRICH und Oswald LORETZ.
Bd. I: *Ugarit und seine altorientalische Umwelt.* 1995 (ISBN 3-927120-17-0). XII + 298 S., DM 120,--; SFr 120,--; ÖS 860,--.
Bd. II: H.-G. BUCHHOLZ, *Ugarit und seine Beziehungen zur Ägäis.* 1996 (ISBN 3-927120-38-3)(im Druck).

Bd. 8 Manfried DIETRICH - Oswald LORETZ - Joaquín SANMARTÍN, *The Cuneiform Alphabetic Texts from Ugarit, Ras Ibn Hani and Other Places.* (*KTU: second, enlarged edition*). 1995 (ISBN 3-927120-24-3). XVI + 666 S., DM 120,--, SFr 120,--, ÖS 850,--.

Bd. 9 Walter MAYER, *Politik und Kriegskunst der Assyrer.* 1995 (ISBN 3-927120-26-X). XVI + 545 S., DM 170,--, SFr 170,--, ÖS 1.190,--.

Bd. 10 Giuseppe VISICATO, *The Bureaucracy of Šuruppak.* 1995 (ISBN 3-927120-35-9). XX + 165 S. DM 80,--; SFr 80,--; ÖS 570,--.

Bd. 11 Doris PRECHEL, *Die Göttin Išhara. Ein Beitrag zur altorientalischen Religionsgeschichte.* 1996 (ISBN 3-927120-36-7). XII + 248 S., DM 102,--; SFr. 102,--; ÖS 734,--.

Ugaritisch-Biblische Literatur (UBL)

Herausgeber: *Oswald* LORETZ

Bd. 1 Oswald LORETZ, *Der Prolog des Jesaja-Buches (1,1-2,5).* 1984 (ISBN 3-88733-054-4), 171 S., DM 52,--; SFr 52,--; ÖS 364,--.

Bd. 2 Oswald LORETZ, *Psalm 29.* 1984 (ISBN 3-88733-055-2), 168 S., - Neuauflage UBL 7.

Bd. 3 Oswald LORETZ, *Leberschau, Sündenbock, Asasel in Ugarit und Israel.* 1985 (ISBN 3-88733-061-7), 136 S., DM 47,--; SFr 47,--; ÖS 330,--.

Bd. 4 Oswald LORETZ, *Regenritual und Jahwetag im Joelbuch.* 1986 (ISBN 3-88733-068-4), 189 S., DM 62,--; SFr 62,--; ÖS 430,--.

Bd. 5 Oswald LORETZ - Ingo KOTTSIEPER, *Colometry in Ugaritic and Biblical Poetry.* 1987 (ISBN 3-88733-074-9), 166 pp., DM 52,--; SFr 52,--; ÖS 364,--.

Bd. 6 Oswald LORETZ, *Die Königspsalmen.* Teil I. *Ps. 20; 21; 72; 101 und 144.* Mit einem Beitrag von Ingo Kottsieper zu *Papyrus Amherst.* 1988 (ISBN 3-927120-01-4), 261 S., DM 82,--; SFr 82,--; ÖS 574,--.

Bd. 7 Oswald LORETZ, *Ugarit-Texte und Thronbesteigungspsalmen.* - Erweiterte Auflage von UBL 2. 1984-. 1988 (ISBN 3-927120-04-9), 550 S., DM 94,--; SFr 94,--; ÖS 650,--.

Bd. 8 Marjo C.A. KORPEL, *A Rift in the Clouds.* 1990 (ISBN 3-927120-07-3), 736 S., DM 110,--; SFr 110,--; ÖS 770,--.

Bd. 9 Manfried DIETRICH - Oswald LORETZ, *"Yahwe und seine Aschera".* 1992 (ISBN 3-927120-08-1), 220 S., DM 76,--; SFr 76,--; ÖS 532,--.

Bd. 10 Marvin H. POPE, *Probative Pontificating in Ugaritic and Biblical Literature. Collected Essays.* Ed. by Mark S. SMITH. 1994 (ISBN 3-927120-15-4), xvi + 406 S. DM 106,--; SFr 106,--; ÖS 760,--.

Bd. 11 *Ugarit and the Bible*. Ed. by G.J. BROOKE, A.H.W. CURTIS, J.F. HEALEY. 1994 (ISBN 3-927120-22-7), X + 470 S., 3 Abb., DM 104,--; SFr 104,--; ÖS 750,--.

Bd. 12 *Ugarit: Religion and Culture. Proceedings of the Edinburgh University International Colloquium 20-23 July 1994*. Eds. N. WYATT, W.G.E. WATSON, J.B. LLOYD. 1996 (ISBN 3-927120-37-5) (im Druck)

Altertumskunde des Vorderen Orients (AVO)

Herausgeber: *Manfried DIETRICH - Reinhard DITTMANN - Oswald LORETZ*
Mitwirkende: *Nadja Cholidis - Maria Krafeld-Daugherty - Ellen Rehm*

Bd. 1 Nadja CHOLIDIS, *Möbel in Ton*. 1992 (ISBN 3-927120-10-3), XII + 323 S. + 46 Taf., DM 119,--; SFr 119,--; ÖS 833,--.

Bd. 2 Ellen REHM, *Der Schmuck der Achämeniden*. 1992 (ISBN 3-927120-11-1), X + 358 S. + 107 Taf., DM 125,--; SFr 125,--; ÖS 875,--.

Bd. 3 Maria KRAFELD-DAUGHERTY, *Wohnen im Alten Orient*. 1994 (ISBN 3-927120-16-2), x + 404 S. + 41 Taf., DM 146,--; SFr 146,--; ÖS 1.030,--.

Bd. 4 Manfried DIETRICH - Oswald LORETZ, Hrsg., *Festschrift für RUTH MAYER-OPIFICIUS mit Beiträgen von Freunden und Schülern*. 1994 (ISBN 3-927120-18-9), xviii + 356 S. + 256 Abb., DM 116,--; SFr 116,--; ÖS 835,--.

Bd. 5 Gunnar LEHMANN, *Untersuchungen zur späten Eisenzeit in Syrien und Libanon. Stratigraphie und Keramikformen zwischen ca. 720 bis 300 v.Chr.* 1996 (ISBN 3-927120-33-2), x + 548 S. + 3 Karten + 113 Tf., DM 212,-- / SFr 212,-- / ÖS 1.500,--.

Bd. 6 Ulrike LÖW, *Figürlich verzierte Metallgefäße aus Nord- und Nordwestiran - eine stilkritische Untersuchung*. 1996 (ISBN 3-927120-34-0)(im Druck)

Eikon

Beiträge zur antiken Bildersprache
Herausgeber: *Klaus STÄHLER*

Bd. 1 Klaus STÄHLER, *Griechische Geschichtsbilder klassischer Zeit*. 1992 (ISBN 3-927120-12-X), X + 120 S. + 8 Taf., DM 40,80; SFr 40,80; ÖS 285,--.

Bd. 2 Klaus STÄHLER, *Form und Funktion. Kunstwerke als politsiches Ausdrucksmittel*. 1993 (ISBN 3-927120-13-8), VIII + 131 S. mit 54 Abb., DM 43,--; SFr 43,--; ÖS 348,--.

Bd. 3 Klaus STÄHLER, *Zur Bedeutung des Formats*. 1996 (ISBN 3-927120-25-1)(im Druck).

Forschungen zur Anthropologie und Religionsgeschichte (FARG)

Herausgeber: *Manfried DIETRICH - Oswald LORETZ*

Bd. 27 Jehad ABOUD, *Die Rolle des Königs und seiner Familie nach den Texten von Ugarit*. 1994 (ISBN 3-927120-20-0), XI + 217 S., DM 38,50; SFr 38,50; ÖS 280,--.

Bd. 28 Azad HAMOTO, *Der Affe in der altorientalischen Kunst*. 1995 (ISBN 3-927120-30-8), XII + 147 S. + 25 Tf./155 Abb., DM 49,--; SFr 49,--; ÖS 350,--.

Bd. 29 *Engel und Dämonen. Theologische, anthropologische und religionsgeschichtliche Aspekte des Guten und Bösen.* Vorträge gehalten während eines Symposiums zu Tartu/ Estland am 7.-8. April 1995, hrsg. von Gregor AHN - Manfried DIETRICH, 1996 (ISBN 3-927120-31-6) (im Druck)

Mitteilungen für Anthropologie und Religionsgeschichte (MARG)

Herausgeber: *Gregor AHN - Manfried DIETRICH - Ansgar HÄUSSLING*

Bd. 8 1994 (ISBN 3-927120-21-9), X + 219 S., DM 51,--; SFr 51,--; ÖS 370,--.

Bd. 9 *In memoriam A. Rupp (1930 - 1993)*. 1994 (ISBN 3-927120-23-5), XXVI + 341 S. + 15 Taf., DM 62,--; SFr 62,--; ÖS 440,--.

Bd. 10 1995 (ISBN 3-927120-32-4), VI + 173 S., 31 Abb., DM 46,--; SFr 46,--; ÖS 322,--.

Bei einem Abonnement der Reihen liegen die angegebenen Preise um ca. 15% tiefer.

Auslieferung durch -
Distributed by:
BDK Bücherdienst GmbH
Kölner Straße 248
D-51149 Köln

Distributor to North America:
Eisenbrauns, Inc.
Publishers and Booksellers
POB 275
Winona Lake, Ind. 46590
U.S.A.